RELIGION IN CONTEMPORARY CULTURE

HARPER'S SOCIAL SCIENCE SERIES
Under the Editorship of
F. STUART CHAPIN

HARPER & BROTHERS, PUBLISHERS, NEW YORK

RELIGION IN CONTEMPORARY CULTURE

A STUDY OF RELIGION THROUGH SOCIAL SCIENCE

PURNELL HANDY BENSON

RELIGION IN CONTEMPORARY CULTURE: *A Study of Religion Through Social Science*

Printed in the United States of America

L-K

Library of Congress catalog card number: 60-7021

Contents

Preface

This is a text in the scientific study of religion, a substantial claim to make since writers in religion more than in other fields have turned uncritically to pieces of driftwood floating in science which might support preconceived ideas, a mood not conducive to objective scholarship. Nevertheless, the author is willing to launch this book from the platform of scientific procedure, and in so doing he endeavors to compartmentalize his enthusiasm for the religious life of mankind in its wide variety of forms. If he is unwittingly pulled off center by this enthusiasm, he invites the aid of other scientific workers to establish more correctly the bearings of religion.

That a writer in social science labors for objectivity scarcely needs saying. His highest loyalty should be to facts and conclusions logically derived from facts. Where matters are disputed within a science, the opposing viewpoints require review. In no field of social science is this objectivity more difficult to achieve than in the study of religious behavior. Religion is enmeshed in human emotion. It is characterized by controversy. Scientists, as all people, are products of the culture in which they live, a culture which gives the scientist his initial concepts and which may indoctrinate with loyalty to a particular religious group or avoidance of religion in general. The problem is to free oneself from biases and gain the necessary facts while one takes a fresh scientific look at the subject matter. The author's religious background is that of a member of the Society of Friends. He agrees with the Hindu leader Mahatma Gandhi that a higher value is to be set upon truth than upon any other principle. He seeks, if possible, to set aside his practical interests while he takes up the task of scrutinizing religion.

An individual who strives for neutrality in writing about religion may be more vulnerable to the charge of partisanship than the frank proponent of a sectarian view. At least the reader knows where the sectarian stands and does not hold him up to an artificial standard. The writer who claims or aims to be objective provokes criticism. He may not satisfy partisans as to the correctness of his description and analysis.

Criticism which is not dogmatic is healthful for scientific inquiry and is to be welcomed in the task of discovering greater truth. The findings of science are always subject to modification in the on-going process of research. The gift of science to mankind is not a set of eternal propositions, but a method of inquiry by which propositions may be tested and refined, scientific method being a procedure which every human being may utilize in pursuing his life purposes. The attitude of "I'm from Missouri" expresses the epitome of science.

Primarily the task of this volume has been to assemble relevant answers, insights, and research contributions of which the author is aware and which have accumulated in the scientific study of religion during the past few generations and especially during recent years. The effort has been made by the author to sharpen this material and to organize it so that its content can be more adequately considered. This is a textbook of concepts and principles for students, researchers, or laymen who wish to reflect upon or act upon the material.

The book seeks to provide information and ideas about religion, representing viewpoints in our cultural heritage about which thoughtful persons would like to be informed whatever their religious preferences may be. Knowledge of these viewpoints does not imply acceptance of them, merely comprehension of what they are. In this respect the book focuses on the need in the American educational system to teach, not a particular faith, but what some of the answers given by different faiths are together with answers submitted by researchers outside of the leadership in organized religious groups. As in most text material in the social sciences, there are few absolutely right or wrong answers, but rather answers with which the student is expected to become familiar and then to select or modify as he constructs his own life scheme. The book calls attention to guiding ideas in the scientific study of religion, the actual route taken being left to the reader. The writer hopes the book may be useful to students in courses about religion given in various departments of instruction. The public whose interest in religion is perennial may also desire to proceed through its pages.

The author's personal debt to teachers, students and writers who have aided him in the formulation of the manuscript is too large to be adequately acknowledged. The Bureau of Research and Survey of the National Council of Churches in the U.S.A. administered a grant in partial support of the project and provided consultative assistance and research resources in fulfillment of the project. Charles S. Estus, Robert Lee, David R. Mace, Paul B. Maves, James A. McClintock, Scott Mitchell, Setsuko M. Nishi, Paul C. Obler, Frederick A. Shippey, Helen F. Spaulding, and Glen W. Trimble have read sections of the manuscript and have made many valuable suggestions. Elaine R. Brown, Catherine S. Faatz, Frances F. Obler, Leona M. Rogers, Wiley K. Rogers, and Charlotte E. Van Valen have shared the arduous task of preparing the manuscript for publication and checking copy. The author's thanks are especially due to Lauris B. Whitman, Director of the Bureau of Research and Survey of the National Council of Churches, who read the complete manuscript and whose efforts and counsel helped bring to a conclusion the lengthy and detailed project extending over a decade. The author has an immeasurable obligation to his beloved wife and family whose sympathetic understanding and generous sacrifices have made his program of study and writing possible.

PURNELL HANDY BENSON

RELIGION IN CONTEMPORARY CULTURE

chapter 1 Introduction

In the unfolding history of ideas philosophy has been the mother of the various sciences. First the physical, then the social, one by one, have taken their place as independent disciplines. This passing from infancy to maturity has not been easy. Philosophy, as the mother, has been reluctant to see her offspring taken away from her. The physical sciences have looked down upon the younger ones as having less right to call themselves sciences.

The turmoil of childhood has been a struggle by each to articulate itself as a science. One of the more recent to mature has been sociology, knowing itself by that name for little more than a century, and having been taught as a college course for about half that time. The latest to give evidence of appearing as a social science is the field of religion, aided by research in sociology, anthropology, psychology, and psychoanalysis. In their study of society and the individual these four have recurringly encountered and described the force and reality of religious ideas and motives in human behavior. Literature from these fields is introduced in this text. The literature has been surveyed in works in sociology by C. Y. Glock, W. J. Goode, T. F. Hoult, Clifford Kirkpatrick, E. K. Nottingham, D. J. Pittman, A. L. Swift, Jr., Joachim Wach, and J. M. Yinger;[1] and in works in psychology by

[1] C. Y. Glock, "The Sociology of Religion," in R. K. Merton, L. Broom, and L. S. Cottrell, Jr. (eds.), *Sociology Today,* Basic Books, 1959, pp. 153–177; W. J. Goode, *Religion Among the Primitives,* Free Press, 1951; T. F. Hoult, *The Sociology of Religion,* Dryden, 1958; Clifford Kirkpatrick, *Religion in Human Affairs,* Wiley, 1929; E. K. Nottingham, *Religion and Society,* Doubleday, 1954; D. J. Pittman, "The Sociology of Religion," in J. B. Gittler (ed.), *Review of Sociology,* Wiley, 1957, pp. 546–558; A. L.

W. H. Clark, G. A. Coe, L. W. Grensted, P. E. Johnson, J. B. Pratt, Orlo Strunk, Jr., and R. H. Thouless.[2]

Religion as one of man's social institutions refers to ideas, aims, activities, and experiences which have become stabilized from generation to generation. Religion as recorded in literature is the most ancient of the storehouses of human lore and learning. From prehistory to the present, man has faced crises of life and death which have turned him periodically to religion. What he has been able to unravel or invent about its mysteries have been so meaningful to him that for centuries the words Bible and book were synonymous. Religion has long been taught as history, literature and philosophy, or simply as the revealed word of God which needed no intellectual justification for its acceptance.

Upon this paternalistic scene religion as a field for study in social science makes its appearance. The youthful presumption of such a contender is an affront to traditional guardians of religious truth. At the same time, other fields of social science which have only recently freed themselves from the intellectual entanglements of religion feel apprehensive if religion again becomes an intruder in the family of sciences. Still, reality is of one piece, from the innermost recesses of the human mind to the outermost reaches of space. Whatever can be experienced, recorded, and verified as data provides building material for the architects of science. If the data of religion are susceptible to common observation and report, they too must yield to science.

In philosophy one finds increasing recognition that the study of religion must become a science. A Quaker writer, D. E. Trueblood, comments in *Philosophy of Religion,* a work which marks the culmination of his preceding writings: "Fortunately, scientific method is not limited to the method of experimentation or to any laboratory technique. Instead, it is a way of facing the relevant evidence, whatever that may be. This is why the spirit of science can be applied to religious inquiry. It is not a perfect

---

Swift, Jr., *New Frontiers of Religion,* Macmillan, 1938; Joachim Wach, *Sociology of Religion,* University of Chicago Press, 1944; J. M. Yinger, *Religion, Society and the Individual,* Macmillan, 1957. Pending publication by the Free Press is a book of readings edited by C. Y. Glock.

[2] W. H. Clark, *The Psychology of Religion,* Macmillan, 1958; G. A. Coe, *The Psychology of Religion,* University of Chicago Press, 1916; L. W. Grensted, *The Psychology of Religion,* Oxford University Press, 1952; P. E. Johnson, *Psychology of Religion,* Abingdon, 1959; J. B. Pratt, *The Religious Consciousness,* Macmillan, 1920; Orlo Strunk, Jr. (ed.), *Readings in the Psychology of Religion,* Abingdon, 1959; R. H. Thouless, *Introduction to the Psychology of Religion,* Macmillan, 1923.

method, and it can never give us the kind of certainty which we find within a mathematical system, but we are satisfied with what we have."[3]

In considerable measure the study of religion as a science has become established. The ethnological studies of anthropology have delineated ideas and values which guide the mind of primitive and modern man. Sociologists, pursuing the strands of social structure, have found these frequently end in the ideological anchors of religion. Freud has examined the doctrines of dogmatic religion from a scientific standpoint and denied that these have scientific validity, an opinion not necessarily relevant for all systems of religion. Freud could not avoid the requirement for the category of the superego, and he acknowledged that what man needs fundamentally is the love of his associates. The voice of conscience and the brotherhood of man which he recognized in his cure of the sick have a familiar ring in the religions of mankind. These are compelling value systems from which even the atheist cannot escape and remain a normal human being.

The intellectual onslaughts of Feuerbach, Tylor, Frazer, Leuba, and Freud upon the traditional dogmas of religion have not made religious-minded persons receptive to the scientific study of religion. In historical retrospect, one can understand how it happened that the critics of religion were the first to enlist scientific tools of inquiry in religious study. Religionists, secure in Olympian aloofness, had no need of the gadgets of science to bolster their faith. The means of sculpture for those who sought to refashion the traditional role of religion were the novel techniques of observation, analysis, and verification developed by scientists. Moreover, those inquiring as scientists were in a position to discover flaws not recognized by self-assured religionists.

The contribution of scientific studies of religion has been preponderantly a positive one. A dean of American sociologists, Talcott Parsons, writes of this contribution:

> In a society where the academic disciplines are perhaps more secularized than the rest of society, there has, as a result of scientific study of religion and society in these disciplines and in history and anthropology, emerged an overwhelming impression of the fundamental importance of religion in human affairs. Like the historian, the sociologist can now say unequivocally that the fairly recent popular positivistic view that religion was essentially grounded in the ignorance and superstition of a prescientific age, and could be expected rapidly to disappear in our era, is definitely in error. The proponent

[3] D. E. Trueblood, *Philosophy of Religion,* Harper, 1957, p. 66.

of this view is the victim of his own ignorance and counter-superstition. True, *many specific features* of historic religions are related to a low level of scientific development and could not persist in a scientific age. But this is not true of the fundamental significance of religion.[4]

If early social scientists unevenly cleared the ground upon which foundations of religion as a scientific study were to be built, this does not belittle the edifice eventually to rise. If religionists do not approve of the structure taking shape, it seems more useful for them to take up the tools of scientific masons and share in the construction than to retreat and deny that the building exists.

The author's opinion is that some of the central concepts and principles of Christianity and other world religions become floors and walls in the new structure. Although fashioned long ago when science was unknown in name, nevertheless these ideas often represent results gained from observing and analyzing the processes and experiences of life. Unless they had been cast in molds conforming to realities experienced, they could not have withstood the millennial erosion of doubt and disagreement. Religious prophets have been social and psychological prescientists in much of what they discovered and recorded. To correct their errors makes more serviceable their truths, which stand all the stronger if supported by scientific inquiry.

It may seem strange to consider God as a scientific concept in psychology, a being unapproachable to many religionists and unidentifiable to many scientists. This fundamental category of human thought and experience requires reconsideration from the standpoint of the data in which it is rooted. Notwithstanding the scientific erasure of theological beings by antagonists in philosophy and science, America has been undergoing its largest religious revival in history under the leadership of Billy Graham. He addresses, not a crowd of uneducated frontiersmen, but a college generation exposed to many years of scientific sophistication. They find, not assume, Christ in their lives. What is the experience to which they refer?

John Dewey found the basis for God in human ideals. William James pointed to man's higher self as the empirical beginning of man's idea of God. If this idea refers to data in man's inward experience, it belongs in the realm of psychological and social science with respect to its verifiable aspects. A French sociologist, Emile Durkheim, following W. Robertson Smith, a Scottish

[4] Talcott Parsons, "Sociology and Social Psychology," in H. N. Fairchild (ed.), *Religious Perspectives in College Teaching,* Ronald, 1952, p. 335.

Biblical scholar, examined the social basis for man's experience of God. His findings not carefully qualified, Durkheim has often been ignored as an analyst of religion by social scientists who considered his work inadequate and by the religiously orthodox who regarded it as profane. The task of scientific explanation for the prevalence of theistic belief is one which recurs. The Swiss psychiatrist Carl G. Jung has concluded from his case studies that an autonomous complex functioning in human personality gives man his experience of God. A recent contributor on the scene of the scientific study of religion is P. A. Sorokin, whose studies of altruism provide a turning point in the subject matter of sociological inquiry.

Religious ideas also rise above the planes of science by the pathways of philosophy. When these ideas go beyond what science can show by empirical methods, science cannot pursue the answers. The limit where science must cease is the lower boundary where philosophy begins. The questions of immortality and the nature of God outside human experience are meaningful ones to which philosophers address themselves, the human mind insisting upon probing the implications of such questions.

We must recognize that these questions are outside the scope of religion as a social science, except as the latter records descriptively that man does have such questions to which he gives intelligent though speculative answers, and that these answers play a meaningful part in his social and personal existence. It is part of the task of empirical study of culture to record the prevailing philosophies which human beings hold. These systems of ideas are important ingredients of religion. The effort is made here to describe these features without facing the philosophical issues of their validity, it not being a purpose of the writer to become involved in philosophical inquiry outside of the methodology of science.

In this text we develop the theme of Robertson Smith and Durkheim that social experience is the ground of religion. In social science the task of religious study is twofold: (1) to compile a cultural record of religious activities, beliefs, and motivations, and (2) to analyze the inner workings of religion in human personality and group life, what religion is, what it does, and why man is a religion-building animal. In the plan of this book these two topics are considered together. Cultural data require theory for their interpretation, and theory requires data for its demonstration and proper qualification.

The description of religion is restricted to the Western world in the twentieth century, specifically the scene in the United States. To the extent that other cultures are similar, the findings may have broader application. The author speaks of religion as he sees it in the land where he lives, since what is nearer is clearer to him. He does not minimize the great currents of religion elsewhere, many of which have reached the shores of America to the enrichment of its life. Occasional reference is made to religions of American Indians.

Religion is primarily important to people because of its involvement in their thoughts, goals, and feelings. An understanding of religious processes therefore requires more interpretation than other topics of social science. This text is intended to be a work of interpretation of religious motives and ideas in ways in harmony with empirical data.

Much of the material presented is in the nature of theory only partly tested by scientific study and requiring further research. It seems best to offer interpretations, rather than nothing, even though these are not fully substantiated. Where scientific work has not yet assembled its data, the individual may find it useful to refer to facts from his own social experience or to facts reported by his cultural heritage. Such facts have their limitations, but they may be more useful than no data at all.

A piece of writing, if successful, is no more than a transitional stage in human understanding along the pathways of scientific progress. There never can be finality in the movement toward scientific perfection. Whenever humanity allows itself to rest lazily on its intellectual oars, it may be swept backward by the eddies into the swamp of unknowing from which it emerged in the past. Each generation must regain for itself the essential insights of mankind, for the most which the preceding generation can bequeath are mute volumes in library stacks. Knowledge does not spring from the printed page, but only comes to life through active and persistent exercise of reflective abilities aided by eagerness for experience. The cutting edge of these abilities is kept sharp by the quest to go beyond the preceding generation. The flame of man's desire for more abundant understanding must perpetually burn.

No culture in the world today has a monopoly on truth. The insights given to human beings in different lands emerge from social experience and mental equipment shared by all human beings. But the tongues they speak are diverse, and it becomes necessary to probe the choice of words to the experiential meaning which underlies verbal variation and is a common possession of the peoples of the earth. The attitude expressed in the following is appropriate: "God speaks to man in many tongues, and all of them are tongues of fire."

The task of assigning credit to others for ideas which they have formulated is one which requires extensive survey of their writings. As cultural streams move forward, ideas whose appearance is imminent may appear simultaneously in the writings of two or more thinkers. Parallel developments may take place within cultures at opposite sides of the globe. Limitation of time available for scholarly survey has restricted the author primarily to writers who speak from or to those living in contemporary American culture. The historical search for who thought of what first may satisfy little more than idle curiosity. More is learned by rediscovering in experience the insights open to humanity than by exhaustively combing the libraries of history as clerks or scribes. The former effort gives creative understanding, while the latter effort, if it goes beyond maintaining normal continuity with the past, dissipates itself in endless clerical labor and gives no more than a pale reflection of genuine understanding. The reader of this text may find too much intrusion of particular authorities to make the material as understandable as it might be. Religious study is in process of establishing itself as a social and psychological science, and during this process the diverse intellectual roots should be traced where possible. Still, what seems of more importance than giving a full exposition of the authorities in the past, except as these speak to the present, is to deal adequately with those who are spokesmen for the contemporary generation. A distinctive generation of scientific students of religion have made their appearance on the scene of world history. Their views, whether completely valid or not, are revelatory of the nature of contemporary culture.

The student who disagrees with a prevailing view in social science is encouraged to continue his search. He may unearth new facts or insights which will serve mankind more securely tomorrow. Yet it remains his task to become familiar with various theories which are found in social science today. Excerpts from writings of social scientists, including psychologists and psychoanalysts, are introduced at intervals in this text to give their ideas and conclusions a more authentic flavor. Preceding each section of chapters are brief pictures of American religion. These contribute perspective for chapters which follow and confront the student with data requiring explanation or interpretation. They provide a series of facets of American religious culture not otherwise encompassed by the textual presentation. The works from which quotations are taken contain more extended materials useful for collateral reading. Where innovations are made it is important to begin with concepts and principles already articulated since these are conceptual tools shared in common with others. Beyond knowing what these are, how the student makes up his mind is no one's prerogative besides his own.

part I Scientific Study of Religion

NATIVE AND CONTEMPORARY RELIGIONS

Crow Indian

At the time of the great Sun festival brave men—and only such—were entertained with that prized delicacy, buffalo tongues. Warriors about to raid a hostile camp would go to Sore-tail for instructions, and when they returned laden with spoils, the choicest of the booty went to Sore-tail's lodge till he ranked as the wealthiest Crow within the memory of man. Why had he become rich while Small-back remained horseless except for the little nag a generous brave had in sheer pity donated to him? Why was Bell-rock the greatest of all chiefs and Yellow-crane rated a good-for-nothing poltroon? The young man knew, for from a boy he had had the answer dinned into his ears: to become great, to make sure of success in any of life's critical situations, one must gain the blessing of some supernatural power. A few favored persons were lucky enough to be visited by the spirits in their sleep or in some other way that involved no effort; but the majority had to earn their vision through pain and hardship. The ambitious warrior, the mourner filled with the lust for vengeance, the spurned lover, and the youth chafing from a sense of his family's poverty, must mortify their flesh and thus rouse the compassion of the supernatural powers.

The procedure was fairly fixed. A would-be visionary would go to a lonely spot, preferably to the summit of a mountain. Naked except for a breechclout and the buffalo robe to cover him at night, he abstained from food and drink for four days or more if necessary, wailing and invoking the spirits. Usually some form of bodily torture or disfigurement was practised as an offering to the supernatural beings. Most commonly, perhaps, men would hack off a finger joint of the left hand, so that during the period of my visits to the Crow (1907–1916) I saw few old men with left hands intact. The Sun was generally the being supplicated, and the following may serve as an example of a typical prayer:

> Hallo, Old Man, I am poor! You see me, give me something good. Give me long life; grant that I may own a horse, that I capture a gun, that I strike a

> blow against the enemy! Let me become a chief, let me own plenty of property!

But although the Sun was called, he rarely appeared. The actual visitants are occasionally connected with the Sun as his messengers or symbols, but in general they are conceived as in no way related to him. According to a usual pattern, they present themselves in human guise, but before they leave their true nature is revealed, either by the words of their song or their re-transformation or by some special instruction. The visitant adopts the suppliant as his child and proceeds to give him specific directions. If martial glory is sought, the spirit may give a dramatic performance of combat, himself equipped in sharply defined fashion, defying the hostile darts and laying low the enemy. The implication is that if the spirit's newly adopted child shall scrupulously imitate his patron's appearance and follow any special admonitions conveyed to him, he will gain his ends.

An illustration or two of visions actually reported by my informants will make the matter clearer.

When Medicine-crow was a young man, he fasted for four days, offered a finger joint to the Sun, and prayed for horses. A young man and a young woman suddenly came towards him, each holding a hoop with feathers in one hand and a hoop with strawberries in the other. The woman said, "We have come here to let him hear something." While Medicine-crow was wondering what she had in mind, her companion went to the other side of the ridge and soon reappeared, driving a herd of horses. The woman followed suit, also returning with horses. Both wore crowns of a certain kind. One of them said, "I have shown you all these horses. I am the sacred Tobacco. I want you to join the Tobacco society with these crowns." The young woman told him not to allow guns at the tobacco planting.

As a result of this experience, Medicine-crow not only came to own a great many horses but also founded a new chapter of the great ceremonial organization known as the Tobacco society, making all his followers wear such crowns as had been revealed to him and forbidding the use of firearms in connection with the ritual.

While Medicine-crow's experience is typical of communications that lead to ceremonial prominence and wealth, that of Scratches-face represents a popular form of war vision. He, too, fasted and cut off a finger joint, which he offered to a mythical character called Old-woman's-grandson, who is sometimes identified with the Morning-star. This was the prayer uttered on this occasion:

> Old-woman's-grandson, I give you this (joint), give me something good in exchange . . . I am poor, give me a good horse. I want to strike one of the enemies and . . . I want to marry a good-natured woman. I want a tent of my own to live in.

After his sacrifice he heard footsteps but could not see anyone. He fell asleep and heard a voice: "What are you doing? You wanted him to come. Now he has come." Then he saw six men riding horses, one of them seated on a bobtail, and this one said, "You have been poor, so I'll give you what you want . . . I am going to run." The trees around there suddenly turned into enemies and began to shoot at the horsemen, who rode away but returned unscathed. The rider of the bobtail said to Scratches-face, "If you want to fight all the people on the earth, do as I do, and you will be able to fight for three or four days and yet not be shot." The horsemen began to ride east. . . . The enemies attacked them once more, but the rider of the bobtail knocked them down with a spear. A storm came up (explained as the Thunder), and hailstones big as a fist knocked down the enemies.

In consequence of his blessing Scratches-face struck and killed an enemy without ever getting wounded. He also obtained horses and married a good-tempered and industrious woman.[1]

Urban Protestant

On a shaded street in an area of homes will be found the typical church. The building, whether of early or recent date, never seems exactly adequate for the demands which are made upon it; the stage in the recreation room was built without rear exits, the Sunday school classrooms, while separated from one another by partitions, are not soundproof, the acoustics in the auditorium are poor, the ladies' parlor is badly in need of redecorating. Yet in spite of its deficiencies and the somewhat musty odor which characterizes the basement dining-room it is a familiar and beloved structure in which its people feel at home. The governing board has its quota of interesting personalities: the cautious member who is sure that discretion is the better part of valor, the man who prides himself on saying exactly what he thinks, "even to the pastor himself," the vivacious woman who always has some contribution, more or less valuable, to make to the discussion, the plain hard-working men and women who say little but carry their assignment of responsibilities faithfully.

The church school, which meets at half-past nine each Sunday morning preceding the church service, is divided along the conventional lines for beginners, primaries, juniors, intermediates, and seniors, with one or two adult classes meeting simultaneously. The opening exercises for all from the intermediates up may be enlivened by an orchestra, and rousing hymns are sung under the supervision of a leader, the quality of whose voice does not reach the high pitch of his enthusiasm. The teaching staff is never entirely satisfactory to the church school board, in spite of intermittent efforts at teacher training. It is difficult to induce capable persons to accept classes, and it is equally difficult to secure tactfully the resignations of inept teachers. So the staff is a motley group, with members ranging from timid young girls who have been persuaded that it "isn't hard to teach primary children" to a benevolently firm elderly gentleman who conducts the adult mixed class through the mysteries of Job and Daniel. There are winsome children who speak pieces on Children's day; there are bad and troublesome junior boys who solve the school's discipline problem by drifting away during the intermediate age (some of these are recaptured in the Boy Scout troop, which flourishes under the leadership of a serious young college student); there are senior boys and girls developing an interest in each other and romance.

The young people's society is the pride of the minister's heart, for he has worked hard to create and strengthen it. The church board is distressed, however, by the fact that the young people do not stay after their meeting for the evening service, but instead drive off in the family cars, perhaps for petting parties. Nevertheless, they are a loyal crowd and will undertake almost any job the minister requests of them. A prob-

[1] Reprinted from *Primitive Religion* by R. H. Lowie, pp. 3–6, by permission of Liveright, Publishers, N.Y. Copyright (R) 1952, Robert H. Lowie.

lem is created by a few of the members who do not realize that they are no longer young people and who annoy the latter by attending their meetings and attempting to assume leadership.

The women's auxiliary is the liveliest organization in the church, holding general meetings twice a month and social or sewing meetings for subgroups at least once a month. The president is determined to make the general sessions "educational" and persuades local and city leaders to address the women. The most important function of the society, if one would judge not by statement of purpose but by practice, is financial, and the church dinners and banquets which are prepared not only furnish the occasion for much sociability among the women but also swell their contributions to pay off the church debt. There are petty feuds and personal quarrels among them at times, but in crisis situations they pull together and give an assuring aspect of solidarity to the church. It is a matter of comment that fewer men attend services than women. An effort to interest more men in the church has resulted in the establishment of a men's club, which holds meetings spasmodically. These are moderately successful, but it is noticeable that on "ladies' nights" the attendance of men is much greater.

The worship service on Sunday mornings is a semi-dignified occasion. The sanctuary is not particularly conducive to a spirit of reverence; it is essentially an auditorium, with bright direct lighting and large colored windows conspicuously dedicated to the memory of deceased benefactors. There is a general rustling and whispering as members enter, greet their friends and impart bits of information to their neighbors a pew or two forward. This is covered fairly well by the organ music, but is disconcerting when the organist pauses between selections. A last-minute announcement of the foreign missionary meeting is handed to the minister during the singing of the first hymn and is included by him in the announcement period, which effectively breaks the unity of the service. The volunteer choir sings an anthem with a pleasing degree of accuracy and feeling, and an offertory solo is executed by the favorite soprano. The sermon is rather long and its outline is somewhat vague; but the preacher has lived earnestly and suffered deeply, and his illustrations bring salutary tears to the eyes of his listeners. Many thank him with evident sincerity at the close, and go home from this effective though technically imperfect service with a determination to lead more Christlike lives. The typical church. One is sometimes alarmed that it accomplishes so little, and again amazed that it contributes so much to the lives and souls of people.[2]

The objectives of the church as listed by various ministers include the following:

> The true understanding that the church is the body of Christ through which by the word and sacraments, as the means of grace, men, women, and children are to be brought into saving relationship with him and through which it is his purpose to usher in his kingdom. . . .
>
> To maintain a warm and effective evangelistic program; to use the best educational methods; to reach, hold, and train youth in

[2] Reprinted from *City and Church in Transition* by M. H. Leiffer, pp. 158–161, by permission of Harper & Brothers. Copyright by Harper & Brothers.

Christlike attitudes; to devise means by which religious enthusiasm may express itself in action. . . .

To break down denominational barriers and serve the whole community; to be of service to all in special times of need.

Conserve the youth of this section of the city. Develop Christian character which applies itself to individual and social problems. A major emphasis this month on (1) personal adequacy, (2) world peace.[3]

These two descriptions, one an instance of native American Indian religion, the other of contemporary religion as imported and modified by white migrants from European nations, suggest the large range and variety of manifestations of religion throughout the world. While the pattern of religion interwoven with the cultural fabric varies endlessly from culture area to culture area, common strands are found running through the entire tableau. The needs of people which prompt them to religion are universal. The drives for success, for economic well-being, for good luck, for happiness, for salvation in its broadest sense, transcend the coördinates of time and place. That the Crow Indians seek these things through visions of supernatural powers and the middle-class American through his neighborhood church, are individual variations in religious expression.

Can religion be studied scientifically? Is this not a contradiction in terms? Religion, suffused with sentiment and dogma, seems the opposite of science. There is a question of what science can and what it cannot study. In what sense, if any, can science study theological or supernatural beliefs?

The techniques whereby science proceeds require examination. How sound are the findings of social scientists about religion? Disagreement exists in social science, even as among people generally. Where scientists disagree in their results, they then review their methods. The validity of findings in social science about religion rests upon the soundness of the methods of inquiry employed. To appraise the findings, the methods need to be weighed.

In no other phase of human life and religion does it seem more essential that scientific investigators follow carefully prescribed methods, since nowhere else is truth so vulnerable to prejudice and emotion. Those who presume to use the name of science in defending their assertions about religion must be very clear as to their meaning of what the word *science* means. So strong is the tendency toward dogmatism in this area that those who speak have a special obligation to establish the scientific character of their work.

Texts in social, as well as physical, science give increasing attention to steps of procedure for obtaining scientific results. Our initial topic in Part I is to consider where and how social, including psychological, science may proceed in its study of religion.

[3] *Ibid.*, pp. 162–164.

chapter 2 Science and the Supernatural

Man's Interest in the Supernatural

Human beings in every culture have been intrigued by fathoming the mysteries of the supernatural side of life. Man's span of life experience carries him up to the point of death, when all suddenly ceases. Animation goes out of the body, which lies an inert mass wherever it is placed. Decomposition rapidly sets in. For reasons of human sensibility the body must be buried or burned. Life goes out with the abruptness of a candle flame extinguished in the darkness.

Man's experience tells him what life is like. He knows from experience the hard facts, as well as the delights of his earthly existence. But nothing in this experience can tell him what death is like. Is it a state of nothing, of nonbeing? Is the journey of life continued elsewhere in the space-time continuum? Are human beings compensated for what they have lost, or penalized for what they have taken from others? No man has ever gone to the land of the dead and returned with a report which others can verify. Houdini, the master magician, left $10,000 for any one who could communicate with his spirit after death. There have been no takers of that reward.

As a moving picture is broken in the middle of a dramatic plot, so death takes human beings wherever they are, whatever they are doing, at work, at play, in their sleep or in their old age. Disgruntled spectators coming home from a movie whose ending they could not witness feel powerfully impelled to speculate how the play ended. So it is with death. The curiosity of human beings demands that they know what lies beyond this life. They cast their reasoning powers again and again against the citadel of the supernatural, seeking to see through the veil of death.

Man's experience carries him up to the present instant of time. What lies beyond the present moment of time? Will Richard be successful in his courtship of Marianne? Will he pass the bar examinations? Will he earn a secure living in his new job? Man must wait and see.

History slowly unfolds. Since World War II the world has hovered between peace and war. Which way will the balance swing? Is there ultimate hope for lasting peace? Is progress the destiny of mankind? With the aid of scientific observation and prediction man looks into the future of the history of the race. After his powers of observation and analysis are exhausted, what then? Man taxes his imagination when his empirical faculties fail.

Man looks backward from whence he came. Science has found that before man were lower species of animals, before these were spineless worms, before these, a sea of slime, before the sea, an incandescent planet, before incandescence, darkness, before darkness, what? The infinity of the past and the infinity of the future are riddles beyond the ability of the scientific mind. Someday science may solve these riddles. Short of that day man still demands answers.

Man looks at his puny mind and wonders whether the universe contains other minds greater than his. If so, such other minds may know and control the universe. They may be its first cause. They may contain the destiny of the future. If there is a cosmic mind, perhaps it is benevolent. Man would like to think that an all-powerful mind is benevolent toward him, that God protects man in life, preserves him in death, gathering him into His arms for an eternity of bliss after the struggle and strife of life have ceased. The great questions of death, destiny, and divinity are problems of the supernatural about which man feels he must know.

With the advance of orderly science, man's interest in the supernatural has waned but not disappeared. Science has pushed the frontiers of knowledge far back in the past and far ahead in the future, but beyond the fringe of knowledge is an unknown area. Does this area of the infinite dissolve in a cosmic mind? The stark facts of death are as inscrutable now that the average length of life is seventy as when that length was seventeen among people in a Stone Age of development. Does life after death bring one into unity with divinity? Sacred theologies are insistent with their answers. Millions believe supernatural beliefs with an emotional intensity which science could hardly dislodge even had it the facts for such refutation, which frequently it does not have.

Even the flow of events, often capricious, which man does experience does not satisfy his intellectual craving. He cannot understand the capriciousness of misfortune. Especially when events bring disaster as their consequence, does man seek to foresee or to escape by a supernatural route. If he takes a new job on Friday, will he fail? If he carries a left-hind foot of a rabbit, will it protect him from the malevolence of fate? If he opens a letter with a strong enough will for good news, can it contain anything else? Man thinks of lifting his arm, and the thought controls the blob of protoplasm which is his arm. Does the mind have any other control over matter? If faith is great enough, can it move a mountain? Thus man's imaginative faculties inject a supernatural element directly into the humdrum existence of daily life, man seeking through magic to set aside the immutable laws of nature. Must these work their inexorable outcome, or can man by supernatural practices prevent that outcome?

THE SUPERNATURAL WHICH FALLS OUTSIDE EXPERIENCE

In the past ten generations science has risen to great prominence and now dominates the cultural scene. Eagerly students interested in the supernatural side turn to science, thinking that its tools are now available for unraveling the absorbing questions of death, destiny, and divinity. They hope they will get the "lowdown" on spiritualism, "the scientific line" on Christianity, indeed answers to all of the questions on their list of life's important matters.

To avoid disappointing those who turn to science for an oracular instrument to divine the supernatural, let it be said at the outset in this scientific inquiry into religion that science can go so far and no farther. When we analyze more carefully what we mean when we use the word *supernatural,* we find that science and the supernatural are for the most part two exclusive categories, and the one often can tell us little or nothing about the other.

Sociologists, anthropologists, and others studying human culture have found in the progress of their research that they must define what they mean by the word *supernatural.* Many of the beliefs interwoven in the cultural fabric are beliefs about supernatural phenomena. The scientific task of studying what is believed has pushed scientists to the point of defining what lies outside of science, namely the supernatural.

In meaning the word signifies above or beyond the natural. What is the natural world? It is the world conforming to orderly laws which can be studied and repeatedly verified by common experience. This definition of the natural realm permits one to distinguish several senses in which the concept of the supernatural is used, senses which are not entirely separate but which refer to various kinds of nonnatural events.

One definition ascribed to *supernatural* is in the sense of what exists outside of human experience altogether. What happens to the personal thread of existence after death is a supernatural matter. Perhaps nothing happens, in which case there is no supernatural existence of the soul, but at least the possible category can be defined.

Those who believe there to be a vast cosmic mind extending outside the narrow confines of our experience also have a supernatural belief of something outside human experience. The commonly accepted view of God's infinite qualities outside our experience is a belief about a supernatural reality.

Science rests upon data which can be verified by any properly trained observer. This means data grounded in experience and conclusions closely reasoned from these data. The supernatural by definition is a category of reality outside human experience. If the reality is outside, the scientific instruments for probing experience are as useless as a plow at the polar regions. They simply do not apply. They cannot even start an analysis except where data are given by experience. If there are no data, there can be no science.

Role of Philosophy in Religious Study

Science with its empirical starting point has nothing to say about the truth or falsity of supernatural beliefs outside the compass of experience. They may or may not be correct. They refer to a reality which, if it exists, is as remote as the far side of the universe, and disputes about it have no place in science, belonging rather to philosophy.

Philosophy seeks plausible answers where science cannot yield them. Is it more reasonable to believe that human consciousness continues after death in another plane, or that it does not continue? Some philosophy argues that an event that has happened once is more likely to occur again than not to occur again. Having lived once, the individual is more likely to live again in the unfolding processes of the universe than not to do so.

Is it more reasonable to believe that a cosmic mind is the central force and guiding principle of the universe, or that no such mind exists? The affirmation of the existence of a God outside the empirical world is more than a childlike fancy. It is a conclusion of scholars who carefully reason that in no other way can an intelligible explanation of the complexity and harmony of the universe be given. If one were traveling in a dense forest and came upon a house and garden, one might reasonably infer that a mind was somewhere about. In the same way, the travels of science through the universe strongly suggest that somewhere there is a creative mind at work. What is seen seems to be the product of a mind rather than the product of impersonal laws of chance. The comments of the psychologist William James are of interest in relation to the possibility of a supernatural world. "I *can,* of course, put myself into the sectarian scientist's attitude, and imagine vividly that the world of sensations and of scientific laws and objects may be all. But whenever I do this, I hear that inward monitor of which W. K. Clifford once wrote, whispering the word 'bosh!' Humbug is humbug, even though it bear the scientific name, and the total expression of human experience, as I view it objectively, invincibly urges me beyond the narrow 'scientific' bounds."[1]

Other philosophers come to different conclusions. The point to be made here is simply that philosophizing is intellectually respectable, indeed a highly exacting discipline of the mind, even if it directs its attention to the possibility of realities outside of the domain of science. It is philosophy, rather than science, to which one turns in seeking answers about phenomena which are supernatural in the sense of what may exist outside of present-day human experience.

RELIGIOUS REVELATION

Another use of the concept *supernatural* is concerned with what is experienced by a privileged few but not by all. The qualities often imputed to religious revelation fall under this heading of the supernatural. We read of Moses and the burning bush:

Now Moses was keeping the flock of his father-in-law, Jethro, the priest of Midian; and he led his flock to the west side of the wilder-

[1] William James, *The Varieties of Religious Experience,* Modern Library, 1936, p. 509. Permission to reprint granted by Paul R. Reynolds & Son, 599 Fifth Avenue, New York, N.Y.

ness, and came to Horeb, the mountain of God. And the angel of the Lord appeared to him in a flame of fire out of the midst of a bush; and he looked, and lo, the bush was burning, yet it was not consumed. And Moses said, "I will turn aside and see this great sight, why the bush is not burnt." When the Lord saw that he turned aside to see, God called to him out of the bush, "Moses, Moses!" And he said, "Here I am." Then he said, "Do not come near; put off your shoes from your feet, for the place on which you are standing is holy ground." And he said, "I am the God of your father, the God of Abraham, the God of Isaac, and the God of Jacob." And Moses hid his face, for he was afraid to look at God.[2]

Again, we read in the New Testament of Paul's conversion:

"As I made my journey and drew near to Damascus, about noon a great light from heaven suddenly shone about me. And I fell to the ground and heard a voice saying to me, 'Saul, Saul, why do you persecute me?' And I answered, 'Who are you, Lord?' And he said to me, 'I am Jesus of Nazareth whom you are persecuting.' Now those who were with me saw the light but did not hear the voice of the one who was speaking to me. And I said, 'What shall I do, Lord?' And the Lord said to me, 'Rise, and go into Damascus, and there you will be told all that is appointed for you to do.' And when I could not see because of the brightness of that light, I was led by the hand of those who were with me, and came into Damascus."[3]

These are supernatural events in the experience of special persons. The ordinary individual may have been present, but could not see or feel what was uniquely revealed to Moses or to Paul. Religious revelations of a private character fall under this heading of the supernatural, although the term *revelation* may also refer to what the ongoing collective experience of mankind discloses.

That modern man is also prone to visions is shown by a mimeographed communication which came to the author a few years ago from a faith healer.

The year of 1949, 6 A.M., February 23, 1949, I, Avak, was in bed and the following vision was revealed to me:

A map was drawn on the sky approximately twenty feet wide and twenty feet long. Upon this sight, I recognized it as the map of the United States of America, the name of which was written across it in large letters. At the same time, another map was drawn with every detail and written in large letters, it said, "Moscow, Russia." Then followed another map, upon which was written, "Berlin," in dark letters.

[2] Exodus 3:1–6. All Biblical references are to *The Holy Bible,* Revised Standard Version, Nelson, 1952.

[3] Acts 22:6–11.

Another appeared quite near to Russia, but closer attached to the United States, and upon this map was written, "South America." After this followed a map of England, near to the United States. Then many other small maps appeared all around the large maps without names on them, so I didn't know what countries were represented.

After seeing these maps, a voice came to me from Heaven saying, "Look at these maps and watch very carefully and see what is going to happen." While I was studying and marveling the great drawings, I noticed the moon as it traveled on its regular route. It was suddenly snatched and placed under those maps, between Heaven and Earth. Then suddenly it lost its brightness and became dark all over. While I was amazed at that sight, there appeared the gleaming sun, which was just about to set in the horizon. The sun also was snatched as the moon, and was placed under those maps as though it were suspended between Heaven and Earth. Then suddenly the bright sun lost its shine and changed to a blood-red color; it burst into flames and those flames poured upon the Earth.

The same voice that spoke to me before said again, "Did you observe what was happening?" Then, "The whole world will burst into flame without notice," the voice said.

At that time there appeared streets with people holding copies of those same maps and they were distributing them among themselves and talking about the happening event. Two persons were standing by me and I asked them to go and get some of these maps and distribute them among the people. Just as they started to go, I stopped them first to ask permission from God. As in a reply, the same voice said, "You have my permission to go and execute."

The above revelation is absolutely the truth and I feel it is my duty to tell everyone. This is the will of God and has to be fulfilled. There is no other way to prevent this, but to pray and repent.[4]

What can science say about these special experiences? If they have no natural causes which can be scientifically controlled, they are not verifiable by repeated observation. Science rests not only upon experience, but upon those features of experience which can be verified again and again by trained observers. It can be argued that past revelations of religious history therefore are outside the domain of scientific observation and study. As to the plausibility of these, one may turn to philosophy and religious history. Intellectual effort is expended in theological schools in assessing the plausibility of various revelations reported in history. If there is a cosmic mind, would that cosmic mind reach into the consciousness of human leaders and tell them the plan of the universe?

[4] Mimeographed circular, March 3, 1949, received by the author from K. Chaachou, Miami Beach, Florida.

Another view is that science knows enough concerning human motivation and experience to determine whether religious revelations are in point of fact experiences produced by natural causes in personality and environment. People have dreams and visions whose occurrence is explicable in terms of laws of psychology, an occurrence theoretically duplicable if the proper social and psychological conditions are present. Mystical experience may be explained in terms of the conditioning of the religious seer. Moses, brooding over the desperate condition of his people, or Paul, torn by inner conflict and suffering a nervous disorder, might react with psychological violence and experience visions. The occurrence of these is a stable psychological fact apart from the validity of the ideas implanted during them.

An interesting point of philosophy arises in connection with the scientific explanation of the visions of religious prophets. Even if it is assumed that their revelations are scientifically explained as products of psychological conditioning, the philosopher may still reason that a cosmic mind chose the medium of an exceptional mind to reveal its will to mankind. This would be otherworldliness integrated into the framework of natural laws.

In contrast to concepts of religious revelation as supernatural or abnormal is the concept of this as a natural, normal phenomenon. There is a view in Judaism which regards revelations to prophets as not having a privileged character, but rather as being products of intuition through which God reveals his will to a well-disposed and well-schooled individual. A corresponding view in Christianity considers the experience of Christ's spirit to be one which any human being with faith in the power of that spirit may have. In this more general sense, the content of religious experience falls entirely in the domain of verifiable phenomena. The science of psychology can explore, analyze, and determine the laws to which such religious experiences conform, in which case these experiences are not properly called supernatural.

MAGIC

A third sense in which the term *supernatural* finds application in the study of human belief is in connection with magic, a fallacious procedure for arresting or altering what people expect to be the usual course of events. People who practice magic believe, of course, that it will or might work. Are you dying of incurable cancer? The specialist in magic will utter spells or administer potions to facilitate recovery. Such magic has been found to be widespread among nonliterate people surviving in a late Stone Age of development. Curiously enough, magic is even found among supposedly scientific urban dwellers. Get after that cold with a remarkable remedy purchased at the dime counter! The doctor who dispenses pills for an ailment he cannot control is much more appreciated by his patients than the doctor who says he is sorry, he can do nothing. So people take the pills with a firm belief that they will aid recovery. People do not call such procedures magic, but they conform to the definition of magic. Neither does the primitive always distinguish between magic and utilitarian procedures. To him both are effective in bringing about desired results. The imputation of error is a judgment of science.

Magic is one kind of supernatural belief which can be subjected to scientific test. The patent nostrums of the credulous ill among our population are periodically refuted by the careful experiments of laboratory science. However, it is outside the field of social and psychological science to test the truth of physical details of magic, this being left to the physical scientist, if he chooses to say anything about it. Is magic anything more than faulty science? Sometimes the distinction is difficult to discern. Manufacturers of patent medicines may claim scientific authority for the effectiveness of their drugs which actually may do the human body more harm than good. Those who take them may think that they are being scientific. Then again, those who are ill may attach a mysterious potency to their private pills which they are convinced surpass any ordinary remedy of medical science and halt the course of disease in a miraculous manner. Sometimes therapeutic methods, such as faith healing or physical manipulation, possess some soundness, but acquire magical attributes when followers insist that they work for supernatural reasons or that they will cure anything.

The difference is that magical beliefs are not born of cold scientific effort, but rather are products of wishful thinking which ignores systematic inquiry. The medicine man who knows he must cure an epidemic sweeping the tribe mixes his potions with the overpowering feeling that they have to work. In our society the insistence of sick people that they take something which will make them well makes them ready buyers of products which science knows are ineffective. The advertiser does not deceive himself, but finds it easy to mislead a public prone to believe in magic. Therefore magic is not scientific error, but is a program which obstinately sets itself in opposition to science and which may claim greater potency than science itself in overturning the usual laws of life. The error is not one which occurs during the pursuit of science but which arises from deliberate disregard of science. Magic is not simple ignorance, as in the beginnings of science, but it is opposition to the ordinary ways by which experience is understood. It seeks to circumvent the expected order of events. Belief in it appears most readily when the expected order is a matter of chance. There is a disregard of the laws of probability as these apply to unlikely events, rather than of laws which have one hundred percent application. Magical beliefs appear most often when people's desires are intense, as in relation to danger, disease, or death.

Magic is much more common among primitive peoples than modern. Among these the concept of magic as we describe it may be lacking or implicit in the thinking of primitive people. To the primitive both magic and everyday knowledge work. The distinction is one of subtle shadings about which the primitive reflects little although he acts upon magical assumptions. The reality to which "extraordinary" refers may be something "outside" the fixed world of space and time. In this way magical ideas may be blended with ideas of what goes on outside human experience altogether. The prominence of wishful thinking in the face of ordinary results characterizes magic. Moreover, far from being erroneous, primitive magic may be sound, as in the use of correct therapy to cure sickness. But the therapy is part of magic when regarded by its practitioner as an extraordinary procedure which overcomes the expected course of disease, a procedure which contradicts the daily facts of life, rather than extending or integrating them.

It is beyond the scope of this text to review the many intriguing attempts of humans, both ancient and modern, to make magic work. Not only magic, but divination, astrology, spiritualism, shamanism, and witchcraft have a perennial capacity for survival. It is as if human beings recurringly cannot believe that science has properly approached the study of reality, and instead believe that they discover some new channel of heretofore unknown truth. A fascinating description of magic and allied efforts is given by William Howells.[5]

Mana

Somewhat similar to magic is mana, an impersonal power rather than a procedure, widely believed by primitive people to

[5] William Howells, *The Heathens,* Doubleday, 1948.

reside in objects or persons under special circumstances. A. A. Goldenweiser's description illuminates the concept introduced by Codrington. "By means of numerous illustrations, Codrington showed that among the various tribes of the South Seas, mana, as a religious concept, occupies a distinct and clearly defined position; it indicates power which is supernatural and impersonal. Mana itself is not an animal or a human being, nor a ghost or spirit. It is just power, magical potency. Although impersonal in itself, it can work its effects with equal facility through natural objects or beings, or through men, spirits, or ghosts."[6]

A lucky arrow which will find its mark with uncanny accuracy, or a warrior who seems invincible even when outnumbered, are examples of having mana. Such things or persons are gifted with a power which apparently defies ordinary explanation. Something of this concept of mana was attached to Harold "Red" Grange, the galloping ghost of the gridiron a generation ago. He was believed to be unstoppable by tacklers in front of him, capable of breaking loose behind his own goal line for a touchdown run when his team was losing. He was believed by watching crowds to be a man of destiny who could not be overcome. Likewise, the home-town girl who astonishes her neighbors by making good on nation-wide television is thought by them to have mana or something similar to it when they assume that her lucky stars destined her for success over all rivals.

The line between magic and mana is not always clearly evident. In magic, the supernatural power resides in the procedure followed. Anyone who follows the correct formula can make magic work. In mana, only the person or object having the special supernatural power can produce the result. A spirit medium, a sacred feather, or a good-luck charm need not depend upon incantation or formula. They work by their own inward power, by whomever used. How are we to classify a left-hind foot of a rabbit? This is magic, in the sense that one must go through the procedure of carrying a bit of fur for good luck. But it is mana in that this particular piece of rabbit's anatomy has the supernatural power to ward off evil. Magic and mana are further related in that magical procedures may be used to give an object or a person mana. Nor is the line between mana as a supernatural power and mana as a natural psychological power always easily drawn. What is thought by some to be success supernaturally achieved may actually result from the operation of intangi-

[6] A. A. Goldenweiser, *Anthropology,* Crofts, 1946, p. 221.

ble psychological qualities. While the primitive who speaks of mana makes no distinction of this kind, scientific principles of psychology may be involved in the production of unusual results.

Supernatural Intervention

Narrowly defined, mana refers simply to things which are capable of extraordinary effects. In this sense an arrow with mana has no special ingredient or essence apart from its potency in reaching its mark. The primitive mind, like our own, tends to view as an object any relationship which is not fully understandable. It is difficult to convince contemporary persons that ordinary physical force is not a separate substance but merely expresses the relationship between a cause and its effects. Those not physicists often think of electricity as some mysterious substance rather than a relationship of space and motion between particles. Likewise, the primitive who believes in mana is apt to think of this supernatural force as an actual substance or agency which can be created, extracted, or transferred from one thing to another. The commoner who touches a chieftain may gain some mana from him, but at the chieftain's expense. Hence a taboo may prevail keeping commoners and chieftains separate. When mana is thought of as a supernatural essence existing outside and beyond the world of experience, we have a merging of the first and third categories of the supernatural which have been described. Specifically, what is believed is that there is an intervention or intrusion from another world outside of experience, a supernatural one, into this world producing events in experience which contradict the usual laws of causation. A concept which refers to intervention in the physical world by a personal supernatural agency is that of "miracle." A familiar one reported in the Old Testament is Joshua asking God to make the sun stand still until the battle was finished.

"Then spoke Joshua to the Lord in the day when the Lord gave the Amorites over to the men of Israel; and he said in the sight of Israel, 'Sun, stand thou still at Gibeon, and thou Moon in the valley of Aijalon.' And the sun stood still, and the moon stayed, until the nation took vengeance on their enemies. Is this not written in the Book of Jashar? The sun stayed in the midst of heaven, and did not hasten to go down for about a whole day. There has been no day like it before or since, when the Lord hearkened to the voice of a man; for the Lord fought for Israel."[7]

[7] Joshua 10:12–14.

In this episode God intervenes in the ordinary course of physical events and holds the sun still in its course across the heavens or else the earth stopped revolving. Whatever one thinks of the plausibility of such a happening, at least the concept of supernatural intervention as a component of religious belief can be defined. Myths often refer to supernaturally caused events in the past. In another context, a more familiar one, the notion of supernatural intervention persists in the functioning of human personality. Religious revelation in which unusual insights or visions come to the individual, if regarded as supernatural phenomena, implies intervention by something in a world beyond. A common concept of religious worship is that God intervenes in response to prayers to change the life of the individual, giving him fortune or fortitude not explicable by natural psychological laws. This is a merging of the first and second categories of the supernatural.

J. B. Pratt has analyzed the various types of relationship, found in religious beliefs, between the supernatural world outside of experience and the natural world within experience.[8] Besides the direct intervention just described of the supernatural in the realms of physical events and inward experience, a second concept assumes instead a harmonious correspondence between the supernatural and natural worlds. In this view God does not interrupt natural psychological laws, but functions through them. He bears the same relationship to the universe as the human mind does to its body, which is that of a parallelism or functional correspondence between spirit and matter. In this view worship and prayer are understood to take place by natural psychological laws, but they also involve harmony with God's supernatural will. In this sense the supernatural world is an unexperienced extension of the world of natural law. A third concept of the relationship between the supernatural and natural worlds is that the two have no causal connection whatever. If the supernatural exists, it is a world entirely apart from this one. What happens in the natural world has no effect upon it, and vice versa. For all practical purposes the natural world is the only one which exists or is known.

To be distinguished from supernatural views of God, whether of miraculous intervention or simply of functional harmony between God and the universe, is the naturalistic concept of God. In this approach God is considered to be an object experienced

[8] J. B. Pratt, *The Religious Consciousness,* Macmillan, 1956, pp. 37–39, 442–443.

in the natural psychological processes of religion. Such statements as "God is love," "God is the totality of our ideals," "God represents the noblest aspirations of the human race," and "God is altruism," define God as a natural part of human personality and group life. If the terms *love, ideals, aspirations,* and *altruism* are based upon demonstrable psychological data, the God referred to is as much a real part of the world of science as any psychological reality can be. A naturalistic concept of God may be combined in religious thinking with supernatural views of larger aspects of God's nature beyond human experience, aspects which are essentially unexperienced extensions of the natural world of experience.

Magic and Religion

As we have noted, religious beliefs include views of man's origin and destiny on this earth and in life hereafter. Since these views go outside science, they are classed as supernatural. The supernatural enlargement of man's existence is one of the satisfying strands of religion to which man clings tenaciously.

Since religion already has one foot in the realm of the supernatural through philosophical theorizing, it is to be expected that religion frequently takes a hand in magic and mana. Freed from the fetters of empirical reality in one category of the supernatural, the human mind readily roams in categories of the supernatural which conflict with science. The tribal shaman easily combines the functions of practicing magic and communicating with the world of spirits whose aid is sought in performing magic or obtaining mana. Not only is man a species who practices magic or relies on mana, he imputes supernatural powers to spirits or gods whom he believes inhabit his world. These may be propitiated or controlled by the appropriate rites. In such ideas we have a blending of "other-world" and "this-world" supernatural phenomena. The following description of magical beliefs of the Papago Indians of southern Arizona illustrates such beliefs:

> The Desert People believe that sickness and other misfortunes come from offending one of the many supernatural forces which menace humans. From early childhood they are taught what to do and what not to do in order to maintain the right relationships with these forces.
>
> Certain rites must be performed for every individual: if a baby is not taken to a medicine man a month or so after birth, he may fall sick or die. If he does undergo the proper rite, he will be healthy, a good worker, and a swift runner. The girl who does not consult the medicine man at her first menstruation may be consumed by fire and

may bring misfortune to all her relatives. Even some of Presbyterian Papago feel uneasy unless this ceremony is performed.

Dead persons are potential threats to health and good fortune, and care is taken to avoid offending them lest their ghosts return to bring sickness upon their living relations. Until about thirty years ago, the Papago buried their dead in little stone replicas of houses on a hill near each village. Personal property was buried with the corpse—a man's saddles and bridle, his tools and clothing, and any ceremonial paraphernalia he might have; the baskets a woman had made and any favorite possessions; the toys of a child. Food was often interred with the body. Then the house where the death had occurred was torn down, and the name of the dead person was mentioned no more. . . .

All animals are endowed with supernatural power, which they may use to help humans, but, if offended, to send sickness. This possibility, together with the fact that it may be a ghost, makes any animal a potential threat, hence the Papago fear animals and take great care not to offend them. If you imitate the bobwhite's whistle, the Desert People believe, your house will burn down. If rabbit blood touches your body or eyes, you will have sores or become blind. The breath of dogs will bring illness. Some animals are especially dangerous; the wild horse, for example, is associated with evil. Others are dangerous to children. These are only a few instances of widely prevalent animal superstitions.

Humans may escape the wrath of animals through avoidance. Children are taught not to play near gopher holes and to keep their distance from all other wild animals. Even those killed for food are handled as little as possible. But if one must be near animals, he may use magic to protect himself. For example, men who break wild horses take magical precautions against acquiring horse sickness.[9]

Through its historical evolution, religion seems frequently to be woven in one piece with magic, men turning to each for similar reasons. The powers of gods may be magiclike or manalike in nature. This might lead to the mistaken impression that religion and magic are inseparable phenomena, that religion is based only upon magical beliefs produced by wishful thinking.

In Chapter 5, the topic of religion will be circumscribed in a task of definition not undertaken at this point. Yet, with reference to magic, it can be stated in anticipation of later treatment that the beliefs which compose religious ideology may or may not be scientific. Certain religious movements, such as the Ethical Culture Society or Buddhism, are essentially naturalistic in outlook. The approach of Christian Science to neurosis through spiritual therapy has sound scientific basis. Much of the benefit

[9] A. Joseph, R. B. Spicer, and J. Chesky, *The Desert People,* University of Chicago Press, 1949, pp. 77–78.

which Catholics, Protestants, or Jews derive from their religious exercises is practical and demonstrable by means of everyday experience. Magic is no more necessarily mixed with religion than it is with medicine, a branch of knowledge with which it also has been intertwined. It would be a misleading simplification to think of religion and magic as identical categories, and although they may become jointly involved, separation of their concepts should be maintained.

Misuse of the Term Supernatural

Human beings may engage in activities whose results are believed to be supernatural and inexplicable in scientific terms, yet which are actually soundly based upon orderly laws of experience. Quinine was thought by its primitive discoverers to have magical properties, more recently shown by science to be matters of fact.

What are sometimes thought of as privileged religious revelations may actually be duplicable in the experience of other properly disposed and trained individuals. Faith healing is thought of by some as a supernatural matter in which the sciences of medicine or psychology play no part, but sound psychiatric basis for the healing usually exists. "The psychotherapeutic value of the medicine man's rites should not be underrated. When the doctor is thought to have supernatural power and has proved it by curing many patients, a sick man will have confidence that he too will be cured. In any sickness this is half the battle. Government doctors on Indian reservations are coming to see this point and to make use of the medicine man rather than to decry him."[10]

Accordingly, the occasional claim of religion that its beliefs or practices are supernatural may not stand under scientific scrutiny. This is an important point of definition to emphasize. Not all that is called supernatural as the term has been defined here actually is supernatural. It is the privilege of human beings to define terms as they wish. If, however, the definition restricts what science is capable of doing, then the discrepancies in the definition ought to be disclosed.

It would seem a service to human beings if religious lore which has traditionally been called "supernatural" is actually shown to be within the verifiable experience of human beings. For if the lore is found to be demonstrable, not supernatural, this makes it available, not to a fortunate few, but to the great mass of mankind to understand and to employ. Where religious work-

[10] *Ibid.*, p. 80.

ers actually employ sound scientific principles, it is valuable to realize that the effects achieved are not supernatural, but are scientifically verifiable and achievable by all under the appropriate conditions. The practical workings of religion become understood and usable by others not initiated into the mysteries of the religion. Furthermore, the effectiveness of one procedure compared with another can be tested empirically so that the psychological usefulness of the procedure can be maximized.

CAN SCIENCE STUDY RELIGION?

If science has nothing to say about the supernatural realm, how much basis is there for social science to study religion? Shall the tasks of religious inquiry be left to philosophers and theological schools? At this point we should define the province of social science. This province is human behavior and motivation. Shall the social scientist cease his study as soon as this behavior or motivation becomes religious? This does not seem sensible, since the religious phases of society and personality may exercise much influence over other human behavior and motivation, and the secular phases of society and personality may be quite influential in shaping the religious pattern.

Domain of Social Science

Social science, especially sociology and anthropology, sets for itself the study of culture. This concept refers to patterns of behavior, thinking, and desiring learned from other people and the personality growth based upon such learned patterns. Religion is largely learned from other persons, and therefore stands squarely in the domain of social science. What people who profess religion do, think, and desire can be studied by the same empirical methods employed for studying deeds, thoughts, and desires in general.

It may be contended that such scientific study of religion does not reach its vital features. If religion is to be understood primarily through acquaintance with the supernatural, empirical study will accomplish little more than routine description of rituals related to supernatural realities. In advance of empirical study, one cannot assert whether it will or will not be profitable. The scientific hope is to go beyond a cataloguing of rituals and statistics of membership to a disclosure of the real meaning and impact of religion in human life. Religious behavior becomes comprehensible through study of the social beliefs, needs, and feelings of participants, just as political opinion and interest are meaningful in grasping political events.

In recording what people believe, it is appropriate to describe what they believe about supernatural things as well as what they believe about the solid facts of their existence. While the validity of supernatural beliefs may not be tested by science, it still remains an important task of empirical science to describe what these beliefs are. Furthermore, the scientist seeks to go beyond description to the discovery of laws of interaction. The cause-and-effect connection of supernatural beliefs with other facts of social existence, the interplay which goes on between religion and the rest of culture is a vital area of inquiry in social science and presupposes the empirical study of what people's religious beliefs are.

While science is excluded from inquiry into the supernatural in the sense of what exists beyond human experience, this does not mean that its treatment of religion loses track of questions of greatest interest. True, death continues a mystery to be speculated upon by philosophy. But life remains. The fruition of the finer qualities of human existence, here and now, endures as the absorbing subject for scientific inquiry. It is the author's conviction that the most important features of religion affecting man's contemporary existence are those which can be observed by science. The heart of religion is found in what it can do for human beings in this life, not in the next. What it can do in this life remains in the verifiable domain of scientific inquiry. While no inside track to the supernatural can be offered in social-scientific study, the solid pathways of social achievements of religion can be reviewed and analyzed. Following scientific examination of the facts and laws of religious life, one rightly expects to have gained a fuller understanding of the potentialities, as well as the limitations, of religion.

Emile Durkheim has summarized the relationship between religion as a way of acting and science as a method of knowing.

> It is said that science denies religion in principle. But religion exists; it is a system of given facts; in a word, it is a reality. How could science deny this reality? Also, in so far as religion is action, and in so far as it is a means of making men live, science could not take its place, for even if this expresses life, it does not create it; it may well seek to explain the faith, but by that very act it presupposes it. Thus there is no conflict except upon one limited point. Of the two functions which religion originally fulfilled, there is one, and only one, which tends to escape it more and more: that is its speculative function. That which

science refuses to grant to religion is not its right to exist, but its right to dogmatize upon the nature of things and the special competence which it claims for itself for knowing man and the world. As a matter of fact, it does not know itself. It does not even know what it is made of, nor to what need it answers. It is itself a subject for science, so far is it from being able to make the law for science! And from another point of view, since there is no proper subject for religious speculation outside that reality to which scientific reflection is applied, it is evident that this former cannot play the same role in the future that it has played in the past.

However, it seems destined to transform itself rather than to disappear.[11]

SCIENCE AND THE STUDY OF VALUES

A viewpoint which restricts the study of religion as a social science is the contention that values are outside the natural world and therefore outside the scope of scientific inquiry. For some scholars, both scientists and nonscientists, the realm of values is to be considered supernatural or at least beyond the scope of empirical science. Religion, being a system of values, cannot in this view be studied by science, at least in respect to its value aspects. This viewpoint has been stated by one of the leading defenders of mysticism in modern times, the Quaker philosopher Rufus Jones. The following passage from one of his last works is a plea to scientific-minded persons to recognize the validity of religious experience and sets forth the claim that religion is an affair of values outside natural causation or even descriptive science.

It needs to be pointed out, first, that there is a vast field of human interests with which the scientific method is incapable of dealing. And this vast field of human interests needs to have an equal place in institutions of higher learning along with this mighty method of approach we have been calling *science*. Science can deal adequately only with what comes within the field of observation, with what can be described and explained in terms of antecedent causes, or at least in terms of absolutely accurate description, preferably in mathematical terminology. It speaks with very slight authority, and is outside its proper field, when it undertakes to deal with what we may rightly call *intrinsic values,* such as beauty, moral insight, *love* of the purest and highest order, consciousness of non-sensuous universals, mind that knows that it knows, i.e., self-conscious mind, and the amazing in-

[11] Emile Durkheim, *The Elementary Forms of the Religious Life,* Free Press, 1947, p. 430.

sight that the spirit within us frequently has direct intercourse with a pervasive Spirit, that seems to us to be the ultimate and eternal reality of the universe, which is in fact the very heart of religion. There is, furthermore, an extraordinary body of literature of revelation, which has had a major transforming influence in fashioning the highest types of civilization that our world has so far known. This, too, belongs in the list of intrinsic values, the insights of which cannot be dealt with by the scientific method. Here is a whole range of life-imparting *values,* with which science is not at home and about which it speaks but haltingly.

Unfortunately scientists, though not usually those of the highest order, have in our time assumed that the scientific method is the only method of knowledge. They have quietly taken for granted that there is nothing in the universe which cannot be brought under their method of treatment, and they have consequently been giving their students a greatly reduced universe. The effect of the scientific method has been so extraordinarily successful in bringing order and explanation into what a short time ago was an unknown universe, full of mysterious gaps, that it becomes easy and natural to leap to the conclusion that the laboratory can furnish the final word, not only about "the choir of heaven and the furniture of earth," meaning the visible universe, but about what I have called ultimate realities and intrinsic values. The result has been that in the field of higher education the great moral and spiritual issues of life have been seriously neglected, and the realities of religion have become more or less dubious, because the focus of attention has been in other directions.[12]

One has the impression in reading Jones's works analyzing mysticism that he very capably described religious experience, citing numerous cases, and drawing principles of cause and effect from these. His defense of knowledge gained from this analysis was made with a narrow view of science, and hence he considered himself nonscientific. Not realizing the extent to which he was himself a religious psychologist, he did not appreciate that the discipline of scientific method does not stop with the external world but steps by introspection and case studies into the interior world of thought and feeling. Since the science with which he was familiar did not appear to deal satisfactorily with religious experience he concluded that it never could do so. However, social science at least appears capable of describing what people say their values are, whether it appraises these values or not.

The stipulation that social science cannot make value judg-

[12] R. Jones, *A Call to What Is Vital,* Macmillan, 1948, pp. 5–6.

ments was put forward by Emile Durkheim and Max Weber at an earlier time when sociology was struggling to establish itself as a rigorous science. It now appears that this early view is too restrictive and that many values are appropriately measured and analyzed by empirical science. Full agreement, however, does not obtain among social scientists on this question. The opposing arguments are primarily questions: "How can you observe values?" "How can you measure values?" "How can you establish laws of values?" To these questions we will return.

Values as an Impediment to Science

From one standpoint, science should avoid values in pursuing its inquiry. If a scientist wants one result very strongly, rather than another, because the first would be valuable to him, he risks coming to mistaken conclusions. The values held by those carrying on scientific research may affect the quality of their observation or analysis if the results which might be found impair the values they cherish. For this reason, by a feat of mental gymnastics, the scientist suspends his desires while the judicial side of his mind analyzes the facts. He sets aside the personal values he holds in order that these may not distort his scientific judgment. This is important if results of scientific quality are to be achieved.

Descriptive Study of Values

To set aside one's values during the steps of scientific analysis does not mean that values themselves may not be data in the inquiry. The social sciences cannot avoid studying human values since these are in the fabric of social behavior. If nothing else, an exacting descriptive approach records what the values are which people in various cultures have, what they desire in life. An instance of a descriptive study of American values is that made by Sister Frances Jerome Woods, *Cultural Values of American Ethnic Groups.*[13] However sociologists and anthropologists view the status of values in scientific inquiry, they commonly give descriptions of the values which people hold. A major study of values by anthropologists has been in progress at Harvard since 1949.[14]

[13] Sister Frances Jerome Woods, *Cultural Values of American Ethnic Groups,* Harper, 1956.

[14] W. L. Thomas, Jr. (ed.), *Current Anthropology,* University of Chicago Press, 1956, pp. 300–301.

Scientific Value Judgments

C. A. Ellwood has affirmed the need of sociology to make value judgments.

Human relations are world-wide, not only in space but in time also. If sociologists are to function in the present world they must think in terms of the spiritual unity of mankind. They cannot afford to overlook any human relationship; the integration not simply of the city, or of the local community, or of the nation, but of the whole human world is their concern. Any sociology that fails to see the functional unity of mankind, and the need of world-wide social adjustments is hardly abreast of developments in our human world. Such problems may be too difficult for scientific solution. That is another question. But they should not be ignored, if we wish sociology to function in the present human world—to have even a little to say about world-wide human relations.

But the spiritual unity of mankind is not simply a matter which concerns the present. Human relations stretch back into the past and project themselves into the future. The social behavior of men, cultural sociology has demonstrated, is largely a matter of the tradition of their groups. These group traditions are obviously now in deadly conflict. Sociology ought to be a systematic procedure for arriving at reasoned value-judgments as to the relative social worth of these traditions. It should expose the facts upon which they are based, and it should critically judge their functioning in human relationships. A sociology which is not a criticism of institutions has hardly any social value. If possible, emotional value-judgments of customs and institutions should be replaced by scientific value-judgments based upon the facts of human experience.

Indeed, in one sense the whole mission of sociology as a science is to bring about a transition from arbitrary and emotional traditions to scientific traditions in guiding social behavior. There need be no fear that the real values in past social traditions will be destroyed by scientific examination and criticism. They may be, to be sure, if social scientists are not aware of the facts of history and the lessons which those facts teach. But at bottom science is not an attempt to destroy anything; it is an attempt to understand, to control, and to use for human advantage. A sociology which understands its human mission will undertake this task.

But the continuity of civilization and of civilizing values is, after all, not the main practical problem of scientific students of human relations. What we call civilization has been filled with too many errors, too many value-judgments not based upon all the facts of experience, for sociologists to be over-zealous about the continuity of human cultures. Inevitable questions of intelligent rational changes in human relations will arise. If the social sciences are worth anything, they should afford guidance in the bringing about of rational social changes. The advocates of the use of force in bringing to pass social changes have not only so far won out that they wish to suppress criticism of the institutions of certain groups, but some even talk openly of a war after the present one to settle the relations between classes.[15]

Can the social sciences go further than description and make value judgments? Can they specify conditions for the realization of values? Can they affirm not only what values people do seek but also what values they should seek? C. C. Bowman in sociology has developed the view that science can inform people what means they should seek in order to achieve goals which they have.[16] Starting from the values which people do have, it becomes possible to point out what things are necessary means to these values. Whatever is instrumental is in turn valuable to the recipient. It then becomes a matter of scientific judgment to declare what things would be valuable to persons who have certain basic values in their scheme of life aims.

Whatever can be described can also be studied from the standpoint of laws and relationships. If values can be described, a causal science of values becomes possible. To state laws about values is to make general value judgments about classes of things. The study of what is of greatest value to people is to be empirically pursued. Not only what people do seek but what they should seek for maximum fulfillment of desire is a legitimate topic for scientific inquiry.

An anthropologist, David Bidney, has written a repudiation of cultural relativism, the notion that whatever values a culture contains are best for that culture. Understandably, cultural values depend upon environmental circumstances, but some values represent better modes of adaptation to the physical and social environment than do other values. It is an appropriate task for anthropology to discover and demonstrate universal laws of cultural values so that mankind as a whole can move forward.

If anthropology is to attain the stage of making significant generalizations concerning the conditions of the cultural process and the

[15] C. A. Ellwood, "What's the Matter with Sociology?" *American Sociologist,* February, 1943, quoted in H. E. Barnes, *An Introduction to the History of Sociology,* University of Chicago Press, 1948, pp. 866–867.

[16] C. C. Bowman, "Evaluations and Values Consistent with the Scientific Study of Society," *American Sociological Review,* June, 1943, pp. 306–312. A representative discussion of the status of values in theoretical writings of sociologists is given by W. L. Kolb in H. Becker and A. Boskoff (eds.), *Modern Sociological Theory in Continuity and Change,* Dryden, 1957, pp. 93–132. For a discussion by a Catholic sociologist, see P. H. Furfey, *The Scope and Method of Sociology,* Harper, 1953, chaps. 1, 2, 4.

values of civilization, then comparative studies of culture and their values must be made with a view to demonstrating universal principles of cultural dynamics and concrete rational norms capable of universal realization. . . . I suggest that anthropologists show their respect for human reason and science by cooperating with other social scientists and scholars with a view to envisaging practical, progressive, rational ideals worthy of winning a measure of universal recognition in the future.[17]

It is commonly accepted in social research that what is meant by a value is something which is desired or which leads to the fulfillment of desire.[18] This may be immediate or remote in producing fulfillment of the desire. The realization of aims or desires, the experience of making compelling ideas an actuality, seems the essence of value. Three elements involved are the desire, the thing which realizes it, and the feeling tone which accompanies realization. The psychological elements involved bring value squarely within the realm of psychology in which the analysis of the inner workings of desire is a central topic.

The critic outside social science may say, "How do you know that realization of desire is valuable?" This seems to be straining at semantic difficulty. If people commonly employ the term *value* to refer to realization of desire, then it seems justifiable in analyzing the culture and personalities of people to employ the term with this meaning. Of course the peculiar conditions of life which, according to religious teaching, permit larger fulfillment of spiritual desires than of self-seeking ones merit scientific study.

Causal Studies of Values

Fulfillment of desire is a topic within the scope of psychology and sociology. Empirical inquiry can be pursued into the conditions under which the maximum fulfillment of desire takes place, that is, for achieving maximum value. How to find fulfillment in marriage has become an absorbing topic in social science. Sociologists and psychologists such as E. W. Burgess, H. J. Locke, and L. M. Terman have carried on a series of studies into the attitudes and other personality traits which are favorably related to satisfying personal relationships in married and fam-

[17] D. Bidney, "The Concept of Value in Modern Anthropology," in A. L. Kroeber (ed.), *Anthropology Today,* University of Chicago Press, 1953, p. 698.

[18] Besides Bowman, *op. cit.,* see, for example, S. C. Dodd, "On Classifying Human Values: A Step in the Prediction of Human Valuing," *American Sociological Review,* October, 1951, pp. 645–653.

ily living.[19] In these studies the level of satisfaction or success is assessed by the answers to searching questions such as: "How happily married are you?" or "Do you think you would be more happily married to someone else?" Points are assigned to the kinds of answers given and the points totaled into a score which reflects the approximate degree to which the couple are happily and successfully married.

Attention is increasingly being given to the study of vocational satisfaction. The conditions of work which make tasks easier for the employee, including types of personal relationship between supervisor and employee which invite the latter's good will and increase his efficiency and job satisfaction, are topics of intensive empirical inquiry. The incentives which hold the employee's loyalty to his work and the social significance he is able to find in his routine of duties receive careful analysis so that work may be more interesting and meaningful to the participant.

Reference to this research is relevant in the study of religion because religion is a source of incentives for work or family life. The investigator is inevitably led to consider what role religion plays in satisfaction on the job or in matrimony. Moreover, if satisfaction in employment or matrimony can be studied scientifically, it follows that satisfaction derived from religious activities themselves can also be studied. In short, the feelings fostered by religion become a legitimate subject for scientific inquiry. Such feelings have traditionally been thought of as the privileged province of mysticism and supernatural revelation. It may come as a novelty to some to realize that psychology and other social sciences turn their attention to the scientific study of this topic.

An aim in such study is not simply a description of how persons feel about their religion, but a determination of what kinds of religious patterns contribute most to personality fulfillment. Religion thus becomes scientifically appraised according to what it can or cannot do to help people to find more meaningful lives.

One phase in the study of values is to consider the kinds of means which most nearly realize the desires of people. Determination is made not only of the means which people do seek, but also of the means which they might seek if they knew of them.

[19] E. W. Burgess and L. S. Cottrell, Jr., *Predicting Success or Failure in Marriage,* Prentice-Hall, 1939; E. W. Burgess and P. Wallin, *Engagement and Marriage,* Lippincott, 1953; H. J. Locke, *Predicting Adjustment in Marriage,* Holt, 1951; L. M. Terman, *Psychological Factors in Marital Happiness,* McGraw-Hill, 1938.

Disclosing what these means are enables people to change their situation in the direction of more fulfillment of their desires. The judgment involving "should" or "ought" is a statement that the value of a new means is greater than the value of a present means for realizing desire. With reference to religion, some modes of life contribute to greater satisfaction of man's psychic needs than others. The value judgments in religion pertain to things of greater value to human beings than the means which they currently use in pursuit of their aims.

Another approach in value analysis is to examine desires which are in conflict within the individual or between individuals. The values taught in certain religions are in conflict with those of pleasure seeking and self-seeking. Which needs are greater, satisfaction of man's spiritual desires or his material desires? Religion contends that the spiritual needs are more fundamental to maximum personality fulfillment. The problem is also one of the conflict between desires of the moment and those of a lifetime. Religion advocates curtailing immediate impulses in order that greater total fulfillment of desires may eventually take place.

An extension of this approach considers ways in which desires can be transformed. Some of these are more firmly rooted in man's physiological and social nature than others. Even the strongest of physical needs is susceptible to modification in intensity or quality of its expression. The value systems of people can be changed not only by giving them new means but also by giving them new desires. A secular example of this is found in the influence of advertising. Brand preference can be created by improving a product or by increasing the public's desire for the product. The author has been working with a research model for analyzing consumer preference which illustrates the dual ways in which values can be modified.[20]

Man is not a passive pawn of his desires. He can remake his desires as well as his environmental means for satisfying them. He can become to a large extent the kind of human being he wants to be. He can be the creator of culture, rather than merely its creature. A criterion for the optimum shaping of motivation is how the life of man can gain the maximum experience of goal realization. What kind of personality structure must he have

[20] P. H. Benson, "A Model for the Analysis of Consumer Preference and an Exploratory Test," *Journal of Applied Psychology,* October, 1955, pp. 375–381; "Optimizing Product Acceptability through Marginal Preference Analysis," in E. R. Ott (ed.), *Quality Control and the Consumer Conference,* Rutgers, 1957, pp. 67–94.

to find the maximum values inherent in the physical and social universe? The universe has such value for him, and a major task assumed by religion and education is to help him achieve the essential worth of his existence.

The practical question in personality fulfillment is that of finding the form into which the desires given by heredity and social experience can best be changed and of devising the means in educational or religious development by which reconstruction can best be accomplished for a life of maximum realization. This question is one of both research and institutional implementation. Limitations in human nature require recognition, as well as potentialities and resources for development. Factual studies are accumulating, but much more remains to be done.

Problems in the Study of Values

At this point other questions about the naturalistic study of values appear. Is there sufficient uniformity from one person to another for a conclusion to be made that what is valuable for one would be valuable for another? If there is no uniformity, there can be no laws, and if no laws, the science of values would be of an inferior, descriptive order at best.

It will clarify the problem of uniformity of desires to point out that the variation in desire from individual to individual is not the issue. It is quite evident that people are not alike in their desires any more than they are identical in other features of their personalities. The scientific question is one of whether there are laws governing the process of fulfillment of desire. Are there some desires, such as spiritual ones, which are capable of greater fulfillment than others? Are there desires whose acquisition is preferable from the standpoint of potential realization to other desires?

The question of whether uniform laws can be discovered cannot be settled in advance of the investigation. It remains for analysis such as that attempted in this text to show whether systematic principles concerning realization of desire in religion can be established. Already, with reference to the psychology of desire in general, psychiatrists and psychologists have been active in their observations and pronouncements. In the field of mental health, it is evident that persons who live in situations which block fulfillment of their desires, or who fail to develop desires in harmony with the opportunities of life, are distressed, disturbed people. Living for others instead of oneself is advocated.

Of more fundamental methodological concern are the questions of whether desires can be observed, or, if so, of whether they can be measured. The objection is raised by some students of values that values cannot be studied by empirical science since they cannot be observed, let alone measured. If values are defined in terms of the psychology of desire fulfillment, they can be observed if desires can be observed. They can be measured if desires can be measured. The question of how behavioral science can proceed in the observation of desire is considered in the chapter on research techniques in the study of religion. The thesis is presented that desires can be observed and measured by prevailing techniques of psychology.

Supernatural Values

There is an obvious level at which science cannot concern itself with values, and this is when desires refer to things in the realm of the supernatural, defined in terms of what is outside human experience altogether, as where desires are believed to be realized in life after death. The problem of whether there are higher values outside life on this planet is a philosophical one. While important in religion, the problem can be approached by social science only to the extent of describing the philosophical questions which human beings have and the answers which they record in their religious systems. Value defined in terms of supernatural purposes or results cannot be dealt with by science other than to describe what people's desires or beliefs are. We cannot assert that values in general can be scrutinized by science, only those which have an empirical reference. Supernatural values are the proper subject for philosophical treatment. Philosophy is to be acknowledged as a partner of science in the investigation of religious phenomena.

Recapitulation of Scientific Study of Values

In drawing together the various conceptual threads concerning the study of values, the following statements represent the viewpoint of this text. (1) By value is meant the experience of realizing desire or the means to this experience. This definition says nothing of the relative merits of spiritual goals or personal wants in the larger picture of total life fulfillment, which provides an important topic for empirical study. (2) When the object of desire is outside the empirical world, study of the object belongs to philosophy, but description and analysis of the desire fall within the science of psychology. (3) When the object of desire is within verifiable experience, both the object and the desire can be studied by the procedures of science. (4) Values may be studied and value assertions made from several standpoints, depending upon what aspect of the psychology of desire is involved. The values which people do hold, as shown by their desires and beliefs, may be described, and the formation of values may be shown in terms of the psychology of desire and belief. Conclusions can be drawn concerning means to fulfillment of desire, means not yet known to people. Conclusions can be drawn about how people will find greater values in their experiences when their desires are remade in the direction of larger potential fulfillment. In scientifically declaring an object to be of value, it should be indicated whether the statement is about a desire which an individual now holds, or about a more effective means to such a desire, or about an object which becomes valuable if a new desire capable of more complete fulfillment is acquired.

chapter 3 Nature of Scientific Study

Historical Conflict of Scientific and Religious Authority

It is illuminating in a study of religion to sketch the nature of science. From the time of man's earliest self-conscious efforts at reconstructing the nature of himself and the universe in which he lives, reason and religion have come into recurring conflict. The conflict appears sharper in the twentieth century than ever before. Two cultural giants, science and religion, are engaged in a struggle for the control of men's minds. This struggle may be unnecessary. There may be a higher ground of reconciliation between the ideologies of science and religion in which each adjusts itself to realities of the other. Whatever view one takes of the opposing sides, it is necessary to see modern science in its correct cultural perspective if one is to appreciate the total canvas upon which religion also is painted.

Traditionally, religion has tended to speak with dogmatic authority, claiming absolute truth given by God, rather than to invite inquiry and discussion. To some extent this dogmatic attitude persists in the popular mind with reference to science, but among scientists the notion that science confers authority simply by virtue of the name or position of the scientist who speaks is repugnant. The authority of science is found instead in the varying degrees of compulsion which hard facts or subtle processes of inference impose upon the human mind. Of course there are occasions, as in the operating room of a hospital, when one accepts the authority of medical science. Yet, if one wished, one could enroll in a medical school, undergo the requisite training, and embark upon a program of treatment and research which would prove or disprove prevailing medical practices. The authority in such a case would again be that conferred by data and logical reasoning, and this above all else is the only effective scientific authority by which others can be influenced.

SCIENCE AS A WAY OF KNOWING

Before initiating the study of religion from a scientific viewpoint, it is desirable to fix clearly in mind what scientific inquiry involves, especially since doubt may exist concerning the applicability of such study to religious phenomena.

Science is not a body of dogma, but a method for investigating situations to obtain correct conclusions about them, and it refers also to the conclusions which are thereby accumulated. Even the method itself is not dogmatic. One can, if one wishes, investigate the effectiveness of scientific techniques by scientific observation and analysis. So scientific method uses itself to study itself. Out of such study has emerged a set of basic concepts and principles of procedure which by common agreement are understood to be scientific. They are scientific in the sense of having been found to be more likely to lead to accurate conclusions than alternative procedures.

Fundamental to an understanding of scientific method is realization that it is a way of knowing, a way of getting to know things which one did not know before. In this sense, all people are scientists, whether efficient or not. We all observe. We all reason. The housewife studying cuts of meat in a grocery acts in the role of a scientist making predictions about the palatability of foods. The small boy who digs up a hill of ants to investigate their social life is also a scientist of sorts.

Dewey's Approach

An advocate of the scientific study of religion, John Dewey has done more than any other thinker in America to emphasize the essential similarity of (1) knowing as a psychological process, (2) scientific research, and (3) sound educational procedure. Concerning the relationship between getting knowledge in science and acquiring knowledge from one's livelihood, he says: "Moreover, there is no difference in logical principle between the method of science and the method pursued in technologies. The difference is practical; in the scale of operations conducted; in the lesser degree of control through isolation of conditions operative, and especially in the purpose for the sake of which regulated control of modifications of natural existences and energies is undertaken; especially since the dominant motive of large-scale regulation of the course of change is material comfort or pecuniary gain."[1]

People are unequal in their abilities to discover truth about themselves and their environment. Science has a more specialized meaning than that which characterizes common-sense procedures which most people follow in orienting themselves to reality. Scientific method can be defined as the most efficient procedure known for gaining accurate, generalized ideas of what man and his universe are like. The various steps involved in scientific method are the same steps involved in the psychological process of gaining knowledge, that is, gaining correct ideas of past, present, or future experience. In Dewey's view the act of experimentation is central in both scientific and life procedures.

> While the traits of experimental inquiry are familiar, so little use has been made of them in formulating a theory of knowledge and of mind in relation to nature that a somewhat explicit statement of well-known facts is excusable. They exhibit three outstanding characteristics. The first is the obvious one that all experimentation involves *overt* doing, the making of definite changes in the environment or in our relation to it. The second is that experiment is not a random activity but is directed by ideas which have to meet the conditions set by the need of the problem inducing the active inquiry. The third and concluding feature, in which the other two receive their full measure of meaning, is that the outcome of the directed activity is the construction of a new empirical situation in which objects are differently related to one another, and such that the *consequences* of directed operations form the objects that have the property of being *known*.[2]

In other words, to gain knowledge the actor makes systematic changes in his situation to see what consequences will follow. The changes and the consequences provide him with cause-and-effect information.

> The rudimentary prototype of experimental doing for the sake of knowing is found in ordinary procedures. When we are trying to make out the nature of a confused and unfamiliar object, we perform various acts with a view to establishing a new relationship to it, such as will bring to light qualities which will aid in understanding it. We

[1] From *The Quest for Certainty* by John Dewey, pp. 84–85. Copyright 1929. Used by permission of G. P. Putnam's Sons and Allen & Unwin Ltd.

[2] *Ibid.*, pp. 86–87.

turn it over, bring it into a better light, rattle and shake it, thump, push and press it, and so on. The object as it is experienced prior to the introduction of these changes baffles us; the intent of these acts is to make changes which will elicit some previously unperceived qualities, and by varying conditions of perception shake loose some property which as it stands blinds or misleads us.

While such experimentations, together with a kind of experimental playing with things just to see what will happen, are the chief source of the everyday non-scientific store of information about things around us, forming the bulk of "common-sense" knowledge, the limitations of the mode of procedure are so evident as to require no exposition. The important thing in the history of modern knowing is the reinforcement of these active doings by means of instruments, appliances and apparatus devised for the purposes of disclosing relations not otherwise apparent, together with, as far as overt action is concerned, the development of elaborate techniques for the introduction of a much greater range of variations—that is, a systematic variation of conditions so as to produce a corresponding series of changes in the thing under investigation. Among these operations should be included, of course, those which give a permanent register of what is observed and the instrumentalities of exact measurement by means of which changes are correlated with one another.[3]

In this description of common-sense knowing and of scientific procedure Dewey does not sufficiently stress the role which thought processes play in the acquisition of knowledge. Elsewhere he develops more adequately the creative part played by intellectual effort. He does this by describing the rehearsal in the mind of the consequences of possible actions before deciding upon any one of them.

Our first problem is then to investigate the nature of ordinary judgments upon what it is best or wise to do, or, in ordinary language, the nature of deliberation. We begin with a summary assertion that deliberation is a dramatic rehearsal (in imagination) of various competing possible lines of action. It starts from the blocking of efficient overt action, due to that conflict of prior habit and newly released impulse to which reference has been made. Then each habit, each impulse, involved in the temporary suspense of overt action takes its turn in being tried out. Deliberation is an experiment in finding out what the various lines of possible action are really like. It is an experiment in making various combinations of selected elements of habits and impulses, to see what the resultant action would be like if it were entered upon. But the trial is in imagination, not in overt fact. The experiment is carried on by tentative rehearsals in thought which do not affect physical facts outside of the body. Thought runs ahead and foresees outcomes, and thereby avoids having to await the instruction of actual failure

[3] *Ibid.*, p. 87.

and disaster. An act overtly tried out is irrevocable, its consequences cannot be blotted out. An act tried out in imagination is not final or fatal. It is retrievable.[4]

Experimenting in the imagination as to the possible consequences of alternative life actions can be applied to the subject matter of religion. The scientific approach to life is to anticipate the consequences of various aims and actions and thereby to select what is of optimum benefit to the individual and to society. When this imaginative reconstruction is undertaken by a scientist as part of a research program, he endeavors to anticipate the results of possible experiments to avoid, if possible, the need for carrying them through. What is involved is the deductive application of principles of cause and effect already established. When these are put together, new consequences can be deduced.

The part played by thought processes is more creative than is suggested by the foregoing. This part refers to the way in which new ideas emerge from experience. Much of what we know is given directly by experience, but much more requires reflection and comparison with other experiences for its features to come into our awareness. Essentially there is a transition from raw, concrete experiences to carefully formulated abstract ideas.

The importance of the intellectual transition from concrete to abstract is generally recognized. But it is often misconceived. It is not infrequently regarded as if it signified simply the selection by discriminative attention of some one quality or relation from a total object already sensibly present or present in memory. In fact it marks a change in dimensions. Things are concrete to us in the degree in which they are either means directly used or are ends directly appropriated and enjoyed. Mathematical ideas were "concrete" when they were employed exclusively for building bins for grain or measuring land, selling goods, or aiding a pilot in guiding his ship. They became abstract when they were freed from connection with any particular existential application and use.[5]

The Process of Differentiation

C. G. Jung has frequently referred to the process of differentiation by which unconscious ideas and motives submerged in concrete experience develop toward the scene of conscious awareness, but more complete description should be given of this

[4] John Dewey, *Human Nature and Conduct,* Modern Library, 1930, p. 190.

[5] Dewey, *The Quest for Certainty, op. cit.,* pp. 153–154.

process than is contained in either his or Dewey's writings. Abstraction as a deliberate process is to be distinguished from involuntary differentiation. It is a psychological fact that experience is an ongoing unity. Only if that unity is broken down analytically into its elements do we become aware of its elements. The experience of a religious service is a single general impression until one reflects that the organ is loud, the singing amateurish, the minister inspiring, the prayer moving, and so on. The service must be intellectually dissected for its component features to be known. Similarly, other features in the complex of religious life require isolation in the field of attention in order for them to become known by the individual.

Some of these elementary components are cause-and-effect relationships or generalizations about the way things happen. Others are structural relationships which join things together. Others are constituent variables of position, quality, or number. These principles and elements become resolved out of the concrete oneness of experience partly by actual manipulation of events experienced and partly by imaginative construction. The latter is more than a replication of past overt experimentation and consists of new syntheses from which new conclusions emerge. Out of the variation of experience by external means or internal imagination are abstracted new ideas and insights which the individual did not previously possess. These become differentiated from the prior experience and from each other by becoming associated with characteristic verbal symbols which are used to evoke them when thinking is to go on. In this differentiation, form cannot be isolated from quality. That is, the "grin of the Cheshire cat" does not exist apart from the cat. However, the idea of a black-and-white square can perform the function of squareness in thinking. Ideas of form stress formal detail with quality indistinct, and ideas of quality stress qualitative distinctiveness with little formal detail. The verbal symbols associated with these ideas are recalled whenever the formal or the qualitative aspects are encountered. Whether it is a cat or a child who grins, the word *grin* is recalled in commenting on the experience. If ideas and their symbols correctly represent the component features of experience, we call them knowledge.

A continuous interplay goes on between our ideas and our perceptions of objects in experience. The ideas we have enable us to perceive events in an intelligible, organized way by sensitizing us to key features in which we are interested and of which we become aware. If one has an idea of what a friend looks like, one can pick him out in the congregation. If not, one sees only the congregation. Thus what we are able to experience is in part a product of ideas which we already have. At the same time, the ideas which we have develop out of past experience. From the various experiences with our friends and our thinking about them we acquire ideas of the behavior of our friends. In the same way, scientific ideas pave the way for collecting data by providing principles for selection and classification, and new scientific ideas result from data obtained and reflected upon in the process of research.

Knowledge, Past and Present

In the thought of Dewey, science as a creative way of knowing stands in opposition to what was considered knowledge in the ancient and medieval worlds, largely a deductive system of immutable ideas, encrusted with tradition.

> The work of Galileo was not a development, but a revolution. It marked a change from the qualitative to the quantitative or metric; from the heterogeneous to the homogeneous; from intrinsic form to relations; from esthetic harmonies to mathematical formulae; from contemplative enjoyment to active manipulation and control; from rest to change; from eternal objects to temporal sequence. . . .
>
> The revolution opened the way to description and explanation of natural phenomena on the basis of homogeneous space, time, mass and motion. . . . Heavenly bodies and movements were brought under the same laws as are found in terrestrial phenomena. The idea of the difference in kind between phenomena in different parts of space was abolished. All that counted for science became mechanical properties formulated in mathematical terms: the significance of mathematical formulation marking the possibility of complete equivalence or homogeneity of translation of different phenomena into one another's terms.[6]

While the revolution has taken place in the realm of physical science, according to Dewey two kinds of knowledge continue in the social realm, empirical and dogmatic. "The idea of a two-realm scheme persisted for moral and religious purposes; it vanished for purposes of natural science."[7] The significance of this for the scientific study of religion is that one is apt to embark upon such study still profoundly influenced by the older, dogmatic conceptions of what to expect about religion. Such prejudgments profoundly interfere with the process of scientific

[6] *Ibid.*, pp. 94, 97.
[7] *Ibid.*, p. 95.

deliberation. One of the conditions of the scientific process of knowing is freedom of the mind from emotional attachment to prejudgments. Such predisposition distorts the ideas derived from experience and may even inhibit experience or artificially create experiences which would not otherwise exist. This provides a problem which we examine under the heading of scientific procedure.

SCIENTIFIC PROCEDURE

The Problem of Prejudice in the Social Sciences

As we have seen, one of the reasons why scientists sometimes seek to avoid any contact with values is that these are potent sources of error in scientific inquiry. Especially in social science there exists risk of the researcher's personal interests or prejudgments distorting his thought processes. The sociologist who believes that not every worker is entitled to a private dwelling unit for his family is less likely to carry on an objective survey of congested housing than the sociologist who has little emotional concern one way or the other. The biased individual is more likely to call housing adequate when it is actually unfit. If errors exaggerate his statistical findings he is less likely to worry about discovering such errors, feeling, perhaps, that as long as the errors do not overestimate the need for public housing, little reason exists for disclosing them.

The physical scientist has no feeling of sympathy for an electron or a chemical compound, although his professional pride may be at stake if he obtains one result rather than another. The social scientist typically studies values or things closely related to values. Inevitably many of the things which he studies impinge upon either his interests as a human being or the interests of those who pay for or publicize his research. People tend to believe what they wish to believe. The impact of human emotion upon the scientific process when man studies himself is far-reaching.

The mind of the social scientist can be influenced not only by wishful thinking, but also by the uneven effect which past experiences have upon his opinions. To illustrate this point, consider again the role of the physical scientist. Before he walks into his laboratory or peers through his instruments he has had no contact during childhood and adolescence with his subject matter. His mind is a blank upon which data have not yet recorded themselves. He can receive his data with complete impartiality. In contrast the student of social science has grown up in a situation which gives him some data about human life, but not all. If he grows up in a ten-room apartment on "easy street" his empirical view of life is entirely different from the boy who is reared in a two-room flat in a tenement section. Each of the two has had a different set of data impressed upon him while growing up. When either comes to study the problem of housing, the data which are newly acquired must withstand the one-sided influence of earlier conditioning. Human beings reach adulthood with neither a balanced set of social data in their experience nor an absence of any data at all, but a one-sided set of data for which scientific study must somehow compensate.

Nor is the problem simply one of getting adequate data. Before the individual matures and takes his place in society he has been subjected to teaching by his culture nearly every day of his life. He is continually indoctrinated with conclusions which society has already reached. He believes whatever vested interests with an ax to grind propagandize him to believe. Indeed, he could not live unless he took over ready-made many of the beliefs of society. By the time he reaches a course in social science he already has definite opinions about many of the things he is to study.

The answer to this problem of objective study is not found in abandonment of all that life has taught, for life must go on from day to day upon whatever premises the individual believes. Rather, the answer is provided by the act of setting aside one's prejudgments while one takes a fresh look at the subject matter. One holds one's opinions in abeyance while restudying the data and rethinking one's conclusions. The chances are that, after such analysis, most of the former opinions will continue to be acceptable, with perhaps some modification. In a few cases a drastic revision of one's beliefs may be required. If such revision carries one nearer to a reliable set of social beliefs, such revision will be worth the individual's effort since he can then base his decisions and actions upon sound, rather than deceptive, premises and thereby more nearly achieve his life goals.

The groundwork of the problem of prejudice in scientific study is more easily traced before one considers the emotionally explosive subject of religion. It is a little easier to accept the notion in general of temporarily setting one's personal beliefs aside before raising the question of religious beliefs to which people are frequently either greatly attached or else by which they are strongly repelled. All that has been said about the problem of prejudgment in social scientific study applies in particular to religion. The beliefs taught us by our religion are very important to the individual involved. Somehow we must place these beliefs, so to speak, on a siding, while the train of scientific investigation is allowed to proceed. After that train has verified the sureness of the route, that system of beliefs may again be set in motion, with such reconstruction as is necessitated by the scientific inquiry. Only by such courageous facing of new facts and new ideas may the human mind progress toward greater truth.

Descriptive Science

In explaining the basic steps which all science shares, we are doing so in terms of (1) the psychology of knowing, (2) the kinds of things, descriptive or causal, which science seeks to know, and (3) the steps which are indispensable for accurate knowledge.

The psychology of knowing tells us that we experience before we know. In scientific terms we gather data. This is often listed as an initial step in scientific inquiry. However, one does not gather data until one has first decided upon a topic about which data are sought. So first of all the scientific investigator must get a problem. This means to tell himself what he does know and what he does not know so that he can then proceed to fill in the unknown territory in his knowledge.

In religious study such a problem might be the description of store-front religion. In congested urban areas with a floating population, a new pattern of church has become evident. This is a church without a steady congregation located in a store on a business street. In the windows and over the doorway will be signs and slogans such as "Jesus Saves," or "The Wages of Sin Are Death," or "All Welcome." Through most of the week the store location is closed or devoted to business use, perhaps real-estate or burial insurance. Services are held several evenings a week and several times on Sunday. While a service is in progress, a loud-speaker pipes the proceedings out to the sidewalk to attract passersby. Inside, the self-styled minister who holds forth may possess a scholastic degree granted by a board of bishops he has nominated himself from his supporters, or perhaps no degree at all. When not at his religious work, he may likely be a vacuum-cleaner salesman or a haberdasher. Sundays he turns his vocal talents to religion.

People impoverished in body and soul who hunger for the "good old-time religion" crowd into his meeting place, especially if he has a reputation for oratory. He leads the service, offers some of the prayers, and gives the sermon. Organ music is provided in canned form, and singing is enthusiastic. The minister is paid by money taken up in the collection plate. For a Sunday's work he may earn twenty dollars. If his reputation grows for keeping people happy or for healing the sick, his financial return may be very much greater. He then rents a large church, or may even own it himself. He buys time on the air and broadcasts his services, appealing also for funds to his radio audience. His congregation is unstable, here today and gone tomorrow. After people feel that the minister has talked himself out, they drift elsewhere to some other store-front church. Or he may himself move to another part of the city, relying upon the fresh appeal of his services to attract a new crowd.

Data are gathered by the scientist's direct observation of the religious proceedings, or they may be obtained secondarily from the reports of participants or other witnesses. After gathering data the investigator analyzes them. He manipulates his ideas in such ways that he becomes aware of things in the data which he did not know before. By turning the data over in his mind he formulates concepts which represent to him certain general features of the data. *Concept* is the scientific term for an idea derived by the mind from the data presented to it. Before the data can be accurately and illuminatingly described, concepts must be formulated of what a store-front church is, of how it differs from more conventional churches with a regular congregation, of the role of the minister in a store-front church, and of its techniques of financial operation. Clear definitions of these features are written out after the concepts have been abstracted from the data.

However, concepts not only are derived from the data; some elementary concepts must precede the gathering of data. No data at all can be obtained without advance formulation of some of the concepts needed for carrying on observation. A child, for example, lacking concepts for social and psychological study, would be unable to report matters of scientific interest. To the degree that the investigator has sensitized himself to his material by gaining clear concepts, his observations become the more comprehensive. Just as ideas both precede experience and also result from experience, so also concepts, which are scientific ideas, are needed before any data are gathered, and after data are assembled new concepts become differentiated.

Having formulated concepts of basic things in the data, the investigator may next classify the data. This means to group the data together according to which data possess a basic characteristic, and which lack this characteristic. Having grouped the data, he may then count how many instances he finds of data which have a certain characteristic and how many instances lack this characteristic; this step involves the act of enumeration. The purpose of classification is to summarize the data as briefly yet as completely as possible.

The grouping of data of store-front churches would take place by putting similar churches together or by grouping similar participants in the same descriptive classes. Grouping might be effected by income level, occupation, marital status, age, or former religious affiliation of participants. Size of congregation, presence or absence of faith healing, and type of appeal of minister would be ways for classifying the churches themselves. After grouping similar store-front churches together, or classifying participants, the number falling in each category are then counted, and the data thereby become enumerated.

An essential step of scientific work remains to be performed. This is the step of verification. The original investigator repeats his work again at every step to see if possible error can be circumvented. The definition of the problem is reëxamined. Data are rechecked and concepts are reconsidered. Statistical grouping and counting of data are redone. Other investigators, especially if they have reason to doubt the novelty of the initial findings, likewise will repeat the work step by step. The nature of this coöperative verification upon which the authority of scientific knowledge depends is described by Dewey.

> In spite of science's dependence for its development upon the free initiative, invention, and enterprise of individual inquirers, the authority of science issues from and is based upon collective activity, cooperatively organized. Even when, temporarily, the ideas put forth in science by individuals sharply diverge from received beliefs, the method used is a public and open method which succeeds only as it tends to produce agreement, unity of belief among all who labor in the same field. Every scientific inquirer, even when he deviates most widely from current ideas, depends upon methods and conclusions that are a common possession and not of private ownership, even though all of the methods and conclusions may at some time have been initially the product of private invention. The contribution the scientific inquirer makes is collectively tested and developed and, in the measure that it

is coöperatively confirmed, becomes a part of the common fund of the intellectual commonwealth.[8]

The outcome of this painstaking repetition is the kind of knowledge called scientific, not knowledge which is infallible or unchangeable, but knowledge believed more likely to be correct than any other alternative conclusion. We recognize that scientific knowledge is not, strictly speaking, defined as absolute in its truth, but rather consists of knowledge reached by procedures leading more nearly to true knowledge about the world of experience than any other procedures would succeed in doing. The methods of science are selected on the basis of their effectiveness in producing correct knowledge. This effectiveness is the reason for requiring such steps in scientific procedure as repeated verification.

Let us recapitulate what we have said so far about scientific procedure in the form of an outline:

1. Formulate a problem.
2. Gather data.
3. Formulate concepts.
4. Enumerate data in terms of concepts.
5. Verify preceding steps.

In scientific work it is not necessary that one step be finished before proceeding to the next. Frequently the scientist decides during formulation of his concepts to gather more data. And, as was pointed out, the formulation of at least some concepts must precede all gathering of data.

Having completed the foregoing steps, the investigator has knowledge of a purely descriptive character. He has knowledge which is accurately and efficiently summarized. He lacks knowledge of causal character. The hope of the scientist is to discover relationships of correlation or causation between things which he studies so that these things can be predicted or controlled.

Causal Science

The discovery of relationships of causation or correlation involves a repetition of the five basic steps with concepts of causation or correlation characterizing the inquiry, instead of concepts of purely descriptive classifications. First, one must have a problem: What is the relationship between two factors? For instance, what is the relationship between recency of migration and participation in store-front religion?

[8] John Dewey, "Science and the Future of Society," *Intelligence in the Modern World,* Modern Library, 1939, p. 359.

Next, data about the two factors must be gathered. Data may be gathered from events naturally occurring, or by experimental control new situations of data may be provided without waiting for natural processes to yield them. Such experimental control of social situations frequently is not possible but changes foreseen may artificially create new situations which can be studied as if a real experiment were in progress.

Third, a hypothesis must be formulated of the relationship between the factors. A hypothesis is an idea (i.e., a concept) of a cause-and-effect (or a correlation) relationship between two things. For example, the hypothesis may be that the more recent the migration, the more frequent the participation in store-front religion. The hypothesis is an idea which may or may not be correct. This is why it is considered hypothetical until proven or rejected. It is impossible to test a causal relationship without having first formulated a hypothesis of such a relationship.

Fourth, the data are grouped according to those which support the hypothesis and those which negate it. People in store-front congregations and outside of such congregations are classified according to recency of arrival in the city or neighborhood. Every instance of one factor is examined to see if the other factor is present and every instance of the other factor is studied to see if the first has also been present. Then the instances for and against are counted. If no exceptions are found, the relationship is considered a causal law. If the relationship falls short of such causal perfection it may be recorded as a relationship of association or correlation, and the degree of association or correlation measured by a statistical coefficient. The relationship is called functional when cause and effect vary in magnitude with each other. The formulation of the relationship by mathematical symbols permits a large range of different situations to be summarized in a single equation with much economy of language and logic. How accurately the formula succeeds in representing the data is measured by the correlation coefficient. If the association or correlation is zero, the hypothesis is entirely rejected and an alternative hypothesis is then considered.

Before the hypothesis is accepted as a law, the work of establishing it must be repeated by the same and by other investigators. If they are all able to verify its existence, then it may be given the status of a law. If elements of verification are partially lacking, it is usually given the name of theory. A theory is a scientific principle which is not yet fully proven or to which there are unexplained exceptions. Scientists are cautious in elevating their theories to the status of laws without ample verification.

Many of the causal principles in social science are, in the technical view of scientists, called theories or models. This does not mean they consist of idle speculation. Rather there are substantial bodies of data gathered in support of them. Sometimes they are generalizations which can only be stated in terms of the percentage of time they are found to hold in various situations. Much social-scientific generalization consists of statistical relationships, even when the language is nonstatistical, as in employment of adverbs such as *sometimes, usually, always,* or *never.*

Theory and model building frequently proceed by means of introspective insights or deductive conclusions which touch firm, verifiable facts of behavior only at some points but not at all those needed for complete proof. It seems more congenial to the social scientist to call scientific principles of this type theories, even though the experience of most ordinary persons would demonstrate them to be dependable laws of life.

Dependence on Assumptions

In the controversy between religion and science, the religionist sometimes argues that science makes assumptions, so religion is also entitled to make assumptions. It is appropriate to examine the nature of the assumptions which science makes.

An important class of assumptions consists of principles in the process of being examined empirically. In model construction, it is customary to state a list of assumptions. These are acts not of faith, but of intelligent insight. They are retained in the category of assumptions only for so long as their disposition is in doubt. Eventually they come to be proved as acceptable as scientific principles, or else discarded as unfitting hypotheses. The methodological principles whereby science proceeds are initially in their evolution assumptions without empirical basis. As soon as they have justified themselves in terms of empirical results, they are no longer ventures of speculation, but are demonstrated by successful research activity, the same as any other psychological principles of the process of knowing come to be demonstrable scientific conclusions.

There are also philosophical assumptions which scientists take for granted. One of these is the conviction of scientists that other people have thoughts and feelings. This cannot be demonstrated empirically. No one can get inside another person's mind to see what experiences go on there. One must rely upon the reports of others that they do have feeling states. Along the same line, it is a matter of inference that people with the same physiological capacity, past conditioning, and social situation experience equal degrees of desire. This is an assumption of the uniformity of nature, not provable empirically in every instance, but taken for granted by the scientist on the basis of what instances he can observe. For example, he infers that the curvature of the far side of the moon resembles that of the near side which he sees. Prior to rockets he could not prove his inference by direct observation of the far side. But his assumption of the uniformity of nature leads him to believe in the continued operation of the same physical laws in unobservable situations. The same type of reasoning is followed in concluding that similarly constituted persons who are in the same situation experience similar feeling states.

It can be maintained that the only assumption made by science which cannot be immediately verified by the data of experience is that of the uniformity of nature. Others would increase the list of assumptions. The point with reference to science is that its assumptions are peculiar to it and play a necessary part in the methodology of science. The circumstance that some assumptions are necessary is not an "open sesame" for either science or religion to make any assumptions wished. In particular, if religion seeks to emulate the intellectual status of science, it should make no assumptions except those which science makes. Otherwise religion moves outside the realm of scientific demonstration into that of philosophy or some other form of speculation.

This text does not attempt to be a work in the philosophy of science, and those desiring answers to philosophical questions raised about science are referred to works in philosophy. This work in religious science, like other scientific projects, takes the assumptions of science for granted and presupposes the right which any science enjoys of defining its subject matter by scientific criteria and of employing methods which meet scientific standards. The attempt to answer problems outside the purview of the practicing scientist is not made. Outside this practical scope philosophy is an essential partner of all science in the investigation of the assumptions used by science which cannot be proved by empirical data. What is necessary to insist is that religious science not be held uniquely accountable for assumptions employed by motivational and behavioral scientists in general.

Legitimate questions about these assumptions can and should be raised, but they belong to philosophers in the division of labor of human learning.

SOCIAL SCIENCE AND THE INDIVIDUAL

Growing Nature of Scientific Truth

Scientists, especially social and psychological ones, are extremely reluctant to close the door of inquiry upon a principle in declaring it to be a law. Too often have they been mistaken in doing so in the past. Man and his universe are too full of potentialities for discovery for scientists to venture far from the category of theory in affirming their present conclusions. It is well that they strive so vigorously to keep the doors open for new truth. The outlook for a culture which is smug and complacent in its possession of eternal truth is pathetic because of the stagnation and decay which inevitably set in.

Frequently principles are called theories because of disputes among scientists when ordinary persons who use the principles would be entirely satisfied as to the reliability of these as laws. Many of the principles discussed in this text are called theories because they are disputed by men trained as social scientists. This does not mean that the individual student need remain in a state of suspended doubt until scientists have managed to achieve unanimous agreement. Theories are important as a basis for action because they may be much superior to no knowledge at all. If the student finds that the so-called theories actually seem to be laws according to all that he is able to discern in his experience, he is entitled to rely upon them as if they were laws in pursuing his life purposes. Life cannot wait for the final formulation of generations of meticulous scientists. This is true of physical science as well as of social.

Some scientists, in spite of their careful training, may commit errors in their thinking because of the influence of cultural indoctrination or emotional disposition upon the workings of their minds. Rather than wait for perfection in the minds of all scientists, most persons are satisfied to ignore occasional disagreement among social scientists where it seems evident that such disagreement by a few might result from variations in background.

However, the existence of disagreement is a continual challenge to seek greater accuracy of results. Furthermore, such disagreement should be vigorously encouraged whenever it appears hesitant or unpopular, since the existence of continuing disagreement presents the only possibility whatever for the discovery of newer and greater truth. If scientists ever reach the point of complete agreement, human progress is dead. The human race can welcome, as the lifeblood of civilization, a continuing condition of disagreement without restriction as to subject matter. The wider and sharper the disagreement, the more nourishing the accompanying blood stream of ideas.

Of course science is more than a method; it is also a body of conclusions which have been reached through the application of the method of science. Its conclusions rest upon the testimony of the ablest minds through human history. This does not mean that the findings of science are fixed and immutable. They are subject to change and growth. To the extent that science is a body of truth, it is a body of growing and developing truth. Its present findings are acknowledged to be approximations, the best approximations available, but still imperfect. As scientific enlightenment moves forward, the lines of accuracy become more closely drawn. Science continually approaches but never reaches absolute precision.

Periodically, puny man has reacted emotionally to his inability to find absolute precision of truth. In a fit of frustration, he may declare there is no truth, that all is changing and relative. Or he reacts with stubborn rigidity in defense of what principles he has. He declares them to be given directly by God, perfectly articulated, incapable of improvement since they have already achieved the ultimate in truth. Such emotional insistence does not confer any higher measure of scientific worth upon man's social and religious conclusions. However he chooses to think wishfully about them, they still remain products refracted through the prisms of his mind. In a larger sense, he may feel the voice of absolute truth defining reality for him, yet his sacred writings are, after all, merely his own writings, and no better at any stage of human history than his ability at that time to discern truth and to write. However perfect and precise the orderly laws and processes of the universe may be, as man comes to see them, he does so with a greater or lesser margin of error.

Rather than deceive himself into thinking that the truth which he has is perfect, man is wiser to keep the doors open to further enlightenment by continued seeking for something more precise. He need not abandon the social or religious wisdom of the ages, nor its apparent origin in a mind greater than his. He can simply acknowledge that in accepting and using it he will keep on the lookout for more definitive wisdom.

Status of Religious Knowledge

If social science is unable to propose absolutely complete and correct laws of human life, what is its usefulness for human beings? Before considering applications of social science to religious study and decision, let us review the present status of scientific and of traditional religious knowledge.

Each religious group possesses a sacred literature, sometimes of recent origin, but often of remote antiquity. This literature is customarily declared by the orthodox to be absolutely true and infallible, having been given by God to mankind. Since God would not deceive human beings, it follows that complete reliance may be placed upon his word. The declaration that the Bible contains what God told men is meaningful in the sense that men of the time when events in the Bible took place felt within themselves spiritual impulsions and ideations which they considered to be the spirit of God expressing itself to them. Assuming this was the case in the preparation of scripture, the circumstance remains that the Bible contains what men claim God disclosed to them. The claim of any human being about events experienced is susceptible to question. Claims of the writers of Christian scripture may be valid in some respects and not in others. In some current theological analysis it is recognized that, while God speaks to man in scriptural record, the record itself, having been based upon experiences reported by man, is susceptible to error. Scripture is then to be reëxamined in terms of historical context or present-day experience in order for the particular nature of what was experienced to be known. This latter viewpoint is scientific in seeking by orderly examination of facts to establish conclusions which may be drawn. However, the scientific study of the Bible is in its beginning stages, as far as integration with fields of psychology, sociology, and anthropology are concerned.

As far as is known, none of the gospels were written down until some time after Jesus was crucified. In the interim there was unavoidable dependence upon memory and hearsay. It is possible that all which happened during Jesus' life was correctly remembered and accurately recorded, but this is no more than a possibility. Each part of the material claimed to be true because it is the word of God requires reëxamination in the light of present psychological and social study. Following this cleansing bath by scientific analysis, essential principles in the Bible may remain validly viewed as the disclosure of a divine spirit. Other principles may come to be discarded in the light of scientific study.

The Bible is a compendium of diverse types of knowledge, only some of which are approachable through science. Insofar as it is a work of philosophy or speculative theology, it necessarily follows that empirical science is of no assistance in resolving where truth and error rest. Much of the Bible falls under the heading of poetry or literature whose content more nearly approaches historical fiction or legend than case material for scientific history, sociology, or psychology. On the other hand, the Bible contains sociological and psychological principles which have varying degrees of scientific adequacy. Some of these principles, in view of present scientific knowledge, are palpably erroneous statements of human nature or society. Others are suitable hypotheses for further investigation. Still other principles have sufficient evidence in support of them, either within Biblical accounts or from present data, to be considered part of scientific knowledge. In summary, the Bible contains a blend of empirical knowledge and philosophy, case material and fiction, truth and error.

The nondemonstrable, the undemonstrated, and the demonstrably false material in Biblical scripture need not overshadow the extensive system of empirical principles which are contained in it and which have been and continue to be of large usefulness to the human race in its religious pursuits. One repeatedly finds the Bible to declare that a spiritual power is found in the individual's life. A psychologist would be insensitive if he did not sense that there is something thereby declared which merits close study. Exactly what the power is may be more accurately describable by scientific study than by scripture. At least its existence cannot be rejected until extensive and careful research someday shows that nothing of the kind exists in human life and action. It is true that in current scientific controversies the existence of a spiritual power is questioned or denied by some. But it is questionable whether their researches have continued long enough or deeply enough to overbalance either the testimony of milennia of historical experience or the findings of contemporary psychologists and sociologists, such as John Dewey, Emile Durkheim, or C. G. Jung, who find a psychological power functioning in religious phenomena.

What has been said in reviewing the status of the Bible as knowledge might arouse expectations that scientific study of religion today has produced knowledge of superior status. In considering the researches of the past half century one is obliged to conclude that they provide in the aggregate a minor store of findings compared with what is offered by the Bible. The results are generally superior in accuracy to those set forth in scripture, but some findings suffer from the divergence of opinion concerning them. Scientific knowledge does not achieve full dependability until repeated studies lead to consensus. This text, like others, seeks to advance and define the frontiers of scientific conclusions about religion. Nevertheless, abstract scientific statements do not take the functional place of religious writing which portrays principles in concrete form. The human mind grasps with difficulty and soon loses touch with conceptual abstractions with which it comes in contact. In contrast, what is set forth in dramatic literature and poetry lives in the sentiments of mankind in a vivid and real way. On the other hand, systematic rather than traditional study of religion is needed to extend knowledge concerning it. Scientific study permits the reader to select in a discriminating manner the portions of the Bible on which he can rely. The student can then turn to his Bible with fresh illumination and can receive clearer and stronger inspiration from its passages.

Eventually social science may make advances comparable to those in physical science. What science and scripture now have to offer as religious knowledge is a mixed array which requires discriminating judgment in the selection of sound material. Usually scientific knowledge is accurately qualified by its expositor so that the degree of validity attached to it is known to the reader. Where scientific matters are in dispute, consideration of the cultural background and professional skill of proponents is relevant, as well as the weight of data and logical reasoning, unless the reviewer is a scientific expert in his own right. The more universally verified is the information which social science is able to assemble, the larger the reliance the individual may place upon it. Some social insights are supported by centuries of observation and study, and a relatively high degree of certainty can be attached to them.

The problem facing the student of the Bible is that of knowing what may be considered reliable and what is to be questioned or discounted altogether. Religious denominations do not agree among themselves, although the differences may be verbal ones. As sacred scripture stands, the separate evaluation of parts of it is not self-evident. One criterion is the amount of consensus prevailing in the group in which one lives. This is hardly a satisfactory criterion for the scientific researcher, but it provides a rough guideline for the inquiring individual. Some measure of truth is reflected in doctrines firmly declared by large numbers of people to have basis in their experience.

Another criterion is the scientific expertness of those whose concurrence supports the knowledge in question. Expertness is not to be ascribed to those spokesmen whose facility is merely verbal, but rather to those whose capacity for creative understanding is demonstrated. However, consensus and expertness are nothing more than checks against error. They are not a full guarantee of truth.

A third criterion is the individual's own judgment as he assesses principles in his program of study and decision. In this program the scientific and religious writings of others are of indispensable aid. In a lifetime of study the individual could not reconstruct by his own efforts the vast material accumulated through centuries. During his study the individual can gain ability to evaluate conclusions from a scientific standpoint. The particular ways in which material in science is useful to the individual provide the next topics for examination.

Social Science as a Guide to Religious Study

The student who approaches written material finds that there are alternative ways of studying it. One of these is to commit material to memory, retaining words by rote. The student who memorizes may make himself into a parrot who has no idea of what he is saying. With abundant libraries and mechanical aids for recording verbal material, such as microfilming, tape recording, and electronic memory devices, it is superfluous to commit to memory anything which is more readily accessible by other means. While in some situations, such as delivering a speech or making a sales presentation or giving verbal counsel, memory powers are an asset worth cultivating, little excuse exists for the emphasis in religion placed on committing to memory so-called infallible teachings. Most of the time the availability of books and notes makes memorizing unnecessary. Of much greater value is time spent in gaining understanding through reflection and problem solving.

In an approach which contrasts with that of memory, teaching and written aids to study set problems for the student to think about. He is given concrete examples or data from which he can derive concepts and principles. Then he is given propositions which other minds have discerned. He can use statements of these as a check upon his own conclusions. In much the same manner as a mathematics text sets problems and gives answers at the end as a check, a text in social science can be regarded as setting forth problems for the student to think about and answers furnished by other minds as a check upon the student's own thinking. If the student memorizes the answers, the experience of problem solving for him is lost. Statements of principles are verbal guideposts pointing to inward realities which the student can, by patient reflection, uncover. The psychological process of abstraction whereby he gains insights from concrete experience is facilitated by verbal cues which guide and stimulate his own thinking. In using verbal descriptions as signposts for his psychological journey, he must not consider collecting the signposts as a genuine substitute for taking the intellectual journey. Words must not be mistaken for ideas, labels for realities. To become a proficient parrot is to descend, not advance, along the ladder of human evolution. The student is expected to verify the truth of ideas for himself. Even an agency with the concept of authority possessed by the Catholic Church expects the individual to follow the light of his conscience in or out of the church. The emphasis in modern education is primarily upon developing the individual's ability for scientific observation, analysis, and conclusion. Knowledge can be found, when needed, from a book or an expert. But no substitute exists for the individual's possession of a scientific mind to aid him in life.

Dewey's comments upon training the power to think have acquired the standing of a classic in educational science.

> . . . there is no single and uniform power of thought, but a multitude of different ways in which specific things—things observed, remembered, heard of, read about—evoke suggestions or ideas that are pertinent to a problem or question and that carry the mind forward to a justifiable conclusion. Training is that development of curiosity, suggestion, and habits of exploring and testing, which increases sensitiveness to questions and love of inquiry into the puzzling and unknown; which enhances the fitness of suggestions that spring up in the mind, and controls their succession in a developing and cumulative order; which makes more acute the sense of the force, the *proving* power, of every fact observed and suggestion employed. Thinking is not a separate mental process; it is an affair of the *way* in which the vast multitude of objects that are observed and suggested are employed, the way they run together and are *made* to run together, the way they are handled. Consequently any subject, topic, question, is intellectual not *per se* but because of the part it is made to play in directing thought in the life of any particular person.

For these reasons, the problem of *method* in forming habits of reflective thought is the problem of establishing *conditions* that will arouse and guide *curiosity;* of setting up the connections in things experienced that will on later occasions promote the flow of *suggestions,* create problems and purposes that will favor *consecutiveness* in the succession of ideas . . . an illustration or two drawn from failure to secure proper conditions will indicate more clearly what is meant. Children are hushed up when they ask questions; their exploring and investigating activities are inconvenient and hence they are treated like nuisances; pupils are taught to memorize things so that merely one-track verbal associations are set up instead of varied and flexible connections with things themselves; no plans and projects are provided that compel the student to look ahead and foresee and in the execution of which the accomplishment of one thing sets up new questions and suggests new undertakings. The teacher may devise special exercises intended to train thinking directly, but when these wrong conditions exist, special exercises are doomed to be futile. The training of thought can be attained only by regulating the causes that evoke and guide it.[9]

Further comments of Dewey's have particular application to the question of whether students who are not interested in religion should be taught it and whether those who are interested should be indoctrinated with one religion or educated about religion in general.

If we generalize from such a commonplace case as the education of artisans through their work, we may say that the customs, methods and *working* standards of the calling constitute a "tradition," and that initiation into the tradition is the means by which the powers of learners are released and directed. But we should also have to say that the urge or need of an individual to join in an undertaking is a necessary prerequisite of the tradition's being a factor in his personal growth in power and freedom; and also that he has to *see* on his own behalf and in his own way the relations between means and methods employed and results achieved. Nobody else can see for him, and he can't see just by being "told," although the right kind of telling may guide his seeing and thus help him to see what he needs to see. And if he has no impelling desire of his own to become a carpenter, if his interest in being one is perfunctory, if it is not an interest in *being* a carpenter at all, but only in getting a pecuniary reward by doing jobs, the tradition will never of course really enter into and integrate with his own powers. It will remain, then, a mere set of mechanical and more or less meaningless rules that he is obliged to follow if he is to hold his job and draw his pay.

Supposing, again, that our imaginary pupil works for and with a

[9] John Dewey, *How We Think,* Heath, 1933, pp. 55–57.

master carpenter who believes in only one kind of house with a fixed design, and his aim is not only to teach his apprentice to make just that one kind of house, but to accept it with all his soul, heart and mind as the only kind of house that should ever be built, the very type and standard model of all houses. Then it is easy to see that limitation of personal powers will surely result, not merely, moreover, limitations of technical skill but, what is more important, of his powers of observation, imagination, judgment, and even his emotions, since his appreciations will be warped to conform to the one preferred style. The imaginary case illustrates what often happens when we pass from the education of artisans to that of artists. As a rule a carpenter has to keep more or less open; he is exposed to many demands and must be flexible enough to meet them. He is in no position to set up a final authority about ends and models and standards, no matter how expert he may be in methods and means. But an architect in distinction from a builder is likely to be an "authority"; he can dictate and lay down what is right and wrong, and thus prescribe certain ends and proscribe others. Here is a case where tradition is not enhancing and liberating, but is restrictive and enslaving. If he has pupils, he is a "master" and not an advanced fellow worker; his students are disciples rather than learners. Tradition is no longer tradition but a fixed and absolute convention.

In short, the practical difficulty does not reside in any antagonism of methods and rules and results worked out in past experience to individual desire, capacity and freedom. It lies rather in the hard and narrow and, we may truly say, uneducated habits and attitudes of teachers who set up as authorities, as rulers and judges in Israel. As a matter of course they know that as bare individuals they are not "authorities" and will not be accepted by others as such. So they clothe themselves with some tradition as a mantle, and henceforth it is not just "I" who speaks, but some Lord speaks through me. The teacher then offers himself as the organ of the voice of a whole school, of a *finished* classic tradition, and arrogates to himself the prestige that comes from what he is the spokesman for. Suppression of the emotional and intellectual integrity of pupils is the result; their freedom is repressed and the growth of their own personalities stunted. But it is not because of any opposition between the wisdom and skill of the past and the individual capacities of learners; the trouble lies in the habits, standards and ideas of the teacher.[10]

It is with respect to religious matters that the viewpoints of this discussion are most often ignored in contemporary culture. Traditionally religion assumes dogmatic authority, leaving little or no latitude for independent judgment as a check against error. Traditionally religion has regarded itself as antiscientific or at

[10] John Dewey, "Individuality and Freedom," *Intelligence in the Modern World,* pp. 621–623.

least unscientific, insufficient attention being given in religious schools to developing the analytical equipment of the individual, so that he can follow religion more scientifically in personal living. Traditionally religion teaches by rote rather than by developing concepts in the individual's mind, usable in his own life. It is necessary to underscore these points if instruction in religion, the last citadel to be invaded by the rise of science, is to alter its ways. If religious leaders highly prize understanding among their adherents, they will welcome the aid which scientific method and the psychology of education offer in fostering a genuine grasp of religious realities.

The steps of study by the student parallel those of scientific research. Before selecting a course of instruction, the student realizes this encompasses an unfilled area in his knowledge. The prospectus for the course is a statement of problems not yet resolved by the student. In the work of the course he collects or is provided data, and he also draws upon his own experiences for these. From this empirical material he formulates concepts and principles which represent the data with fidelity. If detailed accuracy is sought, he examines the statistical extent to which each concept or principle prevails. In proceeding through these scientific steps he is at the same time verifying the work of scientists. Not infrequently a discerning student makes a genuine contribution to scientific knowledge by modifying or augmenting material offered during a course of instruction. Alert teachers learn much from their students during class discussions. In modern education the activity of study and the application of scientific method become one and the same, whether the topic is religion or arithmetic. Sometimes this aim of education becomes obscured by the obsession for grades and degrees and the artificial performance necessary to get them, but the achievement of this aim is a gold mine to the individual who acquires a mind trained in more efficient problem solving.

The student of this text is counseled to regard it not so much a summary of viewpoints in social science about religion as an opportunity for him to exercise his mental powers in the field of religion, checking the opinion of experts against his own judgment, and acquiring social concepts useful in life pursuits. Concepts are illuminating ideas which enable him to observe, analyze, and represent situations to himself. Not only are these a feature of scientific training, but they are necessary in practical living. An ethical power which is a verbalism is nothing. But an ethical power which is grasped by the experience of the individual and impresses itself upon him as his own insight is a meaningful guide to action. The acquisition of genuine concepts in place of verbal phrases is all-important in religion, as in all social living.

Dewey and others have maintained that study is not limited to libraries or classrooms. Action nearly always involves thinking about the course of action to follow. Problems of students are to be brought into the school curriculum, and the school curriculum should impart study techniques which enable people to face life problems in post-school years. These observations apply as much to the search for religious meaning of life as they do to the resolving of secular affairs. Furthermore, abstract principles and concepts gain a more accurate setting in one's knowledge through being applied to practical situations. For example, from reading one grasps as a generality that religious exercise alters motivation. Through actual performance the individual perceives how much religious exercise produces various degrees of change in motivation. From experience as well as by research procedure the individual learns, in a relationship of two variables, the degree to which one variable changes as a result of changes in the other. The detailed meaning of general principles read in books becomes apparent when these are applied and examined in the concrete context of life.

Social Science as a Guide to Religious Decision

During life the individual faces many questions for him to decide. What church shall he join? What political program shall he support? Whom shall he marry? What vocation shall he follow? When moving, shall he permit his home to be purchased by a minority group member? These are questions with religious aspects, and the individual frequently turns to religion for help in getting answers. Religion offers general help in the form of techniques for clarifying or strengthening ideals involved in the process of decision. Also, it prescribes behavior patterns and their consequences, and guides decisions of the individual.

The teachings of religion are an area which has been only partly explored by systematic empirical research. The individual cannot yet expect to turn to social science for full guidance in religious matters. He can turn to religious wisdom, assembled in his culture from a prescientific era. While this is incomplete and sometimes erroneous, it often constitutes as reliable a guide as can be found. Someday social science may afford clear-cut answers to questions of life decision, answers from organized research which are more incisive than the individual could gain by his own efforts alone. Nevertheless, the greatest contribution of social science rests not in its counsel to the individual nor in its prescriptions for a perfect society, but in a procedure of inquiry which is available to every individual in pursuing his life purposes. It is not possible for science to anticipate all of the individual's situations with ready-made answers. With the method of science the individual can become a creative agent, discovering new truth and constructing decisions of his own as he goes through life. In analyzing his problems he makes abundant use of concepts, principles, and findings established by social scientists, putting these together in terms of immediate data which confront him.

The incomplete nature of religious knowledge is one reason why the individual cannot abdicate from his independence of judgment. Another reason for holding fast to independence of judgment derives from the errors made by institutional leaders exposed to various pressures. Where those who give leadership in social policy stand to retain power or protect status by what they propose, the individual should examine proposals critically. Although they are made with good intentions, they may be influenced by interests of institutional survival. To put the matter bluntly, democracy cannot survive unless its citizens are willing to think through basic decisions or at least to know enough to check aspects of answers proposed by others. Failure in this regard makes voting meaningless and paves the way for a benevolent or malevolent dictator to control the government.

The same problem may arise in connection with institutional power sometimes held by church leaders. Rather than accept such leadership uncritically, the individual should be prepared to make up his own mind about the religious matters confronting him. His protection against misguidance by those who claim absolute authority is to think out the religious and social questions which face him. Even those whose religious dedication is profound may be mistaken in their opinion. The fact that religious leaders in the past have sometimes insisted upon absurdities is a caution to each generation to do its own thinking. Sometimes religious thinking is influenced by survival needs of religious institutions. Rather than acknowledge past mistakes, it may be more expedient to make no new pronouncements except ones in harmony with past edicts, laying a wall from the past in the path of future development. An individual does well to rethink the judgments of those who speak from positions of institutional leadership. The reliance which may be placed upon the authority of a physician or consultant to the individual is in a somewhat different plane. These are disinterested experts, not personally involved in the relapse of the patient or the collapse of his schemes. They usually stand to gain by giving the best advice possible, the individual therefore reposing confidence in their authority.

Realizing the vulnerability of the human mind to error, one suspects the quality of judgment of those who judge human beings to be infallible. Indeed, the assertion of infallibility may be meaningless in scientific work. Most statements can only be expressed in terms of probabilities and margins of error. In science complete certainty and absolute precision are unfamiliar terms. Although scientific truth is superior in its dependability to any other form of truth, the door to improved knowledge is always kept open by science.

On the other hand, human beings accept many prescriptions for action from others while growing up. Especially in religion a long program of religious exercise and development is needed before the individual gains sufficient experience to decide for himself the correctness of religious principles. Consequently, independence of judgment is often appropriately suspended by the individual until the years of requisite study and experience have been undergone. In the interim the individual proceeds with a faithlike conviction that the program tendered to him by his mentors is sound. He follows written or oral counsel of others, at the same time endeavoring to comprehend this counsel as fully as possible. Because of the hazard to the individual's own achievements a completely experimental attitude toward life may be impractical, although wherever feasible modern education expects the individual to learn by experience and insight.

After the individual reaches adulthood, verification of many principles of social science continues beyond his reach since his time is taken by more immediate tasks. It seems impossible for any individual to verify every principle which he uses in making daily decisions. He necessarily relies upon the authority of others in using these principles. Increasingly, scientific research aids the individual in making effective decisions or predictions about alternatives, and he finds it desirable to accept voluntarily this type of counsel.

Since authorities are sometimes in conflict or in error, especially in religion, the question arises of how to decide which authority to follow. The professional scientist makes it his responsibility to verify everything. An obvious procedure for the individual is to rely upon a check of part of the principles in the written authority employed. If sample checks at random indicate validity, reasonable ground exists for accepting the remainder without full verification. Furthermore, if authoritative writing is to grow in its adequacy and accuracy, it seems inescapable that successive portions of it will perennially be reexamined and subjected to further test in the light of more complete data yielded by life situations. While retaining the major portion of the body of written knowledge, innovations can be considered. By studying the effects of minor alterations in variables, the question of whether larger alterations are needed can be approached.

Protestantism arose as a modification of traditional Catholic principles. Some branches of Protestantism are in a state of ferment as new approaches to religion are being examined by laymen and scholars alike, while other branches retain religious stability comparable to that of Catholicism. Protestantism appears to have too great a propensity to innovate in some respects while not enough in others. Innovations in substantive conclusions are more frequent than those in methods of analysis. The reluctance to employ scientific procedure and to rely upon an empirical theology are key questions in contemporary religion. The problem of both maintaining and developing culture is one of balance. Christianity arose as a series of innovations within Judaism, but excessive innovation was discouraged by Christian leaders. Jesus is quoted as saying: "Then if anyone says to you, 'Lo, here is the Christ!' or 'There he is!' do not believe it. For false Christs and false prophets will arise and show great signs and wonders, so as to lead astray, if possible, even the elect. Lo, I have told you beforehand. So, if they say to you, 'Lo, he is in the wilderness,' do not go out; if they say, 'Lo, he is in the inner rooms,' do not believe it."[11]

Dewey suggests a procedure for adjusting what is taught in schools to the requirements of common sense. While he refers to students of education, the import of his remarks has general application to religious teachings.

> I knew a teacher in a training school for teachers who used to tell his students, "If you find that what I am telling you, or what another teacher here tells you, gets in the way of your common sense, of your use of your own judgment in an actual school situation, forget what you have learned and rely upon what your own judgment tells you is the best thing to do under the circumstances."

[11] Matthew 24:23–26.

I never understood this saying to mean that the teacher thought that personal common-sense judgments and intuitions were the sole and sufficient guides of the teacher, or that he regarded the principles and facts which were taught to those in training of no practical value. I imagine that what he said was a negative way of stating that the value of the science, the history and philosophy of education acquired in the training school, resides in the enlightenment and guidance it supplies to observation and judgment of actual situations as they arise. If, in any particular case, the students saw no connection between what they had learned and the school situation, instead of trying to derive a rule from what they had learned they should depend upon their judgment as that had been developed by theoretical learnings and as these might operate unconsciously. In short, it was a way of saying that the value of definite instruction with respect to educational matters consists in its effect upon the formation of personal attitudes of observing and judging.[12]

No uniform rule can be given for how much the individual shall rely upon his own judgment in planning his course of action and how much upon the judgments offered by his culture, specifically by science. The more highly trained the individual is and the greater his mental endowment, the more independence of judgment he can safely exercise. The more thoroughly the testimony of the best minds in history is united in showing principles to be sound guides to human welfare, the larger is the reliance which the individual (but not the professional scientist) can place upon them.

From another standpoint, insights from the group are not useful to the individual unless he thinks them out and makes them his own. Action cannot be intelligently guided except as it is illuminated by insights which the actor possesses. The reason why vocational and marital counselors encourage advisees to develop their own insights is that a continuing pattern of successful action is not possible unless this is guided by means of insights possessed by the advisee. The contribution of wisdom from culture is not so much a mechanical control of the individual's actions as it is a series of suggestions of ideas for him to think about and fit into his own program of action.

In selecting guiding ideas from his culture, the individual needs to be on guard against ideas which are promoted merely because they serve someone's self-interest, rather than the purpose of human enlightenment. In the contemporary era, the ideas and values in our culture have come to be prefabricated for us, like our cars or our clothes. Our personalities receive their

[12] John Dewey, *The Sources of a Science of Education,* Liveright, 1929, pp. 30–32.

stamp from the assembly line dies of television networks controlled by corporate interests. These interests are not, generally speaking, motivated by our welfare. They are principally interested in making money or increasing their power. An unceasing stream of mental and emotional contamination from these vested interests floods our psychic and social worlds. These commercially motivated purveyors of culture place the independence of human reason in severe jeopardy. At the same time these purveyors intensify the need for each individual to think out and carry out his own decisions, resisting indoctrination by those who would twist truth to their own use. C. Wright Mills, a penetrating social analyst at Columbia University, comments on the difficulty of the problem:

> The role of reason in human affairs and the idea of the free individual as the seat of reason are the most important themes inherited by twentieth-century social scientists from the philosophers of the Enlightenment. If they are to remain the key values in terms of which troubles are specified and issues focused, then the ideals of reason and of freedom must now be re-stated as problems in more precise and solvable ways than have been available to earlier thinkers and investigators. For in our time these two values, reason and freedom, are in obvious yet subtle peril.
>
> The underlying trends are well known. Great and rational organizations—in brief, bureaucracies—have indeed increased, but the substantive reason of the individual at large has not. Caught in the limited milieux of their everyday lives, ordinary men often cannot reason about the great structures—rational and irrational—of which their milieux are subordinate parts. Accordingly, they often carry out series of apparently rational actions without any ideas of the ends they serve, and there is the increasing suspicion that those at the top as well—like Tolstoy's generals—only pretend they know. The growth of such organizations, within an increasing division of labor, sets up more and more spheres of life, work, and leisure, in which reasoning is difficult or impossible. The soldier, for example, 'carries out an entire series of functionally rational actions accurately without having any idea as to the ultimate end of this action' or the function of each act within the whole. Even men of technically supreme intelligence may efficiently perform their assigned work and yet not know that it is to result in the first atom bomb.[13]

Choice of a Church

To encounter new ideas in religion sometimes makes church changing or church leaving seem attractive, when the net gain

[13] C. Wright Mills, *The Sociological Imagination,* Oxford University Press, 1959, pp. 167–168.

in novelty is a fraction of the solid worth one possesses in the religious group where one already belongs. As the science of religion advances, the prospect of constructing a religious system entirely upon abstract scientific principles of psychology and sociology seems intriguing. What is overlooked is the illumination given to a religious system by historical achievements and personalities of leaders recorded in sacred literature, representing religious principles in poetry and story. In comparison with this literature the abstract principles enunciated by science are feeble fare for religious devotees. These principles have as much relation to practical problems as chemical equations of the physiologist have to the practical business of eating, sleeping, and working. Scientific understanding is a powerful ally of any enterprise, but its aid must be held in proper balance with appropriate vehicles for communicating ideas. For those who have grown up in the sacred writings of a particular religious tradition, abstract science by itself offers no acceptable substitute. However, if these writings are reconsidered in the light of scientific knowledge, their religious value is enhanced through deeper understanding of their content. The viewpoint advocated by this text is one of fidelity by each to the cultural traditions and historic memories which are the living realities in his religion. While some of these may not be believed, as long as the individual perceives validity in the major premises he is counseled to remain within his religious tradition. The author happens to be a Protestant, but if he had grown up in some other stream of religious culture, he would probably continue his membership in it, apart from what scientific study led him to believe, since he sees essential validity in the principal religious denominations of the world.

Because of deeply embedded cultural ties of which one may scarcely be aware, spiritual uprooting is a major surgery to perform upon personality. William Howells, an anthropologist, has described the serious crisis precipitated when outsiders sought to change the religion of the Polynesians.

> I am only trying to reveal how a naturally evolved religion fits into the life of a people by showing what happens when it is amputated. When the missionaries put a stop to something Polynesian they did not replace it with something else Polynesian but with something non-Polynesian, so that soon the religion which was part of the culture was not there any more. Now a three-legged stool with one leg taken off is not a two-legged stool—it is no stool at all. That is why the life in fact disintegrated.

To put it more abstractly, people must have lives which are wholes; they must live by a philosophy, which is a system of values or ideals. Ritual, we have seen, expresses and preserves values, putting them in religious terms which are familiar and meaningful to the people. But ritual, patterns of culture, and properly fitted lives all grow up gradually, and new religions and rituals will not convey as much to a whole people as old ones to which they are used. Decline and decay, on the other hand, especially with outside help, can be much more rapid. And when values and ideals have little left to represent them, and the people have no way of being communally aware of them, their life will most certainly become disorganized and apathetic.[14]

Human personality is sustained by the culture to which it belongs. With cultural uprooting, personality structure becomes weakened. It seems important for the religious-minded individual to retain and strengthen social ties with the group to which he already belongs. If he deepens his thinking about this group and its ideas, he will more fully appreciate what he already has. If he prefers somewhat different religious exercises or modes of thinking, he can engage in these in addition to those with which he is already familiar. By gaining a scientific understanding of the reasons why people think as they do, he can appreciate the ways in which their thinking is valid. If he feels the need for change, he can seek to bring this change about step by step where he already is. Religion, like all of human life, undergoes growth however strong the institutional restraints appear to be. It grows from within its existing forms, which may be crystallized in sacred scripture but which gain their expression in the fluid, changing minds of men.

[14] W. Howells, *The Heathens,* Doubleday, 1948, pp. 267–268.

chapter 4 Research Procedures in the Study of Religion

DIFFERENCES BETWEEN PHYSICAL AND SOCIAL SCIENCES

Achievements

The physical sciences are older than the social, and their achievements are greater. When one thinks of the marvels of science, one thinks almost immediately of the accomplishments of modern medicine in the conquest of death and disease, or of the miracle of supersonic flight, or of the unleashing of atomic energy for wartime or industrial purposes. We live in a world which would seem like a story of magic to the ancients with their slow, hazardous modes of existence. These achievements are overwhelmingly those of the physical sciences.

Ask the average man what science has done, and he will recite these triumphs of physics, chemistry, and biology. His view of what science is vividly portrays a white-frocked technician in a laboratory behind a maze of glassware, electric wires, and sensitive instruments. It is not easy for the layman to grasp the fact that the social researcher with his notebook watching what people do and say is as much a scientist as the physicist.

Social research has had to establish itself in the popular mind as actual science. It has had to meet the criticism of some physical scientists, successful in their own field, who narrowly construe science in terms of what they do themselves and who occasionally try to prove that social study is not and cannot be a science. It was stated in the first chapter that behavior and inward motivation accompanying behavior can be studied scientifically. Let us examine this assertion more carefully.

Unity of Science

The arguments about whether social research is science need to be reviewed in a text on religion because the arguments are voiced with renewed intensity when religion is raised as a topic for scientific inquiry. The mistrust which some have of scientific study of behavior, thought, desire, and satisfaction in general becomes vociferous when religious behavior, thought, desire, and satisfaction are made the subject of inquiry. To allay this mistrust, it is necessary to recognize the essential nature of science and then to determine whether social science correctly conforms to this nature. Important differences exist between the procedures of physical and social science. Do any of these differences make a difference as to the status of social research as a science?

In the preceding chapter the essential steps of science as an accurate and orderly way of knowing were outlined. None of these restricts the scientist to the study of physical objects in space. Karl Pearson, a biological statistician, upon whose mathematical work many social scientists have built, points out that the unity of science is found in its method, not in the particular subject matter to which that method is turned. The method may be applied to any subject matter whatever, provided that subject matter is verifiable. It follows that anything in the common experience of human beings and which they jointly can confirm may be made the focus of scientific inquiry in an effort to describe accurately the uniform features of this experience and to discover the laws which govern its changing features. Potentially, science includes not only atoms and electrons or nerve currents and muscle contractions, but people as total organizations of physical substance, and the thinking, feeling, and desiring which people experience and which enable us to understand the complexity of their behavior.

Quantity versus Quality

Physical science possesses features in its subject matter which make its discovery of laws different from the search for laws in social science. Let us see what these features are.

A student is impressed by the predominantly quantitative nature of the subject matter studied in physical science. Spatial objects possess dimensions which can be measured in terms of numbers. Position, direction, motion, and so on are quantitative variables readily lending themselves to mathematical formulation. In contrast, social science is confronted by qualitative material, such as opinion, thinking, feeling, and desire. Even behavior, which is spatial in character, is frequently best dealt with in qualitative rather than quantitative terms.

This distinction is a matter of degree, not absoluteness. Time is a quantitative dimension which the social, as well as the physical, scientist utilizes. Such numerical variables as age, family size, income, and mobility in space are all studied in social science, as well as variables provided by counting statistics. On the other hand, and this seems quite important in the argument, the subject matter of physical science is frequently qualitative and structural. Biology and geology deal with structures not always reducible to simple quantities, and which are described by means of words, not mathematical formulas. True, the aim is to reduce verbal description to mathematical formulation. The same aim prevails in social science, where remarkable steps have been taken toward putting qualitative variables into quantitative formulation by means of mathematical scaling. The advantage of mathematical formulation is its simplicity in describing or analyzing a complex situation, a single formula summarizing a large mass of data.

Experimental Control

To consider another feature of physical science, one is profoundly impressed by the effectiveness of its experimental procedures in the discovery of laws. By means of experimental control with laboratory apparatus, a scientist is able to create the data he wants when he wants them, a circumstance of immeasurable value in looking for cause-and-effect relationships. In contrast, the social scientist testing a law must frequently content himself with searching for data as these are afforded by events naturally occurring. Human beings will not submit to experimentation with their life activities in any fundamental way. Can one envisage an atheist mother surrendering one of her twin sons to the local church so that a scientist might carry on a controlled experiment to determine the effect of religious teaching upon personality development? Such experimentation would settle many of the obscure questions of the actual effect of religion, but is often no more than an intriguing possibility for the social scientist to speculate about.

The real value of experimental control rests in the ability of the investigator to eliminate all extraneous influences from the situation he is studying, thus settling conclusively what is cause and what is effect. As far as human beings are concerned, even if they agree to experimentation, it is not possible to separate people from their digestion nor to sever their emotional ties. Break a human being down into elementary variables, and you no longer have a living, functioning human being. Experimentation is undertaken in social science with much success, but falls short of the fundamental purpose of completely separating a complex situation into its component parts. Social experimentation usually must assume that variables not taken into account remain static or can be ignored rather than bringing them under full experimental control. Therefore the relationships found between variables apply only under the narrowly defined conditions under which the experimentation went on. The inability of social science to make more rapid progress toward a general system of laws may largely be attributed to the difficulty in behavioral study of employing the experimental method to eliminate extraneous variables or to control them throughout their range of possible variation.

Would it mean that social study is not scientific if it fails to discover laws? It does establish many laws and develops many statistical generalizations. It employs ingenious mathematical analysis of data as a substitute when overt experimentation is not possible. It relies upon insight and introspection as a means of constructing theoretical generalizations which can then be empirically tested. Social science makes possible much prediction and control of human life, although many of its predictions or prescriptions have substantial margins of error. On the other hand, some branches of physical science, such as meteorology, are conspicuous by their failure to discover laws upon which reliable predictions can be based. These branches, like social science, must frequently content themselves with descriptive accumulation of data, letting the achievement of general laws wait. Even if social science were primarily a descriptive rather than a causal science, it would remain a science because of its systematic procedures for obtaining and classifying data.

It is sometimes claimed that human behavior and human motivation are too complex for study, that no laws can be discovered. It is even asserted that no laws exist, so chaotic and capricious does human life seem. However, what is involved appears to be less a matter of complexity than a lack of procedures comparable to those in physical science for dealing with situations complicated by large numbers of variables.

Social science has an approach of its own for disentangling the complex features of human behavior. This approach is based upon the study of processes inwardly experienced, such as thinking and desiring. Social scientists can only partially experiment with their data, but they can do something which physical scientists cannot do. They can talk to their material and obtain reports concerning the interior side of human life. Social science is distinctive in that it studies the data of inner, as well as outer, experience. What is meant by the designation of data as inner or psychic, the usefulness of these data, and techniques for studying them are topics to which we next turn.

Psychic Experience in Religion

The characteristics of religion of greatest interest are those which reach into the inward experience of participants. Peace of mind, peace of soul, faith, emotional security—these are affairs of the psychic world. Only by devising adequate procedures for their study can we make progress in analyzing and understanding religion. It is simpler to give examples of this type of experience than it is to define and differentiate it from experience of the external world. The problem of differentiation is complicated by use of the term *subjective* to describe the experience. This term is used as synonymous with *psychic* since the experience is peculiarly the property of the subject rather than others around him, but it has multiple meanings. The word *subjective* is used in another sense in scientific work to describe procedures which are not reliable, unbiased, and free from prejudice, that is, which are not objective. Because of possible ambiguities, it seems more satisfactory from a scientific standpoint to reserve the term *subjective* to characterize experiences which seem prejudiced, ideas which do not refer to describable things, or conclusions which are affected by individual vagaries of observation or analysis. By avoiding the term *subjective* as a general classification, the question of how much and in what circumstances the facts of psychic experience are to be admitted as scientific data is not prejudged.

The problem of explaining the role of psychic experience in social research is also confused by the disagreements as to what role, if any, this type of experience should perform in scientific study. Some recognize its existence but would relegate its analysis to philosophy, which traditionally has delved into introspective material. On the other hand, this would divorce study of inner experience from its practical applications, such as the psychoanalytic treatment of mental disorder. A few extremists have denied the existence of inner experience, claiming they never have any, contending that such words as *thought* and *desire* are circumlocutions for visually or aurally observed data. J. B. Watson, a figure associated with behaviorism through the years, denied that thought or consciousness can be observed or is available for verification. For him the process of thinking simply consists in subvocal talking. Mental life is to be studied only as this is manifested in vocal or other behavior. The reduction of imagination to vocal responses or to physiological functioning of the nervous system does not explain away the fact that people do have ideas. A critic of Watson once asked him whether he had an idea of what he was talking about. Watson replying that he certainly did have an idea, the critic pointed out that Watson had admitted ideas whose observation he rejected. Perhaps the principal reason why the existence of conscious thought has been denied is that the thinker is often aware only that thought is going on, not that different parts of the process can be distinguished by him. Frequently ideas are too weak to be recognized as psychic objects. However, they readily become associated with verbal stimuli through which they can be manipulated and thought about. This intimate connection of ideas with verbal symbols may explain the readiness of Watson to regard thinking as subvocal talking.

Varying degrees of emphasis upon behaviorism have persisted in sociology and psychology, as evidenced by the writings of F. H. Allport, C. L. Hull, G. A. Lundberg, M. F. Meyer, B. F. Skinner, and J. B. Watson.[1] These men usually contend that social science must restrict itself to data perceived by the senses. Psychic experience, being non-sensory, cannot be considered as data. However, verbal reports about inner experience are permissible as data, but not as communication of data. The distinction is tenuous and not well maintained in practice.

With reference to learning theory, Skinner maintains that to understand a speaker is to talk as he does. On the face of it, this may appear absurd, since the speech of children in imitation of

[1] F. H. Allport, *Social Psychology,* Houghton Mifflin, 1924; C. L. Hull, *Principles of Behavior,* Appleton-Century, 1943; G. A. Lundberg, *Social Research,* Longmans, Green, 1942; M. F. Meyer, *Psychology of the Other-One,* Missouri Book Company, 1921; B. F. Skinner, *The Behavior of Organisms,* Appleton-Century, 1938; *Science and Human Behavior,* Macmillan, 1953; *Verbal Behavior,* Appleton-Century-Crofts, 1957; J. B. Watson, *Psychology from the Standpoint of a Behaviorist,* Lippincott, 1921. For recent discussions, see G. A. Lundberg, "The Natural Science Trend in Sociology," *American Journal of Sociology,* November, 1955, pp. 191–202; C. E. Osgood and Charles Morris, "Language in the Objective Mode," *Contemporary Psychology,* August, 1958, pp. 209–214.

adults has little relation to comprehension. From the standpoint of perceived behavior, however, an understanding person does speak and act as do other understanding people. But what place is there in this behavioristic view for explaining to the new student how to gain useful insights? He gains these by fixing attention upon relevant imagery and ideas which he selects for consideration and upon which he reflects. The key point for educational development is that his attention be directed away from the symbols to their meanings in his psychic world. Then and only then does differentiation of imagery into more sophisticated levels of thought take place.

Among those researchers who argue in their writings for the inclusion of data from inner or psychic experience in research are Herbert Blumer, C. H. Cooley, C. A. Ellwood, P. H. Furfey, William James, C. G. Jung, G. F. Stout, N. S. Timasheff, and Max Weber.[2] Their viewpoints are generalized and expanded below. They do not subscribe to the subterfuge that facts of inner experience are admissible for scientific study only because communications about them are data. Of course all data in science are contained in verbal reports of some type, qualitative or numerical. These men argue that the facts of inner experience are themselves data, whether anyone reports them or not. They make a distinction between communication of introspective data and data of introspective communication. They admit both types of data for scientific study. For precise versions of the extent to which they employ psychic data in scientific work their works should be consulted.

Some aspects of psychic experience are vague and elusive, being difficult to detect. Much of this type of experience is on the fringe of conscious awareness or is fused with concrete sensory material in an overtone of meaning. Even when considered alone, such psychic objects as ideas, especially if they are abstractions from experience, have a colorless or qualityless nature. They are distinguishable from each other by being associated with visually or aurally perceived verbal symbols. These

[2] H. Blumer, "What Is Wrong with Social Theory," *American Sociological Review,* February, 1954, pp. 3–10; C. H. Cooley, "Roots of Social Knowledge," *Sociological Theory and Social Research,* Holt, 1930; C. A. Ellwood, *Methods in Sociology,* Duke University Press, 1933; P. H. Furfey, *The Scope and Method of Sociology,* Harper, 1953; W. James, *Principles of Psychology,* Dover, 1950; C. G. Jung, *Psychology and Religion: West and East,* tr. by R. F. C. Hull, Pantheon, 1958; G. F. Stout, *Analytic Psychology,* Macmillan, 1898; N. S. Timasheff, *Sociological Theory,* Random House, 1957; T. Parsons, "Max Weber: Methodology," *The Structure of Social Action,* McGraw-Hill, 1937.

symbols are used to evoke and guide them during the process of reasoning. Despite their weak appearance they may be of supreme importance in the solution of complex problems or in the integration of various segments of personality into a harmonious whole.

Religious experience, consisting of mental and emotional states, has been called "ineffable" or indescribable by William James. The point is that the individual may be aware only that psychic experience is going on, not that it can be concretely differentiated into recognizable parts any more than thinking in general can be differentiated except by association of different mental states with distinct symbols. On the other hand, imagery composed of copies of experiences just perceived is composed of readily recognizable ideas. Through frequent usage and association with symbols, imagery retrogresses into a qualityless state, differentiated only by the characteristic verbal symbols with which the ideas making it up have become associated. The status of psychic or inner experience in scientific research is more easily considered with reference to clear-cut concrete images. Consideration of the scientific status of psychic material is indispensable to an evaluation of what can or cannot be accomplished by applying scientific techniques to religious material. This topic necessarily claims somewhat extended attention.

The reality with which imagery impresses itself upon human experience is unmistakable. One readily imagines on a hot summer day while seated in the classroom listening to a dull lecture how pleasant it would be to spend the day at the beach. The boy friend or girl friend, the drive down, the hot sand, the cool water, languishing on the beach, and memories of sunburn course through one's mind almost as realistically as if one were actually on the outing. If one is not able to take the desired vacation, it remains purely a matter of imagination. It is not a real vacation about which one is thinking. But it is an undeniable fact that one does have a picture of such a vacation in one's imagination. Therefore ideas may be psychological facts, even though the things to which the ideas refer are fictitious and nonexistent. It is a factual matter that human beings do have interior experiences, whether their internal impressions are sense or nonsense. Jung affirms the adequacy of data of psychic experience for scientific investigation.

It is an almost absurd prejudice to suppose that existence can only be physical. As a matter of fact, the only form of existence of which we have immediate knowledge is psychic. We might well say, on the contrary, that physical existence is a mere inference, since we know of matter only in so far as we perceive psychic images mediated by the senses.

We are surely making a great mistake when we forget this simple yet fundamental truth. Even if a neurosis had no cause at all other than imagination, it would, none the less, be a very real thing. If a man imagined that I was his arch-enemy and killed me, I should be dead on account of mere imagination. Imaginary conditions do exist and they may be just as real and just as harmful or dangerous as physical conditions. I even believe that psychic disturbances are far more dangerous than epidemics or earthquakes. Not even the medieval epidemics of bubonic plague or smallpox killed as many people as certain differences of opinion in 1914 or certain political "ideals" in Russia.

Although the mind cannot apprehend its own form of existence, owing to the lack of an Archimedean point outside, it nevertheless exists. Not only does the psyche exist, it is existence itself.[3]

Comparison of Psychic and External Experience

Compared with objects perceived in space, thoughts are usually dim and vague. They are largely under the control of the will, although an obsessive desire or image may recur in spite of our efforts to think of something. In contrast with psychic experience, sensory perceptions of objects in space impress themselves vividly and clearly upon the individual. They cannot be done away with by an act of will. They are there in space for all to see. The status of sensory data in science is secure.

These distinctions in terms of vividness, clearness, or control by the will are relative, not absolute conditions. What one perceives in a darkened room may be as weak and indistinct as thought. People who "see" ghosts may be those whose imagination exceeds their sensory processes in intensity. The influence of motivation over perception has been extensively studied, it being found that what people are interested in largely determines the characteristics they perceive. Psychic patterns fuse with sensory details in the activity of perceiving. To secure a reliable rule for differentiating internal from external data we must seek further.

Such a rule appears to exist in the stimulus origin of the experience. What is called outer or sensory experience comes into existence as a direct result of a stimulus occurring outside the human body. On the other hand, we note that in the case of inner or psychic experience, such as a recalled image, the

[3] Jung, *op. cit.,* p. 12.

stimulus originates within the body itself. This stimulus may itself be a delayed result of a previous external stimulus, but the immediate physical basis for the inner experience does not occur outside the body. As far as the experience itself is concerned, no discernible difference may exist between a vivid hallucination and an actual sensory impression, except that in the first case there is no external stimulus and in the second case there is.

Of course other persons confirm the sensory perception but not the hallucination, since no external stimulus exists for the latter. The relationship of the experience of one person to the experience of another provides another means for distinguishing inner from outer experience. In the case of external experience, two persons see the same object, a table, simultaneously. Both see something brown and flat on four legs. What one experiences the other also experiences. While it is true that their perspectives differ somewhat, most of the features of the table are the same, and, what is of key importance, the details of the table are experienced simultaneously. If the table is moved, the sensory impression of each is synchronized with the sensory impression of the other. If the table is rattled, they both hear it rattled at the same time.

On the other hand, two persons rarely have the same inner experiences at precisely the same time. In a class of students some may be following what the instructor is saying while others are daydreaming. Of the daydreamers, one may be thinking of a day at the beach, another a drive to the mountains. Their imagery is not synchronized as is their experience of the common world of objects in the classroom. Each has his own personal world of thoughts, desires, and feelings. The essence of inward experience is the individual unfolding of this world, while external experience is characterized by the simultaneous unfolding of the same stream of objects seen in space by different persons.

Verification of Data from Psychic Experience

The admissibility of data from psychic experience into the boundaries of social science depends upon the verifiability of these data. Data of the outer world are easily verifiable because each investigator may have a "look-see" at the same time. They can compare notes from instant to instant. Since each is talking about what is happening at the same point of time, it is relatively easy for each to point out to the other what he is seeing.

In comparing internal experiences, one student in medical school may experience a glowing vision of professional success at one time and a second medical student experience the same at still another. They do not experience their hopes and enthusiasms at the same instant of time. Does this mean that they could not mutually verify the pleasant anticipation which success in a medical career engenders? If they both experience the same elements of anticipation, each could corroborate these internal feelings, it not being necessary that each experience his vision of a professional future at the same instant of time. As a matter of fact, in the study of external data scientific investigators rarely trouble themselves to look at their objects of study simultaneously. They could if they wanted to, if each doubted the observational powers of the other, but simultaneous observation is not necessary for verification. The essential feature of verification is that each of two persons reports experiencing the same data. If each has the same experience, it is possible for both to report and describe that experience, regardless of simultaneity of the experiences of each. It therefore seems incontestable that internal data can be verified, provided the internal experiences of human beings have characteristics in common. The only way to determine whether these common features exist is to investigate the internal experiences of different persons. If such inquiry verifies that there are similarities from person to person, the knowledge in question becomes admitted to the status of science. When there are differences in conclusions, each investigator is called upon to analyze in full detail in terms of elemental characteristics exactly what the object is which he finds. Furthermore he is obligated to specify the particular locus where the object is to be found. This locus is specified by pointing out the space, time, or other structural relationships between the object and other phenomena on which investigators do agree. Continued collaboration in examining the psychic experience of others and of oneself is required until consensus is achieved.

By this pattern of procedure a considerable amount of psychic data and analysis have already been recorded in social science. Every culture contains inward features in respect to the values and beliefs which people in that culture experience in common. By interrogating a representative group of persons in the culture or by participating in the culture oneself it becomes possible to establish rather closely what the particular values and beliefs held by persons in that culture are. In the study of religious conviction and feeling social science proceeds in the same manner to determine what common psychic elements of religion are experienced by the group. Religion is largely a shared experience, and it is the common nature of psychic experience which not only gives people the conviction that their religious objects are public but also makes scientific verification of religious experience possible.

Scientists in a philosophical mood sometimes debate the question of whether two people can ever be certain that they are talking about the same object, especially one in inward experience, since neither has direct access even to the external experiences of the other. All one has are sensory impressions synchronized with those of others or ideas similar to those of others. The conclusion that the words of the other portray the same experience as one has oneself is a matter of inference. One might say for the sake of argument that a mischievous elf causes me to have a sensation of red when others have a sensation of green. As long as I use the word *green* to refer to my experience, neither I nor others will ever know that the colors have not been switched in my perceptual apparatus. This apparently childish quibble brings out something of research importance in the study of data from the inner experience of others. The objects in their inner experience are not conveniently synchronized with my state of thinking as are the objects which we all see in a common world of space perception. The conclusion that the person with whom I am talking actually reports the same object in inner experience which I think he does is a matter of inference. He may be a poor observer of his inward processes or he may desire to mislead me. I would be a naïve scientist if I took everything which people say about their beliefs, feelings, or purposes at its face value. Somehow I must accurately reconstruct from what people do tell me and from their actions what is the actual content of their inner world. The intriguing philosophical question of whether any inferences about the existence or nonexistence of the external or internal experiences of others can be proved by my experience need not concern us. Sensory and psychic data have the same scientific status in this respect.

Laws of Psychic Experience

Not only are similarities in descriptive features sought, but social science also seeks to see if the same uniform laws govern the psychic reactions of each person. This, of course, does not mean laws in the sense of political edicts, but rather cause-and-effect connections between psychic objects of people and their hereditary constitution, learning experiences, and social and geographic environment.

The figure of speech offered by William James of the "stream of consciousness" is an illuminating one. This stream of psychic as well as sensory experience flows steadily on through life like a river. A hydrologist in the study of rivers seeks for principles which relate variables of depth, width, sedimentation, curvature, gradient, and velocity to each other. In the same way the investigator into the stream of experience seeks for relationships which connect such variables as quality, intensity, form, and duration with each other. Ultimately religious experience may be reducible to such systematic terms, although description at present takes place at a simpler conceptual level. What are familiarly called spiritual laws by the religious-minded are actually principles dealing with the functioning of processes in the interior religious life.

Laws of psychic experience, whether of a general psychological scope or of a specific religious application, are obtained as insights by reflecting upon the content of inward experience, either that of others or of oneself. While necessitating much time and patience for their satisfactory observation, objects in inner experience such as thoughts and desires actually appear to be encompassed by a simpler system of principles than the network of cause-and-effect relationships involved in the complexities of overt behavior and its environment. With the aid of little experimental control beyond that possible in the manipulation of inner content, principles of thinking and motivation seem to be more readily detectable than laws of human behavior apart from inner experience. If the greater availability of laws of inner processes is doubted by anyone, let him take a sheet of paper and write on it all of the laws of human life of which he can think. What he will note first is that what he is able to write consists primarily of principles referring directly to inward processes, and second, the statements about behavior, excluding the trivial ones such as eating breakfast after awakening from sleep, represent statements demonstrated at the expense of considerable research effort compared with the task of reflecting upon commonsense aspects of inward experience. Intuitive principles from inward experience form the major propositions in schools of psychoanalysis, in the folk wisdom of culture by which scientists themselves for the most part live, and in the teachings of religions. As insights, these principles frequently stand in need of more precise development, but even as they stand, they indicate the possibilities of new and profitable directions for building psychological and social theory. The principles receive added verification when it is found that the behavior they predict actually takes place.

As far as research into human behavior is concerned, these psychic principles constitute hypotheses for testing and research. The genius of principles from inward experience is that these point to key variables in behavior with which the inner variables are intimately associated, and the psychic principles spotlight the relationship between the behavior variables. This relationship can then be studied exhaustively and made more precise by case studies or mathematical analysis. Without the benefit of introspective insights, the investigator would not know which of innumerable behavior variables are fruitful for study through being causally or functionally related to each other. Principles from inward experience tell him the variables whose more exact formulation is required and whose functional relationships he can usefully test. In the first stage of a psychological survey, it would not be possible to construct a sensible questionnaire without aid in the choice and wording of questions given by reflections from inward experience.

An example or two may serve to make clear the assistance which is provided by study of inner experience for behavioral research. A scientist from a strange land (and most scientists come from strange lands in their first approach to research problems not previously experienced by them) has available to him a mass of behavior data about life in an American town. By using a duplicating machine and the mails or canvassers he can collect answers to countless questions and thereby multiply his data. Let us suppose part of the vast array of data include whistles blown and people running. Are these two events of chance connection? By searching for the inward meaning of these actions, the scientist readily discovers that they have a common factor, getting to a fire to put it out. The pieces of behavior can at once be fitted into a known system of principles of motivation. Similarly, bell ringing and incense burning in religious ritual fall into a coherent pattern when their inward meaning in terms of desires, beliefs, hopes, and faith is known.

While some behavioral scientists disavow the aid of insights from inner experience, it can sometimes be seen that the behavioristic theories which they espouse are in effect projections of their unconscious thought processes. What transpires involuntarily as part of the scientific procedure merits a formal place in order that its contribution to behavioral study may be properly assessed and fully utilized. Yet, as far as religion is concerned, the assistance which psychic study gives to analysis of behavior is only part of its importance for religion. The heart of religion is the interior life. Until science has succeeded in unraveling this, it cannot be expected to displace insights accumulated by generations of religious seekers from a prescientific era. Physiological psychology, such as that which has been conducted in Russia, is to be commended for its treatment of functioning of the nervous system.[4] However, the practical control over one's own actions or those of others is through evoking ideas or appealing to wants in psychic life. Unless these are accurately understood in terms of systematic principles, control over people through psychological knowledge is not possible except in certain physical respects.

REPORTING PSYCHIC FEATURES OF RELIGION

Scientific techniques for studying experience in religion do not differ from those employed for investigating thinking and motivation in economics, politics, education, or family life, our review of these applying to social phenomena in general. Nor is it necessary to distinguish between psychology and other social sciences concerned with data from inner experience. How shall the investigator study what goes on there? He cannot see into the mind of another to learn by direct observation the thoughts and feelings of another. If he is studying objects in space, he has only to go and look for himself since he knows that what he sees is what others also see. The standard procedure of social and psychological science is to enlist the aid of the individual as an observer. Ordinarily a scientist prefers to do his own observing. If he is unable to do this, even the physical scientist may rely upon data reported by nonscientists.

Sometimes data from inner experience have been recorded by subjects in letters or autobiographical accounts. The most notable collection and analysis of such case studies in religion was made a half century ago by William James in *The Varieties of Religious Experience.* In this project he drew considerably upon the work of others, putting their results together with fine literary style. A current series of case studies is described by

[4] B. Simon (ed.), *Psychology in the Soviet Union,* Stanford University Press, 1957.

P. E. Johnson in *Personality and Religion*.[5] Frequently social scientists interrogate their subjects where the subjects live. Pauline Young's *Pilgrims of Russian Town* is a field study by a sociologist, and numerous studies of primitive religions have been made by anthropologists through field work.[6]

Interviewing

Many of the techniques of social science are concerned with the special problem of how to secure as complete and accurate information as possible from the respondent. Formidable problems of observation and report arise. Things in the interior experience of people do not endure as do external objects, which can be depended upon to be "there" when looked for. Frequently the flow of ideas can only be caught and reported in recollection. Memory is subject to flaws. The social scientist not only gets his data second-hand from the subject, but the subject frequently makes his report second-hand because he reports not what he experiences at the time of the interview but what he remembers of experiences at an earlier time.

Even when the subject is engaged in the particular experience which he is reporting, it must be noted that things in this experience are typically dim and vague. When one turns one's attention self-consciously to report them, the shift in the field of attention may cause them to disappear altogether.

Furthermore, some kind of appeal must be made to the subject to gain his coöperation. Human beings do not typically wish to spend time talking with scientific busybodies. The appeal for the subject's coöperation may be financial, but this increases the cost of scientific work. The appeal may be to vanity or sympathy, but these may cause the subject to exaggerate his experiences. If the subject interviewed is applying for admission to school or employment, he tends to say what will improve his standing with the interviewer. The best appeal seems to be in terms of helping the cause of science. If the subject responds to this appeal, he realizes the importance of strict accuracy in scientific work.

Assuming the subject's readiness to coöperate, it is still neces-

[5] P. E. Johnson, *Personality and Religion,* Abingdon, 1957.

[6] Pauline Young, *Pilgrims of Russian Town,* University of Chicago Press, 1932. Among numerous examples of anthropological studies of religion is A. Radcliffe-Brown, *The Andaman Islanders,* Free Press, 1948. Among sociological researchers into contemporary denominational life are J. H. Fichter and Marshall Sklare, whose works are cited later. A new scientific journal, the *Review of Religious Research,* appeared in 1959.

sary to ask him questions. In some research, the subject is simply told to start talking about anything he wishes, but the communication may then lead slowly, if at all, to the things which the scientist wishes to know. The difficulty in asking questions is that ideas are planted by phrasing of the questions which would not otherwise be in the subject's mind. General questions which merely call attention to topics for reporting are preferable to specific ones. If specific questions are asked, careful judgment is required in formulating questions in a neutral manner. Even neutral questions, however, carry overtones of suggestion which may influence the subject's account of himself in subtle ways. The scientific interviewer tries to strike a balance between completeness and accuracy of report, realizing that for completeness he must ask many questions, and that for accuracy he must ask as few questions as possible.

The stressing of techniques to the student helps make plain that those engaged in religious, as well as other social, research do not proceed haphazardly to gain the opinions and experiences of others, but seek to do so as accurately and completely as possible. At times cross-questioning may be necessary to determine how consistent the subject is in his reports. Interviewing is a scientific technique calling for a large amount of skill in securing information of scientific value from respondents untrained in scientific reporting.

Written Questionnaires

A form of interrogation in which the personal equation of the interviewer is eliminated is provided by the printed questionnaire, personal equation meaning the distortion of data owing to uncontrolled variations in the attitudes of different interviewers. With written interrogation, all subjects are asked identical questions in exactly the same way. The replies may be in the form of alternative answers to be checked, in which case statistical summarizing of replies is made easier, although some sacrifice in accuracy is thereby made since the individual may not feel that any of the alternatives offered fit his case. Furthermore, printed questions with uniform types of answers introduce distortions in proportion to the respondent's lack of objective self-knowledge. As an example of questionnaire research into religious experience, the reader is referred to the study of religion among college students reported by Gordon Allport in *The Individual and His Religion*.[7] The first major such study is that of re-

[7] G. W. Allport, *The Individual and His Religion,* Macmillan, 1950.

ligious conversion made by E. D. Starbuck, entitled *The Psychology of Religion.*[8]

Psychological Measurement

Where standardized questions are asked, statistical techniques may be employed for rating or ranking subjects along a scale according to the quality or intensity of their opinions or feelings. Much of the social research now current has been concerned with devising such social barometers or thermometers for measuring variable factors in the subject's experience. Although little has been done in religious research along this line, there seems to be no reason why the same mathematical principles cannot be applied.

One problem of particular importance to religion is the measurement of desire. In order for there to be a universal system of values applying to all human beings, there must be uniform ways of measuring desire and the things which bring about its fulfillment. A special research interest of the author has been in the measurement of consumer desire, applications of which can be made to any field of motivation. By the use of the methods which have been developed step by step in psychometrics during the past three decades, it is possible to measure the intensity of desires in a way which satisfies the same conditions as physical measurement except for physical separability of quantities. A desire cannot be cut into two lengths as sections of a foot rule, but numerical values are assigned to various degrees of desires so that the equivalence of different combinations of desires is correctly shown and the part which desires play in functional relationships to other variables arithmetically described. It becomes possible to say in a meaningful way that one desire or its satisfaction is twice the intensity of another, and a calculus of the greatest good of the greatest number from the standpoint of spiritual fulfillment becomes at least theoretically possible. Explanation of the measuring procedures is beyond the scope of this text, but their nature is basic to a science of values, and the reader is referred to current literature.[9]

[8] E. D. Starbuck, *The Psychology of Religion,* Scribners, 1899.

[9] P. H. Benson and J. H. Platten, Jr., "Preference Measurement by the Methods of Successive Intervals and Monetary Estimates," *Journal of Applied Psychology,* December, 1956, pp. 412–414; A. L. Edwards, *Techniques of Attitude Scale Construction,* Appleton-Century-Crofts, 1957; J. P. Guilford, *Psychometric Methods,* McGraw-Hill, 1954; H. O. Gulliksen, "Measurement of Subjective Values," *Psychometrika,* September, 1956, pp. 229–244; S. S. Stevens, "On the Psychophysical Law," *Psychological*

If it is recognized that self-seeking desires are self-defeating with respect to their potential fulfillment and that a spiritual way of life premised upon desiring the welfare of others permits a maximum experience of self-realization for all human beings, then the measurement of desire and of its accompanying feeling of fulfillment occupies a central place in religious science. The particular conditions under which religious development optimally proceeds can be made the subject of research investigation. It cannot be said that something is good simply because it is desired, but it is possible to conduct research into the type of spiritual aspirations out of which human personality is most appropriately constructed and to indicate the social and educational means for developing such personality within the capacities conferred by heredity. A hierarchy of experiences which are desired can be constructed on a uniform numerical basis, although much practical research remains to be done before this is accomplished. It goes without saying that the intensity of people's desires shifts according to circumstances in the backgrounds of individuals or in their opportunities for fulfillment. Yet the way is opened by the metric techniques to establishing laws about human desire and the conditions of its realization. It is possible to speak of measuring human values, that is, things which fulfill desires, and of formulating laws governing values. Obvious distinctions exist between what people think will fulfill their desires and what actually will, and between the values which people do hold and those which would give them a larger experience of fulfillment of desire if they did hold them. Such distinctions and relationships are features studied in an empirical science of values.

Participant Observation

Human subjects are not easily accessible for interrogation. When they do consent to come into an office where interviewing takes place, something of the luster of their lives is lost by taking them out of their natural situation. Like shells of the sea, they look a neutral gray after being wrested from their habitat. Consequently, social scientists employ participant observation in an effort to capture more fully the real qualities of life. In participant observation one becomes a member of the group being studied—an employee, a neighbor, a churchgoer, or a dweller in

Review, May, 1957, pp. 153–181; L. L. Thurstone and L. V. Jones, "The Rational Origin for Measuring Subjective Values," *Journal of the American Statistical Association,* December, 1957, pp. 458–471.

the criminal underworld. By this means the investigator sees and hears for himself. The range of his questions may be widened by his participant location, and the answers he gets are frequently more genuine. He can examine his own experience as a group member to appreciate more fully its psychological feelings.

The participant role is not a garb to be easily donned. Time is required to gain the confidence of the group and develop understanding of its common life. Especially in religion, participation is slow to produce meaningful results. Since religious life, according to its creed, may require a lifetime to develop, a congregation must be joined and followed in its precepts and practices for many years in order to appreciate the qualities of life thereby created.

The casual visitor to the religious services in an Orthodox Jewish synagogue would find them incomprehensible, so also would the uninformed individual who witnesses Catholic Mass without intimate instruction about the meaning of its various acts. Such visitation amounts to looking into a church through the outside of stained-glass windows. One must go inside to see them in their full beauty and significance, and the same should be said of religious ritual in general. One must be "on the inside" through sympathetic understanding of the feelings and purposes of the religious group to gain intelligent meaning of its strange procedures.

INTROSPECTION AS AN AID TO SCIENTIFIC RESEARCH IN RELIGION

Need for Trained Introspection

The average individual in reporting his interior experiences is only able to report his concrete impressions in a casual way. These experiences contain many component elements of which the individual is little aware, if at all. He is aware of the totality as it streams through his mind. What that totality contains can only be learned by more searching analysis.

It is a property of all inner experiences that if the individual allows his mind to dwell upon them extensively, they tend to break up into simpler parts which the individual can then observe and report. This is the typical experience of abstraction which every human being has when he analyzes a complex situation, such as religion, to himself. He keeps mulling it over in his mind until its salient features emerge as new insights in his consciousness. At first he is only aware of the total configuration; then he becomes aware of separate characteristics out of which the configuration is compounded.

If the individual receives training in fixing his attention upon his interior experience, he is able to report much that would otherwise escape his notice. The average subject lacks the motivation or training for such introspection. The question then arises, if it is appropriate for the scientist to study the personal experiences of other persons, why may he not also study his own experiential world? Which is preferable, to rely only upon reports by untrained subjects, or to employ also the reports made by trained scientists? The answer seems plain: it is equally, if not more, justifiable to utilize reports from trained introspectionists than from ordinary persons.

In the study of religion, introspection seems especially fruitful because many of the pertinent elements of religious experience and motivation can be disclosed through introspective analysis more effectively than by relying only upon direct reports by untutored participants. The average student will find that religion becomes more intelligible to him to the extent that he introspects his own experiences. The religious seers of the past evidently gained much of their insight through prolonged reflection and analysis of religious experience.

Although present investigators have shown reluctance to embark upon introspective projects of self-analysis, it is widely admitted that introspection may be a fertile source of hypotheses which can then be subjected to test by other means than introspection. If introspection is useful at all as a source of hypotheses, this apparently is an argument in favor of its being carried on as systematically as possible, if only in the quest for hypotheses to be tested by other methods.

It is quite possible that many of the most important scientific insights about religion or man's mental and emotional life generally are incapable of being subjected to completely rigorous test. When this limitation exists, investigators may choose between no knowledge or introspective knowledge. Rather than castigate the faultiness of a scientific technique such as introspection, it may be preferable to gain as much proficiency as possible in assembling verifiable knowledge by its aid.

Difficulties in Introspection

Yet we must recognize that introspection, by which is meant self-observation by the scientist, has not been in good standing in recent decades. During the nineteenth century a considerable amount of work was done in psychology by introspection, most of it in the study of processes of sensory perception, but some of it also concerned with the principles of association and recollection of ideas. William James's *Principles of Psychology* was a highpoint reached by introspective psychology in America. Concerning methods of investigation in psychology he wrote:

> *Introspective Observation is what we have to rely on first and foremost and always.* The word introspection need hardly be defined—it means, of course, the looking into our own minds and reporting what we there discover. *Every one agrees that we there discover states of consciousness.* So far as I know, the existence of such states has never been doubted by any critic, however skeptical in other respects he may have been. That we have *cogitations* of some sort is the *inconcussum* in a world most of whose other facts have at some time tottered in the breath of philosophic doubt. All people unhesitatingly believe that they feel themselves thinking, and that they distinguish the mental state as an inward activity or passion, from all the objects with which it may cognitively deal. *I regard this belief as the most fundamental of all the postulates of Psychology,* and shall discard all curious inquiries about its certainty as too metaphysical for the scope of this book.[10]

Work in psychology with introspection led to intense and seemingly insoluble disagreements. An endless variety of conflicting reports were made by investigators. The subject matter proved to be difficult to work with because of its vagueness. Introspection of thoughts is especially elusive since thoughts are frequently colorless and nonvisual, primarily controlled by symbols viewed or recollected. To a considerable extent psychologists ceased their arguments and inquiries and simply abandoned introspection in favor of more tangible lines of investigation. Introspection was not disproved; it simply became ignored. With that cessation of introspection there also took place a declining interest on the part of psychologists in inner experience in general, by whatever techniques studied, and to a lesser extent sociology was similarly affected. More recently the study of preference and satisfaction in school, vocation, and marital life has increased scientific interest in the study of inward experience.

The two principal arguments against introspection appear to be difficulty and disagreement. Yet neither of these has for long been accepted in science as a valid argument against research in a complex area. Where there is difficulty of techniques, scientists seek through study and practice to improve their techniques.

[10] William James, *Principles of Psychology,* 2 vols., Dover, 1950, Vol. I, p. 185.

Where there is disagreement, they continue their inquiry, carefully reviewing their methods and findings step by step until agreement can be reached. No inherent reason appears to exist why introspection cannot be fully restored to the equipment of social and psychological scientists if they choose to take it up systematically. James's comments on the status of introspection seem as sound today as when they were written by him.

> . . . our general conclusion [is] that *introspection is difficult and fallible; and that the difficulty is simply that of all observation of whatever kind.* Something is before us; we do our best to tell what it is, but in spite of our good will we may go astray, and give a description more applicable to some other sort of thing. The only safeguard is in the final *consensus* of our farther knowledge about the thing in question, later views correcting earlier ones, until at last the harmony of a consistent system is reached. Such a system, gradually worked out, is the best guarantee the psychologist can give for the soundness of any particular psychologic observation which he may report. Such a system we ourselves must strive, as far as may be, to attain.
>
> The English writers on psychology, and the school of Herbart in Germany, have in the main contented themselves with such results as the immediate introspection of single individuals gave, and shown what a body of doctrine they may make. The works of Locke, Hume, Reid, Hartley, Stewart, Brown, the Mills, will always be classics in this line; and in Professor Bain's Treatises we have probably the last word of what this method taken mainly by itself can do. . . .[11]

It seems clear that verification of facts of psychic experience in religion is similar to verification of other facts of experience. Observation is continued until a consensus is reached among observers as to the data they find. Whatever religious realities are thereby disclosed in the psychic world have status as scientific data.

Introspective Technique

It is not easy to state the details of how introspection is to be carried on. Simple reporting of sensory impressions is much easier than analyzing processes of thinking and desiring. If one meditates for long intervals of time upon one's inner experiences, one finds that they tend, of their own accord, to become differentiated into component elements, becoming associated with verbal symbols used with them. It is helpful with new material to vary the content about which one reflects. New content is recalled by symbols or ideas of symbols. This variation causes

[11] *Ibid.,* Vol. I, pp. 191–192.

differential association of a residual component with a symbol of its own. In tracing problems similar to ones covered, steady concentration is effective. In approaching new problems, note taking on the progressive results of introspection stimulates further differentiation of material. It is desirable to repeat and continue one's introspection until no new elements are forthcoming. When this plateau of stability has been reached, one has reasonable assurance that one has a clear grasp of the psychic elements involved at that level of analysis.

The process of introspection into one's individual world seems to be the same thought process which one carries on in the study of ordinary problems or situations outside of oneself. One thinks about external problems by means of thoughts derived from experience and recalled to mind by verbal symbols. These thoughts become resolved into their key elements by repeated reflection upon them. When one can find out nothing more by thinking about a problem, one assumes that the more important strands of the problem have been seen by the mind. The activity of study is therefore similar to introspection, except that introspection directs one's study to objects of the interior world, rather than to reflecting upon thoughts of events in the world of objects. Subjecting inner experience to analysis by abstraction can be referred to as introspective analysis to differentiate it from the bare reporting which characterizes simple introspection of sensory perceptions or inward experiences.

The foregoing is a general description of introspective or intuitive analysis. In application to concrete problems, multiple use is made of previous literature, source materials and fresh data in stimulating and guiding reflection upon psychic materials. C. W. Mills has given a description of details of the craftsmanship involved in the search for new ideas and hypotheses.[12] The stage in research of formulating these overtowers all else in scientific development in the social sciences. The mechanical details of data collection and statistical analysis are minor phases compared with the development of psychological insight and the construction of frameworks of theory.

Since introspective analysis is a psychological process which each student must perform for himself, the futility of learning conclusions by rote is readily seen. Verbal instruction is of value only insofar as it guides the mind in the process of abstracting components from psychic materials. Large amounts of time are

[12] C. W. Mills, *The Sociological Imagination,* Oxford University Press, 1959, pp. 195–226.

needed to accomplish difficult acts of abstraction. This is an opportunity often denied the reflective student who is harrassed by recurring course assignments, papers, and examinations. In place of the dizzy whirlpool of facts and words in which students are often immersed, leisure for reflection is of paramount importance to intellectual development. This is especially important in religious study, where the distillation and weighing of alternative concepts or hypotheses can hardly be encompassed by a one-semester course of study. What is gained in a single course of study is intended to make more effective a process of inquiry and development which can extend life long.

PSYCHOANALYTIC STUDY OF RELIGION

Rise of Psychoanalysis

During the first third of the twentieth century, psychology was preoccupied with study of physiological and behavioristic aspects of personality, and interest within psychology in the inner or psychic side of personality was at a minimum. Meanwhile, three other scientific disciplines turned to this neglected field for inquiry. Sociology and anthropology investigated internal features of culture, delineating ways in which people in groups think and feel, as well as how they act. Psychoanalysis, with nineteenth-century medical roots in the treatment of mental disorder, rapidly moved toward a total study of human personality, with principal attention being given to pathology of the interior life of the individual. Drives, impulses, and inner conflicts, which can be meagerly dealt with, if at all, in terms of the surface data of behavior, became leading topics for investigation. While the starting point was the treatment of neuroses and psychoses, the conclusions have been of general significance for an understanding of normal as well as abnormal personality. More recently, the findings have become increasingly merged, along with some from sociology and anthropology, in the field of psychology. The latter field still pays occasional and nominal respect to its former principle of excluding all except external data from its domain, but implicitly, at least, many of the inner implications from related disciplines have become embodied in its main stream.

Sigmund Freud and C. G. Jung, both leading figures in psychoanalysis, have been very much interested in the relationship of religion to mental disorder and have analyzed different aspects of that relationship. In his clinical studies, Freud found ways in which religious institutions harmfully repress individual development, emphasizing the inflexible wall of repression built around the sexual urge. Jung has been interested in the aid which religious participation gives the individual in the achievement of personality integration. Less conflict than is generally realized exists between the views of these two men because they are concerned with different aspects of religion. Because of religion's relationship to mental health, it follows that psychoanalysis, an active branch of science studying mental health, is an important area in the scientific study of religion.

Field of Psychoanalysis

In speaking of psychoanalysis, we are to keep in mind that the word may be used in two senses. In its broader meaning, psychoanalysis refers to the methods and theories developed by Sigmund Freud and those who came after him, some in strong disagreement with him, for scientific study of personality in general, especially its psychic conditions, and particularly its unconscious aspects. In the restricted sense, psychoanalysis is an intensive form of case study and treatment of individual mental disorder originated by Freud. Other psychoanalysts, such as Alfred Adler and C. G. Jung, have developed different methods of treatment, which they do not call psychoanalysis. It is in the sense of psychoanalysis as a science of people in general, rather than a program of individual treatment, that the approach of psychoanalysis in the study of religion is considered here.

Debate goes on as to the exact meaning of various psychoanalytic categories, but the general approach seems to have established itself as a science, notably because of its effectiveness in predicting and controlling the course of mental disorder. The major assumption is that behavior is not only guided by thoughts and impulses of which the individual is conscious, but behavior is also under the influence of forces operating in the unconscious mind. Since much religious activity takes place under the influence of unconscious motives, the analysis of the unconscious phases of the subject's life plays an important part in the study of religion.

Study of the Unconscious

In the development of psychoanalysis, it early became apparent that those features of interior experience of which the individual is conscious provide inadequate ground for an understanding of human beings, especially those who are emotionally sick. Attention was focused on desires once experienced and now repressed, and on impulses never consciously felt by the individual because thwarted in their normal development. These things came to be recognized as important psychic determinants of behavior. Since these either had been consciously experienced in the past or could be consciously experienced in the future but were not in consciousness in the present, they were designated as "unconscious" ingredients of personality.

The *unconscious* refers to things which are latent but not yet apparent in experience, or to things which have been experienced but are not now accessible for recall, having become forgotten or repressed. The reality of the unconscious is assumed in the present because of its effects upon ongoing behavior and experience. Symptoms or actions betray the existence of forces in the mind of which the person is unaware.

To speak of unconscious phases of interior experience seems at first sight a contradiction in terms. We are either conscious of what we experience in our thoughts and feelings or else we are not conscious of it, meaning that it is not in our experience. Actually the relationship of conscious to unconscious is not simple and categorical. Certain things may be on the fringe of consciousness, as when we successfully maneuver a car through traffic while concentrating upon conversation with a passenger. Awareness of other cars and traffic hazards is said to be "subconscious." Technically, we are responding to these stimuli while conversing, but they operate below the threshold of actual awareness. An individual who suffers a blow on the head or who is under the influence of alcohol may nevertheless find his way home subconsciously and the next day remember nothing of the episode, it having left no discernible trace in his experience.

In another sense there are things actually in our experience, but we are not conscious of them as distinct objects. Much of the learning process of human beings has to do with making explicit what is at first only implicit in our experience. The schoolboy who looks at a diagram of the Pythagorean theorem has all of the perceptual experience needed to proceed with his proof. But this experience comes to him initially as a totality. The distinct parts and their relationships which he must discover are at first blended together in this totality. He is aware of the totality, but not of its components one by one. He discovers these by reflection. As he ponders his problem, the elements eventually emerge as separate insights. Can we say he did not experience them before? He experienced them, but not separate one from the other. After he abstracts them, he experiences them one at a time. He sees them step by step in a way which leads to proof that the sum of the squares of the legs equals the square of the hypotenuse of the right triangle.

According to psychoanalysis, the motives of human beings as these are thought about by the individual develop through the same process of abstraction. Initially our motivations are buried in total experiences, part of vague, undifferentiated urges. Gradually motives become differentiated as distinct impulses of which we are separately aware. The child who first imitates her mother's love by caring for a doll is having a social experience out of which her own love for a child will eventually develop. A child caring for a doll cannot be said to have a conscious motive of love for another's well-being. After continuing years of development, such a motive finally emerges as a distinct impulse. The child, by that time an adolescent, then experiences a conscious desire to take care of others. The process of emergence tends to take place of its own accord, but is facilitated by educational experiences and by introspective reflection upon one's inward nature. Prior to their emergence into conscious awareness, and sometimes thereafter, motives are not integrated into a unified personality structure. The integration is accomplished through cultural indoctrination with patterns of organization and by the individual as his own architect consciously selecting and putting together those components of which he seeks his personality to be built. The Swiss psychiatrist C. G. Jung has dwelled at length in his clinical studies and writings upon the part which religious activities play in the development and organization of motivation and belief. He and Gardner Murphy in the United States have both centered attention upon the concept of differentiation in personality development. To dynamic ideas and motives Jung has given the term *archetypes,* and their development in personality is Jung's principal concern. These universally compelling psychological forces become distinct entities after they have separated from the common core of psychic and social experience which all human beings have. Where do these exist before their emergence? They are technically within our experience, but since this experience is at first a totality, we are not aware of these motives. If they influence our behavior, they do so without our being aware of them, without our knowing why we act. Some complexes of ideas and motives remain mostly in the unconscious. Symbolic images in culture for influencing them have an important place in social control. Jung has given to this kind of unconscious motivation the term *collective uncon-*

scious. The adjective means that all human beings share the same common storehouse of experience out of which specific motives may emerge. Jung ascribes a hereditary origin to the collective unconscious, which has been a topic of strong debate among psychologists.

Analysis of processes in the collective unconscious occupies particular importance in religious study since compelling ideas central to religious activity come out of this unconscious realm. These are frequently among the most advanced abstractions of which the human mind is capable, although religion remains of deep consequence to masses of people whose facility for abstraction does not equal that of the trained scientist. In the event that education and social development have not overcome this limitation, religion speaks to the unconscious condition of people, influencing and directing their subterranean longings which they poorly articulate, if at all. An understanding of the functioning of religion in addressing itself to unconscious needs and in bringing these needs to conscious expression presupposes a knowledge of the dynamics of unconscious mental and emotional processes. Religion is not only concerned with the interior life, it is an affair of the unconscious.

Sometimes the emergence of motivations from the collective unconscious is thwarted by personal frustration or adverse cultural teaching. If the emergence is blocked, nervous disturbances of a mild or a serious character may result. When thoughts or desires become repressed, a third category of unconscious material is defined. By this is meant that they become logically contradicted by other thoughts or experiences which are more powerful. A desire may be blocked by circumstances which make its realization impossible, as when one is rejected by the girl courted in matrimony. Or a desire may be blocked because it conflicts with another desire dominating the individual's mind, as when a professional career crowds out maternal goals. In either case the frustrated desire is partially or completely pushed out of consciousness by the ascendant experiences. As long as the blocked motivation continues to press for attention, the subject may experience dissatisfaction, unhappiness, or nervousness.

Eventually the motive may be forgotten and pass out of the mind altogether. If the individual is frequently reminded of his blocked desire, it is not forgotten and may continue in the individual's unconscious mind as a threat to his mental and emotional stability. The blocked desire may reappear infrequently in conscious experience or may not appear at all. It may have once been conscious or it may never have emerged from the unconscious realm. Freud calls repressed material which can become conscious by the term *unconscious,* Jung's term for this category being the *personal unconscious,* the impulse failing to appear in conscious experience because of individual circumstances of repression. Both the collective and individual unconscious are assumed to be component parts of the personality system, just as all motivations, whether functioning in inward experience or not, are components grounded in the structure of the nervous system. The criterion for the special distinction made between the conscious and unconscious portions of personality is accessibility of the psychic object for recall.

Psychoanalytic Procedures

Concepts and techniques of psychoanalysis as a method of scientific inquiry merit careful examination and appraisal, since upon their validity depend findings of psychoanalysis in the study of religion. The techniques employed include introspection, which Freud and Jung acknowledge as a source of insights into the dynamics of personality, although neither attaches full importance to the technique as a systematic scientific procedure. Jung indicates that by patient self-study the individual can reduce material in the collective unconscious to contents of which he is consciously aware, although few are capable of undertaking such a project without counsel from others skilled in their understanding of personality. Repressed material blocked by other experiences is not available for introspection as long as the blocking continues. Psychoanalysis is distinctive for its development of techniques for discovering the content of the unconscious portion of personality.

The technique elevated by Freud to a systematic procedure for learning the content of the unconscious domain is dream analysis. The theory underlying this approach is that desires of which the individual is not aware reveal themselves in a symbolic manner in the dream life of the individual between sleeping and waking. Upset digestion or nervous tension may provide the stimulus for the dream state, but the pattern which the dream assumes is a function of forces in the unconscious. Garbed in picturesque symbols, these forces enact their drama in the episode of the dream, which may profoundly reveal key elements in the individual's psychic make-up, elements he is unable to grasp in his waking life. The interpretation of dreams is not new with psychoanalysis. One recalls the role played by dreams in religious prophecy in the Old Testament.

The symbolism of dreams may be elaborate and variable from dream to dream. Usually a series of dreams, plus knowledge of the individual's actual circumstances, are needed to unfathom the content of his unconscious mind. A simple illustration of how a dream foretells what is happening in the individual's mind is furnished by the following. The subject dreams that he is walking in an orchard, enjoying the shade and sweet fruit to eat. Abruptly he reaches the edge of the orchard and stands in the glaring sunlight.

In this dream, fruit symbolizes pleasures, especially sexual ones. The sun, also circles or other perfect geometric figures, symbolize the experience of God. What the dream shows is that the subject is enjoying life as he samples pleasure after pleasure, but that eventually this course of life must reach an end, the individual then standing face to face with his God, from whose piercing light he cannot escape. The dream forewarns the individual of what is in store for him if he follows his present life pattern. The example given here is an oversimplification, since usually many dreams are needed for reliable interpretation of the individual's unconscious life.

A second technique developed by Freud for discovering the content of the unconscious mind is free association. The patient may recline on a couch without facing the interviewer and is instructed to describe whatever comes into his mind, relaxing any tendency to direct his thinking. One thought suggests another. The stream of associated ideas carries out some of the hidden contents of the unconscious mind. Ideas whose appearance might be expected from the flow of thought but which are resisted by the patient give additional clues to what is repressed and what does the repressing. As an aid to stimulating the patient's flow of ideas in revealing directions, Jung devised a free-association word test. Key words are read as stimuli, the individual being instructed to reply as quickly as possible with the first thought suggested by the stimulus. In theory those thoughts near the borderline of consciousness may be drawn forth by the stimulus momentarily, before the individual for conventional reasons refuses to recognize them. Still another variant is the confessional interview in which the respondent is encouraged by the analyst's sympathetic reaction to pour out his feelings as completely as possible. In the talking-out process, material otherwise repressed tends to be carried along with the conscious thoughts. The unconscious pieces tend to form a pattern, and the skilled analyst can then determine what the content of the unconscious mind is.

An approach of increasing interest in the past two decades is provided by the Rorschach ink-blot test, the thematic apperception test, and other projective devices. The interpretations which the respondent gives of irregular ink blotches or of suggestive pictures whose story is told by the respondent reveal patterns of thinking beneath the surface. These devices are also useful in determining conscious attitudes which the respondent might not otherwise communicate because of their impropriety.

The interests and techniques of the psychoanalyst are not limited to probing unconscious processes. Unconscious events require being fitted into the total life scheme of the individual for their proper understanding. Psychoanalysis reiterates the essential unity of personality as a dynamic system. The life history of the individual, as he or his associates relate it, gives essential information. In approaching conscious areas of inward experience, psychoanalysis uses any appropriate reportorial techniques found also in psychology, sociology, or anthropology. A comprehensive exposition of principles and techniques of psychoanalysis is given by Ruth Munroe,[13] and shorter summaries in relation to other theories of personality are found in a recent work by Calvin S. Hall and Gardner Lindzey.[14] A synthesis of Jung's concepts has been made by Jolande Jacobi.[15]

EXTERNAL PROCEDURES FOR STUDYING RELIGION

Approaches to inner experience such as interviewing, introspection, and dream analysis are only some of the means for studying religion or any other social phenomena. Other lines of inquiry are possible which employ external data. Study of the individual's behavior, his situation, and his physiological make-up may supplement techniques for studying inward aspects of his life or may be utilized by those researchers who wish to avoid all involvement in the analysis of inner data. As has been noted, speech reactions or replies to questionnaires can be treated as external data, rather than as reports by the subject about inward data. Statistical surveys of membership, belief, and ritual afford

[13] R. Munroe, *Schools of Psychoanalytic Thought,* Dryden, 1955.

[14] C. S. Hall and G. Lindzey, *Theories of Personality,* Wiley, 1957.

[15] J. Jacobi, *The Psychology of Jung,* tr. by K. W. Bash, Yale University Press, 1951.

important findings concerning externals of religion. These surveys utilize interviews and questionnaires to collect data about external aspects of life, such as people's activities and the group situations in which activities take place.

Usually a sharp line cannot be drawn between procedures which use inner data and those which rely upon outer data. The former may suggest hypotheses for analyzing the latter, and the latter may be used as a factual basis for making inferences about the former. Not only speech reactions but actions of the individual reveal what his desires and beliefs are. As is said in a court of law, people are presumed to intend the natural and probable consequences of their actions. If a parishioner dozes during the sermon, the minister knows the parishioner comes to church for some other purpose than to hear it. Or if a boy takes money from the collection box, it is evident he does not believe honesty to be the best policy, whatever he says to his Sunday School teacher.

A basic principle of personality development is that motives and beliefs are products of situations in which the individual has lived. As is said epigrammatically, love begets love and violence begets violence. A knowledge of such situations provides the basis for inferring what the present attitudes of the individual are. If inferences from behavior, past experience, and verbal reports by the subject all lead to the same picture of his interior make-up, a high probability of correct conclusions is achieved.

Behavior data have particular usefulness in researching principles about the interior processes of personality. As initial insights, these principles are vague theories, such as the epigram just cited. In analyzing a case study, these principles are put together in a chain of deductions pointing to a program of therapy and its outcome. One of the tasks of a psychiatrist or case worker in a prison is to make predictions concerning the likelihood that an inmate will commit no further crime after his release. Information in the background and behavior of the individual, as well as what he says about himself, form the basis for inferring a picture of the individual's actual life aims and belief. From his motivation the conclusion is reached as to whether he is prone to further crime and under what circumstances. After release, the offender's subsequent record confirms or upsets the prediction. If the prediction is not supported, the deductive reasoning which led to it must be adjusted to explain the actual result. This enables the researcher to place the principles of motivation in a more precise context and to narrow the margin of error in future predictions about other cases. The same type of analysis is involved in evaluating the effectiveness of a religious program upon the personality development of members of a church congregation. General principles of religious development known first as intuitions from inner experience receive more precise statement in terms of actual cases of individuals whose lives reflect these principles.

In mathematical analysis of behavior data, the researcher seeks to incorporate results from a series of cases by stating the relationship between variables found in the cases. While scientific progress in this direction has so far been somewhat limited, especially as far as religious behavior is concerned, the research opportunities seem largely undeveloped. No inherent reason exists why mathematics might not be applied to problems of religious psychology as well as other kinds of motivational situations. The effect of analyzing either single cases or a group of mathematically related cases is to make more precise the general intuitive principles stemming from the interior life.

Of most importance is the added verification which facts of behavior give to theories evolved from study of inner experience. It has been said half humorously of ministers and social workers that since they keep the score of the behavior problems solved in their community, they are generally satisfied with their efforts. Especially in religious expression, human beings seem prone to think wishfully concerning the principles in which they believe. Whether these principles are valid is shown by careful examination of the life activities to which they lead. Spiritual principles which are unrealistic receive a valuable correction when the lives of religious-minded persons are studied to see what happens in the working out of these principles.

To summarize, neither external nor internal analysis of religion is sufficient by itself. Each performs tasks which are of assistance to the other. In the study of human beings analysis of inner experience provides the framework of theory, pointing to key variables in behavior and relationships between them. Analysis of external data utilizes, calibrates, and verifies the framework of theory. The two approaches provide a coöperative means for forwarding effective scientific research into motivation and behavior.

Apart from formal research projects into the lives of others, the scientific-minded student has abundant opportunities in his own life for discovering, testing, and verifying principles of religion or any other principles related to the growth and functioning of human personality. The methods of scientific inquiry are ones which he can apply directly to himself and his life program. His testimony and that of others provide a realistic verification which adds to the pronouncements of science. Whether a meaningful, satisfying way of life has been found by the individual is disclosed by reports he makes after encountering realities in his inward experience.

APPROACH OF ANTHROPOLOGY

Cultural anthropology is an example of how procedures for studying internal and external features of human life may be combined in social science. Statistical analysis, projective testing, participant observation, and case reports all find application in the study of cultures of primitive peoples. Although informative and illuminating studies have been conducted of modern industrial culture by anthropology, its distinctive work consists in the study of human groups who are preliterate and preindustrial. Fragmentary remains permit some reconstruction of cultures from prehistoric times. In widely scattered localities of the globe have been found contemporary peoples in a late Stone Age or at least a nonliterate stage of development. They are loosely called "primitive" since their cultures suggest an earlier stage in linear development than industrial. In some features the so-called primitive culture may be more advanced with reference to utilitarian values than our own with its preoccupation with such obsessions as keeping the front lawn trimmed and rolled like a putting green or endlessly polishing a waxed floor as soon as footprints appear upon it, activities which the primitive might regard as a senseless waste of time. The shrinking of cultural boundaries owing to improved transportation and communication is transforming these Stone Age cultures, but already careful documentation of hundreds of such groups has been accomplished by anthropology. A major contribution is provided by the incisive concepts which anthropologists have developed for analyzing religion, concepts much used by psychologists and sociologists.

Advantages

Several reasons make study of primitive cultures useful in gaining a scientific understanding of human behavior. The societies involved are often small in size and self-contained because of their relative isolation from other societies, which makes the scientific task simpler than in the study of the complicated cultures of today. The analysis of religious needs may be more readily carried out in the study of an uncomplicated way of life. Especially in the study of religion, one finds that present-day systems of thought and behavior are elaborate historical products, changed many times by interaction with other streams of ideas, lacking the delimited character of primitive religions. Frequently primitive mythology portrays human impulses and ideas with concrete clarity.

In the induction of general principles one finds that the number of primitive cultures greatly exceeds the few major cultural systems of the modern world. The statistical demonstration of principles therefore becomes more adequate. At the same time, a large diversity of primitive cultures are available for comparative study under different conditions of economic survival. The nature of religion when the arts of writing are not available to record custom and belief can be examined.

The study of primitive cultures helps the student to appreciate the possibility of human life proceeding with religious and ethical patterns widely different from those to which he is accustomed. He is thereby encouraged to hold a more flexible attitude toward his own customs and to realize that they are not necessarily the only ways nor even better ways of living. At the same time, where the student finds in primitive religion some of the same elements also present in his own religious culture, he can with firmer confidence recognize things which are universal in all religion, irrespective of time or place. W. A. Lessa and E. Z. Vogt have performed a valuable service by collecting in one volume a wide range of studies by anthropologists of primitive religion.[16] William Howells has brought together results from anthropological studies of religion in a very readable account.[17]

Limitations

Despite these advantages, limitations arise in the study of primitive cultures which sometimes make an extension of findings from such study to religion of today of doubtful validity. Preliterate, prescientific, preindustrial culture is not like the culture in which we live. What is true of primitive religion may not be true of the great historical religions of the modern world. Since preliterate societies depend upon word of mouth for the handing down of religious ideas, it follows that their systems of

[16] W. A. Lessa and E. Z. Vogt, *Reader in Comparative Religion,* Row, Peterson, 1958.

[17] William Howells, *The Heathens,* Doubleday, 1948.

philosophy are not clearly articulated and refined by the type of critical thought which written literature makes possible. Religious thinkers today are not the naïve imaginers of the preliterate, Stone Age epoch.

In particular, religion today has encountered a cleansing intellectual force which primitive man never knew, namely the discipline of scientific thought. Under the impact of science, the supernatural phases of religion have tended to recede until they assume the proportions of respectable philosophical inquiry.

Primitive religions usually contain greater amounts of supernaturalism in the form of magic or phenomena from the world of spirits. The tendency of some anthropologists to define religion in terms of a belief in supernatural powers as the essential ingredient may miss the practical, social character which religion is coming to possess in contemporary America. The ghost worship of primitive man helps us to see the persistence of similar patterns in our own culture, but should not be mistaken for the major focus of existing religion.

The industrial revolution has strongly necessitated a social concern by people for larger numbers of other people than ever before. This social consciousness is dictated by the need for harmonious coöperation with millions of other people involved in the same system of division of labor. As the world becomes one vast network of social, political, and economic relationships, religion of a constructive type takes an interest in defining the positive responsibilities of each human being toward others which it did not before possess.

The improvements in communication and transportation, the unfolding of scientific discovery, the harnessing of vast power, and the advent of a large and complex industrial organization are all features of a rapidly changing world. The principal limitation in extending the study of primitive culture to modern seems to be the static formalism of the former. In the early cultures things are done and minds are dominated by patterns which change slowly. One can more or less sharply sketch out the customs and rules of a primitive tribe, authoritative for all its members. Their culture rests on their heads like a large slab of ice.

In contrast, life today is fluid and rapidly changing. The traditional cultural controls are weak. People are emancipated. They think for themselves. They must think for themselves because they live in a world which continually confronts them with new decisions. The uniqueness of the role of each person in the complicated division of labor necessitates that each decide for himself, the tribe being unable to formulate his behavior pattern for him. The individual is believed to be capable of a more satisfying life if he does formulate his own life pattern. The emphasis now is upon the development of the internal capacity of each human being to think and act responsibly for himself and his group, not to act in slavish imitation of custom. Even if rules can be formulated, it is believed best for the individual if he learns to think for himself. True, religion lags more than the rest of contemporary culture behind this ideal. Yet, in the analysis of religion we must recognize that it has changed from its prehistoric pattern in a gradual accommodation to a world of change and individual action.

part II Nature of Religion

FORMS OF RELIGIOUS EXPRESSION

Indian Ghost Dance

The original Ghost Dance was not complex, consisting usually of outdoor dancing in a circle and singing, and of bathing. Promising return of the dead, and boding no good for the Whites, it nevertheless did not preach any action but dancing. Then there was another conflagration, and it started, incredibly enough, in exactly the same place as the first, among the Northern Paiutes at Walker Lake in Nevada. Here a shaman, a "dreamer," had a vision and organized a dance. His name was Wovoka, or Jack Wilson, and he was the son of a shaman who had actually been associated with Wodziwob, the 1870 prophet.

During an eclipse, probably January 1, 1889, amid the excitement which this caused his fellow Paiutes, Wilson went into a trance. He was taken up to heaven, he said, where he saw God, who showed him all the dead, playing their old games in a land of plenty, all happy and all young. God commanded him to go back and preach to his people, telling them to live in peace with one another and the Whites, to work hard, and to avoid lying, stealing, and war. This would bring them after death to the beautiful other world, and God gave him a dance for the people to perform, which would take them to heaven more surely and quickly.

Wilson came back to earth, and in January 1889 he held a Paiute dance and at once attracted much attention among the Paiutes and neighboring tribes. The dance spread quickly both through Paiute missionaries and through visitors from distant tribes who had heard of the prophecy. It crossed over the Rockies to the east, and in the Plains it ran wild.

The Sioux were then the largest and most intransigent of the tribes, but in 1890 they were suffering both privation and the misery of seeing their way of life strangled. In 1868 they had agreed to stay on a reservation which was most of South Dakota, in return for food, cows, doctors, teachers, and other benefits. When gold miners rushed into the Black Hills on the reservation, the Indians reacted, Custer made his Last

Stand, and the government in the ensuing "agreement" took a third of the reservation away. Then the government took half of what was left, and the best half.

Word of the Ghost Dance came in 1889. The Sioux were greatly excited and, responding to the preaching of one of the delegates, Short Bull, organized dances on the Rosebud reservation at once. The dance itself took a more virulent form: faithful dancing was necessary, and would cause not only the return of the dead and of great herds of buffalo, but also the absolute annihilation of the Whites, through a great landslide which would cover them up forever. In dancing, while the Indians were to carry no arms, nor any metal, they were to wear "ghost shirts," dance shirts cut in Indian style, which were believed to be bullet proof.

The agent at Rosebud did not like the look of things, and ordered Short Bull to stop the dances, and the Indians obeyed. But the dance was the very flame of new hope to the Sioux, and probably nothing could have kept it from spreading. In June a large dance was held, with ghost shirts, on adjoining Pine Ridge reservation. Red Cloud had announced his belief in the Ghost Dance and urged his people to take it up. In August two thousand Indians met for another dance. The Pine Ridge agent went out to stop them, but they took up their guns and said they would fight with their lives for their new religion. Back on the Rosebud reservation the dance broke out once more in September, again under Short Bull; again the agent managed to stop it, but when he had to leave for a short while, dancing burst forth anew. The dance was carried in October up to Standing Rock, on Sitting Bull's invitation; here also the reservation agent tried to stop it, but Sitting Bull declared flatly that he would keep the dances going.

On December 29, surrounded on all sides by soldiers, Big Foot's people at Wounded Knee were asked to turn over their arms. They did not do this willingly or promptly, and soldiers started searching the tipis, causing confusion and nervousness among the Indians. A medicine man, Yellow Bird, began urging the warriors (in Sioux) to resist, reminding them that their ghost shirts made them invulnerable. At last an Indian brought a rifle from under his blanket and fired a shot, and immediately there was a violent toe-to-toe battle, with the government troops using two pound shells; in a very few minutes sixty soldiers and almost all the Indian men were killed, and the soldiers, who were raw, shot down many women and children who were trying to run from the scene; about two hundred and twenty Sioux were later found dead on the field.[1]

The Kingdom of Father Divine

"Father Divine is God!"

Whether whispered, spoken, sung, or shouted hysterically, these words are believed by hundreds, even thousands, of people. They may be heard almost any afternoon or evening at the main kingdom of heaven, which forms part of a crowded street in New York's Harlem. During the past few years the street has been more crowded than ever, for now Father Divine's cars and buses with their placards of "Peace," "We thank you, Father," and "Father Divine's Peace Mission" are lined along the curbing. Nearby laundries, cafeterias, and small shops, otherwise like most of their kind, display signs of "Peace," "Special attention given to Father Divine children," "I thank you." On Saturday and Sunday afternoons and evenings moving crowds fill the side-

[1] Abridged from *The Heathens,* by William Howells, pp. 270–277. Copyright 1948 by William Howells. Reprinted by permission of Doubleday & Company, Inc.

walk in front of kingdom headquarters. Sooner or later most of the people are inside.

The doors of the kingdom are always open. In the small corridor, leading to the upstairs assembly hall, we face a brightly colored sign: "The relation of your conscious mentalities is but the reconception of God's omniscience." The hall itself is filled with believers, sitting on simple wooden benches. Most of them are Negroes, with a sprinkling of whites. White visitors are easily recognized. They are given seats or ushered to the platform at the front of the hall.

The room is filled with crude banners. High overhead is stretched in silver letters: "Father Divine is Dean of the Universe." The followers (or "children," as they call themselves) are singing the verse:

Father Divine is the captain
Coming around the bend
And the steering wheel's in his hand

The song has five verses. Singing is accompanied by a small brass band. No one officially leads the "children." It is unnecessary. A few already know the song, and the rest soon catch the simple rhythm. The crescendo increases with each verse.

At the end of this song, a large, middle-aged colored woman testifies how Father cured her bad knee, which specialists had been unable to help. Some listen; others close their eyes and moan. Shouts of "Isn't it wonderful!" "He's so sweet!" and "We thank you, Father!" are frequent. One or two hysterical Negroes walk around dazed and shouting, occasionally falling. The testimony ends with the first line of another song, sung with great feeling by the testifier. It is immediately picked up by others. The band catches the tune. Soon all are singing:

One million blessings,
Blessings flowing free,
Blessings flowing free,
There are so many blessings,
Blessings flowing free for you.

We turn to our colored neighbor and ask him when Father Divine is coming. He looks at us blissfully and says, "He's here." "Where?" He points at random: "He's there, there, everywhere. He's in your heart." Another follower notices our dilemma and advises us to go downstairs to the banquet table. Father speaks there, if he speaks at all. Many have already gone down. It is about 11 P.M.

The banquet hall is filled. A large, horseshoe table takes up most of the space, and around it are seated about a hundred children. Another hundred or more are standing in the crowded spaces nearby. There is one place conspicuously vacant at the head of the table, near which sit several well-dressed Negroes and one white. We are told they are Angels. They seem more self-possessed, more patient, more intelligently alert than the rest. On the table, in front of the Angels, are great platters of turkey, chicken, cold cuts, fruit, and bread. The air is close and sticky.

This room, too, is lined with banners, proclaiming such sentiments as: "Father Divine is the only redemption of man"; "Father Divine is God and a little child shall lead them."

In return for the benefits they receive, supposedly everything the children have is

Father's—their money, their services, their thought, their love. Those who come to live in one of the numerous kingdoms give Father their property, their insurance, their extra clothes, their savings—everything. Most of those who live outside the kingdoms give him something, after providing minimum needs for themselves.

Parents who join the kingdom are separated as man and wife. They generally leave their children behind in the outer world to fend for themselves. More frequently a single parent (usually the mother) enters the kingdom, forgetting and giving up completely children and spouse. Worldly habits, such as smoking and drinking, are taboo. There is no cohabitation in the kingdoms. The general, positive attitude is sufficiently dynamic to overcome these specific, worldly behavior patterns. All signs of bodily afflictions, such as glasses, trusses, or crutches, are thrown away. Ailments are forgotten. No medical or dental attention is allowed.

With the disappearance of the old identity goes all thought of race, color, or vocation: "All God's children are equal"; "In God's sight there is no difference in color." No one is allowed to use the words "black," "white," or "Negro" in the kingdom. One speaks of "a person of the darker (or lighter) complexion."[2]

Jehovah's Witnesses

Jehovah's Witnesses is the fastest-growing religious movement in the world. In fifteen years it has tripled its membership and today has 591,556 active members in 162 countries. Its 1957 yearbook, which has just appeared, reports the distribution of 55,735,715 copies of its magazines, an increase of 19 million over the previous year. To supply the demand for religious literature the movement has printed 130,992,362 Bibles and books in more than a hundred languages.

Another startling evidence of Witness growth is found in Brooklyn. If you have not been on Columbia Heights during the past few years you are in for a surprise. The once reviled and lowly Witnesses have put up an impressive eight-story building with a two-story cupola that would do credit to any traditional denomination anywhere in the U. S. A.

Open the sparkling doors at 124 Columbia Heights and walk up the stairs. If you have time for nothing else, at least go into the thick-carpeted reception room and stand for a moment at one of the massive windows. You are now looking out across the East River at a gorgeous view of the New York skyline. You are standing on the spot where the home of Henry Ward Beecher once stood. What is more, you are standing in the nerve center of a group which believes with all its heart that its members are God's chosen people, believes it with a devotion that puts to shame the apathy of many of us old-line Protestants.

I say this is the nerve center. But it may be that the real center of this closely knit, hierarchical crusade for Jehovah is located a few blocks away at the gargantuan printing plant which rises like a mighty fortress at the foot of Brooklyn bridge. Upon its towering walls is inscribed: Read The Watchtower and Awake!

Watchtower and *Awake* are, as everyone knows, the monthly publications of the Witnesses. You have seen them when a Witness came to your door on his house-to-house round. You may have spied them in racks in public places. You have caught

[2] Abridged from Hadley Cantril, *The Psychology of Social Movements*, New York, Wiley, 1941, pp. 123–129.

glimpses of these 5-cent journals held up in the hands of devotees on street corners—men and women who defy wind and rain and rushing crowds to witness for Jehovah God. . . .

Every Witness is a minister. Every minister is a house-to-house visitor. Every visitor is a trained servant. I dare say that no other religious movement has each state, each county, each city, each block and each street in America as thoroughly graphed as has Jehovah's Witnesses. No other headquarters knows with such unerring accuracy what its minister members are doing, where and how they are serving, what they are earning and what they are thinking. They operate as a unit, as an army. In fact, the local group used to be called a company, the person in charge was the captain, and the place of meeting was and still is the "Kingdom Hall."

You see, the rank and file Witnesses believe that we are living in the last days. They are little Noahs calling the unheeding millions into the ark. They are the latter-day prophets crying to the unhearing to prepare for the fearful day of Armageddon. (They expect it some time between 1970 and 1980.) They are not unaware that the end of the age and the dawning of the millennium has been predicted in every century since the beginning of the Christian era. One Witness talked to me glowingly about the fact that Lactantius, the "Christian Cicero" of the 4th century, declared that the blood of Armageddon would flow in his time. No matter. The signs were never truer than they are today that the Son of God is waiting in the shadows to slay the wicked and to turn the world over to the righteous.

This is why their society was formed, to serve as Christ's army when he comes. For this purpose ministers and missionaries are trained in a five months' course at the Watchtower Bible School of Gilead near Ithaca, New York. Because of the immensity of this millennial event, it is said, much of the work at Brooklyn must be secret, even mysterious.[3]

Ghost dancing, feasting, and witnessing are not the familiar forms of religion we experience among our neighbors in church, yet they are vital manifestations of religion in America. To see the more dramatic and more extreme forms gives the student some perspective in comprehending the many dimensions of religion, which does not always take the customary form of praying, singing, and preaching typical of the hour-long service in the average local church. Powerful emotional forces are latent in human personality which periodically spring forth in religious expression in novel patterns of behavior, even in settled denominations.

In answering the question "What is religion?" our answer must encompass not only the traditional liturgy to which we are accustomed, but also the impulsive and untraditional behavior of cults. Our definition must be broad enough to include significant variations, yet not so broad that religion is watered down in its definition to include all of life. In developing cause-and-effect explanations for why human beings are religion-building and religion-practicing animals, we must explain not only those who are church members

[3] Marcus Bach, "The Startling Witnesses," *Christian Century*, February 13, 1957, pp. 197–198.

by habit, but also those who break with the past in fresh and dynamic ways. The capacity of religion to reappear again and again in new forms shows that its power is not simply one of survival, but of revival as well. The explanation of this power in terms of cause and effect is a challenge to the scientific ingenuity of the student of religion. Our initial phase of inquiry into religion and contemporary culture is to develop answers which have been given to questions about what religion is and to describe the principal forms which it takes on the American scene.

Our first scientific task in approaching the study of religion is to consider its general nature. Definitions have been freely coined by numerous writers. These often represent alloys compounded out of various aspects of religion. From these compounds, with the aid of empirical studies of religious experience and behavior, we endeavor to extract the common metal of religion, if such be isolable. After determining the nature of religion in general, we next look at religion in America.

chapter 5 What Religion Is

After hearing a scholarly lecture well received by its academic audience, an evangelical Christian was heard to remark about the talk: "It certainly didn't feel like religion." Therein lies a dilemma. If the analysis of religion is scientific, the analysis is supposed to be devoid of feeling, intellectual inquiry not being an emotional process. By being empty of feeling, analysis of religion fails to arouse concretely the true meaning of religion and may seem thereby to miss the mark.

A purpose of religion is to stimulate and to organize the feelings of people toward life so that they find importance and inspiration in what they do. In order for religion to accomplish this effectively, there should first be accurate awareness of the social and psychological factors in the processes involved. When these things are known and used by the individual, reconstruction of the feeling aspects is possible. If stone and lime mined from the ground do not at first convey the aesthetic impression of an attractive home, this does not mean they may not come to form the materials of one. Out of studious searching for the elements of religion emerge the materials for religious reconstruction of life. In seeking to establish a definition of religion, the student gains a clearer awareness of the basic realities involved.

Nor is intellectual apprehension fully possible without participation in religion. Unless there is content from one's life for the categories of religion, these are verbal labels for empty concepts. One can as easily explain to a child the meaning of sexual love as convey to one outside the domain of religion what it means to those inside. A concrete idea of religion requires living in accordance with patterns which produce an experience of religion. Nevertheless, an effective start can be made toward a definition without having experienced all of the elements needed. Those categories for which insights are available from personal experience can be described, and adjacent categories labeled and located to be filled in later. As one's definition becomes more developed, ways become clearer for gaining a more complete experience and definition of it.

Nor can verbal delineation in the early portion of a text provide much more than an abstract skeleton to be filled in concretely as the text proceeds. In his youth, the author asked a Sunday School teacher for a definition of religion, to which she replied that religion was what she was teaching. There is some validity in such an answer, since the task of definition is essentially an unfolding one. During the description, the subject matter becomes delimited and specified, and the longer the description is continued, the more incisive the definition. The casual reader may prefer to skim or skip sections in this chapter at first, returning to them later in detail. For the serious or advanced student, it seems useful to offer a somewhat historical and scholarly development of the concepts of religion and the religious being which is a focus of worship as these concepts have crystallized in social and psychological science.

Definition of Definition

In a chapter devoted to the task of definition, it would be useful to define what we mean by the process of definition. First, as to purpose, definition has as its role the specification of a topic with sufficient exactness that affirmative propositions may later be stated with reference to that topic. A distinction is usually made between a description of the topic sufficient to provide a definition and additional description which provides substantive knowledge about the topic. In some branches of learning, definition is regarded as a purely intellectual exercise quite apart from data experienced, and principles are deduced by logical manipulation of definitions and assumptions. This is not the meaning of definition in science nor the use to which a definition is put. Rather, the act of defining calls attention to certain elements in experience, specifies what these are in relation to other things known or defined, and assigns labels to these elements. The term *designation* conveys more of the scientific meaning of *definition.*

The words used to phrase definitions refer to elements in experience. The definition consists of verbal labels in one-to-one correspondence with the contents of the bottles of experience to which the labels refer. Yet reality is not found so neatly separated in containers. The contents are fused into a mass of experience which must be broken down by analysis. Part of the cracking process is achieved by experimental inquiry or by sifting through data occurring naturally; part is accomplished by the psychological process of abstracting elements from experience. When the subject matter is pondered on for a sufficient length of time, its essential elements emerge in the awareness of the investigator. These elements are the things to which the words in the definition refer.

A definition of religion incorporates elements of both interior experience and behavior. On the internal side, religion is an affair of emotion, feeling, aim, and belief. On the external side, religion involves behavior ranging from rituals performed to the details of daily activities permeated to a greater or lesser extent by the influence of religion. A circumscription of the topic of religion is therefore not a simple matter but necessitates delineating a complex affair in such a way that it is differentiated from other life activities.

Mutually Understood Meanings of Terms

The elements in motivation and behavior to which religion refers can be specified by means of psychological and social terms. The definition of religion consists in a putting together of these terms in a way which specifies the constituents of religious phenomena to the exclusion of nonreligious phenomena. The unique concurrence of general descriptive categories provides the definitive specification required.

For the definition to be effective, the terms involved must have well-understood meanings. The careful choice of words rich in familiar meaning facilitates communicating the nature of religion to others. On the other hand, words which are most vivid in meaning are frequently those which have multiple meanings. The social scientist chooses his words carefully from among the terms which everyday language affords and then proceeds to assign carefully specified meanings to his terms. The task of defining religion introduces terms whose meanings also must be defined by employing still other terms whose meanings must be understood. The task of definition would be endless if it were not assumed at some point that words used in the process of defining are already known to those in communication.

The most precise terms, but not those which are most clearly intelligible, are provided by the language of mathematics. *Structure, quality, space, time, variable,* and *function* are mathematical terms with specific meanings. A goal only partially realized in social and psychological research is to describe human life by means of these abstract concepts. One advantage is that ambiguity of meaning can more fully be resolved. If there is a question as to whether an alleged phenomenon exists, the question can be settled by stating what, when, and where the phenomenon is. Independent investigators then know where in internal or outward experience to direct their attention to verify its existence. The unnecessary proliferation of terms in social and psychological science, many of which are synonyms for ones already in use, can be halted by the precise assignment of meanings. If all who innovate a term or emphasize a new aspect in their definition would do so by using the fundamental language of mathematics, the perennial practice of introducing new words for old ideas would disappear. A second advantage is that mathematical terms permit concise summarizing of relationships between variables. An array of data can be encompassed by a single formula.

It would hamper the flow of communication among people generally if such exact definition were insisted upon most of the time. Yet where differences in understanding arise, it becomes an obligation to state one's view as precisely as possible, in order to establish the common ground of agreement and to delineate the area of difference which remains for further inquiry and verification. In such circumstances it may be necessary to resort to a technical vocabulary to specify what is being talked about. If a definition developed in this text falls short of having sufficiently complete specification, the obligation for more exact definition is assumed by parties involved in the disagreement caused by imperfect definition.

The empirical elements in terms of which religion is defined for the most part are in the inner world of desires and beliefs, and hence are not easily verifiable by those who require that they see and touch what they accept scientifically. Instead, tedious processes of abstraction and inference must be carried through, nor is performance of these processes a guarantee in advance that agreement will be reached by different investigators. The background of previous experience occupies a substantial role in determining whether individuals come into possession of those psychological elements which are the empirical counterparts of religious terminology. It is difficult, although theoretically possible, for one who has had no concrete experience of religious participation to put together elements from his other experiences in order to construct an imaginative concept of what religion is like. An outstanding sociologist, E. W. Burgess, who has specialized in the study of matrimony is himself a bachelor. But intellectual grasp is facilitated if some first-hand acquaintance with the subject matter is possessed.

One of the controversial areas in religious study pertains to the existence and nature of God. If introduced as a topic for scientific treatment beyond describing someone as having a belief in God, it must be made clear what the elements are in experience to which the term *God* is applied. If outside of experience, the questions are those of philosophy, not science. If within verifiable experience, then hypotheses can be stated in experiential terms for verification and acceptance or rejection.

Scope of Definitions

When a definition serves the purpose of marking the boundaries of a field for inquiry, the question of how widely or how narrowly the boundaries are to be drawn cannot be answered arbitrarily. It is desirable to widen the definition sufficiently to include all relevant phenomena, but not to allow it to become so broad that the definition produces a vast and unworkable field for inquiry.

A tendency has prevailed among devotees of some religions to identify their particular system of beliefs and practices with the true religion and to regard faiths different from their own as lacking in some important element or even as not genuinely religious at all. When *The Varieties of Religious Experience* appeared fifty years ago, a clergyman of the time remarked that William James should have called his book *Wild Animals I Have Known,* owing to the inclusion of forms of religion different from Christianity. Another example of sectarian definition is given by Parson Thwackum in Fielding's *Tom Jones*. "When I mention religion, I mean the Christian religion; and not only the Christian religion but the Protestant religion; and not only the Protestant religion, but the Church of England." A definition drawn in so restricted a form is ethnocentric to an extreme degree and lacks scientific utility. Excluded are not only the historical religions of the world, whose influence through acculturation has been extensive, but also omitted is the rich variety of religions of primitive peoples which contain much of the same social and ethical content found in so-called advanced religions.

At the other extreme are definitions of religion so broad that they include virtually all of life. Erich Fromm writes: "I understand by religion any system of thought and action shared by a group which gives the individual a frame of orientation and an object of devotion."[1] Under this definition, politics might be considered a religion. In between extremes of breadth and narrowness are definitions of religion so numerous as to overwhelm the student who seeks a simple, direct answer to the question: "What is religion?" The task of formulating a single satisfactory definition might appear insurmountable. However, the task is instructive, when systematically pursued, since it calls attention to various aspects of religious phenomena. There are unifying threads among the definitions, and our purpose is to weave these into a working picture of what religion is.

Needless to say, religion does not become something by declaring it to be so. The realities remain the same, whatever words are selected to describe or delimit them. If in the process of definition, phenomena such as magic or mana are excluded, which have been included by some investigators, this does not deny the reality of these phenomena nor the importance of studying them. The exclusion merely means that the definer finds distinctions between them and religion, and that for a more specific and less ambiguous vocabulary it is desirable to institute separate categories rather than lump closely related phenomena together. It is also important in the definition to differentiate between what is always present in the thing defined and what may or may not be present.

RELIGION AS A BELIEF IN SPIRITUAL BEINGS

Tylor's Definition

A starting point in the task of building a definition of religion is the concept formulated by E. B. Tylor, and from this we consider the sequence of developments in anthropology. Tylor, an Englishman, may be considered the first social scientist, apart from historians, to make an extensive study of religious behavior and belief. A century earlier David Hume, the Scottish empiricist philosopher, had contended that religious behavior, like any

[1] Erich Fromm, *Psychoanalysis and Religion,* Yale University Press, 1950, p. 21.

other behavior, should be the topic of scientific study. Tylor is also credited with founding cultural anthropology as a scientific discipline and with being the first to define the concept of culture basic in social science today. Systematic methods developed in history and allied fields were confronted by data of isolated tribes reported by travelers, merchants, and missionaries. Darwin's theory of the biological evolution of man as a species turned attention to earlier forms of man's institutions evident in the life of contemporary primitive peoples. In *Primitive Culture,* published in 1871, Tylor assembled an extensive collection of ethnological data in testing and illustrating his concepts and hypotheses about religion and culture.

In his studies of primitive peoples, he encountered widespread beliefs in human spirits inhabiting the body and surviving after death and in spirits inhabiting natural objects as their bodies or moving freely through the universe. The belief in a world inhabited by spiritual beings was named by him *animism,* and he formulated as a minimum definition of religion the belief in spiritual beings, ranging from the souls of the departed dead to the great gods of the universe.[2] Here appeared to be a key characteristic of all religions, primitive, ancient, and modern. The theology of the Crow Indians illustrates this world of spirits.

The Crow Indian approached the universe with a sincere humility that contrasted sharply with his personal pride towards fellow-tribesmen. He evinced that sense of absolute dependence on something not himself, which Schleiermacher and Feuerbach postulate as the root of the religious sentiment. By himself man was nothing, but somewhere in the world there were mysterious beings greater than he, by whose good-will he might rise. The significant fact to an individual was that during a spell of ecstasy he had come into contact with something supernatural, and that something was his God while everything else sank into a relatively subordinate position. . . .

The Sun was to a marked degree the recipient of offerings and the object of supplication. Before setting out on a raid, men would vow to give him eagle feathers or fox skins; the hide of an albino buffalo was invariably consecrated to the Sun with a prayer for longevity and wealth; and to erect a little booth for sweating oneself was considered a ritual in his honor. It is therefore not at all remarkable that the Sun should be the first being normally addressed by the seeker of a vision. The remarkable thing is rather that he so rarely came. "Sometimes," said White-arm, "the Sun himself appeared to the visionary, but mostly animals came. These I do not think are related to the Sun at all. When

[2] E. B. Tylor, *Religion in Primitive Culture,* Harper, 1958, p. 8.

men are praying, the Sun is first thought of, but generally other beings appear.". . .

The Sun, to be sure, means more to a greater number of persons than any one other spirit; he approaches more nearly than any other our notion of a Supreme Being. Yet what astonishing conceptions cluster about him, and in what chaos is Crow theology concerning the most elementary definition of his identity! The most trustworthy witnesses can not agree as to whether he is identical with Old-Man-Coyote, the hero of Crow folklore; nay, in a single cosmogonic myth there is constant vacillation on this point. Now Old-Man-Coyote is in many episodes of his cycle a typical trickster, wallowing in grossness and buffoonery. . . .

Yet even if the Sun be wholly dissociated from Old-Man-Coyote, he remains an odd sort of a supreme being. In fact, he is not really supreme at all: there is nothing to preclude his being worsted by Morning-star or the human hero of a traditional tale. Again, he looms as the creator by having some birds dive into the sea for the submerged earth and by fashioning human beings out of mud; but he is not the source of *all* being. Apart from cryptic Old-Man-Coyote, the sacred Tobacco (usually identified with a star) and the sacred Rock appear as entities of explicitly independent origin. Finally, from an ethical point of view, he is sometimes benignant but also turns malevolent towards the whole tribe when his mistress is seduced by a boy hero, and is even represented as boiling and eating the flesh of brave warriors.[3]

Omissions in Tylor's Definition

Tylor's equating of religion with animism omitted elements which succeeding scientists of religion regard as important. He declared that man installed spirits to explain the capricious behavior of physical objects of the universe, literally by animating them. Animism for Tylor stemmed from man's intellectual need to explain the inexplicable. This interpretation of why man engages in religion is too limited, as will be considered in a later set of chapters on causation of religion.

Tylor's concept of religion failed to stress the menacing or beneficent power which man believes spirits to have, nor did it include man's feelings and practices about his religion. The person who believes but feels and does nothing is not religious in the usual sense. Having peopled his world with spirits, primitive man lived in alternate moods of fear and gratitude toward spirit beings. When food failed or pestilence struck, he was tormented by worry over his relationship to spirit beings. Was he behaving

[3] From *Primitive Religion* by Robert H. Lowie. By permission of Liveright, Publishers, N.Y. Copyright (R) 1952, by Robert H. Lowie.

properly toward them? Had he done the right thing to gain their favor? Then again, when food was plentiful and sickness absent, he felt at home in the company of his spirits and experienced joy at their benevolence. The forces of nature being a hard master, he came to regard spiritual beings with awe and reverence for their power over life and death. He developed religious attitudes of humility and self-effacement toward them. At those times when natural spectacles of solar eclipses or storm winds startled him, he experienced a thrill of excitement. Sometimes this emotional thrill would be recreated by dancing in the form of a religious revival meeting. These various shadings of feeling are conspicuous in religious phenomena.

Because man is a creature with feelings, he is impelled to act by them. If he does not feel right with the spirit beings, he offers sacrifices, tortures himself, anything to show loyalty to or gain the favor of spirits who control his fate. When spirit beings appear to shower favor on him, he shouts, jumps, and dances with delight. He expresses his religious feelings in crowd behavior. He offers prayers of gratitude, at the same time imploring his gods not to forget him in the future. An important feature of religion is provided by what man does toward his world of spirits, that is, his religious behavior.

Within two decades after Tylor, an extensive and carefully compiled study was made of magic and religion by J. G. Frazer, another British anthropologist. He defined religion in terms of beliefs and behavior. "By religion, then, I understand a propitiation or conciliation of powers superior to man which are believed to direct and control the course of Nature and of human life."[4] It might be said that Tylor by implication recognizes feelings experienced and behavior expressing feelings as elements of religion, but these were given little attention in his analysis of religion as meeting an intellectual need.

Inclusion of Religious Experience

The feeling element in religion was insufficiently considered in the work of either Tylor or Frazer. A third British scholar, R. R. Marett, appears to have been the first anthropologist to give sufficient attention to this element and to provide a well-rounded concept of religion. Writing in 1909 in *The Threshold of Religion* in answer to Tylor, he says: "My theory is not concerned with the mere thought at work in religion, but with religion as a whole, the

[4] J. G. Frazer, *The Golden Bough,* Macmillan, 1941, p. 50.

organic complex of thought, emotion and behavior."[5] The following passages elaborate this concept.

> Definitions of words are always troublesome; and religion is the most troublesome of all words to define. Now for the purposes of anthropology at its present stage it matters less to assign exact limits to the concept to which the word in question corresponds, than to make sure that these limits are cast on such wide and generous lines, as to exclude no feature that has characterised religion at any moment in the long course of its evolution. Suffice it, then, to presuppose that the word stands for a certain composite or concrete state of mind wherein various emotions and ideas are together provocative of action. . . . Now for most persons, probably, the emotional side of religion constitutes its more real, more characteristic feature. Men are, however, obliged to communicate . . . by the way of ideas solely. Hence, if for no other reason, the ideas composing the religious state tend to overlay and outweigh the emotional element, when it comes to estimating man's religious experience at its widest. . . .
>
> . . . we must, I think, in any case admit the fact that in response to, or at any rate in connection with, the emotions of awe, wonder, and the like, wherein feeling would seem for the time being to have outstripped the power of "natural," that is reasonable, explanation, there arises in the region of human thought a powerful impulse to objectify and even personify the mysterious or "supernatural" something felt, and in the region of will a corresponding impulse to render it innocuous, or better still propitious, by force of constraint, communion, or conciliation. *Supernaturalism,* then, as this universal feeling taken at its widest and barest may be called, might, as such, be expected to prove not only logically but also in some sense chronologically prior to animism, constituting as the latter does but a particular ideal embodiment of the former.[6]

Goldenweiser, writing in 1922, calls attention to the "thrill" which he finds as the essential characteristic of religion as well as magic.

> Experiences with the supernatural are accompanied by a peculiar exaltation, a *religious thrill.* It is true that in religion or magic, as actually practiced even by primitives, this thrill is not always there. This is due to the tendency of such emotions to "evaporate" (Marett) when the procedure becomes habitual and formalized, a mere something to be gone through and over with. But the "live" religious or magical situation is characterized by the presence of these emotions; the at-

[5] R. R. Marett, *The Threshold of Religion,* Methuen, 1909, p. xii. Later writings of Marett emphasize social and ethical aspects of religion. See *Faith, Hope, and Charity in Primitive Religion,* Macmillan, 1932; *Head, Heart and Hands in Human Evolution,* Holt, 1935.

[6] Marett, *The Threshold of Religion, op.cit.,* pp. 3–4, 10–11.

mosphere is charged with mystic potency, and man responds. In this, then, lies the common ground of magic and religion.[7]

The emphasis upon experience suffused with emotion is not new in religious study, as Marett recognizes in referring to the British-American psychologist William McDougall. "This position is set forth more lucidly and plausibly [in *An Introduction to Social Psychology*] than in any other psychological treatise known to me. His account of the emotions that underlie religion is especially illuminating."[8] The experiential side of religion was emphasized by William James in *The Varieties of Religious Experience* in 1902. For centuries philosophers have been much concerned with the experiential aspects of religion. These historical details illustrate the difficulty of tracing scientific ideas to their innovators. One can more readily describe the stand taken by influential scholars at a given period of time than assign credit for antecedent discoveries forgotten by succeeding generations in the welter of words inscribed since the writing of thoughts first began. In our present treatment we are limiting ourselves primarily to scholars self-consciously writing in the social-scientific tradition.

RELIGION AS A BELIEF IN SUPERNATURAL POWER

Role of Power in Religion

Another aspect which should be included in the concept of religion is the power of spirits or other objects of religious attention to influence human life. If spirits were nothing but clouds in the skies, man would ignore them. Because he believes that they have great power for human good or harm he feels and acts as he does toward them. By something having *power* is meant that strong effects result from that something. The concept of power is rooted in the cause-and-effect relationship between that which is said to have power and the results which take place. The modern scientific concept of force or power, following Hume, is not that of an isolable ingredient contained in a powerful object, but rather is that of the observed results to which the object inevitably leads. Power simply expresses the relationship between an object and the effects which follow from it. Since these effects are in the nature of changes in variables, the concept of power can be defined mathematically in terms of the derivatives

[7] A. A. Goldenweiser, *Anthropology,* Crofts, 1946, p. 218.
[8] Marett, *op. cit.,* p. xi.

of variables. The power of a spiritual being is defined empirically by the changes brought about by that being in human life.

In the scientific era, Frazer and Codrington played important roles in defining religion in terms of powers superior to man. In Frazer's definition previously quoted, the verbs *propitiate* and *conciliate* limit his conception of powers to ones which are personlike. Frazer's conception is essentially an investment of the doctrine of belief in personal spirits with powers attributed to such spirits. Yet there is no reason why the concept of power in religion must be attributed only to a personal religious object. The concept of power in the physical world refers to impersonal force. It would prelimit the domain of religion if it is stipulated in advance that the powers to which man adjusts are always personal, rather than impersonal also. Buddhism, Confucianism, and Ethical Culture are religions in which impersonal ethical values provide the central focus for belief and activity. These values are regarded as potent in their beneficial effects on human life. In a sense, these values are personal since they are attributes which prevail or are sought in human personality, a sense which is examined more fully later. Rather than prejudge the situation, we preferably define religion in terms of a belief in superior powers, personal or impersonal.

On the other hand, the definition of religion in terms of power requires description of the type of power involved in order to avoid including adjustments to all of the powers of the environment. Conscious of this requirement, scholars have attempted to designate the kind of power central in religious belief and activity by various categories, supernatural, sacred, or psychological. After Tylor and Frazer the development of religious study in anthropology was in terms of the concept of the supernatural based upon the notion of mana which emphasizes the idea of unusual potency. Religion is then defined in terms of a belief in supernatural power and practices based upon this belief.

Belief in Mana

About the same time as Frazer's study of magic and religion appeared, R. H. Codrington in 1891 first described mana, which played a fundamental role in the life of the Melanesians in the South Pacific.

If a man has been successful in fighting, it has not been his natural strength of arm, quickness of eye, or readiness of resource that has won success; he has certainly got the *mana* of a spirit or some deceased warrior to empower him, conveyed in an amulet of stone round his neck, or a tuft of leaves in his belt, in a tooth hung upon a finger of his bow hand, or in the form of words with which he brings supernatural assistance to his side. If a man's pigs multiply, and his gardens are productive, it is not because he is industrious and looks after his property, but because of the stones full of *mana* for pigs and yams that he possesses.[9]

Mana appears in numerous religions under various names. In Hinduism it is *darshan;* in Christianity it is known by its result, divine grace, literally a God-given quality; among American Indian tribes it is called *manito* by the Algonquins, *wakanda* by the Sioux, *orenda* by the Iroquois, and *maxpe* by the Crow. Religion is primarily a system of beliefs, practices, and experiences concerned with the utilization of special powers which man thinks he possesses or has discovered.

It [mana] is the common element in ghosts and gods, in the magical and the mystical, the supernal and the infernal, the unknown within and the unknown without. It is the supernatural or supernormal, as distinguished from the natural or normal; that in short which, as Jevons phrases it, "defeats reasonable expectation." Or perhaps another and a better way of putting it, seeing that it calls attention to the feeling behind the logic, is to say that it is the awful, and that everything wherein or whereby it manifests itself is, so to speak, a power of awfulness, or, more shortly, a power (though this, like any other of our verbal equivalents, cannot but fail to preserve the vagueness of the original notion). Of all English words awe is, I think, the one that expresses the fundamental religious feeling most nearly. . . . we admit wonder, admiration, interest, respect, even love perhaps, to be, no less than fear, essential constituents of this elemental mood.[10]

Among anthropologists in America, Goldenweiser has sharpened the relationship of mana to spirit.

In retrospect, the *mana* idea must be welcomed as a genuine addition to our understanding of early religion, nay of all religion. There is, of course, no point in juxtaposing *mana* and spirit, as to chronological priority; what is important is to realize that the idea of spirit must be supplemented by that of power (*mana*), if primitive religion, or any religion, is to be understood. *Mana* supplies the dynamic principle, whereas spirit, as such, is but a concept of form or being. . . . From this it follows that the idea of supernatural power—impersonal, formless in itself, but withal, a power and supernatural—must be coupled with spirit in all interpretations of religion.[11]

[9] R. H. Codrington, *The Melanesians,* Oxford, 1891, p. 120.
[10] Marett, *op. cit.,* pp. 12–13.
[11] Goldenweiser, *op. cit.,* p. 225.

Max Weber, a German sociologist writing about the same time as Marett and Goldenweiser, uses the term *charisma* to designate the exceptional quality inherent in supernatural events. He also brings out the philosophical and meaningful aspect of the supernatural for human beings. Talcott Parsons, a leading expositor of Weber's writings in America, characterizes Weber's views as follows:

The fruitful starting point [in primitive religion] is rather the observation that religious as distinct from secular actions involve qualities, forces, etc. which are exceptional, removed from the ordinary (*ausseralltäglich*), to which a special attitude is taken and a special virtue attributed. This exceptional quality Weber calls *charisma*. It is exemplified in such conceptions as mana.

From this conception of things "set apart" can easily arise that of a "world" of entities different from that involved in the ordinary affairs of everyday life—in this sense and only this, a "supernatural" world. The ways in which these entities may be conceived and the character of their relations to the "natural" world are most various. They may, for example, be distinguished as "personal" and "impersonal," but Weber does not for present purposes lay great stress on these distinctions; the important thing is the difference of attitude toward these entities, however conceived, from that toward everyday things. They tend to issue in two types of entity; in so far as this supernatural world is involved in the individual personality itself, it becomes the "soul," or if outside the individual, "gods" or "demons." Whether or not the conceptions are anthropomorphic is of secondary importance. The ordering of the relations of these entities to men is what Weber designates as the realm of religious action.

One further element of this complex is important. This quality of special apartness, charisma, is often attributed to objects, acts, human beings, which in other respects belong to the everyday world or are closely related to it. This quality is in some sense a manifestation of these supernatural forces or entities. Some distinction between the natural and the supernatural elements in these concrete things is imperative. Among the possible interpretations of the relation of the two elements is that the former symbolizes the latter. As Weber says, "Now not only do things play a part in life which are merely there and happen, but also which have a 'meaning' and are there because of this meaning. With this, magic, from the direct action of forces, becomes symbolism." However different the "native" interpretation of this may be from our own self-conscious symbolism, here is an element of fundamental importance.

From this basal idea Weber draws one of his fundamental theses, that the first effect of "religious ideas" on action including economic action —an effect everywhere present—is to sanction the stereotyping of tradition. "Every magical procedure which has been 'proved' efficacious is naturally repeated strictly in the successful form." That is extended to the whole realm of symbolically meaningful actions. . . .

They [religious ideas] are ideas concerning not merely *how* the world works, but *why* in a teleological sense; they concern the "meaning" of the world. From this point of view religious ideas are inseparably bound up with human interests and vice versa. Weber has shown how the problem of evil, especially suffering, forms a central starting point for the formulation of the question of meaning. Conversely, what human religious interests *can* be, comes to be defined in terms of the conception of the meaning of the world.

This mutual relation is not altogether a completely relativistic circle. It is possible to say, in general, what kind of meaning and of interest is involved. The meaning is just that involved in the above teleological sense. If a friend is killed in an automobile accident the "how" is usually fairly clear in a scientifically satisfying sense. It is true that our knowledge of the physiology of death is by no means complete—and the friend of the deceased is not likely to be in possession of more than a small fraction of that knowledge. But this is not what is problematical to him. It is rather the "why" in a sense relative to a system of values. The question is, what purpose or value could his death serve? In this sense such an occurrence is apt to be felt as particularly meaningless.

The "meaning" in question, then, is that which is relevant to a teleological value context, not to a scientific explanatory context. The interests are those in the ultimate-value achievements with which we identify ourselves. In this connection it must be noted that the religious ideas Weber is primarily concerned with are not as such exclusively value ideas, or ends of action. They are rather rationalized interpretations of the meaning of the world, including a complete metaphysical system. Out of these fundamental metaphysical postulates, then, is to be derived what meaning the world *can* have for man and, from this, in turn, what his ultimate values can "meaningfully" be.[12]

Supernatural or Natural Power?

Few, if any, will contest the importance of the supernatural in a definition of religion. The philosophizing through which the world gains greater meaning to man is fundamental to religion. Furthermore, supernatural events conceived as occurring in the world itself have often played a significant part in religious history. Whether religious attitudes are to be limited to objects in the supernatural category is another matter. It seems arbitrary and restrictive of scientific inquiry to define religion in terms of the supernatural if exhaustive empirical study has not disclosed

[12] Reprinted from *The Structure of Social Action* by Talcott Parsons, by permission of McGraw-Hill Book Company, pp. 564–566, 667–668. Copyright 1937 by McGraw-Hill Book Company.

the occasion for this. The question would be more easily resolved if Marett and those following him gave a more incisive definition of what they mean by supernatural.

In exploring the meaning to its limits, we may first recite Codrington's definition of mana, quoted with approval by Marett.[13] "It is a power or influence, not physical, and in a way supernatural; but it shows itself in physical force, or in any kind of power or excellence which a man possesses." It is "what works to effect everything which is beyond the ordinary power of men, outside the common processes of nature." This appears to identify supernatural with the extraordinary and uncommon. As noted previously, Marett cites Jevons' characterization of that which "defeats reasonable expectation." Lowie, illustrating Marett's concept of the supernatural, writes:

> When a Hopi Indian in Arizona raises corn where a white tiller fails, when a Papuan boatwright constructs elaborate buildings without nails or metal implements, when a Polynesian carves the most aesthetic patterns with a shark's tooth, he is solving his everyday problems not only competently but with elegance. All these activities, however, though sometimes curiously associated with (to our mind) irrelevant considerations, belong in the main to what Dr. Marett would call the *workaday* world, i.e., the domain of reason, of normal experience, of an empirical correspondence of cause and effect. But everywhere there is, in addition to such practical rationalism, a sense of something transcending the expected or natural, a sense of something Extraordinary, Mysterious, or Supernatural.[14]

If we mean by supernatural merely the unexpected experience in terms of statistical frequency, we are not going outside the world of natural law. If, however, we mean events which contradict natural law, we are confronted by one form of the supernatural. The major import of Marett's description of religion as followed by Goldenweiser and Lowie is apparently in the sense of emotional experiences caused by the impingement of happenings believed to be supernatural. If this is the case, a definition of religion in terms of supernatural belief would be unduly limiting.

On the other hand, Marett does not seem to go as far as Goldenweiser and Lowie in losing sight of the normal, psychological aspects of mana. We read in one of Marett's later works:

> To sum up, then, it would appear that the religious faith of the savage is not merely a will to believe a lot of nonsense. Nor, again, is it simply a will to take his world as he finds it, because in order to live

[13] Marett, *op. cit.,* p. 120; Codrington, *op. cit.,* pp. 118–119.

[14] R. H. Lowie, *op. cit.,* pp. xv–xvi.

up to such a hard world a man has to be fit, and fitness depends on *mana*. Now *mana* stands at once for miracle and *morale;* and who will say that the savage is not right in identifying the two. With wonder and positive awe he discovers, as we all may do, that the moral order is capable of supplying out of itself the motive—the "drive"—necessary to evoke moral action on the part of Man. This revelation comes, however, to the primitive man in a special way. So concrete-minded is he that he is bound to be more or less of a pantheist. He encounters the divine stimulus here, there, and anywhere within the contents of an experience in which percepts play a far more important part than concepts. The civilized man, on the other hand, thanks to a far wider system of communications which entails a free use of mental symbols, favors a more abstract notion of deity, seeking to grasp it in the unity of its idea rather than in the plurality of its manifestations.[15]

This passage sets forth a psychological concept of mana which places it within the domain of verifiable experience. The term *supernatural* then falls in the context of religious usage wherein the category is applied to the world of inward or spiritual experience as opposed to the outer world of objects in nature. This is a common usage of the term *supernatural* among mystics whose preoccupation is with their inward world of feeling. Yet this usage is not to be encouraged because of the ambiguity between what is not found in outward experience but which can be scientifically studied, and what is not found in common experience and which is outside the domain of science altogether.

We may also note a perennial tendency of each generation of people who fail to rediscover the inward sentiments and ideas of the religion of their forebears. This is a tendency to place in an artificial category of the so-called supernatural those realities recorded from the past which cannot be readily verified through experience and study. So the God who reigned in the inward world of yesterday may be relegated to the speculative realm of today. Like a child who alternately finds and loses his possessions, man alternately discovers his God in experience and then puts him away in a supernatural closet. A problem of religious education is to keep alive in people's consciousness the supreme religious realities upon which devotion is focused. Religious leaders, as well as social scientists, manifest the tendency to regard religious objects as supernatural when these cannot be rediscovered in the natural realm.

W. H. Clark, the author of a recently published study in

[15] R. R. Marett, *Faith, Hope, and Charity in Primitive Religion,* Macmillan, 1932, pp. 144–145.

the psychology of religion, speaks for the tradition in scientific inquiry which would keep the study of God out of the empirical realm and who would define religion in terms of a belief in a super-experiential reality. Following a review of definitions of religion, he writes:

> It should be noted that many of these definitions, as we would expect, make reference to "higher powers" or God. But the reader must understand that the psychologist, *as a psychologist,* has no business in assuming the existence of God as a fact, or in trying to prove His existence or to disprove it. This is the function of the theologians. This conviction explains why some psychologists, like Allport, strive to omit references to the divine in their definitions. When the psychologist does refer to God, or an equivalent idea, it simply reflects the fact that the idea of the divine or of some supersensible power usually, though not always, is found among those who are self-consciously religious. Consequently, any reference to God by the psychologist of religion is simply by way of describing the consciousness of the individual, or what the person reports it to be. . . .
>
> With the full recognition that we are on ground where the experts disagree, and thus well aware of the hazards involved, we will venture our own definition. It is our feeling that religion can be *most characteristically* described as *the inner experience of the individual when he senses a Beyond, especially as evidenced by the effect of this experience on his behavior when he actively attempts to harmonize his life with the Beyond.* This is not proposed as a definition to end all discussion, but is simply by way of informing the reader what the author has in mind, or rather in the back of his mind, when he discusses religion. For religion is too large and inclusive a term to be stringently confined within any definition suitable for the use of a psychologist, and we may be using the term occasionally in a less rigorous sense, as will be explained later on in the discussion.
>
> It will be noted that religion is first of all described as something inward, and secondly in such terms as to suggest that the essential experience partakes of mystical qualities; for the term *Beyond* stands for what is felt to be a supernatural or supersensible force, most probably personal in nature, apprehended by a psychological process of which the individual can give no very adequate account.[16]

Omissions Made by a Supernatural Definition of Religion

If the concept of supernatural is defined to include only things outside of experience or contrary to laws of experience, a definition of religion in terms of supernatural beliefs omits religions having little or no supernatural quality about them. Buddhism and Confucianism in their pure forms are avowedly antisuper-

[16] W. Clark, *The Psychology of Religion,* Macmillan, 1958, pp. 21–22.

natural. Buddha insisted that all which men need to know about religion is to be found in the world of experience. He rejected the efficacy of prayers to Gods or spirits. He challenged the priests of the times by asking which one of them by praying to the river could make one bank reach the other so a man might walk across dry-shod. The religious mood of America, as described by Will Herberg, is increasingly a practical religion of social belonging without supernatural implications.[17]

Nor are we on satisfactory ground if we restrict the concept of religion to unusual experiences. More frequently than otherwise, the emphasis in the religions of the East is upon quiet meditation and serenity, not emotional display. One of the strong trends in denominational religion in America is away from emotionalism to calmness and stability of religious feeling. There is no emotional excess in Christian Science as a rule for everyday health, nor in Quaker principles for everyday living. The most naturalistic and least emotional of all are perhaps members of the Society for Ethical Culture, a small though active group of intellectuals banded together in various cities for religious activity based upon idealistic principles.

Among social scientists analyzing religion, M. J. Herskovits has turned away from the current of thought which limits religious belief to supernaturally conceived objects. In his text on anthropology he comments:

> The less spectacular phases of everyday religion, which are certainly of no lesser importance, are, in point of fact, the ones that pervade religious behavior. All men, at all times, have sensed frustration and fear when faced with problems that their own human resources could not solve. Such frustrations and fears come not alone with dramatic displays of nature, with thunder and lightning and hail, with blizzards, and insect pests, and drought. They also arise, in everyday life, in the give and take of human relations, in encounters with fellow humans who deny, forbid, dominate, challenge, or inflict pain.[18]

RELIGION AS A BELIEF IN A HIGHER POWER

Herskovits' Definition

A wider definition is proposed by Herskovits through dropping the supernatural qualification from the concept of power in religion.

[17] Will Herberg, *Protestant-Catholic-Jew,* Doubleday, 1956, Chap. 11.
[18] M. J. Herskovits, *Man and His Works,* Knopf, 1948, pp. 375–376.

We must, then, recognize that, however frequent a concomitant of religion supernaturalism may be, any definition drawn in terms of it lacks a requisite comprehensiveness. If, in addition, we recognize further that an adequate definition must take into account the everyday functioning of religion in terms of its more placid manifestations as well as its more dramatic elements, then, in these terms, we may think of religion as *belief in, and identification with a greater force or power.* The belief may so pervade attitude and action as rarely to enter the stream of conscious thought, except in moments of crisis when it is called upon to steady a world that seems to be falling about one's head; or, under more commonplace circumstances, when tradition and conviction assure success in some undertaking; or in effecting a cure, or insuring a good crop by the performance of established rites. The greater force or power that stands for order and protection in the life of the individual may be a supernatural being or beings, an impersonal force, a concept such as society, or science. It is enough that man have faith in its unfailing potentialities, that he feel that it is to be called on when needed, that it will not fail him when his own resources are insufficient.

Above all, religion implies the emotional response to the power that rules the universe, however it may be conceived. Though the supreme religious experience, the "thrill," is felt by relatively few persons, and by them but sporadically, yet the raw material of emotion is ever present, and on a less intense scale is experienced by all those whose emotional susceptibilities are keyed to a religious response.[19]

This definition does not restrict religion to spiritual beings which are propitiated or conciliated. It is sufficiently general to encompass Buddhism or Ethical Culture (power of ideals). It also includes socialism (power of economic coöperation), progressive education (power of child-centered curriculum), Federation of American Scientists (power of science), and National Association for the Advancement of Colored People (power of interracial justice). *Greater* apparently means greater than other forces or powers which human beings control or influence.

Problem of Breadth in Herskovits' Definition

The question arises of whether all of these powers are to be considered religious objects. They are powers toward which human beings may take a serious or devoted attitude. Of the attitude toward science, Herskovits relates:

In our mechanistic culture, where there is progressively less place for supernaturalism as a functioning element comparable to the man-

[19] *Ibid.*, p. 377.

ner in which it is operative in an Indian tribe, the emotional drive, the deep faith in the transcendental importance of what is undertaken, the dedication to the experimental tradition that marks the scientist in his laboratory, is essentially religious in its psychological orientation. The thrill that comes when the formula is discovered to be correct, when the last stroke of the adding machine proves the validity of the mathematical calculation, is no different from that experienced by the nonliterate man when he comes face to face with his spirit.[20]

To be devoted to an object, to identify oneself with it, and to find a thrill in experiencing it are psychological characteristics of other human activities, such as romantic love or drug addiction. Some limitation of definition seems needed to exclude devotion to motor cars, jet propulsion, and atomic energy, which are important powers in contemporary life, in order that religion does not become synonymous with compelling enjoyments of life. When there is an element of personification of the power, then activities approach those of a religious nature. Drug usage may play a role in a few bizarre religions, and the following passage illustrates the context in which such usage may involve a religious attitude.

O just, subtle, and all-conquering opium! that, to the hearts of rich and poor alike, for the wounds that will never heal, and for the pangs of grief that "tempt the spirit to rebel," brings an assuaging balm;—eloquent opium that with thy potent rhetoric stealest away the purposes of wrath, pleadest effectually for relenting pity, and through one night's heavenly sleep callest back to the guilty man the visions of his infancy, and hands washed pure from blood;—O just and righteous opium! that to the chancery of dreams summonest, for the triumphs of despairing innocence, false witnesses, and confoundest perjury, and dost reverse the sentences of unrighteous judges;—thou buildest upon the bosom of darkness, out of the fantastic imagery of the brain, cities and temples, beyond the art of Phidias and Praxiteles, beyond the splendors of Babylon and Hekatompylos; and, "from the anarchy of dreaming sleep," callest into sunny light the faces of long-buried beauties, and the blessed household countenances, cleansed from the "dishonors of the grave." Thou only givest these gifts to man; and thou hast the keys of Paradise, O just, subtle, and mighty opium![21]

On the other hand, defining religion in terms of higher powers which are personified in some manner by those who are devotees does not adequately describe ethical-culture religions in which the higher powers are social values or social ideals. In consider-

[20] *Ibid.*, p. 377.

[21] Thomas de Quincey, quoted in A. J. Rosanoff, *Manual of Psychiatry and Mental Hygiene*, Wiley, 1947, p. 404.

ing how to classify these religions we turn to the line of development of religious concepts in psychology.

RELIGION AS A BELIEF IN AN UNSEEN HIGHER POWER

The attempt to define religion in terms of scientifically verifiable elements of experience goes back to Schleiermacher in the early nineteenth century, who defined religion as a "feeling of absolute dependence."[22] This concept is closely related to that of a higher power, in that dependence implies a power upon whom one depends. Since Schleiermacher did not qualify the type of dependence or power involved, his definition encounters the same problem of generality as that of Herskovits' more recent one. While the feeling of utter dependence conveys much of the religious mood of God worshipers, by itself the definition is inadequate. Hegel was led to remark that by this definition Schleiermacher's dog was more pious than his master. Nevertheless, Schleiermacher's concept prevailed until the evolution of religion became a preoccupation of British anthropologists, whose concepts of religion have been recounted. Schleiermacher's concept has been popular with those who view God as a supernatural reality outside human experience and beyond empirical study. What remains for psychology is the attitude of the religious devotee toward his supernatural religious object.

In the late nineteenth century, American psychologists, among them G. S. Hall, E. D. Starbuck, J. H. Leuba, G. A. Coe, and William James studied the development of religion in the life of the individual, specifically the phenomenon of religious conversion. This work began with that of G. S. Hall in 1881.[23] Although not the first of this group of psychologists, James was the most illuminating writer among them, reproducing and popularizing ideas and results gained by others. James's and Schleiermacher's concepts of religion or similar ones with modification have been prominent in religious psychology to the present time.

James's Definition of Religion

Reducing Herskovits' definition to a supernatural residue seems inadequate. We now explore another direction for limiting its scope, following the lead of William James in stressing the "unseen" nature of the higher powers with whom man deals

[22] F. Schleiermacher, *The Christian Faith,* 1821–1822, ed. by H. R. Mackintosh and J. S. Stewart, Scribner's, 1928, p. 12.

[23] G. S. Hall, *Adolescence,* Appleton, 1911, Vol. 2, p. 292.

in his religions. "Were one asked to characterize the life of religion in the broadest and most general terms possible, one might say that it consists of the belief that there is an unseen order, and that our supreme good lies in harmoniously adjusting ourselves thereto. This belief and this adjustment are the religious attitude."[24]

In applying this definition, James indicates that the unseen order is one of higher energy or power capable of producing results of human importance. "Union or harmonious relation with that higher universe is our true end. . . . Prayer or inner communion with the spirit thereof—be that spirit 'God' or 'law'—is a process wherein work is really done, and spiritual energy flows in and produces effects, psychological or material, within the phenomenal world."[25] We can summarize James's concept by defining religion as a system of beliefs in an unseen order of higher power and of adjustments to this order for human good.

According to James, the adjustment is more basic if by an individual practicing religion in solitude than if by a group meeting together. "In one sense at least the personal religion will prove itself more fundamental than either theology or ecclesiasticism. Churches, when once established, live at second-hand upon tradition; but the *founders* of every church owed their power originally to the fact of their direct personal communion with the divine. . . . Religion, therefore, . . . shall mean for us *the feelings, acts, and experiences of individual men in their solitude, so far as they apprehend themselves to stand in relation to whatever they may consider the divine.*"[26]

The antichurch attitude of James is not related to his major analytical contributions, but this has slowed the acceptance of his work by organized religion. In contrast to James's individualistic approach, Emile Durkheim restricts religion to group expression of it, as did Robertson Smith. "A religion is a unified system of beliefs and practices relative to sacred things, that is to say, things set apart and forbidden—beliefs and practices which unite into one single moral community called a Church, all those who adhere to them."[27] Durkheim's effort to define reli-

[24] William James, *The Varieties of Religious Experience,* Modern Library, 1936, p. 53.

[25] *Ibid.,* p. 475.

[26] *Ibid.,* pp. 31–32.

[27] Emile Durkheim, *The Elementary Forms of the Religious Life,* tr. by J. W. Swain, Free Press, 1947, p. 47. Also see Howard Becker's treatment of the *sacred,* "Current Sacred-Secular Theory," in Howard Becker and Alvin Boskoff (eds.), *Modern Sociological Theory,* Dryden, 1957, pp. 133–185.

gion in terms of the concept of sacred is apparently unsatisfactory, since the latter concept is not well defined. In the narrow sense, "set apart and forbidden" comprises only one aspect of some things in religion. The trend in religious development among many persons at the present time is in the direction of self-determination and individual development of religion rather than submitting to ordering and forbidding. In the broad sense, sacred appears to be synonymous with religious, which fails to provide a real definition. However, Durkheim's emphasis upon the group nature of religion is a corrective to James's individualism, the latter seeming to be more of a predilection than a proved principle.

Supernatural and Psychological Beings in Religion

The usefulness of the concept of unseen is that it subsumes both supernatural and inward realities of religion. When man projects personal characteristics upon the universe outside him, he believes in supernatural personal beings. When he refers to Zeus as king of Olympus or God as creator of the universe, he believes in characteristics imputed to a cosmic mind. This is the supernatural type of religious belief to which the definition applies. James's interest was in God, supernaturally conceived. The definition apparently covers the worship of physical objects, as among the Crow Indians, since such worship implies supernaturally conceived qualities of an invisible and psychological nature in the objects to which personal appeal can be made. At the same time, the definition is not so broad as to include the entire range of man's beliefs about and adjustments to visible forces of the universe. These forces are seen in that they evidence themselves in observable changes in motion or position and are known by abstraction from concrete physical data.

On the other hand, when people believe in spirit possession or that God or the devil inhabits their personalities as a phenomenon of inward experience, leading them to perform actions of kindliness or viciousness, this is an inward type of religious belief. People find within themselves motivational complexes which they personify and regard as independent realities within their own personality system. In this way the individual may feel the will of God as if it were an independent will, operating within him. C. G. Jung has called attention to the existence of such psychological forces in awareness of gods. "Religion is a relationship to the highest or most powerful value, be it positive or negative. The relationship is voluntary as well as involuntary, that is to say you can accept, consciously, the value by which you are possessed unconsciously. That psychological fact which wields the greatest power in your system functions as a god, since it is always the overwhelming psychic factor that is called 'God.' "[28]

While we can distinguish two classes of spiritual beings, supernatural and psychic, the two are frequently blended in the processes of religion. Freud among others has pointed out that man projects upon the universe his own inward dispositions. "Spirits and demons were nothing but the projection of primitive man's emotional impulses; he personified affects, populated the world with them, and then rediscovered his inner psychic processes outside himself."[29] Among a list of gods of the Ifugaos of Luzon reported by R. F. Barton are many which are obvious projections of traits of human personality. Some of those involved in the debtor-receiver relationship include: Fast Beating of the Heart from Fear, Gasp of Fear, Fear in the Lungs, Gentleness, Cooling of Fever, Rattling of the Teeth, Too Steep to Climb, Slowness, Craziness, Concession, Leaning on Something, Soften the Debtor Up, Slamming Down Payment at Once, Agreed On, Consolation, Overflowing and Overflowing, Dammed Up.[30]

The frequent confusion between supernatural and psychic beings does not imply that all supernatural ideas are projections of human impulses. Intelligent philosophy is free from emotional structuring. Its principles about things beyond experience are what appear to be the most plausible conclusions which can be inferred from the fragmentary evidence within experience. This philosophy applies the procedures of scientific method to problems where data are perpetually incomplete. The chains of reasoning are therefore inadequate. Man contents himself with such philosophy in his religion since the alternative is to hold no opinion at all concerning the unverifiable but meaningful questions of life beyond death and God beyond experience. In this philosophizing, man frequently identifies the portion of God's will or spirit which he feels in experience with the vast reality of God whose existence outside of experience he assumes. From this viewpoint, he believes that the two manifestations of God are parts of the same unified whole.

[28] C. G. Jung, *Psychology and Religion: West and East,* tr. by R. F. C. Hull. Bollingen Series XX, Bollingen Foundation, Inc. Pantheon, 1958, p. 81.

[29] Sigmund Freud, *Totem and Taboo* in *The Basic Writings of Sigmund Freud,* tr. by A. A. Brill, Random House, 1938, p. 878.

[30] R. F. Barton, "The Religion of the Ifugaos," *Memoirs of the American Anthropological Association,* No. 65, 1946, cited in William Howells, *The Heathens,* Doubleday, 1948, p. 217.

RELIGION AS ETHICAL CULTURE

Dewey's Approach to Defining Religion

The eminent American philosopher and psychologist John Dewey is critical of attempts to define religion and in particular raises objection to the concept of unseen because of its supernatural overtones.

However, in the *Oxford Dictionary* I find the following: "Recognition on the part of man of some unseen higher power as having control of his destiny and as being entitled to obedience, reverence and worship." This particular definition is less explicit in assertion of the supernatural character of the higher unseen power than are others that might be cited. It is, however, surcharged with implications having their source in ideas connected with the belief in the supernatural, characteristic of historic religions.[31]

For we are forced to acknowledge that concretely there is no such thing as religion in the singular. There is only a multitude of religions. "Religion" is a strictly collective term and the collection it stands for is not even of the kind illustrated in textbooks of logic. It has not the unity of a regiment or assembly but that of any miscellaneous aggregate. Attempts to prove the universality prove too much or too little. It is probable that religions have been universal in the sense that all the peoples we know anything about have had *a* religion. But the differences among them are so great and so shocking that any common element that can be extracted is meaningless.[32]

In reality, the only thing that can be said to be "proved" is the existence of some complex of conditions that have operated to effect an adjustment in life, an orientation, that brings with it a sense of security and peace. The particular interpretation given to this complex of conditions is not inherent in the experience itself. It is derived from the culture with which a particular person has been imbued. A fatalist will give one name to it; a Christian Scientist another. . . . The determining factor in the interpretation of the experience is the particular doctrinal apparatus into which a person has been inducted. The emotional deposit connected with prior teaching floods the whole situation. It may readily confer upon the experience such a peculiarly sacred preciousness that all inquiry into its causation is barred.[33]

The actual religious quality in the experience described is the *effect* produced, the better adjustment in life and its conditions, not the manner and cause of its production. The way in which the experience operated, its function, determines its religious value. If the reorientation actually occurs, it, and the sense of security and stability accompany-

31 John Dewey, *A Common Faith,* Yale University Press, 1934, p. 3.
32 *Ibid.,* pp. 7–8.
33 *Ibid.,* p. 13.

ing it, are forces on their own account. It takes place in different persons in a multitude of ways. It is sometimes brought about by devotion to a cause; sometimes by a passage of poetry that opens a new perspective; sometimes as was the case with Spinoza—deemed an atheist in his day—through philosophical reflection.[34]

Any activity pursued in behalf of an ideal end against obstacles and in spite of threats of personal loss because of conviction of its general and enduring value is religious in quality. Many a person, inquirer, artist, philanthropist, citizen, men and women in the humblest walks of life, have achieved, without presumption and without display, such unification of themselves and of their relations to the conditions of existence. It remains to extend their spirit and inspiration to ever wider numbers. If I have said anything about religions and religion that seems harsh, I have said those things because of a firm belief that the claim on the part of religion to possess a monopoly of ideals and of the supernatural means by which alone, it is alleged, they can be furthered, stands in the way of the realization of distinctively religious values inherent in natural experience.[35]

The identification of religion with pursuit of values or pursuit of ideals has been a recurring theme in the history of religious study. The historical forerunner of this type of definition given by Immanuel Kant is that the essence of religion is not metaphysical knowledge but devotion to moral duty. The difficulty with this line of definition is that religion becomes equivalent to the practice of ethics, as Dewey acknowledges. Still, Dewey recognizes the deep importance of processes for developing ethical personality but does not note when these become religion.

Examination of the practices in religion discloses that these often involve the cultivation of ethical attitudes and responses. Religion is then not the practice of ideals so much as it is the acquisition and cultivation of ideals so that life more fully expresses these. When the required motives have been developed in personality, the idealistic behavior to which Dewey refers makes its appearance. Religion is therefore both a preparation for living and the business of living.

Nor is the preparation to be thought of as essentially supernatural. While supernatural devices have been relied upon by men in various religions, the development of ideals as motives takes place more effectively by understandable psychological processes. What these processes are and their involvement in worship and prayer receive consideration in later chapters. On

[34] *Ibid.*, p. 14.
[35] *Ibid.*, pp. 27–28.

the other hand, the supernatural aspect of religion should not be discounted. The type of philosophy which one constructs as an interpretation of the universe affects the development and pursuit of ideals. To the extent that this philosophy incorporates ideas of God and immortality, ideals may be affected by supernatural elements in religion.

To identify religion with ethics not only seems a large dilution of meaning, but the identification involves the assumption that all religions contain idealistic behavior. That individuals may manage to believe in and practice religion without achieving visibly ethical behavior seems apparent. At the same time, some of the most notable humanitarians have been persons who deliberately shut religious belief and exercise out of their lives. Their humanitarianism may have been transmitted to their personalities by a previous generation whose values were cultivated through religious development, but they are ethical without giving evidence of religious interest or participation.

Ethical Culture Religion

A small religious group with meetings built around the purpose of cultivating ethical values are the Ethical Culture Societies organized in twenty-three American cities with a total membership in 1957 of six thousand. The first such society met in New York City in 1876, the founder being Dr. Felix Adler, the son of a rabbi. Dr. Henry Neumann has been a contemporary spokesman for the movement.

> The societies conduct weekly meetings, chiefly on Sunday mornings. . . . At these meetings, Leaders and guest-speakers discourse on problems of the inner life, or on questions of current social importance, or on both. Forums, classes, institutes, meetings of Men's Clubs, Women's Clubs, Young People's Associations afford occasion for discussion of these matters and of practical ways to deal with them. Sunday classes for boys and girls are of special help with children of intermarriage because the ethical interest unifies where creed (or ancestral affiliation such as the Hebrew) may separate. Leaders are empowered to conduct marriage services; they officiate at funerals and naming-ceremonies; and they offer personal counsel to members and non-members.
>
> The Ethical Culture Society is to us a religious society in the sense of giving us a cause entitled to chief claim upon our energies, our most inclusive fellowship, our most satisfying way of reading life's meaning, our best long-run incentive, our deepest assurance and hope. As in some traditional ethical religions, we hold that human behavior is good according as it is animated by faith in a supreme excellence, that at all times the test of such faith is conduct, and that the truest way to

cooperate with the noblest life in the universe is to ennoble the life of man.[36]

Nor can we commit ourselves to the belief that the best ethical behaviors require trust in a Creator. We think that the best in the God-belief itself points to a very different truth. The very progress from a god of magic to a God who expects mankind to do justice and mercy indicates how ethical thinking and ethical practice decide what kind of God-belief, if any, people will reach. Likewise, the best in the belief in immortality is the hunger for continued fellowship and the desire that human goodness shall grow to perfect flower. At their best these beliefs are ethically motivated. Their finest outcome is ethical practice.

On these traditional beliefs, we leave our members free to decide for themselves. Experience has taught us that most of those who come to us do so because they want a fellowship where the conviction is stressed that first-rate living can and should be sought because of its own inherent appeal that human spirits, human hands, must do the necessary labors and that the most deeply satisfying meaning of life is to be found in the process of such striving and in the reflections which it enlightens. Because this is an experiment in a new way of living, Ethical Societies are needed to organize, direct, and inspire such efforts.[37]

A large group of persons in conventional churches, among them many Unitarians and Universalists, seem to accept the principles of the ethical culture movement by their ignoring the question of a personal God and giving nominal support to traditional forms of worship while recognizing that talks and discussions are means for cultivating personal and social values. God becomes at most a deistic concept of philosophy. This variety of religion regards the ideals and values of human beings as the prime movers of civilization. These are higher forces to be aroused and set in motion. They make the difference between war and peace, between economic destitution and economic abundance. Since these psychological powers are part of the unseen world of inward experience, they satisfy James's definition of religion.

The late A. Powell Davies was a leading spokesman for Unitarians, an influential denomination in America. Many Unitarians accept the importance of a personal God and can be classified as liberal Christians. Justice W. O. Douglas writes of Davies' views as follows:

Dr. Davies had little tolerance for doctrines. In an address at Harvard in 1954 he said:

[36] H. Neumann, "Ethical Culture," in V. Ferm, *Religion in the Twentieth Century,* Philosophical Library, 1948, p. 333.
[37] *Ibid.,* p. 334.

"It is significant, I think, that although thousands have been done to death for heresy—that is to say, for not believing the official doctrines—no one, through all the Christian centuries, has ever been tried by an ecclesiastical court for not loving his neighbor as himself or for transgressing the Golden Rule. This means that it has been more important to the churchmen that people should accept their speculations on matters concerning which almost nothing is known than that they should follow the teaching and example of Jesus."

He once wrote a friend, "I do not think that morality depends upon any particular system of religious doctrine. The ecclesiastical imperialism which claims that there cannot be a universal good society until Christian doctrine is accepted is both mischievous and grotesque. What is needed is the identification of the spiritual and moral values in all the great provinces of religious culture (and outside them), so that the world may have a common basis for its united life."

He had a like quarrel with psychiatrists. In a sermon delivered April 17, 1949, he said:

"We hear that what we must do to get peace of mind is to get rid of our conscience. For guilt feelings are not examined to discover whether they indicate the presence of a soul; it is taken for granted that they indicate the presence of a neurosis. Sometimes they do; but not as often as the shallow diagnoses of modern days would indicate. There *should* be guilt feelings; just as a sick body gives warning of its sickness through pain, so does a sick soul. And spiritual opiates are not the answer. They ease the pain only to kill the soul."

Dr. Davies pleaded for the removal of the supernatural from religion:

"There is no God in the sky. God is in the heart that loves the sky's blueness. There is no army of angels, no hosts of seraphim, and no celestial hierarchy. All this is man's imagining. But there is angelic purity of motive, and seraphic joy, and a celestial heightening of the human spirit."

Though Dr. Davies rejected religious convictions based on dogma or creed and stood firm for "the reasoned beliefs of a free mind," he was the first to defend the principle that "the right of private judgment" must be "scrupulously upheld." It was for that reason he always insisted "upon tolerance for convictions opposed to my own. I may at a later time come to accept some other convictions than I hold at present, and so I should be humble and attentive in the presence of views from which at the moment I differ."[38]

Influencing Higher Powers in Religion: Leuba's Definition

In the problem of defining the limits of religious phenomena, the question remains of whether the category *unseen* may not

[38] W. O. Douglas (ed.), *The Mind and Faith of A. Powell Davies,* Doubleday, 1959, pp. 29–30.

open the definition of religion to any activity stemming from human motives, since these are unseen forces in the functioning of personality. The cravings for sex or food are very powerful. Shall these higher forces be considered religious when people engage in love-making or feasting? If this is done, then religion becomes a general designation for any intense activity of human life.

The needed distinction is evident in the Ethical Culture Society. The attitude of members toward ethical powers is one of cultivating them, that is, intensifying them through group assemblies or individual pursuit. The additional qualification needed in James's definition is that the adjustment made to the higher powers is one of *psychologically influencing* them for human good, or at least attempting to do so. No confusion then exists between an ethical assembly and a house party of fun-making young people. In the former, *modification* of desire is central, while in the latter, *satisfaction* of desire is of primary interest. In the former, the adjustment is by influencing the aims of conduct, while in the latter the adjustment is by selecting appropriate means to fulfilling desires. To take another illustration, if people simply play golf they merely express impulses for athletic and social activity. If, however, a movement is organized to intensify the desire to play golf among members and outsiders, the movement becomes a cult, religious in one respect.

To the extent that progressive education, with its purpose of influencing social values of children, utilizes a higher psychological power, it is a form of religion, although not in all of its aspects. Furthermore, religion is distinguished by periodic revival of values and attitudes through religious exercises, as Durkheim pointed out, and not simply by developing social traits in the growing personality. To be fully religious, the cultivation pertains to psychological powers acknowledged as supreme or at least superior to other motives. It is true that this leaves the door of definition open to include orgiastic cults; yet on the other hand, it must be recognized that such cults have played an important role in ancient and primitive religions. The devotees behave toward their sexual or bucolic spirit as if he were a god. When church people today tell themselves that ethical values or spiritual powers are more important to them than any other forces of their existence, we have the essence of a religious attitude toward such higher powers. Max Weber's and J. M. Yinger's reference to religion as being concerned with ultimate values conveys the idea of supremely important powers.

When the adjustment to which James's definition refers consists of influencing higher beings, the definition includes worship, prayer, sacrifice, or any form of propitiation of a psychological or supernatural being. In regard to a supernatural being the psychological influence cannot be empirically demonstrated and is instead assumed or attempted. The following prayers for rain and for fair weather are examples of supernatural prayer.

O God, heavenly Father, who by thy Son Jesus Christ hast promised to all those who seek thy kingdom, and the righteousness thereof, all things necessary to their bodily sustenance; Send us, we beseech thee, in this our necessity, such moderate rain and showers, that we may receive the fruits of the earth to our comfort, and to thy honour; through Jesus Christ our Lord.[39]

Almighty and most merciful Father, we humbly beseech thee, of thy great goodness, to restrain those immoderate rains, wherewith thou hast afflicted us. And we pray thee to send us such seasonable weather, that the earth may, in due time, yield her increase for our use and benefit; through Jesus Christ our Lord.[40]

With respect to a religious being considered as an aspect of human personality, the influence is upon psychological forces within the field of scientific study. Cultivation of spiritual power within the individual is a vital phase of religious exercises such as worship, prayer, and meditation, which are found among the rituals and practices of contemporary religious groups in America as well as elsewhere. The definition of religion given by J. H. Leuba comes close to incorporating the psychological influence by man of higher powers, both natural and supernatural, found or believed to exist in religious life. "Religion is that part of human experience in which man feels himself in relation with powers of psychic nature, usually personal powers, and makes use of them."[41]

Buddhism

Of special interest in America from the standpoint of ethical-culture religion are the Buddhist churches with a domestic membership of around 70,000. Most of these are Americans of Japanese ancestry who brought their religion with them from their native country.[42] Five centuries prior to the Christian era a Hindu prince, Gautama Buddha, left his wealth, wife, and in-

[39] *Book of Common Prayer,* 1936, p. 40.

[40] *Ibid.*

[41] J. H. Leuba, *A Psychological Study of Religion,* Macmillan, 1912, p. 52.

[42] Robert P. Jackson, a sociologist who has studied Buddhism in America, collaborated with the author in preparing the brief account given here.

fant son for a life of self-denial, charitable works, and meditative study. The spiritual fruit of this life is a profound system of teachings which have spread through India, China, Japan, and many parts of the world. The present membership is difficult to estimate because of the capacity of Buddhism to influence or fuse with other religions with which it has come in contact, but this is estimated as between 200 and 500 million. Nor has Buddhism emphasized ecclesiastical organization or formal conditions for membership. It represents a way of life which the individual follows by faith, meditation, and self-discipline more than a corporate way of worship. The Buddhist churches in America, as have many elsewhere, have instituted formal readings and liturgies adapted to temporal and cultural context, and some mutual interaction with Christianity has taken place.

Although prescientific in its origin, Buddhism is of deep significance for the scientific study of religion. As a way of life it reacts against supernaturalism, and its teachings are directly based upon individual exploration of the interior life. In the best tradition of causal science the four noble truths of Buddha declare: (1) Life contains suffering, discord, jealousy, and angry contention. (2) The cause of this suffering is ignorance and self-seeking desire. (3) The suffering can be ended by removing its cause. (4) The way to this removal is the Eightfold Path of Righteousness. The path consists of eight facets: right understanding, right purpose, right speech, right conduct, right livelihood, right endeavor, right thought, and right meditation. These are elaborated in a catechism for Shin-shu Buddhist Sunday Schools.

What do we mean by right understanding?
Ans. Right understanding means that we should try to learn and understand the teaching of our Lord Buddha.
What do we mean by right purpose?
Ans. Right purpose means that we should have an ideal and try to live up to it.
What do we mean by right speech?
Ans. Right speech means that we should guard our tongue and say only truthful and kind words.
What do we mean by right conduct?
Ans. Right conduct means that we should reverence our religion, respect our parents and teachers. We should be truthful and honest, polite and sincere, compassionate, moral, and temperate.
What do we mean by right livelihood?
Ans. By right livelihood we mean that we should earn our living in a way that will harm no one.

What do we mean by right endeavor?

Ans. By right endeavor we mean that we should try to become better and better in every way.

What do we mean by right thought?

Ans. By right thought we mean that we should be very careful of our thoughts because our words and our actions arise from our thoughts.

What do we mean by right meditation?

Ans. By right meditation we mean that we should keep the teaching of the Lord Buddha constantly in mind and often repeat his holy name. [This is the *Nembutsu.*]

In more sophisticated explanation of the Eightfold Path, right purpose or aspiration is defined with regard to the ultimate human goal, nirvana, the state of being resulting from following the Eightfold Path. Right speech, right conduct, and right livelihood mean actions harmless to pursuit of that goal by oneself or others. Right endeavor means no ill-directed or aimless effort. Right thought pertains to ideas beneficial to one's endeavor. Right meditation means concentration upon Buddha as a spiritual principle and upon the achievement of Buddhahood. Those interested in gaining a detailed understanding of Buddhism and the parent religious culture from which it evolved, Hinduism, are referred to recent interpretations written by spokesmen under the editorship of K. W. Morgan and published under the sponsorship of the National Council on Religion in Higher Education.[43] A small volume of references comparing Buddhism with a Quaker's view of Christianity is that authored by Teresina Havens.[44]

The Eightfold Path of Righteousness is a program for the individual to pursue and practice, and the resulting experience is one of peace and happiness. The listing of the rules does not bring out the psychological dynamics, which are found by the individual when he follows the program. These dynamics are not easily summarized because of the shifting and multiple forms and vocabularies which Buddhism has taken in its growth in various parts of the globe. Essentially there are two psychological forces making for religious growth. One of these is self-power, emphasized in some forms of Buddhism such as Zen, exercised by the individual through seeking self-enlightenment, and, as far as Shin-shu is concerned, displaced by a greater

[43] K. W. Morgan (ed.), *The Religion of the Hindus,* Ronald, 1953; K. W. Morgan (ed.), *The Path of the Buddha,* Ronald, 1956.

[44] Teresina Havens, *Buddhist and Quaker Experiments with Truth,* Religious Education Committee, Friends General Conference, 1958.

power as spiritual life develops. The central being or power in Shin Buddhism is Amida, the personification or manifestation of compassion, accepted by the individual through a life of kindness and love toward all living beings, a power exemplified most fully in the life of Buddha himself. The principal saying of Shin Buddhists is the *Nembutsu,* which expresses unconditional faith in Amida Buddha, not a creed and which might be translated as "I have faith in the power of enlightened love." This is repeated during religious services and by the individual at frequent times during daily life.

Historically, Buddhism rejects the demonstrable existence of supernatural gods, although it cannot be overlooked that in Buddhism's fusion with various religious cultures, supernaturalism and even naïve superstition have been practiced by nominal Buddhists with only a thin veneer of the actual teaching in their lives. In varying degrees Amida Buddha as a principle of love is personified as a psychological God, not supernatural. Uniformity of belief concerning the personal or impersonal nature of God is not found. Even though personified, God has not typically been the object of prayer as in the usual historical sense of verbal appeal to a person. In its different wings Buddhism has placed alternate stress upon a prescribed path for salvation and upon an informal, intuitive, often unverbalized experience of study, development, and spiritual attainment. The emphasis in American Buddhism seems a little more upon the latter than the former. In the latter, nirvana, the goal, is a state of being which is considered to be "not conceivable" by persons still attached to non-Buddhist forms of religion. Buddhism is an open door to developing various beliefs in and out of religion. The Zen form has furnished a point of departure for a group of American intellectuals who are resigned to life and whose ideas are esoteric and humanistic.

Buddhism has been reluctant to call itself a scientific religion since science is frequently taken by others to mean a preoccupation with material realities, incidental to spiritual enlightenment. The realities of Buddhist religion are found in the interior or psychic world. If systematic study of the inner world is called a science, then Buddhism is a scientific religion. Although lacking formal research projects and the contemporary ritual of scientific method, the emphasis upon individual exploration, discovery, and verification of religious principles is strongly scientific in tone. In the onward development of religions of the world,

Buddhism may be expected to give and to gain much in the scientific study of religion.

Religion Defined in Terms of Its Functions

Since a prominent feature of religion is the cultivation of ethical values, the scientific investigator may be inclined to define religion in terms of the result achieved by such activity, namely the intensification of ethical values in the life of people. The desired results from the standpoint of maintaining human life which are produced by the institutions in which human beings engage, such as family, economic order, government, school, and church, are functions of the institutions. These functions may be *latent* or unconsciously brought about, as well as *manifest* or intended consequences of the institutional activity. Corresponding to each institution are characteristic human needs met by the institution. The effort is made in sociology and anthropology to define institutions in terms of their functions.

Defining religion in terms of its functions first requires the definition of a set of functions to be considered uniquely religious. But the determination of such functions is characterized by substantial difficulties. A. W. Eister in discussing the problems of analyzing religious institutions in complex societies remarks:

> . . . there appear to be a number of difficulties that impede the effort to designate theoretically the functions that religion, or religious institutions, perform in complex societies such as our own. This paper holds that (1) specification of expected functions of religious institutions—either on purely logical grounds or on the basis of generalization from empirical evidence—is less precise and likely to be less readily accomplished than for almost any other major area of social organization (economic, political, family, communicational, institutions), and that (2) any attempt to apply most of the available functional theories of religion to complex societies rather than to primitive ones is more likely to lead to frustration than to fruitful understanding or insight.[45]

The various functions found by investigators are not uniformly present in all religions. As a world-wide social movement, Communism displays some qualities of religion, such as the endeavor to construct a new way of life and its reliance upon mis-

[45] A. W. Eister, "Religious Institutions in Complex Societies: Difficulties in the Theoretic Specification of Functions," *American Sociological Review,* August, 1957, pp. 387–388.

sionary endeavor, but it as strongly rejects the functions claimed by religious orthodoxy as it is criticized by other religious groups for being dysfunctional. In the cross fire of argumentation it is unlikely that particular functions or dysfunctions of either type of religion will be disclosed. Basis for defining just what religion is in terms of its functions is not easily apparent, and different groups are prone to call other groups irreligious.

The intensification of ethical values which is connected with religion is lacking in the religious life of some people. Nor does it seem satisfactory to broaden the intensification to include a larger range of human motives than ethical drives, since the intended influence may be entirely directed to supernatural beings. If the definition is recast in terms of attempted functions, the definition is no longer a functional one in the sense of results produced by activity, but is a definition in terms of activity short of functions achieved. In particular, a functional definition excludes human efforts to deal with supernatural beings except as these efforts have incidental results for the maintenance of human life in the verifiable world. It is possible to give a scientific definition in terms of functions which can be verified by science, but not in terms of supernatural results, such as placating angry gods, preparing the soul's way to heaven, or union with the dead.

Nor is there agreement as to what are the functions of religion in maintaining present human society. We have referred to an important one found in many religions, that of intensification of altruistic motivation. Other important ones are included in the definition by J. M. Yinger, a current social scientist whose contributions in the sociology of religion are well recognized.

> What, then, are the functions that distinguish religion as a human activity? To try to answer this question is essentially the task of this book; hence the highly condensed statement appropriate to a definition can only hint at problems that receive fuller treatment in later chapters. Paul Tillich has said that religion is that which concerns us ultimately. This can be a good starting point for a functional definition. While there are important disagreements concerning the "ultimate" problems for man, a great many would accept the following as among the fundamental concerns of human societies and individuals: How shall we respond to the fact of death? Does life have some central meaning despite the suffering, the succession of frustrations and tragedies? How can we deal with the forces that press in on us, endangering our livelihood, our health, the survival and smooth operation of the groups in which we live—forces that our empirical knowledge is inadequate to handle? How can we bring our capacity for

hostility and our egocentricity sufficiently under control that the groups within which we live, without which, indeed, life would be impossible, can be kept together?

Put in this way, these questions appear to be self-conscious and rational. They are more appropriately seen as deep-seated emotional needs, springing from the very nature of man as an individual and as a member of society. The questions appear first of all because they are felt—the death of a loved one wrenches our emotions, the failure to achieve that for which we yearn saddens and bewilders us; the hostility between ourselves and those around us infuses our social contacts with tension and prevents the achievement of mutual values. Religion may develop an intellectual system to interpret and deal with these questions, but they express first of all an underlying emotional need, not a group of rationally conceived problems.

Religion, then, can be defined as a system of beliefs and practices by means of which a group of people struggles with these ultimate problems of human life. It is the refusal to capitulate to death, to give up in the face of frustration, to allow hostility to tear apart one's human associations.[46]

Perhaps the type of element one would like to see stressed more strongly in a functional description of religion is its capacity for going beyond the negative control of hostile impulses to the creative enrichment of human life through a spiritually exhilarating existence. This is an experience highly esteemed by the religiously devout, but cannot be regarded as universally sought or attained in religion.

A further question which is recognized by Yinger is that of how religious activities shall be distinguished from nonreligious activities serving the same functions.

Religion, of course, is not alone in attempting to deal with the ultimate problems of human life. Rational efforts are important in all societies. Moreover, there are many individual emotional responses to insecurity and the problem of evil in addition to religion. Even in the healthiest and wealthiest and most rational of societies, however, secular responses cannot eliminate the problems of suffering, evil, and hostility. Realizing the gap between their hopes and the realities of their existence, men everywhere seek *closure* by a leap of faith that says: this need not, this will not, be true. Some time, some place, some how, suffering and evil will be defeated. (The enormous variation in conceptions of time, place, and method measures the range of religious expressions.)

The Persistent Functions of Religion. In this sense, religion can be thought of as a kind of residual means of response and adjustment. It

[46] J. M. Yinger, *Religion, Society and the Individual,* Macmillan, 1957, p. 9.

is an attempt to explain what cannot otherwise be explained; to achieve power, all other powers having failed us; to establish poise and serenity in the face of evil and suffering that other efforts have failed to eliminate. "When other helpers fail, when comforts flee," man can give himself over to despair, or he can seek relief by the leap of faith. Most people have chosen the latter, and have preferred, in Reinhold Niebuhr's words, "a citadel of hope built on the edge of despair," to acceptance of ultimate defeat.[47]

In this definition, Yinger follows Knight Dunlap, a psychologist who has extensively analyzed some of the functions of religion. "Religion is the institution, or feature of culture, which undertakes, in the service of mankind, those functions for which there is no other institution or for the undertaking of which no other institution is as yet adequately prepared."[48] An apparent difficulty is that for some the ultimate resort in the face of death or frustration is psychotherapy, for others the study of philosophy apart from religious practice, for others an absorbing hobby, and for still others alcohol as a solvent of problems. While the functional description given of religion is certainly illuminating concerning characteristics which religion often possesses, the problem of differentiating religious from nonreligious activity remains, as far as conceptual definition is concerned.

Unquestionably there are unique functions which religion can perform or at least which it can perform in a manner superior to other modes of human adjustment, for otherwise religion would not possess such deep and perpetual roots in human nature. A basic task of the scientist is to search for and describe the functions of religion. As an initial step, it is helpful to know the particular kind of activity whose functions are to be investigated. The achievement or nonachievement of functions of such activity provides hypotheses for research. The sequence followed in the present text is first to define religion, and then to seek to determine the nature and extent of functions which religion brings about.

A Definition of Religion

The foregoing considerations lead us to the following definition: Religion is a system of (1) beliefs in an unseen order of higher power, (2) activities to influence this higher power psychologically to meet human needs, and (3) experiences accom-

[47] *Ibid.*, p. 10.

[48] K. Dunlap, *Religion: Its Functions in Human Life,* McGraw-Hill, 1946, p. 321.

panying these things. The higher power is either a psychological component within personality or else a supernatural being to whom psychological traits are imputed. Since beliefs, aims, activities, needs, and experiences are simultaneously involved in whatever occupies human beings, they are included in the definition. The key elements in the definition are the unseen order, the higher power, and the psychological influence attempted or achieved. This definition does not imply that numerous other practices of a magical or secular nature may not be mixed with religion, nor that a variety of functions, manifest and latent, may not result. Unless exceptions are found which necessitate abandonment or amendment of the definition, it can be accepted as usable, and it is the definition employed in the present text.

chapter 6 Religion in America

The formulation of a definition of religion has delineated several aspects of religion: beliefs, activities, and experiences. In the case of most religious groups in America, these three are expressed in a larger system of secular activities, aims, and beliefs, such as what people think or do about social questions or everyday affairs as a result of their religion. From this broader perspective we ask in this chapter: What are the principal beliefs, aims, practices, and experiences of religious denominations? The separation of the four categories is not easy, since aims involve beliefs, practices stem from beliefs and aims, beliefs may be rationalizations for practices, and all provide experiences. At this point, we merely seek an overview, various details being taken up in succeeding chapters. Some of these data provide the basis for scientific analyses made, and some of the data are left for analyses by the student.

A statistical indication of the relative prevalence of various religious systems is relevant to a description of these systems. Church membership has increased absolutely and proportionately to a point not previously reached in American history. In 1958, 110 million members were reported by churches to the *Yearbook of American Churches*. These include 61.5 million Protestant, 39.5 million Roman Catholic, 5.5 million Jewish, and 2.5 million Eastern Orthodox.[1] It should be recognized that Protestant churches generally enumerate only those 13 years and older, while Roman Catholics count all baptized persons, however young.

[1] *Yearbook of American Churches,* National Council of the Churches of Christ in the U.S.A., 1960, p. 273.

The Problem of Generalization

The task of generalizing is difficult. Frequently the differences within groups are larger than those between them. One of the three main cultural streams, the religion of Jews, is divided into three tributaries: Orthodox, Conservative, and Reform Judaism, the latter making a break with the past comparable with that of liberalism in Christianity. The second stream, Roman Catholicism, reveals some cleavage between official church doctrines and beliefs and practices of communicants. The third stream, made up of the Protestant churches, branches into six large groups, to which four-fifths of the Protestants belong, and nearly three hundred tiny rivulets. Cutting across the denominational lines of Protestantism are several major currents of belief and practice, ranging from Fundamentalism to Liberalism and back to Neo-orthodoxy, of greater significance than individual church names. Of further importance are still other streams, such as those of the Eastern Orthodox Churches, the Mormons, the Christian Scientists, and the Buddhists and Mohammedans in America. Of very substantial importance are the views and behaviors of the two-fifths of the population affiliated with no church, but who possess various degrees and kinds of religious or philosophical ideas.

In an overview, it seems desirable to present the more traditional points of view, since these are more stable, while the recent currents are vacillating and subject to change. In 1941 a pocket volume, *The Religions of Democracy,* containing three essays by recognized scholars speaking for Jews, Catholics, and Protestants, was published under the sponsorship of the National Conference of Christians and Jews as an aid to intercultural understanding in America. The preface states: "Without debate or argument and with the single purpose of making clear the faith by which men live and the kind of conduct that such faith requires, its authors offer their contributions to the cause of concord and understanding." To employ the statements of such men or records in sacred scripture as factual basis for the study of beliefs and practices is not only the fairest representation of religious views in a controversial field, but this procedure is sound anthropology or sociology. One turns for authoritative statements about the religion of the tribe to the shaman or priest and his sacred books, if he has these. We begin by reviewing the religions of Jews, Catholics, and Protestants, with excerpts from the reports by L. Finkelstein, J. E. Ross, and W. A. Brown in

The Religions of Democracy. These reports are more indicative of aims and beliefs which issue from scripture or religious teaching than they are of practices actually observed. In contemporary culture, disregard of religious teachings is more common than faithful observance. Yet examination of these traditions provides a useful corner from which to look out upon the religious scene generally.

RELIGION OF JEWS

The first selection describes traditional aspects of Judaism.

Judaism is a way of life which endeavors to transform virtually every human action into a means of communion with God. Through this communion with God, the Jew is enabled to make his contribution to the establishment of the Kingdom of God and the brotherhood of men on earth. So far as its adherents are concerned, Judaism seeks to extend the concept of right and wrong to every aspect of their behavior. Jewish rules of conduct apply not merely to worship, ceremonial, and justice between man and man, but also to such matters as philanthropy, personal friendships and kindnesses, intellectual pursuits, artistic creation, courtesy, the preservation of health, and the care of diet.

The decisions regarding right and wrong under given conditions are not left for the moment, but are formulated with great care in the vast literature created by the Jewish religious teachers. At the heart of this literature are the Hebrew Scriptures, usually described as the Old Testament, consisting of the Five Books of Moses (usually called the *Torah*), the Prophets, and the Hagiographa. These works, particularly the Five Books of Moses, contain the prescriptions for human conduct composed under Divine inspiration. The ultimate purpose of Jewish religious study is the application of the principles enunciated in the Scriptures, to cases and circumstances which the principles do not explicitly cover.

Because the preservation of the Divine will regarding human conduct is basic to all civilization, none of the commandments is more important than that of studying and teaching the Law. The most sacred object in Judaism is the scroll containing the Five Books of Moses. Every synagogue must contain at least one copy of it. The scroll must be placed in a separate Ark, before which burns the eternal light. The position of this Ark in the synagogue is in the direction of Jerusalem; everyone turns toward the Ark in prayer. When the scroll is taken from the Ark for the purpose of reading, all those present must rise. No irreverent or profane action may be performed in a room which contains a scroll, nor may a scroll be moved from place to place except for the performance of religious rites.

At the present time, the Jewish people have no living central authority comparable in status to the ancient Sanhedrin or the later academies. Therefore any decision regarding Jewish religion must be based on the Talmud, as the final résumé of the teachings of those authorities when they existed. The right of an individual to decide questions of religious Law depends entirely on his knowledge of the Bible, the Talmud, and the later manuals based on them, and upon his fidelity to their teachings. Those who have acquired this knowledge are called rabbis. There is no sharp distinction in religious status between the rabbi and the layman in Judaism. The rabbi is simply a layman especially learned in Scripture and Talmud. Nor is there any hierarchical organization or government among the rabbis of the world. Yet some rabbis, by virtue of their especial distinction in learning, by common consent come to be regarded as superior authorities on questions of Jewish Law. Difficult and complicated issues are referred to them for clarification.

The central doctrine of Judaism is the belief in the One God, the Father of all mankind. The first Hebrew words which a Jewish child learns are the confession of faith contained in the verse, "Hear, O Israel, the Lord is our God, the Lord is One," and every believing Jew hopes that as he approaches his end in the fulness of time, he will be sufficiently conscious to repeat this same confession. This monotheistic belief is subject to no qualification or compromise.

Another doctrine, which has become universal in Judaism, is the belief in the incorporeality of God, i.e., the belief that God has no physical, visible form.

A third doctrine, equally important, is the timelessness and omnipresence of God. As one of the Talmudic sages states, "God is the place of the Universe; the Universe cannot be regarded as His place."

The essential element in the synagogue is, of course, not the building, but the community. Public worship may be conducted in a building, or out of doors. But it can be held only in the presence of a congregation, which theoretically consists of a minimum of ten heads of households. For the purpose of prayer, and because of the difficulty in finding ten heads of households in very small communities, ten males (over thirteen years of age) are considered heads of households. The assembly of ten such people is called a *minyan* (quorum) sufficient for public service.

Any adult male Jew may lead the congregation in public prayers. The rabbi participates simply as a member of the congregation.

While according to the Jewish faith God's presence can be felt at any time and place, there are times, just as there are places, which through their associations have become especially propitious for communion with God. Of these the most important are the holy days and the fast days. The holy days, according to the Jewish ritual, are the *Shabbat* or Sabbath, celebrated on the seventh day of each week, *Pesach* (Passover), *Shabuot* (Pentecost), *Rosh Ha-Shanah* (the Jewish religious New Year's Day, *Yom Kippur* (Day of Atonement), and *Sukkot* (Tabernacles).

In order that these days may be devoted as completely as possible to the spiritual life, work is forbidden on them. This prohibition includes not only all gainful occupation, but also household tasks.

As a result of these various prohibitions, the Sabbath and festivals become virtually periods of cessation of all labor on the part of observant Jews. Because of the difficulties involved in maintaining this rigid discipline in an industrial society like our own, many Jews otherwise very observant, do not refrain from all labor on the Sabbath. Nevertheless, even among these a large number set aside the free hours of the day for spiritual contemplation and prayer, and mark the Sabbath with the ceremonials devoted to it.

The significance of each festival is enhanced through the natural and historical interpretations associated with it. All of them are intended to increase man's faith in God by reference to His revelation in the natural order, and also in the succession of human events. Their symbols are particularly significant in an industrial and commercial civilization, where man tends to be separated from nature; and their reflection of the Divine purpose in history gives one strength in times of international crisis, and fills one with humility in moments of peace and prosperity. The purpose of the festivals may thus be said to place human life in both its cosmic and historical perspectives. They enable Man to see himself both as part of Nature and as distinguished through the providence of God.

Like every other authentic experience, training, or ambition, piety cannot stop short of the home. If religion were to be merely ecclesiastical, it would soon cease to be that, too. The psalmist who was told "Let us go up to the house of the Lord," rejoiced because in his own house the reality of God was never forgotten. Throughout Jewish history indeed the attempt to reproduce in the home the order and mood of the place of worship has never been relaxed.

In a sense, every detail of home life is an expression of the pattern of sanctity. Jewish homes, for example, are generally expected to contain the basic religious texts like the Bible, usually accompanied at least with the commentary of Rashi, the Talmud, perhaps an abbreviated code (the short Shulhan Aruk), some of the magnificent moralistic works, and of course the Prayer Book—which is actually one of the most extraordinary anthologies of Jewish classical literature.

Similarly, the various family festival celebrations with their rituals constitute activities which bring the divine message very close to the Jew. It is an insensitive Jewish child indeed who forgets the beauty of the Seder at Passover, or the kindling of the lights during Hanukkah, or the sight of his mother kindling the Sabbath lamps at dusk. These and like activities collaborate to make holiness a familiar emphasis and delight.

Part of the daily pattern of sanctity is formed by the so called dietary laws. As is well known, Jewish law prohibits the eating of certain foods. These prohibitions are enumerated essentially in Leviticus, chapter 11, and again in Deuteronomy, chapter 14. No vegetable growths are prohibited; but of animal life the Law permits fish which have scales and fins, certain types of fowl, and only those quadrupeds which chew their cud and have cloven hoofs.

Virtually every prophet in Scripture has predicted that in the fulness of time, man will gain a more complete understanding of God, and will inaugurate a reign of justice and peace on earth. According to the interpretation of this prophecy in the Talmud and later writers, this age of universal peace will be established by a great, but humble teacher of the lineage of David: the Messiah. Reform and many conservative Jews, on the other hand, expect that the Messianic age will come about through the gradual enlightenment of men, and through the work of many thinkers and teachers. All agree that the age will be one of profound and universal faith in God, recognition of human brotherhood, and an unprecedented knowledge of the universe. There will be no discrimination between persons because of sex, origin, faith, occupation, nationality, or any other reason. The evils of human origin will have been overcome; those inherent in Nature will be mitigated through further knowledge and increased piety. In this world of brotherly love, there will be no room for pride in achievement, nor for memories of past bitterness and oppression.[2]

RELIGION OF CATHOLICS

We turn next to excerpts from an account by a Catholic.

The Roman Catholic Church, according to the definition of the Baltimore Catechism, "is the congregation of all those who profess the faith of Christ, partake of the same Sacraments, and are governed by their lawful pastors under one visible Head." Then it goes on to say that "the Pope, the Bishop of Rome, is the visible Head of the Church." And though as a general thing the conscience of the individual Catholic will tell him that the Pope is right, *if* an individual were convinced that he should not do what the Pope commands, theologians say that the individual would be bound to follow his conscience.

For one who has the use of reason the only way to attain salvation is by living up to one's conscience. And the Catholic position is that anyone believing in God and supernatural sanctions who lives up to his conscience will be saved; whereas anyone who without repentance dies after having seriously transgressed his conscience will be lost.

Although the human mind by the light of reason can arrive at certain religious truths, such as the existence of God, there are other religious truths which by itself it cannot reach. And for ease and certainty in knowing any religious truths the generality of mankind needs the

[2] Abridged from L. Finkelstein, J. E. Ross, and W. A. Brown, *The Religions of Democracy,* Devin-Adair, 1941, pp. 3–4, 10, 12–13, 20, 41, 42, 50, 56, 84–86, 89.

assistance of God's Revelation. In a strict sense, Revelation is a supernatural imparting by God of truths which man could not know simply by his unaided natural reason; in a broader sense Revelation is any truth made known supernaturally by God; in a still broader sense it is the making known of religious truth even by natural means—"the heavens show forth the glory of God." (Psalms XVIII.1) God's Revelation in the strict sense is contained principally in the canonical books of the Bible.

The average man, of course, is not capable of deciding between the claims of various books or portions of books to a place in the Bible. Catholics confronted by the massive fact of the Church and believing that the Church was established by Christ with authority to teach, accept from the Church a decision as to what writings are inspired and therefore part of the Bible. After long years of controversy in regard to particular books, the Council of Trent finally decided the canon of the Old and of the New Testaments for Catholics, and put both sections of the Bible on the same basis. Both are equally the Word of God. And as the Word of God they contain no error.

By saying that the Bible is inspired, Catholics mean that God moved the will and enlightened the intellect of the various writers in such a way that He can be truly called the Author of what they wrote; that they wrote what He intended should be written for the instruction of His Church, and wrote only what God wanted them to write.

Tradition, in its technical sense, is also part of Revelation. Before the first book of the New Testament was written naturally there was no New Testament. But there was a teaching of the Apostles, and Catholics believe that this apostolic teaching was Revelation.

This teaching of the Apostles which is not a part of the Scriptures is "Tradition," and it forms a source of Catholic belief. As far as what is officially binding upon the faith of all Catholics, Revelation was closed with the death of the last Apostle. Of course God can and possibly does make revelations to individuals now living. However, the Pope or the Church cannot make such private revelations part of the *De Fide* Catholic Creed.

But though the deposit of faith was closed with the death of the last Apostle, our understanding of Revelation may grow. This accounts for the definition of additional dogmas, such as that of the Immaculate Conception of the Mother of Christ or of the infallibility of the Pope, as late as the nineteenth century. Catholics do not believe that the ordinary individual Catholic is gifted by God with infallibility in interpreting the Scriptures. But they do believe that God has given infallibility to one individual, the Pope, in his official capacity as Head of the Church. When ordinary means of scholarship fail, he will decide between two or more interpretations.

The God of Catholicism is a personal God possessing intelligence and free will, and it is because we have intelligence and free will that we are said to be made in His likeness. Unlike us, however, God is a pure spirit possessing no body, and so is not subject to the limitations of matter.

God is infinite, possessing all perfections in an infinite degree. He is everywhere whole and entire; He is all good, and infinitely benevolent. God has always existed in one eternal now. For Him there is neither past nor future but only present— "I am who am."

Both the Trinity and the Incarnation are mysteries of faith—that is, no human mind can fully understand them. Just how there can be Three Divine Persons and only one God cannot be completely explained. All that can be done is to make a little clearer, perhaps, what we actually believe. We are, of course, staunch monotheists. We believe that there is only one God, and that only He is to receive divine worship; but we also believe that there are Three Persons in this one God, the Father, the Son, and the Holy Ghost, each co-equal with the other two.

Each human being is said to be born with original sin, not in the sense that he commits this sin in the same way that he commits other sins during his life, but in the sense that he does not have the supernatural gifts which he would have had if Adam had been faithful to God.

But the Second Person of the Trinity became man not only to die in atonement for human sins, but also to furnish us an example of perfect living and to give us additional Revelation of God. During His public ministry He chose certain Apostles who were to continue teaching His Revelation to all nations and to administer the Sacraments, which He had established. They and the disciples who accepted the new Revelation formed a true society, with head and members. One of them, Peter, had a primacy of governing and of deciding the correct interpretation of God's Revelation, as, for instance, in accepting gentiles into the society.

Though they are not all specifically mentioned in the Apostles' Creed, there is a supernatural help, a Sacrament, for each of the great experiences of life—seven in all. For birth there is Baptism; on attaining the use of reason, Confirmation—each to be received but once. Corresponding to the food for the body is the Eucharist, while the medicine for the soul curing the sickness of sin is the Sacrament of Penance. Under ordinary circumstance the Eucharist may be received as often as once a day; Penance may be received as often as desired. Marriage was raised by Christ to the dignity of a Sacrament and made indissoluble except by the death of one of the spouses. Those who devote themselves to the priesthood receive Holy Orders. Finally, for the last great adventure, the passing into eternity through death, there is for those who have obtained the use of reason and so can have sinned, the Last Anointing, or Extreme Unction.

Only absolutely pure souls can enter Heaven, and only those dying with unforgiven mortal sin go to Hell. Those who die with the stain of venial sin, or the remains of forgiven mortal sin, for a time endure a state, Purgatory, which is neither Heaven nor Hell, until they have been purged or purified for entrance into Heaven.

In general, a Sacrament is an outward sign of invisible grace established by Christ. All grace is a supernatural help given by God. But the reception of the sacramental grace depends upon the recipient's dispositions.

The Mass is not only a re-enactment of the institution of the Eucharist at the Last Supper, it is also a re-presentation of the sacrifice of Christ on the cross to His heavenly Father. Hence the Mass has great values of satisfaction, worship, and petition.

The Mass is a public act of worship which the faithful who have attained the use of reason are bound to attend on Sundays and holy days of obligation. But, as has been said, no ecclesiastical law binds under a proportionately serious inconvenience, and there are many circumstances which excuse the individual from attendance at Mass.

The Body and Blood of Christ, since it is a living Christ, are present whole and entire under the appearances of bread and the appearances of wine. Those who receive these appearances (whether of bread only, or of bread and wine) receive the whole Body of Christ.

In the Solemn Mass with its various incensings, an appeal to every sense has been used to achieve the one result of drawing the worshipper closer to God. For those with even a modicum of sympathy and understanding for the sublime subject matter of the Mass it is the most marvelous drama, not excepting the classic Greek, which human genius has ever united the arts to expound.

In fact, in spite of the seeming complexity of the Catholic religion and its frank use of externals, the essence of Catholicism can be summed up in that one phrase, "Thy will be done!" Everything in the Catholic Church, though to an outsider it may seem distracting and irrelevant, is directed to the purpose of bringing the human will into conformity with the divine will. The essence of sin consists in the individual setting his will against God's will; and, contrariwise, the essence of virtue consists in the individual making God's will his own.

The externalism of the Catholic Church is evident to every observer. A Catholic is bound to attend the liturgical public worship of Mass every Sunday, he is encouraged to say vocal prayers every day, he receives certain outward signs in the Sacraments, he venerates the relics of the Saints, he uses the sign of the cross, holy water, and other sacramentals. But the spiritual benefit for him of any of these things depends upon his own inner disposition.

And a balance is kept between the external and the inner spirit. For the Catholic is also encouraged in a direct cultivation of the interior life through mental prayer as contrasted with vocal prayer. Members of religious communities have by their rule a certain time set aside each day for meditation on the truths of religion, the incidents of Christ's life, the application of Christ's example to themselves. Lay Catholics are also encouraged to practice such meditation and to make a retreat of several days when they separate themselves as far as possible from all worldly distractions.

Catholicism should affect every phase of life. Fortunately the American separation of Church and State does not mean the subjection of the Church, or religion, by the State, its confinement to the sacristy, while political, economic, and social activities are freed from the teachings of religion on all these questions.

It is the American tradition that religion is more than attendance at church on Sunday, and that it has a perfect right to express itself on the morality of business and political acts. Catholicism has always accepted this American tradition. It is catholic (with a small "c") as embracing the whole of life in its scope.[3]

RELIGION OF PROTESTANTS

The concluding essay is by a Protestant.

With their Catholic fellow-Christians, Protestants recognize that God is Triune and confess Him in the words of the ancient Creed as "Father, Son and Holy Spirit." With them, they believe that God reveals Himself in nature, in history and in the soul of man; but above all, through His Son Jesus Christ, the second person of the Trinity who for us men and for our salvation became man, being conceived by the Holy Ghost, born of the Virgin Mary, was crucified under Pontius Pilate, rose again from the dead on the third day, manifested Himself to His disciples after His death as their living Lord and will come again with glory to vindicate His authority and establish His Kingdom.

Luther was a monk and, as he himself tells us, one who took the monastic discipline seriously. It was concern for his soul's salvation which had led him to abandon the world for the cloister and that concern made him meticulous in the fulfillment of all his appointed duties. "If ever a monk could have been saved by his monkery," he tells us, "that monk was I." But the penances he practised and the austerities he underwent brought him no peace. On the contrary they made him the more conscious of the imperfection within. Like St. Paul he found two men within him struggling for the mastery, and do what he would the baser had the upper hand.

Then it was that to Luther there came the conviction that he was on the wrong track. It was through a word of the Apostle Paul that the insight came: "The just shall live by faith." Luther perceived that all his striving availed him nothing. He was sure that there was another way, a simpler way: the way of trust which Paul's words pointed out to him; the way of which Jesus, as he understood Jesus, had spoken, the way of the child that does not earn or deserve, but simply receives and is thankful.

[3] Abridged from *ibid.*, pp. 97, 107–112, 114, 117, 119–121, 124, 135–138, 153–154, 156–157, 160.

With this conviction of Luther we reach that which is distinctive in Protestant piety, the experience of a relation to God which is antecedent to and independent of all merit, a relation which makes direct contact possible and so renders all churchly mediation superfluous.

This does not mean that the Christian is under no obligation to do good works, but only that his motive for doing them is altered. He does them not to gain advantage for himself, but to express gratitude to God who has called him to holiness, and desires for him that he should perfectly realize the life of love.

The way in which man lays hold of the salvation made possible through Jesus Christ is faith. This saving grace which lies at the very heart of the Protestant conception of religion is defined in the Westminster Confession of Faith as due to "the work of the Spirit of Christ in the hearts of the elect. It is ordinarily wrought by the ministry of the Word by which also and by the administration of the sacraments and prayer it is increased and strengthened."

The Protestant view of the nature of the Christian life culminates in the view of its goal. Protestants, Catholics and Jews agree that God has made man an immortal spirit and that the life begun here will continue after death.

The sharpest contrast meets us in the conception of the life after death. Catholics interpose between the final stage when there will be only Heaven and Hell an intermediate state called Purgatory, in which all those who have not died in mortal sin will have the opportunity to complete the period of disciplinary suffering which is their due. Protestants recognize only two states for the sinner after death: heaven and hell; although they, too, make place for an intermediate period in which those who have died await the full consummation of the last day. This intermediate period, however, involves no change in moral status. In Protestant teaching, the moral issues of life are finally determined at death.

By contrast, Protestant worship seems to the Catholic to be formal and bare. The pulpit takes the place of the altar. The minister is first of all preacher and only incidentally priest. And while the sacraments have their place they are celebrated seldom and without the elaborate pomp and ceremony with which the Catholic Church surrounds them.

This more formal character of Protestant worship is a natural result of its history as a reforming movement. From the first, Protestantism has appealed to the intelligence of its worshippers. The minister is not there to tell his congregation what they do not know; rather to remind them of those simple but essential truths which God has made known to his children through the Bible: truths equally accessible to each worshipper if he will study God's revelation for himself.

Protestants recognize two external means through which God's grace is mediated and two only: the Word and the sacraments. By the Word, is meant the contents of the Gospel as authoritatively set forth in the Bible and transmitted to succeeding generations by the preaching of the spoken Word. By a sacrament the Protestant understands "a holy sign or seal of the covenant of Christ immediately instituted by God to represent Christ and His benefits and to confirm our interest in Him as also to put a visible difference between those who belong to the Church and the rest of the world, and solemnly to engage them to the service of Christ according to His Word."

Only two such sacraments are regarded by Protestants as having scriptural authority: Baptism and the Lord's Supper. "Baptism is a Sacrament of the New Testament, ordained by Jesus Christ, not only for the solemn admission of the party baptised into the visible Church, but also to be unto him a sign and seal of the covenant of grace, of his ingrafting into Christ, of regeneration, of remission of sins, and of his giving up unto God, through Jesus Christ, to walk in newness of life." The Lord's Supper is the "Sacrament of Christ's body and blood, to be observed in His Church unto the end of the world, for the perpetual remembrance of the sacrifice of himself in his death, the sealing all benefits thereof unto true believers, their spiritual nourishment and growth in Him, their further engagement in, and to all duties which they owe unto Him; and to be a bond and pledge of their communion with Him and with each other as members of His mystical body." While it is not a repetition of the sacrifice of Christ, but only a commemoration of it, it is not a mere memory but a means through which "worthy receivers outwardly partaking of the visible elements in this Sacrament, do then also inwardly by faith, really and indeed, yet not carnally and corporally, but spiritually, receive and feed upon Christ crucified, and all benefits of his death: the body and blood of Christ being then not corporally or carnally in, with, or under the bread and wine; yet as really, but spiritually, present to the faith of believers in that ordinance, as the elements themselves are to their outward senses."

Protestants give first place to the devotional reading of the Bible as the most effective means of cultivating a life of prayer. In public worship Protestants put the sermon in the central place. This is not because they wish to magnify the preacher but because the sermon is the most effective way to bring to the attention of the worshipper the central teaching of the Bible and to draw its consequences for the personal Christian life.

Like Catholic piety, Protestant piety should begin in the home. It finds its characteristic expression in family worship. At no point has Protestantism departed more widely from its original ideal than in the widespread neglect of family prayers. This neglect is all the more serious because Protestants have not ordinarily at their disposal those visible reminders of the claims of their religion which play so large a role in Catholic piety—the Crucifix, the Rosary, pictures and statues of the Saints and of the Virgin, and the like.

In the normal Protestant home, religious training begins early. The child is taught to read the Bible and it may be to learn parts of it by heart. As soon as he is old enough he is taken to Sunday School where he receives systematic instruction in the principles of his religion.

Later he accompanies his parents to Church and when he reaches years of discretion becomes a member of a Communicant's Class and after having been examined by bishop, minister or session as the case may be, is admitted to the Communion.

A further mark of the difference between Catholic and Protestant piety is the absence from the latter of the devotion paid to the Virgin and the Saints.

This is due in part to historical reasons. As the Protestant Reformers found no scriptural authority for the central place given to the Pope, so they found no such authority for the unique place given by Catholics to the Virgin Mary. While they reverenced her as the Mother of their Lord, they found no warrant in Scripture for belief in her sinlessness. More than this they saw in the doctrine of the Immaculate Conception, and in the title given to her in much Catholic literature, "Mother of God," a tendency to break down the line of demarcation which separates Jesus Christ as God Incarnate from all other creatures, a tendency against which they feared that the distinction made by Roman Catholic theologians between different kinds of worship did not provide a sufficient safeguard.

It is not an easy ideal to which Protestants feel that God has called them but one which demands every power of heart and mind and will. Detachment is required, an inner detachment which is all the more difficult because of the lack of outward helps such as are supplied by the rules of the Catholic religious orders, or even the general rules of the Catholic Church. Selfish desires must be mastered, legitimate instincts must be sacrificed, so that the soul may dedicate itself to its primary task. Protestants, like Catholics, attain this detachment by means of contemplation and prayer. In the solitude of his room at night, or in the stillness of the early morning, the man who must act comes into touch with ultimate reality, and waits for the insight which will guide him on his way. The true test of his piety is found in what happens when he rises from his knees and goes out to meet his fellow men.[4]

The foregoing description is primarily of Orthodox or Conservative Protestantism. To supplement this with a view of Liberal Protestantism found among different Protestant groups, we turn to the informative account given by J. P. Williams in his book about religious groups in America, *What Americans Believe and How They Worship,* from which the following material is excerpted.

Trying to describe Protestantism is like trying to describe the United States: one can say almost anything about it—and almost anything one says can be shown to be false in some particular. Protestants

[4] Abridged from *ibid.,* pp. 194–196, 198, 201–202, 204–206, 209–210, 212–213, 227–228, 230, 232.

range in belief all the way from the supernaturalism of the right-wing Lutherans to the agnosticism of the left-wing Unitarians. Protestants range in worship forms all the way from the complexity of the high-church Episcopalians to the simplicity of the silent-meeting Quakers. Protestants range in emotionalism all the way from the restraint of the Congregationalists to the exuberance of the Pentecostals.

Most present-day Protestants are not Biblical literalists. They believe that the Bible contains the divine word, that it is the revelation of God, that it should be studied by every Christian. But they do not look to the Bible for scientific truth, nor necessarily for historical accuracy.

Protestant Liberals more than other Christian groups stress the right of individuals to decide for themselves what is true in religion. The belief in freedom from theological domination by creeds, councils, bishops, pastors amounts to about the most basic religious conviction. Theological divergence among Liberals is, accordingly, great.

Liberals strive to be attuned to modern thought, which is dominated by science. Every contemporary religious thinker must deal with science in some way. A few reject it completely. Others, recognizing its threat to traditional supernaturalism, build compartments in their minds and refuse any commerce between their ideas of science and their religion. The Liberals, however, strive to make science their ally not their enemy; they take science into the very citadel of religion. Science is a new confederate in the battle for truth; thus Liberals hold that no vital religion can ignore scientific discoveries.

The majority of Liberals hold to the traditional Christian teaching that God is personal; that is, He is more like a person, than like a tree, or a machine, or electricity, or any other thing He might be likened to. Liberals react sharply against the crude anthropomorphism which pictures God with hands and feet and a long white beard; yet most of them do hold that His chief characteristic is mind. He is conscious both of Himself and of us, and cares for us.

A considerable proportion of the Liberals reject the Trinity and with it the deity of Jesus. On the other hand, a considerable number of Liberals consider belief in the Trinity to be essential. But they wish to define it in modern terms—perhaps in terms like the following: "It is entirely rational to believe in the First Person, the Creator, and in the Third Person, the Spirit of God in the world. Moreover, the basic affirmation of the Christian religion is that God is like Jesus, not that Jesus is like God."

Liberals have many different beliefs about prayer. The practice of praying for help of a physical nature has, for the most part, been given up by them. Liberals hold that God would not answer, say, prayers for good weather or for the alteration of the course of physical disease. However, most Liberals believe that prayer for help of a spiritual sort is rational. Thus prayers for wisdom or for patience to endure difficulty are thought to be rational. Liberals stress the value of prayers of "communion." In such prayers, the worshiper seeks to conform himself to God's Will, not to bend God to the worshiper's will. It is the worshiper who must change.

Some of the Protestant Liberals do not believe in immortality; according to them life after death is something about which man can have no knowledge. A few Liberals would contend that the belief is unimportant; "One world at a time," they say. But most Liberals hold that faith in a future life is both important and rational. They think it is important in order that men may have an adequate perspective from which to make moral judgments. They think it is rational because a God who conserves the matter and energy of the universe so carefully that none is destroyed, would not destroy the human mind which is a much higher manifestation of creative power than either matter or energy. Liberals have given up belief in hell and in the Devil; but most of them believe in heaven. However, they profess no knowledge of what heaven is like.

Out of Liberalism sprang what is called the Social Gospel, the belief that religion must deal more effectively with social injustice. Many Christians believe that the function of the Church is to develop Christian convictions in the hearts of individual men who in turn will put these convictions into operation in politics and business. Followers of the Social Gospel contradict this point of view; they declare that society as well as individuals must be saved; that a healthy individual cannot develop in a poisoned environment. Consequently, many of the Liberals are much exercised over the problems of war, poverty, and racial discrimination.

Optimistic Liberalism dominated the theological field until the bitter realities of living in a world smashed by war demanded a change. Theologians began to be "realists." They lost faith in the capacities of man to work out his own salvation; they declared man to be naturally evil; they attacked the scientific method as a means of dealing with the basic religious problems; they even lost faith in the power of reason to guide man to supreme values. European theology turned definitely toward the dogmas of traditional supernaturalism.

Neo-orthodoxy attacks Liberalism's faith in reason. Reason is a human instrument. It can no more settle the problems of basic *religious* faith than could the mind of a chimpanzee settle the problems of physics. Reliance on reason is but another instance of man's arrogance.[5]

It is much easier to characterize the religious beliefs of churchgoers who profess adherence to a set of doctrines than it is to find out what people think about religion who do not go to any church at all. Jerome Nathanson, a leader in the Society for Ethi-

[5] Abridged from J. P. Williams, *What Americans Believe and How They Worship,* Harper, 1952, pp. 88, 96, 103–104, 106–110, 112.

cal Culture reports observations concerning the approximately two-fifths of the population in the United States who are not church members.

> Why are so many Americans members of no church? Has religion failed them?
>
> There is no simple answer. Many of those who do not belong to any church have taken the hard rather than the easy road, for they have withstood great pressure in order to stay out of groups it is so easy to join, and for which high approval from neighbors and community is given. . . .
>
> We must realize that the overwhelming majority of our 64,000,000 are not *anti*-religious. To be sure, some of them profess atheism openly —but they are a very small fraction of the total. And some are agnostics—those who say they simply do not *know* whether there is or is not a God, or a heaven and hell, or a life hereafter. They hold that to go to church without real conviction and unquestioning faith is hypocritical, a profanation of the religious idea. . . .
>
> Do the 64,000,000 Americans who refuse to "believe" in this way have anything in common—except the fact that they do not go to church? Yes. They share an important attitude—the idea that it is possible to be "religious," moral, decent, without joining a group and worshiping *en masse*. They believe the individual can get as close to the idea of God as any cleric or institution can bring him. They hold the high faith that men are responsible for what they do with their lives, how they think and live. They do not feel the need for "official" forgiveness or rituals or catechisms to make them men of virtue. They try to lead a life which is honorable, productive, satisfying, right, good—for *them*. (It may or may not be right or good for someone else.) A good life, to their minds, does not depend upon church attendance. They believe, as did some of the greatest men the human race has produced, that personal morality is not dependent on organized religion.[6]

Needless to say, short summaries cannot do justice to the richness of detail in the religions of contemporary American life. The separation of religious phenomena into categories of belief, aim, practice and experience is an analytical one, these components being fused in concrete religious experience. The student will find it a useful exercise to go through the preceding accounts and to list particular beliefs, aims, practices and experiences which he finds. Some of these details are dealt with at greater length in further chapters of this text. Additional descriptions

[6] Jerome Nathanson, "What Do They Believe?" in Leo Rosten (ed.), *A Guide to the Religions of America,* Simon and Schuster, 1955, pp. 166–170.

of Judaism, Catholicism and Protestantism are given on pages 12–14, 206–208, and 592–597.

Beyond the summary descriptions given by way of introduction, more detailed analysis will be made of denominational characteristics in succeeding chapters. It is desirable at the outset to describe more fully an important aspect by means of which Judaism, Catholicism and Protestantism in their various branches are to be compared. This aspect consists of beliefs which adherents have about the sources of their religious knowledge, a topic which receives treatment in the next section.

BELIEFS ABOUT SOURCES OF RELIGIOUS KNOWLEDGE

By knowledge is meant ideas which are accurate representations of reality, usually recorded in written literature or possessed by individuals regarded as authoritative in matters of knowledge. Less narrowly defined, knowledge refers to ideas commonly believed to be true representations of reality, and it is in this sense that we consider what various groups believe to be the sources of their religious knowledge.

In tracing the sources which religious adherents give for their knowledge, it is illuminating to keep in mind that all knowledge is either derived from experience or thinking of people, or comes through communication with those who have knowledge. From this standpoint a useful distinction is made between knowledge which religious experience teaches, and knowledge obtained by communicating with others. The sources of religious knowledge fan out in many roots when one considers the numerous individuals, past and present, from whose experiences and communications knowledge may be drawn.

Religious groups do not agree as to the relative weight to be assigned the various roots of knowledge. Some insist that their sacred scripture is a complete and accurate repository of their religious knowledge, others vest ultimate authority in their living religious leaders, and still others assign primacy to religious experience which the individual possesses as the genuine source of religious knowledge, at least for him. Some believe their sacred scripture to have been communicated literally by God in a supernatural revelation, and others conceive its factual basis to be religious experience of a kind capable of being verified by human beings in any generation.

Communication with a spiritual being is a special category requiring more detailed consideration as a source of religious knowledge. This category is exemplified by mystical experiences, hearing of voices, visions, dreams, or meditations in which ideas are revealed verbally or pictorially or as insights to the religious seeker. To him these ideas seem to come as an authoritative communication from outside himself. He may believe them to be supernaturally revealed to himself or a privileged few alone, or he may consider them to be given to all properly disposed persons and susceptible to general verification.

Whatever supernatural interpretation is attached to such communication from a spiritual being, from a scientific standpoint the communication consists of ideas appearing in the recipient's mind. The ideas are believed by the psychologist to appear for entirely natural causes operating in the recipient, being derived from his previous experiences through abstraction, inference, or imagination. From a scientific standpoint the communication can only be analyzed as a kind of experience. It is understandable that the religious mystic who does not comprehend the laws governing the generation of ideas might believe that the sudden rush of insights above the threshold of consciousness is a direct communication from outside himself.

The validity of beliefs derived from such an experience is partly a psychological question and partly a philosophical one. The question is a psychological one with regard to whether the ideas alleged to be knowledge are securely grounded in verifiable experience. The question is a philosophical one if it is asked whether these ideas spring ultimately from a cosmic mind outside of experience which chooses the medium of psychological processes and laws for the revelation of religious ideas, or if the vision is assumed to be not duplicable and beyond science, whether the spiritual communication is credible from the standpoint of philosophical criteria. From a scientific standpoint, any experiential phenomenon is regarded as duplicable, given conditions which are controllable, and the allegation that it is supernatural is subject to scientific scrutiny. However, we are here concerned only with what is believed to be the source of religious knowledge.

In tracing religious beliefs to their supposed source, we are not at the moment concerned with the program of religious education or indoctrination or social control whereby beliefs are transmitted to each generation by the preceding one. Nor are we concerned with actual factors which produce beliefs. We are interested rather in the source or origin to which each religious group attributes its beliefs, whether supernatural revelation or common experience, whether received by individuals in the past or in the present, whether recorded in sacred literature or communicated by contemporary leaders or found by the religious seeker within his own life experience.

With these conceptual distinctions about sources of religious knowledge before us, we may classify examples of religion described in the summaries according to what are believed to be the sources of their knowledge.

Judaism

First among the written sources of religious knowledge to which Jews may turn is their Holy Scripture (referred to by Christians as the Old Testament). Central in scripture is the Torah, or Five Books of Moses. (In a general sense Torah also means teaching or law as the will of God.) Next is the Talmud, which is a record of teachings and traditions stemming from scripture. Containing a further codification of Jewish law, together with information and folklore on a large variety of topics, the Talmud is a vast collection of material covering Jewish life and development up to the sixth century of the Christian era. In addition to the Bible and the Talmud are comprehensive commentaries prepared by Jewish scholars down to the present time.

These authoritative sources are not always in agreement, and different strands of Judaism are interwoven in history. In the Middle Ages two influential spokesmen for these were Maimonides, who, emphasizing an intellectual approach, wrote out a statement of articles of faith, and Crescas, who said that religion flowed from the heart, seeking a recovery of the intuitive emotional religion of the ancient prophets. Thus intellectualism and mysticism as sources of knowledge prevail side by side in Judaism as in other religions.

In studying religious literature, the individual is aided by the rabbi of his congregation, who is a learned teacher without priestly functions. Extensive graduate training is required of rabbis before ordination. Depending upon the rabbinical school attended, rabbis vary in their teaching and interpretation of Judaism. In Orthodox congregations, to a large extent in Conservative ones, and less so in those of Reform Judaism, rabbis are accepted as authoritative sources of religious knowledge, and they in turn depend for their knowledge upon religious literature. The trend in recent years is one of declining influence of rabbis among their congregations.

As followers of doctrines written and taught, Jews are expected to find verification in their own experience of the living spiritual realities portrayed. It is through study, reflection, and experience that they are expected to make religious doctrines their own. The extent to which this is done varies from person to person and place to place, as is the case in most religions. Most Jews believe that the ongoing testimony of contemporary life corroborates, at least to some degree, their historically derived beliefs.

Many Jews believe further that ongoing experience is a source of further religious knowledge. They regard historical experience as a progressive revelation of God's will continuing at the present time. Based upon fresh experience in the modern era, new movements have arisen within Judaism. One of these, Reform Judaism, arising in Germany and the United States in the nineteenth century, departs furthest from the traditional authority of Hebrew scriptures, making far-reaching accommodations to the social setting in which Jews find themselves, yet seeking to retain essential religious and ethical concepts of Judaism. "To stress the common bond with their countrymen, the vernacular was substituted for Hebrew as the chief language of prayer and the study of Hebrew was either eliminated or subordinated to a minor place in the religious curriculum. Whatever savored of social segregation or emphasized ritual distinctiveness, such as the dietary laws and numerous other observances, was opposed on doctrinal grounds and by the denial of supernatural authority to ceremonial law in the Bible and later sacred literature."[7] As a countermovement, Conservative Judaism retains many but not all of the traditions of Orthodox Judaism and has less literal emphasis upon scripture than Orthodox Judaism.

Hebrew is not only retained as the language of prayer, but is also highly valued as a national bond of union, as a vehicle in which the Jewish soul is revealed historically, and as an instrument for preserving the living Hebraic consciousness. Conservative Judaism does not seem committed to a literal interpretation of the Sinaitic revelation, but it does acknowledge the authority of the Bible and the Talmud and deals reverentially with the customs and ceremonies that developed during the later centuries. The Torah is revered as a program of living as well as an idealized concept of divine wisdom. Particular stress is laid on home ceremonies, the observance of the dietary

[7] A. A. Neuman, "Judaism," in E. J. Jurji (ed.), *The Great Religions of the Modern World,* Princeton University Press, 1947, p. 279.

laws, the Sabbath, and the holy days according to the traditional laws and customs.[8]

In Orthodox Judaism is found the greatest reliance upon the authority of the Bible and the Talmud as sources of knowledge and belief, these being regarded as revealed by God and literally true, especially the Torah. "The chief theological distinction of Orthodox Judaism is its adherence to the principle of literal revelation and its denial of the principle of historic evolution as applied to the theory and practice of religion."[9]

These different movements evidence the degree of variation which is possible within Judaism upon a basis of considerable harmony and mutual acceptance. Individual members of congregations are not excluded if they hold beliefs which disagree with those of the majority. "Wide as are some of their differences in belief and practice they are not separatist sects but differing members of one religion. They are united not only by kinship and history and the bonds of a common destiny but also by a deep and abiding faith in religious principles which they hold to be immortal and which they cherish for the happiness of humanity."[10]

In history, experience of the Jews has been the source of Hebrew literature. Further excerpts from A. A. Neuman's essay explain its role.

> This people, one of the smallest and oldest historic nations—now scattered over the globe—out of the depth of its own experience, attained to a lofty and unique vision of God, man, and the universe, and translated that vision into a program of living. That vision and that way of life constitute the philosophy and the precepts of Judaism. . . .
>
> Slowly and painfully over the course of many centuries it was beaten out of the historic experiences of the nation, illumined by the vision of its prophets and sages. The prophets of Israel, profound mystics, who envisaged God the Infinite, who perceived that His Spirit filled the universe, and who spoke in His Name with the warmth, intimacy, and conviction of personal revelation, were not detached individualists or universalists. They were essentially national heroes of the Jewish religious genius. The problems, sins, failures, and sorrows of their people were the starting-point of their spiritual brooding.
>
> The Jewish people did not learn to know God through either syllogism or dogma. They happened upon God. As a sensitive child who awakens to the mysteries and wonders of nature, so were the early spirits of Israel in their awareness of God. Their God-perception was

[8] *Ibid.*, p. 280.
[9] *Ibid.*, p. 281.
[10] *Ibid.*

the result of intuition rather than reason and it unfolded as a psychological process. . . .

To the ancient Hebrews, then, the knowledge of God was not a matter of transmitted knowledge to be classified or codified, but a growing awareness of His Being through growth and experience, a spiritual sensitivity which eluded definition. To know God in the Biblical sense did not mean intellectual perception or cognition, but a soul-stirring emotional reaction due to the impact of His Will on the human being.[11]

The issue of whether religious experience is "supernatural" has not penetrated Judaism to the degree that it has done so in Christianity. Religious experience is usually taken at its face validity without insisting that the question of whether it is natural or supernatural be settled. Jews have not set science and religion in opposition to the degree which many Christians have done. With a less evangelical concern and a wider tolerance of disagreement among followers, there has been more room for religion and science, and especially religion and psychology, to grow side by side. Less occasion has arisen in Judaism to buttress belief with supernatural sanction against the inroads of science. However, in Orthodox Judaism and to some extent in Conservative Judaism, supernatural revelation, as opposed to reproducible experience, is a source of essential religious ideas in the Torah.

Roman Catholicism

Referring to the summary from the essay by J. E. Ross, we note that Catholicism, like Judaism, is recorded in two principal sets of documents, Holy Scripture and writings which elaborate Holy Scripture. The first of these comprise the Old and New Testaments, and the second is incorporated in declarations made by religious councils and popes at various times in Catholic history. The development of doctrine proceeds within the framework of principles believed to be contained in the Bible and in Tradition, the latter made up of oral teachings by Jesus' apostles which were eventually written down but omitted from the Bible as not having adequate claim to inclusion by church leaders. The doctrines pronounced since the Bible do not constitute a growth in religious revelation, but rather a growth in Catholic understanding of revelation which occurred at the time of Jesus and the apostles. Catholic doctrine is further elaborated in scholarly writings by various individuals, foremost among them being

[11] *Ibid.*, pp. 224, 225, 231, 232.

Thomas Aquinas, who, writing in the thirteenth century, gave a comprehensive and systematic exposition of Catholic ideas which had developed by his time.

Unlike the Talmud of Judaism, which reached a close fourteen centuries ago, authoritative literature in Catholicism continues to be formulated by council and papal pronouncement, Catholics believing that Jesus gave the church the authority to do this. Under specially defined circumstances, the pope is believed to speak with infallibility on principles of faith and morals which have been revealed in Scripture or in Tradition. While it is not entirely clear to others which declarations are covered by the principle of infallibility, these are accepted by loyal Catholics as final and authoritative statements, anyway.

Unlike Judaism, Catholicism has a central organization headed by the pope which assures basic uniformity of teaching and guidance by the priesthood. Although lay members of the Catholic church may lag or diverge from published church doctrine, there are no divergent movements within Catholicism comparable to those in Judaism or Protestantism. Principles reside securely in the Bible and in official interpretations of the Bible. Final authority for defining doctrine rests with the pope, who is aided by a large organization of scholars and, as Catholics believe, by divine assistance. The scriptural basis for papal authority is contained in a statement by Jesus: "And I tell you, you are Peter, and on this rock I will build my church, and the powers of death shall not prevail against it. I will give you the keys of the kingdom of heaven, and whatever you bind on earth shall be bound in heaven, and whatever you loose on earth shall be loosed in heaven."[12]

Church statements stem from the Bible, and this in turn is believed by Catholics to consist of error-free communication from God in that he is the author of what was written. Of the leading religions in America, that of Catholics seems most outspoken in its insistence that religious doctrines in the Bible were given by supernatural revelation, by which is apparently meant that compelling ideas appeared in the minds of the writers of scripture which are not explainable by natural psychological laws.

A view more compatible with science would be the philosophical assertion that the revelation of ideas in the Bible proceeded from a God outside of experience coupled with the scientific acknowledgment that this revelation took place within the framework of natural psychological processes. It seems possible as a

[12] Matthew 16:18–19.

future development that contemporary religious doctrines about the supernatural may move in this direction in adjusting themselves to the requirements of modern psychological science. It should be kept in mind that the question of whether the ideas revealed are true or false is independent of whether they initially make their appearance as ideas within the framework of natural psychological processes. However, the supernatural origin ascribed to certain ideas is a vital matter for Catholics.

It is expected in Roman Catholicism that much of the doctrines will be fully understood by the faithful and through realization in daily living thereby become a part of their verifiable experience. The individual is encouraged to follow his conscience within principles laid down by the church, which gives Catholicism an inward vitality of intellectual as well as social growth not fully appreciated by non-Catholics who consider only the authoritative organization of the church. While the opportunity for religious and moral innovation is limited, the literary, artistic, scientific, and religious achievements of Catholics have been extensive through the ages.

It is significant that the largest growth of Protestant Christianity has taken place among Catholics or their descendants. If the individual's conscience conflicts with teachings of the Catholic Church, he is expected to follow his conscience, rather than the church. But this does not mean he is believed to have correct knowledge, rather that genuine religious growth cannot proceed in mechanical imitation of doctrines which the individual's conscience does not support.

The obstacles to continuing historical development of religious principles are substantial. Being convinced that their doctrines are error-free, Catholics recognize no need for changing them. If the individual Catholic finds results from experience and reflection which diverge from doctrines of the church, he is judged to be in error, and if the error is sufficiently gross, he is excluded from the church. The practical effect of this is that the individual Catholic is not a source of new church doctrine as in the branches of Judaism and Protestantism believing in progressive revelation of religious doctrines, although in a minor way the individual Catholic may through acquiring a position of importance as a scholar in the church contribute to the shaping of church doctrine. A further difficulty is that certain religious principles are expressly declared to be mysteries which human beings are incapable of understanding. These have been supernaturally revealed to the apostles of Jesus and through them transmitted in fixed form to the Catholic Church. In declaring these to be beyond human understanding, encouragement is lacking to conduct scientific inquiry to augment knowledge concerning them. Offsetting the disadvantage of excluding new ideas is the advantage to Catholics of being assured that their doctrines are stable and dependable from generation to generation, not being upset by every wind which blows across the seas of psychoanalysis. Still, all religious doctrines undergo some change with time.

Eastern Orthodoxy

The sources of religious knowledge in Eastern Orthodox churches in America and their parent countries are distinctive and merit consideration. The distinctions provide much of the ground for the conflict between Eastern and Western branches of Christianity which culminated in a final separation in 1054. The differences are subtle, though profound, and we quote from a European theologian, Joseph L. Hromadka, who has been a visiting professor in America.

> Eastern theology has not defined any doctrine of the Church. Retrospectively, her theologians argue that a definite doctrine of the Church is impossible just as a definition of life itself would make no sense. The Church of Christ is the original, primary reality preceding any human thought and action; the light which enables us to see; the truth which mediates any knowledge of what is true and right; the love which brings us in touch with our fellow men and fills us with human understanding and compassion. The Church as the primordial reality resists any dogmatic definition; the real being exists beyond human abstractions and categories. Unless we share in it, and find ourselves part and parcel of the mystical fellowship embracing all the members of the body of Christ we are incapable of understanding and apprehending the Church. . . .
>
> The theologians of the East like to speak of the Church as the continuation of Christ's incarnation and of Pentecost. Through the incarnation the eternal Son of God entered the realm of history and nature, broke the dividing line which separates the realm of the immortal, uncreated deity from the created, sinful, mortal, perishable world. The incarnation as the reality of the divine regenerating life did not cease to exist within our life and history with the resurrection and ascension of Christ; it is present in its original, real, and life-creating nature within the mystical, sacramental, and liturgical fellowship of all believers, in their mystical love for one another. The life of the Church is the life of the Incarnate Christ, the life of the Truth.
>
> Hence we may understand some of the emphases of Eastern Ortho-

doxy: First, the Church is only One, as Christ can have only one body. It is useless to argue about the relation of the visible and invisible Church. The Church is both, continuing in the unity of the divine and human nature of Christ. . . .

Second, the Church has the final norm and criterion of truth in herself. There is no higher authority beyond the Church since the Church is the primary reality, the source and fountain of all redemptive knowledge and life. Not even Christ should be understood and looked upon as authority to which the Church is subordinated. The Church *is* the Incarnate Christ, His life is her life; there is no dividing line between His God-manhood on the one hand and the Church on the other. Christ does not live and act outside of the Church. After His incarnation, the Church is the only mode of His existence. The Christ outside the Church, the Christ of modern rationalism or moralism is an artificial construction, without life and without power. An appeal to Christ against the Church contradicts the very reality of the heavenly life. The same is true of the authority of the Holy Scriptures. The Bible of the Old and New Testament has no normative validity outside the Church. It is the Church that created the canon, not vice versa. The Scripture certainly is the eternal revelation of God, and has its unique value. Nevertheless, it is only a part of the living tradition of the Church. . . .

Third, strictly speaking there is no specific office or instrument of infallibility. In the Roman Church either the Pope alone or the Pope with the Ecumenical Council are the divinely instituted channels of infallible authority, of the *Potestas magisterii.* Not so in the Eastern Church. Of course, the believers cannot live without the light of definite dogmatic formulas, liturgical and sacramental order. They must hear and know the voice of truth lest they get lost and confused. The Church has an unambiguous, unqualifiedly valid confession of faith, a doctrine concerning God, Christ, salvation, and eternal life. The seven Ecumenical councils were official gatherings of the Church acting, speaking, and defining the Creed under the guidance of the Holy Spirit. Historically or empirically, these councils of all bishops represented the Church and have been interpreted as infallible spokesmen of the whole Church. Yet, the theologians of the East more and more energetically object to this interpretation, and insist upon the fact that the Church as a whole, is an organic, mystical body of all believers, and has been the medium, instrument, and embodiment of the infallible truth of Christ. True, some doctrines and dogmas were defined and promulgated by the councils; however, it was not until the whole Church accepted, and incorporated, them into the living tradition that they proved to be authoritative, infallible manifestations of the divine Truth. The patriarchs of the East replied to the letter of Pope Pius IX in 1849 in this spirit: Only the Church as the living organism of all believers, laymen as well as bishops, can claim infallibility and protect the integrity of dogma and the purity of the liturgy.

The Church *lives* the truth, *has* the truth; an individual believer can have a real knowledge of it not by memorizing and accepting the formally promulgated doctrine but by living in communion with the body of the Church. . . . The claim of exclusive dogmatic or doctrinal authority by clergy, episcopacy, or the Pope amounts to an arrogant, heretic, disruptive self-separation from the Church.

Hence the conviction that the Church can grow and expand solely in a spiritual way. She has no right and means to force anybody to join her and to accept her truth. She invites into unity and fellowship but without judging or condemning the recalcitrant. The Church rejects any legal form, order and discipline—the law and legal power are at variance with the nature of the Church. The Eastern Church claims to be hierarchic, but not hierocratic, her authority being spiritual and mystical, not legal and jurisdictional.[13]

Two things may be noted which make the Eastern Orthodox churches deeply conservative. One of these is that the church in unity speaks truthfully and infallibly, or stated negatively, nothing new can be added in doctrine which is not accepted by the united church. The other circumstance is that the church as the living Christ continues to speak in harmony with scripture, hence departure from tradition is slow and difficult. The emphasis, however, upon a living experience today as the source of religious truth introduces potentialities for growth, even if slow and gradual. It seems possible that the Eastern Orthodox churches may adjust more flexibly to changing conditions in science and in economics than the Catholic or the Fundamentalist Protestant churches, whose basic principles are bound within the covers of the Bible to a greater degree. The problem of conflicting views in Eastern Orthodoxy is minimized simply by being denied, Christ speaking with infallible authority today as yesterday and not contradicting himself. If men think they find contradictions, it is they who are mistaken, not Christ.

Protestantism

In contrast with these difficulties of adjusting to new discoveries and insights in psychology and philosophy, we find the main stream of Protestantism more flexible in its ampler willingness to discard past errors or restrictions in thinking in favor of fresh experience. Increasingly, the authority of God in the present speaks more powerfully to members of Protestant churches than the authority of God in the past. By their attitudes and doc-

[13] J. L. Hromadka, "Eastern Orthodoxy," in E. J. Jurji (ed.), *The Great Religions of the Modern World,* Princeton University Press, 1947, pp. 289–293.

trines concerning sources of religious knowledge, Protestants as well as Jews seem better adapted to incorporate contributions from the scientific study of religion into their ideologies. Here, however, generalization is difficult, since Protestants represent the refraction of the rays of God through the prism of humanity, and the resulting spectrum ranges from intransigent Fundamentalism to evanescent Modernism. Furthermore, Protestantism is in a state of flux and the ultimate developments within the organized body of Protestantism cannot be securely predicted. Judging by the trend of cultural drift through a century since the popular publication of Renan's *Life of Jesus,* a scientific approach to religion is gaining ascendant authority, but countercurrents of antiscientism are periodically in evidence.

Protestants made their appearance as dissenting groups within the Catholic Church during the sixteenth century and have since undergone internal divisions and indigenous developments. Since there are alternative forms of dissent, there are alternative forms of Protestantism. The early Protestants rejected the authority of the pope but continued to accept the Bible as supernaturally revealed under divine inspiration and therefore the infallible word of God, a viewpoint continuing strong in Protestantism to the present time. Harnack, a prominent writer in the first part of the twentieth century, declared: "Christianity is a revelation which is to be believed, an authority which is to be obeyed. . . ."[14] The individual, rather than the pope, is expected to interpret the meaning of scripture. Bible study since the Reformation has assumed large importance for Protestants. It is not believed by traditional Protestants that a devout follower of Christ will be led into error in interpreting his teachings. Christ or the Holy Spirit is active in the life of the believer to aid him in interpreting the Bible. In varying degrees, Protestants are aided by their religious leaders or supplementary literature in understanding the Bible.

Fundamentalists at the present time retain these beliefs concerning the literal truth of the Bible. Billy Graham is a leader of these people in many contemporary churches. The effect of insisting upon inflexible scriptures as a source of religious knowledge is similar to the restraining influence of Catholic doctrines in that progressive development of principles through science or creative insights is not possible. Catholic doctrines are more detailed in their instruction of individual belief than are the

[14] A. von Harnack, *The Expansion of Christianity in the First Three Centuries,* tr. and ed. by J. Moffat, Putnam, 1904, Vol. I, p. 299.

scriptures, but accepting the latter as immutable restricts intellectual growth in religion to improving one's understanding of what has already been revealed nearly two thousand years ago.

Liberal Protestants have a different attitude toward the Bible. They regard it reverently as man's major source of religious knowledge. They do not believe that all of it, or for some, that any of it, was communicated as the word of God. Rather, they consider the Bible as the product of man's efforts to discover and write down religious truths. In this sense, the record of man's religious knowledge is a growing one, being added to by literature, philosophy, psychology, and the social sciences. What is the source of religious knowledge for the liberal Christian? The particular balance between individual experience, authority of leadership, psychology, literature, and traditional doctrines varies from one Protestant to another. It would be a fairly accurate generalization to say that the individual is expected to study the Bible, read scholarly writings in philosophy and science, listen to the guidance of his pastor and of his neighbors, learn from spiritual experience, and then to rely upon the path of understanding opened by these things.

The trend in Protestantism for a century or more has been away from rejecting as members those who differ in their religious beliefs from other members. At one time Protestant congregations took considerable notice of the correctness of the moral behavior or religious beliefs of their members. Now this is a minor issue of membership in most churches. Full opportunity to follow one's own convictions without inconvenience, unless these are decidedly unpopular, such as holding communist beliefs, generally prevails in Protestantism.

Of the different Protestant groups, Quakers have attached more importance to spiritual experience of the individual as the primary source of religious knowledge. For them the Bible is a record of knowledge, but is to be used not as a source book, but rather as a guidebook together with the counsel of friends in finding the "Inner Light" of Christ in one's own life experience. The latter is the authentic source of religious knowledge for Quakers. Emphasis is placed upon a meditative type of worship, without aid of scriptural readings or a set pattern of vocal ministry, during which members seek to discern, share, and follow the spiritual realities in their lives. This meditative experience is also found occasionally among other Protestant groups and in Catholic religious retreats but has been directed to a considerable extent by a planned program or by reading scriptural material. In the case of Quakers for a century and a half little conflict between the Bible and individual experience arose. In the nineteenth century several separations occurred in which the authority of individual experience was a critical issue. At the present time Quakers are preponderantly liberal in theology and seem receptive to new ideas from psychology if they thereby feel that God is speaking to them through their inward experience.

The Neo-orthodox are reacting against Protestant liberalism. The "essential" doctrines of the Bible are accepted as basic matters of Christian faith, supernaturally revealed by God. However, these doctrines were written down or translated by men who as scribes might err. Hence scientific evaluation of Biblical writings is an important task. Properly evaluated, these writings approximate the word of God. But the Neo-orthodox do not entirely agree as to what the "essential" doctrines are, nor concerning the net result of scientific scholarship to establish the validity of Biblical texts. From a practical standpoint, the writings of contemporary theologians among the Neo-orthodox are accorded considerable respect and authority by ministers and laymen who seek to bring their thinking and spiritual experiences into harmony with these writings. Neo-orthodoxy, at the risk of oversimplification, combines a liberal methodology with traditional Christian faith. If any current may be said to be dominant among Protestants, especially the clergy, it is Neo-orthodoxy. Yet many do not like to be labeled.

Besides the Fundamentalists, the Neo-orthodox, and the Liberals are the Conservatives who fit somewhere between Orthodoxy and Liberalism, and the Modernists who are out beyond the Liberals in their departure from traditional scriptural authority and their espousal of religious ideas from new currents in psychology and philosophy. While these five groups can be arranged in a linear series according to their degree of emphasis upon the Bible as a source of knowledge, they differ from each other qualitatively in ways which cannot be arranged along a single dimension. For example, Fundamentalism and Liberalism seem respectively to be religions of spiritual and social feeling, while Neo-orthodoxy and Modernism emphasize intellectual development of religion.

In summary, the core of sacred scripture in Judaism and in Christianity continues to be an important source of religious knowledge. However, this appears to be shrinking in exclusive importance compared with the growing body of writings in the past few hundred years. Liberal and modernist groups in Judaism and in Christianity are the ones whose religious literature most lacks well-defined doctrines. On the other hand, this literature can, by its flexible concept of authority, more readily accommodate itself to and benefit from fresh insights in the psychological and social sciences.

NORTH AMERICAN INDIAN RELIGION

In recognition of the religious creativity of the American Indians, it is appropriate to consider their beliefs side by side with those of other Americans. In doing this, we recall that the traditional patterns of Indian culture are in transition under the impact of European and industrial ways of living. The religious systems of the American Indians are to be viewed as a phase of their history, not strictly contemporary. These nonliterate systems provide illuminating contrast with religions whose substance has for thousands of years been recorded in writing. Numerically speaking, American Indians are a small and scattered minority, approximately 400,000, the states containing more than 10,000 being New York, Wisconsin, Minnesota, North Dakota, South Dakota, Oklahoma, New Mexico, Arizona, California, Montana, and Washington. These are the remainders of tribes about twice this population who roamed or lived in sparse communities north of Mexico at the coming of Columbus. These, together with Indians in Central and South America, are believed to have migrated from Siberia via Alaska in successive waves starting near the close of the last glacial era about 15,000 years ago. They brought with them an advanced Stone Age technology. Adapting themselves to new surroundings, they became agriculturalists or continued as hunters or food gatherers as circumstances permitted. Their cultural achievements are extensive.

> The Indians, whose existence in the Western Hemisphere covers scarce a tenth or even a twentieth of the time man and his hominid forerunners have lived on earth, nonetheless developed cultures which, for variety in form, differences in the complexity of different aspects, and types of adjustment to habitat compare with the cultures of any other large region anywhere. In this period, they domesticated the enormous variety of plants they were found to have by the European explorers who had first contact with them. They had, in Central and South America, developed the technique of pottery-making to a degree unsurpassed elsewhere. From what is now New Mexico, southward to Peru, great aggregates of population formed political units, and had a standard of living that impressed all the early Europeans.[15]

[15] M. J. Herskovits, *Man and His Works,* Knopf, 1948, p. 130.

The differing times of migration and places of settlement meant that even if the cultures of the Indians were once homogeneous, they did not remain so. Yet common elements in the religions of different tribes are evident. One of these is the guardian spirit. The extent to which this feature can be attributed to a single origin, and the extent to which it came into being as a result of shared physiological, geographic, or group conditions is a difficult question to answer. Of its fundamental place in the American Indian religion, Goldenweiser writes: "Of all religious phenomena in North America, the most general as well as varied are the beliefs and practices centering in the cult of the guardian spirit. In essence, these cults are rooted in a faith in supernatural power, personal or impersonal."[16]

For a description of religious ideas and practices among Indians we turn to a valuable essay by Ruth Underhill, from which excerpts are taken.

Most Indian religious attitudes have worldwide counterparts, and some seem so fundamental that they may have been brought by the first paleolithic immigrants. Among these are the concepts of mana and taboo. The Melanesian word mana has been standardized by anthropologists to refer to a widespread primitive belief in some invisible force pervading the universe. It can be focused on any object, animate or inanimate, endowing that object, for the time being, with supernatural power. Sacred places, objects used in ceremony, or human beings under certain circumstances can be imbued with this power. The Siouan word *wakan,* the Iroquoian *orenda* and the Algonquian *manitou* all refer to it, and many other tribes have the concept if not the name.

As a corollary, the focus of power was dangerous to one not in a sacred state. This is the familiar concept of taboo which is as worldwide as that of mana. It regards the focus of power as untouchable, not because it is unclean, but because it belongs to the supernatural world with which contact may be dangerous. To meet the situation, an age-old technique has been developed whose remnants are visible even among modern people. Briefly, it requires that anyone who has been in contact with a supernatural power, either voluntarily or involuntarily, must negate the danger by withdrawing both from human society and from bodily activity. As interpreted by various Indian groups, this can mean seclusion; fasting; abstaining from speech, sleep, looking at the sun or at fire, touching the head (the most important part of the body), or touching the lips with water.

This technique, in whole or in part, was used by many Indian groups at the life crises of birth, puberty, and death. These were occasions

[16] A. A. Goldenweiser, *Anthropology,* Crofts, 1946, p. 242.

when an uncontrollable biological event swooped in to affect human life. Those under its influence were considered subject to supernatural power, and they practised the techniques which would keep them safe and also keep others safe from them. Such an attitude was found most often in the food-gathering and hunting groups where organization was simple. With agricultural groups, who had a wealth of ceremonies, the seclusion rules, especially those for women, were often obscured or omitted.

Here we must differentiate between girls' and boys' puberty. The acknowledgment of maturity for boys, as we shall see below, is usually accompanied with ordeals and initiations undertaken on the boy's own initiative. A girl's puberty, without any effort on her part, fits her to perform the miracle of childbirth. The menstruant and the parturient are considered under such strong supernatural influence that, unless they withdraw, they would be in danger themselves and would certainly bring danger to men. This attitude is particularly true of the hunting and food-gathering groups.

Withdrawal in some degree was practised by the bereaved after a death, and sometimes by enemy slayers, murderers, even whale killers. Here there is an explanation. There is danger from the soul of the departed which either wishes to take a loved one with it for company or to injure its killer.

A belief in spirits and a purposeful attempt to conciliate them is found in every Indian tribe. Spirits of the dead, just mentioned, did not play the all-important part sometimes found in the Old World. True, some far western tribes imagined them as stealing the souls of the living and so causing illness. A few thought of them as acting the part of guardian spirits, and others conceived of them as reincarnated in children. As a rule, it was thought that the average dead person existed in the afterworld only until the last person who remembered him on earth was gone. A few might be elevated to powerful spirits or gods.

This afterworld was a shadowy place to which both good and bad went indiscriminately. Days of withdrawal were often observed by mourners or corpse handlers while souls were supposedly on their journey thither, and they were supplied with food for this journey. Some tribes also supplied their dead with goods to keep them contented so they would not return. To this end, too, their dwellings were often destroyed and their names never mentioned. This belief and practice cause difficulty for Indians in going to hospitals, for many have died there, but the building stands replete with supernatural danger. They also make it difficult for white men taking census because names of the dead must not be mentioned.

Other spirits were those of animals, plants, and natural phenomena. To most Indians, there was no sharp dividing line between these and human beings. The Sioux spoke of all living things as the two-leggeds, the four-leggeds, and the wingeds. All these had life and must be treated as fellow beings. So must even the plants and Mother Earth who bore them. A Comanche on being urged to plow and reap objected: "Shall I stab my Mother's breast and cut my Mother's hair!" True, agricultural tribes did dig the earth, but usually they had a tradition of a supernatural visitant, perhaps the corn plant, which had bidden them to do so. Every act connected with planting was a religious ceremony. Every wild thing, too, was treated with consideration. The Papago woman asked permission of the plants which she plucked for basketry. The Zuni apologized to the deer he killed.

The spirits were approached in two very different ways and were closely connected with the economics of a tribe and its degree of organization. The two ways are vision and ceremony.

The vision took numberless forms among the different tribes and was sought under varying circumstances. With the Woodland Algonquians of the East, the Salish of the Northwest and some Plains tribes, it was sought at puberty. Here, every boy (and a few girls) hoped for supernatural help to guide his career and ensure success. To that end he practised seclusion and fasting, sometimes repeatedly, but *before* the supernatural experience, not after as with women. Sometimes he added ordeals to gain the spirits' pity and show his courage. In fact, this was a religious ritual based on a definite theology, not a blind observance of taboo. It served as a substitute for boys' initiation ceremonies, rare in North America.

The puberty vision followed a standard form for which the boy was well prepared. An animal appeared in its human guise and took him to its village in the forest or under the sea or perhaps delivered instruction on the spot. This consisted of a song to be used when power was needed and usually a fetish which was given or which he must find or make. With the fetish went a rudimentary ritual which must be followed on pain of losing power or being injured by it. Even an unimaginative youth was likely to achieve such a vision after repeated trials. Often he had some supervision from an older man or a whole group of them. If his hallucination was not of acceptable form he was likely to be told: "That was a false spirit. Try again."

The most usual rituals were often for the sake of weather and crop growth. For the latter, there might be two or three rituals, corresponding to the life crises of birth (planting); maturity (green corn) and death (harvest). Others were special pleas for rain, rituals to help or to celebrate war raids, and pilgrimages to obtain blessing—the Papago salt journey or the Pawnee Hako and great ceremonies "to keep the world in order."

Each tribe had its own series of ceremonies and its own fostering spirits, often those of the plants themselves. There is not enough space here to name all the ritual acts worked out, but they fall within a large common framework. This included purification of the participants, which might mean all those present or only officiants. It might be by a sweatbath, as with the Sioux; vomiting, as with the Navaho and

Creek; or confession, as with the Iroquois. There were offerings to the spirits: tobacco, food or, in the Southwest, the feathered wands called prayersticks. There was little blood sacrifice. Individual Plains Indians sometimes cut off a finger to gain the spirits' pity. A dog was ritually killed and eaten by some tribes, and the Pawnee killed a human captive to help the crops. The concept of vicarious sacrifice in Christian belief seems, therefore, strange to many Indians.

After Christian teachings had become somewhat familiar, there was a series of what I may call amalgamation religions. These did not contemplate the conquest or disappearance of the whites. Instead, they aimed at peaceful living for the Indians under the new conditions. Though they often kept old Indian customs and eschewed Christian theology, they included definite ethical teachings. The need for such teaching was obvious since Indian groups were breaking up, and the old clan and family influence was not sufficient to control behavior. Above all, liquor was making its inroads, and the new preachers demanded total abstinence as well as peaceful and upright living.

Among such preachers was Handsome Lake of the Iroquois, 1799–1815, who was profoundly influenced by Quaker missionaries. In the Southern Puget Sound country, in 1881, John Slocum founded the Shaker religion, a compound of Christian elements and Indian style vision. Both of these cults are still functioning. The most widespread of all was the Peyote religion, many of whose adherents were brought together in 1918 as the Native American Church. Like other cults, Peyotism involved a combination of old Indian practices with social ethics. It had no one prophet, although several Southwestern tribes tell of a suffering individual who had a vision after the old pattern. He saw the peyote plant in human form, was given the directions for a ceremony and ethical maxims, and was bidden to teach these to his people for their salvation.

Peyote (Mexican peyotl) is a small globular cactus with a root like a carrot found growing on both sides of the Rio Grande. It contains a number of alkaloids, the chief being mescaline, and has the power of producing hallucinations with intense and varied colors. It was used by Mexican Indians, notably the Huichol in elaborate ceremonies.

The Peyote religion teaches an ethical doctrine much like those of the monotheistic religions. However, it eschews specific Christian theology, its exponents often stating that while Christ came to the whites, peyote came to the Indians. This is an obvious reaction to the subordinate place so often given to the Indian converts in a church organization. Indians resent being treated as inferiors in religion as elsewhere.

Their meetings, which have been attended by a number of anthropologists including myself, are like some Protestant prayer meetings, where the program includes singing, prayer, and testimonials. They are held in a tepee strewn with white sage in the Plains manner and with a half-moon shaped earthen altar as in some Kiowa ceremonies.

During the evening, a drum and rattle are passed around clockwise, one man singing a song, supposedly of his own composition, while a man on one side of him drums and on the other rattles. Meanwhile heads of the cactus, usually dried, are passed around, each person expecting to eat eight during the evening. After midnight, when the round had been made once, there are testimonials from individuals who have been helped to follow "the straight road," giving up liquor and other faults. At dawn comes a token meal of old Indian foods, then prayers asking God's help for Indians, whites, and all the world.[17]

To this review of religious ideas and practices of American Indians can be added a quotation from Goldenweiser pointing up the nature of the search for an experience of a guardian spirit.

To acquire a guardian spirit is the Indian's most sacred quest. When a boy approaches maturity, when "his voice begins to change," he repairs to the woods, where he builds for himself a crude hut or tent. Here he lives in isolation, takes frequent purgatives and eats sparingly. His thoughts are bent on the supernatural experience he is about to face. When he has reached a high state of purity, physically and spiritually ("so the spirits can look through him," says the Indian), the desire of his soul is realized: the guardian spirit appears to him in a dream or vision. The spirit may appear in animal, bird, or human shape, or it may be a monster creature told about in myths. The guardian spirit bestows upon the novice a supernatural gift or several such and, having given him advice as to a proper life to lead, disappears. Henceforth, the youth stands in an intimate personal relation to the spirit, appeals to it for protection, and is warned by it when danger impends. If the spirit is an animal or bird, the youth may have to abstain from eating or killing individuals of that species; this taboo, however, is not found in all Indian tribes.

This generalized representation of the guardian-spirit quest does scant justice to this central cult of the North American Indians and its many cultural ramifications.[18]

And it may be remarked that Christianity is also pervaded by the guardian-spirit idea. In a general sense, the holy spirit or spirit of God is protective in nature, guiding and safeguarding the individual from harm. In a more specific way people speak, sometimes half seriously, of a man being protected by his "guardian angel." The approach of the Indian to his spirit world

17 Abridged from Ruth Underhill, "Religion Among American Indians," *The Annals of the American Academy of Political and Social Science,* May, 1957, pp. 127–136, by permission of the American Academy of Political and Social Science. Copyright 1957 by the American Academy of Political and Social Science. Dr. Underhill is at present at work on a book in which the material in this essay will be expanded and developed.

18 A. A. Goldenweiser, *op. cit.,* p. 242.

is more individual while that of Christianity is more through group religious activity. Nor should the ethical content of the religion of American Indians be minimized. Protestant missionaries in early America found that a common ground could be found with Indians in their ideas of the Great Spirit. George Fox, a Quaker leader, describes a religious discussion.

> And there was a doctor that did dispute with us, which was of great service and occasion of opening much to the people concerning the Light and the Spirit. And he so opposed it in every one, that I called an Indian because he denied it to be in them, and I asked him if that he did lie and do that to another which he would not have them do the same to him, and when he did wrong was not there something in him, that did tell him of it, that he should not do so, but did reprove him. And he said there was such a thing in him when he did any such a thing that he was ashamed of them. So we made the doctor ashamed in the sight of the governor and the people; and he ran so far out that he would not own the Scriptures.[19]

Sources of Religious Ideas in Orally Transmitted Beliefs

There being no writings among the American Indians historically considered, no sacred scripture exists to which men can turn to settle their questions. Sacred objects have special meanings and provide the nearest approximation to written doctrine, their details serving as reminders of stories or principles in religious tradition. Without these objects, ceremonial practices would be on a par with spoken language as far as assuring permanence of beliefs from generation to generation is concerned.

The authority of oral religious traditions among Indians is strong, overlapping that which elders hold over the younger generation. Religious leaders exist who, as shamans, are much more authoritative than persons whose experiences in the spirit world have been meager, but almost no organized priesthood like that of a conventional church is found among the pre-Columbian North American Indian tribes. In spite of the lack of written creeds or institutional leadership, the religious beliefs and practices remain fairly stable from generation to generation until confronted by European culture. This stability seems less dependent upon oral transmission than upon continuance of environmental and physiological factors which provide perennial roots for religious beliefs, a principle evidenced by the widespread character of some Indian religious beliefs.

[19] J. L. Nickalls, *The Journal of George Fox,* Cambridge University Press, 1952, p. 642.

The major source for the beliefs held by tribes and individuals appears to be the distinctive experiences encountered in the quest for help from the spirit world. While naturalistic explanation of these visions and dreams is required by scientific analysis, an imaginative interpretation is placed upon them by Indian devotees. What the guardian spirit reveals or tells a man to do is absolutely authoritative for him. The scrupulous care with which clues from visions or dreams are obeyed is hardly exceeded by that of the followers of any church which has a well-organized priesthood and doctrine.

In inquiring why such reliance is placed upon the capricious flow of experience during semiconsciousness, an answer which seems plausible is that such psychic states possess a high degree of validity. The rise of psychoanalysis has shown the scientific importance of dreams in telling man about himself and in giving him answers to problems whose elements are buried below the threshold of consciousness. Much of the guidance which Indians receive from their visions and dreams has a reasonable quality about it. The supernatural sanction given to communications with the spirit world helps to gain acceptance for religious wisdom. The supernatural chaff mixed with the kernels of truth is largely innocuous, and apparently cannot be readily screened without spiritual and social wisdom being lost. The emphasis which Indians place upon inward spiritual experience is imposed by a lack of written scripture to which they might turn for authoritative direction. While lack of writing handicaps orderly intellectual progress, this lack has the effect of keeping Indians closer to the source in experience from which religious doctrines are ultimately developed.

part III Functioning of Religion

TWO FORMS OF RELIGIOUS PRACTICE

Christian Science

Christian Science is the system of religious thought and the denomination founded by Mary Baker Eddy in 1879 as the outcome of her discovery of this religious truth at Swampscott, Massachusetts, in 1866, and her publication of the first edition of its basic textbook, *Science and Health with Key to the Scriptures,* in 1875. From childhood Mrs. Eddy had been deeply religious and a profound student of the Bible, and had long been inclined to attribute all causation to God, and to regard Him as infinitely good, and the Soul and source of all reality. But in 1866 a lifetime of ill-health was climaxed by what was regarded as a fatal injury from which she recovered almost instantaneously after reading an account of healing in Matthew's Gospel. That seeming miracle set her mind to work. It appeared to her as a divine revelation, the prophecy of a revolution in human thinking, and an inspired call to action. She describes (in her brief autobiography *Retrospection and Introspection*) how she withdrew from society for about three years "to ponder [her] mission, to search the Scriptures, to find the Science of Mind that should take the things of God and show them to the creature, and reveal the great curative Principle,—Deity."

Christian Science is not new: it is as ancient as God-like thinking and spiritual perception. Why then did it need to be "discovered"? Mrs. Eddy replies: "Our Master healed the sick, practised Christian healing, and taught the generalities of its divine Principle to his students; but he left no definite rule for demonstrating this Principle of healing and preventing disease. This rule remained to be discovered in Christian Science."

But what of the demand of Christian Science to be rated as not only *a* Science but *the* Science? Certainly Christian Science claims not only to have searched for truth, but to have found Truth, to have reduced this basic knowledge of Truth to a system which is eminently communicable; to have brought to light general or fundamental laws, and to have made this organized system of knowledge available in work, life and the search for truth.

Is Christian Science, then, a rather thin modern broth of Deism? When Mrs. Eddy was asked directly, Do you believe in God?, she replied: "I believe more in Him than do most Christians, for I have no faith in any other thing or being. . . . To me God is All. He is best understood as Supreme Being, as infinite and conscious Life, as the affectionate Father and Mother of all He creates."

But how can a Christian Scientist speak of healing unless he believes in a human material body which seems to demand healing? Of course man has a body. But that body is not material or physical. Human body and human mind are merely two aspects, outer and inner, of the same appearance. Human belief constructs this human body, controls it, afflicts it, and finally destroys it. Never was that body material; it was always a mortally mental concept,—although appearing to the human senses as an aggregation of organic cells. Hence the possibility of utilizing spiritual power, right thinking, spiritual prayer, to heal what appears to the corporeal senses as a sick, diseased, broken body, but which must be conceived as a sick, disordered, lawless, and fearful human mind.

In this process of attaining daily *rapport* with divinity and ultimate unity or salvation, prayer is a method recognized by most of the great religions. Curiously enough, however, some uninformed critics have charged that Christian Science dispenses with prayer.

No prayerless religion would provide that every church service must include a period for silent prayer and the audible repetition of the Lord's Prayer. Note further that Mrs. Eddy directs in the Church Manual that members of her Church should "daily watch and pray to be delivered from all evil, from prophesying, judging, condemning, counseling, influencing or being influenced erroneously." Moreover, in that same Manual she enjoins that it shall be the duty of every member of this Church to pray each day the prayer which now has attained wide acceptance: " 'Thy kingdom come;' let the reign of divine Truth, Life, and Love be established in me, and rule out of me all sin; and may Thy Word enrich the affections of all mankind, and govern them!"

We have repeatedly emphasized that Christian Science is a religion, and not just a new-fangled form of medicine or faith healing. Yet healing is the irrefutable witness that Science does embody the word and works of Christ Jesus the Way-shower and is thus able to "reinstate primitive Christianity and its lost element of healing." Hence every genuine Christian Scientist is expected to be a healer. But it was entirely natural that certain among them should feel the special qualifications for and an urge to devote their time and energies to healing on a full-time basis. *The Christian Science Journal* at present lists over 10,000 such practitioners serving throughout the world.[1]

The foregoing passage describes a system of religious practice whose adherents in the United States now number approximately a half million. In less than a century The Church of Christ, Scientist has grown through adversity into a large and influential urban denomination. It has strong appeal to those who suffer nervous or emotional illness for which the program of religious therapy of Christian Science proves remarkably effective. By concentrating attention upon Divine Love, sick personalities become rebuilt on a new level of integration about a spiritual force.

[1] Abridged from A. J. Todd, "Christian Science," in V. Ferm, *Religion in the Twentieth Century*, Philosophical Library, 1948, pp. 357, 361, 362, 364–368, 373.

A different approach to absorbing spiritual power into human life is provided by the sacramental system of Catholics, the largest religious group in the United States, as well as the largest religious group in the world. The principal and most often repeated rite in this system is the celebration of Mass. Preliminary to the series of chapters on the functioning of religion we note the nature of this dramatic religious act.

Catholic Mass

The priest faces the altar again and, remaining in the center, says, "*Oremus*"—"Let us pray." Now begins the sacrificial part of the Mass. So far the Mass has been principally instructive in order to put the people in the proper disposition for what is to follow. In the early centuries at this particular point of the Mass non-Catholics and candidates for baptism were asked to leave. What was to follow was only for the initiated.

While the priest has been saying this prayer, ushers have been taking up a collection from among the congregation. In the early days of the Church the faithful offered instead of money bread and wine for the church, the priests, and the poor. This collection is taken up only on Sundays and holy days.

The priest takes the veil and the pall off the chalice and puts them to one side. In some churches a bell is rung at this point to mark the beginning of this more solemn part of the Mass. Now the celebrant removes the paten (sacrificial plate), which covers the chalice. On the paten rests a large round wafer of unleavened bread—the Host. This the priest elevates before him, offers it to God, and then places it on the altar. He picks up the chalice and . . .

Going to the right side, where the altar boys have been waiting with a cruet of water and one of wine, takes the wine cruet and pours into the chalice a little wine, which symbolizes the divine nature of Christ. Then he blesses the water, which symbolizes the human nature of Christ, and carefully pours a drop or two into the chalice.

He returns to the center, where he raises the chalice and, as he did with the Host, prays that almighty God will accept it "for our salvation and that of the whole world." Then he puts the chalice down, covers it with the pall, and, bending low, professes his own and the people's humility before God. Standing erect again, he invokes the blessing of the Holy Spirit and makes the sign of the cross over the chalice and the Host.

Now he goes to the right side, where the altar boys have been waiting with water, a basin, and linen. He washes and dries his fingers, reciting meanwhile six verses of Psalm 25 (Psalm 26 in non-Catholic versions of the Bible).

Returning to the center, he bows and asks the most blessed Trinity (God the Father, God the Son, and God the Holy Spirit) to accept this sacrifice for the honor of God and the saints and for the salvation of the people.

Turning to face the people, he says, "*Orate, fratres*"—"Pray, brethren," begging the congregation to add their prayers to his own that the sacrifice may be acceptable to God the Father almighty. The altar boys make the response in the name of the people.

Still at the center, he reads silently one or several prayers, which vary with the feast of the day, placing the offering of the sacrifice under the patronage of Our Lord.

He concludes the last prayer aloud so that the faithful may ratify it:

V. *"Per omnia saecula saeculorum"*—"World without end."

R. *"Amen."*

V. *"Dominus vobiscum"*—"The Lord be with you."

R. *"Et cum spiritu tuo"*—"And with thy spirit."

V. *"Sursum corda"*—"Lift up your hearts."

R. *"Habemus ad Dominum"*—"We have lifted them up unto the Lord."

V. *"Gratias agamus Domino Deo nostro"*—"Let us give thanks to the Lord our God."

R. *"Dignum et justum est"*—"It is meet and just."

The priest continues aloud with the preface, a prayer developing the idea of thanksgiving in the light of the feast of the day and of the season, asking that with his prayer and those of the people all may be permitted to join the heavenly choirs praising God face to face: "And therefore with the angels and archangels, the thrones and dominions, and the whole host of the heavenly army we sing the hymn of thy glory, saying again and again . . ." Bowing humbly before the altar, he continues in the sublime words of Isaias the prophet and of the Psalms: "Holy, holy, holy, Lord God of hosts. Heaven and earth are full of thy glory. Hosanna in the highest. Blessed is He that cometh in the name of the Lord. Hosanna in the highest." This is called the Sanctus.

A bell is rung three times by one of the altar boys at the words "Holy, holy, holy." This is the signal for the people to kneel, since the action on the altar now begins to penetrate more deeply into the mysteries of the heavenly court.

The priest is no longer free to turn and beg the prayers of his congregation. He is preoccupied with the approaching sacrifice.

He kisses the altar and makes the sign of the cross three times over the bread and the wine. He prays now for the universal Church, for the Holy Father, for the bishop, for those who need his prayers or to whom he has promised a remembrance, and finally for those who are assisting at the Mass (a Catholic never merely attends Mass; he assists at Mass). The celebrant goes on to unite himself and his people with the Virgin Mary and the saints, adoring God, with Christ, in heaven.

The bell is rung once as the priest extends his hands over the bread and the wine—called the oblation. This ringing of the bell is to warn the people that the consecration (the changing of the bread and wine into the body and blood of Christ) is about to take place.

The priest prays again for the acceptance of the offering. Again he makes the sign of the cross three times over the bread and the wine together; then he makes the sign of the cross separately over the Host and over the chalice. The Church is now very still, the people around you intent on the altar. In an instant—according to the belief of those around you—the priest will transform the bread into the body of Christ and the wine into His blood. The change will not be visible, but we have Christ's word for it that the change will take place.

The celebrant bends over the Host and pronounces the sacred words: "Take and eat ye all of this; *for this is my body."*

He genuflects in adoration before the Host, which has become God between his fingers, and the bell is rung. He raises the Host high so that the faithful may adore their Savior, and the bell is rung again. He genuflects again, and the bell is rung a third time.

Without pausing, he goes on to the consecration of the wine in the chalice: "Take and drink ye all of this; *for this is the chalice of my blood, of the new and eternal Testament: the mystery of faith: which shall be shed for you and for many unto the remission of sins.* As often as ye do these things, ye shall do them in remembrance of me."

Again he genuflects, adoring the blood of Christ before him, and the bell is rung. He raises the chalice for the adoration of the people, and the bell is rung again. He genuflects again, and the bell is rung the third time.

This is the essence of the sacrifice—this mystical separation of Christ's body and blood. The priest has with the sword of his miraculous words made a cleavage, as it were, yet Christ lives whole and entire under the appearance of the bread and the wine. Christ the victim rests immolated (sacrificed) on the altar before him. This is a mystery whose roots are in eternity. We accept this mystery on the word of God Himself.[2]

The foregoing lines describe the heart of the supreme act of worship by Catholics, the reënactment of the sacrifice of Jesus Christ for the salvation of mankind. As part of the Mass, prayers are said to God for the living and the dead, the faithful eat a portion of the bread which has been transformed into God, and they are thereby recipients of God's grace. In this sacrament it is emphasized in Catholic teaching that the higher power of religion is outside natural explanation. The events during Mass through which the power of God comes to mankind are accepted as mysteries beyond the ability of human comprehension.

While having deep respect for the religious rites of Catholics and others for whom acts of worship are considered to be beyond scientific understanding, nevertheless scientific students of religion endeavor to advance the frontiers of empirical analysis of religious activity as far as science can go. Supernaturally located, the higher power of religion lies outside the scope of science, and nothing can be done in cause-and-effect analysis except to describe the effects which appear in the observable world. On the other hand, the assertion that the power is supernatural does not thereby discourage the scientist of religion from investigating whether this is really so. If the power is found to be psychological, residing in the world of inward experience, both it and the effects which result from it can be examined by techniques of scientific inquiry.

In offering this empirical analysis, no presumption is made that those to whom thoroughgoing reliance upon science in religion is unsound are to agree. Rather, the concern of the scientist is to foster understanding among those who are willing to rely upon scientific study to gain religious truth. In this effort, science merely asks the same tolerance for itself in matters of religion which religious devotees expect for themselves. The attempt is made in this text to represent different religious viewpoints which exemplify ways of believing and worshiping in contemporary culture. Where these viewpoints are defended by intellectual processes outside the scope of science, the in-

[2] R. Ginder, *For the Visitor at Mass,* The Queen's Work, 1940, pp. 10–15.

terested student will turn to writings by those whose field for thought is larger than science permits. For this larger inquiry, which lies beyond this text, writings in history, theology, philosophy, and sacred literature are relevant.

The series of chapters in Part III analyze the basic functioning of religion. The inquiry begins with an examination of viewpoints concerning what is meant by "higher power." Efforts to define an empirical psychological power are reviewed. The second chapter in Part III examines the processes whereby this psychological force or power functions in human personality. The third chapter probes the nature of the social and psychological adjustment which people make to the higher power in religion, considering ways in which they evoke its functioning.

The term *function* recurs at intervals through the text, and attention is given now to its various meanings, discussed at length by R. K. Merton.[3] The most clear-cut usage is in the mathematical sense of one variable being a function of another. In this sense the values of one variable are mathematically related to the values of the other. The distance required to brake an automobile to halt is a function of speed. One can also say that the distance needed for stopping is a function of the type and size of brakes. This suggests a second and more concrete usage of the term *function*. Brakes are necessary to the safe operation of a car. What is their ultimate purpose? More basic than merely depriving a car of its motion when the foot is applied to the pedal is the need to preserve life and limb by avoiding collision with objects. In a deeper sense, the safety of passengers is a function of the braking system, being mathematically determined by the efficiency of this system. Here the interest is in the result produced by the brakes in satisfying the desire of people for safety. The usual sense in which the term *function* is used is to describe the results of an activity. They are its function, which may be the satisfying experience produced by the activity or an essential means to such experience. This is the customary usage in this text in speaking of the functions of an institution. A third usage arises when one speaks of the functioning of an activity or a personality or an institution. This refers to the process or way in which the situation operates to produce results. Rarely are functional relationships between variables simple. The unfolding of variables in their interrelationship to each other constitutes their functioning. Finally, the variables and their interrelationships are called a *functional system,* or more briefly, a *system*.

Taking the Catholic Mass as an example of these ideas, one can speak first, in a purely mechanical sense, of the functional relationship between movement of lips and vocal sounds produced, a relationship describable in mathematical terms. The importance of Mass, from the standpoint of participants, is found in the effects which it produces in the lives of people, as well as in its supernatural implications for God. In science, of course, we limit ourselves

[3] R. K. Merton, *Social Theory and Social Structure,* Free Press, 1957, pp. 19–84.

to empirically verifiable functions. In this respect, we can speak of the satisfaction and the psychological enrichment in the lives of participants, which amount to a fulfillment of religious needs. The scientifically curious observer will ask how Mass functions to bring about such results, seeking to know the psychological processes involved. In a scientific sense, he will speak of the Mass as being central in the Catholic system of worship, a system which embraces psychological and social variables in their interrelatedness.

It is easy to recognize that these usages are similar, and the student may wonder why refinement in definition is given. The possibility of confusion arises when the functional hypothesis is examined, namely that religion produces results satisfying basic human needs. Religion is a functional system, apart from whether its consequences are beneficial or otherwise. It is necessary to see from the context whether speaking of religion as functional refers in a neutral manner to the existence of a system of variables or whether the reference amounts to a declaration of the functional theory of religion, that it plays a basic role in meeting human needs.

In analyzing the functioning of the higher power defined in the initial chapter of Part III, we are specifically concerned with the way in which it functions in the overall personality system and with the effects which it brings about in the personality system. The basic hypothesis concerning the higher power of religion is that it functions to fulfill human needs in ways not otherwise achievable. In this functioning appropriate adjustment by human beings is typically required for the full benefits of the power to be achieved. Effects of the higher power depend upon activities of prayer and worship. The functioning of religion refers to these adjustments which influence the higher power as well as to its operation in people's lives. While James among others has contended that religious institutions hinder rather than facilitate this adjustment, that is, they are dysfunctional, most investigators do not agree. In any event, the individual practicing religion in solitude as James recommends depends upon literature and instruction provided by the group in which he lives, whether this is a church or not. The scientific question is not one of either religion in solitude or religion in company, but rather it is one of how much coöperation the group can appropriately give the individual and how much solitude is beneficial to him, or more generally, when religion performs functions and when it performs dysfunctions. The following chapters describe the higher power of religion from an empirical standpoint, the way in which it functions in people's lives, and the adjustments which they make in influencing it. Besides the basic functioning of religion in human personality, there are other consequences of religion for human needs in generating social, political, and economic activities. These consequences are considered in later chapters. Furthermore, supernatural beliefs play a fundamental functional role in most religions. Since this function is closely related to the rationalizing tendency of human beings, it is considered in connection with the causation of religious culture. Part III restricts itself to the basic functioning of religion with reference to the altruistic motivation which religion fosters. Later chapters analyze dysfunctions of religion.

chapter 7 Description of the Power in Religion

In the preceding chapter a review was given of beliefs and activities prevailing among religious groups in America. At the core of these beliefs are those concerning the existence of God and other spiritual beings. In our definition of religion these consist of beings believed by devotees to possess higher power than other things in or outside of the universe. In describing the nature of religion beyond giving a definition or providing examples, our attention turns to the nature of this higher power and its involvement in religious activities. In our definition little has been said concerning this power and the means followed to influence it. While some religions are concerned with a plurality of higher powers, the predominant view in American religion is of one higher power. Central to the major religions of America is a supreme being and acts of communication with this being. What can be said from an empirical standpoint about these things?

EMPIRICAL ASPECTS OF THE HIGHER POWER

The beliefs which people hold are empirical psychological facts apart from whether the beliefs are true, false, or unprovable from an empirical standpoint. In factually generalizing about beliefs concerning God, we distinguish between those which are not exposable to empirical test and those which pertain to observable matters. Under the first heading are beliefs about what God did in creating the universe or what he will do in life hereafter. Also there are beliefs concerning what God supposedly can do but never does in this world. Thus God is referred to as "all-powerful—he can do anything if he wishes to." As long as the power remains potential rather than actual, the most which can be accomplished from the standpoint of empirical study is to note that people do believe in the existence of such a higher power.

With respect to beliefs about what God does do in the daily life of this world, we are on more testable scientific ground. What God as a higher power is believed to do for people is demonstrable at least from the standpoint of supposed effects. The major things which God is believed to accomplish for people in this life include protection from chance misfortune, health, happiness, success in human endeavors, and personality development. Some of these categories overlap. The first of them refers to the miraculous setting aside of physical laws of probability, such as bringing good weather, and is in the same category as magic, performed by a supreme being instead of by a person. The remaining categories—health, happiness, success involving personal abilities, and personality development—are largely psychological phenomena. Indeed, we may correctly say that the overwhelming proportion of effects attributed to God as a higher power in human life are psychological in nature, and the psychological domain is the realm in which God is principally believed to rule.

As empirical features of the higher power in religion, we next note how people believe God acts to bring about his effects. There are two principal ways in which he is believed to act. One of these is for him to proceed without human beings' taking the initiative to appeal to him. In this role God is believed to act as a judge of human events and to impose appropriate rewards, punishments, or compensations according to what people deserve or what their situation requires. These benefits or deterrents are sometimes believed to take the form of physical consequences, but more typically they refer to things with a psychological basis, such as sickness, pain, health, happiness, and personal or group achievement.

In the other role, God is influenced by human intervention. In essence the human act is one of communication addressed to God. In various ways human wants or thanks for past needs met are made known to him or his presence invoked. These things are done through worship in which gestures, posturing, sacramental swallowing of wafers or wine, and other actions are combined with verbal appeal or acknowledgment. They are also done through singing sacred music and through silent meditation in which thoughts are directed to God and inaudible prayer or communion with God takes place. It is to be noted that these approaches are psychological in nature, as should characterize approaches made to a being endowed with personal or psychological attributes.

Psychological Questions

A significant observation about theological beliefs is that they are mostly about psychological attributes. The topic of the higher power in religion is a suitable one for psychology to analyze. Nor have all psychologists been reluctant to undertake this analysis. Most of the observations and conclusions to which we now direct our attention arise in psychology and psychoanalysis, with some scattered findings about the higher power in religion contributed by sociology and anthropology, fields which border psychology and occasionally reach into it.

A fundamental question for scientific inquiry is posed by the belief that a higher power in religion produces beneficial effects on human life. This is a hypothesis about cause and effect, that a power exists and effects follow in the lives of those affected by the power. In the scientific sense, an effect is something which always follows from an antecedent condition known as its cause. The cause-and-effect relationship is shown by the invariable sequence which the events follow. If the cause and effect can be measured, then the relationship shown is that an increase in the cause is followed by an increase in the effect.

Religious groups assemble considerable evidence of different kinds to support their conclusion that beneficial psychological results occur. Psychologists analyzing religion also report these effects, although they find them in various degrees, ranging from effects which are slight or negligible to ones which are striking in intensity. Findings in psychoanalysis parallel and extend those in psychology, the beneficial role of religion in psychotherapy being widely recognized. At the same time, psychologists and psychoanalysts have noted that religion is not uniform in its benefits, but may impose damaging stress and strain upon personality, may restrict or inhibit normal growth and adjustment to life situations, and may afford escape mechanisms which enervate personality. Sociologists and anthropologists have approached religion from the standpoint of the functions which it performs in human life. Agreement is substantial that beneficial functions are performed by religious institutions. At the same time, dysfunctions are noted, such as restrictions upon personality development, internal value conflicts in personality, clashes between conflicting religious ideologies, religious prejudice and discrimination, and religious ideas which are a divisive instead of an integrative factor in family life. With respect to causing harm, as well as good, religion is no more impeccable than politics. It can be beneficial or harmful, depending upon the details of the religious pattern involved. Just as the benefits of most governments outweigh their evils, so those of most religions outweigh their deficiencies. In neither case need one become an anarchist, since discernible defects are frequently correctible.

The research problem is not one of whether the hypothesis of beneficial effects is true in general, but rather it is one of how large are the effects, what in religion is responsible for the effects, and how can they be augmented and harmful countereffects avoided. In order to examine carefully a relationship of cause and effect, it is necessary to define fully the objects which are considered to be cause and effect, and then to observe what happens when the cause is present and when it is absent. The effects attributed to religion afford no particular problem of definition. The primary question of definition is that of specifying the higher power hypothesized as the cause, which is the task of this chapter. This power is believed by some religious psychologists to exist outside the verifiable empirical realm, in which case it is impossible to demonstrate both cause and effect by science. Another view is that beneficial effects occur in religion for reasons other than a higher power but that a belief in it is satisfying to followers of religion. This view is one testable by science. A third view is that an empirically definable power functions in religious phenomena. We turn initially to an overall review of these three types of theories.

TYPES OF CAUSAL EXPLANATION FOR RELIGIOUS EFFECTS

Supernaturalist

We consider first scientists who hold supernatural beliefs. A scientist speaking as a supernaturalist is not drawing upon his competence as an empirical investigator, but rather speaks from the chair of a philosopher. In this category may be noted William James and other religious psychologists since James who are convinced that the psychological effects of God are results of supernatural intervention, a viewpoint entering psychology from Christianity.

> The further limits of our being plunge, it seems to me, into an altogether other dimension of existence from the sensible and merely "understandable" world. Name it the mystical region, or the supernatural region, whichever you choose. So far as our ideal impulses originate in this region (and most of them do originate in it, for we find them possessing us in a way for which we cannot articulately account), we belong to it in a more intimate sense than that in which we belong to the visible world, for we belong in the most intimate sense wherever our ideals belong. Yet the unseen region in question is not merely ideal, for it produces effects in this world. When we commune with it, work is actually done upon our finite personality, for we are turned into new men, and consequences in the way of conduct follow in the natural world upon our regenerative change. But that which produces effects within another reality must be termed a reality itself, so I feel as if we had no philosophic excuse for calling the unseen or mystical world unreal.
>
> God is the natural appellation, for us Christians at least, for the supreme reality, so I will call this higher part of the universe by the name of God. We and God have business with each other; and in opening ourselves to his influence our deepest destiny is fulfilled. The universe, at those parts of it which our personal being constitutes, takes a turn genuinely for the worse or for the better in proportion as each one of us fulfills or evades God's demands.[1]
>
> What the more characteristically divine facts are, apart from the actual inflow of energy in the faith-state and the prayer-state, I know not. But the over-belief on which I am ready to make my personal venture is that they exist. The whole drift of my education goes to persuade me that the world of our present consciousness is only one out of many worlds of consciousness that exist, and that those other worlds must contain experiences which have a meaning for our life also; and that although in the main their experiences and those of this world keep discrete, yet the two become continuous at certain points, and higher energies filter in. . . . I suppose that my belief that in communion with the Ideal new force comes into the world, and new departures are made here below, subjects me to being classed among the supernaturalists of the piecemeal or crasser type.[2]

The supernaturalism of James is more sophisticated than that of many religiously orthodox persons. The comments of J. B. Pratt from the standpoint of psychology on this general form of supernaturalism cast light upon its implications for science.

[1] William James, *The Varieties of Religious Experience,* Modern Library, 1936, pp. 506–507. Permission to reprint granted by Paul R. Reynolds & Son, 599 Fifth Ave., New York, N.Y.

[2] *Ibid.,* pp. 509, 511.

This is, of course, the view held by the Roman Catholic Church and the many learned writers on mysticism who represent it. More important still, this is the view of most of the mystics themselves. In the ecstasy, say they, the soul comes face to face with God and receives from God revelations, comfortings, assistance which it can carry back into the world for the help of all the faithful. This hypothesis is usually based upon a dualistic view of the universe as consisting of the two realms of Nature and of Grace, each with its own laws; and the contact of the soul with the Supernatural realm in the mystic union is regarded as more or less miraculous.[3]

I do not see that this view of the Supernatural can be proved false. There are too many seeming gaps in our experience, too much that is unexpected and unaccountable in our lives, for us to be able to demonstrate in them an unbroken causal chain. As a fact, to be sure, this view of the Supernatural so far as it concerns the outer world has been largely given up;—and, it must be added, with no great harm to the cause of religion. In the inner world, however, it is still defended, and the theologian and philosopher are perfectly free to accept and vindicate it. But the psychologist is not free to do so. If the Supernatural breaks in upon the natural, psychology as a science is *so far forth* impossible. The theological explanation is no explanation for the psychologist, because it is not capable of being confirmed by experience. And for psychology, or any science, to admit that there are any facts incapable of being explained, incapable of being regularly connected with the other facts of experience, would be a surrender of its fundamental presuppositions. For its own protection science must *act as if* this view of the Supernatural and its interruptions of the natural were false. It cannot take cognizance of interruptions.[4]

The theory that events occur in this world caused by realities in another is in effect a declaration that things happen in this world without any causes in this world. In particular, James contends that ideals have their origin in the supernatural, whereas most psychologists conclude that ideals, like other components of personality, come into being through the causal processes of personality development. These causes are utilized in controlling the development of personality in the educational process. J. H. Leuba joins Pratt in rejecting on scientific grounds the supernaturalism of James.

Should God act in this manner, nothing ought to be easier for the psychologist than to show in the life of feeling and of thought disturbances not depending upon known natural causes. The student of religious life would be in the position of the astronomer who knows that certain stars are affected by forces of which he does not yet under-

[3] J. B. Pratt, *The Religious Consciousness,* Macmillan, 1920, p. 442.
[4] *Ibid.,* pp. 38–39.

stand the source. The fact is that, in proportion as psychology advances, the apparent anomalies of the religious life are more and more completely explained according to known laws.[5]

In James's supernaturalism we are rejecting a fundamental assumption of science, that events occur in a uniform order of cause and effect within the empirical world. A scientist should be open-minded about the assumption of the uniformity of nature. What Shakespeare has Hamlet say, "There are more things in heaven and earth, Horatio, than are dreamt of in your philosophy," applies even more to science whose dimensions and presuppositions are narrow and restrictive. However, this open-mindedness in science extends to the eager search for fresh data which demonstrate that events occur uncaused by realities in this world, that is, which happen contrary to known laws. Supernaturalists in recorded literature have assembled some evidence to show that the beneficial effects attributed to God are not explicable in terms of antecedent conditions in personality or its environmental situation. The most striking cases are those of faith healing, such as the following cure reported by L. D. Weatherhead, which took place after the patient bathed in the spring at Lourdes.

Mademoiselle C.D. was born in 1906. In 1922, at the age of sixteen, she was diagnosed as having tuberculous peritonitis and was treated with sunlight therapy. In 1924 she developed a right-sided pleurisy. In 1928 her tuberculous peritonitis flared up again and an exploratory operation was performed. She was subsequently moved to a sanatorium for tuberculous cases. In 1931 she developed an internal tuberculous abscess, and in 1934 involvement of her kidneys was confirmed by her passing blood and tubercle bacilli in her urine. Her general condition deteriorated, and in 1935 she was operated on again for intestinal obstruction due to pressure on the intestine from enlarged tuberculous glands. Towards the end of 1935 she also developed signs of involvement of the membranes covering the brain (meningitis). In 1936 she developed severe renal pain from further involvement of the kidneys. At the end of this year she was discharged from the sanatorium, being regarded as incurable. In 1939 tuberculosis of the right lung developed and was confirmed by X-rays. In 1940 the glands in her abdomen resulted in severe intestinal colic, and she developed a high fever. There were definite cavities now present in the right lung, and, in addition, she had septic tuberculous sinuses opening into the skin. In 1941 an attempt was made to collapse her right lung, but adhesions prevented this. She had lost a great deal of weight and had confirmed

[5] J. H. Leuba, *A Psychological Study of Religion,* Macmillan, 1912, p. 242.

tuberculosis of the lung, kidneys, peritoneum and intestinal glands. The prognosis seemed to be hopeless.

She was taken to Lourdes on October 6, 1941. At 2 P.M. on October 7 she entered the bath, and at 7 P.M. a medical examination showed her urine to be clear of tubercle bacilli. She had no pain in the abdomen and her body seemed to have changed, in that it was supple instead of tense. She was later examined by Dr. Y., who reported that there was now no cough, that the sputum and gastric juice were negative for tubercle bacilli, and that she had no fever and no pain in the area of the kidneys.

The patient was subsequently examined by eight doctors, and the most stringent tests for tuberculosis were applied, and the conclusion reached that the patient's body was entirely free from tuberculosis.

She has been re-examined at Lourdes at yearly intervals since her cure, and the last report of her was to the effect that she was a normal healthy woman. Mademoiselle C.D. is recorded as having been cured miraculously through the offices of the Blessed Virgin.[6]

It is of scientific interest to speculate whether the healing described was a rare but chance occurrence, or whether some psychic power of mind over body was involved, or whether there was an actual suspension of physical laws of disease through supernatural intervention. At any rate, this is one of numerous cases reported of the escape from seemingly inevitable disease or death. But such evidence is imperfectly articulated from the standpoint of research design. Only 2 percent of the sick patients who bathe at Lourdes come back cured. A valid experimental test would divide the prospective patients at random into two groups, one of which would take the cure, the other serving as a control to learn the incidence of recovery by chance circumstances. Until confronted with adequate evidence, one must as a scientist question the type of supernaturalism which goes counter to the main stream of scientific principles. The more plausible explanation of the cures at Lourdes is that psychological healing is involved, the overcoming of fear being one of the powerful factors in recovering from destructive illness. The body of scientific evidence that the beneficial effects of religion stem from natural causes is considerable and is reviewed at some length in this book. To the extent that this evidence shows the higher power of religion to be a natural phenomenon, the hypothesis of independent supernatural causation is thereby excluded.

It should be noted, however, that from a philosophical standpoint this does not disprove the type of supernaturalism which

[6] From *Psychology, Religion and Healing,* by Leslie D. Weatherhead. Copyright 1951 by Pierce and Smith. By permission of Abingdon Press.

can be harmonized with science. If a cosmic mind in its operations possesses the same parallelism and synchronization with the natural universe as the human mind possesses in relation to its body, such a philosophical view of God is compatible with science. But such supernatural parallelism is superfluous from the standpoint of scientific explanation, however meaningful it may be in philosophy. The chain of causes and effects in the natural universe forms a closed series sufficient by itself. From a practical standpoint the causal process can be entirely controlled through use of natural causes as means of manipulation.

The views of psychologists who believe in supernatural intervention are given little further attention here since the achievement from their scientific study amounts to a description of what man does to influence the higher power and of the effects which are produced. This description differs little from that given by natural scientists studying the same religious behavior. Those religious psychologists who follow the pattern of William James in mixing science and the supernatural are to be commended for their pursuit of difficult problems, and their investigations should certainly be encouraged. At the present time their substantive findings seem too few and too speculative to warrant their inclusion in an introductory scientific work such as this, although it must be recognized that they have a substantial following in the reading public. In particular, James's supernaturalism is defended by him on pragmatic rather than scientific grounds. In *The Will to Believe* in 1897 he declared that when a hypothesis can be neither proved nor disproved, it has a claim to be believed if accepting it produces beneficial results.[7] On this basis the existence of God is to be believed because the belief works. This is philosophy, not science.

Rationalist

The most frequent answers given in psychological and social science to the question of what produces the beneficial effects of religion involve no introduction of supernatural influences into the natural world. Within the category of answers for which scientific investigation is by itself sufficient we note two subgroups of naturalists, who may be referred to as rationalists and empiricists and who constitute important schools of scientific thought about religion. The rationalists usually acknowledge the worth-while effects of religion but trace them to natural causes

[7] William James, *The Will to Believe,* Dover, 1956.

other than a higher power inside or outside of personality which can be meaningfully called *God*. They conclude that the belief in God is beyond empirical validation, and the empirical task which remains is to explain how human beings happen to have such a belief and the useful functions which this belief performs in improving human life. The belief is explained as a rationalization produced by various intellectual or emotional forces in personality. Rationalists usually make no attempt from a scientific standpoint to prove or disprove the correctness of religious beliefs, recognizing that these may stem from logically sound philosophical reasoning. The circumstance, however, that man feels so overwhelming a need to build philosophy to make meaningful the gaps in his experience is an important factor, apart from whether his philosophy is adequately demonstrated. At its broadest the approach of rationalists extends to a study of the mental processes whereby a particular religious philosophy is achieved and considers the personality needs which are served. Those who may be called rationalists are not in agreement and represent various colors of thought along a band. The separation of rationalists and empiricists from each other is frequently artificial since eclectics draw upon both types of analysis in their explanation of religious beliefs.

Among the rationalists are found classical anthropologists, such as Tylor and Frazer, who have delineated psychological compulsions which lead primitives to develop their religious and magical beliefs, and sociologists who find the basis for religious beliefs and practices in the functions which are thereby served. Also included are psychologists, such as Freud who attributes the belief in God to the wish by the growing adolescent to find a substitute for the human father who no longer shelters the child in adulthood, and predecessors of Freud, L. A. Feuerbach and Wilhelm Wundt. Rationalists, apart from Freud, have usually been intellectually content to permit human beings to hold speculative beliefs or even those palpably erroneous. Their concern has merely been to show how human beings happen to possess such beliefs. Some rationalists are emphatic in underscoring the functional importance of religion as an indispensable system of thought, feeling, and action.

An important sector of causation of religion is developed by rationalists in social science. To a greater or lesser extent, all religions have been permeated by a rationalizing tendency, an overwhelming desire to make over the universe as the man-child would like it to be. He does this by creating enough assets in the form of philosophically assumed realities to counterbalance the ugliness and unpleasantness which sometimes characterize human life. We return to the causes which produce religious rationalization in a later chapter.

Related to scientists who explain why man has religious beliefs are philosophers whose concern is to establish logical reasons why religious beliefs about empirically unprovable phenomena are valid. In the first instance the analysis is in terms of psychological traits of man as a philosopher, and in the second instance these traits are exhibited during the construction of philosophy. Supernaturalists who philosophize fall under the latter heading. James's pragmatism is an example of his role as a philosopher. Another American religious psychologist to be classified in both science and philosophy is J. B. Pratt, whose concern in science is to explain why man builds religious philosophy and whose concern in philosophy is to demonstrate spiritual realities underlying intuitive impressions. A sociologist who has stoutly defended religion from both scientific and philosophical standpoints is C. A. Ellwood. He argues that the content of religious beliefs is philosophical, but that religious beliefs are justified from a scientific standpoint because of the demonstrable human values which they serve. He views God as the hypothesis of a moral power assumed to fit observed facts of human life. The God whom he affirms without undertaking an adequate demonstration is largely what empiricists affirm through analysis of experience of human beings.[8]

Empiricist

Turning to empiricists, we are confronted by scientific investigators who conclude that religious beliefs are not simply constructs of the imagination but are derived from the inward experience of man. Their view of the beneficial effects of religion is that these are caused by the operation of psychological forces which, through conscious or unconscious thought processes, give man a concept of a supreme power or God. For the most part such a concept is handed down and modified from generation to generation, and people are dimly or partially aware of the psychological antecedents out of which it has developed. A psychological task of large magnitude is presented by the discovery of the psychological variables whose functioning is reflected in the concept of God in different religions. The conclusion

[8] C. A. Ellwood, *The Reconstruction of Religion,* Macmillan, 1925.

of empiricists is that among the ideas and motives which function within personality is a dynamic system which performs the role of the higher power in religion. These ideas and motives are found in inward experience, they have their physiological basis in the brain and nervous system, and they express themselves in behavior. With reference to the pantheon of spirits and deities which human beings have at intervals in history or prehistory discovered within themselves, there exist a series of dynamic complexes which give empirical reality to these spirits or deities.

Empiricists usually recognize that man also engages in much philosophizing about the higher powers of religion, attributing to them many empirically unprovable characteristics. This is man's effort to construct a meaningful web between the psychological realities he discovers within himself and the universe outside. Empiricists introduce much of the analysis of rationalists in explaining why man builds speculative systems about his psychological nature. Although empiricists are not in agreement among themselves, they find a minimum platform in their principle that psychological forces in personality provide man with an empirical basis for his belief that there is a higher power to which he turns and which gives him psychological help.

The trend among empiricists is from merely noting that man has an empirical basis for his theological beliefs to conducting empirical analysis to define as fully as possible what the higher power operating in personality is and what its relationship to the rest of personality is. This project is necessary in order to delineate fully the empirical basis for religious beliefs and activities. Inevitably through this project religious psychologists become theologians in an empirical sense, even though religious leaders or laymen are reluctant to acknowledge a psychological approach to God. Apart from the question of what verbal label is appropriate in the scientific sense to refer to religious reality, the empiricist is drawn into the question of what this reality is and how maximum benefit may result from its functioning. If the analysis shows there to be a distinctive manifestation for which other psychological terms do not suffice, some sort of verbal label must be assigned. A psychologist more widely known for his work in mathematical models, R. B. Cattell, invented a scientific term, *Theopsyche,* but the designation has not gained acceptance since it means much the same as what many others mean by the word *God.* The prospect of a scientific theology is relatively new to religionists and social scientists alike. In this developing situation one is well advised from a scientific standpoint to entertain no preconceived conclusions, but to proceed with analysis patiently until new points of arrival become clearer. No inherent reason exists why man's religious ideas cannot continue to function in the context of psychological science as they have in past centuries, and it would not be unusual if the scientific method of inquiry, which has unearthed so much about the physical universe, also contributed something new to an understanding of man's religious life.

What is done in the remainder of this chapter and the two following ones is to note the developing stems and leaves of thought among empiricists and to attempt to bring some of these things to a clearer stage which they may be expected to reach. Individuals whose writings within science are relevant in this development include E. S. Ames, R. B. Cattell, G. A. Coe, John Dewey, Emile Durkheim, L. A. Feuerbach, G. S. Hall, William James, C. G. Jung, J. H. Leuba, D. C. Macintosh, P. A. Sorokin, W. Robertson Smith, and H. N. Wieman. These write from the standpoint of psychology except Durkheim and Sorokin (sociology), Macintosh (empirical theology), and Robertson Smith (biblical criticism). The writings of most of these men cover the past fifty years. Owing to the reciprocal influence they have upon each other, an arrangement of their work by chronology is not especially meaningful. It is more effective to view their work as providing a general movement from which various details can be culled which demonstrate particular points.

Historical Background of Empiricist Analysis of Religion

Before proceeding with major developments, mention may be made of several men whose work marks the transition of empiricist analysis of religion from philosophy to psychology and sociology, since such mention provides a fuller historical setting. David Hume, the eighteenth-century Scottish empiricist philosopher, was an early pioneer in the scientific study of religion, using the data of both history and religious experience to examine the beliefs and practices of religion. A German contemporary, Immanuel Kant, found the essence of religion in devotion to moral duty to one's fellow men and argued that consciousness of moral commands implies a God whose will is present in moral commands. While this line of analysis is a form of rationalist philosophy, it comes close to identifying God's will with the moral imperatives which man experiences within himself, a dominant viewpoint in current empiricist religious psychology. F. E. D. Schleiermacher, a younger contemporary of Kant, considered the essence of religion to be a feeling of absolute dependence. This experience of dependence implied the existence of a higher power or God as a cause of the feeling. These developments in philosophy are significant as attempts to derive the existence of God from the empirical facts of religious experience.

The somewhat nebulous work of another German philosopher, Hegel, also contains important elements of empiricist analysis of religion. His esoteric view of humanity inhabited by a divine oversoul of which individual souls are manifestations found more concrete expression in the work of Comte, Robertson Smith, and Durkheim. His concept of God as consisting of ideals in the process of becoming received fuller development at the hands of Feuerbach, Dewey, and Leuba. The voluminous work of Hegel has been succinctly summarized in one volume by W. T. Stace. He describes Hegel's view of God as follows.

> This individual human mind, in its immediacy, its particularity, its finiteness, is *not* God. It is precisely because of its immediacy, particularity, and finiteness, that it feels and knows itself as separate from God, as alienated from Him. It is only by renouncing and giving up its particularity that it can enter into union with God. I, as this particular ego, with all my selfish impulses, my foolish whims and caprices, am essentially *not* the universal mind, but only a particular mind. Nevertheless the universal mind is in me, and is my essential core and substance. We have already seen, in the spheres of morality and the state, how the individual mind has to forego its personal ends, adopt universal ends, and thereby develop the universal mind within itself. And the universal mind is none other than the mind of God, who is, therefore, my inner core and essence in so far as I can give up my particularity and rise to the height of the universal. It is not held to be either pantheism or blasphemy to say that God is in the hearts of good men; and this is the Hegelian position.[9]

Ludwig Feuerbach, also a German, was a provocative pioneer in empiricist thought who identified God with man and supposed he had thereby dispensed with the need for most traditional religious ideas. Much of religion for Feuerbach was wishful thinking, foreshadowing studies by Tylor, Wundt, and Freud. He was a sharp critic of orthodox religious ideas, a characteristic which has made him popular with agnostics but has alienated much of his positive contributions from the main stream of religious psychology in church circles. His critical commentary, *The Essence of Christianity,* contains basic empiricist developments,

[9] W. T. Stace, *The Philosophy of Hegel,* Dover, 1955, pp. 489–490.

but his ideas are not presented with scientific appeal. He is more to be classed as a speculative theorizer than as a psychologist of religion.

The work of a nineteenth-century German theologian, Albrecht Ritschl, preceding empiricist religious psychology is distinctive in its contribution. While denying that study of religious experience can be a science, he also claimed it did not belong to speculative philosophy. He sought to establish it as a field independent of both science and philosophy, an area of human consciousness in which value judgments are revealed, those which make up Christian doctrine. This divorce of intuitive religious knowledge from philosophy went far to open the door for scientific examination of religious experience. Leuba grasped the door opened by Ritschl to insist that study of religious experience belongs to psychology. Leuba summarizes his argument by saying: "This section has come to its logical conclusion: the claim that 'inner experience' is independent of psychological science remains unsubstantiated. I trust it has become clear that the hope to lift a theology based on inner experience out of the sphere of science is preposterous; since whatever appears in consciousness is material for psychology."[10] The study of interior religious life which was for Kant and Schleiermacher a branch of philosophy and for Ritschl neither philosophy nor science becomes for Leuba, Jung, and other religious psychologists the scientific study of religious motivation and experience. Nevertheless, Ritschl's viewpoint about the separate domain of value judgments has widely persisted in social science as well as theology. Ernst Troeltsch and Max Weber in sociology have maintained a similar separation between empirical social study and the analysis of religious values. In recent decades social scientists have shown increasing readiness to test value judgments by empirical investigation.

Two nineteenth-century attempts to make theological study an empirical science were those by Auguste Comte and Gustav Fechner, a French sociologist and a German psychologist, who each proclaimed a scientific religion for humanity. The cult of Comte takes enlightened humanity for its God and has satirically been called Catholicism minus Christianity because of the elaborate ecclesiastical organization proposed. Known principally for his fundamental research in psychological measurement, Fechner sought through this to give religious study a more secure footing in psychology. Actually his analysis of religion is as much phi-

[10] Leuba, *op. cit.*, p. 242.

losophy as it is psychology. William James acknowledges his intellectual debt to him. Although their empirical accomplishments in the study of religion were slight, Comte and Fechner helped to localize the components of the higher power of religion in society and in the individual, conceptual approaches now refined to theoretical importance in the scientific study of religion. Moving nearer the present, Durkheim's social analysis of religion owes much to Comte. Dewey's work builds upon the social and idealistic concepts of religion proposed by predecessors, notably Kant, Hegel, and Comte.

Beyond the sources described here, the roots of religious empiricism spread out in many directions and reach into ancient and modern cultures, the history of ideas repeating itself as well as succeeding itself. Several works of descriptive and bibliographical assistance in the history of religious psychology may be noted, those of E. A. Burtt, G. A. Coe, and D. C. Macintosh bearing directly on this theme, and those of E. G. Boring and F. B. Karpf affording more general background in psychological and social science.[11]

While the empiricist controversy has moved from a philosophical setting to a scientific one, it continues among philosophers, recent participants in the debate being F. R. Tennant (antiempiricist), and D. L. Scudder and D. E. Trueblood (pro-empiricist).[12] Primary factors in the shift of religious study from philosophy to science have been the growing recognition of interior experience as a topic for scientific study and the growing competence of scientific procedures to deal with research problems of religion. Early milestones in scientific achievement were the studies of primitive religion made by Tylor, Spencer, and Frazer, and that of eastern religions by M. Müller. Following these studies, the interest of psychologists turned to the phenomenon of religious conversion, especially as this occurs in Christianity. Are the benefits of conversion claimed actually achieved? Is God a secure fact of inner experience or a supposition? By the turn of the twentieth century, psychologists of religion were considering these problems, and at the same time

[11] E. A. Burtt, *Types of Religious Philosophy,* Harper, 1939; G. A. Coe, *The Psychology of Religion,* University of Chicago Press, 1916; D. C. Macintosh, *The Problem of Religious Knowledge,* Harper, 1940; E. G. Boring, *A History of Experimental Psychology,* Appleton-Century-Crofts, 1950; F. B. Karpf, *American Social Psychology,* McGraw-Hill, 1932.

[12] F. R. Tennant, *Philosophical Theology,* Cambridge University Press, 1935, 2 vols.; D. L. Scudder, *Tennant's Philosophical Theology,* Yale University Press, 1940; D. E. Trueblood, *Philosophy of Religion,* Harper, 1957.

psychoanalytic study of religion and personality was making rapid progress in the hands of Freud and his followers. The stage was set for social and psychological science to turn its tools to analysis of empirical aspects of the religious power in man's existence, whatever this might be.

Empiricist theories have generated considerable counterargument within the framework of scientific discussion as well as outside. Theologians and religious leaders have been slow to turn over their subject matter to a branch of science or even to let science have a look at it. At the same time, those already established in psychological and social science have looked questioningly at the work of empiricists in religious psychology. Rationalists, especially, have been critical of empiricist analysis, although no necessary conflict exists when it is recognized that religious belief may come out of both need and experience. Because of the scientific questions involved in the controversy and its practical interest to followers of religion, the debate within science is reviewed in some detail.

Importance of the Empiricist Controversy

That we now turn to this difficult and perplexing topic, in which tangible data are so obviously lacking, is not simply a line of inquiry pursued from curiosity. If it is indeed the case that God, or something to which human beings refer when they talk about God, is a category of human personality, then our scientific obligation to confront and to characterize that category from an empirical standpoint is clear. We propose in a scientific inquiry to describe religion, all of its empirical aspects, both interior and exterior. Since it is evident that man's ideas of God are very compelling aspects of his religions, we need to exhaust the opportunities for examining their empirical basis before halting the inquiry. To study religion without considering the empirical extent of this central reality may be likened to a description of a wedding which takes no note of the bride except what others think about her. However she is hidden beneath veils and flowers, her role is central. In a practical vein, to study government without analyzing the intangible power in the minds of people by which it is maintained would give a fragmentary view of political science. To study religion without examining the nature of the power utilized in religion would similarly yield an incomplete understanding of religion.

Metaphors aside, the topic is difficult and perplexing since it extends into the heart of the problem of describing man's inward experience when definitive indices of this in external behavior are lacking to an unusual degree. Man pursues food or sex, and the nature of his desire can at once be inferred. Man pursues God, and neither the desire nor its object can be found in the external world of sense perception so confidently relied upon in many matters of scientific inquiry. Yet the quest for the nature of man's experience of God differs in degree, not in kind, from the quest for delineating other aspects of his inward experience which psychology and psychoanalysis endeavor to explore. One must proceed as well as one can along the obscure pathways in inward experience, getting definite bearings at those occasional points where facets of observable behavior provide bench marks. These provide partial checks upon the accuracy of the route traveled and increase its precision, but they do not illuminate the untraveled road ahead. One relies upon introspective study of one's own interior processes and those of others to follow the continuing route of insight. Religious experiences are a commonplace possession, but the intellectual resolution of such experiences into the components of thought and motivation is less easily achievable. Years of effort may be required before the individual student can with confidence say that he does or does not discern the specific elements fused in the concrete inward experience.

The apparent reason why religious doctrines function effectively when taken on faith is that the individual is assured that the component elements are actually contained in his interior experience even though he is unable intellectually to abstract them. By attributing the doctrines to a supernatural origin, the uncertain task of their rediscovery in inward experience is avoided. As far as the concrete religious experiences are concerned, these can be regained by acquiring the appropriate beliefs and attitudes and following the prescribed exercises and rituals. Intellectual analysis of religious experience becomes unnecessary to the achievement of such experience. Offsetting the easy security of ready-made dogma, the advantages of intellectual analysis are large: more effective control over religious life, retention by the individual of self-determination, an open highway to the discovery of deeper religious truth in the future, and firmer conviction given by adequate proof. Notwithstanding the recurring effort to give religious principles supernatural sanction which obviates need for demonstration, the human mind has a restless curiosity to prove or disprove the puzzling doctrines of religion.

It does not occur to the primitive mind that it is necessary to prove the existence of gods or spirits. These are taken for granted and passed along from generation to generation through custom and experience. The intellectual demonstration of the existence of God is a latter-day development which can be attributed on the one hand to man losing touch with the simple emotional experiences from which his gods took form, a loss apparent when written literature became a substitute for realities in experience. On the other hand, as man's capacity for systematic speculation grew and he became accustomed to philosophical argument, he became self-conscious of the need for proof of his religious imagery. From either standpoint, he came to feel it necessary to prove the existence of that which he lost or could not firmly grasp.

The arguments for the existence of a religious being have usually been philosophical in character, man seeking to regain the spiritual realities of tribal existence by that route which he traveled in projecting his imaginative systems of theology. In various ways from Plato to the present, philosophers have endeavored to show by the artifices of systematic speculation that a reasonable interpretation of life or of the universe implies logically the existence of God. Succeeding thinkers culminating with Kant showed that none of these arguments, however plausible or ingenious, is logically rigorous. In the past century the ground of the argument shifted away from philosophy toward science, and it is at this point where we begin our consideration of it.

Our immediate task is to specify what the higher power is to which effects in religion are attributed. The higher power is identified by some of the investigators analyzing it with what people speak of as God. For the moment any theological implications do not concern us. We seek rather for the psychological and social elements in which the higher power or what is referred to as God consists. Preceding investigators have not adequately separated the task of empirical definition from the task of predicating theological characteristics, and in quoting from their historic and authoritative writings, definitions are not always distinct from predications. We return in later chapters to the question of what may be causally or functionally demonstrated about the phenomenon considered to have characteristics of force, power, or dynamism, these terms being similarly used by those analyzing the higher power of religion.

THE HIGHER POWER AS A MOTIVATIONAL SYSTEM

In 1902 James endeavored to set forth the most which psychology can say concerning religious experience, drawing his conclusions from case studies, and at the same time to indicate where the "over-beliefs" from philosophy begin. Far from settling the mounting questions, James's work opened these for wider discussion. His views provide a useful historical starting point in reviewing the questions involved.

James's Concept of the Higher Self

In the processes of religious behavior James finds that a "higher self" functions as a system within human personality. That this self exists in the form of interior feelings and attitudes does not, in James's view, detract from the factual quality of its existence. Concerning the firm status of interior data he says:

> That unsharable feeling which each one of us has of the pinch of his individual destiny as he privately feels it rolling out on fortune's wheel may be disparaged for its egotism, may be sneered at as unscientific, but it is the one thing that fills up the measure of our concrete actuality, and any would-be existent that should lack such a feeling, or its analogue, would be a piece of reality only half made up.
>
> If this be true, it is absurd for science to say that the egotistic [interior] elements of experience should be suppressed. The axis of reality runs solely through the egotistic places—they are strung upon it like so many beads. To describe the world with all the various feelings of the individual pinch of destiny, all the various spiritual attitudes, left out from the description—they being as describable as anything else—would be something like offering a printed bill of fare as the equivalent for a solid meal. Religion makes no such blunder. The individual's religion may be egotistic, and those private realities which it keeps in touch with may be narrow enough; but at any rate it always remains infinitely less hollow and abstract, as far as it goes, than a science which prides itself on taking no account of anything private at all.
>
> A bill of fare with one real raisin on it instead of the word "raisin," with one real egg instead of the word "egg," might be an inadequate meal, but it would at least be a commencement of reality. The contention of the survival-theory that we ought to stick to non-personal elements exclusively seems like saying that we ought to be satisfied forever with reading the naked bill of fare.[13]

By *self* is meant a portion of the individual's personality of which he is aware, and by *higher* is meant what is ideal or more

[13] James, *op. cit.,* pp. 489–490.

valuable from the standpoint of the individual and the group. It is the kind of self to which people aspire and the kind of life they would like to lead more fully than when living under the influence of the lower self which is self-seeking. The higher self may be manifested simply as higher ideas and impulses, or as a general experience the individual feels comes from God, or as a psychic power given by Christ. Cases of each of these in relation to the lower self are cited by James. The first is a document concerning a young man in love with a girl whom he did not respect.

For two years of this time I went through a very bad experience, which almost drove me mad. I had fallen violently in love with a girl who, young as she was, had a spirit of coquetry like a cat. As I look back on her now, I hate her, and wonder how I could ever have fallen so low as to be worked upon to such an extent by her attractions. . . . Although for a year we took our meals at the same boarding house, so that I saw her continually and familiarly, our closer relations had to be largely on the sly, and this fact, together with my jealousy of another one of her male admirers and my own conscience despising me for my uncontrollable weakness, made me so nervous and sleepless that I really thought I should become insane. I understand well those young men murdering their sweethearts, which appear so often in the papers. Nevertheless I did love her passionately, and in some ways she did deserve it.

The queer thing was the sudden and unexpected way in which it all stopped. I was going to my work after breakfast one morning, thinking as usual of her and of my misery, when, just as if some outside power laid hold of me, I found myself turning round and almost running to my room, where I immediately got out all the relics of her which I possessed, including some hair, all her notes and letters, and ambrotypes on glass. The former I made a fire of, the latter I actually crushed beneath my heel, in a sort of fierce joy of revenge and punishment. I now loathed and despised her altogether, and as for myself I felt as if a load of disease had suddenly been removed from me. That was the end. I never spoke to her or wrote to her again in all the subsequent years, and I have never had a single moment of loving thought towards one who for so many months entirely filled my heart.[14]

James describes this situation as one of a divided self. "This seems to me an unusually clear example of two different levels of personality, inconsistent in their dictates, yet so well balanced against each other as for a long time to fill the life with discord and dissatisfaction. At last, not gradually, but in a sudden crisis, the unstable equilibrium is resolved, and this happens so unexpectedly that it is as if, to use the writer's words, 'some outside

[14] *Ibid.,* pp. 176–177.

power laid hold.' "[15] The next case cited from James is an autobiographical document of Tolstoi.

I remember one day in early spring, I was alone in the forest, lending my ear to its mysterious noises. I listened, and my thought went back to what for these three years it always was busy with—the quest of God. But the idea of him, I said, how did I ever come by the idea?

And again there arose in me, with this thought, glad aspirations towards life. Everything in me awoke and received a meaning. . . . Why do I look farther? a voice within me asked. He is there: he, without whom one cannot live. To acknowledge God and to live are one and the same thing. God is what life is. Well, then! live, seek God, and there will be no life without him. . . .

After this, things cleared up within me and about me better than ever, and the light has never wholly died away. I was saved from suicide. Just how or when the change took place I cannot tell. But as insensibly and gradually as the force of life had been annulled within me, and I had reached my moral death-bed, just as gradually and imperceptibly did the energy of life come back. And what was strange was that this energy that came back was nothing new. It was my ancient juvenile force of faith, the belief that the sole purpose of my life was to be *better*. I gave up the life of the conventional world, recognizing it to be no life, but a parody on life, which its superfluities simply keep us from comprehending.[16]

The third case refers to the higher self in Christological terms.

One Tuesday evening I sat in a saloon in Harlem, a homeless, friendless, dying drunkard. I had pawned or sold everything that would bring a drink. I could not sleep unless I was dead drunk. I had not eaten for days, and for four nights preceding I had suffered with delirium tremens, or the horrors, from midnight till morning. I had often said, "I will never be a tramp. I will never be cornered, for when that time comes, if ever it comes, I will find a home in the bottom of the river." But the Lord so ordered it that when that time did come I was not able to walk one quarter of the way to the river. As I sat there thinking, I seemed to feel some great and mighty presence. I did not know then what it was. I did learn afterwards that it was Jesus, the sinner's friend. I walked up to the bar and pounded it with my fist till I made the glasses rattle. Those who stood by drinking looked on with scornful curiosity. I said I would never take another drink, if I died on the street, and really I felt as though that would happen before morning. Something said, "If you want to keep this promise, go and have yourself locked up." I went to the nearest station-house and had myself locked up.

I was placed in a narrow cell, and it seemed as though all the demons

[15] *Ibid.*
[16] *Ibid.*, p. 182.

that could find room came in that place with me. This was not all the company I had, either. No, praise the Lord; that dear Spirit that came to me in the saloon was present, and said, Pray. I did pray, and though I did not feel any great help, I kept on praying. As soon as I was able to leave my cell I was taken to the police court and remanded back to the cell. I was finally released, and found my way to my brother's house, where every care was given me. While lying in bed the admonishing Spirit never left me, and when I arose the following Sabbath morning I felt that day would decide my fate, and toward evening it came into my head to go to Jerry McAuley's mission. I went. The house was packed, and with great difficulty I made my way to the space near the platform. There I saw the apostle to the drunkard and the outcast—that man of God, Jerry McAuley. He rose, and amid deep silence told his experience. There was a sincerity about this man that carried conviction with it, and I found myself saying, "I wonder if God can save *me?*" I listened to the testimony of twenty-five or thirty persons, every one of whom had been saved from rum, and I made up my mind that I would be saved or die right there. When the invitation was given, I knelt down with a crowd of drunkards. Jerry made the first prayer. Then Mrs. McAuley prayed fervently for us. Oh, what a conflict was going on for my poor soul! A blessed whisper said, "Come"; the devil said, "Be careful." I halted but a moment, and then, with a breaking heart, I said, "Dear Jesus, can you help me?" Never with mortal tongue can I describe that moment. Although up to that moment my soul had been filled with indescribable gloom, I felt the glorious brightness of the noonday sun shine into my heart. I felt I was a free man. Oh, the precious feeling of safety, of freedom, of resting on Jesus! I felt that Christ with all his brightness and power had come into my life; that, indeed, old things had passed away and all things had become new.

From that moment till now I have never wanted a drink of whiskey, and I have never seen money enough to make me take one. I promised God that night that if he would take away the appetite for strong drink, I would work for him all my life. He has done his part, and I have been trying to do mine.[17]

James's conclusions concerning the existence of the higher self in personality are given in the following citations.

The individual, so far as he suffers from his wrongness and criticizes it, is to that extent consciously beyond it, and in at least possible touch with something higher, if anything higher exist. Along with the wrong part there is thus a better part of him, even though it may be but a most helpless germ. With which part he should identify his real being is by no means obvious at this stage; but when stage 2 (the stage of solution or salvation) arrives, the man identifies his real being with the germinal higher part of himself; and does so in the fol-

[17] *Ibid.,* pp. 198–199.

lowing way. *He becomes conscious that this higher part is conterminous and continuous with a MORE of the same quality, which is operative in the universe outside of him, and which he can keep in working touch with, and in a fashion get on board of and save himself when all his lower being has gone to pieces in the wreck.*[18]

The "more," as we called it, and the meaning of our "union" with it, form the nucleus of our inquiry. Into what definite description can these words be translated, and for what definite facts do they stand? It would never do for us to place ourselves offhand at the position of a particular theology, the Christian theology, for example, and proceed immediately to define the "more" as Jehovah, and the "union" as his imputation to us of the righteousness of Christ. That would be unfair to other religions, and, from our present standpoint at least, would be an over-belief.

We must begin by using less particularized terms; and, since one of the duties of the science of religions is to keep religion in connection with the rest of science, we shall do well to seek first of all a way of describing the "more," which psychologists may also recognize as real. The *subconscious self* is nowadays a well-accredited psychological entity; and I believe that in it we have exactly the mediating term required.[19]

Let me then propose, as an hypothesis, that whatever it may be on its *farther* [supernatural] side, the "more" with which in religious experience we feel ourselves connected is on its *hither* side the subconscious continuation of our conscious life. Starting thus with a recognized psychological fact as our basis, we seem to preserve a contact with "science" which the ordinary theologian lacks. At the same time the theologian's contention that the religious man is moved by an external power is vindicated, for it is one of the peculiarities of invasions from the subconscious region to take on objective appearances, and to suggest to the Subject an external control. In the religious life the control is felt as "higher"; but since on our hypothesis it is primarily the higher faculties of our own hidden mind which are controlling, the sense of union with the power beyond us is a sense of something, not merely apparently, but literally true.[20]

Disregarding the over-beliefs, and confining ourselves to what is common and generic, we have in *the fact that the conscious person is continuous with a wider self through which saving experiences come,* a positive content of religious experience which, it seems to me, *is literally and objectively true as far as it goes.*[21]

By *subconscious* James apparently means what is usually designated by the term *unconscious.* The idea that an assumed

[18] *Ibid.,* pp. 498–499.
[19] *Ibid.,* p. 501.
[20] *Ibid.,* pp. 502–503.
[21] *Ibid.,* p. 505.

supernatural power introduces effects into the natural world through the medium of unconscious self is credited by James to F. W. Myers. We are not concerned with this supernatural theory except to the degree that it impinges on science. As far as James's empirical findings go, beneficial effects on personality take place. We are interested, however, in learning from what in the natural world these effects might arise.

James's supernaturalist conclusion, as was previously cited, is that the power lies outside the natural world and that human beings have access to it through prayer and faith. Let us examine this conclusion to see if we are brought to it by failure of natural causation. From an empirical standpoint it is acknowledged by James that the power operates through a psychological object, the higher self. This is the same as saying that the higher self is a link in the chain of causation between the supernatural power and the natural effects. That which is a link in a process of causation is itself a cause, and consequently the higher self is at least an instrumental cause of the beneficial effects upon personality.

What other causes are involved? If we fall back on supernatural explanation, the additional causes required to produce the effects on personality are outside the empirical realm. It is unnecessary to accept this explanation until the search for adequate causes in the natural realm has failed. A fundamental principle of science is that natural causes can be found for all changes taking place in the universe. Assuming that this principle is valid for personality processes, we are entitled to say that the higher power is contained entirely within human personality or the environmental influences which shape personality. The overwhelming weight of psychological opinion is that personality does conform to principles of natural causation, and research analysis will be reviewed which shows the higher power to be a part of a system of natural causation. The view that the power is contained in personality or its social environment is at least in harmony with James's data. Until data arise which occasion a reversal of judgment, it seems more appropriate to assume that the power is in the natural world than to assume that it is not.

We here define personality as the overall system of the individual's inward experience, behavior, and physiological make-up, and the natural environment refers to social and physical objects which are outside of this particular system. By system is meant a set of events which are related by cause and effect, or in the mathematical sense, which are functionally related variables. The personality system is part of a larger social system involving a plurality of persons. Within the personality system are complexes of causally related motives, ideas, and responses. Each motive and its related ideas and responses constitutes a motivational system.

The case studies in which the higher self has been described refer to aims, beliefs, and activities for a better life. Consequently the higher self is a motivational system. Whether the higher self contains all of the components of the higher power has not yet been shown by James's data or our interpretation of them. However, by reasoning from James's data, we conclude that the higher power is at least in part a motivational system. Just what the elements in this system of power are, how human beings have access to the system by religious procedures, and what the chain of causation between the power and its effects in transforming personality remain to be shown from other source material than that of James.

Dewey: The Power in Religion as That of Ideals in Process of Realization

John Dewey, E. S. Ames, and H. N. Wieman were a group of three philosophically oriented psychologists associated together at different times at the University of Chicago. Dewey, the eldest of the three, appears to be the initiator of their ideas, his writings containing recurring references to naturalistic religion, but his principal work in the field, *A Common Faith,* was not published until 1934. The major portion of his career was spent at Columbia University following a ten-year stay at Chicago which began in 1894 about the same time that Ames came to Chicago for his doctorate. Ames remained to teach philosophy and to serve as pastor at the University Church of the Disciples of Christ, and *The Psychology of Religious Experience* was published by him in 1910. H. N. Wieman became professor of the philosophy of religion at the University of Chicago Divinity School in 1927. His wife, Regina Wieman, is coauthor of his principal work, *Normative Psychology of Religion,* published in 1935. Also an associate of the group is D. C. Macintosh, a Baptist minister from Canada who took his doctorate at Chicago in 1909 and went on to write and to teach at Yale in theology as an "empirical science," as he called it. Critical of most other empirical viewpoints, he quotes Wieman's work with approval. The present author also studied at Chicago and has been influenced by this group.

Although philosophers in background, Dewey, Ames, and

Wieman proceed self-consciously as psychologists to base their concepts and conclusions upon empirical data. These data, for the most part, are not systematically compiled as case studies, but represent data contained in personal experience and in surrounding culture. The data are of a type accessible to students in their own lives. The procedure of analysis used by the three men is in part introspective, carried out by focusing attention upon their inward experiences as well as those of others. As a systematic procedure, this intuitive approach has made uneven progress in psychology generally. Although introspection is formally rejected by some psychologists, it is unusual to find a treatise in motivational psychology in which introspection does not at least play a role in the formulation of hypotheses, and often the role is evident in the theoretical interpretation of data by reading into these data meaningful realities from the inner experience of the investigator. The opinion of the present author is that introspection affords a technique indispensable to psychology in general and religious study in particular, and that the technique should be systematically practiced, rather than informally or unconsciously introduced in a manner which augments, rather than diminishes, the difficulty of securing reproducible results from its use.

Dewey is strongly critical of supernaturalism in religion, declaring that religious principles should be cast in psychological terms. In clearing away the dogmas of tradition he refers to these as "the useless lumber that blocks our highways of thought."[22] He insists upon the primacy of experience as the source of knowledge, not passive experience, but experience which comes to the individual during the ongoing process of solving the problems of living. Personal conviction comes not from what others say, but from the authority of one's ideals as these emerge during living.

> Conviction in the moral sense signifies being conquered, vanquished, in our active nature by an ideal end; it signifies acknowledgment of its rightful claim over our desires and purposes. Such acknowledgment is practical, not primarily intellectual. It goes beyond evidence that can be presented to *any* possible observer. Reflection, often long and arduous, may be involved in arriving at the conviction, but the import of thought is not exhausted in discovery of evidence that can justify intellectual assent. The authority of an ideal over choice and conduct is the authority of an ideal, not of a fact, of a

[22] John Dewey, *Contemporary American Philosophy,* Macmillan, 1930, Vol. II, p. 26.

truth guaranteed to intellect, not of the status of the one who propounds the truth.[23]

. . . new methods of inquiry and reflection have become for the educated man today the final arbiter of all questions of fact, existence, and intellectual assent. Nothing less than a revolution in the "seat of intellectual authority" has taken place. This revolution, rather than any particular aspect of its impact upon this and that religious belief, is the central thing. In this revolution, every defeat is a stimulus to renewed inquiry; every victory won is the open door to more discoveries, and every discovery is a new seed planted in the soil of intelligence, from which grow fresh plants with new fruits. The mind of man is being habituated to a new method and ideal: There is but one sure road of access to truth—the road of patient, coöperative inquiry operating by means of observation, experiment, record and controlled reflection.[24]

The argument that because some province or aspect of experience has not yet been "invaded" by scientific methods, it is not subject to them, is as old as it is dangerous. Time and time again, in some particular reserved field, it has been invalidated. Psychology is still in its infancy. He is bold to the point of rashness who asserts that intimate personal experience will never come within the ken of natural knowledge.[25]

With this psychological emphasis upon the source of religious knowledge, Dewey proceeds to develop the empirical nature of God as consisting of the union between man's ideals and what is being actualized by human effort, a concept related to Hegelian thought and introduced by Dewey in 1887.[26] In this concept Dewey refers to a motivational system embracing components of aim, belief, activity, and experience in the ongoing achievements of human beings. What is significant is that Dewey does not refer to static ideals contemplated as ideas but to ideals as motivating forces while these are producing action and are in process of fulfillment. A motivational system is alive and dynamic, engaged in doing something, not static and inert.

Ends, purposes, exercise determining power in human conduct. The aims of philanthropists, of Florence Nightingale, of Howard, of Wilberforce, of Peabody, have not been idle dreams. They have modified institutions. Aims, ideals, do not exist simply in "mind"; they exist in character, in personality and action. One might call the roll of artists, intellectual inquirers, parents, friends, citizens who are neighbors, to show that purposes exist in an *operative* way. What I have

[23] John Dewey, *A Common Faith,* Yale University Press, 1934, pp. 20–21.
[24] *Ibid.,* pp. 31–32.
[25] *Ibid.,* p. 35.
[26] John Dewey, *Psychology,* Harper, 1887, p. 244.

been objecting to, I repeat, is not the idea that ideals are linked with existence and that they themselves exist, through human embodiment, as forces, but the idea that their authority and value depend upon some prior complete embodiment—as if the efforts of human beings in behalf of justice, or knowledge or beauty, depended for their effectiveness and validity upon assurance that there already existed in some supernal region a place where criminals are humanely treated, where there is no serfdom or slavery, where all facts and truths are already discovered and possessed, and all beauty is eternally displayed in actualized form. . . .

Moreover the process of creation is experimental and continuous. The artist, scientific man, or good citizen, depends upon what others have done before him and are doing around him. The sense of new values that become ends to be realized arises first in dim and uncertain form. As the values are dwelt upon and carried forward in action they grow in definiteness and coherence. Interaction between aim and existent conditions improves and tests the ideal; and conditions are at the same time modified. Ideals change as they are applied in existent conditions. The process endures and advances with the life of humanity. What one person and one group accomplish becomes the standing ground and starting point of those who succeed them. When the vital factors in this natural process are generally acknowledged in emotion, thought and action, the process will be both accelerated and purified through elimination of that irrelevant element that culminates in the idea of the supernatural. When the vital factors attain the religious force that has been drafted into supernatural religions, the resulting reinforcement will be incalculable.

These considerations may be applied to the idea of God, or, to avoid misleading conceptions, to the idea of the divine. This idea is, as I have said, one of ideal possibilities unified through imaginative realization and projection. But this idea of God, or of the divine, is also connected with all the natural forces and conditions—including man and human association—that promote the growth of the ideal and that further its realization. We are in the presence neither of ideals completely embodied in existence nor yet of ideals that are mere rootless ideals, fantasies, utopias. For there are forces in nature and society that generate and support the ideals. They are further unified by the action that gives them coherence and solidity. It is this *active* relation between ideal and actual to which I would give the name "God." I would not insist that the name *must* be given. There are those who hold that the associations of the term with the supernatural are so numerous and close that any use of the word "God" is sure to give rise to misconception and be taken as a concession to traditional ideas. . . .

Whether one gives the name "God" to this union, operative in thought and action, is a matter for individual decision. But the *function* of such a working union of the ideal and actual seems to me to be identical with the force that has in fact been attached to the conception of God in all the religions that have a spiritual content; and a clear idea of that function seems to me urgently needed at the present time. . . .

One reason why personally I think it fitting to use the word "God" to denote that uniting of the ideal and actual which has been spoken of, lies in the fact that aggressive atheism seems to me to have something in common with traditional supernaturalism. I do not mean merely that the former is mainly so negative that it fails to give positive direction to thought, though that fact is pertinent. What I have in mind especially is the exclusive preoccupation of both militant atheism and supernaturalism with man in isolation. . . . A religious attitude, however, needs the sense of a connection of man, in the way of both dependence and support, with the enveloping world that the imagination feels is a universe. Use of the words "God" or "divine" to convey the union of actual with ideal may protect man from a sense of isolation and from consequent despair or defiance.

In any case, whatever the name, the meaning is selective. For it involves no miscellaneous worship of everything in general. It selects those factors in existence that generate and support our idea of good as an end to be striven for. It excludes a multitude of forces that at any given time are irrelevant to this function. Nature produces whatever gives reinforcement and direction but also what occasions discord and confusion. The "divine" is thus a term of human choice and aspiration. A humanistic religion, if it excludes our relation to nature, is pale and thin, as it is presumptuous, when it takes humanity as an object of worship.[27]

Dewey describes a psychological reality which is the acknowledged God of many persons in America who follow his thinking. He also believes that he correctly describes the empirical content of the God in whom traditional Jews or Christians believe, a topic for inquiry to which we return later. Ames's work, like that of Dewey, is revelatory of American culture in exemplifying the religious orientation of persons who accept his teaching or read his writings, as well as calling attention to the nature of the power in religion. From Ames's work in the psychology of religion the following passage refers to the idea of God as the higher power of religion and describes this idea as a motivational system.

The idea of God, in so far as it is a live idea in consciousness, carries with it this dynamic character. The attitudes and tendencies which it sets up when brought to the focus of attention depend upon the social

[27] John Dewey, *A Common Faith,* pp. 48–54. Reprinted by permission of Yale University Press. Copyright 1934 by Yale University Press.

relations and processes which operated in the formation of the idea in the individual or in the group from which he derived it. A person's idea of God may be taken as comprehending the highest ideal interests known or felt by him. It stands therefore for concrete purposeful activity and effort in those directions. Calling this idea to mind means putting one's self in an attitude consistent with the interests which controlled its formation. Therefore in a despotic society where sovereignty is idealized, to think of God means to humble one's self, to take on the postures and employ the phrases which a menial uses in the presence of his lord. The ritual and psalms of many oriental peoples illustrate this type of reverence and worship. But where the idea of God is the embodiment of ideals arising from democratic social movements, its presence in the mind expresses itself in motor reactions indicative of respect for the welfare of all members of society. The thought of God is then accompanied by impulses toward social conduct. In other words the idea of God, like any other general idea, signifies a system of habits, and in this case, as elsewhere, the presence of the idea has for its normal effect the initiation of those habitual attitudes and endeavors.[28]

Wieman calls attention to the growing nature of man's experience of God, and at the same time is more explicit concerning the affectionate motivation of which this experience consists.

This growth of meaning and value in the world is God. There are five grounds on which this claim rests.

1. Growth of meaning commands our supreme devotion and highest loyalty by right of its worthfulness.
2. It creates and sustains human personality.
3. It carries human personality to whatsoever highest fulfillments are possible to it.
4. It has more worth than personality, hence human personality finds its highest destiny in giving itself to this growth to be mastered, used and transformed by it into the fabric of emerging values.
5. The greatest values can be poured into human life only as we yield ourselves to the domination and control of this growth. When we try to dominate and use it, we lose these values.[29]

One of the most common cases of this superhuman growth is found in the friendship and love that grows up between two or more persons. When two complex personalities meet in such a way that the meanings of the one begin to modify and be modified by the meanings of the other, new activities are elicited in the individuals concerned, quite beyond any plan or intent in their minds. Also new activities, unforeseen by them, are elicited from their operative environment, in re-

[28] E. S. Ames, *The Psychology of Religious Experience,* Houghton Mifflin, 1910, p. 313.

[29] H. N. Wieman and R. W. Wieman, *Normative Psychology of Religion,* Crowell, 1935, p. 51.

sponse to these new activities in their respective ways of living. Some of these new activities in the several persons and their environment enter into connections of mutual support and mutual control. They do this not because of any planned effort on the part of the persons, but because the human organisms so function in relation to one another and with other features of environment, and the environment with them, that such connections develop. Thus the world takes on a richer body of meanings and values than it had before. Such is the creative process by which a friendship or a love or a beloved community grows.

Such enrichment of the world is a genuine creation in the sense that these meanings did not pertain to the existing world at all, prior to this kind of interaction between the persons and their operative environment. They were, of course, possibilities. But they could not be foreseen or known in their specific nature until this particular interaction occurred. This augmented enrichment of the world was not produced by men except that human personalities entered into the total process by which this greater system of value was brought forth.[30]

Sorokin: The Higher Power in Religion as That of Altruism

Ideals are motivating desires for something better. While ideals may refer to specific achievements in art, science, and literature, as well as in social welfare, their ultimate purpose is more abundant life for human beings, and in this way they become synonymous with altruistic motivation. While Dewey emphasizes ideals from the standpoint of goals in process of realization, others have dwelt primarily upon the altruistic nature of ideals and have analyzed them in terms of the process of human love rather than as aims for achievement. Wieman more than Dewey or Ames defines the higher power or God in terms of altruistic process. The idea that God is love is almost as old as human history. This thesis is a fundamental proposition of the religions of the world.

Russian thinkers in whose work the scientific study of altruism has deep intellectual roots are Feodor Dostoevski, N. F. Fedorov, V. S. Solovyev, and Leo Tolstoi. Those who ponder the loyalty of Russian people to their common good can usefully investigate the impact of such writers. A leading scientific student of altruism in the contemporary generation is P. A. Sorokin, of the Harvard Research Center in Creative Altruism, who comes out of this Russian tradition. Sorokin's activity in sociology has been much more extensive than his present preoccupation with altruism would indicate. Of Sorokin's remarkable achievements as a so-

30 *Ibid.,* p. 59.

ciologist, N. S. Timasheff writes: "Among the analytical sociologists of our time, one must be singled out, we believe, to be given first rank in creative ability, erudition, and command of the prerequisites of a system of scientific thought. This scholar is Pitirim A. Sorokin."[31]

Sorokin possesses more talent for developing large systems of far-reaching theories in support of which encyclopedic data are gathered than he does for painstaking narrowing of hypotheses and focusing particular segments of data upon them. For this reason some of Sorokin's contemporaries have overlooked the deeper significance of his pioneer studies in altruism. He also has developed his vocabulary of concepts with considerable independence of what has been done in psychoanalysis, psychology, and sociology. Lacking a common universe of discourse, a meeting of scientific minds becomes more difficult. One of the reasons for the persistent, if pedantic, attempt in this text to represent the concepts and theories of other writers, even though their pronouncements might be reformulated in simpler and more understandable ways, is that for better or worse their conceptual contributions represent the working tools of collaborators in the same fields. If these tools are cast aside in favor of new systems, the bridge of continuity with other workers is broken.

Whatever details of methodology or vocabulary in Sorokin's work to which exception may be taken, none can deny the creative nature of his insights nor the prolific and indefatigable way in which he has collected empirical materials supporting these insights. His research explorations into human love are almost without a precedent or a parallel in modern times.[32] Those who dwell upon shortcomings in his work would spend their time more effectively if they addressed themselves to his same field of inquiry and kept at it until they have something better to offer. Sorokin quotes a psychologist, A. H. Maslow, who is concerned by the lack of research accomplishment in understanding love.

Unfortunately, we know about "love energy" much less than about light, heat, electricity, and other forms of physical energy. "It is

[31] N. S. Timasheff, *Sociological Theory, Its Nature and Growth,* Random House, 1957, p. 235.

[32] P. A. Sorokin *Altruistic Love: A Study of American "Good Neighbors" and Christian Saints,* Beacon, 1950; (ed.), *Explorations in Altruistic Love and Behavior,* Beacon, 1950; (ed.), *Forms and Techniques of Altruistic and Spiritual Growth,* Beacon, 1954; *The Ways and Power of Love,* Beacon, 1954. A predecessor in sociology who defended the functional value of Christianity was C. A. Ellwood. See his *Christianity and Social Science,* Macmillan, 1923; *The Reconstruction of Religion,* Macmillan, 1925; *The World's Need of Christ,* Abingdon Press, 1940.

amazing how little the empirical sciences have to offer on the subject of love," correctly says A. H. Maslow. "Particularly strange is the silence of the psychologists. Sometimes this is merely sad or irritating, as in the case of the textbooks of psychology and sociology, practically none of which treat the subject. . . . More often the situation becomes completely ludicrous. [As a rule] the word 'love' is not even indexed [in psychological and sociological works]."[33]

Sorokin cannot be considered a sentimental unrealist. His scientific contributions to the topic of altruism grow out of his experiences as secretary to Kerenski and later an exile of the Russian Revolution, which have left him a pacifist, rather than a militarist, and out of a lifetime of scholarly achievement in sociology. The focus of Sorokin's research is less upon religion than upon altruism as a pattern of interpersonal and intergroup living. He analyzes altruism as a general social phenomenon rather than limiting consideration to its part in religion, although he affirms that the power in religion is that of altruism and strongly emphasizes the importance of religious exercises in fostering altruism. In this chapter we are concerned with empirical definition of what is considered to be the higher power in religion in order that in subsequent chapters the effects attributed to this power can be properly traced. In a chapter entitled "The Manifoldness of Love and Its Main Aspects," in *The Ways and Power of Love,* Sorokin reviews a number of ideas any one of which might be construed as defining altruism. The closest to a workable definition is provided in the section "The Psychological Aspect of Love."

Psychologically the experience of love is a complex consisting of emotional, affective, volitional, and intellectual elements. It has many qualitative forms, covered by such terms as: empathy, sympathy, kindness, devotion, admiration, benevolence, reverence, respect, adoration, friendship—to single out a few. Each of these "shades" of love as psychological experience has its own "color." These experiences are opposite to those of hatred, enmity, dislike, envy, jealousy, antipathy, and other forms of hate. *In any genuine psychological experience of love, the ego or I of the loving individual tends to merge with and to identify itself with the loved Thee.* The greater the love, the greater the identification. The joy or sorrow of the loved person becomes joy and sorrow to the loving person. Genuine sharing of all the values of life follows. Sacrifice for the loved person becomes a sacrifice for the person himself.

[33] Sorokin, *The Ways and Power of Love, op. cit.,* p. viii. The Maslow quotation is from a symposium on love: Ashley Montagu (ed.), *The Meaning of Love,* Julian Press, 1953.

In other words, *love as psychological experience is "altruistic"* by its very nature; whereas the opposite *experience of hatred is inherently selfish.* In a genuine love the loved person is experienced always as the *end* value; in egoistic experience the other person is always only the *means* value. Aristotle and V. Solovyev have pointed out very clearly this characteristic of love *versus* the egoistic experience of hatred and pseudo-love. In a real love or friendship a friend is "one who does what is good (or what he believes to be good) for another for that other's sake, and one wishes his friend to . . . live for that friend's own sake," and not because the friend gives him pleasure or is useful to him. Pseudo-friendship, motivated by pleasure or utility, takes the other person as a means and not as the end value.[34]

This love is not limited in its effects to kindly deeds. It fosters growth in the individual. In an expanding way, growth for more effective altruism is part of the system of motivation. Sorokin has devoted lengthy attention to growth aspects of love, the subtitle of one of his works being *Types, Factors, and Techniques of Moral Transformation,* and the main title of another being *Forms and Techniques of Altruistic and Spiritual Growth.* At one point he tersely states his conclusion: "Love not only cures and revitalizes the individual's mind and organism; it proves itself to be the decisive factor of vital, mental, moral, and social well-being and growth of an individual."[35]

After reviewing the contributions of the foregoing investigators concerning the nature of altruistic motivation as the power utilized in religion, it is appropriate to generalize a concept of this motivational system. By altruistic motivation is meant that the individual wants to fulfill the wants of others as ends in themselves, not as means to his getting others to do something for him. Their wants become internalized in his personality so he is motivated to act for the satisfaction of their wants as if they were his own. This motivation is a system of interrelated variables of desire, belief, temperament, and action. The stability of altruism as a category in scientific research has been demonstrated by a statistical study of personality variables correlated with altruism carried out by R. W. Friedrichs.[36]

Obviously there are degrees and varieties of altruism. People may love their families, their friends, their communities, or the entire human race. An optimum way exists in which each individual can live for the well-being of others. In this optimum way

[34] *Ibid.,* pp. 9–10.

[35] *Ibid.,* p. 65.

[36] R. W. Friedrichs, *An Exploratory Study of Altruism,* Ph.D. Thesis, University of Wisconsin, 1957.

the individual possesses the correct combination of aims, plans, enthusiasms, beliefs, and activities which his capacities permit. This optimum way of life constitutes the highest of which the individual is capable when dominated by a desire to live for others and properly educated and experienced in the appropriate means to follow. When controlled by altruistic aims and beliefs he chooses and follows the best he is able to do with the counsel and help of others. This is altruism in its fullest practical form. It is a system of motivation containing within itself power for the performance of altruistic actions. This is a growing, not a fixed, pattern of motivation since it contains the aim for something better and the belief that by further effort and experience ways can be pursued which are superior to those followed today. In a religious context, the motivational system includes the aim of spiritual development toward more effective altruism and convictions of how this development can come about.

In identifying altruistic ideals as the effective force in religion, Dewey, Ames, Wieman, and Sorokin seem to be saying what has been said in the religions of world history without the equipment of science. What is significant about the scientific study of religion is less what science finds out which is new than it is the discovery that much of what has been said in religion in the past is confirmed by scientific study. Thus science in its systematic inquiry becomes of one piece with insights from a prescientific era which affirm the power of love in human affairs. Although more is involved for science to amplify, many scriptural ideas cease to be supernatural, philosophical, or poetic generalities and become instead psychological statements. Scientific method with its fascination for intellectual nicety can sometimes miss the simple, homely details of love, a term easily misunderstood by academic-minded psychologists on the one hand and by romance-conscious students on the other. For an apt description of altruism in its fullest meaning, one is inclined to go back almost two thousand years to a description then given.

> If I speak in the tongues of men and of angels, but have not love, I am a noisy gong or a clanging cymbal. And if I have prophetic powers, and understand all mysteries and all knowledge, and if I have all faith, so as to remove mountains, but have not love, I am nothing. If I give away all I have, and if I deliver my body to be burned, but have not love, I gain nothing.
>
> Love is patient and kind; love is not jealous or boastful; it is not arrogant or rude. Love does not insist on its own way; it is not irritable or resentful; it does not rejoice at wrong, but rejoices in the

right. Love bears all things, believes all things, hopes all things, endures all things.

Love never ends; as for prophecy, it will pass away; as for tongues, they will cease; as for knowledge, it will pass away. For our knowledge is imperfect and our prophecy is imperfect; but when the perfect comes, the imperfect will pass away. . . . So faith, hope, love abide, these three; but the greatest of these is love.[37]

THE HIGHER POWER AS A SOCIAL SYSTEM

The altruistic motivation within a single personality is a modest spark for arousing religious enthusiasm of the group. The simultaneous functioning of social ideals in the lives of many generates the degree of power expected of a central reality in religion. The shared aspect of altruistic motives has drawn recurring attention by social philosophers and social scientists. One of the conceptual labels which has arisen to designate the shared quality of group ideals is *group mind.* While this term has occasioned some misunderstanding, it aptly stresses the integration of altruistic motives of individuals into a larger social system of aims, ideas, and activities. In the empirical analysis of the higher power in religion, the question arises of how the higher power in each personality is related to the higher power in other personalities. We turn to this topic by first noting historical roots of the question and its analysis.

The question involves analysis of the group to which the individual belongs. Thomas Aquinas, a profound social thinker of the Middle Ages, some of whose insights are still outstanding, defined society as a union of men for a common purpose. Locke and Hobbes in the seventeenth century and Rousseau in the eighteenth differentiated the will of the group from the will of the individual in their analysis of political life. Hegel in the early nineteenth century developed a concept of the state as a reality existing beyond its people and a concept of God as the absolute spirit of which human spirits are manifestations. Lazarus and Steinthal gave Hegel's incipient social concepts more concrete setting in their study of folk psychology, and Wundt also developed a group psychology. A few years after Hegel, Comte brought his social and religious ideas closer together in advocating a religious cult in which humanity was the object of worship. Although impractical and ill articulated, Comte's thinking about this adumbrates Durkheim's empirical analysis of tribal

[37] I Corinthians 13:1–10,13.

spirits and God in terms of society. Also influencing Durkheim were Le Bon's analysis of crowd psychology and Robertson Smith's study of the religion of ancient Semitic peoples. Robertson Smith showed how man's idea of God is shaped by prevailing political and social organization and how that which is believed to be God's will is the group's will. Robertson Smith was removed from his professorship because of his modernist theological views expressed in articles which he wrote for the *Encyclopaedia Britannica,* but he was later made its editor and achieved popularity as a scholar.

Durkheim: Society as the Higher Power in Religious Worship

Recognized as an important contributor to the concepts and methods of social research, Durkheim wrote during the last of the nineteenth and the first of the twentieth centuries at a time when the methodology of sociology was not yet well developed, and some of his formulations are incomplete. Nevertheless, he is acknowledged to be one of the most forceful thinkers in the scientific study of religion. Two of Durkheim's concepts relevant in the study of religion are society and *conscience collective,* the latter a French term not to be translated literally. In the precise limits of his concept of society, Durkheim seems somewhat vague, but he apparently means the overall system of interacting personalities of people in the group. As an organized system of beliefs, wants, ideas, values, meanings, and activities, society is a social reality *sui generis,* that is, of its own nature, representing something more than a sheer collection of unrelated individuals. Society is a force constraining the individual, either through compulsion or the subtler though more powerful appeal of sentiments which the individual shares with others in the group. He feels society as a reality exterior to him, to which he must adjust his organic wants. Durkheim so strongly stressed the nature of society as a system distinct from, exterior to, and constraining upon individuals that his concept of society has been caricatured by critics as a mind without a body. While he did not adequately guard himself against such misinterpretation, it is clear from his statements that he did not think of society as a concrete entity existing apart from the individuals who compose society. He merely wished to stress the existence of social relationships which an aggregate of isolated individuals does not possess.

The French word *conscience* means both conscience and consciousness. The overtone of meaning which the words *social awareness* have come to have in popular speech, implying both perception of and sensitivity to the needs of others, is perhaps a suitable translation. *Conscience collective* then means collective awareness of and collective feeling for the group. The adjective *collective* refers to the shared quality of social perceptions and sentiments, called by Durkheim "collective representations" of society. Like Freud's superego, *conscience collective* includes both social compulsion and social feeling.

Durkheim's concluding major work, *The Elementary Forms of the Religious Life,* first published in 1912, sets forth his thesis about the nature of the religious object which men worship. This object, conceived of by men as a tribal spirit or God, is society, rather than *conscience collective* or altruistic motivation, which society as a system of interior realities includes. God becomes identified with the group in general, rather than its ideal aspirations alone. Durkheim's astonishing conclusion has seemed to most religionists to be a crude confusion between society and its ideals. It may be said in explanation that Durkheim analyzed data from a central Australian group of primitive tribes in a late Stone Age of development. These people did not distinguish moral ideals from their usual mode of living. They apparently thought of themselves as identical with the tribal spirit whom they worshiped, rather than thinking of this as something above and beyond the present life of the group. This identification seems understandable in a group whose aim is not improvement but survival, although absurd in a group which is capable of abstracting the concept of altruism from its social life. On the other hand, the confusion persists sufficiently in contemporary life for nationalism to assume characteristics of a religion when the nation is regarded as an object of devotion and a source of mystical strength to its people. A perennial weakness of man is his inclination to accept a status equal to that of his gods or else to pull them down to his own level.

The data upon which Durkheim bases his analysis were collected by other investigators. The people whose religious life he analyzes practice totemism, a type of worship involving an animal or plant with which the people consider themselves affiliated. Durkheim observes that the totem is, first, a name for a tribe; second, an emblem or image of the totemic spirit or god; and third, an animal or a plant. These three: society, the spirit, and the animal are an indivisible trinity to the totem worshiper, who thinks of his tribe, the spirit, and the animal as one and the same being whom he worships.

Each clan has its totem, which belongs to it alone; two different clans of the same tribe cannot have the same. In fact, one is a member of a clan merely because he has a certain name. All who bear this name are members of it for that very reason; in whatever manner they may be spread over the tribal territory, they all have the same relations of kinship with one another. . . .

In a very large proportion of the cases, the objects which serve as totems belong either to the animal or the vegetable kingdom, but especially to the former. Inanimate things are much more rarely employed. Out of more than 500 totemic names collected by Howitt among the tribes of south-eastern Australia, there are scarcely forty which are not the names of plants or animals; these are the clouds, rain, hail, frost, the moon, the sun, the wind, the autumn, the summer, the winter, certain stars, thunder, fire, smoke, water or the sea.[38]

The tribes of Central Australia, especially the Arunta, the Loritja, the Kaitish, the Unmatjera, and the Ilpirra, make constant use of certain instruments in their rites which are called the churinga by the Arunta, according to Spencer and Gillen, or the tjurunga, according to Strehlow. They are pieces of wood or bits of polished stone, of a great variety of forms, but generally oval or oblong. Each totemic group has a more or less important collection of these. *Upon each of these is engraved a design representing the totem of this same group.* A certain number of the churinga have a hole at one end, through which goes a thread made of human hair or that of an opossum. Those which are made of wood and are pierced in this way serve for exactly the same purposes as those instruments of the cult to which English ethnographers have given the name of "bull-roarers." By means of the thread by which they are suspended, they are whirled rapidly in the air in such a way as to produce a sort of humming identical with that made by the toys of this name still used by our children; this deafening noise has a ritual significance and accompanies all ceremonies of any importance. . . .

In fact, every churinga, for whatever purpose it may be employed, is counted among the eminently sacred things; there are none which surpass it in religious dignity. This is indicated even by the word which is used to designate them. It is not only a substantive but also an adjective meaning sacred. . . . Profane persons, that is to say, women and young men not yet initiated into the religious life, may not touch or even see the churinga; they are only allowed to look at it from a distance, and even this is only on rare occasions.[39]

On the other hand, the plant or animal whose name the clan bears may be seen and touched by everybody. The churinga are preserved in a sort of temple, upon whose threshold all noises from the profane life must cease; it is the domain of sacred things. On the contrary, the

[38] Emile Durkheim, *The Elementary Forms of the Religious Life,* tr. by J. W. Swain, Free Press, 1947, pp. 102–104.

[39] *Ibid.,* pp. 119–120.

totemic animals and plants live in the profane world and are mixed up with the common everyday life. Since the number and importance of the interdictions which isolate a sacred thing, and keep it apart, correspond to the degree of sacredness with which it is invested, we arrive at the remarkable conclusion that *the images of totemic beings are more sacred than the beings themselves.*[40]

A member of the Kangaroo clan calls himself a kangaroo; he is therefore, in one sense, an animal of this species. "The totem of any man," say Spencer and Gillen, "is regarded as the same thing as himself; a native once said to us when we were discussing the matter with him, 'That one,' pointing to his photograph which we had taken, 'is the same thing as me; so is a kangaroo' (his totem)."[41]

So we must be careful not to consider totemism a sort of animal worship. The attitude of a man towards the animals or plants whose name he bears is not at all that of a believer towards his god, for he belongs to the sacred world himself. Their relations are rather those of two beings who are on the same level and of equal value. The most that can be said is that in certain cases, at least, the animal seems to occupy a slightly more elevated place in the hierarchy of sacred things. It is because of this that it is sometimes called the father or the grandfather of the men of the clan, which seems to show that they feel themselves in a state of moral dependence in regard to it. But in other, and perhaps even more frequent cases, it happens that the expressions used denote rather a sentiment of equality. The totemic animal is called the friend or the elder brother of its human fellows. Finally, the bonds which exist between them and it are much more like those which unite the members of a single family; the animals and the men are made of the same flesh, as the Buandik say. On account of this kinship, men regard the animals of the totemic species as kindly associates upon whose aid they think they can rely. They call them to their aid and they come, to direct their blows in the hunt and to give warning of whatever dangers there may be. In return for this, men treat them with regard and are never cruel to them; but these attentions in no way resemble a cult.[42]

Just as a man who belongs to the Crow clan has within him something of this animal, so the rain, since it is of the same clan and belongs to the same totem, is also necessarily considered as being "the same thing as a crow"; for the same reason, the moon is a black cockatoo, the sun a white cockatoo, every black-nut tree a pelican, etc. All the beings arranged in a single clan, whether men, animals, plants or inanimate objects, are merely forms of the totemic being. This is the meaning of the formula which we have just cited and this is what makes the two really of the same species: all are really of the same flesh in the sense that all partake of the nature of the totemic animal.[43]

[40] *Ibid.,* p. 133.
[41] *Ibid.,* p. 134.
[42] *Ibid.,* pp. 139–140.
[43] *Ibid.,* p. 150.

Thus the totem is before all a symbol, a material expression of something else. But of what?

From the analysis to which we have been giving our attention, it is evident that it expresses and symbolizes two different sorts of things. In the first place, it is the outward and visible form of what we have called the totemic principle or god. But it is also the symbol of the determined society called the clan. It is its flag; it is the sign by which each clan distinguishes itself from the others, the visible mark of its personality, a mark borne by everything which is a part of the clan under any title whatsoever, men, beasts or things. So if it is at once the symbol of the god and of the society, is that not because the god and the society are only one? How could the emblem of the group have been able to become the figure of this quasi-divinity, if the group and the divinity were two distinct realities? The god of the clan, the totemic principle, can therefore be nothing else than the clan itself, personified and represented to the imagination under the visible form of the animal or vegetable which serves as totem.[44]

This social view of God parallels and extends a statement made two decades earlier by Robertson Smith, a statement related to ideas of Frazer concerning totemism and kinship in *The Golden Bough.*

Some of the most notable and constant features of all ancient heathenism, and indeed of all nature-religions, from the totemism of savages upward, find their sufficient explanation in the physical kinship that unites the human and superhuman members of the same religious and social community, without reference to the special doctrine of divine fatherhood. From this point of view the natural solidarity of the god and his worshippers, which has been already enlarged upon as characteristic of antique religion, at once becomes intelligible; the indissoluble bond that unites men to their god is the same bond of blood-fellowship which in early society is the one binding link between man and man, and the one sacred principle of moral obligation. And thus we see that even in its rudest forms religion was a moral force; the powers that man reveres were on the side of social order and tribal law; and the fear of the gods was a motive to enforce the laws of society, which were also the laws of morality.[45]

Since the primitive tribes whom Durkheim analyzed did not differentiate between society and its ideals but were concerned principally with survival, he found little opportunity for regarding *conscience collective* rather than society the higher power of religion. The locus of the higher power in religion is shifted to society, of which *conscience collective* is the internalized representation in the personalities of individuals.

[44] *Ibid.*, p. 206.

[45] W. Robertson Smith, *The Religion of the Semites,* Meridian, 1957, pp. 52–53.

The general conclusion of the book which the reader has before him is that religion is something eminently social. Religious representations are collective representations which express collective realities; the rites are a manner of acting which take rise in the midst of the assembled groups and which are destined to excite, maintain or re-create certain mental states in these groups. . . .

Collective representations are the result of an immense cooperation, which stretches out not only into space but into time as well; to make them, a multitude of minds have associated, united and combined their ideas and sentiments; for them, long generations have accumulated their experience and their knowledge. A special intellectual activity is therefore concentrated in them which is infinitely richer and complexer than that of the individual. From that one can understand how the reason has been able to go beyond the limits of empirical knowledge. It does not owe this to any vague mysterious virtue, but simply to the fact that according to the well-known formula, man is double. There are two beings in him: an individual being which has its foundation in the organism and the circle of whose activities is therefore strictly limited, and a social being which represents the highest reality in the intellectual and moral order that we can know by observation—I mean society.[46]

Positive altruistic implications can be seen in Durkheim's analysis of religion, in particular when the individual identifies his will with the will of the group and makes this will his own.

Since it [society] has a nature which is peculiar to itself and different from our individual nature, it pursues ends which are likewise special to it; but, as it cannot attain them except through our intermediacy, it imperiously demands our aid. It requires that, forgetful of our own interests, we make ourselves its servitors, and it submits us to every sort of inconvenience, privation and sacrifice, without which social life would be impossible. It is because of this that at every instant we are obliged to submit ourselves to rules of conduct and of thought which we have neither made nor desired, and which are sometimes even contrary to our most fundamental inclinations and instincts.[47]

Examining some of the same data as Durkheim, R. R. Marett places an idealistic interpretation upon totemism. "Some primitive folk, such as the Arunta of Central Australia, make up for a miserable environment by spending half their time in a transcendental region where they commune with their ideal selves in the shape of reincarnating totemic ancestors, and after their

[46] Durkheim, *op. cit.,* pp. 10, 16.
[47] *Ibid.,* pp. 206–207.

own Stone-Age fashion taste something of life's inner meaning, though with never a God in sight."[48]

Durkheim's analysis of the social basis of religion is less an explanation for the belief in God based on ethical power than it is a theory that gods and spirits, benevolent and malevolent, have their empirical roots in society.

But, it is said, what society is it that has thus made the basis of religion? Is it the real society, such as it is and acts before our very eyes, with the legal and moral organization which it has laboriously fashioned during the course of history? This is full of defects and imperfections. In it, evil goes beside the good, injustice often reigns supreme, and the truth is often obscured by error. How could anything so crudely organized inspire the sentiments of love, the ardent enthusiasm and the spirit of abnegation which all religions claim of their followers? These perfect beings which are gods could not have taken their traits from so mediocre, and sometimes even so base a reality.

But, on the other hand, does someone think of a perfect society, where justice and truth would be sovereign, and from which evil in all its forms would be banished forever? No one would deny that this is in close relations with the religious sentiment; for, they would say, it is towards the realization of this that all religions strive. But that society is not an empirical fact, definite and observable; it is a fancy, a dream with which men have lightened their sufferings, but in which they have never really lived. It is merely an idea which comes to express our more or less obscure aspirations towards the good, the beautiful and the ideal. Now these aspirations have their roots in us; they come from the very depths of our being; then there is nothing outside of us which can account for them. . . .

But, in the first place, things are arbitrarily simplified when religion is seen only on its idealistic side: in its way, it is realistic. There is no physical or moral ugliness, there are no vices or evils which do not have a special divinity. There are gods of theft and trickery, of lust and war, of sickness and of death. Christianity itself, howsoever high the idea which it has made of the divinity may be, has been obliged to give the spirit of evil a place in its mythology. Satan is an essential piece of the Christian system; even if he is an impure being, he is not a profane one. The anti-god is a god, inferior and subordinated, it is true, but nevertheless endowed with extended powers; he is even the object of rites, at least of negative ones. Thus religion, far from ignoring the real society and making an abstraction of it, is in its image; it reflects all its aspects, even the most vulgar and the most repulsive. All is to be found there, and if in the majority of cases we see the good victorious over evil, life over death, the powers of light

[48] R. R. Marett, *Head, Heart and Hands in Human Evolution,* Holt, 1935, p. 100.

over the powers of darkness, it is because reality is not otherwise. If the relation between these two contrary forces were reversed, life would be impossible; but, as a matter of fact, it maintains itself and even tends to develop.[49]

This societal theory of religion is inadequate unless one assigns a causal role also to hereditary and other factors in religion, inasmuch as such things as theft, trickery, lust, war, sickness, and death to which Durkheim refers are not simply societal phenomena and may be primarily physiological. In reviewing his work, one is impressed by the forceful way in which he assembles facts to substantiate his conclusions and by his ability as a theorist. On the other hand, his concepts of the nature and causation of religion provide an incomplete picture from the standpoint of a social or psychological scientist.

Elsewhere in his writings Durkheim treats the concept of altruism in a manner similar to the development of the concept given in a previous section. B. P. Dohrenwend has compactly summarized Durkheim's references to this concept.

Altruism, on the other hand, is a "state of impersonality in the social unit." Here "the individual has no interests of his own." He is rather "trained to renunciation and unquestioned abnegation. . . ." Duty and honor are of paramount importance. Ego is "blended with something not itself . . . the goal of conduct is exterior to itself, that is, in one of the groups in which it participates." Military societies and some "primitive" societies afford examples of this state.[50]

R. B. Cattell: God as the Mind of the Altruistic Group

In 1920 W. McDougall published a work of social psychology entitled *The Group Mind.* In this he analyzed the organization of the mental and emotional life of the group, with particular reference to the psychology of nationalism. R. B. Cattell uses the concept of the group mind as the starting point in his examination of religion entitled *Psychology and the Religious Quest.* Better known for his work in factor analysis of personality traits, his essay, containing empirical concepts for scientific study of religion, has gained limited attention among psychologists. He argues the usefulness of McDougall's concept for religious study.

There are already in psychology certain conceptions and some experimental research results which offer a basis for an entirely new and

[49] Durkheim, *op. cit.,* pp. 420–421.

[50] B. P. Dohrenwend, "Egoism, Altruism, Anomie, and Fatalism: A Conceptual Analysis of Durkheim's Types," *American Sociological Review,* August, 1959, p. 467.

constructive scientific approach to religion. The first and most important of these comes from social psychology. It is the notion of the Group Mind, which McDougall developed in 1920, without, however, dwelling upon implications for religion. . . .

Elements of the modern conception of a group mind are found in Hobbes, Hegel, Bosanquet, and others. The essence of the notion is that in any organized group of human beings there exists a super-individual mind, built up from, yet greater than, the sum of the individual minds. . . .

What do we mean when we speak of any individual mind? We mean that the individual is alive, that he responds to stimulation, that he has emotions and appetites, that he acts and wills to do certain things, that he decides between different courses of action, that his behavior shows evidence of memory and of some constant habits and sentiments which constitute his personality. If we are not behaviorists —it is of no great relevance to the detection of mind—we also assume that he is conscious. Further, as biologists, we expect the behavior characteristic of mind to be invariably associated with some physical grey matter, either in one mass as in the vertebrates or in more scattered masses as in the invertebrates.

Now consider any group—from a ship's crew or a football team to a nation. The group, if in a healthy state, acts in a unified way towards some definite end, as an individual does when sane. It responds as a whole to external stimuli. It shows evidence of emotion and heightened excitability, which you can perceive in an individual by his pulse or his language. Similarly you can perceive in a football crowd a common wave of emotion, reddening a thousand faces, or read in the newspapers of a nation the more wild expressions which mirror a heightened feeling tone. The behavior of a nation reveals idiosyncrasies of habit and native temperament as does that of individuals. . . .

The question of group mind structure, though a fascinating one, cannot be approached here more than to observe that most mental features of the group mind are carried in the individual minds. The individual mind mirrors in miniature the group mind, yet no individual mind, not even the comprehensive minds of politicians, or of literary or scientific men, can subtend the whole range of awareness of the group mind. Nor can any individual mind, however great its feeling or desire to act, equal the power and intensity and richness of feeling included in the group mind. . . .

But the important thing is that the elements of the group mind should be in communication, by sight, speech, writing, telephone, or other means, so that each portion of nervous tissue can react appropriately to whatever is affecting all the others. Whether the portions of grey matter are separated by interstitial tissue and communicate by nerve threads as in the brain or are separated by brick walls and communicate by electric wires as in the group mind is of little consequence. Nor are the idioms of communication important providing they are appropriate to the mental experience to be transmitted: lovers may communicate by hand pressures and mathematicians by symbols: each maintains a group awareness of some form of initially individual excitation.

Naturally there are different types of group mind just as there are different kinds of individual mind, and the less organized kind of group mind, the crowd, is lower than any individual mind, unless we look for the latter far down in the scale of animal evolution.[51]

. . . the existence in common speech of terms for the group mind, its feelings, attitudes, and behavior, indicates that something exists which is most conveniently handled in thought in this way. When we say, "Great Britain is distinctly uneasy over the situation," or "The committee has decided to act in such and such a manner," we mean that groups of people have experienced certain thoughts, feelings, and attitudes and possess an organization capable of putting their decisions into effect. We are speaking of no mythical, ideal entity present only in verbal thinking, but of certain agglomerations of matter and consciousness quite as real as any individual.[52]

In describing the group mind as a social system, Cattell recognizes that the group mind is not like the individual mind in having a unified field of consciousness. The mind of the group is made up of contiguous, rather than continuous, fields of consciousness, even though these possess a single purpose. However, he points out that an individual may display the unusual phenomenon of a split personality in which two streams of consciousness apparently function within a single brain and nervous system, and he also calls attention to the divided character of conflicting impulses found within a single personality as well as in the mind of the group.[53]

From a common-sense standpoint, the group mind may be said to exist whenever individuals are considered to be acting as a group. More precisely, by the criteria cited, the group mind includes all aspects of people's personalities which are involved in their reaction to a common stimulus, a reaction which takes place through their being in communication with members of the group. The group mind excludes reactions to stimuli not shared by the group. The profound involvement of the lives of many individuals in objectives of the group means that most, if not all, of their personality systems may be contained within the group mind. The person whose life, for example, is completely inte-

[51] R. B. Cattell, *Psychology and the Religious Quest,* Nelson, 1938, pp. 62–65.

[52] *Ibid.,* p. 68.

[53] *Ibid.,* p. 66.

grated about group religious purposes is entirely a functioning participant in the group mind.

The concept of group mind encountered opposition when McDougall introduced it, on which Cattell comments as follows in a research paper which develops concepts and procedures for study of traits of the group mind.

It is of historical if not of scientific importance that McDougall's penetrating pioneer analysis of the 'group mind' was badly received by a certain section of American psychologists. In the descendants of this sectional opposition the allergic reaction to his expression is still so strong as to paralyze thought, and writers who pander to irrationality have for years operated with McDougall's concept by circumlocutions. The rejection was not due to opposition to Hegelianism, for McDougall's able philosophical preamble explicitly refuted Hegelian mysticism and accepted Hobhouse's searching anti-idealist criticisms. The probably correct, but more trivial explanation was that this contribution to social psychology was launched at an unfortunate moment. For a large number of callow students in psychology were unable at that time to recognize any manifestations of mind unless formally, or often actually, reduced to the twitching of a dog's hind leg.[54]

Cattell suggests another term as expressing the basic idea of the group mind. "Examination of many possible verbal roots indicates *syntality* as best indicating the 'togetherness' of the group, while having sufficient suggestive parallelism to 'personality' and 'totality.' Further, we may perhaps speak appropriately of the syntality of a group as inferred from the 'synaction' of its members—the group action defined below. Syntality covers dynamic, temperamental and ability traits of the group."[55] Cattell then develops a theoretical model of concepts and methods for study of group mentality. In a subsequent paper he applies this approach in isolating ten dimensions of the mentality of nations,[56] which suggests the usefulness of a corresponding study of religious groups.

While avoided by some social scientists, the concept of group mind appears to have usefulness for the study of persons acting as a group, since the concept indicates the close psychological unity of the whole system of motivation and behavior. It is out of

[54] R. B. Cattell, "Concepts and Methods in the Measurement of Group Syntality," *Psychological Review,* January, 1948, pp. 50–51.

[55] *Ibid.,* pp. 48–49.

[56] R. B. Cattell, "The Dimensions of Culture Patterns by Factorization of National Characters," *Journal of Abnormal and Social Psychology,* October, 1949, pp. 443–469; also "The Principal Culture Patterns Discoverable in the Syntal Dimensions of Existing Nations," *Journal of Social Psychology,* November, 1950, pp. 215–253.

the situation of the group mind in general that Cattell finds God as a social-psychological reality to emerge.

What size and structure are necessary in a group before the higher characteristics of group spirit emerge? If God emerges from the group mind, at what point of its evolution does this significant event occur; or have we to deal wholly with a continuous change, only to be described appropriately by the formulae of mathematical covariation? Again, is the group mind for all practical purposes to be identified with our living fellow-men, so that the modern tendency to substitute service to the group for service to God will receive support from our present analysis? . . .

The present introductory investigation of the group mind and its place in thought would not be complete without emphasis on the great dependence of the characters of the group mind upon those appearing in individual minds. It might be asserted, for instance, that the group mind has most of the qualities assigned to God, except his benevolence and concern for the individual. Great societies have sometimes had little concern for the lame, the halt, and the blind. But no great society since the emergence of Christianity—since this new pattern of God spread through the whole of society—has shown ruthless indifference. The group mind may have, on a right basis of population, many of the qualities of God. Benevolence, love, and hatred of unnecessary suffering must be present in individual minds if they are to suffuse the group mind. Similarly, purposiveness in the group mind largely, but perhaps not entirely, emanates from individual minds. At least it is clear that the miracles performed by small groups of enthusiasts—by, for example, the early Christians or Garibaldi's thousand volunteers—come of closely unified and intense individual consciousnesses. Nevertheless, in the end there is something beyond individual minds. The fabric of thought, the noble virtues, the lofty laws of good living acquire a power greater than that of men themselves.

First the qualities must exist in the individual, but to this must be added each individual's awareness of others in the same state. Communication is essential. Men who love goodness, truth, or beauty, if they are to sustain and be sustained by the faith and purpose of the group mind, must know, and preferably not by intuition alone, that other men, however few, or remote in space or time, are working with the same faith towards the same beloved goals. A universal awareness of the universal pattern is essential to its existence. . . .

God truly emerges from the group mind only at that stage of development when an adequate conception of his nature, origin, functions, and capacities grows up in a sufficient number of human brains. Beyond this point we may call the group mind the Theopsyche, to indicate its divine properties.[57]

[57] R. B. Cattell, *Psychology and the Religious Quest*, pp. 80–83.

It is apparent that Cattell is discussing God, not deities in general. To summarize, God is the mind of a group which is altruistic in its motivation. The altruistic motivations of the members of such a group constitute a functional system in which the single aim of seeking the welfare of others is dominant. The thinking, desiring, believing, and acting of the group are integrated about this aim. This social system of motivation is the higher power of religion. For any one individual the altruistic motivation within his personality is the power directly influencing him. As far as the behavior of the group is concerned, the entire social system of altruistic motivation in the group is the power influencing it.

Cattell does not deal adequately with his question of whether religion is merely to be identified with serving one's fellow men, a question which cannot be answered until the role of worship is analyzed. But Cattell does make the following affirmative statement about love of God and love of man.

> A scientific approach to this problem of human energies in relation to the Theopsyche and the Universal Reality therefore leads to the conclusion that the brotherhood of man is not a full expression of the moral trend which exists in living matter. The magnificent solidarity of the human race, the self-effacing love of man for man in the sufferings and death which accompany our strange, great adventure, is one of the noblest spectacles in the pageant of life. There is only one thing nobler and that is the undefeated spirit of the lonely individual, striving for his comrades of the future in the face of the taunts and misunderstandings of his fellows, sincerely loving those who hate him, serenely prepared for whatever fate may hold. For the love of God includes the love of man, heightened in so far as they strive towards what is God. But the love of man need not include the love of God; it may be arrested at a mutual condonation of man as he is, pleasure-loving, static, semi-bestial.[58]

With reference to the idea that there is something spiritually greater than the love of man, a further comment may be made. Whatever may be the altruistic motivation of which the individual is capable in living for others now, he is capable of something higher in his future thinking, desiring, and acting. Similarly, the human race is capable of continuing development. Devotion to God as consisting of unfolding potentialities is more creative of value than devotion to man. Exclusive preoccupation with specific needs circumscribes the horizon of the actor, while

[58] *Ibid.*, p. 140.

concentration upon a developing state of altruistic thinking and acting opens the door to further opportunities.

The achievement of future opportunities is facilitated by systematic inquiry, by the individual in his own life, and by the researcher in his scientific programs. Concerning research needs, Cattell comments:

> Our questioning should be concerned to find out, for example, what changes in the behavior of individuals and groups follow upon their appreciation of the reality of the Theopsyche; to understand first how defective, relatively, is the adjustment of those who work with some personalized symbol of God; to discover the way in which the science of the Theopsyche is best taught to the young. There are a whole set of questions concerning the effect of religious belief or its absence upon spending and the economic stability of groups. The incidence of delinquency, neurosis, and insanity is clearly likely to have important relations to the group outlook and to the ratio between speed of progress and changing adjustments to the Theopsyche. . . .
>
> Does the continual drip of advertisements of bad taste wear away some stone of social conscience or sensitivity? What are the measurable effects of beautiful surroundings in terms of finer moral behavior? Which improvements in political, economic, and recreational life are barred by the limitations of inborn mental capacity in the species of men which constitute the group? And in what manner do various features of group life—its kindliness, its interest in culture, its susceptibility to change, its freedom from economic panic, its freedom from physical disease, depend on the summation of small inborn or acquired traits in individuals? . . .
>
> These are but a fraction of the questions regarding group mechanisms needing solution if we are even to begin to understand the superbly intricate workings of the Theopsyche; but few of them can possibly be answered in more than a tentative fashion today. A great research has to be organized which is nothing less than an experimental study of God. To introduce the idea that God should be regarded as a legitimate object of experimental investigation is not to imply or invite any diminution of that reverence towards God which has dominated religious thought and which, as far as we know, is a sane and desirable emotional relationship in well-adjusted societies and individuals.[59]

The designation of a psychological force as *God* requires scientific justification for this use of the word *God,* with all the added overtones of meaning. Consideration of whether this verbal usage is scientifically appropriate is reserved until Chapter 9. For the present chapter, no more is meant by the word *God* than the so-

[59] *Ibid.,* pp. 154–155.

cial or psychological power to which empirical reference is made by the analysts whose work is introduced.

THE HIGHER POWER AS AN UNCONSCIOUS SYSTEM

Experiences of the group mind, of altruistic motivation, or of an ideal of group perfection are emergents from the social experience of human beings. Before these things appear in the consciousness of individuals, they are fused with other elements in psychic experience from which they become differentiated through reflection, education, or the passage of time. Prior to appearing as separate awarenesses, they are said to be in the unconscious side of experience in the sense that the individual is not aware of them except as he is conscious of the totality of experience containing them as component parts. Furthermore, social ideas when present in conscious awareness are largely experienced symbolically and do not have the recognizable qualities of concrete images, but rather are weak, colorless, and evanescent. One can readily imagine a human face and then abstract the eyes from the mental picture and think of them exclusively. The abstraction of social or religious ideas takes place in a more difficult manner, and one relies much upon symbols to gain hold of the ideas and to control their appearance in consciousness.

The significance of the unconscious mind of the human race for religion or for any field of endeavor can hardly be overestimated. The unconscious realm is the vast reservoir of new ideas, except those which come directly from new experiences of the external world. The method of experimentation in science furnishes fresh data, but the implications which can be abstracted from the data of either the external or internal world seem a limitless capacity of the human mind. The unconscious side of personality contains much more than the unfulfilled ideals of which people are aware and to which they aspire. It contains countless ideals, plans, and possibilities as yet unthought of. This inexhaustible capacity of the unconscious mind appears to be the basis for the infinite possibilities traditionally ascribed to God.

Approach of C. G. Jung

Nearly all of the writers to whom reference has been made in this chapter indicate the unconscious source of altruistic motives which provide man with an experience of God. More than any of these, C. G. Jung has analyzed religious experience and motivation as a system linking conscious and unconscious elements. His conclusions are drawn from clinical studies of the motivation of persons seeking help because of malfunctioning of their system of conscious and unconscious impulses and ideas.

Jung was the son of a pastor in the Swiss Reformed Church, which at least partially explains his interest in religion. Nearly twenty years younger than Freud, Jung worked closely with him in the initial growth of the psychoanalytic movement, serving as first president of the International Psychoanalytic Association in 1910. A few years later Jung broke with Freud because of their divergent concepts and theories and founded his own school of "analytical psychology" in place of psychoanalysis. Prominent among the issues which divided them was the role of religion in personality development. Concerning the role of Jung in psychology, C. S. Hall and G. Lindzey state: "Carl Jung is acknowledged to be one of the greatest living thinkers. For over half a century he has devoted himself with great energy and singularity of purpose to analyzing the far-flung and deep-lying processes of human personality. Now in his ninth decade of life, Jung is still actively engaged in research and writing. His writings are voluminous and the extent of his influence incalculable."[60]

It is not easy to give systematic quotations from Jung to illustrate all of his ideas. His writings are extensive and his findings distributed in various works. His anatomy of personality, while a profound scientific contribution, seems unnecessarily encumbered with mythological terms and symbolic references from literature which make readability difficult and which sometimes might be said to require interpretation by the reader as if they were dream material. Jung's basic system of psychology is, however, clearly defined and has been concisely presented by Jolande Jacobi in *The Psychology of Jung* and by C. S. Hall and G. Lindzey in *Theories of Personality*. An illuminating exposition of Jung's principles of religious psychology has been assembled by Hans Schaer in *Religion and the Cure of Souls in Jung's Psychology,* published by the Bollingen Foundation, which sponsors Jung's writings in America. Currently, Jung's works with his later revisions are being published in English by this foundation. Another review of Jung's work is that made by C. A. Meier, one of his leading disciples, in a series of lectures given at

[60] C. S. Hall and G. Lindzey, *Theories of Personality,* Wiley, 1957, pp. 77–78.

and published by Andover Newton Theological School in 1959, entitled *Jung and Analytical Psychology.*

Of his scientific approach to religion, Jung writes:

Although I have often been called a philosopher, I am an empiricist and adhere as such to the phenomenological standpoint. I trust that it does not conflict with the principles of scientific empiricism if one occasionally makes certain reflections which go beyond a mere accumulation and classification of experience. As a matter of fact I believe that experience is not even possible without reflection, because "experience" is a process of assimilation without which there could be no understanding. As this statement indicates, I approach psychological matters from a scientific and not from a philosophical standpoint. Inasmuch as religion has a very important psychological aspect, I deal with it from a purely empirical point of view, that is, I restrict myself to the observation of phenomena and I eschew any metaphysical or philosophical considerations. I do not deny the validity of these other considerations, but I cannot claim to be competent to apply them correctly.[61]

Spiritual Drive

In analyzing human motivation Jung endeavors to correct the one-sidedness of Freud's emphasis upon pleasure seeking as the basis of human behavior and also the one-sidedness of Alfred Adler, who stressed the will to power and superiority. We quote from Jacobi's summary.

Jung recognizes the decisive role that sexuality and will to power play among men. Consequently there are numerous cases in which the illness is referable to disturbances in one of these driving factors and which must therefore be approached from a Freudian or an Adlerian point of view. But while with Freud mainly the pleasure principle, with Adler the will to power act as explanatory principles, Jung regards other equally essential factors besides these as motivating elements of the psyche and therefore rejects decisively the postulate that the predominant role in all psychic disorders belongs to one driving factor alone. Besides these two assuredly significant ones there are for him still other highly important drives, before and above all that which belongs to *man alone*—the spiritual and religious need inborn in the psyche. This view of Jung's is an essential point in his theory, which distinguishes it from all other theories and determines its prospective-synthetic direction. For "the spiritual appears in the psyche likewise as a drive, indeed as a true passion. It is no derivative of another

[61] C. G. Jung, *Psychology and Religion: West and East,* tr. by R. F. C. Hull. Bollingen Series XX, Bollingen Foundation, Inc. Pantheon, 1958, pp. 5–6.

drive but a principle *sui generis,* namely, the indispensable formative power in the world of drives."[62]

The system of motivation operating in religion is designated by Jung as "spiritual" or "religious" rather than "altruistic." Perhaps the former terms are to be preferred if altruism is regarded in a limited context as referring simply to impulses of charity. Part of altruistic motivation in its full sense is a striving for more of this motivation so that increased altruistic living takes place. This striving in turn involves recognition of the tendencies of motivation to grow and of the ways in which growth takes place, that is, recognition of altruism as a psychological power which induces people to stimulate its growth through spiritual or other exercises in development. The term *spiritual* excludes purely self-seeking motives for engaging in spiritual activities, but it includes activities motivated by the basic aim of increased altruism. The higher power in religion thus encompasses spiritual efforts to express more of that power. *Spiritual* for Jung also includes various impulses and compulsions besides altruistic which induce people to cling to religious beliefs and to engage in religious behavior. However, the major motive in the spiritual system is for worth and meaning beyond self-seeking.

Unconscious Motivation

In Jung's analysis the motivational power in religion is experienced unconsciously as well as consciously, referred to by people as their experience of God or of the will of God. "Unconscious experience" is not a contradiction in terms. Important features of interior experience, such as one's urges and assumptions, may be buried in the everyday experiences of living. The individual is then unaware of what he wants or why he acts as he does. Thus a boy may unknowingly be attracted to marry a girl because she looks like his mother, although that thought may never have occurred to him, or more subtly, he may be attracted because the girl's temperament is like that of his mother. All that he is aware of is that he is in love, but the psychologist can see the unconscious motivation from childhood which fixes his matrimonial choice.

It is to be kept in mind that Jung employs the concept of the unconscious in a way different from Freud, who restricts its

[62] Jolande Jacobi, *The Psychology of C. G. Jung,* tr. by K. W. Bash, Yale University Press, 1951, p. 80.

meaning primarily to psychic material repressed by conflicting desires or pressure of circumstances. The roots of Jung's concept of the unconscious are contained in views of Kant and Hegel concerning ideas in process of historical appearance and also in the work of the physician and psychologist, C. G. Carus. The psychic material of which Jung speaks is that which is as yet unborn in the individual's awareness, not that suppressed after its appearance. The material may, of course, be both unborn and repressed in a personality whose development is frustrated. Since the unconscious source of ideas and impulses is a common storehouse in the personal and social experience of mankind, Jung refers to this source as the *collective unconscious*. His term *archetype* refers literally to the ancient pattern in which images and motivations of every generation fall. Jung's theory of the hereditary origin of the collective unconscious has been criticized, a problem of religious causation to which we return. This theory is incidental to describing the unconscious aspects of personality explored by Jung.

In the life development of the individual many of the unconscious components of personality are gradually brought into conscious awareness and integrated with the rest of personality, or if too obscure to be raised to consciousness, they may be incorporated in cultural images which bring them partially into consciousness and reorient personality about them. Sometimes these images are half-truths, such as the Santa Claus image symbolizing generosity. Images are an essential part of social experience, fused with our perceptions of ourselves and others. That they are images does not at all mean that they are imagined. We live by means of real mental pictures of the motives of ourselves and others. We do not conceptualize these motives in the abstract, but almost always think of them in terms of concrete actions and situations.

Prior to integration the unconscious contents are unorganized materials, and after integration they become linked with stable purposes and habits so that they find effective expression in the individual's life. One of the aims of education is to make manifest what is latent in the individual's personality. The experience of God involves unconscious spiritual motivation which appears in experience in the form of imagery, as illustrated by the following quotations from Schaer.

> It will have become apparent from our exposition so far that Jung does not speak of God as an *idea,* but that when he speaks of God at all he means something quite different. God is not thought or con-

trived, nor is he apprehended and exhausted by our ideas: he is *experienced.* And as long as what a man experiences of God is alive, he is influenced by it. . . . Jung associates the God-image with the power of imagination. Imagination is an actualization of the contents of the unconscious, which do not belong to the empirical [exterior] world and are of an archetypal nature. . . . The God-image that men make for themselves in idea is likewise a work of imagination—that is to say, it is not so much a matter of knowledge of some fact external to man as of the expression of a psychic fact, the best possible formulation of some psychic actuality which we have to exteriorize in order to grasp at all.[63]

In his practice Jung has observed people during the period when a new intuition of God was taking shape in them. He tells us—in the case we have already mentioned, of the patient whom he could help only by continuing the analysis and who had to discover a new meaning for her life *by herself*—how certain contents gradually appeared in her dreams which could not be interpreted at all save as a new God-image. At first, the dreams seemed to indicate the person of the analyst, since they showed him in superhuman proportions and thus had all the appearance of typical transference-dreams so very familiar from the literature of psychoanalysis. But in time Jung became convinced that this could not be the right interpretation, and that a new God-image was clearly being sought in the dreams—that is, a new God-symbol was taking shape. The dreams disclosed a veritable God-seeking, a lusting after God. Gradually a God-image of archaic character was crystallized out, evidently formed in the unconscious. As though in inner harmony with this, the patient developed a new, distinct, and spiritually stable mode of life. Jung gives literary examples of such a renewal of God—above all, in Spitteler.

Here, too, it must not for a moment be supposed that the individual is creating God; it is simply that the supra-personal functions of the psyche are creating the God-image. The evolution of this is not a conscious act of will, as far as the individual is concerned, but, at most, an event which he can actively experience; he cannot determine the course it is to take. A man may recognize or repudiate his God and fight against him, but he cannot ever be rid of him. This can be seen with many converts and atheists. Nietzsche was never able to carry his conflict with Christ to a successful conclusion in the sense of turning to something new and positive. Goethe, on the other hand, never attempted to deviate from his God-image, but strove to deepen it all his life.

From the psychological point of view, therefore, God manifests himself as an autonomous complex of considerable strength and intensity. The God-symbol is ultimately the expression of life's intensity

[63] Hans Schaer, *Religion and the Cure of Souls in Jung's Psychology,* tr. by R. F. C. Hull. Bollingen Series XXI, Bollingen Foundation, Inc. Pantheon, 1950, pp. 137, 139.

at its highest, and is thus always stronger than consciousness. It can do more than the conscious will can do, for it partakes of the "objective psyche": the material of the unconscious. That is why God is always experienced as power at first and never as idea.[64]

One great innovation strikes you at once in Jung's psychological researches into religion: that is the significance he attaches to the unconscious in religious life. As we have seen in our sketch of Jung's views, he holds that the unconscious is just as important as the conscious mind. This is unconditionally true of religion also. . . .

Thus Jung traces back to the unconscious the "inner voice" so important to every religious person, the voice of revelation. "Revelation," says Jung, "is an opening of the depths of the human soul, a 'laying bare,' a psychological mode pure and simple, which says nothing about what *else* it could be. That lies outside the bounds of science." What is at the bottom of these processes Jung refuses to conjecture; but this much is certain for him, that what we experience as revelation comes from the unconscious.[65]

The process is less mysterious than it seems. What is involved is the psychic differentiation of experience into its component characteristics which appear in the mind as insights into experience. The process is a creative one since things come into conscious awareness which were previously in the unconscious mind and not known to the individual. In religious revelation, according to Jung, implications are extracted from experience by the innate ability of the mind to generate new insights. For profound ideas or motives, this creative process is slow and difficult, sometimes not accomplishable by people. Even though people may be unable to derive key elements from their experience of their motivation, these key elements may be important in the functioning of personality. Because of the importance of spiritual ideas and inclinations, some means of designating these and influencing them is necessary in religious life. This means is afforded by what Jung calls "symbols."

Symbols in Religion

For Jung a symbol is not a verbal label, as when the word *Jesus* has as its meaning a particular religious leader. This is the customary usage of the word *symbol*. By symbol Jung means a mental image which contains within itself an essential idea, its meaning. Thus the image of Jesus as a shepherd contains the idea of God taking care of people. The idea is concrete rather than abstractly articulated. It is difficult for people to conceive of

[64] *Ibid.*, pp. 145–146.
[65] *Ibid.*, pp. 61–63.

a God who takes care of people. They cannot see God, who is either a philosophical construct or else an abstract characteristic of the personality system. The pictorial image of a shepherd presents vividly and concretely the idea of an effective caretaker. This idea is the meaning of the image. The image does not bring the characteristic fully to consciousness as an abstract idea of a power taking care of one. Such an idea may lie beyond the ability of the individual to conceptualize although he might readily repeat the words empty of meaning. The image brings the characteristic into conscious experience by presenting the characteristic in pictorial form. It is not brought fully and precisely to consciousness, since it is fused with the image of a shepherd taking care of sheep.

Taken literally, symbolic images are readily refuted by logic. But such logic overlooks the vital meaning contained in the allegory. To insist literally "the Lord is my shepherd" would make of oneself a sheep. Less literally, to insist that God is a person with a body raises the question of where he resides, on a space platform perhaps. To Protestants the Catholic dogma of the bodily ascension of Mary into heaven seems incredible. But Jung points out that the question is not one of physical possibility but of psychic necessity. God as a father omits divine maternal qualities. Prayer to the Virgin Mary, even though this is merely intercessory, expresses the maternal idealism which the worshiper feels must be found in divine reality. "As to the psychological elements of the symbol, Jung says: 'The living symbol is the formulation of an essentially unconscious fragment, and the more universal this fragment is the more universal the effect of the symbol, since it will touch a chord in each of us. . . . Only when the symbol grasps this primitive factor and brings the expression of it to the highest pitch does it enjoy universal effect. Therein lies the tremendous and at the same time the saving power of a living social symbol.' "[66]

Those who are able to think abstractly use symbolic images merely as aids to understanding, not taking them literally, or perhaps if the images seem too naïve, dispense with them entirely. Yet the usefulness of symbols for periodically bringing to the worshiper's mind a heightened sense of God must not be overlooked. Religious rituals contain these symbols. For example, the communion service presents to perception the physical elements of bread and wine, symbolizing the body and blood of Jesus, a pictorial way of reminding the worshiper of the supreme

[66] *Ibid.*, p. 84.

sacrifice of Jesus and of making vivid the experience of his spirit and life. The infusion of God's power into the personalities of worshipers is symbolized by physically consuming the bread and wine. If the worshiper is unable to think of God's role in the abstract, the experience of taking communion at least gives him an indirect insight in which this religious reality is fused with concrete components in the experience of the worshiper.

In the history of the world's religions, symbolic images in mythology, literature, and art have come into being as spontaneous creations by man in response to and as an expression of the spiritual impulsion he feels within himself. These include geometric designs which figure prominently in religious architecture, such as circles, spirals, crosses, squares, rosettes, or detailed elaborations of these figures. Called *mandalas,* these figures symbolize the wholeness or completeness of personality which results when the God-archetype is accepted and incorporated into the total personality. Other symbols of deity are light, fire, and water, and also personality types in mythology which are projections of motivational complexes in the unconscious.

Paralleling the development of religious symbols in history, the mind of the individual periodically recreates such symbols for himself. He may know nothing of the church or religion, but nevertheless the same symbols spontaneously make their appearance in his dreams. If he is set a projective task of drawing whatever figures come into his mind, he recreates on paper the crosses or rosettes of church art if under the influence of unconscious religious motivation. Such images express unconscious strivings of the individual. They are parts of his personality system. His dreams reënact themes from mythology or sacred history. These dreams portray aims, hopes, beliefs, and attitudes in his unconscious mind, things which are largely independent of his conscious will. They are components of a motivational system which is partly conscious (present as distinct images) and partly unconscious (contained implicitly within the images). To the extent that the symbols are spiritual and altruistic in content they express components in the system of motivation which is the power functioning in religion. The reality of the power exists in the images by which the inward motivation represents itself.

In Jungian dream-analysis—as is evident from all that has been said before—the psychological phenomenon generally denominated the SYMBOL plays a central role. . . . The psychic images, in the dream as in all their other manifestations, are at once reflection and essence of the dynamics of the psyche. They are at once reflection and essence of the dynamics of the mind, just as in the case of a waterfall the waterfall is at once reflection and essence of force itself. For without force, i.e., physical energy (which in itself is only a working hypothesis), there could be no waterfall, whose essence it therefore is; but simultaneously it reflects too in its form of being this energy, which without the waterfall, in which it becomes visible as it were, would be wholly inaccessible to observation and verification. . . . The symbols have at the same time expressive and impressive character, on the one hand expressing internal psychic happenings pictorially, and on the other hand —after having been transformed into images, having been "incarnated" as it were in an imaginary material—through their meaningful content influencing these same happenings, thus furthering the flow of the psychological processes. For example, the symbol of the withered Tree of Life, which was meant to convey the idea of an over-intellectualized existence that had lost its natural instinctive basis, would on the one hand express this meaning pictorially before the very eyes of the dreamer, and on the other hand, by thus presenting itself to him, impress him and thereby influence his psychic dynamism in a certain direction.[67]

A further phase to be kept in mind is that ideas after differentiation may still retain a colorless, qualityless character. They are evidenced by the characteristic words or actions associated with them. More than this, the individual is merely aware that psychic experience is going on. This is especially characteristic of spiritual experiences. The emergence of these from undifferentiated experience, the collective unconscious, does not reach the level of awareness except as the individual is aware of words or actions associated with these psychic states. Symbols in Jung's sense are of enormous importance in expressing or making conscious contact with these qualityless psychic states. Does the individual then become conscious of these states? He may not in the usual sense of the word conscious. The individual becomes aware of a characteristic word or action and the psychic component associated with it. The latter may possess no observable identity except its capacity to evoke symbols or stimulate behavior connected with it.

At this point it is relevant to refer to Sorokin's conceptual treatment of the unconscious in psychoanalysis. He directs sharp criticism against Freud for stressing repressed biological impulsion as a major factor in behavior. At the same time, Sorokin does not take account of the divergent development which Jung

[67] Jacobi, *op. cit.,* pp. 123–124.

gives of the concept of the collective unconscious as the concrete ground of undifferentiated experience from which spiritual ideas and ideals, as well as all creative thought, grow. Sorokin formulates a concept of the "supraconscious" to refer to these things after their appearance in consciousness. In reading Sorokin's works, the student will find it helpful to keep in mind that Sorokin uses the term *supraconscious* to refer to psychic material whose source Jung calls the *collective unconscious*. The two men are talking about the same phenomenon, one before emergence and the other after.

It seems probable that both Freud and Jung press an artificial separation between unconscious and conscious processes. Many ideas and impulses seem to function alternatively above and below the threshold of awareness. Only in moments of acute preoccupation does the average individual distill the contents of his mind into clear-cut images. Still, life moves on in a variegated totality of ongoing experience. The circumstance that dreams so often refer to consciously experienced tensions in personality, as well as those of which the individual is not consciously aware, indicates this interweaving of conscious and unconscious experience. It seems typical of pathological persons whom Freud and Jung treated that psychic barriers exist which prevent the easy flow back and forth of ideas and impulses from the unconscious to the conscious fields of personality.

A feature of the normal process of growing up is for the convictions and goals of adulthood to develop out of the collective unconscious, take their place and function on the conscious scene of personality. Jung places upon people the responsibility, with the help of others, of discovering and following the implications of their unfolding pattern of life. When they fail to do this, important ideas and powerful motivations may remain subterranean and operate in an uncoördinated manner in the individual's life. The unconscious aspects of the higher power in religion are, as far as possible, to be brought into consciousness where they can function effectively in human personality, and to the extent that they cannot become fully conscious are influenced and expressed through religious behavior.

While other empiricists whose work has been reviewed restrict themselves primarily to an account of the social and altruistic components of man's experience of God, Jung broadens his approach to account for malevolent spirit beings in religion and he also includes the genesis of religious rationalizations. Thus theological ideas with supernatural referents arise as contents of the collective unconscious of mankind. The manner of their origination, Jung points out, does not tell anything concerning their validity, which is a question left to philosophers and theologians. Nor do the contents of the collective unconscious operate in a uniform way, as evidenced by the variability in the world's religions. The particular theological concepts of a group depend upon the circumstances and history of its development. Man may speculate or err in the cosmological, spiritual, or theological interpretations which he places upon religious forces in his personality field, but the forces are real nonetheless. The empirical basis for other higher powers of religion besides the monotheistic one so far reviewed should be discussed more fully. The next chapter considers the functioning of the higher power of monotheistic religion in relation to destructive forces which underlie the devils and evil spirits of primitive religion, and religious rationalizations are considered under the heading of causation of religion.

Others in psychoanalysis besides Jung have interested themselves in the constructive role of religion and altruism in human personality. Alfred Adler and Erich Fromm are two of these.[68] Although their work does not focus as sharply upon the functioning of religion as does that of Jung, they are sympathetic towards the role which religion can play. Fromm supports humanistic over authoritarian forms of religion. In the past two decades psychoanalysis has moved toward more of a social psychological point of view. C. S. Hall and Gardner Lindzey describe the developments, to which passing reference is made here.

> Among those who provided psychoanalytic theory with the twentieth century look of social psychology are . . . Alfred Adler, Karen Horney, Erich Fromm, and Harry Stack Sullivan. Of these four, Alfred Adler may be regarded as the ancestral figure of the "new social psychological look" because as early as 1911 he broke with Freud over the issue of sexuality, and proceeded to develop a theory in which social interest and a striving for superiority became two of its substantial conceptual pillars. Later, Horney and Fromm took up the cudgels against the strong instinctivist orientation of psychoanalysis and insisted upon the relevance of social psychological variables for personality theory. Finally, Harry Stack Sullivan in his theory of interpersonal relations consolidated the position of a personality theory grounded in social processes.[69]

[68] Alfred Adler, *What Life Should Mean to You,* Little, Brown, 1931; *Social Interest,* Putnam, 1939; Erich Fromm, *Man for Himself,* Rinehart, 1947; *Psychoanalysis and Religion,* Yale University Press, 1950; *The Sane Society,* Rinehart, 1955; *The Art of Loving,* Harper, 1956.

[69] Hall and Lindzey, *op. cit.,* p. 115.

The problem of man's relations to society is one of great concern to Fromm, and he returns to it again and again. Fromm is utterly convinced of the validity of the following propositions: (1) man has an essential, inborn nature, (2) society is created by man in order to fulfill this essential nature, (3) no society which has yet been devised meets the basic needs of man's existence, and (4) it is possible to create such a society.

What kind of society does Fromm advocate? It is one ". . . in which man relates to man lovingly, in which he is rooted in bonds of brotherliness and solidarity . . . ; a society which gives him the possibility of transcending nature by creating rather than destroying, in which everyone gains a sense of self by experiencing himself as the subject of his powers rather than by conformity, in which a system of orientation and devotion exists without man's needing to distort reality and to worship idols."[70]

[70] *Ibid.*, p. 130.

chapter 8 Functioning of the Higher Power

The analysis so far of the major psychological power operating in contemporary religion has been directed to defining from an experiential standpoint what the power is whose religious effects are to be investigated. This power has been described as a system of altruistic motivation which is social as well as individual, and unconscious as well as conscious. In the present chapter we consider in what sense the system has the characteristics of a higher power by examining some of its effects on personality systems of which it is a part, effects which depend in part upon the performance of religious exercises. We make an analysis of the processes through which it produces its results, that is, an analysis of its functioning. In later chapters causes and effects in religious phenomena are examined in further detail.

EFFECTS OF ALTRUISTIC MOTIVATION

Sorokin: The Sociology of Love

Functioning of altruistic motivation in human life can be referred to succinctly as the ways and power of love, incorporated in the title of a principal work of P. A. Sorokin, *The Ways and Power of Love,* from which we draw some initial observations. The power of altruism has various aspects, only some of them relevant to an analysis of the inner workings of religion. Sorokin indicates the manifold extent of this power in his preface.

Now more than ever before I believe in the following truths, which are fully confirmed by our experimental studies:

Hate begets hate, violence engenders violence, hypocrisy is answered by hypocrisy, war generates war, and love creates love.

Unselfish love has enormous creative and therapeutic potentialities, far greater than most people think. Love is a life-giving force, necessary for physical, mental, and moral health.

Altruistic persons live longer than egoistic individuals.

Children deprived of love tend to become vitally, morally, and socially defective.

Love is the most powerful antidote against criminal, morbid, and suicidal tendencies; against hate, fear, and psychoneuroses.

It is an indispensable condition for deep and lasting happiness.

It is goodness and freedom at their loftiest.

It is the finest and most powerful educational force for the ennoblement of humanity.

Finally, only the power of unbounded love practiced in regard to *all human beings* can defeat the forces of interhuman strife, and can prevent the pending extermination of man by man on this planet. Without love, no armament, no war, no diplomatic machinations, no coercive police force, no school education, no economic or political measures, not even hydrogen bombs can prevent the pending catastrophe. Only love can accomplish this miracle, providing, however, we know well the nature of love and the efficient ways of its production, accumulation and use.[1]

While many in scientific work would, as a matter of personal conviction, agree with Sorokin's summary of the importance of altruistic love, it does not appear that the principles involved have all been adequately demonstrated or explored by scientific procedures. The confirmation is less full than Sorokin represents, and there is question of how far proof by actual experimentation can proceed in the study of any sector of human motivation. What human beings have felt or known intuitively for generations as part of folk wisdom provides much unfinished business for social and psychological scientists.

Altruism as an Integrating Force in Society

Like any other form of motivation, altruism is a functional system composed of wants, beliefs, and responses. The immediate and obvious effect produced by motivation as a force is found in the behavior which it brings about. Desires, whether altruistic or any other kind, have a persistent, compelling character which continues to stimulate the personality system to activity until the situation satisfying the desire is achieved. Altruism, as any motivation, possesses power of this kind. In the

[1] P. A. Sorokin, *The Ways and Power of Love,* Beacon, 1954, pp. vii–viii.

case of enlightened altruism, the power brings about social good, integrating society through relationships of mutual aid. Human life is superior in quality because of the myriad of individual acts of affection and aid which human beings have performed for each other in all societies, primitive, ancient, and modern. In the case of outstanding personalities, the results can be extensive. The following case of Asoka, a historic Hindu leader, illustrates the direct extent of the power of altruistic motivation.

After his accession to the throne in 273 B.C. Asoka, like his predecessors, spent the first twelve years of his reign in wars of consolidation of his Indian empire. The conquest of the province of Kalinga in 261 B.C. was his last war. From Asoka's own inscriptions we learn that the horrors and miseries of wars aroused in him a deep remorse, a sense of profoundest shame, and an understanding of the utter futility of war as a means of pacification and of social improvement. As a result, in 261–260 B.C. he was converted to Buddhism, as a lay disciple, and in 259 he entered a Buddhist order as a monk. This date marks the complete transformation of Asoka and of his policies. The successful emperor-warrior changed into a zealous apostle of peace, compassion, love, and good works. He began now to preach, to practice, and to carry on "the policies of goodness, mercy, liberality, truthfulness, purity, and gentleness,"—especially towards the conquered peoples—and the policies of liberation from "depravity, violence, cruelty, anger, conceit, and envy." Specific duties required from his followers and officials were: nonslaughter of animate beings, noninjury to "existing creatures"; hearkening to father and mother; reverence to teachers; liberality and seemly behavior towards friends, acquaintances, fellow men, and ascetics; compassionate and seemly conduct towards slaves and servants; and "small expense and small accumulation."

His *works of charity* consisted in planting the roads with shade trees and orchards, building rest houses and watering sheds, and digging wells; in construction of hospitals and dispensaries (for men and animals), in distribution of medical drugs, in planting medicinal herbs and fruit trees; in outright grants of money and organized relief to the poor, the aged, the helpless, prisoners, the infirm, and needy people generally.

His *political administration* was marked by the complete cessation of wars and establishment of undisturbed peace—internal and external—and by the organization of a special class of high officials (Dharma-Mahamatras) whose duties were concerned solely with the temporal and spiritual welfare of the people. All political officers were to follow Asoka's example in their personal behavior. They were exhorted to carry on the policy of good will, sympathy, and love to their own people, as well as to the peoples of the bordering territories. The officials thus were missionaries and moral leaders. One of their main functions was to be "peacemakers" between all sects, races, parties, and peoples, building their mutual good will and decreasing their enmities. Asoka revised the existing law and judicial administration, making these more just, human, and uniform. He made himself available for the business of the people at any and all times, and so on.

Asoka's *cultural activities* resulted in spreading mental and moral education among the people; in reconstructing the fine arts, particularly the art of the stage. The amphitheaters were used, among other things, for dramatization of the enjoyments which would follow from a life of virtue, from improvement of economic conditions of the people, and so forth.

To sum up: here we have a striking example of a peaceful, *love-motivated* social, mental, moral and aesthetic reconstruction of an empire. Was Asoka's experiment successful? It certainly was. He secured internal and external peace in his empire, not only up to his death in 232 B.C., but for an additional thirty to forty years after his death—that is, for a period of some sixty to seventy years.[2]

Allowing for exaggeration which occurs as events recede in time, the altruistic achievements following from Asoka's life are still an impressive record for any political or social leader to emulate. Such episodes can be duplicated from other times in history, and they are occurring today in the lives of those statesmen devoted to the peace and happiness of humanity. When some are striving for altruistic aims, other persons are stimulated to similar desiring and acting, which accounts for the multiplying effects of personalities in social movements. The influence of generosity is especially seen in the dispelling of social conflict through kindly actions toward opponents. Sorokin cites a series of fifty-one cases of how love stops aggression and enmity.[3]

Altruism as an Integrating Force in Personality

The aspects of altruism just described indicate nothing unique about its connection with religion. A distinctive power of altruistic motivation is found in its ability to integrate personality. Sorokin comments upon its curative effect upon mental disorder.

The power of love, sympathy, empathy, and understanding appears to be the main curative agent in diverse therapies of mental disorders. How curative the various psychiatric techniques actually are is exceedingly difficult to establish. The difficulties are due to a lack of objective criteria of improvement, diagnosis, record-keeping, etc. Various attempts to measure the curative effects of diverse psychiatric therapies give discrepant results from a very low percentage of

[2] *Ibid.*, pp. 66–68.
[3] *Ibid.*, pp. 48–58.

patients, with temporary and slight improvement, up to some 40 to 60 percent of cases in psychoneurotic, sexual, and character disorders; and much lower percentages in epilepsy, migraines, stammering, chronic alcoholism, and psychoses.

Regardless of the uncertainty and contrariety of the curative results of various psychiatric methods, on one vital point the psychiatrists seem to be in essential agreement, namely, *that the main curative agent in all the diverse psychiatric techniques is the "acceptance" of the patient by the therapist, the rapport of empathy, sympathy, kindness, and love established between the therapist and the patient.* In other words, the essence of curative therapy consists in the patient's exposure to the "radiation" of understanding, kindness, and love of the therapist, instead of the atmosphere of rejection, enmity, reproof, and punishment the patient is usually living in.[4]

What is involved is the internalization or activation of altruistic motives in personality about which the personality becomes restructured. Essential in this restructuring is the role of durable convictions and beliefs of the individual about the effectiveness of altruism as a way of life, what religionists call "faith." Of the role of faith a recent and popular writer in religious psychology, P. E. Johnson, states:

Religion and psychotherapy meet in recognizing faith as essential to mental health. Whatever the orientation of the counselor or therapist, no one who understands the predicament of man in our time will deny that faith is a basic requirement for healthy living. Faith may not mean the same thing to everyone, and yet whatever you believe will make a difference in how you behave. Faith is more than belief, for it involves the whole attitude of a person toward his world, his emotional response and purpose to deal with the total situation which he confronts. As such it permeates all of life, affecting a person's concept of himself and his relationship to other persons. The quality of personal faith is a determinant second to none in human behavior.

Faith is important for mental health because it is the antidote to anxiety. As we come to understand how anxiety pervades human experience from birth to death we become aware of the magnitude of the problem it presents. Anxiety, as we have seen, disturbs emotional security, blocks learning, distorts perceptions, and upsets interpersonal relations. To cope with anxiety a person may entrench himself behind rigid barriers and with the best of intentions deceive himself as to the real situation. Plagued by anxiety he may misconstrue the meaning of other persons' behavior or fail to communicate his own meanings effectively. In seeking to counteract the devastating effects of anxiety, psychotherapy aims to provide a relationship of trust essential to mental health.

[4] *Ibid.*, pp. 62–63.

Such faith arises in a secure and permissive interpersonal relationship wherein one may explore his anxieties more openly and develop more trusting emotional responses which can be generalized to other relationships.[5]

The major process for religion in the functioning of the power of altruism is its integration of personality. The activities of religion today are ones which aid this process. The purpose of the present chapter is to analyze the process of integration and to consider ways of stimulating the process through religious exercises to be examined in more detail in later chapters. Besides Sorokin and Johnson we review the viewpoints and findings of Durkheim, Dewey, and Jung concerning the functioning of psychic power utilized in religion.

Durkheim's Theory of the Power of Society

After identifying the Australian tribesman's god with the group to which he belongs rather than specifically with its altruistic ideals, Durkheim indicates the nature of the effects of this power on lives of members of the group. This power reaches and influences people's personalities through their consciousness of society. Power is exercised by society over people, according to Durkheim, in several ways. One of these is the sense of profound dependence which people have upon the group for their continued existence.

In a general way, it is unquestionable that a society has all that is necessary to arouse the sensation of divine in minds, merely by the power that it has over them; for to its members it is what a god is to his worshippers. In fact, a god is, first of all, a being whom men think of as superior to themselves, and upon whom they feel that they depend. Whether it be a conscious personality, such as Zeus or Jahveh, or merely abstract forces such as those in play in totemism, the worshipper, in the one case as in the other, believes himself held to certain manners of acting which are imposed upon him by the nature of the sacred principle with which he feels that he is in communion. Now society also gives us the sensation of a perpetual dependence.[6]

Besides the power which society exercises over its members because of their social dependence upon it, society has the power which moral commands possess. This power has two forms: that of authority backed by penalties and that of altruistic appeal.

[5] P. E. Johnson, *Personality and Religion,* Abingdon, 1957, pp. 222–223.
[6] Emile Durkheim, *The Elementary Forms of the Religious Life,* tr. by J. W. Swain, Free Press, 1947, p. 206.

Even if society were unable to obtain these concessions and sacrifices from us except by a material constraint, it might awaken in us only the idea of a physical force to which we must give way of necessity, instead of that of a moral power such as religions adore. But as a matter of fact, the empire which it holds over consciences is due much less to the physical supremacy of which it has the privilege than to the moral authority with which it is invested. If we yield to its orders, it is not merely because it is strong enough to triumph over our resistance; it is primarily because it is the object of a venerable respect.

We say that an object, whether individual or collective, inspires respect when the representation expressing it in the mind is gifted with such a force that it automatically causes or inhibits actions, *without regard for any consideration relative to their useful or injurious effects.*[7]

The effects of the power Durkheim describes are individual strength and social unity.

But a god is not merely an authority upon whom we depend; it is a force upon which our strength relies. The man who has obeyed his god and who, for this reason, believes the god is with him, approaches the world with confidence and with the feeling of an increased energy. Likewise, social action does not confine itself to demanding sacrifices, privations and efforts from us. For the collective force is not entirely outside of us; it does not act upon us wholly from without; but rather, since society cannot exist except in and through individual consciousnesses, this force must also penetrate us and organize itself within us; it thus becomes an integral part of our being and by that very fact this is elevated and magnified.[8]

These effects are intensified by the mechanism of crowd psychology. Citing data of Spencer and Gillen concerning the Warramunga, Durkheim describes this mechanism of intensification among primitive tribesmen.

When they are once come together, a sort of electricity is formed by their collecting which quickly transports them to an extraordinary degree of exaltation. Every sentiment expressed finds a place without resistance in all the minds, which are very open to outside impressions; each re-echoes the others, and is re-echoed by the others. The initial impulse thus proceeds, growing as it goes, as an avalanche grows in its advance. And as such active passions so free from all control could not fail to burst out. On every side one sees nothing but violent gestures, cries, veritable howls, and deafening noises of every sort, which aid in intensifying still more the state of mind which they manifest. And since a collective sentiment cannot express itself col-

[7] *Ibid.,* p. 207.
[8] *Ibid.,* p. 209.

lectively except on the condition of observing a certain order permitting co-operation and movements in unison, these gestures and cries naturally tend to become rhythmic and regular; hence come songs and dances. But in taking a more regular form, they lose nothing of their natural violence; a regulated tumult remains tumult. The human voice is not sufficient for the task; it is reinforced by means of artificial processes: boomerangs are beaten against each other; bull-roarers are whirled. It is probable that these instruments, the use of which is so general in the Australian religious ceremonies, are used primarily to express in a more adequate fashion the agitation felt. But while they express it, they also strengthen it. This effervescence often reaches such a point that it causes unheard-of actions. The passions released are of such an impetuosity that they can be restrained by nothing. They are so far removed from the ordinary conditions of life, and they are so thoroughly conscious of it, that they feel that they must set themselves outside of and above their ordinary morals. The sexes unite contrarily to the rules governing sexual relations. Men exchange wives with each other. Sometimes even incestuous unions, which in normal times are thought abominable and are severely punished, are now contracted openly and with impunity. If we add to all this that the ceremonies generally take place at night in a darkness pierced here and there by the light of fires, we can easily imagine what effect such scenes ought to produce on the minds of those who participate. They produce such a violent super-excitation of the whole physical and mental life that it cannot be supported very long: the actor taking the principal part finally falls exhausted on the ground.[9]

Religious dances among American Indians have a similarly intensifying effect upon their religious feelings, as depicted in the Ghost Dance described elsewhere in this text. Although the tribesman is only vaguely aware of the source of the power affecting him, he is profoundly aware of its effects upon him. His awareness of these effects provides the basis, in Durkheim's opinion, for the distinction between sacred and profane. "How could such experiences as these, especially when they are repeated every day for weeks, fail to leave in him the conviction that there really exist two heterogeneous and mutually incomparable worlds? One is that where his daily life drags wearily along; but he cannot penetrate into the other without at once entering into relations with extraordinary powers that excite him to the point of frenzy. The first is the profane world, the second, that of sacred things."[10] Religion becomes a social reality.

Religion ceases to be an inexplicable hallucination and takes a foothold in reality. In fact, we can say that the believer is not deceived

[9] *Ibid.*, p. 215–216.
[10] *Ibid.*, p. 218.

when he believes in the existence of a moral power upon which he depends and from which he receives all that is best in himself: this power exists, it is society. When the Australian is carried outside himself and feels a new life flowing within him whose intensity surprises him, he is not the dupe of an illusion; this exaltation is real and is really the effect of forces outside of and superior to the individual. It is true that he is wrong in thinking that this increase of vitality is the work of a power in the form of some animal or plant. But this error is merely in regard to the letter of the symbol by which this being is represented to the mind and the external appearance which the imagination has given it, and not in regard to the fact of its existence. Behind these figures and metaphors, be they gross or refined, there is a concrete and living reality. Thus religion acquires a meaning and a reasonableness that the most intransigent rationalist cannot misunderstand. Its primary object is not to give men a representation of the physical world; for if that were its essential task, we could not understand how it has been able to survive, for, on this side, it is scarcely more than a fabric of errors. Before all, it is a system of ideas with which the individuals represent to themselves the society of which they are members, and the obscure but intimate relations which they have with it. This is its primary function; and though metaphorical and symbolic, this representation is not unfaithful. Quite on the contrary, it translates everything essential in the relations which are to be explained: for it is an eternal truth that outside of us there exists something greater than us, with which we enter into communion.[11]

The function of religious assemblies and rituals is to evoke the power of society upon which human beings depend. The essential part played by religious activities is to intensify the natural functioning of the social power by heightening awareness of it as a psychic experience. This function of religious activities is examined in Chapter 9.

Durkheim's conclusion that God is society disguised in symbols and myths is generalized by him from the primitive tribes which he studied so that it applies to all religion. This makes his work, valuable if properly qualified, vulnerable to criticism. There is even question of whether the thesis that society is God applies precisely to the particular tribes which Durkheim studied. His data show that tribesmen identify their group with their tribal God. We are concerned not only with what men think is their God or higher power, but with what actually performs the role of a higher power in their religion. Since the group is a stern authority and a beneficent power rewarding the faithful, it is un-

[11] *Ibid.,* pp. 225–226.

derstandable that the group might be regarded as God-like and be made an object of worship. Does the actual power over individuals reside in society as an object? Talcott Parsons has pointed out that it is not society as an object of knowledge which exercises influence over man's behavior.[12] A society for which man cared nothing would be without power over him. The primary source of power over man is the altruistic desire within himself for society's welfare. Altruistic motivation is the force influencing behavior, not simply society as an object in the environment.

The primitive tribesmen studied by Durkheim did not make these subtle distinctions which a scientific analyst is expected to make. The effects which follow from altruistic motivation are not properly attributable to society as an object. Durkheim seems to take over the tribesmen's confusion into his own thinking. Nor does it help to broaden the definition of society to include all social aspects including altruistic motivation, since society then becomes an ill-defined and ambiguous object for cause-and-effect study.

Even if this confusion between society and its ideals is overlooked in the analysis of Australian primitive religion, Durkheim's analysis cannot be extended to religious devotees who clearly direct their attention toward a psychological power distinct from society. It can hardly be maintained that society is God for followers of contemporary monotheism. At the same time the importance of Durkheim's contributions should not be overlooked. Although he partially misplaced the higher power in religion he painstakingly investigated its social and psychological effects. He is usually credited with being the first in social science to establish the function of religious ritual in evoking the social power of group feeling. Furthermore, the work of Durkheim calls attention to religions today in which the object of worship is society and in which society, rather than its ideals, is erroneously believed to be the central power of religion.

Durkheim's observations seem to apply fairly adequately to those who make the state or a political movement their God or at least their supreme value and object of supreme devotion, as pointed out by Imogen Seger.[13] For some Communists the power which the party has over them is the power of a society upon

[12] Talcott Parsons, *The Structure of Social Action,* McGraw-Hill, 1937, Chap. 11.

[13] Imogen Seger, *Durkheim and His Critics on the Sociology of Religion,* Bureau of Applied Social Research, Columbia University, 1957.

which they depend and which demands complete obedience to its policies and decisions. That the party is not called God may be a verbal difference. To some it can occupy the role of God. At the same time, for many the power of Communism is not any group as it is, even the party entrusted with the future, but the moral power which flows from ideals for a better society than that now existent. A subtle though important difference exists between a group and its ideals as a source of moral authority, especially if the ideals are freely defined and pursued by the individual member.

The psychic energy engendered in the individual by the moral power of ideals aids in understanding the dynamic force of Communism in the world today and the essentially religious conflict between followers of different value systems. Since the time when Marx and Engels first sought to organize struggling bands of peasants and workers in Europe, many devotees of Communism have been inspired by the conviction that the moral forces of the universe are on the side of the collectivist way of life.

These things should be said in frank recognition of the appeal which Communism has for millions of the world's peoples, including some individuals among the American intelligentsia. On the other hand, this does not represent the coercive means whereby organized Communism has often defended and extended itself as socially suitable, any more than a moral interpretation of Christianity justifies the warlike means which have sometimes in history been used to defend or extend Christianity. Furthermore, in cults of nationalism the deification of the group is a reappearance of primitive religion.

Dewey's Analysis of Religious Power and Its Effects

In Dewey's analysis, the power of religion is the power of naturalistic, psychological components of personality, and the effect which they produce is a better life adjustment, in terms of both changing social conditions and reorganizing personality. Ames and Wieman maintain similar views. It will be recalled from the preceding chapter that Dewey defined God as the union of the ideal and the actual. In this experience, it is the ideal which has the dynamic power to produce change.

A writer says: "I broke down from overwork and soon came to the verge of nervous prostration. One morning after a long and sleepless night . . . I resolved to stop drawing upon myself so continuously and begin drawing upon God. I determined to set apart a quiet time every day in which I could relate my life to its ultimate source, regain the consciousness that in God I live, move and have my being. That was thirty years ago. Since then I have had literally not one hour of darkness or despair."

This is an impressive record. I do not doubt its authenticity nor that of the experience related. It illustrates a religious aspect of experience. . . .

In reality, the only thing that can be said to be "proved" is the existence of some complex of conditions that have operated to effect an adjustment in life, an orientation, that brings with it a sense of security and peace. The particular interpretation given to this complex of conditions is not inherent in the experience itself. It is derived from the culture with which a particular person has been imbued. . . .

The actual religious quality in the experience described is the *effect* produced, the better adjustment in life and its conditions, not the manner and cause of its production. The way in which the experience operated, its function, determines its religious value. If the reorientation actually occurs, it, and the sense of security and stability accompanying it, are forces on their own account. . . .

If this function were rescued through emancipation from dependence upon specific types of beliefs and practices, from those elements that constitute a religion, many individuals would find that experiences having the force of bringing about a better, deeper and enduring adjustment in life are not so rare and infrequent as they are commonly supposed to be. They occur frequently in connection with many significant moments of living. The idea of invisible powers would take on the meaning of all the conditions of nature and human association that support and deepen the sense of values which carry one through periods of darkness and despair to such an extent that they lose their usual depressive character. . . .

There are conditions we meet that cannot be changed. If they are particular and limited, we modify our own particular attitudes in accordance with them. . . . There are other attitudes toward the environment that are also particular but that are more active. We react against conditions and endeavor to change them to meet our wants and demands. . . . Instead of accommodating ourselves to conditions, we modify conditions so that they will be accommodated to our wants and purposes. This process may be called adaptation.

Now both of these processes are often called by the more general name of adjustment. But there are also changes in ourselves in relation to the world in which we live that are much more inclusive and deep seated. They relate not to this and that want in relation to this and that condition of our surroundings, but pertain to our being in its entirety. Because of their scope, this modification of ourselves is enduring. It lasts through any amount of vicissitude of circumstances, internal and external. There is a composing and harmonizing of the various elements of our being such that, in spite of the changes in the special conditions that surround us, these conditions are also arranged, settled, in relation to us. . . .

It is the claim of religions that they effect this generic and enduring change in attitude. I should like to turn the statement around and say that whenever this change takes place there is a definitely religious attitude. It is not *a* religion that brings it about, but when it occurs, from whatever cause and by whatever means, there is a religious outlook and function. As I have said before, the doctrinal or intellectual apparatus and the institutional accretions that grow up are, in a strict sense, adventitious to the intrinsic quality of such experiences. For they are affairs of the traditions of the culture with which individuals are inoculated.[14]

Jung's View of Religion as Man's Adjustment to a Higher Power

The archetype of altruism or theological impulsion of man is buried in his unconscious, seeking of its own inward dynamic to find expression. Value-seeking tends of its own nature to displace other motives. Furthermore, the experiences implying it deepen through use. The demands of spiritual motivation may go unheeded or be frustrated by conflict with unsympathetic ideas in culture. The college student who first experiences the pangs of spiritual hunger may ridicule his own religious leanings as sentimental or he may associate with a group of intellectuals who loudly proclaim there is no God. All the while, the God-experience is pressing for recognition as a plant beneath a stone. Its power is not to be underestimated. It can crack the stone and disrupt the present fabric of personality in its efforts to make a place for itself and to reorganize personality about itself.

The emphasis in Jung's treatment of religious psychology is on the adjustments which man must make in his own life pattern and social circumstances to avoid the dysfunction which results if religious forces go unrecognized. On the other hand, if allowed to proceed in coming to terms with the rest of personality, they bring permanent interest and meaning into the life of the individual which pleasure seeking is unable to do. Religion consists essentially of man's corporate and individual adjustments to the higher power. While Jung's analysis is a theory of religious function, it is much more than this. It is a theory of mental health in which the need for expressing altruistic and spiritual impulsion plays a commanding role among other needs. Perhaps the best single volume by Jung for introducing the student to his religious theory of mental health is *Modern Man in Search of a*

[14] John Dewey, *A Common Faith,* Yale University Press, 1934, pp. 11–17.

Soul or *Psychology and Religion,* the latter a series of lectures delivered at Yale in 1937 and recently published as the first part of a longer work, *Psychology and Religion: West and East.* In the the former Jung cites some statistics of the cases of patients who have sought his help.

About a third of my cases are suffering from no clinically definable neurosis, but from the senselessness and emptiness of their lives. It seems to me, however, that this can well be described as the general neurosis of our time. Fully two-thirds of my patients have passed middle age. . . .

I should like to call attention to the following facts. During the past thirty years, people from all the civilized countries of the earth have consulted me. I have treated many hundreds of patients, the larger number being Protestants, a smaller number Jews, and not more than five or six believing Catholics. Among all my patients in the second half of life—that is to say, over thirty-five—there has not been one whose problem in the last resort was not that of finding a religious outlook on life. It is safe to say that every one of them fell ill because he had lost that which the living religions of every age have given to their followers, and none of them has been really healed who did not regain his religious outlook. This of course has nothing whatever to do with a particular creed or membership of a church.[15]

The spiritual archetypes are too variable in their occurrence and development in different individuals and in different cultures for a uniform pattern to be recognized or prescribed. Their expression ranges from philanthropy and social action such as pacifism or Communism to diverse spiritual activities such as rigid ceremonial, quiet meditation, or crowd emotion and action. Which of these is the "right" way? According to Jung, there is no one right way which is the same for all. He does not advocate unthinking acceptance of group norms. Each individual is to look continually for the best which is within him and to be loyal to that. If followed, what develops will lead to something better.

The higher power functions to produce healthy or unhealthy personality, depending upon opportunities for its development. As long as dynamic ideas and impulses are ignored in the unconscious, they come into conflict with other ideas and impulses which are present in consciousness. This form of conflict is conceptualized by Jung as a struggle of opposites. Among the series of polarities, that between man's spiritual and selfish urges is a fundamental one.

[15] C. G. Jung, *Modern Man in Search of a Soul,* tr. by W. S. Bell and C. F. Baynes, Kegan Paul, Trench, Trubner, 1933, pp. 70, 264.

Whereas Freud sought to clear away the cake of custom which hampers expression of organic urges, Jung sought to remove cultural restrictions upon spiritual growth. For Jung the conflict is not resolved by rejecting one set of needs in favor of another. Rather, the conflict is met by allowing the conflicting needs to confront each other on the conscious scene of personality and to develop a mutual assimilation, which they tend to do during intelligent reflection. Sexual needs are not suppressed but gain a new orientation in a spiritual context. They become assimilated within a framework of altruistic love and lifelong fidelity to partner and children.

The unconscious ideation and motivation of religion can be integrated with the rest of personality by one of two routes. Symbols, myths, dogmas, and rituals which contain the unconscious contents can be used to influence and channelize these along the lines of their natural development and expression. For example, a fable may concretely portray a story in which honesty is the best policy. A child might be incapable of thinking abstractly about the meaning of the maxim, yet her motivation and behavior may be much impressed by the story. Similarly, an adult may be incapable of thinking who or what God is, yet the story of God incarnated in Jesus' life and actions profoundly moves his behavior. Thus stories and rituals whose meaning is only partly conscious aid in integrating spiritual motives with the conscious side of personality. The Catholic Church is especially effective in this regard. Schaer's comments are to be noted.

> Jung calls it the greatest objectification of psychic symbols the West has ever known, and is of the opinion that the existence of the Catholic Church is an absolute necessity for many people. It gives them the means of getting into *indirect* touch with the unconscious, and it —and it alone—can give them these means. Any other way would be too difficult and dangerous for their psyches, and they find the optimum psychic conditions for this contact only within the fold of the Catholic Church. The very indirectness of the contact protects them from all the incalculable consequences that flow from a direct encounter with the unconscious. The Church absorbs the archetypes, thereby creating a psychic cosmos instead of a psychic chaos.[16]

The "incalculable consequences" are those which result when persons who by temperament or culture have come to depend upon an external authority for guidance abruptly try to think out

[16] Hans Schaer, *Religion and the Cure of Souls in Jung's Psychology,* tr. by R. F. C. Hull. Bollingen Series XXI, Bollingen Foundation, Inc. Pantheon, 1950, p. 161.

and follow life purposes by their own ingenuity. In contrast, the meditative program of Buddhism seeks to direct the individual's attention inward to an intuitive understanding of himself.

Buddhism, too, tries to help man to face his unconscious by training his attention on the self. But Catholicism understood how to do one thing which this method failed to do: it objectifies the whole symbolism of the unconscious, i.e. places it outside the individual. In this way, always provided that the symbols of Catholic dogma and ritual are still effective for him, he is spared any conflict with his psyche, and thus he has no need of any psychology. The whole thing is projected, objectified, and consequently "exorcised" (bound by oath). The Mass shows how subtle are the psychological techniques that the Catholic Church has at its disposal. In the Mass, Christ is shown as a living quantity and reality—he in whom God's sacrifice is consummated over and over again and who can thus offer us salvation anew every day through the transubstantiation. The Mass represents, in objective form, God become man and man become God. Psychologically, too, the exercises of Ignatius Loyola are extremely shrewd. In other religions there are exercises—yoga, for instance. But whereas yoga stimulates *personal* production of symbols and thus brings the practitioner into the closest possible contact with the unconscious, the Catholic exercises replace the personal production of symbols by carefully chosen elements, so that the individual is insulated against the perils of the soul—but also, be it noted, against its beneficent influences. He gets the experience of Catholic dogma, but not of his own psyche.[17]

Catholicism encourages meditation but within the guiding framework of Catholic dogma. The other route besides traditional symbols is through individual meditation and seeking. This is a more difficult route. The introspective quest eventually brings unconscious components into relationship with conscious words or actions. The submerged components in psychic experience become differentiated through their association with words or actions during reflection. They thereby become connected with conscious aspects of personality from which they were previously separated. After becoming related to the conscious scene, these components tend to reorganize other aspects of personality to form with them an integrated whole. The differentiation and reorganization are aided by religious activities, as considered in the next chapter. Religious education can be combined with ritual activity in a mutually supporting manner so that engaging in ritual does not merely influence unconscious religious realities, but aids in holding them in the forefront of consciousness. The meanings which sacred dogmas and ritual possess can be

[17] *Ibid.*, p. 164.

renewed by reflecting upon these meanings. The Protestant and his Bible afford a classic example of relying both upon individual seeking and upon traditional symbolic aid.

The essential concepts and principles in Jung's analysis of personality integration can be discerned in the following passages from Schaer.

The individual is compelled to come to terms with his "within," his soul. We can say that what is now demanded is adaptation to the inner world. Outward adaptation is no easy matter, and inward adaptation makes no lesser demands. We are concerned with a very complicated psychic process which engages the whole man and ultimately all his faculties as well.

The pressing need for this process can show itself in any number of ways. A man often feels that his life has suddenly lost all meaning. At the very moment when he has successfully adapted himself to the world and he can say that his life is at its peak, all at once, stealthily, the question comes: what's the use of all this effort? He then discovers that though he is doing all sorts of valuable things, he is unable to say why, and what the point is. His life has lost its meaning. In Jung's experience very successful businessmen of the American type are sometimes faced with a personal crisis of this sort. . . .

Our experience of life is that it is somehow based on opposites, and we realize that apart from our present achievements there is something quite different—the Other. The material in or through which a man experiences the opposite is different in each case and is probably related to the attitude or function-type of the individual. But however various the forms may be, it is always a matter of the individual's realizing that the opposite, the Other, exists, and that he is faced with the problem of uniting the opposites. . . .

One of the latest efforts at solving it in Protestant theology is Karl Barth's idea of the Absolutely Other, which, as originally formulated, did offer the beginnings of an answer. But Barth's subsequent development and that of the theology associated with him have tended in a direction which can scarcely offer any solution whatever, since the whole opposition between God the Creator and the evil of this world is denied in the assertion that God has nothing to do with this life and this reality, because Creation, thanks to the Fall, has passed clean beyond God's reach. With this people think that the world is rid of the theodicy problem—at the cost, however, of God's having nothing to do with either man or reality. That is not, of course, a solution of the problem of opposites, only an evasion of it, which is satisfying neither religiously nor theologically nor philosophically. . . .

When a man becomes conscious of it in his life, it may happen that the problem of opposites appears as a *personal* problem only to a limited extent. In this case, if he is not yet fully conscious of it, he may find the solution in some existing symbol. In speaking of the transcendental function and the resultant constellation of symbols, we saw that these may be of supra-personal significance, i.e. that in the symbol wherein some religious founder experienced the unity transcending the opposites, other people too may find the same. Every traditional religion has such symbols, and many people find what they need in them. When a man discovers the solution to his personal crisis in a traditional symbol such as may be afforded by a rite, a dogma, a form of worship, he experiences this symbol with all the greater intensity, and it becomes inwardly alive for him. Then, though he may change somewhat, his changing, like the crisis itself, is not something of which he is fully conscious. He simply slips through the crisis, or partially slips through, without really discovering what it is all about. The symbol then in fact becomes for him what Jung has so clearly and tellingly described: the expression of something intuited but not made fully conscious. The individual in question also experiences the whole process of change as a redemption.

If, however, he cannot avail himself of a universal symbol, the process must now set in which Jung calls individuation. This road is by no means easy, and Jung is of the opinion that only an inner need justifies a man in taking it. Otherwise the solution afforded by traditional religion is to be preferred. The process is called "individuation" because it brings about the restoration of individuality, of one's own personality. Personality must be enlarged by making conscious an essential part of what has hitherto been unconscious. The aim is not what we commonly mean by "individualism," or even by an "individualistic" way of looking at things, i.e. a markedly egocentric attitude; it is an extension of personality *beyond* the ego. The ego is the centre, and a complex, of consciousness. It is, however, bound to consciousness and is consequently negative to the unconscious. It does not know what to do about the unconscious and feels it as something totally alien. Individuation consists essentially in recognizing and assimilating the unconscious. Therefore a new centre of personality must come into being, which is not bound to consciousness like the ego but is capable of taking equal account of both consciousness and the unconscious. When we say "must come into being," we are not to be understood as saying that the advent of this new centre can be forced. Normally it simply develops. But the whole psychic process is one of suffering, not an act of will. This new centre Jung calls the "self," and individuation is the way to the self.

The way is long and perilous. It is an encounter with the unconscious, and somehow or other the individual must get into touch with it and accept it. This is not as easy as it sounds. . . . The man who wishes to follow the way of individuation successfully must, above all, be loyal to his own fate. There must be no flinching; always he must do what is necessary. . . .

Surveying as a whole what Jung has to say about the function of religion, we see that religion always relates to man's wholeness. This is true of the primordial religious experience as it appears in the description we give of individuation, and also true of the collective religions which elaborate a system of myths, rituals, forms of worship, and traditional dogmas. Jung emphasizes very strongly the compensatory effect of religion, meaning that religion contains and brings out those things which are not realized in our everyday thinking and doing, but which are none the less innate in us. I would refer once again to the compensatory attitude of early Christianity as regards antiquity. We can say, then, that religion gives expression to that which is present but not realized. That is the reason why so many unconscious elements are at work in religion. Even though consciousness may follow different principles, the unconscious functions are still there. The neurotic proves that these can make themselves felt in a highly disquieting manner. It is always possible, however, for them to work themselves out in religion. Then they cease to disturb, and contribute in no small way to personality. A man's behavior may be influenced very significantly by the archetypes, so much so that they sometimes involve him in courses of action which, from the point of view of making the best of life, must be pronounced meaningless. But when the archetypes are contained in religious symbols, they may be experienced in a meaningful way, so that the archetypes are, in a manner of speaking, exorcized. And even if the myths and symbols harbour all sorts of unconscious elements, these may yet produce a *psychic cosmos instead of a psychic chaos*. All the psychic contents which are touched into life by religion then become related to one another, e.g. the conscious to the unconscious, the spiritual to the natural; all our stirrings and instincts fall into a pattern. The symbols release things in us, create order, and broaden. Psychic functions that might otherwise exert a disturbing influence become positive in their effect. The individual attains to what we described above as *active* experience, which imposes a cosmos on the chaos of his soul.[18]

Of basic importance in a consideration of Jung's theories are the data which he cites in support of them. An unfolding of the contents of the unconscious in the religious history of Judaism and Christianity is described in his essay "Answer to Job."[19] His books are interspersed with frequent data from dreams of patients. These dreams portray conflicts logically implied by the patient's way of life, conflicts of which he is not consciously aware, as pleasure seeking in conflict with spiritual requirements. In one of the cases analyzed the patient suffers a neurosis which is undermining his morale.[20] The patient is an inactive

[18] *Ibid.*, pp. 117–123, 127–129.

[19] C. G. Jung, *Psychology and Religion: West and East,* tr. by R. F. C. Hull. Bollingen Series XX, Bollingen Foundation, Inc. Pantheon, 1958, pp. 355–470.

[20] *Ibid.*, pp. 23–45.

Catholic, a scientist and an intellectual who thinks that religion is an emotional escape for weak-minded persons. Figures in his dreams dramatically enact the conflict going on in his own unconscious mind. In one of the dreams a female figure, the "anima," tells him his present way of life is lost and turns away in tears. Prior to coming to Jung the patient would have ridiculed the notion that he should again attend confession and communion. Jung points out that the dreams are the voice of the unconscious telling him to go back to church. He does so, and the neurosis ceases to threaten him except when he lets himself be disloyal to his experience.

Jung takes dreams at their face value, a mirror of what is hidden in the personality system. They are the voice of the unconscious describing its own contents in a symbolic manner. They are as authentic a report of the unconscious side of personality as interview data are of the conscious side of personality. Referring to another patient, Jung remarks:

> My patient is now very curious how I shall set about getting at the contents that form the root of the obsession. I then inform him, at the risk of shocking him severely, that his dreams will provide us with all the necessary information. We will take them as if they issued from an intelligent, purposive, and, as it were, personal source. This is of course a bold hypothesis and at the same time an adventure, because we are going to give extraordinary credit to a discredited entity—the psyche—whose very existence is still denied by not a few contemporary psychologists as well as by philosophers. . . .
>
> Yet in dreams we find, without any profound analysis, the same conflicts and complexes whose existence can also be demonstrated by the association test. Moreover, these complexes form an integral part of the existing neurosis. We have, therefore, reason to believe that dreams can give us at least as much information as the association test can about the content of a neurosis. As a matter of fact, they give very much more. The symptom is like the shoot above ground, yet the main plant is an extended rhizome underground. The rhizome represents the content of a neurosis; it is the matrix of complexes, of symptoms, and of dreams. We have every reason to believe that dreams mirror exactly the underground processes of the psyche. And if we get there, we literally get at the "roots" of the disease.[21]

The conclusions of Jung, as well as those of Sorokin, Durkheim, and Dewey, concerning the role of religion in the functioning of personality require additional data for their refinement, yet their materials in the aggregate constitute a substantial sci-

[21] *Ibid.*, pp. 22–23.

entific documentation of the effects of the higher power on personality. Within the past two decades an impressive series of data for testing hypotheses about religion has appeared on the scene of American life. These data are from a contemporary religious movement which has exceptional insight and vitality.

A CONTEMPORARY MOVEMENT

We turn to case material about a remarkable group, predominantly business and professional class, which in just over twenty-five years has grown to 250,000 members in 8,000 local groups meeting weekly in 80 countries. It brought together 10,000 persons at its three-day convention in Long Beach in July 1960. What written theology this group possesses comes not from scripture but from the lives of alcoholics. This is a society of alcoholics to help other alcoholics. None except alcoholics are members of it, nor do members concern themselves with the social drinking patterns of others. They expect to adjust to a world in which alcohol is prevalent. The movement is largely an indigenous development, finding new and vivid meaning in traditional concepts of religion and reconstructing these to meet the needs of alcoholics in the contemporary era. This group is Alcoholics Anonymous. Although spiritual in concepts and practices, it is not a separate church, its members participating in services of the conventional churches to which they belong.

Of course the movement has cultural continuity with the past. Its roots are found in the Oxford Group (now known as Moral Re-Armament, an upper-class Protestant evangelical group[22]) ; in the ministrations of the Catholic Church, whose religious workers have been dedicated to helping the alcoholic; in the discoveries of the medical profession; and in the writings of William James and C. G. Jung. But the religious literature of Alcoholics Anonymous is their own, developed by and for alcoholics. *Grapevine,* the monthly magazine, has a circulation of 40,000. The personal work with alcoholics is done entirely by members who give their time without financial remuneration. This unusual enterprise is financed through sale of literature and by passing the hat.

The cure of mental disorder through religious therapy is as old

[22] M. Bach, *They Have Found a Faith,* Bobbs-Merrill, 1946, pp. 123–161; C. S. Braden, *These Also Believe,* Macmillan, 1949, pp. 403–420; A. W. Eister, *Drawing Room Conversion: A Sociological Account of the Oxford Group Movement,* Duke University Press, 1950.

as the world's religions, recurring references to such cures being found in Biblical literature. In the modern epoch, religious groups such as the Salvation Army and the Catholic Church have worked effectively with alcoholics, achieving permanent cures through acceptance by the patient of the saving power of Christ. Nor is the idea of a religious society of alcoholics new. A century ago the Washingtonian Society of alcoholics gained a half million members but became diverted into larger issues of public temperance and other political matters and moved on to eventual dissolution. Alcoholics Anonymous is distinctive in avoiding the incorporation of traditional Christology in its formulated program, although many of its members wholeheartedly accept orthodox Biblical teachings. By using the term *higher power* rather than *Christ* or *Saviour,* it meets the prejudice of many alcoholics influenced by scientific teaching against supernatural, mystical, or dogmatic concepts of religion, or for whom traditional concepts have lost their meaning. In pursuing the religious specialization in alcoholics, the A.A. type of movement reflects the population concentration and division of labor in the modern industrial world and could not be sustained by small agrarian communities of the preindustrial era.

Beyond these cultural factors, A.A. has as its co-founder a leader of unusual practical and spiritual genius. Completely democratic in its organization structure, being little more than an association of local fellowships of alcoholics, A.A. is composed of members who have been inspired by his initiative to realize of their own volition the soundness of the ideas contained in the books he has written. The real transformation of alcoholics comes from within. As in the case of other figures in religious history, he has been instrumental in calling the attention of people to the reality of forces within themselves. His life illustrates the periodic power of spiritual realities to break through the threshold of consciousness and to motivate the lives of men, relatively independently of traditional religious teaching. Known to the outside world only as Bill W., he prefers to lead a life of anonymity beyond his activity among alcoholics. His story is modestly recounted in an autobiographical book, *Alcoholics Anonymous Comes of Age,* preceding works being *Alcoholics Anonymous* and *Twelve Steps and Twelve Traditions.*

A Description of the Fellowship

An issue of the *Annals of the American Academy of Political and Social Science* was recently devoted to a report upon the problem of alcoholism and ways of meeting it. In this issue a summary account is given of Alcoholics Anonymous, from which is drawn the following description of its activities.

Alcoholics Anonymous is a fellowship of compulsive drinkers, both men and women, who join with each other in a mutual effort to remain sober. It was started by alcoholics themselves in their despair and hopelessness and has apparently achieved a success as great as, if not greater than, professionally directed therapies.

At both "open" meetings to which the public is invited and at "closed" meetings for alcoholics only, its members frankly narrate their drinking histories—their "stories"—and explain how the A.A. program enabled them to gain sobriety. State-wide "retreats" to some outdoor spot widen the scope of associations. Members travel in small groups to adjacent communities to tell their "stories" and share their program for sobriety at A.A. meetings there. Often two or three members will hold meetings in prisons or hospitals where they explain the A.A. program to alcoholic inmates.

The fellowship, however, is more than this. Local groups sponsor dances, parties, and picnics. Families of members who attend such events together often form family auxiliaries with scheduled meetings. Individual members get together to eat lunch, drink coffee; they meet after work, to bowl, fish, and play cards. These informal contacts between members extend the relationship developed at the formal meetings. In this network of interpersonal relations, the "Twelve Steps," listed below, are the core of the joint effort to remain sober.

Membership in A.A. depends solely upon whether or not an alcoholic says he is a member. New members are sought through "Twelfth Step Work," that is, carrying the message to other alcoholics. According to the society's definitions, an A.A. group exists whenever two "drunks" join together to practice the A.A. program for sobriety. There are no officers, no hierarchy, no dues. Local secretaries are necessary, but tenure is short. . . .

On a Friday night in a small Midwestern city numerous persons are parking their cars outside a large brick house in the University district. Some of them are wearing casual sport clothes and some are dressed more conservatively; their cars are of all makes and models. Other persons, obviously still in work clothes, are walking from the bus stop toward the house. This is the A.A. clubhouse, and the meeting is scheduled for eight o'clock. But, as one member put it, "We never start then; we have to do some 'coffee-clatching' first."

Inside the meeting hall many more people are standing around and talking in small groups. One man is describing his reaction to telling his "story" last week at the mental hospital, "I saw myself as I used to be, sitting right there in the front row." To others recapitulating last Saturday night's party, a woman is saying, "We had fifty-eight people here. I had a hilarious time and all of it without any booze."

Approximately sixty persons have assembled. A man at the speaker's stand announces that this is the regular Friday night "open" meeting of A.A., and he calls for a moment of silence to be used as each person sees fit. "My name is Jim P. and I am an alcoholic," he begins and explains the general nature of the fellowship. As chairman for this meeting, he has invited two members of a new group in a nearby community to speak this evening. He calls on the first one.

"My name is Dave L. and I am an alcoholic." Dave's "story" is a series of anecdotes embellished with frank humor. Laughter from the group interrupts him frequently. Someone whispers, "If he made it, anyone can. What a lush he used to be!" His excessive drinking landed him in a mental hospital five times. In the process of his alcoholism he went from manager of a chain grocery store to itinerant laborer. His family had forsaken him, and numerous times he heard the ward doctors brand him hopeless. He "hit bottom" after his third attack of delirium tremens. Twice he almost died from them.

Dave had scorned the idea of A.A. when a member came to him during his fourth commitment. "I thought the guy was shooting an angle, but when I finally went to a meeting during the fifth time I was at the hospital, I discovered he wasn't." He repeats several times that he was surprised to learn from A.A. that he was "sick," but that as such he could still be respectable. The idea of a "higher power," a God, was difficult for him to accept. He finished dramatically, telling the group that he has found in A.A. a "bunch of real friends—twice as good as those drinking buddies who pumped me for every cent I had.". . .

At "closed" meetings of fewer members, there is more informal discussion of how the program works—that is, how the members "live this program for twenty-four hours at a time rather than face the hell of living the rest of our lives without the stuff." Members intimately confess their drinking escapades and often disclose personal problems. A point frequently made to newcomers is, "We did it, so can you."[23]

Effectiveness of Alcoholics Anonymous

At a time when Freud's work gained world recognition for its discoveries in the understanding and cure of mental disorders but frequently could not provide the missing links of treatment for curing chronic alcoholism, A.A. developed a group form of spiritual psychotherapy which its leaders report has cured 75 percent of those who have undertaken it. Those who coöperate in the A.A. program tend to be those who are sociable with an ability to adapt to group therapy and who frequently have had normal religious influences in their background. The cases treated by A.A. have not been easy ones. About half of them do

[23] H. M. Trice, "Alcoholics Anonymous," *Annals of the American Academy of Political and Social Science,* January, 1958, pp. 108–110.

not turn to A.A. until they have hit bottom and realized that alcohol has wrecked the lives of themselves and their families. An increasing number have been turning to A.A. in earlier stages of their sickness in anticipation of the final disaster which would otherwise overtake them. For work among the difficult cases, local A.A. groups are functioning (in 1957) in 265 hospitals and 335 prisons. Where formerly only 20 percent of alcoholics paroled from prisons and institutions could make the grade, now 80 percent of those following the program of therapy are reported by A.A. to do so. The skills of medical practitioners and the facilities of hospitals are used by members of A.A. for correction of physiological conditions beyond the scope of spiritual treatment, but the heart of their program of therapy has been developed by and is carried out by alcoholics. They are convinced that only one who has experienced chronic alcoholism can understand and gain the confidence of a fellow alcoholic.

An exact comparison of the effectiveness of the work of Alcoholics Anonymous with other forms of therapy is not easily made. From a precise scientific standpoint, random experimental and control groups should be devised to compare the effectiveness of the spiritual therapy with other possible modes of treatment. Also involved is an exact definition of a chronic alcoholic. The characteristic that the individual does not stop a drinking spree when other participants are back at work can be narrowly or leniently applied. With excessive intake, psychotic behavior expressing delusions and manias may develop. The addict whose intake is prolonged and continuous may suffer death or insanity from impairment of the brain. Approximately two-thirds of the adult population drink occasionally on social occasions, and about 4 percent of the adult population according to the Jellinek formula may be considered alcoholic.[24]

Of those who seek psychiatric or Antabuse treatment for addiction to alcohol, 30 to 50 percent recover after one or more remissions, especially if they come to understand and are cured of the psychological conflicts or are relieved of the social pressures for which alcohol became a pain-relieving drug. How much natural tendencies to recover oneself play a part in cures reported by the medical profession is difficult to estimate. Among members of A.A. it is noteworthy that many have tried other types of treatment and have only been cured after following A.A.

[24] M. Keller, "Alcoholism: Nature and Extent of the Problem," *Annals of the American Academy of Political and Social Science,* January, 1958, pp. 5–6.

therapy. They uniformly report having found a higher power without whose aid alcohol would continue to disrupt their lives. While the primary group values of a closely knit fellowship help alcoholics to keep on the road of sobriety, it is significant that they do not take those who merely want the encouragement of friendship, but require as a condition of their assistance that the alcoholic accept and follow the twelve steps in their program of therapy or something substantially equivalent to them.

Data from A.A.'s Co-founder

The experience of Alcoholics Anonymous might seem to afford an unusual type of data to test psychological principles, but it is by means of extreme fluctuations that the relationship between variables in a functional system is most clearly seen. The experience of A.A. shows to an intense degree the operation of a higher power which in normal situations of life outside the context of acute alcoholism also performs a role of deep significance in the lives of many church and synagogue members, even though these accept in a less conscious and less articulate way the existence of such a power in their religion. First is noted the experience of co-founder Bill W. His narrative is picked up at the point where he has been contacted by an alcoholic changed by the Oxford Group and engaged in its religious work.

I was not in too awful a condition. In three or four days I was free of what little sedative they gave me, but I was very depressed. I was still choking on the God business. Bright and early one morning friend Ebby showed up and stood in the doorway, smiling broadly. I didn't see what was so funny. Then I had a suspicion: maybe this is the day he is going to evangelize me; maybe he is going to pour on the sweetness and light. But no, he made me wait until I asked him. "Well," said I, "what is your neat little formula once more?" In perfectly good humor, he handed it out again: You admit you are licked; you get honest with yourself; you talk it out with somebody else; you make restitution to the people you have harmed; you try to give of yourself without stint, with no demand for reward; and you pray to whatever God you think there is, even as an experiment. It was as simple and yet as mysterious as that. After some small talk he was gone.

My depression deepened unbearably and finally it seemed to me as though I were at the very bottom of the pit. I still gagged badly on the notion of a Power greater than myself, but finally, just for the moment, the last vestige of my proud obstinacy was crushed. All at once I found myself crying out, "If there is a God, let Him show Himself! I am ready to do anything, anything!"

Suddenly the room lit up with a great white light. I was caught up into an ecstasy which there are no words to describe. It seemed to me, in the mind's eye, that I was on a mountain and that a wind not of air but of spirit was blowing. And then it burst upon me that I was a free man. Slowly the ecstasy subsided. I lay on the bed, but now for a time I was in another world, a new world of consciousness. All about me and through me there was a wonderful feeling of Presence, and I thought to myself, "So this is the God of the preachers!" A great peace stole over me and I thought, "No matter how wrong things seem to be, they are still all right. Things are all right with God and His world."

Then, little by little, I began to be frightened. My modern education crawled back and said to me, "You are hallucinating. You had better get the doctor." Dr. Silkworth asked me a lot of questions. After a while he said, "No, Bill, you are not crazy. There has been some basic psychological or spiritual event here. I've read about these things in the books. Sometimes spiritual experiences do release people from alcoholism." Immensely relieved, I fell again to wondering what actually had happened.

More light on this came the next day. It was Ebby, I think, who brought me a copy of William James' *Varieties of Religious Experience*. It was rather difficult reading for me, but I devoured it from cover to cover. Spiritual experiences, James thought, could have objective reality; almost like gifts from the blue, they could transform people. Some were sudden brilliant illuminations; others came on very gradually. Some flowed out of religious channels; others did not. But nearly all had the great common denominators of pain, suffering, calamity. Complete hopelessness and deflation at depth were almost always required to make the recipient ready. The significance of all this burst upon me. *Deflation at depth*—yes, that was *it*. Exactly that had happened to me. Dr. Carl Jung had told an Oxford group friend of Ebby's how hopeless his alcoholism was and Dr. Silkworth had passed the same sentence upon me. Then Ebby, also an alcoholic, had handed me the identical dose. On Dr. Silkworth's say-so alone maybe I would never have completely accepted the verdict, but when Ebby came along and one alcoholic began to talk to another, that clinched it.

My thoughts began to race as I envisioned a chain reaction among alcoholics, one carrying this message and these principles to the next. More than I could ever want anything else, I now knew that I wanted to work with other alcoholics.[25]

In May 1935, Bill W. met Dr. Bob, whom he helped to recovery, and they then worked together in bringing alcoholics to undergo a spiritual cure. The movement grew slowly at first, having reclaimed forty alcoholics after three years and four hundred after five years. Then, gaining attention for its effectiveness, it received nation-wide publicity in the press, magazines, and radio

[25] *Alcoholics Anonymous Comes of Age,* By a Co-Founder, 1957, pp. 62–64. Reprinted by permission of Alcoholics Anonymous Publishing, Inc.

which brought alcoholics to it by the thousands. The movement survived the problems of sudden growth, crystallized its basic policies, and established itself as a world-wide enterprise. To recount the way in which it took root almost spontaneously in numerous communities is a dramatic story beyond the present task of assembling relevant data for research analysis. The famous "Twelve Steps" of spiritual therapy were formulated by gradual evolution out of precepts of the Oxford Group from which A.A. broke away, principles of religious psychology, medical findings, and church teaching. The steps were drafted in final form in 1938 by Bill W., whose forcefulness as a creative thinker is evidenced by them and by the explanation of them which he gives in *Twelve Steps and Twelve Traditions.* The steps, given by A.A. members as suggestions to fellow-alcoholics, are:

1. We admitted we were powerless over alcohol—that our lives had become unmanageable.
2. Came to believe that a Power greater than ourselves could restore us to sanity.
3. Made a decision to turn our will and our lives over to the care of God as we understood Him.
4. Made a searching and fearless moral inventory of ourselves.
5. Admitted to God, to ourselves, and to another human being, the exact nature of our wrongs.
6. Were entirely ready to have God remove all these defects of character.
7. Humbly asked Him to remove our shortcomings.
8. Made a list of all persons we had harmed, and became willing to make amends to them all.
9. Made direct amends to such people whenever possible, except when to do so would injure them or others.
10. Continued to take personal inventory and when we were wrong promptly admitted it.
11. Sought through prayer and meditation to improve our conscious contact with God as we understood Him, praying only for knowledge of His will for us and the power to carry that out.
12. Having had a spiritual awakening as the result of these steps, we tried to carry this message to alcoholics, and to practice these principles in all our affairs.[26]

The part played by the group in this program of therapy has several phases. A fundamental principle is that only an alcoholic can talk effectively to another alcoholic. Meetings which are

[26] *Twelve Steps and Twelve Traditions,* 1953. Reprinted by permission of Alcoholics Anonymous Publishing, Inc.

open to the public enable members of A.A. to tell their experiences with alcohol and about their spiritual recovery. The primary purpose of these meetings is to give other alcoholics an opportunity to learn of A.A. and to contact members if they desire. Another major source of contact is provided by hospitals to which chronic alcoholics usually find their way and in which A.A. members work as volunteers. No pressure is used, the A.A. member simply sharing sympathetically his own experience. The alcoholic must come of his own volition to a realization that he is powerless before alcohol and to a decision that he is going to undertake the program of A.A. He then attends informal group sessions open only to alcoholics at which members explain the program to him and help him get started in following it. No religious ritual is involved. Sometimes a member of the medical profession is present to help in giving advice, the novitiate sometimes being more willing to take the group's ideas when backed as medical prescription.

Case Studies

The following cases, for the most part abridged, from the book *Alcoholics Anonymous,* are statements by members which describe the control by alcohol experienced in their lives and the subsequent freedom gained following a spiritual experience. Printed words do not adequately portray the realism with which these experiences are told at testimonial meetings in direct, unassuming language and producing a dramatic effect upon the listener. The psychological implications of these experiences for an understanding of the higher power in religion require analysis, to which we turn later. The first of these cases refers to a commonplace episode out of which the peculiar condition of alcoholic addiction eventually developed, and it also suggests the presence of hereditary tendency.

[A] I am in another fellow's room at college. "Freshman," said he to me, "do you ever take a drink?" I hesitated. Father had never spoken to me about drinking and he never drank any, so far as I knew. Mother hated liquor and feared a drunken man. Her brother had been a drinker and had died in a state hospital for the insane. But his life was unmentionable, so far as I was concerned. I had never had a drink but I had seen enough merriment in the boys who were drinking to be interested. I would never be like the village drunkard at home. How a lot of people despised him! Just a weakling!

"Well," said the older boy, "do you?"

"Once in a while," I lied. I could not let him think I was a sissy.

He poured out two drinks. "Here's looking at you," said he. I gulped it down and choked. I didn't like it, but I would not say so. No, never! A mellow glow stole over me. Say! This wasn't so bad after all. In fact, it was darn good. Sure I'd have another. The glow increased. Other boys came in. My tongue loosened. Everyone laughed loudly. I was witty. I had no inferiorities. Why, I wasn't even ashamed of my skinny legs! This was the real thing!

A haze filled the room. The electric light began to move. Then two bulbs appeared. The faces of the other boys grew dim. How sick I felt. I staggered to the bathroom—. Shouldn't have drunk so much or so fast. But I knew how to handle it now. I'd drink like a gentleman after this.

And so I met John Barleycorn. The grand fellow who at my call made me "a hale fellow, well met," who gave me such a fine voice, as we sang "Hail, hail, the gang's all here," and "Sweet Adeline," who gave me freedom from fear and feelings of inferiority. Good old John! He was my pal, all right. . . .

It is a cold, bleak day in November. I have fought hard to stop drinking. Each battle has ended in defeat. I tell my wife I cannot stop drinking. She begs me to go to a hospital for alcoholics which has been recommended. I say I will go. She makes the arrangements, but I will not go. I'll do it all myself. This time I'm off of it for good. I'll just take a few beers now and then.

It is the last day of the following October, a dark, rainy morning. I come to in a pile of hay in a barn. I look for liquor and can't find any. I wander to a stable and drink five bottles of beer. I must get some liquor. Suddenly I feel hopeless, unable to go on. I go home. My wife is in the living room. She had looked for me last evening after I left the car and wandered off into the night. She had looked for me this morning. She has reached the end of her rope. There is no use trying any more, for there is nothing to try. "Don't say anything," I say to her. "I am going to do something."

I am in the hospital for alcoholics. I am an alcoholic. The insane asylum lies ahead. Could I have myself locked up at home? One more foolish idea. I might go out West on a ranch where I couldn't get anything to drink. I might do that. Another foolish idea. I wish I were dead, as I have often wished before. I am too yellow to kill myself. But maybe—. The thought stays in my mind.

Four alcoholics play bridge in a smoke-filled room. Anything to get my mind from myself. The game is over and the other three leave. I start to clean up the debris. One man comes back, closing the door behind him.

He looks at me. "You think you are hopeless, don't you?" he asks.

"I know it," I reply.

"Well, you're not," says the man. "There are men on the streets of New York today who were worse than you, and they don't drink anymore."

"What are you doing here then?" I ask.

"I went out of here nine days ago saying that I was going to be honest, and I wasn't," he answers.

A fanatic, I thought to myself, but I was polite. "What is it?" I enquire.

Then he asks me if I believe in a power greater than myself, whether I call that power God, Allah, Confucius, Prime Cause, Divine Mind, or any other name. I told him that I believe in electricity and other forces of nature, but as for a God, if there is one, He has never done anything for me. Then he asks me if I am willing to right all the wrongs I have ever done to anyone, no matter how wrong I thought they were. Am I willing to be honest with myself about myself and tell someone about myself, and am I willing to think of other people and of their needs instead of myself; to get rid of the drink problem?

"I'll do anything," I reply.

"Then all of your troubles are over," says the man and leaves the room. The man is in bad mental shape certainly. I pick up a book and try to read, but cannot concentrate. I get in bed and turn out the light. But I cannot sleep. Suddenly a thought comes. Can all the worthwhile people I have known be wrong about God? Then I find myself thinking about myself, and a few things that I had wanted to forget. I begin to see I am not the person I had thought myself, that I had judged myself by comparing myself to others, and always to my own advantage. It is a shock.

Then comes a thought that is like A Voice. "Who are you to say there is no God?" It rings in my head, I can't get rid of it.

I get out of bed and go to the man's room. He is reading. "I must ask you a question," I say to the man. "How does prayer fit into this thing?"

"Well," he answers, "you've probably tried praying like I have. When you've been in a jam you've said, 'God, please do this or that' and if it turned out your way that was the last of it and if it didn't you've said 'There isn't any God' or 'He doesn't do anything for me.' Is that right?"

"Yes," I reply.

"That isn't the way," he continued. "The thing I do is to say 'God here I am and here are all my troubles. I've made a mess of things and can't do anything about it. You take me, and all my troubles, and do anything you want with me.' Does that answer your question?"

"Yes, it does," I answer. I return to bed. It doesn't make sense. Suddenly I feel a wave of utter hopelessness sweep over me. I am in the bottom of hell. And there a tremendous hope is born. It might be true.

I tumble out of bed onto my knees. I know not what I say. But slowly a great peace comes to me. I feel lifted up. I believe in God. I crawl back into bed and sleep like a child.

Some men and women come to visit my friend of the night before. He invites me to meet them. They are a joyous crowd. I have never seen people that joyous before. We talk. I tell them of the Peace, and that I believe in God. I think of my wife. I must write her. One girl suggests that I phone her. What a wonderful idea.

My wife hears my voice and knows I have found the answer to life. She comes to New York. I get out of the hospital and we visit some of these new-found friends. What a glorious time we have![27]

The next case is of a man who started drinking during Prohibition and gradually increased his consumption, becoming physiologically dependent on alcohol.

[B] Some nights I wouldn't go home at all and when I did go home I was displeased when my wife had supper ready and equally angry when she didn't. I didn't want to eat at all and frequently when I underestimated my consumption of the amount of liquor I brought home, I made extra trips back to town to renew the supply. My morning ration when I started out was five double whiskies before I could do any business at all. I would go into a saloon, trembling like a leaf, tired in appearance and deathly sick, I would down two double whiskies, feel the glow and become almost immediately transformed. In half an hour I would be able to navigate pretty well and start out on my route. My daily reports became almost illegible and finally, following arrest for driving while intoxicated and on my job at that, I got scared and stayed sober for several days. Not long afterward I was fired for good.

My wife suggested I go to my old home in the country, which I did. Continued drinking convinced my wife I was a hopeless case and she entered suit for divorce. I got another job, but didn't stop drinking. I kept on working although my physical condition was such as to have required extensive hospitalization. For years I hadn't had a peaceful night's sleep and never knew a clear head in the morning. I had lost my wife, and had become resigned to going to bed some night and never waking again.

Every drunkard has one or two friends who haven't entirely given up hope for him, but I came to the point where I had none. That is, none but my Mother, and she, devoted soul, had tried everything with me. Through her, people came to me and talked, but nothing they said—some were ministers and others good church members—helped me a particle. I would agree with them when they were with me and as fast as they went away, I'd go after my bottle. Nothing suggested to me seemed to offer a way out.

I was getting to a place where I wanted to quit drinking but didn't know how. My Mother heard of a doctor who had been having marked success with alcoholics. She asked me if I'd like to talk to him and I agreed to go with her.

I had known, of course, of the various cures and after we had discussed the matter of my drinking fairly thoroughly, the doctor

[27] *Alcoholics Anonymous,* 1944, pp. 228–229, 234–237. Reprinted by permission of Alcoholics Anonymous Publishing, Inc.

suggested that I go into the local hospital for a short time. I was very skeptical, even after the doctor hinted there was more to his plan than medical treatment. He told me of several men whom I knew who had been relieved and invited me to meet a few of them who got together every week. I promised I would be on deck at their next meeting but told him I had little faith in any hospital treatments. Meeting night, I was as good as my word and met the small group. The doctor was there but somehow I felt quite outside of the circle. The meeting was informal, nevertheless I was little impressed. It is true they did no psalm singing, nor was there any set ritual, but I just didn't care for anything religious. If I had thought of God at all in the years of drinking, it was with a faint idea that when I came to die I would sort of fix things up with Him.

I say that the meeting did not impress me. However, I could see men whom I had known as good, hard-working drunkards apparently in their right minds, but I just couldn't see where I came into the picture. I went home, stayed sober for a few days, but was soon back to my regular quota of liquor every day.

Some six months later, after a terrific binge, in a maudlin and helpless state, I made my way to the doctor's home. He gave me medical treatment and had me taken to the home of one of my relatives. I told him I had come to the point where I was ready for the remedy, the only remedy. He sent two of the members to see me. They were both kindly to me, told me what they had gone through and how they had overcome their fight with liquor. They made it very plain that I had to seek God, that I had to state my case to Him and ask for help. Prayer was something I had long forgotten. I think my first sincere utterance must have sounded pretty weak. I didn't experience any sudden change, and the desire for liquor wasn't taken away overnight, but I began to enjoy meeting these people and began to exchange the liquor habit for something that has helped me in every way. Every morning I read a part of the Bible and ask God to carry me through the day safely.

There is another part I want to talk about—a very important part. I think I would have had much more difficulty in getting straightened out if I hadn't been almost immediately put to work. I don't mean getting back on my job as salesman. I mean something that is necessary to my continued happiness. While I was still shakily trying to rebuild my job of selling, the doctor sent me to see another alcoholic who was in the hospital. All the doctor asked me to do was tell my story. I told it, not any too well perhaps, but as simply and as earnestly as I knew how.

I've been sober for two years, kept that way by submitting my natural will to the Higher Power and that is all there is to it. That submission wasn't just a single act, however. It became a daily duty; it had to be that. Daily I am renewed in strength and I have never come to the point where I have wanted to say, "Thanks God, I think I can paddle my own canoe now," for which I am thankful.

I have been reunited with my wife, making good in business, and paying off debts as I am able. I wish I could find words to tell my story more graphically. My former friends and employers are amazed and see in me a living proof that the remedy I have used really works. I have been fortunate to be surrounded with friends ever ready to help, but I firmly believe any man can get the same result if he will sincerely work at it God's way.[28]

The concluding case cited is that of an agnostic, and it is significant for its reference to the higher power in non-theological terms.

[C] Why go into the drinking pattern that is so much the same with all of us? Three times I had left the hospital with hope that I was saying goodbye forever. And here I was again.

The first day there I told the kindly doctor that I was a thoroughly hopeless case and would probably continue to return as long as I could beg, borrow, or steal the money to get in. On the second day he told me that he knew of something that would keep me off liquor for life. I laughed at him. Yes, indeed, I would do anything or take anything that would produce such results, but there wasn't anything. On the third day a man came to talk with me. He was an alcoholic who had stopped! He talked about alcoholism and a spiritual way of life. I was deeply impressed by his seriousness, but nothing that he said made sense to me. He spoke about God, and a power greater than one's self. I remember being very careful not to say anything that might shake his faith in whatever it was he believed! I was deeply grateful to him for taking the trouble to talk with me, but what he had was not for me. I had thought much about religion and had come to rather definite conclusions. There was no God. The universe was an inexplicable phenomenon. In spite of my sorry state and outlook, there were many beautiful things in life, but no beauty. There were truths discoverable about life, but no truth. There were people who were good, kind, considerate, but no such thing as goodness. I had read rather extensively, but when people began to talk in such ultimates I was lost. I could find in life no eternal purpose nor anything that might be labeled "divine guidance." War, illness, cruelty, stupidity, poverty and greed were not and could not be the product of any purposeful creation. The whole thing simply didn't make sense. . . .

The next day another man visited me. He, too, had been an alcoholic and stopped drinking. He pointed out that I had found myself unable to handle my liquor problem by myself. He had been in the same position, yet he hadn't had a drink in over three years! He told me of other men who had found sobriety through the recognition of some power beyond themselves. If I cared to I was to consider myself invited to a gathering the following Tuesday where I would meet other alcoholics who had stopped.

With the knowledge I now have, it is hard for me to recall how screwy the whole thing sounded—the blind leading the blind, a union

[28] *Ibid.*, pp. 320–324.

of drunks, all banded together in some kind of a spiritual belief! What could be more idiotic! But . . . these men were sober! Nuts!

I returned to my despairing wife with this incoherent story of a bunch of drunks who had found a cure for their alcoholism through some kind of spiritual exercise and who held regular meetings where, as far as I could figure out, they went through some kind of spiritual exercise! She was very nearly convinced that my mental balance had now been completely and probably permanently destroyed. The only rational support I could find for giving it a try was that it was vouched for by the kindly doctor whom she had met on several occasions at the hospital. That and the fact that nothing else worked. . . .

But to conclude my story: The following Tuesday, hardly daring to hope and fearful of the worst, my wife and I attended our first gathering with former alcoholic slaves who had been made free through the rediscovery of a power for good, found through a spiritual attitude toward life. I know that I have never before been so inspired. It was not anything that happened. Because nothing happened. Nor yet by anything that was said, but more by an atmosphere created by friendliness, sincerity, honesty, confidence, and good cheer. I couldn't believe that these men could have been drunks, and yet gradually I learned their stories, alcoholics every one!

That was, with me, the beginning of a new life. It would be difficult, if not impossible, for me to put into words the change that has taken place in me, I have since learned that with many members the change has been almost instantaneous. This was not the case with me. I was tremendously inspired at first, but my basic thinking was not altered that evening nor did I expect any profound change. I felt that while the spiritual aspect of what these men had was not for me, I did believe strongly in the emphasis they put on the need to help others. I felt that if I could have the inspiration of these gatherings and if I could have an opportunity to try to help others that the two together would reenforce my own will-power and thus be of tremendous assistance. But gradually, in a manner I can not explain, I began to re-examine the beliefs I had thought beyond criticism. Almost imperceptibly my whole attitude toward life underwent a silent revolution. I lost many worries and gained confidence. I found myself saying and thinking things that a short time ago I would have condemned as platitudes! A belief in the basic spirituality of life has grown and with it belief in a supreme and guiding power for good.[29]

EFFECTS OF ALTRUISTIC MOTIVATION ON A.A. MEMBERS

The Hypothesis to Be Tested

In analyzing the data from Alcoholics Anonymous, the hypothesis to be tested is that the higher power which eliminates al-

[29] *Ibid.*, pp. 351–355.

coholic addiction is the higher power described in the preceding chapter, that is, altruistic motivation. This hypothesis is compatible with the supernatural view of philosophy that a God exists beyond experience who functions through and in harmony with psychological laws. It is in conflict with the type of supernaturalism which introduces an independent system of supernatural causation to account for personality transformation.

In offering and defending the hypothesis of a natural higher power, the opinions set forth here are not intended to displace the firm religious faith of those who hold that the transformation in question is a supernaturally caused and not a naturally caused event. Science is not concerned with changing the opinions of churchgoers, but merely with the cultivation of consensus about reality among researchers. If churchgoers find meaning in the insights and discoveries of social and psychological science, it is their privilege to utilize them. If they do not find them helpful, a social scientist who recognizes the vital function performed by supernatural faith would be among the first to insist that the individual retain his original faith intact.

Supernatural Views

Unquestionably many members of A.A. believe that they have been aided by a uniquely supernatural event, and many others accept a naturalistic interpretation. As an organization, A.A. makes no attempt to define whether its members believe in a supernatural or a natural higher power as the source of their recovery. Two prominent sponsors for the movement, a Catholic and a Protestant, apparently subscribe to a supernatural interpretation of the alcoholic's conversion. Without attempting to define the particular type of supernaturalism which they hold, we cite their views here for the implications for science which they may have. We quote first from an address to the 1955 A.A. convention given by Father Edward Dowling, a Catholic priest.

> What experience should we seek? What beliefs should we accept in our quest for God? . . . Bill early wrote a letter—I have it—in which he said, "How far the alcoholic shall work out his dependence on God is none of A.A.'s business. Whether it is in a church or not in a church, whether it is in that church or this church, is none of A.A.'s business." In fact, he implied, "I don't think it's any of the members' business. It's God's business." And the A.A.'s business is charted in the Eleventh Step. Seek through meditation and prayer to find God's will and seek the power to follow it out.
>
> I would like to share with you what I have found to be God's will. . . . We know A.A.'s Twelve Steps of man toward God. May I suggest

God's Twelve Steps toward man as Christianity has taught them to me.

The first step is described by St. John. The Incarnation. The word was God and the word became flesh and dwelt amongst us. He turned His life and His will over to the care of man as He understood him. The second step, nine months later, closer to us in the circumstances of it, is the birth, the Nativity. The third step, the next thirty years, the anonymous hidden life. Closer, because it is so much like our own. The fourth step, three years of public life.

The fifth step, His teaching, His example, our Lord's Prayer. The sixth step, bodily suffering, including thirst, on Calvary.

The next step, soul suffering in Gethsemane; that's coming close. How well the alcoholic knows, and how well He knew, humiliation and fear and loneliness and discouragement and futility. Finally death, another step closer to us, and I think the passage where a dying God rests in the lap of a human mother is as far down as divinity can come, and probably the greatest height that humanity can reach.

Down the ages He comes closer to us as head of a sort of Christians Anonymous, a mystical body laced together by His teachings. "Whatsoever you do to the least of these my brethren so do you unto me." "I can fill up what is wanting in the sufferings of Christ." "I was in prison and you visited me." "I was sick and I was hungry and you gave me to eat."

The next step is the Christian Church, which I believe is Christ here today. A great many sincere people say, "I like Christianity, but I don't like Churchianity." I can understand that. I understand it better than you do because I'm involved in Churchianity and it bothers me too! But, actually, I think that sounds a little bit like saying, "I do love good drinking water but I hate plumbing." Now, who does like plumbing? You have people who like sobriety, but they won't take A.A.

And then, the eleventh step is several big pipe lines or sacraments of God's help.

And the twelfth step, to me, is the great pipe line or sacrament of Communion. The word that was God became flesh and becomes our food, as close to us as the fruit juice and the toast and the coffee we had an hour ago.[30]

Next we quote from the address given at the same convention by an Episcopalian clergyman, the Rev. Samuel Shoemaker.

In the third and fourth chapters of Acts is the story of the healing of a lame man by Peter and John. A lot of the ecclesiastics wanted to know how this came about. The Apostles told them that it was through the name of Christ that this man was healed. The story says, "And beholding the man which was healed standing with them, they could say nothing against it." Now you can fight a theory about an experience, but you've got to acknowledge the experience itself. . . .

[30] *Alcoholics Anonymous Comes of Age,* pp. 257–259.

We act as if character and reasonably good behavior were the end of all existence. The real questions in life which underlie these matters of behavior are definitely of a religious nature. And they have only a religious answer, an answer that comes from God. Where did I come from, and what am I supposed to be doing here, and where do I go when I die? Those are questions which, unanswered, leave us without direction, without moorings, and without values. Science hasn't got any answer to those things, and philosophy only has the answers of good human guesses. Religious faith is the one candle in man's darkness in the mystery of life. If Christ came down from Heaven to represent God and speak for Him, we have got an answer. The lesser revelations to prophets and seers are of the same nature, but not of the same authority—as Father Ed has been suggesting to us—but all truly wise men begin with the acknowledgment of their finiteness, their darkness, and their needs. When we get through to God, by whatever name we call Him, or rather when we let Him get through to us, then we begin finding light and the answer. . . .

Prayer, either private or group or public, is the place where we get in touch with God and God's power. God's power is always there, as there is always potential electricity in a wire that's plugged into a socket that is in touch with a dynamo. But you don't get the power until you close the circuit by turning the switch. Prayer, in ways which to me are theoretically quite unfathomable but which are always open to us actually, turns on the switch, opens up the power by closing the circuit. We do not so much "get what we want" as find out what we should do. Awakening—in the individual or in companies or in nations—always includes discovering the power that is in prayer.

Somehow we never can do this alone. From the first, Christ drew about Him a company. To join Him, you had also to join that company. The church has always been a scratch company of sinners. It is not the best people in the community gathered together for self-congratulation; it is the people who know they have a great need gathered to find its answer in worship toward God and fellowship with one another. The church is not a museum; it is a hospital. That is why we can all belong to it and all should. . . .

To me A.A. is one of the great signs of spiritual awakening in our time. It is experimental in nature, not dogmatic. But none can doubt that God is what has made A.A. what it is today, what inspires it, what keeps it going, what is that perfectly intangible but absolutely unmistakable spirit that we have felt again and again since we have been here in St. Louis. I am thankful that the church has so widely associated itself with A.A., because I think A.A. people need the church for personal stabilization and growth, but also because I think the church needs A.A. as a continuous spur to greater aliveness and expectation and power. They are meant to complement and supplement each other.

I believe that A.A. will go on serving men and women as long as it may be needed, if it keeps open to God for inspiration, open to one another for fellowship, and open to people outside for service. I think A.A. has been wise to confine its organized activity to alcoholics, but I hope and I believe that we may yet see a wide effect of A.A. on medicine, on psychiatry, on correction, on education, on the everpresent problem of human nature and what we shall do about it, and not least of all on the church itself.[31]

A Medical View

A significant contribution to a naturalistic understanding of the spiritual therapy of A.A. is given by a psychiatrist, H. M Tiebout. He describes the alcoholic's personality structure and the effect of religion on it in the following way.

Characteristic of the so-called typical alcoholic is a narcissistic egocentric core, dominated by feelings of omnipotence, intent on maintaining at all costs its inner integrity. While these characteristics are found in other maladjustments, they appear in relatively pure culture in alcoholic after alcoholic. In a careful study of a series of cases, Sillman recently reported that he felt he could discern the outlines of a common character structure among problem drinkers and that the best terms he could find for the group of qualities noted was "defiant individuality" and "grandiosity." In my opinion, those words were accurately chosen. Inwardly the alcoholic brooks no control from man or God. He, the alcoholic, is and must be master of his destiny. He will fight to the end to preserve that position.

Granting then the more or less constant presence of these character traits, it is easy to see how the person possessing them has difficulty in accepting God and religion. Religion by its demand that the individual acknowledge the presence of a God challenges the very nature of the alcoholic. But, on the other hand, and this point is basic to my paper, *if* the alcoholic can *truly accept* the presence of a Power greater than himself, he, by that very step, modifies at least temporarily and possibly permanently his deepest inner structure and when he does so without resentment or struggle, then he is no longer typically alcoholic. And the strange thing is that if the alcoholic can sustain that inner feeling of acceptance, he can and will remain sober for the rest of his life.

. . . in light of Mr. "X's" [Bill W.'s] own experience, a religious or spiritual awakening is the act of giving up one's reliance on one's omnipotence. The defiant individuality no longer defies but accepts help, guidance, and control from the outside. And as the individual relinquishes his negative, aggressive feelings toward himself and toward life, he finds himself overwhelmed by strongly positive ones such as love, friendliness, peacefulness, and pervading contentment, which state is the exact antithesis of the former restlessness and irritability.

[31] *Ibid.,* pp. 263, 266–270.

And the significant fact is that with this new mental state the individual is no longer literally "driven to drink.". . .

The central effect, therefore, of Alcoholics Anonymous is to develop in the person a spiritual state which will serve as a direct neutralizing force upon the egocentric elements in the character of the alcoholic. If and when that state becomes completely integrated into new habit patterns, the patient will remain dry. . . .

In conclusion, it is my belief that the therapeutic value of the Alcoholics Anonymous approach arises from its use of a religious or spiritual force to attack the fundamental narcissism of the alcoholic. With the uprooting of that component, the individual experiences a whole new series of thoughts and feelings which are of a positive nature, and which impel him in the direction of growth and maturity. In other words, this group relies upon an emotional force, religion, to achieve an emotional result, namely, the overthrowing of the negative, hostile set of emotions and supplanting them with a positive set in which the individual no longer need maintain his defiant individuality, but instead can live in peace and harmony with and in his world, sharing and participating freely.[32]

Demonstration of Cause and Effect in Case-Study Analysis

Before amplifying the analysis of Tiebout and religious psychologists whose work has been reviewed, we should first consider how a cause-and-effect relationship is shown. This is a technical question which the casual reader may by-pass. Cause and effect refer to separate stages or successively observed variables of a process which moves from stage to stage in the same way each time the process is repeated. Thus an object dropped falls to the ground in a continuing process of motion. In order to assert reliably that one stage is followed by another, it is necessary to exclude any intervening influences which might become part of the process and alter its course. The demonstration that extraneous variables have been removed from the situation studied may require investigation of a number of cases in which presence and absence of cause and of effect are separately tested to show their firm relationship. However, as in the case of a falling body, if it is apparent to the observer that nothing intervenes to affect the object, the law of gravitation can be demonstrated by a single case.

Cause-and-effect relationships in the life history of an individual or of a group are frequently demonstrated without exhaustive testing for intervening variables. How well inter-

[32] H. M. Tiebout, "Therapeutic Mechanism of Alcoholics Anonymous," *American Journal of Psychiatry,* January, 1944, pp. 469–470, 472–473.

vening variables have been taken into consideration is usually a matter of judgment rather than mechanical control over the situation, since human subjects do not tolerate experimentation of any fundamental character. The judgment exercised is dependent upon an intuitive grasp of the interior processes of motivation which are involved. Familiarity with these processes enables the investigator to know whether successive events being studied are phases of a single process or whether they are unrelated parts of different processes.

Case-study analysis is largely a deductive procedure in which known principles of cause and effect or functional relationship are fitted together to establish a new conclusion. The data in the case fix the terminal points in the chain of reasoning and frequently some of the intermediate points. The intervening chain of reasoning establishes the causal connection between parts of the data, a functional connection which would not otherwise be apparent. In turn, the data usually permit a more precise statement to be made of the cause-and-effect relationship than that specified by the principles fitted together by deduction. The functional relationship is then described by means of more exact sets of conditions than deductive reasoning would ordinarily achieve.

The known principles used in case-study analysis are often initially derived as hypotheses from introspection. Through repeated application to case studies they acquire the status of dependable knowledge. In being applied they also receive calibration, that is they become stated in more precise form to meet requirements of the data than is possible from introspective intuition. Principles used in case studies of individuals or cultures possess varying degrees of validity as knowledge, depending upon the extent to which they have been investigated and applied. When their status is intermediate between hypothesis and demonstrable law, they are referred to as theories. In the analysis of A.A. data, some of the principles to be introduced may be regarded by some as theories, although their validity seems adequate to other investigators.

Analysis of Alcoholism and Its Elimination by Altruistic Motivation

The conclusion that altruistic motivation is the higher power which enables members of A.A. to recover from alcoholism is consistent with the facts from A.A. Those who cease their addiction are those who follow the program of helping other alcoholics, righting injuries done others, and seeking to follow altruistic goals in their life pattern. However, the facts without deductive reasoning to link them causally do not necessitate the conclusion of cause and effect. To show that the conclusion is valid, the intervening causal processes must be traced. Pursuing this pattern of case-study analysis, we describe the principles which form the chain of reasoning which connects altruistic motivation with elimination of alcoholism.

1. The initial principle to be considered is a corollary of a fundamental process. Desires press for satisfaction through what a person thinks at the time is effective behavior. This is a general statement about the relationship of motivation, internally experienced, to resulting activity, externally observed. Human beings want various experiences, and their desires for these call forth behavior which brings the experiences into existence. Applied to altruism, the desires of people to live for others cause them to be active in ways which they believe effectively further the well-being of others. On the other hand, self-seeking or egoistic (in part what Tiebout calls "narcissistic") desires cause persons to engage in behavior which serves their needs without regard for others.

Under certain conditions, egoistic desires seek satisfaction through excessive and continuous intake of alcohol. The particular causal conditions which differentiate the alcoholic from the average self-seeking person are somewhat obscure and sufficient research has not yet been accomplished. However, one of the conditions is an excessive rigidity of desire, making the desire prone to frustration because of its inflexible, exacting character. This condition is shown by Tiebout's point that the alcoholic is characterized by "defiant individuality." Individuals possessing this type of motivation are easily irritated or depressed by their environment and suffer recurring dissatisfaction and disappointment because of their tendency to be combative toward rather than tolerant of unavoidable circumstances. For such persons alcohol provides the relief of a narcotic, relaxing their tensions and taking away their mental discomfort.[33] Concerning such use of alcohol, the psychiatrist E. A. Strecker remarks: "Alcohol is quickly effective in screening unpleasant reality; it is readily obtainable and the pathologic drinker is tol-

[33] J. J. Conger, "Perception, Learning, and Emotion: The Role of Alcohol," *Annals of the American Academy of Political and Social Science,* January, 1958, pp. 34–36.

erated socially until he has fallen to a very low level. In spite of its reputation among the laity as a stimulant, alcohol is always a narcotic."[34]

This is a motivational condition present to some degree in all people and substantially accounts for the popularity of social drinking. Those who continue drinking when the party is over are apparently those whose conflicts are more acute and whose ability to adjust their desires to circumstances is more limited. Furthermore, from a physiological standpoint they may find drinking more effective in its relief than other persons whose capacity for alcohol is less or for whose hang-overs further alcohol does not afford relief as it does for the alcoholic. Alcoholism then appears to be a special form of drug addiction, a form in which physiological susceptibility to alcohol is critical. Intake continues for relief of the physical or psychological distress which alcohol itself creates. Although rigidity of desire and physical allergy to alcohol seem to be widely prevalent among alcoholics, these things are not all of the complex pattern of motivation, conscious and unconscious, which may be involved.

To a certain extent, inflexibility of desire can also characterize ordinary altruistic motivation, since the desire to help others may meet with adverse results to which persons with temperamental rigidity may find it difficult to adjust. At the same time, however, the practical opportunities for giving help and encouragement to others are almost unlimited, being relatively independent of particular conditions. Furthermore, indoctrination by success ideas in culture reinforces self-seeking ambitions in ways which are often beyond achievement, while cultural indoctrination of altruistic motives tends typically to stress simple, readily attainable forms of friendliness and assistance to others. What seems of special significance is that altruism in its highest form as contained in religious teaching excludes all interposition of the individual's will to accomplish results in predetermined ways. Typically, the religious devotee is supposed to perform, not his own will, but God's will. Since the latter as conceived by man is not for what is absurd or impossible but rather for what is in harmony with the laws of the universe, the altruism which is fostered is strongly realistic. To combat circumstances beyond control would dissipate, not maximize, the effectiveness of altruistic motivation. At its highest it is a system of motivation for doing the best of which one is capable.

[34] E. A. Strecker, *Fundamentals of Psychiatry,* Lippincott, 1947, pp. 144–145.

This motivational flexibility is shown by the spiritual attitude of A.A. The third step in its program is "Made a decision to turn our will and our lives over to the care of God as we understood Him," and in explaining this step Bill W. writes: *"Our whole trouble had been the misuse of will-power. We had tried to bombard our problems with it instead of attempting to bring it into agreement with God's intention for us.* To make this increasingly possible is the purpose of A.A.'s Twelve Steps, and Step Three opens the door."[35] A popular prayer with A.A. members is "God grant me the serenity to accept the things I cannot change; courage to change the things I can, and wisdom to know the difference. Thy will, not mine, be done."

The initial cause-and-effect principle involved in the hypothesis that altruistic motivation eliminates alcoholic addiction may be summarized as follows: Egoistic motivation of a person with excessive rigidity of motivation and physical susceptibility to alcohol seeks satisfaction through alcohol. In analyzing the motivation of alcoholism, oversimplification is to be avoided. Besides the factors to which attention has been called, there may be complicated neurotic conditions involved whose correction by psychiatric therapy is necessary for recovery from alcoholism. Some alcoholics may be able to learn a more flexible type of motivation which accepts circumstances without a full shift from egoistic to altruistic motivation. Others may respond to drug therapy, such as Antabuse. Here we are merely analyzing the cause-and-effect relationships involved in the recovery of A.A. members.

2. Turning to a second principle, we first note that the capacity of behavior to satisfy desires is limited and therefore desires for various experiences compete for fulfillment, the stronger ones displacing the weaker and controlling behavior in rough proportion to their intensity and duration. While people often act from combinations of motives such that altruistic and egoistic systems cannot be separated, nevertheless the two types of motives are in competition with each other. Whichever system of motives is experienced as stronger dominates the functioning of personality. The relevant form of this principle in our deductive analysis is that altruistic desires, if sufficiently strong, substantially eliminate self-seeking desires or cause them to be reorganized and expressed in ways subservient to altruistic requirements. The competition between systems of motivation is evident in the inward struggle of the alcoholic to abstain and

[35] *Twelve Steps and Twelve Traditions,* p. 42.

hold to A.A. principles.[36] Whichever system of motives is stronger makes the opposing system subservient to it.

3. The third analytical principle refers to the growth characteristics of altruistic motivation. In the life history of an individual personality, self-seeking desires are dominant during early childhood. Altruism appears later in human development and in varying degrees displaces egoistic motivation. Several reasons why altruism grows in human personality with the passage of years may be noted. Not until the age of approximately 5 years do children display sufficient imagination to comprehend realistically the needs of others, although earlier than this they act imitatively or in response to commands in ways which do meet the needs of others. Not until sympathetic imagination is functioning do they have the type of social experience out of which altruistic desires develop. The social experience becomes proportionately greater the more the individual becomes involved in the division of labor of the intimate groups in which he lives. The practical problems of living necessitate reflecting upon the needs of others in order to gain their coöperation by serving these needs, and these needs become grafted onto the personality during imaginative projection of oneself into the roles of others. Sympathetically experiencing the desire-fulfillment of others instills the desire in oneself for desire-fulfillment of others.

From the standpoint of cultural teaching, altruistic motives are frequently highly esteemed, and exposure to such influence by culture increases the longer one is alive. The system of motivation in personality then becomes patterned according to a clearly articulated value system in which the needs of others may exercise greater influence on the individual's behavior than do his own needs. Since culture is not homogeneous, individualistic values often being propagated by its real, rather than ideal, aspects, the effects of culture upon the development of altruism are mixed in nature. Yet self-sacrificial or heroic actions make their appearance, which cannot be explained except in terms of altruistic motives that become more powerful than even the desire for life itself. Religious exercises play a fundamental role in intensifying altruistic motivation within the individual. A basic force in the growing dominance of altruism is that man seeks the highest value his experience enables him to know.

That altruistic motivation in some form comes to dominate the personalities of many people seems a secure conclusion, how-

[36] S. Vogel, "Psychiatric Treatment of Alcoholism," *Annals of the American Academy of Political and Social Science,* January, 1958, pp. 103–104.

ever intangibly introspective or other research techniques demonstrate the component processes which are involved. An area of scientific uncertainty pertains to why altruistic growth proceeds more fully in some persons than in others. The precise degree to which hereditary capacity, social opportunity, and cultural conditioning are involved is an important research question. Enough of the processes involved can be described to justify the conclusion that the growth takes place within the framework of natural psychological principles.

In the lives of those who successfully follow A.A. therapy, certain factors evidence themselves. In view of the degree of altruistic motivation eventually shown after following the A.A. program, the inference seems justified that this motivation was substantially present prior to undertaking the program, even if this motivation was ignored or merely latent. During the addiction it seems to exist largely in the unconscious portion of personality. Moreover, the blocking of this pattern by alcoholic addiction accounts for much of the frustration and spiritual depression experienced by the alcoholic. The significant fact is that for his recovery he has a latent asset which he can utilize to displace the self-seeking motivation in which his alcoholism is rooted. Since 75 percent of those who undertake the A.A. program are reported ultimately successful, it appears that the majority of people have a sufficient amount of altruistic motivation at least latent in their personalities. It would be of considerable research interest to conduct intensive case studies of the lives of those who fail in the A.A. program in order to determine in what respect their personality assets were inadequate to overcome the factors causing their addiction.

What is the precipitating factor which activates the altruistic motivation which is unconscious or at least subordinate in the life of the alcoholic? The factor which triggers the latent system is the momentous realization that by turning their thinking to this motivational system as part of the twelve steps, alcoholics can escape from painful tyranny of addiction to alcohol. The second step after admitting powerlessness over alcohol is "Came to believe that a Power greater than ourselves could restore us to sanity." This realization is greatly aided by the dramatic recoveries which A.A. members relate to the novitiate. The inrush of altruistic motivation from the unconscious when the alcoholic becomes acutely preoccupied with it produces a more or less intense state of feeling—a spiritual awakening. Of course it is not clearly articulated, at least at first, and is combined with whatever theological concepts the individual may possess. It may not be thought of by the term *altruism,* but merely as something higher and better in which dedication to the lives of others is implicit.

The twelfth step of A.A. is the requirement to help other alcoholics. In so doing, the A.A. member relives again and again the conviction that only by turning to a higher power with its altruistic involvement can security from alcohol be gained. As often as the conviction is renewed, the preoccupation of the individual shifts from egoistic motivation to the higher power and all that it implies. The motivational system involved is renewed and maintained by being turned to, thought about, and acted upon.

Furthermore, other steps, such as taking a moral inventory and the practice of praying for more motivation of an altruistic kind serve to renew and extend this system. The self-inventory in the fourth step helps to bring thinking and desiring into conformity with reality. The eleventh step is "Sought through prayer and meditation to improve our conscious contact with God as we understood Him, praying only for knowledge of His will for us and the power to carry that out." Prayer can be comprehended naturalistically as an internal conversation between component systems in personality. Just as people talk to themselves, so also they talk to the God which is part of them. The validity of this interpretation is examined in the chapter following the present one.

A prayer often used by A.A. members is that of St. Francis.

> Lord, make me a channel of thy peace—that where there is hatred, I may bring love—that where there is wrong, I may bring the spirit of forgiveness—that where this is discord, I may bring harmony—that where there is error, I may bring truth—that where there is doubt, I may bring faith—that where there is despair, I may bring hope—that where there are shadows, I may bring light—that where there is sadness, I may bring joy. Lord, grant that I may seek rather to comfort than to be comforted—to understand, than to be understood—to love, than to be loved. For it is by self-forgetting that one finds. It is by forgiving that one is forgiven. It is by dying that one awakens to Eternal Life. Amen.[37]

Prayer of this kind is a psychological device which strongly brings altruistic motivation into the field of consciousness. If the egoistic influences of culture have erased some of this motivation, it is renewed. If the individual has further capacity for altruistic growth, it is realized.

[37] *Twelve Steps and Twelve Traditions,* pp. 101–102.

An additional factor which plays a vital role is the influence which members of A.A. have upon each other. They help turn each other's attention to the altruistic ideas and impulses which are their refuge from alcohol. If there is a gap or break in the motivational system of a member which might precipitate him into an alcoholic siege, they respond to his aid and help him strengthen the weak point in the fabric of his motivation. They continuously function as group stimuli to kindle altruistic motivation more fully in the personalities of each other. This is much more than surface encouragement to resist alcohol; rather, it is encouragement of the type of psychological power that excludes motivations which induce alcoholism.

The third principle in the chain of deduction may be summarized in the following way: Altruistic motivation becomes sufficiently strong in its inherent power to displace egoistic motivation of the alcoholic and effect his recovery if life conditions have permitted its latent development in sufficient degree, if the alcoholic turns to it from the conviction that it can end the torment of his addiction, and if the alcoholic renews and strengthens his altruistic motivation through appropriate forms of prayer and group activity. After the initial stage of his recovery he is led, by the altruistic desire he has, to continue the therapy increasing the altruistic power functioning in his life.

The conclusion from the three principles in the chain of deduction is that altruistic motivation is the primary cause of recovery by A.A. members from addiction to alcohol. This is not to say that other routes of cure may not be possible, or that in special pathologies other routes of cure may not be medically necessary. For a few drinkers the problem is not one of lack of self-control, but a reason for drinking exists in the desire to be sick and evade responsibilities of life. What is analyzed here is the power or causative agent which produces the recovery of A.A. members. It is to be emphasized that alcoholics do not possess a uniform personality type, and multiple types of therapy may be needed.[38]

The effectiveness of the higher power does not necessitate a particular form which the system of power takes. Members of A.A. turn to God as they understand him. For some members the

[38] Keller, *op. cit.*, pp. 7–8; J. D. Armstrong, "The Search for the Alcoholic Personality," *Annals of the American Academy of Political and Social Science,* January, 1958, pp. 40–47; S. D. Bacon, "Alcoholics Do Not Drink," *Annals of the American Academy of Political and Social Science,* January, 1958, pp. 55–64.

higher power is thought of merely as A.A., the power of a group, which illustrates the type of higher power Durkheim found in religion. Others think of the higher power in terms of the power of human ideals, a concept similar to that of Dewey. Still others see in service to their fellow men the power which makes possible their recovery from alcoholism. Many members simply accept orthodox theological ideas which have come to them from religious denominations without fully defining what these mean. Yet the emphasis upon following the will of God identified with living for others reveals the extent to which their concept of God is integrated with their system of motivation. The degree to which the higher power psychologically considered approximates the God of traditional orthodoxy is a topic to which we return after examining an additional point concerning the functioning of the higher power. This point is to delineate in what sense the power is "higher."

Meaning of "Higher" Power

The analysis so far made has shown that altruistic motivation in various forms is a dynamic power in personality. At the same time, all motives are psychological powers functioning in the overall personality system to produce particular patterns of behavior. The status of altruism and egoism as independent powers is indicated by the following passages from Freud concerning the superego and the id, which are motivational systems conceptualized by him to include areas of personality with some similarity to those of altruism and egoism.

> We can come nearer to the id with images, and call it a chaos, a cauldron of seething excitement. We suppose that it is somewhere in direct contact with somatic processes, and takes over from them instinctual needs and gives them mental expression, but we cannot say in what substratum this contact is made. These instincts fill it with energy, but it has no organization and no unified will, only an impulsion to obtain satisfaction for the instinctual needs, in accordance with the pleasure-principle. The laws of logic—above all, the law of contradiction—do not hold for processes in the id. Contradictory impulses exist side by side without neutralizing each other or drawing apart; at most they combine in compromise formations under the overpowering economic pressure towards discharging their energy. . . .
>
> [The super-ego is] something which enjoys a certain independence, pursues its own ends, and is independent of the ego as regards the energy at its disposal. . . . For us the super-ego is the representative of all moral restrictions, the advocate of the impulse towards perfection,

in short it is as much as we have been able to apprehend psychologically of what people call the "higher" things in human life.[39]

The Christian teacher Paul in somewhat poetic language draws the outlines of egoism and altruism. "For the desires of the flesh are against the Spirit, and the desires of the Spirit are against the flesh; for these are opposed to each other, to prevent you from doing what you would. . . . Now the works of the flesh are plain: immorality, impurity, licentiousness, idolatry, sorcery, enmity, strife, jealousy, anger, selfishness, dissension, party spirit, envy, drunkenness, carousing, and the like. . . . But the fruit of the Spirit is love, joy, peace, patience, kindness, goodness, faithfulness, gentleness, self-control; against such there is no law."[40]

In what sense shall altruistic motivation or any other dynamic system involved in religious behavior be considered a "higher" power? Let us first consider the empirical basis for higher powers in religion which are inimical to man. As articulated in primitive religion, these consist of devils and evil spirits. No consistent list or description of these can be made from one religion to another. In various ways psychic impulses and indispositions are personified, ranging from anger, avarice, cowardice, and passivity through such syndromes as schizophrenia and epilepsy and including a large number of fixations and compelling ideas which appear in human personality. The spirits discovered by man may be in the human body or outside in its environment. When outside, the spirits are projections by the human mind of its own contents upon objects in the external world. This theory forms an important part of the thinking of Jung. He finds man's belief in spirits to have experiential basis in the impulses which man finds within himself. The spirits are real motivational systems within personality. Jung calls attention to the functional role of primitive religion in controlling inimical spirit beings. These are psychic powers within man which threaten the stability of personality unless controlled by something more powerful.

. . . primitive man is a wholly collective being. He has scarcely awakened to his "I-ness"—hence this is still very much imperilled. The contents of the collective unconscious and of the collective psyche are always on the verge of invading the soul and destroying the ego. That is why primitive man is constantly in danger of running amuck or

[39] Sigmund Freud, *New Introductory Lectures on Psychoanalysis,* Carlton House, 1933, pp. 87, 95, 103–104.

[40] Galatians 5:17,19–23.

succumbing to psychic catastrophes of that kind. But since religion is compensatory to the conscious situation, its aim is to help him consolidate his ego. Religion safeguards primitive man against the perils of the soul. Primitive cosmogony as recounted in myths is really a psychic cosmogony, i.e. the image of how consciousness arose and is consolidated.[41]

From this passage it seems apparent that the injurious powers of man's psychic existence are higher in the sense that they are beyond control by conscious volition of the individual, not susceptible to inhibition by recalling opposing ideas or impulses, and requiring the calling into operation of special religious influences. Similarly, spiritual motives may sometimes so dominate the individual that he cannot act otherwise than he inwardly feels he must. The term *numinous* refers to possession of the individual by a psychic force beyond his immediate voluntary control. "Religion, as the Latin word denotes, is a careful and scrupulous observation of [an act of reverence towards] what Rudolph Otto aptly termed the *numinosum,* that is, a dynamic agency or effect not caused by an arbitrary act of will. On the contrary, it seizes and controls the human subject, who is always rather its victim than its creator. The *numinosum*—whatever its cause may be—is an experience of the subject independent of his will. At all events, religious teaching as well as the *consensus gentium* always and everywhere explains this experience as being due to a cause external to the individual. The *numinosum* is either a quality belonging to a visible object or the influence of an invisible presence that causes a peculiar alteration of consciousness. This is, at any rate, the general rule."[42]

The higher powers of primitive religion are psychic forces which are either benevolent or malevolent. The latter are ones which interfere with processes of normal life unless redirected, assimilated, or displaced by benevolent ones evoked through religious exercises. Modern man faces similar difficulty in controlling himself according to the way he would like to be, as illustrated by a statement of Paul, "I do not understand my own actions. For I do not do what I want, but I do the very thing I hate. . . . I can will what is right, but I cannot do it. For I do not do the good I want, but the evil I do not want is what I do. Now if I do what I do not want, it is no longer I that do it, but sin which dwells within me."[43]

[41] Schaer, *op. cit.,* pp. 103–104.
[42] Jung, "Answer to Job," *op. cit.,* p. 7.
[43] Romans 7:15,18–20.

As the previous analysis has indicated, altruistic motivation is the principal power whereby the harmful powers in personality can be controlled through displacement or assimilation. What is true of the alcoholic or of primitive man is equally true of human beings generally. All personalities contain psychological forces requiring control through reorganization to remove them or integrate them about a central purpose and power. The details of this development and its relationship to religious activities form the material of succeeding chapters. The point to be made at the moment is that altruistic motivation is a higher power in the sense that it is, or tends to become, more potent than egoistic motivation. It enables man to control that within himself which is otherwise uncontrollable, disruptive forces over which ordinary volition is impotent. This appears to be the sense in which members of A.A. believe they are saved by a power greater than themselves. The positive power in religion may become numinous, as under the influence of crowd psychology which induces a state of spirit possession, or after prolonged and concentrated religious development by the individual, the latter being more lasting in its effects.

Another meaning of "higher" besides that evidenced by the superior quality of force is the sense in which James speaks of the "higher" self. In this context "higher" means more valuable or more desirable in terms of personality stability in the face of difficulties, relative absence of injurious frustrations, and positive achievement of meaningful and satisfying goals. The higher power in which altruistic motivation consists is higher because of its valuable nature to those who seek to acquire it.

The I *and the* Me *in Religious Motivation*

A principle generally maintained by religionists is that they seek to live in a passive, not an active, grammatical voice. Religious motivation for them is not so much something which they possess as something which possesses them. A classic statement in this respect is that of Paul, who wrote following the ascendance of spiritual motivation in his life: "It is no longer I who live, but Christ who lives in me."[44] This statement becomes psychologically meaningful in the light of analysis by the University of Chicago social psychologist G. H. Mead. Grammatical parts of speech actually reflect underlying components in personality and interpersonal relationships. Mead has undertaken a pioneer

[44] Galatians 2:20.

analysis of the *I* and the *me* as referring to different aspects of personality. Not all of his analysis is applicable to the topic of Paul's statement, but the following comments related to his analysis are relevant.[45]

The essential idea to be noted is that the *I* and the *me* are different steps in a process of causation leading to activity. The *I* is the immediate idea or intention one feels which leads directly to the action performed. "I will eat my dinner," is a statement of the aim one inwardly experiences of eating. In this respect, the *I* refers to the immediate cause in one's personality of the activity of eating. "The food made me feel hungry," is a statement in which the *me* refers to the effect produced in one's personality by a preceding stimulus. Such effects in personality are referred to by the talker in using the term *me*. The *I* does not refer to all causes in personality, only the immediate idea or impulse to act. In the English language when the effect in personality is produced by the *I* as the actor, the pronoun *myself* is used, rather than *me,* a distinction lacking in languages which use *me* in both contexts.

Whatever is an effect may in turn be a cause of something else in a continuing process. The *me* as an effect of prior personality functioning may in turn become the *I* in present activity. The *I* and the *me* are relative terms, depending upon point of view in considering aspects of personality functioning as causes or effects.

We are now able to examine the psychological meaning underlying Paul's statement or the statements in other religions referring to domination by spiritual motivation. In religious development the seeker turns his attention to the system of spiritual motivation which he seeks to have dominant in his life. By concentrating attention upon this system it is stimulated to generate its fullest potentialities in terms of creative ideas and aims. When these appear they lead more or less automatically to altruistic action. Their appearance is the *effect* of the preceding system of altruistic motivation, the power in religion, to which attention has been turned. Since they are an effect they are appropriately designated as the *me* aspect of personality. In Paul's view they are the result of the spirit of Christ functioning in the life of man.

The *I* is involved as a cause in the voluntary step of turning attention through study, meditation, or prayer to the power in

[45] A. Strauss (ed.), *The Social Psychology of George Herbert Mead,* University of Chicago Press, 1956, pp. 246–247.

religion. What follows is less what the individual does actively than what is done to him as a passive participant. When his ideas and aims reach the point of producing action, they might be referred to as the *I,* but from the standpoint of stressing the prior role of the system of spiritual motivation as the cause they are more appropriately regarded as the *me*. The terms *I* and *me* are relative since what is an effect in personality can in turn be considered a cause of something further. From the standpoint of initiating spiritual development and activity, the *I* plays its principal role as the initial step of turning attention to spiritual motivation already experienced or latent in the individual's life. The religious devotee seeks as much as possible for this motivation to intensify and expand itself, which it tends to do of its own inward dynamic when the *I* directs conscious attention to it. Preoccupied with the effects produced by this unfolding motivation, the religious devotee seeks continually to live in the passive voice, letting spiritual motivation grow and work through him. In order to do this he avoids thinking of spiritual ideas and aims in terms of the *I,* an attitude of self-seeking which differs from the higher power in religion as cause. Rather he thinks of them in terms of the *me* in whom effects are produced by the power in religion. In order to utilize the fullest potentialities of this power in his life, he concentrates his attention upon its role as a cause of personality functioning, not upon his role as an actor in the spiritual life which follows.

chapter 9 Influencing the Power in Religion

Intensification of Religious Power

Analysis of the power in religion discloses a motivational system whose development and expression are of benefit to human beings. The preceding chapter analyzed the way in which the higher power functions of its own inherent dynamic, little attention being given so far to steps taken in religious activity to stimulate its growth and expression. The power system is influenced by verbal symbols and ritual acts which evoke its operation. It is characteristic of all religions that steps are taken to influence the higher power in order that it will function more fully in human life. These steps are taken to make numinous more often what would otherwise be of insufficient power to motivate personality in a socially desirable way. Even if the steps do not call forth motivation which is irresistible, an infrequent level of motivation, at least it is expected that the resulting motivation will be of sufficient strength to proceed readily when the individual voluntarily turns his attention to the ideas and aims involved.

Theological opinion insists that the power thus released is not due to a self-seeking act of will, but to God. This seems demonstrable in that altruistic motivation, as well as a self-seeking desire for a more satisfying life, induces the individual to engage in exercises to intensify the altruistic power in his personality. Altruistic motivation is then a necessary condition of its own augmentation. Jung describes how the role of God in religious exercise has been viewed by religionists.

A great many ritualistic performances are carried out for the sole purpose of producing at will the effect of the *numinosum* by means of certain devices of a magical nature, such as invocation, incantation, sacrifice, meditation and other yoga practices, self-inflicted tortures of various descriptions, and so forth. But a religious belief in an external and objective divine cause is always prior to any such performance. The Catholic Church, for instance, administers the sacraments for the purpose of bestowing their spiritual blessings upon the believer; but since this act would amount to enforcing the presence of divine grace by an indubitably magical procedure, it is logically argued that nobody can compel divine grace to be present in the sacramental act, but that it is nevertheless inevitably present since the sacrament is a divine institution which God would not have caused to be if he had not intended to lend it his support.[1]

With the psychological analysis so far made of the power in religion many followers of particular religions may agree. The question they ask, and which must be answered from a research standpoint, is: What is the relationship of the higher power as a social and psychological system to the God in whom people believe and to whom they pray? Is it God? This type of question is related to that asked by social scientists: What is distinctive about prayer and worship as means of verbally influencing altruistic motivation? Granted that these activities contain verbal symbols which indoctrinate or stimulate ideation and motivation, why not use secular patterns of communication to shape and intensify values in people's experience? Why address God? These are formidable questions for science to undertake, yet answers to these questions are already growing in the literature of religious psychology. Answers to these questions ought to show the appropriateness or inappropriateness of communication addressed to God.

Variability in Theological Belief

In approaching the question of who or what God is, we recognize that hypothetically people can select any object, natural or supernatural, and believe and behave toward this object as a god. Supernaturalists in religious psychology such as James believe that the power in religion coming to them from God is supernatural. In related views it may be acknowledged that the power is part of the natural world while the God to whom one

[1] C. G. Jung, *Psychology and Religion: West and East,* tr. by R. F. C. Hull. Bollingen Series XX, Bollingen Foundation, Inc. Pantheon, 1958, pp. 7–8.

prays and who confers the power is supernatural. This type of supernatural explanation introduces difficulties for science similar to those examined in Chapter 7 if God is conceived as intervening in the natural world, altering natural psychological laws.

The scientific quest in religious psychology concerns itself with what the reality in experience is, if any, which people adhering to major monotheistic religions do in point of fact worship, not necessarily what they think they worship. The problem of analysis is complicated by the conviction of some that their God, although he enters experience, is supernaturally revealed and beyond scientific consideration. This is the traditional viewpoint of mysticism. Another complication is the conviction of some that God is entirely outside of experience. The latter group may overlook the existence of God as an object in the unconscious field of their personality systems. For now we are not concerned with describing what people believe, but with tracing the nature of the psychological or social object to which they respond and with which they are in some form of communication.

The circumstance that religious beliefs proliferate into systems of thought about supernatural aspects of divine and human origin and destiny was referred to in Chapter 2. With reference to such philosophical or supernatural concepts science can do no more than describe what the beliefs are which people happen to hold, and perhaps also to point out reasons in human nature or social situations for the genesis of such beliefs. As to the validity of the beliefs, science within its framework of procedure has little to say. In limiting itself to the empirical side of religion, psychology does not exclude the profound importance of superempirical beliefs to mankind. The functional role played by these beliefs in religious experience presents vital questions for scientific analysis.

A purpose of this chapter is to review and extend what has been said by empiricists about God as a social and psychological phenomenon. Views of religious psychologists in opposition to empiricist conclusions concerning God are next given consideration. The reader is left to form his own beliefs concerning the material introduced. With respect to those who are sensitive concerning what inquiring psychologists may say about their theology, it may be kept in mind that such scientists have no interest in altering the religious ideas involved in the sentiments of others, but merely of answering to their own scientific satisfaction what the experiential reality, if any, is to which the religious worshiper is oriented.

The religious psychologists from whose works quotations are made here have undertaken to generalize from their study of religions what are the essential characteristics of God as a psychic object in human experience. The task of assembling data in support of conclusions is difficult because of the intangible nature of the material. The task is admittedly incomplete. In some cases the writers apparently rely upon their introspective experience with religion and at other times upon the religious experiences of others. They also consider doctrines from sacred literature as data revealing the thinking and desiring of followers of religion, a form of data sometimes so commonplace as to obviate detailed enumeration.

The empiricist thesis is that the higher power described in its various aspects is essentially the God to whom worshipers in contemporary monotheistic religion address themselves. Modifications of or exceptions to this thesis arise when human beings in their religious variability select or exclude one or more components of the system of power. Some of these variations have already been indicated: worship of the group, altruism conceived as an ordinary and imperfect motivational system, altruism conceived as the best motivation of which the individual is capable, or altruism as an inaccessible ideal, as well as altruism involved in the cultivation of impersonal ethical values or that involved in worship of a personal God. The description of these patterns of religious motivation and ideas and the detailing of their functioning in human life provide extensive and important topics for study. To undertake more than a brief incursion into this manifold description is beyond the scope of the present work. The manifold dimensions in which the supreme being is cast in different religions are indicated by Sorokin's listing of names given to the altruistic power by various groups of people.

. . . *The supraconscious is the embodiment of the altruist's very highest ideal. It is his highest value.* In this sense it is his Absolute. As to the name, the supraconscious is called by widely different names by various altruists.

1. The most common name for it is that of God or the equivalent, in personified and transpersonal forms: God, Tao, Chit, Jen, Nirvana, Jehova, Ahura-Mazda, Indra, Vishnu, Brahma, Siva, Buddha, God the Father, God the Son, Holy Ghost, Jesus, Allah, Osiris, and so on.

2. Another common name is a term derivative from the name of God and the equivalent: the Divine, the Absolute, the Divine Madness, the Oversoul, the Soul of the World, the Spirit, Heaven, Logos, Sophia, Soul, Atman, and others.

3. Often the supraconscious is called by various abstract metaphysical or mystic terms: the Supra-Essence, the Ever-Living Fire, the Ever-Progenitive Nature, the Infinite Manifold, the Ground, the *coincidentia oppositorum,* the Inexpressible, the Nameless, the Divine Nothing, and so on.

4. Frequently it is called by diverse psychological and ethical terms: genius, inspiration, categoric imperative, moral duty, call of conscience, inner voice, highest social responsibility, social instinct or sentiment, gregarious or paternal instinct, noblest and highest ego, superego, and so on. On the part of the atheistic altruists (see further about them), their highest ideal and value is often called by various "prosaic" names: the greatest happiness, the greatest good, the main pleasure, the most important social value, the deepest emotional drive, the greatest social need, libido, life energy, and the like. These terms denote in such cases something far transcending their literal meaning. In these denotations and connotations the term *matter* often means about the same as the term *God,* for a believer; the term *life energy* becomes co-identical with that of the *supraconscious;* and so on.[2]

As to conclusions concerning the nature of God, two types emerge from psychological analysis. One type of conclusion describes the system of motivation and ideation which consciously or unconsciously provides the members of each particular religious group with the reality of their God. This type also describes how they conceptualize their God in natural or supernatural terms and how they adjust to him in their pattern of religious activities.

The other type of conclusion proceeds further by indicating from an empirical standpoint the particular reality in experience which most effectively performs the role of God and the way in which this reality is correctly conceptualized and appropriately influenced by man. Although the system of religious reality responds when regarded in different ways, the quality of the response depends upon how the lines of reality are drawn, whether narrowly in terms of inaccessible ideals or broadly in terms of human love. The criterion of effectiveness as shown by the historical evolution of man's definition of God is what psychic constellation appears to be most productive of the highest benefits to the human race sought by participants in religion. The quality of the response made by the higher power also depends upon the extent to which man's theological concepts referring to experience correctly represent what is present or latent in experience and upon the resulting adjustment which he makes to the higher power.

[2] P. A. Sorokin, *The Ways and Power of Love,* Beacon, 1954, p. 146.

INFLUENCING AN IMPERSONAL GOD

The type of God discerned by John Dewey, Emile Durkheim, and J. H. Leuba is an impersonal social and psychological power. After eliminating what they consider to be supernatural, philosophical, and legendary qualities of God they find the residue to consist of social and psychological material, not unlike the superego of Freud. Dewey, as has been noted, finds the empirical essence of God to be ideals in process of actualization. Durkheim views society as God. Among these religious psychologists the most outspoken opponent of a personal concept of God is Leuba, whose work will be considered in a separate section. He develops a concept of an impersonal higher power not unlike Bergson's creative force in evolution, although Bergson in addition sets forth a mystical view of a personal God.

The impersonal type of God or higher power obviously characterizes the views of those who profess an impersonal God or who acknowledge loyalty to an ethical force in their lives. Whether they use the word *God* or not may be a verbal difference. Many persons in Protestant churches, as well as in Buddhist churches, Unitarian churches, and Ethical Culture Societies accept views from the standpoint of science given by Dewey or Leuba or similar versions of an impersonal power. A Gallup poll in 1948 in England disclosed that 45 percent of the people questioned believe in a personal God, 39 percent believe some sort of spirit or vital force controls life, and 16 percent are not sure whether there is a God or life force.

Durkheim is often credited with originating the functional theory of worship. His work has been followed by that of Bronislaw Malinowski, A. Radcliffe-Brown, and other anthropologists. His description of the effects of worship has gained historic importance.

> For a society to become conscious of itself and maintain at the necessary degree of intensity the sentiments which it thus attains, it must assemble and concentrate itself. Now this concentration brings about an exultation of the mental life which takes form in a group of ideal conceptions where is portrayed the new life thus awakened; they correspond to this new set of psychical forces which is added to those which we have at our disposition for the daily tasks of existence. A society can neither create itself nor recreate itself without at the same time creating an ideal. . . .
>
> There can be no society which does not feel the need of upholding and reaffirming at regular intervals the collective sentiments and the

collective ideas which make its unity and its personality. Now this moral remaking cannot be achieved except by the means of reunions, assemblies and meetings where the individuals, being closely united to one another, reaffirm in common their common sentiments; hence come ceremonies which do not differ from regular religious ceremonies, either in their object, the results which they produce, or the processes employed to attain these results. What essential difference is there between an assembly of Christians celebrating the principal dates of the life of Christ, or of Jews remembering the exodus from Egypt or the promulgation of the decalogue, and a reunion of citizens commemorating the promulgation of a new moral or legal system or some great event in the national life?[3]

In a similar vein, but placing more stress upon the moral and ideal function of religious activities, R. R. Marett writes of the religious life of primitives:

Religious action is efficacious just in so far as it serves to disengage the ideal meaning from the gross imagery in which the earthbound spirit is bound to express itself. . . . the supreme object of religious faith cannot be the vulgar moving of any material mountains but rather the moving of the human mind, of the inner man, so that it may be turned right round from the materialism that goes with sheer animalism, and thus may envisage and pursue moral justification in the shape of individuality and community jointly purified, enlarged, and, in a word, made real. Such, I venture to suggest, is the lesson to be drawn from the history of religion as a record of the evolution or unfolding of the profoundest purpose manifested in human life; and, though my business is not to play apologist for the savage, but simply to account for the facts about him, I ask anyone who is at pains to study the evidence whether the will to organize self and society until they meet and merge in a divine goodness is not probably as deep-lying and widespread as human nature itself.[4]

Types of Verbalization in Worship and Prayer

The influence of worship or prayer activities upon a natural social and psychological power is limited to the natural effects which verbal stimuli have upon people's impulses and ideas. When words are uttered aloud or given in printed form, they constitute perceptual stimuli which call forth their meanings in the psychic experience of the listener or reader. The meanings consist of impulses and ideas which are made active in the personality system by being called forth by the stimuli. If the

[3] Emile Durkheim, *The Elementary Forms of the Religious Life,* The Free Press, 1947, pp. 422, 427.

[4] R. R. Marett, *Head, Heart and Hands in Human Evolution,* Holt, 1935, p. 140.

impulses and ideas are not latent in personality due to prior expression of them, the verbal stimuli would be relatively ineffective. The minister who preaches "Parents should be kind to their children" is effective, depending upon whether latent impulses toward parental kindness already exist in the personality system of his hearers.

Of fundamental importance in analyzing the effects of verbal stimuli upon the psychological power in religion is a classification of the kinds of verbal stimuli which can be employed. This classification involves two kinds of things. One of these is the personal pronoun by which the power is designated. The power can be referred to in any of the grammatical forms by which parts or all of the human personality can be labeled by oneself or others, such as by the pronouns *thou, you, it, he,* or *she.* In talking to each other, people use the pronoun *you* to indicate the person to whom remarks refer. Psychologists, as well as people generally, in describing parts of personalities use *it* as the pronoun.

The other aspect of the classification of verbal stimuli is the mood of the verb in the sentence constituting the verbal stimulus. This mood may be indicative or descriptive, as in a statement of fact, which is the way people commonly talk about their personality traits. The mood may be imperative or exhortative, as when people encourage each other or, as in talking to oneself, when one encourages oneself to aim or to act. An example of a descriptive statement which is a verbal stimulus is: "Following parental ideals of kindness toward children makes better children." An example of an appeal is: "You be kind to your children." In a theological context the exhortation might be: "May God help you to be kind to your children."

Little research work has been done by religious psychologists in testing the relative effectiveness of different kinds of verbal stimuli, whether personal or impersonal, second or third person, indicative or imperative. Disagreements, however, among churchgoers and nonchurchgoers and among the followers of different patterns of religion in contemporary culture are sharp, and scientific analysts of religion become increasingly drawn into such controversies. Underlying the verbal expressions are the basic issues of whether God exists in human experience or not, and whether this is a personlike or impersonal psychological reality.

The religious services of a group who believe there is no personal God are often similar in pattern to those in traditional churches. Organ music provides a call to worship. Hymns are sung which perhaps avoid personal references or all references to deity and may consist of lines from famous poets. The minister's prayer then avoids personal characterization of God. Instead of thanksgiving and petition, the prayer expresses acknowledgment of God's value-giving nature and verbalizes human striving toward ethical ideals. An illustration of the form of such a prayer is provided by the following words found used in a religious service attended by the author.

> The eternal God of the human race is great and good. Wonderful are the ways of God. In God we live and move and have our being. God is the source of all truth and beauty, the mainspring of the love of man for man. God is the upbuilding force of civilization, the creative power for the ennoblement of the human race. Let us strive for larger fulfillment of our ideals. Let us bring a fuller measure of love into all our relationships, in the home, at work, and in the wider world community of which we are members. Let us always seek for what is best in ourselves in order that we may become perfected in the ways of God, which is the perpetual home of the human race from generation to generation.

Following music, hymn singing, and a prayer, the minister gives a lecture-type or inspirational sermon in which he explains social ideas or exhorts his congregation to greater social achievement. The service closes with the singing of another hymn.

Scrutiny of the particular prayer cited shows that, although the word *God* is used, the pronoun form of subject is avoided in what is said. If the pronoun reference were used, this might be *it* rather than *he* or *you,* although the latter forms of usage, coming down from tradition, have a more familiar sound. A distinctive feature of the prayer is that the mood of the verb is descriptive, not exhortative. This is understandable in the light of the corresponding theological belief, since a being to whom an appeal cannot be addressed is customarily thought of as an impersonal being, not a personal one.

Nevertheless, exhortations are sometimes addressed to an impersonal psychological object, in religion as well as in everyday speech. The greeting more common in former generations of "Peace be with you," is an example of an impersonal appeal to peace as a state of being, although once it was addressed to Pax, the Roman goddess of peace. "Happiness be yours," and "Trouble stay away from my door," are current folk expressions of an impersonal sort. In the same way, the phrase "God be with you," (now contracted to *good-bye*) might be understood as an impersonal form of appeal. The point is that prayers among those who believe in an impersonal God can be meaningfully addressed to a psychic object. "May God help us to become better people," is a prayerful phrase which need not imply belief in a personal God.

J. H. Leuba

In connection with man's approaches to an impersonal God the work of J. H. Leuba merits consideration. One of the early American group of religious psychologists, who began his writing in this field in 1896, he has been the most outspoken opponent in America of a personal concept of God in favor of an impersonal, nonpurposive, ethical force as the supreme reality of religion. "I cannot persuade myself that divine personal beings, be they primitive gods or the Christian Father, have more than a subjective existence."[5]

Before considering Leuba's views concerning the status of God we can usefully examine his methodological approach to the study of God, in which he makes an important contribution in the history of the psychology of religion. The group of religious thinkers following A. Ritschl endeavored to make of theology a discipline which is neither science nor speculative philosophy, yet one which is built upon the data of religious experience. The proponents of the theology of Ritschl did not perceive the full scientific implications of their work nor the need for systematic application of scientific procedure to the data of inner experience. Somewhat similar to the ideas of Ritschl, although lacking his methodological concern, are those of Rufus Jones, a modern Quaker interpreter of mysticism. Rufus Jones was a professor of philosophy at Haverford College, near Bryn Mawr College where Leuba taught psychology, and students probably compared notes they took from the leading defender and leading attacker of mysticism in twentieth-century America.

Leuba insisted that the field of inward spiritual experience, which Ritschl had maintained was distinct from science or metaphysical philosophy, belonged to psychology. This was also the point of view of Leuba's teacher, G. Stanley Hall, and employed by the latter in *Jesus, the Christ, in the Light of Psychology,* published in 1917. This work, which principally analyzes the life and motives of Jesus, considers the spirit of Christ as a heightened awareness of Jesus' life and teachings following his death.[6] Generalizing along this line, Leuba writes in one of the

[5] J. H. Leuba, *A Psychological Study of Religion,* Macmillan, 1912, p. 10.

[6] G. S. Hall, *Jesus, the Christ, in the Light of Psychology,* Appleton, 1917, p. 710.

chapters, "Theology and Psychology," in *A Psychological Study of Religion:*

> My task in this chapter will be to show:—
>
> 1. That belief in the gods of religion and, indirectly, certain other fundamental doctrines, rest, as a matter of fact, upon inductions drawn from the "inner" life.
>
> 2. That religious experience ("inner experience") belongs entirely to psychology—"entirely" being used in the same sense as when it is claimed that the non-religious portions of conscious life belong entirely to science.
>
> 3. That since the gods of religion are empirical gods they belong to science.[7]

If Leuba won the battle for the right of science to study mystical experience, he lost much of the insights from traditional study of mysticism during his effort.

> States of religious consciousness are what they are, irrevocably. They can no more be denied or explained away than any other state of consciousness,—than, for instance, what passes in the mind of a merchant or poet. They have happened; that is the long and the short of it. Science has never attempted to deny that Saint Francis had moments of inexpressible joy,—joy which he held infinitely superior to any "earthly" pleasure; that Bunyan heard voices which he thought belonged to devils or to God; or that George Muller prayed for help and was "lifted up with a sense of the presence of the Almighty within him." Science accepts these as facts of consciousness, and so there cannot be any conflict here between psychology and theology.
>
> A conflict does arise, however, when these persons imagine their experiences to involve the objective or universal validity of certain of their ideas, when they say, for instance, that their experiences attest the present existence of Jesus of Nazareth. . . . Such claims as this pass out of the incontrovertible, subjective sphere into the sphere of science since the affirmation that certain ideas *mean* an objective existence or are universally valid raises the question of the interpretation of experience.
>
> The validity of the religious states of consciousness is precisely of the same sort as that of any other state of consciousness; they are absolute, undeniable, only so long as they are considered merely as the experience of a subject, and no longer. Before the theologians who claim to find in inner experience the data of theology, and on that ground to remove it from all contact with science, may be looked upon as intellectually worthy of consideration, they must explain how they secure objective and universal knowledge. The mystical claim can exist only because of the failure to separate the subjective significance of

[7] Leuba, *op. cit.*, p. 212.

consciousness from the transsubjective meaning which is attributed to some parts of it.[8]

Leuba, in a sense an American Feuerbach, is strongly critical of orthodox religious dogma, and it may be said that empiricists generally have overlooked the profoundly important role which philosophizing about ultimate values plays in religion. They have not exerted themselves to achieve sympathetic reconciliation of their work with the aims and beliefs of traditional organized religion. Jung stands out for his recognition of the role which philosophical beliefs play in answering inner psychic needs, and Ames, a minister as well as a professor, has been an enthusiastic proponent of Christian teaching through the framework of empiricist ideas. The conflict between empiricists and Christian theologians has been sharpened by the failure of Leuba to perceive more than a nonpurposive, impersonal force at the heart of Christianity. Furthermore, Leuba felt responsible for stripping religion of empirically unproved beliefs and of removing a personal God from the religious scene. As scientists of religion, Leuba and Freud are understandable factors in the slowness of religious leaders to accept psychological analysis of their God.

From the standpoint of rejecting personal qualities attributed to God, Leuba ranks with critical rationalists in concluding that such beliefs are wishful thinking and without empirical counterpart. With the elimination of a personlike nature from God, the basis for influencing God by means of personally addressed communication is also removed. Leuba calls the personal qualities "subjective" because he considers them to be sheer beliefs, vagaries of the imagination, rather than objects experienced by the individual in his religious life. The number of cases, however, of persons reporting an experience of a personal God is impressive. Leuba has been at pains to prove that their reports are statements of opinion, not experience. Some of the documents in question are cited below. In excerpting these, opinions which are not part of the data bearing upon the issue of personlike characteristics are omitted. The cases are a Buddhist priest, two teachers of theology, two students, and Rufus Jones's writing about the Religious Society of Friends.

1. By spiritual enlightenment, I mean a man's becoming conscious through personal experience of the ultimate nature of his inner being. This insight breaks, as it were, the wall of intellectual limitation and brings us to a region which has hitherto been concealed from our view.

[8] *Ibid.*, pp. 236–237.

. . . True, it has only a subjective value, which, however, is just as ultimate and actual as sense-perception. Since it is immediate, there is no other way to test its validity than that each experiences it personally, individually, and inwardly. . . . Mere talking about or mere believing in the existence of God and his intimate love is nonsense as far as religion is concerned. Talking and arguing belong to philosophy, and believing, in its ordinary sense, is a sort of hypothesis, not necessarily supported by facts. Religion, however, wants above everything else solid facts and actual personal experience. If God exists, he must be felt. If he is love, it must be experienced.

2. Many times, in the experiences of those whose senses are trained by use to discern good and evil, the still, small Voice sounds in the soul's ear in tones of mystery. Intimations of duty assert themselves so subtly that we cannot put them into words, while of their divine authority we have no doubt; warnings against courses of conduct that to our prejudiced minds seem expedient, yet upon which the unformulated verdict of conscience sets its prohibition. . . . How can we know that anything spoken in Scripture is truth? By the witness of God in the Soul that what is spoken is the thing that is.

3. God is not a phenomenon that we may observe apart from ourselves, or a truth demonstrable by logical reasoning. He who does not feel Him in his heart will never feel him from without. The object of religious knowledge reveals itself only in the subject, by means of the religious phenomena themselves. . . . We never become conscious of our piety externally, we feel religiously moved, perceiving, more or less obscurely, in that very emotion the object and the cause of religion, i.e. God.

4. To be sure, we may be forbidden to speak of 'experiencing God'; it is quite true that I can experience only myself and the modifications of this self. But, similarly, if I cannot say that I have experienced my fellow-men, still there are certain states of consciousness as to the nature and the significance of which I am not deceived; I know when I have the right to say that I know my fellow-being, I know when my feelings are in harmony with his, when our hearts are as one,—and I also know when my soul communes with the Father. Likewise, when I have once met Christ, I recognize him in my hours of pure and lofty meditation. . . . we feel within us a being that is not ourselves; we see born within us new ideas and perceptions, real revelations that do not come from ourselves; we verify each day, and for years have been able to verify in our life, a progressive and continuous guidance which permits us to assert that we do not proceed alone along life's pathway, that our Christian faith is not an illusion.

5. I say to you that I have known God within me, and it was not a dream, an hallucination; never had my reason been more master of itself; and I say to you that there was within me, speaking to me, drawing me close, uniting itself to me, one who was not of myself, who pro-

ceeded not from me, who had penetrated within me and who filled the depths of my being with I do not know what light which was not of this world, causing me to tremble with I know not what emotion, that nothing human will ever give birth to.

6. The fundamental significant thing which stands out in early Quakerism was the *conviction* which these founders of it felt, that they had actually discovered the living God and that He was in them. They all have one thing to say—"I have experienced God."

It [Quakerism] was first of all the proclamation of an experience. The movement came to birth, and received its original power, through persons who were no less profoundly conscious of a *divine presence* than they were of a world in space.[9]

In the foregoing cases the reports by subjects of experiencing something personlike are persistent and seem, as Jung contends, to be matters of experience, not belief. When one examines the substance of Leuba's conclusions about lack of proof of personal characteristics of God, they do not seem to focus well upon the data which he employs. The instance which he cites of religious experience containing the impression of the present existence of Jesus of Nazareth is incidental to the more general feeling of worshipers that they experience something personal in the higher power of religion. Leuba correctly points out that mystics have not adequately documented their sense of a personal presence in their experience of the higher power of religion. Certainly they have not delineated the personlike characteristics which are the basis for their intuition. On the other hand, their general claim has been so widely repeated that it merits close psychological study. At Leuba's stage of investigation it cannot be passed by as a subjective construct of the imagination.

Leuba contends that mystical states can be duplicated by the administration of drugs.

This book began with the examination of experiences regarded by uncivilized man as revelation of, or union with, the Divine. They were submitted to a critical analysis, and recently acquired scientific knowledge of the psycho-physiological effects of certain ecstasy-producing drugs was brought to bear upon them. It appeared that the early mystics owe their belief mainly to delightful impressions of limitless power and freedom, to altered self-feelings, to the impression that the soul is liberated from the body, to automatisms including wonderful sensory hallucinations. Now, every one of these impressions and beliefs can be satisfactorily explained as the result of psycho-physiological forces set

[9] *Ibid.*, pp. 213–217, 221–223, 227.

in activity or inhibited by the drug. We then examined the mystical ecstasies of the Yogin and of a group of Christian mystics. Their own descriptions were compared with non-religious ecstasies—those of poets, of epileptics, of ordinary normal persons.

In all these ecstasies, the same fundamental characteristics were discovered, and we came to the conclusion that there need be no differences between religious and non-religious ecstasies other than those due to a different interpretation—the interpretation being itself the cause of important affective and volitional phenomena.[10]

What Leuba appears to have shown is that some features of mystical states, such as euphoria or emotional release, can be duplicated by drugs. This, however, says nothing of other psychological characteristics, such as those of ethical ideals or those of a personlike force, which cannot be duplicated by drugs. Leuba's own description of the power in religion suggests overtones of mystical feeling and inspiration, but these do not seem invalidated by their partial duplicability by the action of drugs.

Leuba is to be classified as an empiricist because of his conceptual development of the higher power of religion as a psychological phenomenon, an impersonal force. His description of the residue of the higher power of religion after eliminating all that he considers extraneous would be accepted by many thoughtful persons who acknowledge the importance of ethical ideals as the creative dynamic of human life but who do not comprehend a personal God.

The religion of the future will have to rest content apparently with the idea of a non-purposive Creative Force, making of the universe neither an accidental creation nor one shaped in accordance with some preconceived plan. Would man find what he wants in a Power describable as an impetus coursing through matter, and drawing from it what it can, a Power appearing in man in the form of striving consciousness? . . .

There is no question but that humanity idealized and conceived as a manifestation of Creative Energy possesses surpassing qualifications for a source of religious inspiration. Human relationships have always given rise to the noblest activities of man; they have been and remain the very fountain of life. In a religion of Humanity, man's attention would be directed not to a remote, intangible Perfection, but to a concrete reality of which he is a part and the perfection of which depends upon his own perfection. In Humanity each person can regard himself as a link in the chain connecting the hosts of the past with the hosts that are to come. The recognition of this vast relationship would give a

[10] J. H. Leuba, *The Psychology of Religious Mysticism,* Harcourt, Brace, 1925, p. 315.

sense of fellowship and unity, a feeling of responsibility and dignity; it would make a world worthy of one's best efforts. . . .

A religion in agreement with the accepted body of scientific knowledge, and centered about Humanity conceived as the manifestation of a Force tending to the creation of an ideal society, would occupy in the social life the place that a religion should normally hold,—even the place that the Christian religion lost when its cardinal beliefs ceased to be in harmony with secular beliefs.[11]

Evaluation of Empiricist Analysis of an Impersonal God

The scientific aim of those proceeding from an empiricist standpoint is to describe the social and psychological elements in the religious experience of God. Criticisms of the empiricist line of reasoning in general are reserved for the following chapter. Specific comments can be made now on the effort to delineate the God of contemporary monotheistic religion as an impersonal power.

The God or higher power described by Dewey or Leuba obviously conforms to the belief of those who profess such a religious being and who include many members of large denominations as well as of particular religious groups who lean toward this type of theological view. A poll conducted by Leuba among physical, biological, psychological, and sociological scientists in 1933 indicated that only about three-tenths of them believe in a God to "whom one may pray in the expectation of receiving an answer more than the natural, subjective, psychological effect of prayer."[12] The same query asked in 1914 disclosed that approximately four-tenths of the scientists polled profess this theological belief. These figures involve the issue of supernaturalism as well as that of personalism, yet they strongly suggest that numerous persons sharing the views of these intellectual leaders recognize no more than an impersonal God or ethical force in their lives.

Even though people believe the higher power of religion to be an impersonal ethical force, the question may be asked of whether their belief concerning the higher power to which they adjust is correct. In the case of Durkheim's analysis, the circumstance that society is taken to be God does not mean that such worshipers have thereby correctly located the psychological power which they influence and utilize.

[11] Leuba, *A Psychological Study of Religion, op. cit.*, pp. 334–336.

[12] J. H. Leuba, "Religious Beliefs of American Scientists," *Harper's Magazine,* August, 1934, p. 297.

The analysis of God as an impersonal power gets into its sharpest difficulties when it is applied to religious beliefs of those who say they experience a personal God. The contention of impersonal empiricists is that the residue of empirical qualities left after removing supernatural beliefs is an impersonal social and psychological system of motivation. The contention is supported in two ways, by deducing that supposed personal qualities are matters of subjective opinion and by showing that the remainder of the qualities found in religious experience constitute a system of motives or ideals.

Leuba endeavored to demonstrate that the personal qualities of God are matters of belief, not fact. His interpretation is opposed by the viewpoints of a second group of empiricists, among them R. B. Cattell, D. C. Macintosh, and C. G. Jung, whose ideas about this are yet to be reviewed. While some specific details of sacred history to which Leuba refers are matters of religious opinion, these seem to serve as a concrete vehicle for declaring the sense of something personal in the religious experience of an altruistic power. This is the view of Jung, who does not, however, restrict his analysis of religion to any one type of expression of the religious power in individual experience. The evidence in the cases examined by Leuba seems rather to support the view that worshipers find something personlike in their experience of the power in religion. This view merits further analysis to determine what psychological basis it may possess.

Apart from the obvious demonstration that philosophical attributes of God are matters of opinion, not experience, the problem confronts impersonal empiricists of proving that the residue left after nonempirical theological beliefs are removed actually is an impersonal psychological power. It is one thing to propose a hypothesis and another thing to document it. The same type of problem, however, confronts empiricists who maintain that the residue is a personal psychological power. The system of altruistic motivation, whether impersonal or personal, must be demonstrated to correspond with God much as worshipers regard him. In the case of personal empiricists it is necessary to show that the residue includes personlike qualities as well as those qualities of a higher power claimed by impersonal empiricists. In this respect a wider claim must be supported. On the other hand, the personal empiricists have gone further in their research effort to substantiate their claims. Should their claim to establish empirical basis for a personal God fail, their data may at least substantiate the contention of impersonal empiricists.

Importance of the Issue Between Personal and Impersonal Empiricists

The issue of whether the power to which customary prayer and worship are directed is personal or impersonal, is basic to a consideration of the nature of these religious exercises. Either these activities are grounded in realistic psychology, or else they consist of circumlocutions without functional effect upon personality and the group beyond that which ordinary verbalizations would achieve. The question in religious psychology which overshadows all others is whether prayer is oriented to a supposed object beyond human experience, or whether there is a real power within human personality which responds to prayerful activity. The question is not one of popular belief, for all manner of things are believed in the variability of religion, primitive and modern. Rather the question is one of what the object is which makes a naturalistic response to prayer. If it is personlike, personal address is not only appropriate, but more effective. If the object is not personlike, the religious attitudes defined by Dewey or Leuba are the correct ones to hold in a scientific era, and while some kind of impersonal appeal can be voiced to the latent power of human ideals, there is no basis for couching it in terms of the personal pronoun *you* or *thou*.

The question of whether God, psychologically considered, can be viewed scientifically as having the status of a person to be prayed to is one of the most difficult questions confronting the empiricist approach to religion. The question is not one to be by-passed as fanciful or trivial. It has genuine scientific importance. Trueblood comments on the question.

> The proposition that men have genuine intercourse with God may be true, or it may be false, but the proposition is neither manifest nonsense nor an obvious truism. If it can be shown to be actually true that men do have contact not only with other persons and things, but also with the infinite Person, that is a fact of the greatest significance. The very possibility that anything so important *might* be true gives our researches into these matters a necessary mood of seriousness. Since the claim is conceivably valid, there is the heaviest reproach upon those who fail to examine it seriously. When the claim is cavalierly rejected, without a careful examination, this is presumably because of some dogmatic position.
>
> Because the empirical argument is closely allied with the mood and temper of science, it ought to be especially attractive to scientific minds. The reasonable procedure is to look at religious experience

with open-mindedness, as we look at any other datum. If we are truly scientific we approach any experience or report of experience without prejudice and with humility. The scientific temper demands neither that we *accept* the data of experience unreservedly nor that we *reject* it uncritically. We do not know what any experience, whether sensory or nonsensory, is worth until we analyze it, subjecting it to all the appropriate tests that are available.[13]

For many persons in the scientific world the idea that something within the human personality system has personlike qualities places a strain upon the scientific imagination. Nevertheless, the number of voices within the scientific world which support such a view is increasing. Their claims and analyses together with implications of their developing work warrant close study.

While systematic research is far from complete, findings available from various segments of the psychology of religion, as well as from the everyday experience of people, point to the existence of a social and psychological power in religion with personlike qualities. For others an impersonal ethical motivation represents the most which psychology can substantiate in religion, and some of them question the appropriateness of using the word God at all. It is important that the debate go on until consensus is achieved and that it be renewed whenever differences of opinion appear. Nothing is so stifling as religious culture in which there is insistence that ultimate answers have been found, irrevocably. On the other hand, no impediment exists to people developing the conviction born of individual study and experience that a personlike religious reality prevails, irrespective of whether other persons are so situated from a social and intellectual standpoint as to be able to verify it.

Consideration of the Higher Power as God

Concerning the general question of whether God is to be identified with a social and psychological system of power, those who have assembled data with greater rigorousness are Durkheim, by means of anthropological material, and Jung, with psychiatric studies. Durkheim shows effectively that the Australian tribesmen whom he studied regard society and their tribal spirit as one and the same reality. This relates the experience of God to a social power, although somewhat imprecisely as already discussed, nor is the basis for ascribing personlike characteristics shown. Jung establishes that God is an autonomous complex in personality through observing that his subjects use the word *God* in de-

[13] D. E. Trueblood, *Philosophy of Religion*, Harper, 1957, pp. 145–146.

scribing the functioning of an ideational and motivational system within themselves. In the data of his clinical studies Jung finds a one-to-one correspondence between the word or symbol used by people for God and the presence of a characteristic psychological system whose properties are established by the aid of other verbal, dream, or behavior data, although his demonstrations are not spelled out in as clear-cut terms as are desirable from a scientific standpoint. Nor does Jung conclude that psychological analysis of spiritual motivation exhausts the characteristics which may be possessed by a supreme being. Among the works of Jung analyzing the symbolic representation of God as an autonomous system within personality are *The Secret of the Golden Flower* (with Richard Wilhelm) and *Psychology and Religion: West and East.*[14]

Another approach to showing that the higher power psychologically considered is the same as the God in monotheistic religion is to enumerate characteristics of the higher power and to show that these are matched by the characteristics of God reported in religious literature. This literature is not clear-cut and is amenable to varying interpretations. The demonstration of the empiricist thesis that the higher power psychologically described is the God of theology proceeds most readily in the case of those who recognize their God to be found in their experience. These include those who accept the validity of scientific analysis of religious experience and also mystics who deny that their experience is scientifically examinable. In either event the procedure is to show that the characteristics of the power as a motivational system are the characteristics of God reported from religious experience. It is not expected, of course, that the congruence of characteristics extends to philosophically ascribed attributes of God developed in theological speculation. The nature of such attributes falls outside scientific scrutiny. Empiricist analysis is more difficult to pursue in the case of persons who fail to find God in their experience and conceive of him in exclusively supernatural terms. However, there may still be a power which exercises real effects and which is influenced through worship and prayer, a power which actually exists as an unconscious system in the personality field. In this case, if the correspondence is to hold, it is necessary to show that the char-

[14] Richard Wilhelm and C. G. Jung, *The Secret of the Golden Flower,* tr. by C. F. Baynes, Kegan Paul, Trench, Trubner, 1931; C. G. Jung, *Psychology and Religion: West and East,* tr. by R. F. C. Hull. Bollingen Series XX, Bollingen Foundation, Inc. Pantheon, 1958.

acteristics of God believed to be supernatural are to an adequate degree matched by the characteristics of this unconscious system.

We proceed by reviewing and augmenting the description already given of the higher power in religion and at the same time pointing out the correspondence with the characteristics of the supreme being in contemporary monotheistic religion. This is done first for characteristics which pertain to either a personal or an impersonal God and then exclusively with reference to a personal God. The special problem presented by the roots of a supernaturally conceived deity in the unconscious side of personality is considered in a later section. A number of propositions of correspondence may be stated and elaborated in showing the congruence between the power in religion from a psychological standpoint and God as described in sacred literature or reported by contemporary writers.

Altruistic Motivation

As developed in the two preceding chapters, the higher power in religion is an altruistic motivational system. This system of aims and beliefs is seen at its maximum power in the individual when he is thereby motivated to act as effectively for others as his capacities permit. In relating this to the God of human experience, it is necessary to consider the particular pattern of altruistic motivation involved. If the power to be considered equivalent to God is defined in terms of altruistic motivation which is careless, impulsive, or alloyed with self-seeking or in-group preoccupation, the way is opened for self-indulgent love or nationalism to be considered religious. This would not conform to the ethical and spiritual requirements in the traditions of the principal historical religions of the world. On the other hand, if the higher power is designated in too narrow terms of theoretical perfection which a painstaking scientist might discern in retrospective study, the power would become so infrequent in its manifestation in experience as to have little total effect. It seems preferable to risk some fallibility than to view the power in religion merely as an abstract concept of perfection. Its force in religion and in human affairs is larger than this alone. From a practical standpoint the altruistic motivation identified with the power in religion is that which the individual possesses when his aims are for the best and when exercising reasonable judgment while being aided by thoughtful guidance by others in his group. As pointed out in Chapter 7, this system of motivation includes the aim of development toward something better than that of which one is capable in the present. The God corresponding to such a system of motivation would not be infallible, but worse fallibility arises when man insists that he knows for certain the precise attributes of his God's nature and forever after limits human life to growth within a preëstablished mold of divine standards. From a historical standpoint, the God of evolution has not always been right, as imperfections in life amply indicate. The history of the ancient Jews testifies that God as a social force continues to grow in altruistic dimensions from his initial tribal confines in advance of man's achievements toward something nearer a perfect God. Yet the altruism involved is the best of which man is capable after long and earnest effort.

The high ethical attributes in this pattern of altruism are much the same as those identified with God by followers of contemporary religion. A. A. Neuman writes of Judaism: "As God revealed His purposes through the extraordinary experiences of the nation and its prophets, His attributes became manifest to them. He was seen to be the Creator of the Universe, the Father of man, the universal Ruler and Judge. He revealed Himself merciful, long-suffering, and compassionate, but also under the aspects of truth and justice, so that nations as well as individuals are held accountable by these standards. This was natural theology."[15] It is evident in this passage that metaphysical as well as altruistic attributes are ascribed to God, and the congruence with altruistic motivation in people is limited to the latter.

Judaism has developed the concept of God as infinite. The 147th Psalm reads: "Great is our Lord, and abundant in power; his understanding is beyond measure."[16] By tradition both Judaism and Christianity have evolved a concept of God as limitless in possibilities for action, which might seem to introduce a metaphysical, rather than empirical, dimension to God's altruistic nature. The limited quality of human love, however idealistic and widely shared by an entire group, makes it difficult for people to identify God merely with the motivational system actually expressed by human beings. This difficulty is met when it is realized that the unconscious portion of human personality contains limitless possibilities for creative development of new ideas, purposes, and achievements. A reason why

[15] A. A. Neuman, "Judaism," in E. J. Jurji (ed.), *The Great Religions of the Modern World,* Princeton University Press, 1947, p. 232.

[16] Psalms 147:5.

human beings have tended traditionally to think of God as infinite seems to be a recognition of the apparently inexhaustible capacity of the unconscious mind to generate ideas and ideals. The identification of God with a system of motivation both unconscious and conscious, as yet unexpressed as well as expressed, meets more nearly the characteristics given by traditional insights. While this God is much more than human love now known or achieved, he is not beyond the bounds of scientific inquiry. It is precisely such inquiry directed to the interior side of life which is able to bring latent possibilities in the collective unconscious to life.

One of the strongest statements identifying God with altruistic motivation is contained in the First Letter of John in the New Testament. "Beloved, let us love one another; for love is of God, and he who loves is born of God and knows God. He who does not love does not know God; for God is love."[16] Statements of similar meaning can be found in the scriptures of other world religions. When Islamic thought reached a stage where it was threatened on the one hand by those who would make God completely otherworldly and on the other hand by those who would make him pantheistic and indistinguishable from the natural world, a fresh emphasis upon God as will arose. "It is to the everlasting credit of al-Ghazali—the Augustine or Thomas Aquinas of Islam—that he composed and harmonized these contradictory views into a coherent theology. He took the position that Allah is will. Everywhere he cast his glance he caught a vision of His work. Man's kinship to Allah he explained on the basis of sharing in His will through the spirit breathed into every human creature."[17] The principal work of this eleventh-century theologian was called *The Resuscitation of the Sciences of Religion.*

The identifying of God with the altruistic motivation in personality means that God is part of the overall personality system of the individual and, in a larger way, part of the overall social system of the group. This locates the higher power in man, a point contested by some religious thinkers who insist that God or the higher power which benefits man is entirely outside man. Their arguments in religious psychology are given attention in the next chapter on criticisms of empiricist analysis. Scripture in both the Jewish and Christian testaments frequently refers to the spirit of God being *on* or *in* man. The closeness of God and man in Judaism is shown by the statement in Genesis that man

[16] First Letter of John 4:7–8.
[17] E. J. Jurji, "Islam," in Jurji, *op. cit.,* p. 189.

was created in the image or likeness of God,[18] which is to say that something about man is a replica of God. Paul in a passage cited previously speaks of Christ dwelling in him. The meaning of *in* is not physically inside, but within the personality system composed of variables of thought and motivation.

Psychological Power

Altruistic motivation is a power in the sense of being a dynamic system which transforms personality in the direction of stability and goal fulfillment, and which in general brings about an improved quality of human existence. The detailing of the effects of religion has only been partially accomplished through research, yet data available from religious therapy and other sources show that altruistic motivation is a power sufficiently superior to other forces in personality to reorganize, assimilate, or remove these from personality. Effects of altruistic motivation upon the individual personality are only part of the far-reaching influences described by Sorokin in *The Ways and Power of Love*. The nature of this power is what marks it as God-like and which accounts for human beings' regarding it as a God to them. A power which saves a man from the torment of alcoholism, or which transforms life for those who have experienced defeat and despair in their personal relationships, or which in a larger way saves civilization appears to those aided to have the stature of a God. They take such a power seriously and reverently, lest by mistreating it they alienate themselves from its beneficial effects. Recognizing that its gains cannot be achieved by interposing any other will but that in which the power consists, they attend to its functioning with humility. From the standpoint of the dependence of people upon it, the higher power plays the role of a supreme being.

The religious belief that power is a characteristic of God is common. Frequent references are found in scripture to God, or his spirit, as having power to produce psychological results. "Thine, O Lord, is the greatness, and the power, and the glory, and the victory, and the majesty."[19] "He gives power to the faint, and to him who has no might he increases strength. Even youths shall faint and be weary, and young men shall fall exhausted; but they who wait for the Lord shall renew their strength, they shall mount up with wings like eagles, they shall run and not be

[18] Genesis 1:26–27.
[19] I Chronicles 29:11.

weary, they shall walk and not faint."[20] "But to all who received him, who believed in his name, he gave power to become children of God; who were born, not of blood nor of the will of the flesh nor of the will of man, but of God."[21] "For God did not give us a spirit of timidity but a spirit of power and love and self-control."[22]

Influenceable Power

God is believed by religionists to be influenceable by worship and prayer, and by silent meditation in which the worshiper turns his thoughts to God. Worshipers feel the presence of God during their religious activities. In Christianity, for example, Christ or his spirit is believed to be present during the taking of sacramental bread or wine, although Christians diverge in how much this presence is a matter of experience and how much it is a matter of faith. By many it is expected that the presence of Christ's spirit will endure in an effective way for some time after Holy Communion has taken place.

Prayer is the principal means by which it is believed that God is influenced. Jesus told his followers: "Therefore I tell you, whatever you ask in prayer, believe that you receive it, and you will. And whenever you stand praying, forgive, if you have anything against any one; so that your Father also who is in heaven may forgive you your trespasses."[23] In the Letter of James we read: "If any of you lacks wisdom, let him ask God who gives to all men generously and without reproaching, and it will be given him. But let him ask in faith, with no doubting, for he who doubts is like a wave of the sea that is driven and tossed by the wind."[24]

The nature of the influence upon God through worship activities is believed by some to extend to the production of supernatural results, such as the bringing of rain for crops after an appeal to God for help. Most worshipers consider the benefits from God to be primarily of a social and psychological nature in the form of personality changes, larger success in life achievements, protection from personal misfortunes, and increased welfare of the group. The benefits are essentially the intensification of altruistic motivation in members of the group as a result of the spirit of God coming into their lives. In a passage previously cited from Paul's letter to the Galatians, he states: "But the

[20] Isaiah 40:29–31.
[21] John 1:12–13.
[22] II Timothy 1:7.
[23] Mark 11:24–25.
[24] James 1:5–6.

fruit of the Spirit is love, joy, peace, patience, kindness, goodness, faithfulness, gentleness, self-control."

The higher power, as a motivational system, is also influenceable by communication and by turning attention to it. Verbal symbols which are heard or read call forth into consciousness the ideas and impulses in the motivational system to which the symbols refer. The verbal symbols may take the form of preaching, praying, or scriptural reading. Activities which are symbolic, such as religious ceremonies, bring to mind an awareness of altruistic ideas and aims. Prayer and worship are effective in personality development by turning the individual's thinking to altruistic images in the spoken material. They provide verbal patterns which stimulate and channelize growth of the altruistic system, inducing it to become more dominant in the individual's life. Of fundamental importance, prayer as a form of earnest striving or seeking stimulates the emergence of fresh insights and motivations from the collective unconscious. As noted in connection with the experience of members of Alcoholics Anonymous, turning attention to altruistic motivation, whether done meditatively or whether under the impact of communication, renews and intensifies this motivation. The higher power as a psychological system is thus influenceable in the ways in which man has traditionally sought to influence God. Without answering the question of whether the personal form of address or petition is appropriate in appealing to God or the higher power of religion, other characteristics of influenceability correspond in the higher power as a psychological system and in God as traditionally conceived.

INFLUENCING A PERSONAL GOD

Personal Nature of the Higher Power

We next consider whether the personal form of address common in the worship of God is appropriate in influencing the higher power as a motivational system. If not, the most which has been shown is the congruence of the higher power with an impersonal religious reality such as that found in ethical-culture religions often associated with Buddhism, Confucianism, or Taoism, as well as forms prevailing in American culture. While many religious devotees feel intellectually secure in their belief in the impersonality of the religious reality they experience, numerous others are insistent that their God is a person. The altruistic qualities of God cited from Judaism are qualities which God is believed to possess as a person. Apart from trying by tools of science to resolve the difference in belief, the science of religion faces an important causal question in accounting for the intensity of the belief that God is a person. Part of the explanation can be attributed to the psychological need of people for a personal companion during life or after death or to the psychological tendency of people to read a mind into the larger workings of the universe, which seem to exhibit mental design. But the problem of explaining the belief in the personlike qualities of God is obviously simplified if it can be shown that the higher power from a psychological standpoint possesses personlike qualities.

It is equally obvious that nothing physical or visually observable can be involved in such personlike qualities, since motivational systems have no corporeal existence except for their physiological basis in the nervous system of the human body. The belief that God walks among men is now practically nonexistent, except as there is belief that God appears to man as a spirit. Concerning the latter belief, owing to cultural and psychological variables, people differ in the degree to which they are preoccupied with the world of sense perception or with the domain of thought and feeling. Those whose attention is primarily inward can more readily conceive of spiritual realities than those who are principally conscious of things seen in space. Whatever personlike qualities characterize the higher power are more readily conceptualized by those whose awareness of inward processes is stronger. We proceed to examine what these qualities are.

The view of the higher power as possessing some characteristics of personality is not novel in the psychology of religion, although empiricists generally have done little to analyze the concept of a personal God. Cattell states of his group-mind concept of God: "Even the demand of Dean Mathews, that any philosophical construction shall not be substituted for God if it fails to account for the conscious, human, kindly qualities which we intuit in God, is met. For the group mind is something distilled from those essentially human and purposive qualities to which, as the most valuable and significant in our universe, we are drawn."[25]

D. C. Macintosh has channeled the Ritschl tradition of religious study toward science by constructing an empirical theology of a personal God based upon facts of Christian experience. Of

[25] R. B. Cattell, *Psychology and the Religious Quest,* Nelson, 1938, p. 80.

his primary method of analysis he says: "As a first method, then, we may begin with our 'intuitions' as to the reality in question, i.e., with those unreasoned certitudes which are firmly rooted in immediate experience, treating them critically and even skeptically, deducing hypotheses from them, refuting them in the light of experience where this is possible, but otherwise letting them stand for what they still seem to be worth. . . . In apprehending the divine, as manifested in the spirit of the historic Jesus and in the truly 'Christlike' everywhere, we are identifying the divine with certain qualities. . . ."[26] While Macintosh's concepts are somewhat restricted in their doctrinaire orientation and ignore related psychological theory, his work is a noteworthy step in approaching theology as an empirical study. In a later work, *The Problem of Religious Knowledge,* published in 1940, he seems unduly critical of other approaches to making theology an empirical science besides his own and that of H. N. Wieman. His work requires being broadened to take scientific account of facts of religious experience outside of Christianity, yet he has called attention to the feasibility of a science of religion which focuses upon the empirical role of God.

Drawing upon the analysis of the higher power previously developed, we consider more fully its personlike status. The higher power is an independent force in personality which possesses energy of its own and engages in competition, conflict, and cooperation with other motivating forces, tending to displace, integrate, or assimilate them. Being a motivational system, it involves ideas of action, convictions, purposes, and responses. Ira Progoff summarizes Jung's view of autonomous systems within the personality system and in which independent motivational forces or tensions are operating.

> The main characteristic of a tension in the psyche is that its force is exerted beyond the control of the individual. It is autonomous in the sense that it sets energy free independent of the guidance of consciousness. The very fact of its existence as a conflict in the psyche indicates that it is something that consciousness cannot subdue. Energic forces set free by these conflicts, therefore, may operate under their own power and live, as it were, a life of their own within the personality.
>
> Such quantities of released energy have an attracting power that gathers various psychic contents together around them into a "constellation" or "complex." These complexes, acting under their own power, break away from the totality of the personality. As Jung interprets it,

[26] D. C. Macintosh, *Theology as an Empirical Science,* Macmillan, 1919, pp. 159–160.

"the tendency to split means that parts of the psyche detach themselves from consciousness to such an extent that they not only appear foreign but also lead an autonomous life of their own." This means not only that they go out of the control of consciousness, but that they may operate in consciousness within their own terms. They become "autonomous partial systems," and they function like small personalities within the total personality. In itself, this is not necessarily an abnormal condition. Such psychic "splits" are actually necessary if the individual is to specialize the direction of his energies so as to accomplish some particular work. The "autonomous complex" provides, very often, the "flavor" and distinctiveness of an individual's personality. It becomes a danger point only when, operating as a "partial system," it goes too far out of relation to the rest of the psyche, and a condition of unbalance results.[27]

Such an autonomous system possesses a will of its own which seeks realization by means of ideas and actions through which it functions. It has characteristics of a personality within the total personality system of the individual. It is personlike, although lacking in physical identity separate from the individual or from other human beings. In the realm of motivation its status is much like that of any person with whom one interacts. It has characteristics of a person as far as its psychological existence and its influence over other thinking, feeling, and acting of the individual are concerned.

In its social dimension the higher power is located in the personalities of members of the group who have unity of altruistic purpose. In this way the power works toward a single goal of the greatest good of the human race. Manifestations of this power in different individuals are parts of a group system with a single purpose giving rise to the concept of this power as a group mind. Its personlike characteristics transcend individuals who share common pieces of psychological ground with the system. The resulting superpersonality does not possess the unity of a single stream of consciousness but rather that of parallel streams of consciousness in different individuals united by a common purpose and plan. A separate facet of this social system of motivation functions in the personality system of each individual member of the group, although all are affected by the motivation of each other.

These personlike characteristics are much the same as those believed by monotheists to be characteristics of their God. Most persons think of their God as a person with a will, purpose, and

[27] I. Progoff, *Jung's Psychology and Its Social Meaning,* Grove, 1953, pp. 81–82.

plan, and having the means in human beings through whom he works for the accomplishment of his will. Few religionists, if any, would contend that God manifests the same aspect of his will or personality to all people. In this respect, different facets of the divine nature are believed to be revealed to different persons. The group-mind concept is clearly developed in Christianity in that Christ is regarded as a spiritual being transcending the human race. Paul writes: "For as in one body we have many members, and all the members do not have the same function, so we, though many, are one body in Christ, and individually members one of another."[28] That God's spirit is in man as a transcendent influence for justice is affirmed in Judaism. In the Book of Numbers it is written of Moses and the elders: "The Lord came down in the cloud and spoke to him, and took some of the spirit that was upon him and put it upon the seventy elders; and when the spirit rested upon them, they prophesied."[29] God speaking to Isaiah is recorded as saying of the Jews, although some authorities believe the reference is to a single leader: "I have put my spirit upon him, he will bring forth justice to the nations. . . . he will faithfully bring forth justice. He will not fail or be discouraged till he has established justice in the earth; and the coastlands wait for his law."[30] From these citations it appears that the higher power as a social and altruistic system of motivation has the same personlike characteristics attributed to God to the extent that he is found within human experience. When religious devotees speak familiarly of their God as a person, it seems apparent that, if they refer to something they inwardly experience, they are talking about the personlike characteristics of the higher power analyzed here. In respect to these characteristics, the higher power conforms to the role of God as a person.

Forms of Reference to God in Prayer and Worship

While the foregoing line of analysis is convincing to some, there are others, psychologists and religionists, who are unable to accept the concept of the power in religion as personlike. The gulf of feeling which separates the two groups is so wide that it seems unlikely that either side will soon succeed in convincing the other. At the heart of the issue is the capacity to conceptualize a psychological reality in religion as a person, a

[28] Romans 12:4–5.
[29] Numbers 11:25.
[30] Isaiah 42:1,3–4.

capacity which is considerably affected by previous cultural conditioning to which the individual has been exposed. Religionists generally, whether they believe God is found in interior experience or not, readily think of him as a person to be designated by *thou* or *he*. Those to whom worship experience is unfamiliar are apt to think of the psychological power in religion as impersonal and to be referred to by the pronoun *it*, as in the case of other personality characteristics. Ambivalence on the question is evidenced by a group such as the Christian Scientists, who refer to God in personal and impersonal terms, and furthermore, who sometimes use feminine, as well as masculine, gender in referring to God.

The issue is complicated by the circumstance that for many God is someone or something to be appealed to, even if this appeal is regarded as no more than exhortation of one's ideals to become more dominant in one's life. The problem here is that the imperative mood for appeal in the English language has no impersonal pronoun, only *thou* or *you* in voicing the exhortation. Scientific categories of psychological thought are limited in practical expression to the vocabulary of words available. Even if *it* is a more acceptable pronoun in the third person, no neuter pronoun is available in the second person for employing the imperative mood in worship expression.

To most followers of a theistic religion verbal symbols during worship which refer to God as a person seem appropriate in influencing him. Whether others agree with the appropriateness of personally referring to the higher power in religion by *you, thou,* or *he,* it is understandable from a psychological standpoint how it happens that referring to God as a person is a widely prevalent pattern in worship and prayer. In accounting for the existence of this cultural pattern, the empiricist states that worshipers find something sufficiently personlike in the power of religion for them to use a personal pronoun, speaking of God as *he* rather than *it*. As to whether the personal or impersonal pronoun is to be used during religious exercises, it may be noted first, that as long as words are specifically defined and commonly understood, they may be assigned any meaning desired within a cultural group. Religionists generally believe that the personal pronoun more nearly conforms to customary usage from the secular context. As to whether the personal pronoun is more effective in producing results, scientific data are lacking, other than the commonly expressed conviction of religionists that the personal gender is the proper one to use. The question of whether this gender has a proper place in scientific discourse cannot be answered without careful study of the types of meaning involved. It is the present author's conclusion that psychological characteristics of the power in religion are sufficiently similar to those of a person that the personal pronoun is more satisfactory than the impersonal pronoun. This conclusion is accepted by those who find a personal God differentiated in their psychic world.

Analysis of God as a personal being involves the grammatical mood as well as the pronoun used in worship and prayer. The imperative mood of sentence structure is that of a direct address to a person to act, such as in the request "You help me." This is a verbal stimulus which strongly evokes the impulse of aid. If the sentence communicated were simply indicative in mood, it would state, "You are helping me," or "You were helping me," or "If you help me, I will finish soon." These are all assertions of fact. As verbal stimuli, they merely evoke ideas of helping, not the impulse to help, unless this arises in the hearer's mind for other reasons than the statement of fact.

In the context of the distinction between the indicative and imperative mood, the reason why the religionist uses the imperative mood in prayer is readily seen. For him to say to himself, "If I had stronger ideals, I would be a more effective person," would only call into his mind ideas of cause-and-effect relationship. If he lacked any impulse toward stronger ideals, the effect of repeating the statement to himself might be discouraging, rather than encouraging. The point is that the indicative mood from a psychological standpoint is a weak stimulus to personality activity. If the religionist instead says to himself, "Come on, ideals, be stronger in my life," the energizing influence of the stimulus is apparent. The imperative mood in secular life is a strong verbal stimulus to motivation and action. If these are what are sought in religious life, the appropriate stimulus is the imperative mood.

The critic of religious procedure might still ask why the individual does not exhort himself, as in saying, "Come on, fellow, you must have stronger ideals." This is an imperative stimulus which is obviously more effective than a simple statement of fact, "If I had stronger ideals, I would be a more effective person." Here an empiricist may point out that the question of verbal address to a particular area of personality is involved. When the individual realizes that there is one part of his personality system of special importance to be activated, his ideals, he is apt to single out this area for attention in his imperative appeal. The verbal stimulus is more specific if addressed to the higher part of his personality, rather than to his personality in general. The stimulus activates the ideals he already has, which are the most effective source of stronger ideals. Furthermore, the pattern of the verbal stimulus, "Come on, ideals, be stronger in my life," or, "God, grant me more of thy Spirit," conforms specifically to the unfolding process of larger ideals growing from those already existing in the personality system, which makes it a more effective stimulus. That the verbal stimulus utilizes the imperative mood is an added reason for regarding the object to which it is addressed as personlike, since an object capable of responding to the imperative mood suggests a person in the customary sense.

Whether this empiricist line of reasoning will satisfy all critical students of religion is problematic. Nevertheless, prayer as a pattern common in religious culture becomes more understandable in its use of verbal stimuli of personal address effective in generating personality change. Worship as group communion with God is seen as a psychological process whereby the common life of the group is built up by arousing altruistic sentiments and ideals. Some data are available indicating the extent of the influence of religion on personality growth, reviewed in another chapter, and much more research in religion remains to be performed.

Types of Prayer

Prayer is a verbal form of communication with the deity. The verbalization may be vocal or inaudible. In silent prayer the movement of thought corresponds with what takes place when thinking is voiced aloud. Worship is a wider term than prayer and involves overt actions or rituals as part of the process of communication. Since the actions communicate meanings similar to those which verbal symbols possess, the essential nature of worship is disclosed by an analysis of communication in prayer.

The major form of prayer is petition, amounting to a request or an appeal. The tone is not that of a command, for this implies a threat of force, when none exists in the interior side of personality. Moreover, altruistic growth takes place by subordinating egoistic components of personality at the same time as ideals are stimulated. A command as a verbal stimulus would make ego elements more prominent. Humble petition goes furthest in subordinating the ego to the altruistic ideals whose growth is sought. Furthermore, the independence of the rest of the personality system which the power in religion possesses is acknowledged by the act of petition.

When verbal petition is compounded with action, the worshiper may endeavor to do things which immolate his ego or which direct attention to his distress. Flagellation found in the Middle Ages and fasting in Hindu religious practice are forms of ego destruction. In a milder yet effective way, the performance of penance as part of religious practice subordinates the worshiper's will to that of God. Once a punishment, penance in Catholicism now assumes a positive aspect in the prescription for moral transformation imposed by the priest at confession. The trend in contemporary religion is away from special devices to demonstrate the conquest of self and toward altruistic living as a spiritual achievement. Verbal or inaudible petition is a common religious exercise for the individual and for the group. The following, taken from the Episcopal *Book of Common Prayer,* are examples of prayers.

> O gracious Father, we humbly beseech thee for thy holy Catholic Church; that thou wouldest be pleased to fill it with all truth, in all peace. Where it is corrupt, purify it; where it is in error, direct it; where in any thing it is amiss, reform it. Where it is right, establish it; where it is in want, provide for it; where it is divided, reunite it; for the sake of him who died and rose again, and ever liveth to make intercession for us, Jesus Christ, thy Son, our Lord. Amen.[31]
>
> Almighty God, who hast created man in thine own image; Grant us grace fearlessly to contend against evil, and to make no peace with oppression; and, that we may reverently use our freedom, help us to employ it in the maintenance of justice among men and nations, to the glory of thy holy Name; through Jesus Christ our Lord. Amen.[32]

Another common form of prayer is thanksgiving, which is defined in the *American College Dictionary* as "grateful acknowledgment of benefits or favors." The grammatical mood involved in a prayer of thanksgiving is the indicative mood. With deep feeling the source of personality growth is stated to be God or the highest ideals or values one already has or which reach one from the lives of others. It is a truism among worshipers that they do not tell their God anything he does not already know. However, by restating the source of religious growth to oneself one is reminded of the power to which one turns one's thoughts, and this power is sensitized in the personality system to facilitate further growth. In this manner thanksgiving as a feature of worship contributes to the growth of religious personality.

Combined with verbal thanksgiving are often found rituals of giving or sacrifice by worshipers. The giving frequently takes the

[31] *Book of Common Prayer,* 1936, p. 37.
[32] *Ibid.,* p. 44.

form of a money offering collected in behalf of the church. In the worship service of the Mass the death of Christ is offered up by the priest in consecrating the bread and wine which are the body and blood of Christ, a re-presentation of the sacrifice of Christ on the cross to His heavenly Father. Gifts or sacrifice accompanying prayers emphasize the worshipers' acknowledgment of God as the source of power in religion and the profound gratitude which the worshipers feel for the benefits which God bestows upon mankind. An example of a prayer of thanksgiving follows:

Almighty God, Father of all mercies, we, thine unworthy servants, do give thee most humble and hearty thanks for all thy goodness and loving-kindness to us, and to all men; particularly to those who desire now to offer up their praises and thanksgivings for thy late mercies vouchsafed unto them. We bless thee for our creation, preservation, and all the blessings of this life; but above all, for thine inestimable love in the redemption of the world by our Lord Jesus Christ; for the means of grace, and for the hope of glory. And, we beseech thee, give us that due sense of all thy mercies, that our hearts may be unfeignedly thankful; and that we show forth thy praise, not only with our lips, but in our lives, by giving up ourselves to thy service, and by walking before thee in holiness and righteousness all our days; through Jesus Christ our Lord, to whom, with thee and the Holy Ghost, be all honour and glory, world without end. Amen.[33]

A third form of prayer is intercessory, such as prayers by Catholics to saints to intervene with God. Whatever supernatural implications such prayers may have, they have much the same effect upon the personality system as petitionary prayer, since asking for personality growth is often involved. Furthermore, if the individual finds it difficult to think concretely of whom or what he is praying to, the concrete images of saints as people who have lived deeply spiritual or heroic lives aid the worshiper in turning his attention to ideals and values which are a source of personality growth.

Prayer as a Form of Communication

When an individual prays in private, the conversation does not extend outside a single personality field, as far as has been empirically verified. The question arises of whether this is genuine communication, since no transfer of meaning from one mind to another appears to take place. Except for the indefinite

[33] *Ibid.*, p. 33.

amount of influence which can be attributed to extrasensory perception, the direct effects of prayer in isolation do not extend beyond the personality system of the individual.

Communication between persons takes various forms. When a descriptive statement is made, there is a transfer of meaning from one person to another. Often the transferred meaning also undergoes growth in its implications in the other's mind. When an appeal or exhortation is made, the verbal stimulus used typically arouses a new and expanded meaning in the mind of the other. When the other has gained this new meaning, he is able to respond with aid. When one person asks something of another, the other may immediately respond without reflecting upon the original meaning of the communication.

The usual effects of prayer are found in arousal, not transfer, of meaning. When something is asked of God in prayer, the answer appears in the form of new ideas, impulses, or actions in the functioning of personality. The type of stimulus and the effect of the stimulus are the same as in communication between people, although the appeal and the response in the form of an enlarged meaning both take place within a single personality system.

Nor is it unusual that the communication takes place within a single human being. People often talk to themselves in resolving their thinking or in stimulating their motivation. The social psychologist G. H. Mead based his theory of personality development upon the process of internal conversation in "taking the role of the other" in one's mind.[34] According to Mead, verbal interplay takes place between component motivational systems in personality, consisting of the self and of roles in society which the individual or others assume. Inaudibly one verbalizes these roles in thinking of *you, I, they, we, he* and *she* as one rehearses one's participation in group life, developing a sense of what Mead calls the "generalized other." Just as a person can talk to himself, it is psychologically understandable that in religious communication he addresses the higher part of his personality. C. H. Cooley set forth this view of prayer in 1902.

> To pray, in a higher sense, is to confront our moral perplexities with the highest personal ideal we can form, and so to be unconsciously integrating the two, straightening out the one in accordance with the other. It would seem that social psychology strongly corroborates the idea that prayer is an essential aspect of the higher life; by showing, I mean, that thought, and especially vivid thought, is interlocutory in its

[34] Anselm Strauss (ed.), *The Social Psychology of George Herbert Mead,* University of Chicago Press, 1956, pp. 212–261.

very nature, and that aspiration almost necessarily takes, more or less distinctly, the form of intercourse with an ideal being.[35]

G. A. Coe, one of the early group of American religious psychologists and an associate of Dewey at Columbia, discussed the aspect of prayer as internal conversation,[36] and related work was done with this concept by A. L. Strong.[37] The undeveloped germ of the concept was apparently introduced by Feuerbach, from a negative standpoint. Feuerbach said that in prayer man only talks to himself, as if no God, empirical or otherwise, were there to hear, nothing more being involved than talking to an empty room. A wealth of difference exists between appealing to ideals to become more dominant and merely thinking out loud, the difference between the imperative and indicative mood in verbal stimuli.

More may be involved in the psychology of prayer, as Coe indicates, than internal conversation. When a group is assembled in worship activity the verbal stimulation extends outside of individuals to other individuals. A prayer given by a leader in a service is an appeal to God in the psychic experience of all of the participants. The prayer is much broader than internal conversation within the personality system of one individual. The typical form which Sunday or Sabbath worship takes is that of group communication, rather than individual activity alone. Account must be taken of those whose prayers are addressed to a supernaturally conceived being, but the point in empiricist analysis is that the power in religion can be influenced by personal address in a psychologically understandable way, and in this respect the power in religion occupies the role of a personal God. On the other hand, if the power is not conceptualized as personlike by followers of a religion, the term *God* is less used and activities of personal communication are not ordinarily utilized in religious exercises. With or without a personal God, these exercises to renew or intensify altruistic motivation mark the behavior as religious and differentiate it from the practical performance of ethical principles.

The line of analysis developed in this chapter discloses a one-to-one correspondence between the power in religion, psychologically considered, and the traditional God of monotheistic religion. From this correspondence it can be concluded that persons

[35] C. H. Cooley, *Human Nature and the Social Order,* The Free Press, 1956, p. 387.

[36] G. A. Coe, *The Psychology of Religion,* University of Chicago Press, 1916, pp. 302–320.

[37] A. L. Strong, *The Psychology of Prayer,* University of Chicago Press, 1909.

who speak of God are referring to the motivational and ideational system described as the higher power of religion. In addition to the correspondence, different kinds of psychological powers besides altruistic or ideal may be acknowledged in polytheistic and spiritualistic religions. Also, by philosophical theorizing religious followers expand their concepts of God into a supernatural realm to take account of problems of life and death and the origin and destiny of the universe beyond present experience. There the correspondence ceases.

Implications of Extrasensory Perception for Religion

A common practice in religion is for prayer to be made in behalf of others, as when millions of Americans in church services pray for the recovery from illness of the President of the United States, who is probably unaware of most of the prayers in his behalf. In this situation the analysis of prayer in terms of verbal communication inside or outside of the personal system of the individual does not apply. In a somewhat similar type of situation the worshiper believes that he is praying to more of God than is found within his personality system, a situation in which the worshiper, unknown to others, might conceivably make contact with that of God in their lives. This possibility, which seems to be on the fringe of the occult, is less fantastic in the light of recent discoveries in extrasensory perception. As alternative scientific hypotheses, either such prayers are without discernible effects involving the lives of others, or else some form of extrasensory influence between persons takes place during prayer.

Research in extrasensory perception is stoutly defended by a group of workers who have been able to gain the support of some eminent scientists, among them the world-renowned statistician R. A. Fisher and the highly respected psychologist, Gardner Murphy, Director of Research for the Menninger Foundation, who pronounce the findings to be scientifically sound. A common pattern of extrasensory study is for the experimenter at some distance removed from the subject, possibly many miles away, to draw cards from a deck and look at them. The subject attempts to guess by telepathy which card has been drawn. In repeated experiments subjects have achieved better success in calling cards correctly than would be expected by chance. The improvement over chance results is slight but definitely appears in experiment after experiment.[38]

[38] Gardner Murphy, "Trends in the Study of Extrasensory Perception," *American Psychologist,* February, 1958, pp. 69–76.

One of the researchers, W. W. Carington, explains the result as a transference of association of ideas from the experimenter's mind to the subject's mind. If the experimenter is thinking of the zebra on a card and the idea of telepathy at the same time as the subject is thinking of telepathy, then the association of the two ideas causes the subject to think of a zebra.

If this theory is valid, then associations of ideas in prayers of one person affect associations of ideas in the mind of a person for whom prayer is made. Thus a prayer addressed to something psychological within oneself makes some kind of contact with ideals in another person's mind, and the ideals in the other's mind influence the ideals in one's own mind. This sounds like the primitive religionist's view of mana as a power which can be transmitted from person to person by thinking about it. In prayer possibly a cumulative effect occurs when many people are praying together simultaneously. These natural, rather than supernatural, aspects of religion present interesting possibilities for research, most of which is still undone. Meanwhile, the hope or expectation endures in the minds of millions that their prayers reach a God outside of themselves and that such prayers further the well-being of persons unaware of the prayers offered. For others the sheer finding of God within themselves provides spiritual opportunity in abundance. L. Weatherhead, a British religious psychologist, reports several well-authenticated cases of healing through praying for a sick person, one of which is given below.

Dr. Howard Somervell is a Fellow of the Royal College of Surgeons, and was a member of the Mount Everest Expedition (1922), one of the five to reach the 28,000-feet level. He is unlikely to offer a highly-coloured story of a magical effect of prayer. He tells the story of a schoolmaster with tubercular disease, and says:

"The disease is one which medical science reckons to be well-nigh incurable when it has reached this stage. The man was going down hill and daily getting weaker and more feverish. His legs became more and more painful; and after a few weeks we took another X-ray picture and found the disease was worse in that the whole of the bone was involved. There was only one thing to do, and that was to amputate the leg to save the patient's life. . . .

"So we told the poor fellow that there was nothing else to be done. His reply was unexpected: 'Will you give me three weeks? I want to try the effect of praying about it.' We agreed to give him that time, and the next day he went home. In three weeks he turned up true to his promise. He had left hospital feverish, ill, flushed in the face, and only capable of being carried about. He returned in a car, but hobbling with a stick and looking much better. The wound in the leg was not healed, but the leg itself, as revealed by the X-rays, was wonderfully improved, though not yet free from the disease.

"We were amazed. What had he done to make so great an improvement? He told us quite simply that he had been quite sure it was against the will of God for any of His servants to suffer, and that he had before him a life of service to God if only he could keep his leg and his life. So he called his family and friends together and said to them, 'Look here, will you folk unite in prayer for this leg of mine that it be completely healed?' They agreed, and for a week a continuous chain of prayer was kept up by that family. One of them would pray for a quarter of an hour. Then another would take it up, and so on for over a week. In another three weeks he came to see us again. The leg had healed. He was able to walk on it and appeared almost well. A few months later he was back at school, perfectly fit, playing games with the boys, running about on both legs with no sign of disease."[39]

EMPIRICIST ANALYSIS OF ASSUMED SUPERNATURAL POWER

In the case of persons who acknowledge that they experience their God, the empirical correspondence between their God and altruistic motivation is readily described. This can be done notwithstanding the logical extension which people make of their empirical beliefs to supernatural aspects of their supreme being. The correspondence with the altruistic system of motivation extends only to empirical aspects of God. The situation is more complicated for those who believe their God to be outside experience, even remote from it. In this case it might be insisted that the similarity between God remote from experience and a motivational system within experience ends. It is necessary to examine carefully the content of supernatural religious beliefs in order to discern whether the spiritual power referred to exists in psychic experience.

In the quite different case of those who believe that society is their God, it is found that society as a physical group does not contain the higher power of religion, which actually is located in the altruistic motivation with which people approach society. In this case the higher power is erroneously believed to reside in society but actually has its locus in people's altruistic feeling for society. It is impossible to deny people the privilege of believing that society is their God, although it is possible on scientific

[39] From *Psychology, Religion and Healing,* by Leslie D. Weatherhead. Copyright 1951 by Pierce and Smith. By permission of Abingdon Press.

grounds to question whether the seat of the power in their religion is actually society. The answer might influence people to modify their religious concepts to regard a motivational system as their central religious object.

Application of Jung's Principles to an Analysis of Supernatural Beliefs

To return to the situation of those who conceive of God entirely in supernatural terms, we of course recognize that the belief that God has existence outside of experience is philosophically legitimate. It can, however, be appropriately questioned whether the higher power which is ascribed to God and which produces personality transformation does in point of fact exist outside of a natural causal series. People may believe that the higher power is supernaturally located because of their inability to find it within human experience. The circumstance that people do not know that the higher power is inside their experience does not mean that their experience does not contain it, since the differentiation of components of the interior life is not an easy, clear process. A major thesis of Jungian analysis is that vital psychic factors are found in interior experience as unconscious contents. Only if such factors become lifted from ordinary experience by means of symbolic images or else fully differentiated by intellectual analysis do people become aware of their existence. A typical task of psychoanalysis or of what Jung calls analytical psychology is to disclose to the individual what his interior experience contains. This interior experience is dim and evanescent at best, so the demonstration does not proceed with the facile obviousness of disclosing objects which perceptual experience of the exterior world contains.

In locating the higher power of a religion whose beliefs have supernatural reference, let us take as an example such a supernaturally conceived belief of Fundamentalist Protestants as "Jesus saves." The belief requires more detailed statement. Jesus saves those who are aware of his life, have faith in him, and follow his teachings. This attitude can be summarized as one's thoughts being turned to Jesus. The statement of belief is then that Jesus saves those whose thoughts are turned toward him.

The experience of thinking about Jesus' life and teachings is an experience of symbolic imagery which contains an essential meaning, the altruistic system of motivation. The picturesque imagery by which Jesus' life is portrayed is made up of symbols of archetypes of this motivation. The individual may be unaware of the abstract system contained in the imagery of which he is conscious and might even deny the existence of the system. The point, however, is that altruism can be inferred or abstracted from the spiritual experience of following Jesus' life and teachings. Those who address Jesus in their prayers as a supernatural God (and, as far as Jung is concerned, may succeed in so addressing him) actually are heard by or responded to by a psychological system in their unconscious which consists of or is closely related to the system of altruistic motivation. The result is that this system moves nearer conscious awareness and the rest of the personality system becomes oriented around it.

As in the previously analyzed situation of worship of society, the problem is one of misplaced causation. The higher power which "saves" personality is actually contained in the imagery by means of which the life and teachings of Jesus are viewed by the individual. Activating this imagery and allowing it freely to express itself leads to personality changes which altruistic motivation is capable of bringing about in integrating personality about itself. It is to be emphasized that the imagery involved is not static in nature but is made up of dynamic, compelling sentiments. The situation seems less one of turning attention than of the attention being drawn to and fixed by these compelling impulses. The power is not due to the object to which the imagery refers, that is, the historical Jesus. Rather, the power consists of the unconscious psychological forces contained in the imagery. The system unconsciously contained in Christological imagery is the higher power which performs the role of God in the individual's life. Whether he acknowledges this role of psychic power or designates a supernatural reality as his God is immaterial to the functioning of the psychic process. It is unnecessary and indeed impossible to alter belief contrary to the individual's background of conviction. It is possible however, and scientifically necessary, to show that the psychic agency for affecting personality change is contained in the unconscious experience of the individual himself.

It would be incorrect to conclude from this analysis that man is "saved" by his imagery. Such a conclusion would again be an instance of misplaced causation. The imagery is simply the garb in which spiritual motivation dresses itself. The motivation is real and powerful, and essentially from an empirical standpoint it is God. If it did not come to the surface of consciousness in the imagery of Jesus, the shepherd who came to save mankind, it would do so in some other concrete terms, such as the drama in the *Bhagavad-Gita,* a religious epic in Hinduism. The abstract generic qualities of the motivation are universal, whatever the imagery in which the qualities are cast. If no cultural forms existed into which the motivation might be channeled into consciousness, the human psyche would generate its own, as it did during the first stirrings of religious consciousness in primordial times.

Nor is imagery exclusively or even primarily fictitious in its concrete details. Imagery is a common vehicle for awareness of one's motives or those of others. The images by which psychic material is represented are not imagined but usually come from everyday episodes of life. The psychic meaning is the same whether people say they experience God in Jesus alive today or whether they experience him in altruistic human relationships, for the abstract characteristics which can be distilled from the imagery are the same. Of course if the image of Jesus is that of a judge in afterlife, not a loving influence in human affairs, the principles contained in the imagery are not the same. As an example of an everyday experience providing an image of spiritual power, the following may be cited. A man who was asked for what he lived said in reply that when he came home from work his children ran out to meet him and said, "Daddy, whirl me around." For that man "whirl-me-around" became a concrete symbol of family love for which he lived. If the term *Jesus* or *Christ* is made synonymous, not with historical or philosophical details, but with the dynamic power underlying the imagery and contained in it, then Jesus or Christ is a real God to the worshiper.

At first examination, supernatural beliefs suggest a breakdown in the correspondence between God as traditionally conceived and a system of motivation in personality. Then it is realized that the supernatural imagery contains the power performing the role of God. The correspondence goes further than this. Corresponding to an unconscious psychological system is a supernaturally conceived God. When the concept of the "unconscious" and the concept of the "supernatural" are examined, they each are found to mean something which the individual is unable to find in experience, at least under ordinary circumstances. Only when the infrequent privilege of "revelation" arises does the individual meet his God face to face. This can more regularly be duplicated by the individual achieving spiritual insight through orderly processes of study and personality development. The supernaturalists are right that the higher power of religion cannot be directly documented by data from the experience of people. The contents of their inward experience become differentiated with much difficulty and after long development. The differentiation is not into constituents which they know apart from symbols. The psychic contents are qualityless. They are expressed by symbols or else in concrete images and verbal symbols referring to these images. At the same time, Myers and James are right in tracing the source of the power in religion to the unconscious, or as they call it, the subliminal or subconscious life. It remained for Jung to probe the unconscious, to discover the psychic power residing in this, and to make explicit the way in which this power expresses itself in the personality system.

Analysis of the ground for supernatural theological belief is not set forth by Jung in one place as the systematic account undertaken here. All of the concepts and principles, however, are part of Jung's analysis of religion and can for the most part be found in the quotations given here of Jung's work. What is of special importance to stress is that Jung is not interested in eliminating supernatural symbolism. He recognizes, as do most religious scientists, that supernatural referents are beyond science. He regards symbolic imagery as absolutely indispensable to religion. Even if such imagery is de-supernaturalized, it still plays an essential role in bringing to consciousness the unconscious forces in the individual. The parables of Jesus, for example, present essential religious truths in a meaningful, understandable way, not requiring a trained psychologist for their meaning to be grasped. The incidents in the sacred history of any religion provide an effective vehicle for the periodic revival of religious impulses in the collective unconscious and for the reorientation of personality about them. It is for this reason that the author agrees with Jung in counseling those interested in religion to remain within the historical tradition in which they have grown up. No imagery unfamiliar to them can surpass the usefulness of the sacred stories from their own scripture and teaching, especially when it is remembered that this symbolic imagery is shared and repeated by other members of the group with whom they live.

Application of Psychological Concepts to the Trinity in Christianity

The doctrine of the trinity—Father, Son, and Holy Spirit—has persisted so strongly in Christian thought through the centuries that the psychologist is led by analysis of the unconscious basis for religion to seek for the roots of this doctrine in the structure of human personality. Jung has made an exhaustive study of the psychological basis for Christian doctrine.[40] Along such lines a brief interpretation of the trinity can be given. The Spirit is acknowledged to be an aspect of God of which human beings are conscious. This part of the trinity represents conscious experience of the higher power. Christ, the son, is regarded in Christianity as the presence of God in mankind. This part of the trinity refers to both conscious and unconscious aspects of the altruistic system of power in human race. But religionists also commonly believe there to be more of God than comes within the compass of human experience. Questions of creation and immortality receive compelling answers by making the philosophical assumption of more of God's nature outside the present span of human life. So recognition of God as the creator and receiver of man's soul, a philosophical aspect, is involved. The concept of God the father includes this aspect and the Spirit and Christ as well. The trinity can be represented by three concentric circles proceeding from the inner circle of the Spirit of which man is conscious to unknown areas beyond.

This is not to justify a trinitarian concept of God, but simply to interpret its psychological basis, a basis which has received different expression in Judaism with its central concepts of God, spirit, and law, and which is articulated in still other ways in other religions. The explanation of the trinity in Christianity not only makes psychologically intelligible the triune aspects of a supreme being, but also explains the basis for the historic *filioque* controversy which played an important part leading up to the separation of the Eastern and Western branches of the Christian church in the eleventh century. The theological question is whether the spirit proceeds from God *through* the son. The Eastern Orthodox churches have maintained that it does, while the Roman Catholic statement of faith instead says that the spirit proceeds from the father and the son. While the distinction seems subtle, the point is an important one, which is that the spirit of God as a psychological manifestation develops out of the collective unconscious. The contention of the Eastern Orthodox churches expresses a psychological principle which aids the individual in finding the spirit of God in the life and teachings of Christ or in Christ regarded as an altruistic motivational system.

[40] Jung, *op. cit.*, pp. 107–296.

chapter 10 Criticisms of Empiricist Analysis of Religion

The foregoing scientific views of God as a social and psychological manifestation have been repeatedly challenged by spokesmen for organized religious groups, by philosophers, by theologians, and by social and psychological scientists. While philosophical questions are important in their own domain, we endeavor to limit our attention to the debate which has gone on within the scientific tradition. From the skeptical psychology of Hume and Feuerbach a century and more ago to the far-reaching investigations and conclusions of C. G. Jung the debate has been intense, nor is it likely to cease soon.

The Shifting Ground of the Debate

The ground of the debate has moved from the impoverished view of religion which was the most which empiricist analysis by Hume or Feuerbach could produce. It now concerns ambitious efforts of religious psychologists such as Jung to duplicate in the name of science the richness and depth of traditional religion. It is understandable that early attempts to look at religion through the eyes of science would discern little which continued investigations would later disclose. From the start the findings of empiricists have been a challenge to the substance and the authority of the conclusions promulgated by church leaders. In its early stage the ensuing debate was a united effort by the religious community to defend itself against ideas which were primarily inimical to religion. As the fertility of the empiricist approach has been increasingly realized by religious leaders they have utilized its ideas and approaches to religion. The debate in its later stage is between one religious camp in opposition to another, the traditionalists versus the scientists.

At the same time, the debate has gone on between religionists and rationalists such as Freud who sincerely believe that religion is an emotional remnant of primitive thought. Today religious empiricism faces criticism by both orthodoxy and agnosticism. While the attitudes of the latter two groups fundamentally diverge, when their spokesmen enter the scientific arena they are alike compelled to assume the harness of science. It goes without saying that a scientist such as Freud or those who follow closely the roads which he opened are ready to acknowledge that scientists who differ are expected to compare their methods and their results step by step until agreement is achieved. Those devoted to scientific truth are willing to accept new conclusions, whatever their present standpoint. In contrast, religious orthodoxy feels intensely loyal to its conclusions and, if science fails to substantiate these, is often ready to shift the argument away from science or even to abandon intellectual defense altogether. While critics within the cultural stream of science come well equipped in scientific training and tools, critics from outside the world of science tend to lack the training and tools and may find the garb of scientist a distasteful one to assume. Consequently it is not always easy to achieve a common focus of argument upon the same issues, hypotheses, or data.

L. A. Feuerbach

An examination of the criticisms of empiricist analysis of religion can usefully be introduced by considering the work of Feuerbach, as this will clear the atmosphere for more incisive study of issues. His major work, *The Essence of Christianity,* was first published in 1841. If any one can be assigned the designation of being the first empiricist in religious psychology in modern times, Feuerbach might qualify. Yet he did not write in the carefully worded, undogmatic, scientific manner of his predecessor Hume and of those who followed later. Unlike scientists such as Durkheim or Jung he assembles almost no data. His work has been more of a cross to be borne by those who followed than a platform on which they might build. He has been a favorite whipping boy of critics of empiricist analysis, and for some has become a symbol, if an erroneous one, of religious empiricism. Contemporary religious empiricists who acquire ideas from him are reluctant to admit the connection with his work and usually dissociate themselves from the misunderstandings he occasioned. Dislike of his work stems not only from mistaken ideas in his analysis but also from the missionary manner in which he advanced them. Like Freud, Feuerbach felt called upon not only to analyze religion but to change the ideas of others in established churches.

Theologians such as Karl Barth and H. Richard Niebuhr are desirous of perennial resurrection of Feuerbach's writings in order that their whipping boy may be kept alive to receive further verbal blows. In a contemporary edition of *The Essence of Christianity,* Barth gives an introduction and Niebuhr writes a foreword to Barth's introduction.[1] What they and their associates succeed in doing is refuting Feuerbach, not a difficult task, since he was a naïve, dogmatic writer, while the real scientific issues raised in our generation by Dewey and Jung remain largely unfaced. The genealogical connection of recent empiricist analysis with the work of Feuerbach is as distant as the genealogical connection of Jesus with his progenitor Jacob who defrauded Esau of his inheritance. It is to the credit of Martin Buber among theologians that he directs his attention appropriately to Jung, not Feuerbach. On the other hand Barth wrote of Feuerbach: ". . . so long as the talk about 'God in man' is not cut out at the roots, we have no cause to criticize Feuerbach, but are with him 'the true children of *his* century.' "[2] Feuerbach then becomes the excuse for opposing all forms of religious empiricism.

The task arises of restating what Feuerbach did say and of showing from the standpoint of later empiricists wherein his misconceptions lay. He fancied himself a second Martin Luther, but if his writings had been faithfully followed by many, he would have demolished Christianity altogether. This faith as traditionally cherished by a large section of humanity was wholeheartedly taken as his opponent, although he sincerely believed he was laying the basis for an improved version of Christianity. His attacks left Christian leaders no alternative but to counterattack, which they have effectively done through the years, meanwhile missing the less obvious significance of certain features of his work for a genuinely scientific approach to Christianity and religious experience. Feuerbach has few followers except social radicals of yesterday and some humanists of today. Many of

[1] L. A. Feuerbach, *The Essence of Christianity,* tr. by George Eliot, Harper, 1957, pp. vii–xxxii.
[2] *Ibid.,* p. xxx.

these deserted him because of his dogmatism and occasional lapses into forms of cultism and mysticism. Nevertheless he is still widely read, for the power of his writings is strong.

The remarkable character of Feuerbach's work cannot be escaped. He was a genius, if not a mature one. He wrote brilliantly and fluently. He stated his theses and elaborated them in a comprehensive manner. Empiricist ideas pour from his pen in profusion. One has only to reread Feuerbach, an interesting and rewarding task, to find a dozen hypotheses for Ph.D. theses or even for full-length books. In one sense, modern religious empiricism began with the "big bang" of Feuerbach, rather than by trickles and rivulets growing into the present stream of thought. On the other hand, it can also be maintained that the rationalist school of those who would explain religion away as wishful thinking gained its first real burst in Feuerbach.

The overriding limitation of Feuerbach's work is that, apart from supportable empiricist principles which he voiced, it contains a profusion of claims and assertions, unsupported by reasoning, data, or references to the work of others. This tends to insulate his work from main currents in social scientific thought. While he strongly stressed the importance of approaching religion through verifiable experience, at the same time he belittled as wishful thinking the philosophies by which man enlarges his empirical view of the universe and gains perspective into questions beyond the capacity of scientists. Regardless of how the individual may view this religious philosophy, it has an extensive and intellectually strong foundation, and it has usually played an essential role in religious faith and practice. While religion without philosophy occasionally manifests itself, such religion does not last long nor does it ever number the majority of people among its adherents.

Feuerbach occasionally identified God with human ideals, as had Hegel before him. At the same time he repeatedly states that God is man or that God is oneself. The latter is a legitimate hypothesis but is in conflict with the more restricted hypothesis which localizes God in idealistic motivation, nor is it supported by data which define its application as in the case of Durkheim's identification of God with society. Feuerbach speaks of God as love, but then he says love is feeling, missing its altruistic content. Influenced by Kant, he also refers to God as a concept or an idea, a verbal pitfall into which Höffding and Ames stumbled. Feuerbach welcomes the designation of God as purely subjective, with the confusion of meaning which this term entails.

Feuerbach acknowledged God to be personal, but only because man who is God is a person. Prayer is analyzed as self-conversation, but in this prayer man talks only to himself in the usual secular manner. Characteristic appeal to the higher part of man as part of religious worship is lacking in Feuerbach's analysis. Most or all which religionists have sought through the centuries to isolate and define as the distinctive salt of religion, and which empiricists also have tried to identify, dissolves in the rushing waters of Feuerbach's form of religious empiricism. Some excerpts from Feuerbach will suffice to show the spirited quality of his writings and at the same time to indicate the marked contrast between Feuerbach's principles and those advanced by Jung and other contemporary religious psychologists whose work has been considered in preceding chapters.

Certainly, my work is negative, destructive; but, be it observed, only in relation to the *un*human, not to the human elements of religion. . . . I show that the true sense of Theology is Anthropology, that there is no distinction between the *predicates* of the divine and human nature, and, consequently, no distinction between the divine and human subject. . . . Religion is the dream of the human mind.[3]

Thou hast thus no other definition of God than this: God is pure, unlimited, free Feeling. . . . The divine being is nothing else than the human being, or, rather, the human nature purified, freed from the limits of the individual man, made objective—*i.e.,* contemplated and revered as another, a distinct being. All the attributes of the divine nature are, therefore, attributes of the human nature.[4]

Temples in honor of religion are in truth temples in honor of architecture. With the emerging of man from a state of savagery and wildness to one of culture, with the distinction between what is fitting for man and what is not fitting, arises simultaneously the distinction between that which is fitting and that which is not fitting for God. God is the idea of majesty, of the highest dignity: the religious sentiment is the sentiment of supreme fitness.[5]

God is the highest subjectivity of man abstracted from himself; hence man can do nothing of himself, all goodness comes from God. The more subjective God is, the more completely does man divest himself of his subjectivity, because God is, *per se,* his relinquished self, the possession of which he however again vindicates to himself.[6]

Mysticism is deuteroscopy—a fabrication of phrases having a double meaning. The mystic speculates concerning the essence of Nature or of

[3] *Ibid.,* pp. xxxvi–xxxix.
[4] *Ibid.,* pp. 10, 14.
[5] *Ibid.,* pp. 20–21.
[6] *Ibid.,* p. 31.

man, but under, and by means of, the supposition that he is speculating concerning another, a personal being, distinct from both. The mystic has the same objects as the plain, self-conscious thinker; but the real object is regarded by the mystic, not as itself, but as an imaginary being, and hence the imaginary object is to him the real object. Thus here, in the mystical doctrine of the two principles in God, the real object is pathology, the imaginary one, theology; *i.e.*, pathology is converted into theology. There would be nothing to urge against this, if consciously real pathology were recognized and expressed as theology; indeed, it is precisely our task to show that theology is nothing else than an unconscious, esoteric pathology, anthropology, and psychology, and that therefore real anthropology, real pathology, and real psychology have far more claim to the name of theology than has theology itself, because this is nothing more than an imaginary psychology and anthropology.[7]

The highest idea, the God of a political community, of a people whose political system expresses itself in the form of religion, is Law, the consciousness of the law as an absolute divine power; the highest idea, the God of unpolitical, unworldly feeling is Love; the love which brings all the treasures and glories in heaven and upon earth as an offering to the beloved, the love whose law is the wish of the beloved one, and whose power is the unlimited power of the imagination, of intellectual miracle-working.

God is the Love that satisfies our wishes, our emotional wants; he is himself the realised wish of the heart, the wish exalted to the certainty of its fulfillment, of its reality, to that undoubting certainty before which no contradiction of the understanding, no difficulty of experience or of the external world, maintains its ground.[8]

Thus what is prayer but the wish of the heart expressed with confidence in its fulfillment? What else is the being that fulfils these wishes but human affection, the human soul, giving ear to itself, approving itself, unhesitatingly affirming itself? . . .

It is an extremely superficial view of prayer to regard it as an expression of the sense of dependence. It certainly expresses such a sense, but the dependence is that of man on his own heart, on his own feeling. He who feels himself only dependent, does not open his mouth in prayer; the sense of dependence robs him of the desire, the courage for it, for the sense of dependence is the sense of need.[9]

The fundamental dogmas of Christianity are realised wishes of the heart;—the essence of Christianity is the essence of human feeling. It is pleasanter to be passive than to act, to be redeemed and made free by another than to free oneself; pleasanter to make one's salvation

[7] *Ibid.*, pp. 88–89.
[8] *Ibid.*, p. 121.
[9] *Ibid.*, pp. 122–124.

dependent on a person than on the force of one's own spontaneity; pleasanter to set before oneself an object of love than an object of effort; pleasanter to know oneself beloved by God than merely to have that simple, natural self-love which is innate in all beings; pleasanter to see oneself imaged in the love-beaming eyes of another personal being, than to look into the concave mirror of self or into the cold depths of the ocean of Nature; pleasanter, in short, to allow oneself to be acted on by one's own feeling, as by another, but yet fundamentally identical being, than to regulate oneself by reason.[10]

The foregoing passages make it clear that the main principles of empiricist analysis today diverge from those of Feuerbach. When empiricists are spoken of as a group with some measure of consensus it is well to consider in each instance whether Feuerbach belongs in the group or not. Perhaps the most serious implication of Feuerbach's work for the empiricist approach to religion is that it shows what can happen when this approach is followed, but it is equally true of philosophy as a method that it implies no guarantee that all who exercise its skills will thereby achieve reasonable conclusions. Feuerbach's work was an early attempt by empiricist analysis of religion to get off the ground. Later projects have as little relationship to the shortcomings of that attempt as modern air travel has to clumsy machines of the time of the Wright brothers.

Levels of Disagreement

The analysis of religion by empiricists has been challenged at various levels. The most fundamental challenge is to the right of investigation of man's inward conscious and unconscious processes of motivation and ideation to be considered a science. On this question the initial chapters of this text have already stated the case pro and con, and no more will be said at this point. Those in science who wish to do so will continue to by-pass inward experience as an area for systematic study, and those who recognize the importance of this area from a practical and scientific standpoint will continue to advance their studies.

An intermediate group is provided by those who recognize the importance of interior experience in sociological inquiry but who exclude from such inquiry the study of values or value judgments except as a recitation of values or value judgments which people profess to hold. This group consists principally of German sociologists such as Simmel, Troeltsch, and Weber and those in

[10] *Ibid.*, p. 140.

America allied with their viewpoints such as Parsons and Becker, the latter excluding objects referred to by religious values from the natural domain. By these the study of values is either left to rationalist philosophy or to the special branch of knowledge which Ritschl endeavored to install. Since God or the higher power of religion is a supreme value they would exclude from science study of what this supreme value is with reference to empirical evidence. The arguments against empirical study of value judgments or other internal analysis of values are principally in the form of questions. How can you observe values? How can you measure values? How can you verify values? Answers to these questions were developed in initial chapters. We now consider questions in connection with specific criticisms of empiricist analysis of religion, which are about to be examined.

DIVERGENT FINDINGS

We turn now to scientific opinions of those who acknowledge the status of the study of inward experience as a science but whose findings about inward experience diverge from those of empiricists. The separation of scientific thinkers pro and con into empiricists and rationalists represents an oversimplification. Rationalists, seeking to explain the why and wherefore of religion, are very much guided by empirical data as they find them to be. The term *empiricist* refers to the theory that man believes in God because he finds the basis for God in his own psychic nature. Obviously there are many other reasons why man is a religion-building animal, some of them contained in his propensity to rationalize his emotional needs into a system of believing what he would like to believe, and others contained in his intellectual tendency to construct a congruous and meaningful interpretation of the universe. When it is recognized that man espouses religion for multiple reasons, no necessary conflict exists between the views of empiricists and rationalists. Historically, however, certain men whose explanation of religion is rationalist, such as Freud, who points to man's emotional rationalizing, and J. B. Pratt, who directs attention to man's philosophical rationalizing, have been critical of empiricist analysis. As far as the views of supernaturalists in religious psychology are concerned, to the extent that they develop opinions within a scientific framework, they restate arguments against religious empiricism similar to those brought against it by men whose explanation of why religion exists is rationalist. However, supernaturalists reject the interpretation of religion in terms of emotional rationalism and offer rationalist defense of religion in philosophy. Many philosophers, among them J. B. Pratt, are not supernaturalists in the sense of believing in antiscientific intervention by a supernatural power, although they may admit the possibility of this occurring.

Through the years perhaps the foremost critic, sympathetic to religion, of empiricist analysis has been Pratt. He is foremost at least from the standpoint of the effectiveness of his scholarship and the influence of his scientific writings in circles of religious psychology. His leading work, *The Religious Consciousness,* first published in 1920, is still in print.[11] One whose writings focus less sharply upon views of empiricists and more upon those of religionists in general is Freud, whose influence upon the general public as well as the scientific world, owing to the popularity of his writing, has been very large. A third figure already considered, J. H. Leuba, accepts part of the empiricist analysis of religion but rejects conclusions concerning personality aspects of God. Numerous other writers in the United States and in Europe have also participated in the debate. A review of their writings alone would provide material for several volumes and is a task beyond the present writer's capacity. Those whose approach to religion is in the anthropological tradition of Tylor and Frazer have been critical of Durkheim's analysis on a number of grounds only partly related to the validity of empiricist analysis, and their viewpoints are considered in connection with causal explanations of religious behavior and belief. Freud's work begins earlier than that of Pratt, as well as being antagonistic to religion, while that of Pratt is the reverse. It is to Freud's work that we first give attention.

Freud

In the scientific world the most outspoken opponent of religious viewpoints in their various forms has been Freud. His unsympathetic attitude grew out of research into dysfunctions of religion such as its rigid restraints upon personality functioning, leading to mental disorder. At the same time this attitude of antagonism goes far in accounting for the reluctance of religionists to accept the aid of psychological research in understanding or maintaining religious principles. Despite the brilliant scientific achievements of Freud in other aspects of personality analy-

[11] J. B. Pratt, *The Religious Consciousness,* Macmillan, 1920.

sis, he appears to many religious psychologists to have failed almost entirely in gaining a correct understanding of healthy religion. Freud's life and work illustrate the importance of the dictum that performance of scientific procedure is not in itself a guarantee of successful results, nor is it wise to take for granted the findings of any scientist without carefully looking at and verifying his conclusions. To paraphrase scripture, "Not all who cry 'science,' 'science,' shall enter the kingdom of truth."

Freud's background of medical training, plus his scientific achievements in psychoanalysis, and his skill as a lecturer and writer have caused his views on many matters of psychology including religion to receive wide attention. References to religion appear at many places in his writings, and religion is the major topic of several of his works: *Totem and Taboo, The Future of an Illusion,* and *Moses and Monotheism.*[12] The second of these sets forth Freud's conclusions concerning the intellectual status of religion. He attacks religion as wishful thinking, which to some degree for some persons it unquestionably is. He seeks to undermine the soundness of all religion by exposing the motives of those who believe in God. In answer it may be pointed out that the motives, faulty or not, which bring man into possession of a belief do not answer the question of whether the belief is true or false. For example, a critic of socialist ideas might say that they are the product of rebellious childhood, but this would neither prove nor disprove their economic truth. Likewise, for Freud to dwell upon man's childlike need for a spiritual father has nothing to do with whether such a father exists. The genesis of religious belief is an important topic for scientific inquiry, but it must be clearly separated from questions of truth or falsity of religious belief, a separation acknowledged by most scientific students of religion. Furthermore, in considering the thesis that God is a motivational system within the personality system it is important to distinguish clearly between Freud's view of God as a fictitious idea *produced by* self-seeking motivation and Jung's view of God as *identified with* idealistic motivation. Both things are psychic in nature, but one is a motivational system and the other merely an idea resulting from a motivational system.

We return to the topic of causation of religious belief in a later chapter and turn now to Freud's other arguments concerning the

[12] Sigmund Freud, *Totem and Taboo* in *The Basic Writings of Sigmund Freud,* tr. by A. A. Brill, Modern Library, 1938; *The Future of an Illusion,* tr. by W. D. Robson-Scott, Liveright, 1949; and *Moses and Monotheism,* tr. by Katherine Jones, Knopf, 1939.

logical status of religion. The focus of the following passages is upon dogmas derived from uncritical mystical experience and from supernatural speculation, rather than simply upon empiricist analysis of experience, but there is considerable applicability to the latter, and Jung's support of religion is a target of Freud.

If all the arguments that are put forward for the authenticity of religious doctrines originate in the past, it is natural to look around and see whether the present, better able to judge in these matters, cannot also furnish some evidence. The whole of the religious system would become infinitely more credible if one could succeed in this way in removing the element of doubt from a single part of it. . . .

One must now mention two attempts to evade the problem, which both convey the impression of frantic effort. One of them, high-handed in its nature, is old; the other is subtle and modern. The first is the *Credo quia absurdum* ["I believe because it is absurd"] of the early Father. It would imply that religious doctrines are outside reason's jurisdiction; they stand above reason. Their truth must be inwardly felt: one does not need to comprehend them. But this *Credo* is only of interest as a voluntary confession; as a decree it has no binding force. Am I obliged to believe every absurdity? And if not, why just this one? There is no appeal beyond reason. And if the truth of religious doctrines is dependent on an inner experience which bears witness to that truth, what is one to make of the many people who do not have that rare experience? One may expect all men to use the gift of reason that they possess, but one cannot set up an obligation that shall apply to all on a basis that only exists for quite a few. Of what significance is it for other people that you have won from a state of ecstasy, which has deeply moved you, an imperturbable conviction of the real truth of the doctrines of religion?

The second attempt is that of the philosophy of "As If." It explains that in our mental activity we assume all manner of things, the groundlessness, indeed the absurdity, of which we fully realize. They are called "fictions," but from a variety of practical motives we are led to behave "as if" we believed in these fictions. This, it is argued, is the case with religious doctrines on account of their unequalled importance for the maintenance of human society. This argument is not far removed from the *Credo quia absurdum*. But I think that the claim of the philosophy of "As If" is such as only a philosopher could make. The man whose thinking is not influenced by the wiles of philosophy will never be able to accept it; with the confession of absurdity, of illogicality, there is no more to be said as far as he is concerned. He cannot be expected to forgo the guarantees he demands for all his usual activities just in the matter of his most important interests. I am reminded of one of my children who was distinguished at an early age by a peculiarly marked sense of reality. When the children were told a fairy tale, to which they listened with rapt attention, he would come forward and ask: Is that a true story? Having been told that it was not, he would turn away with an air of disdain. It is to be expected that men will soon behave in like manner towards the religious fairy tales, despite the advocacy of the philosophy of "As If."[13]

It is characteristic of the illusion that it is derived from men's wishes; in this respect it approaches the psychiatric delusion, but is to be distinguished from this, quite apart from the more complicated structure of the latter. In the delusion we emphasize as essential the conflict with reality; the illusion need not be necessarily false, that is to say, unrealizable or incompatible with reality. For instance, a poor girl may have an illusion that a prince will come and fetch her home. It is possible; some such cases have occurred. That the Messiah will come and found a golden age is much less probable; according to one's personal attitude one will classify this belief as an illusion or as analogous to a delusion. Examples of illusions that have come true are not easy to discover, but the illusion of the alchemists that all metals can be turned into gold may prove to be one. The desire to have lots of gold, as much gold as possible, has been considerably dampened by our modern insight into the nature of wealth, yet chemistry no longer considers a transmutation of metals into gold as impossible. Thus we call a belief an illusion when wish-fulfillment is a prominent factor in its motivation, while disregarding its relations to reality, just as the illusion itself does.

If after this survey we turn again to religious doctrines, we may reiterate that they are all illusions, they do not admit of proof, and no one can be compelled to consider them as true or to believe in them. Some of them are so improbable, so very incompatible with everything we have laboriously discovered about the reality of the world, that we may compare them—taking adequately into account the psychological differences—to delusions. Of the reality value of most of them we cannot judge; just as they cannot be proved, neither can they be refuted. We still know too little to approach them critically. The riddles of the universe only reveal themselves slowly to our enquiry, to many questions science can as yet give no answer; but scientific work is our only way to the knowledge of external reality. Again, it is merely illusion to expect anything from intuition or trance; they can give us nothing but particulars, which are difficult to interpret, about our own mental life, never information about the questions that are so lightly answered by the doctrines of religion. It would be wanton to let one's own arbitrary action fill the gap, and according to one's personal estimate declare this or that part of the religious system to be more or less acceptable. These questions are too momentous for that; too sacred, one might say.

At this point it may be objected: well, then, if even the crabbed

[13] From *The Future of an Illusion* by Sigmund Freud. By permission of Liveright, Publishers, New York, pp. 48–51.

sceptics admit that the statements of religion cannot be confuted by reason, why should not I believe in them, since they have so much on their side—tradition, the concurrence of mankind, and all the consolation they yield? Yes, why not? Just as no one can be forced into belief, so no one can be forced into unbelief. But do not deceive yourself into thinking that with such arguments you are following the path of correct reasoning. If ever there was a case of facile argument, this is one. Ignorance is ignorance; no right to believe anything is derived from it. No reasonable man will behave so frivolously in other matters or rest content with such feeble grounds for his opinions or for the attitude he adopts; it is only in the highest and holiest things that he allows this. In reality these are only attempts to delude oneself or other people into the belief that one still holds fast to religion, when one has long cut oneself loose from it. Where questions of religion are concerned people are guilty of every possible kind of insincerity and intellectual misdemeanor. Philosophers stretch the meaning of words until they retain scarcely anything of their original sense; by calling "God" some vague abstraction which they have created for themselves, they pose as deists, as believers, before the world; they may even pride themselves on having attained a higher and purer idea of God, although their God is nothing but an insubstantial shadow and no longer the mighty personality of religious doctrine. . . .

It does not lie within the scope of this enquiry to estimate the value of religious doctrines as truth. It suffices that we have recognized them, psychologically considered, as illusions. But we need not conceal the fact that this discovery strongly influences our attitude to what must appear to many the most important of questions. We know approximately at what periods and by what sort of men religious doctrines were formed. If we now learn from what motives this happened, our attitude to the problem of religion will suffer an appreciable change. We say to ourselves: it would indeed be very nice if there were a God, who was both creator of the world and a benevolent providence, if there were a moral world order and a future life, but at the same time it is very odd that this is all just as we should wish it ourselves. And it would be still odder if our poor, ignorant, enslaved ancestors had succeeded in solving all these difficult riddles of the universe.[14]

Comment on Freud

With Freud's rejection of supernatural doctrines we do not concern ourselves in science, since their appraisal is a philosophical question. However, many would agree that Freud has not given the topic adequate, if any, philosophical analysis. Concerning doctrines based upon religious experience, there seems sufficient reason for Freud to question from a scientific standpoint

[14] *Ibid.*, pp. 54–58.

the claim of *uncritical* mysticism to have succeeded in demonstrating valid knowledge. While the emphasis upon inward experience as a source of knowledge is compatible with science, the opinion of some mystics that their experiences are not communicable nor replicable by others is antiscientific in tone. Science insists that its knowledge be verifiable. If mystics believe that no dependable way exists whereby others can verify their communion with God, the knowledge of such persons falls outside of science, whatever status it may have in philosophy or supernatural doctrine.

The opinion that mystical experience is not duplicable nor describable is understandable when the difficulties involved in the development of inward processes are recognized. To those who do not grasp the psychological principles involved, the achievement of inward spiritual experiences does seem capricious and beyond control. Science, however, seeks to make orderly and controllable phenomena once thought to be beyond human understanding or design. In fulfilling this goal, religious psychology seeks to wrest from mysticism whatever facts or achievements are susceptible to scientific treatment and to integrate these into a larger framework of scientific principles. This would provide the basis for scientific mysticism. While some mystics sincerely believe that science cannot do this, nevertheless the scientific problem is there, and its solution is of benefit to religious devotees generally by enabling spiritual experiences of a few to be more widely shared.

The implication in Freud's statement that religious study of inward experience is to be identified with historical mysticism which sets itself outside reason's jurisdiction seems unnecessary, since there are alternative approaches to inward experience, just as there are both scientific and occult approaches to explicable facts of the external world. Yet the question remains of how religious experiences achieved by some can be verified as scientific facts if others, such as the investigators themselves, do not possess them. The key to Freud's difficulty in not accepting scientific verification of religious beliefs is his failure to recognize that people only have the sought-for experience if the required conditions for religious development have been met. These may involve temperamental disposition and capacity, but of more fundamental importance are social experiences in which the basis for altruism is laid and experiences of religious education which draw out from the collective unconscious the latent materials for spiritual experience.

Freud's hostility toward religion separated him from religious participation and development. Trueblood comments upon the inadequacy of a scientist whose conclusions exceed his experience and competence.

A distinguished physiologist asserts that he does not believe in God; that throughout his life he has never had any sense of the presence of God, and many are impressed by this. Here was a highly intelligent person with a finely trained mind, and the negative evidence provided by his testimony must be given considerable weight. But wait a moment! Are we so sure? Before we give this testimony *any weight at all* we need to know much more. Did the scholar in question submit himself to the kind of situation in which he could expect to be aware of God's presence, if God really is? This scholar would not have expected an opinion concerning physiology to be worthy of attention unless the person announcing the opinion had undertaken a great deal of training in that field. All great things are hard, and there seems no reason to suppose that it would be easier to know God than to know the laws and elements of His creation.[15]

In many persons, as Jung has shown in clinical cases, the seeds of spiritual experience remain dormant but can be demonstrated by depth techniques which probe the unconscious. Until these seeds have the opportunity to grow under favorable conditions of development and expression, the experiences in which religious beliefs are grounded do not appear. No one would argue that no such thing exists as the experience of having a million dollars because not all persons have that experience. Neither can it be properly contended that there is no such thing as specific content in religious experiences merely because not all persons have these. No data in any field can be demonstrated by science except under specified conditions which cause the data to appear in someone's experience, and the data of the higher power or God are no exception. The empiricist approach to religion maintains that under suitable conditions within the reach of all willing to undergo these conditions certain spiritual experiences will take place. In these experiences can be found data to verify the substantial part of religious beliefs. The scientific point is that these experiences are replicable and verifiable under definable conditions. The circumstance that they may not be experienced by all does not detract from the factual nature of their occurrence for others, but rather calls attention to the importance of the scientific task of defining the conditions under which they come into being. In answering rationalist critics, Jung reaffirms

[15] D. E. Trueblood, *Philosophy of Religion,* Harper, 1957, p. 73.

the validity of religious experience which makes its appearance following psychotherapy.

The well-meaning rationalist will point out that I am casting out the devil with Beelzebub and replacing an honest neurosis by the swindle of a religious belief. As to the former charge, I have nothing to say in reply, being no metaphysical expert. But as to the latter one, I beg leave to point out that it is not a question of belief but of experience. Religious experience is absolute; it cannot be disputed. You can only say that you have never had such an experience, whereupon your opponent will reply: "Sorry, I have." And there your discussion will come to an end. No matter what the world thinks about religious experience, the one who has it possesses a great treasure, a thing that has become for him a source of life, meaning, and beauty, and that has given a new splendour to the world and to mankind. He has *pistis* and peace. Where is the criterion by which you could say that such a life is not legitimate, that such an experience is not valid, and that such *pistis* is mere illusion? Is there, as a matter of fact, any better truth about the ultimate things than the one that helps you to live? That is the reason why I take careful account—*religio!*—of the symbols produced by the unconscious. They are the one thing that is capable of convincing the critical mind of modern man. And they are convincing for a very old-fashioned reason: They are *overwhelming,* which is precisely what the Latin word *convincere* means.[16]

A more controversial point dwelled upon by Freud and others is, in Freud's words: "Again, it is merely illusion to expect anything from intuition or trance; they can give us nothing but particulars, which are difficult to interpret, about our own mental life, never information about the questions that are so lightly answered by the doctrines of religion." In other words, the fact that persons have a religious experience does not mean that the ideas which are part of this experience are thereby shown to be true. In the view of rationalists, whether sympathetic to religion or not, the fact that God is experienced as a compelling idea does not mean that God is thereby experienced. This seems the most influential scientific argument brought by rationalists against empiricists, and a careful examination of its several aspects is warranted to see where the truth rests.

J. B. Pratt

The argument against religious empiricism has been stated historically in cogent form by J. B. Pratt, from his standpoint in

[16] C. G. Jung, *Psychology and Religion: West and East,* tr. by R. F. C. Hull. Bollingen Series XX, Bollingen Foundation, Inc. Pantheon, 1958, pp. 104–105.

favor of the defense of religion by philosophical reasoning. Roots of the argument against religious empiricism are deep in the history of philosophy. Within the past two centuries J. G. Fichte and other German philosophers have been much exercised by it. It is an indication of the growth which psychology and sociology have undergone that the argument can now be considered from the standpoint of recognized scientific criteria. Pratt's writings have deeply influenced a generation of religious psychologists. In 1950, thirty years after publication of his *The Religious Consciousness,* he offered in *Eternal Values in Religion* a concluding statement of his criticism of religious empiricism and of the support which philosophy in the form of "critical realism" gives to religious belief.[17] In spite of Pratt's attack upon empirical theology, in actuality he is not far removed from taking facts of religious experience as information about God if properly interpreted by philosophy. His argument against religious empiricism becomes weaker and less conclusive in his later work. We pick up the vein of his thought where he addresses himself to E. S. Ames. Ames was a more outspoken proponent of religion from an empiricist standpoint than Dewey, the first in the Chicago group of empiricists. The relation of psychology to theology was described by Ames as follows:

> If reality is given in experience (and where else could it be given?) then the science of that experience furnishes the reasonable and fruitful method of dealing with reality, including the reality of religion. The psychology of religion possesses, therefore, the greatest possible significance. It does not merely prepare the way for theology, but in its most elementary inquiries, it is already dealing with essentials of theology and the philosophy of religion. On the other hand, the philosophy of religion in its most ultimate problems and refined developments does not transcend the principles of psychology. The idea of God, for example, which is the central conception of theology, is subject to the same laws of mental life as are all other ideas, and there is but one science of psychology applicable to it. Modern psychology emphasises the fundamental unity of mental life. The psychology of religion is only the application of the principles of the one science of psychology to religious experience. It does not limit itself to certain phenomena, such as emotion, or to the working of particular "faculties" or instincts, but attempts to deal vitally with the totality of human nature as involved in religion, and with every stage of the religious development.[18]

[17] J. B. Pratt, *Eternal Values in Religion,* Macmillan, 1950.
[18] E. S. Ames, *The Psychology of Religious Experience,* Harper, 1910, pp. 26–27.

In referring to God as an idea, although he means by God more than this, Ames opened the way for Pratt's persuasive attack on the empiricist approach as Ames stated it.

On reading passages like this from enthusiastic representatives of the new functional psychology one comes away wondering not that they have included so much but that they have included so little within their capacious science. Why stop with the various branches of philosophy? Why not also reduce physics, chemistry, astronomy to functional psychology? What, indeed, are the physical sciences but formulations of experience—and is not psychology the science of experience? The same arguments hold in the case of physics that held for metaphysics. Surely if "the idea of God is subject to the same laws of the mental life as are all other ideas," the same may be said with equal truth of the idea of the solar system. And this, I think, makes clear both the fallacy and the danger of this "pragmatic" view. Psychology studies the *idea* of God and the *idea* of the solar system and stops there. But neither astronomy nor theology means to limit its study to our ideas. They both mean to be objective—and it is hard to see why one should be denied this privilege if it be granted to the other. And if objectivity be denied to theology, the dangers that inevitably result are evident. Theology becomes purely subjective,—a description of the way we feel; the idea of God is substituted for God and hence becomes the idea of an idea, or a confessed illusion; and the psychology of religion, having absorbed all that was objective in religion, finds it has nothing left to study, or at best becomes a branch of abnormal psychology. "This method," writes Boutroux, "if it succeed, will lead sooner or later to the abolition of the fact itself, while the dogmatic criticism of religions has striven in vain for centuries to obtain this result. . . . Contrary, then, to the other sciences which leave standing the things that they explain, the one just mentioned has this remarkable property of destroying its object in the act of describing it, and of substituting itself for the facts in proportion as it analyzes them."

The psychology of religion must then, in my opinion, take a much humbler position than that which some of its devotees desire for it. It must content itself with a description of human experience, while recognizing that there may well be spheres of reality to which these experiences refer and with which they are possibly connected, which yet cannot be investigated by science.[19]

It is perhaps unfortunate for the empiricist tradition that Ames did not take proper precaution in his choice of words to make it clear that God in the empiricist view is much more than an idea. Ames was influenced by the Danish psychologist and philosopher, Harald Höffding.[20] The latter regarded ideas of God

[19] J. B. Pratt, *The Religious Consciousness,* Macmillan, 1920, pp. 41–42.

[20] Harald Höffding, *The Philosophy of Religion,* tr. by B. E. Meyer, Macmillan, 1906.

as equivalent to God since they perform the role of God in the conservation of values. What Höffding seems to overlook is that ideas derive their force from the psychic object of which they are a representation. For Dewey, however, God is the union of the ideal and the real, a process in experience in which human ideals become actualized, and in fact a dynamic system of thinking, motivation, and behavior. This system is one of ideation as well as motivation. Ideas of a world becoming are contained in it. Its substance is psychic, just as the substance of personality in general is psychic. Yet, as a motivational system it has physical roots, even as the personalities of people are grounded in their physiological being. All of this adds to much more than the "idea of God" which Ames at times appears to equate with God. Pratt is of course right that Ames fails to distinguish between God and the idea of God, or, in other words, between a motivational system and an idea of a motivational system. By incanting the ill-chosen words, "idea of God," as the central religious reality Ames opened the door for waters of confusion to swirl over more critical issues in the controversy.

In a later portion of his principal work Ames develops the dynamic aspect of God as a motivational system, as was quoted in the chapter defining the higher power of religion. "A person's idea of God may be taken as comprehending the highest ideal interests known or felt by him. It stands therefore for concrete purposeful activity and effort in those directions." Rejecting a metaphysical idea of God or the logical validity of philosophical proofs of God's existence, Ames does describe in some detail the motivational situation to which the idea of God refers.

> The chief difficulties concerning the truth of ideas arise from attempts to estimate their validity out of relation to the only situations in which they can be true or false, that is the situations involving conduct. The idea of God has been treated in this way. It has been taken apart from the social experiences and the genetic processes in which it arose, and then has been subjected to various ingenious manipulations to determine whether it be true! It is somewhat comparable to seeking the meaning of a word after removing it from any context by repeating the sound, counting the letters, or analyzing the ink with which it is written. The mediaeval and Cartesian arguments for the "being of God" are largely just such inapt endeavors. As Kant demonstrated, they are full of fallacies and labor in vain to produce the desired results. No such static, transcendent, non-empirical reality is conceivable by us: much less are its existence and nature demonstrable. The psychological solution of the difficulty lies in another direction, as already indicated. Perhaps the case is analogous to the experience of a child who looks behind the mirror for the reality

answering to the image which he sees. Before he can solve the puzzle of the reflected image he must seek for it in another place and by a different method. The reality to which the image leads is not within the image alone, as phenomenalism might say; neither is it behind and beyond the mirror as the realist and the absolute idealist might say; but it lies on this side of the mirror, within the actual world of men and things. The idea of God, when seriously employed, serves to generalize and to idealize all the values one knows. Our actual interests move in the social world and within the vast order of nature. In the simplest reflections upon the facts of life one is led deep into the labyrinth of the natural and of the human worlds. The idea which gathers into itself the interests and values of our daily concerns must therefore signify what are for us the greatest realities in nature and in human experience. To the plain man as he uses the idea of God, in contrast with a passive formal attitude toward it, the idea involves a living process, law or movement, in the working of which human needs are satisfied, justice and truth established, and distant ideals attained. Even the oath of the profane man has an echo of the tremendous dynamic force of the word. It is the biggest word he knows. The reality answering to the idea of God, it may be said, must include, at its best, all that is involved in the deep instinctive historical and social consciousness of the race. It signifies the justice which government symbolizes, the truth which science unfolds, and the beauty which art strives to express. The "attributes" in the conception of God are as numerous as the ideal interests of those who use it, for it signifies the totality of our purposes and values.[21]

Pratt is unmoved by Ames's characterization of God and apparently confuses an empirical view of conduct with a pragmatic view of it.

If the idea of God be what Professor Ames has here described and no more, the religious consciousness should welcome his book as the final and complete refutation of all possible atheism. For if by God we mean merely our human values then not even the fool will venture any longer to say in his heart, There is no God. By one clever stroke of pragmatic logic and functional psychology Professor Ames seems to have accomplished what all the long line of philosophers and theologians have attempted in vain. But I fear the religious reader of "The Psychology of Religious Experience" will find cold comfort after all when he learns that the only God who exists is just human society's longings and ideals and values, and that He cannot even *mean* anything more than that. And even after Professor Ames and Dr. King and their colleagues have made use of all the appliances of the latest structural psychology in the analysis of the God-idea and found in it only personal and social attitude and various human values, the re-

[21] Ames, *op. cit.*, pp. 317–318.

ligious soul, I fear, will remain stupidly unconvinced. "I know," he will say, "what I mean by the justice which government symbolizes, the truth which science unfolds, and the beauty which art strives to express. And I know that while these may be included within my idea of God, I mean by God something besides these things. I mean by God 'an existence of some sort' (in spite of Dr. King), a real Being who dwells not only 'within the actual world of men and things,' but, if you will, 'behind the mirror.' "

I feel convinced that such a response to Professor Ames and his school would be quite justified. Important as is the pragmatic element in the God-idea it is not the only element. And the attempt to prove it such is both bad psychology and bad epistemology. Bad psychology because it neglects altogether certain real elements in the religious consciousness, whether found in philosopher, priest, or humble worshiper,—men who through all the ages have truly meant by "God" something more than the idea of God, something genuinely transcendent. Bad epistemology because based ultimately upon a viciously subjective view of *meaning,* a view which would identify our objects with our ideas of our objects, and which, carried to its logical conclusion, would result in solipsism.[22]

RECONCILIATION OF VIEWPOINTS

Can a Scientific Answer Be Found?

At this point the student of the rationalist-empiricist debate concerning the status of God as a verifiable phenomenon may be thoroughly perplexed as to what, if anything, of a conclusive nature is offered by scientific analysis. If large groups of eminent scholars in social and psychological science disagree after spending their lives arguing the controversy, how can the casual student with a few years' background of scholarly effort be expected to settle the question for himself?

In pondering whether a scientific answer can be found, it should be noted that we live in a time when the science of religion is being rocked by disputes comparable to those which divided physicists several hundred years ago, who debated whether the earth was round or flat and whether the earth or the sun was the center of the solar system. If those living at that time despaired of an answer when scientific scholars could not agree, consensus on the basis of evidence never would have been achieved concerning what appear now to be simple questions. Furthermore, it may be seen that the contemporaries of Columbus and Copernicus were ensnared by conceptual shackles im-

[22] Pratt, *The Religious Consciousness, op. cit.,* pp. 208–209.

posed by the culture of their day. It seemed absurd that the earth could be round, for else people on the bottom would fall off. It seemed absurd that a ball of the earth's size could hurtle through space around the sun when to the passengers all appeared quiet and still. It seemed much easier to think of the sun as a ball of light moved by God around the sky. In our age of space travel we have grown up in a culture which has long since come to contain reasonable understandings of these things. The time is now being reached when present-day human beings are struggling through the evidence from inward experience to achieve commonly shared and dependable understandings about religion. The debate is one going on in religious psychology and it has seemed scientifically relevant to review it in a study of religion through social science even though its full consequences are not yet entirely clear.

To a future generation the present controversy may seem pedestrian. To us who live today, it is a matter of profound issues. The controversy is important to those whose unconscious needs impel them to seek for a God on whom they can count. It is also important to those whose ways of life ignore religion and whose intellectual honesty would be at stake if it is true that a demonstrable God places certain social and psychological demands upon people in opposition to accepted modes of seeking satisfaction in life. Behind the ideological clash of empiricists and rationalists are powerful desires which by understandable processes of rationalization hinder human minds in their pursuit of truth. Perhaps the dichotomy of desires is not sharp and an appropriate integration of man's spiritual and physical needs can be achieved, but even so, such integration would require recognition that man cannot live effectively by whim and that man must seriously examine and come to understand himself, voluntarily giving up some things which are appealing in the short run for others which are enduring in the long run.

Nor are the everyday wants of human beings the only ones affected by the debate. Also at stake are the professional interests of those who have invested their lives in training for behavioral research. If this training, as in the case of many eminent scientists, has been confined within the boundaries of visually observable data, such professional persons may not welcome confrontation by a type of analysis which requires years of additional study in a different direction, that of psychoanalysis or introspection. Still other professional interests are possessed by leaders of organized religion. For these the scriptures have usually been adequate as they stand. What strange speaking in tongues is it which obligates the scholar of religion to receive training in the advanced techniques of psychological analysis and mathematics now coming to the foreground in behavioral science? Yet how else can such a scholar answer for himself whether human values are measurable, and in what sense? How can he develop within his own mind the degree of differentiation of conceptual components required for verification unless he devotes, not two years of postgraduate study, but ten years of study? His role is comparable to that of a brain surgeon who reaches the age of thirty-five before he begins to practice, so comprehensive are the successive steps of training from the first year of medical school through the final year of internship on the staff of a neuropsychiatric clinic. If this is the price which knowledge demands of human beings, what else can be expected of the large majority of people except to live uninformed about the storms of religious controversy which blow overhead?

The answer to the last question seems to fall along the following lines: Few persons in a lifetime of subsidized study can think through to their own intellectual satisfaction all of the issues of religion and psychology, yet the major ingredients can be identified and accepted. In preparing for more effective living, the skills of writers and educators serve the public in directing attention to those things which are more important for reflection and in supplementing the knower's first-hand acquaintance with part of the questions by giving him findings about related facets, such as the measurement of human motivation. These are technical matters in which it is appropriate to accept assistance from specialists.

The educational task is complicated by the lack of agreement among representatives of ideological schools. Still, there is agreement as to what problems merit attention by the individual, such as the existence of the empiricist-rationalist debate. In time people may be expected to think and rethink their way through this controversy to the level where general understanding is reached. No short cut can be found. The world will experience intellectual travail until it has assimilated into its culture dependable data and lines of reasoning which enable it to see reliably whether the earth is flat or round, and whether the sun goes around the earth or the earth around the sun. The present text is an effort to facilitate resolution of contemporary controversies in the study of religion to the extent that the concepts and principles of social science, including psychology, are applicable.

Comment on Pratt

With fresh resolution, we look again at the empiricist-rationalist controversy. In essence, Pratt and other religious psychologists allied with him say the empiricist God is at best a petty one, and at worst merely a subjective figment of the human mind, a piece of imagination, an illusion.

The past thirty years of research by C. G. Jung and his associates go far in bringing to light definitive answers. Unfettered by tradition and guided by the facts of man's psychic nature as these are isolated and discovered through psychoanalysis, Jung has been brought to definitive conclusions. Starting from a standpoint close to that of Freud, he has been compelled to recognize the functioning of religious realities in the overall personality system. These realities are often submerged in the collective unconscious, where they influence behavior and give man peace or distress, depending upon his adjustment to them. These realities form the basis for a system of concepts interpreting the effects of religion upon personality.

Concerning how high is the stature of God as a social and psychological manifestation, the answer is given by the degree of power of which such a God is capable. How much of a power is a question for scientific research. Some of this research is reported at various places in this text, and much more of it is needed. Science may not show the effectiveness of altruistic motivation as a center for the integration of personality and of society to be as great as that of God in mythology, but at least science shows a demonstrable power. One may belittle the power, but not so the alcoholic who can find nothing else which will reclaim him from the grip of alcoholic addiction. To him that power is God in actuality. To many others altruistic motivation is the prime mover of civilizations through centuries. Perhaps such a God is not all-powerful as far as is shown by human experience, but at least there is demonstration of a power which is effective in the redevelopment of human nature and in the reconstruction of social and economic organization.

What Freud says in another context, education, applies to broader resources of human development, including altruistic motivation. Speaking to the orthodox religionist, Freud says:

> . . . our god *Logos* is not perhaps a very powerful one; he may only fulfil a small part of what his forerunners have promised. If we have to acknowledge this, we shall do so with resignation. We shall not thereby lose our interest in the world and in life, for we have in one

respect a sure support which you lack. We believe that it is possible for scientific work to discover something about the reality of the world through which we increase our power and according to which we can regulate our life. If this belief is an illusion, then we are in the same position as you, but science has shown us by numerous and significant successes that it is no illusion.[23]

One may choose between a God who is scientifically unproved, remote from human experience, who proceeds in mysterious and supernatural ways, and in the understanding of whose ways scientific effort can offer little to help man in his adjustment, or one may turn to a God, a psychological power, the existence of which can be shown, which is a direct and intimate part of human experience, and the adjustment to which can be aided by techniques of scientific inquiry.

The more perplexing question raised about empiricist analysis of religion is that of subjectivism. To a scientist disinterested in practical affairs, the charge that his analysis of religion introduces subjective terms is of no concern. It is sufficient for him that he has isolated motivational variables which form the basis for religious belief. Whether partisans brood over subjectivity of religious reality is not his worry. The situation is different for one who would like to resolve the anxiety of religious leaders about a religious reality with a subjective taint. The prospect that God is only a product of imagination is a specter which chills the religionist who looks for more reality in God than the vague potency of an idea or an ideal. The principal objection to accepting the empiricist analysis of God as a social and psychological reality has been the cry "subjective." Durkheim and Macintosh have evidenced discomfort at the allegation, and Jung also has bent in the philosophical wind while declaring his view that God is a psychological fact. One surmises that a possible reason why Durkheim so strongly insisted that God is to be identified with society, rather than with social consciousness, is the subjective hue carried by the latter in contrast with the objectivity of the former.

A Philosophical Question

After Macintosh published his work on theology as an empirical science, his work was beset by Pratt and others who complained of the subjectivist implications in it. Macintosh's defense has been in terms of philosophical reasoning, set forth in

[23] Freud, *op. cit.*, p. 95.

The Problem of Religious Knowledge, published in 1940.[24] This reasoning follows that employed in philosophy to show securely that objects in space keep on existing when no one experiences them. This philosophical problem may seem absurd when one first thinks of it, since what could be more obvious than that the table in front of oneself must be there when no one is looking at it, for otherwise why would it be seen each time someone looks for it? From the standpoint of strict empiricism, the existence of the table is shown by our sensory perceptions. When our attention is occupied elsewhere, we cannot directly prove by the data of experience that some capricious spirit has not meanwhile borrowed the table from the scene, taking care to return it whenever someone wants to use it or look at it. Philosophers delineate the chain of deductive reasoning which leads to the common-sense conclusion that the table is still there even when no one is looking at it. The reasoning proceeds in various ways for different philosophers, but the conclusion is the same, that underlying our sensory perceptions are permanent objects.

If it is proved that something exists to give the table substance besides our sensory images of it, then it may be argued that these sensory images are characteristics of the sensory apparatus of the perceiving subject, could be duplicated by hallucinations, dreams, or drugs, and are not properties of the object at all. In this way some philosophers have abruptly found themselves lost in a dream world, not knowing for a certainty whether anything else exists besides the mental condition of the subject. If philosophers can so easily become lost in the world of tangible objects, they can much more easily do so when investigating objects in inward experience, such as motives and beliefs. Hence Macintosh is desirous of establishing the objective existence of the God whom man finds in his inward experience.

In Macintosh's view the experience of God bears the same relation to an objective reality as sensory perceptions do to their external objects. In either case the experience may be transitory, but the object giving rise to the experience is permanent. "It is not from the mere idea of God that we can prove the existence of God, but from a consciousness of God which is at the same time an experience of God."[25] "One of the criticisms most commonly made against proposed scientific empirical theology is that its

[24] D. C. Macintosh, *The Problem of Religious Knowledge,* Harper, 1940, chap. 12.

[25] D. C. Macintosh, *Theology as an Empirical Science,* Macmillan, 1919, p. 97.

religious realism is dogmatic in *presupposing* 'the real existence of God.' In reply it might be maintained that the religious expert has the same *logical* right to presuppose it as the physicist has to presuppose the existence of electricity. *That* it is, is sufficiently sure on the basis of prescientific experience; scientific method is to be employed to find out more exactly just *what* it is."[26]

Unlike Macintosh, Jung does not interest himself in the philosophical effort to prove the permanence of objects underlying sensory or psychic experience. His concern for philosophical questions about the reality of objects apart from experience has been so slight that he was occasionally willing to concede the subjectivist argument brought from a philosophical standpoint against the existence of God as an object in religious experience. In the Terry Lectures which he gave at Yale in 1937 he remarked:

> It would be a regrettable mistake if anybody should take my observations as a kind of proof of the existence of God. They prove only the existence of an archetypal God-image, which to my mind is the most we can assert about God psychologically. But as it is a very important and influential archetype, its relatively frequent occurrence seems to be a noteworthy fact for any *theologia naturalis*. And since experience of this archetype has the quality of numinosity, often in very high degree, it comes into the category of religious experiences.[27]
>
> The thing that cures a neurosis must be as convincing as the neurosis, and since the latter is only too real, the helpful experience must be equally real. It must be a very real illusion, if you want to put it pessimistically. But what is the difference between a real illusion and a healing religious experience? It is merely a difference of words. You can say, for instance, that life is a disease with a very bad prognosis: it lingers on for years, only to end with death; or that normality is a general constitutional defect; or that man is an animal with a fatally overgrown brain. This kind of thinking is the prerogative of habitual grumblers with bad digestions. No one can know what the ultimate things are. We must therefore take them as we experience them. And if such experience helps to make life healthier, more beautiful, more complete and more satisfactory to yourself and to those you love, you may safely say: "This was the grace of God."[28]

Macintosh commented on these passages: "In the end, Jung, still entangled in the subjectivism of religious psychologism himself, strongly desiderates religious realism in his patients if he is to effect their cure. . . . As we propose to show in a later part of our present discussion, the therapeutic and dynamic religious

[26] Macintosh, *The Problem of Religious Knowledge, op. cit.,* p. 192.
[27] Jung, *op. cit.,* p. 58–59.
[28] *Ibid.,* p. 105.

realism which is apparently psychologically impossible for Jung himself, but which, fortunately, is psychologically possible to many another, may prove, on adequately critical grounds, to be theoretically permissible and even positively reasonable."[29]

Elsewhere as in "Answer to Job," Jung is less hesitant about psychology showing God to be a fact. He joins other empiricists in his unequivocal affirmation of God as a factual component of human personality.

> . . . I have been asked so often whether I believe in the existence of God or not that I am somewhat concerned lest I be taken for an adherent of "psychologism" far more commonly than I suspect. What most people overlook or seem unable to understand is the fact that I regard the psyche as *real*. They believe only in physical facts, and must consequently come to the conclusion that either the uranium itself or the laboratory equipment created the atom bomb. That is no less absurd than the assumption that a non-real psyche is responsible for it. God is an obvious psychic and non-physical fact, i.e. a fact that can be established psychically but not physically.[30]

Least troubled by the subjectivist issue is Dewey, who maintains that all experience is reality and is to be taken at its face value without looking for hypothetical realities behind experience. "Things are what they are experienced as."[31] Sensory impressions are real; they are given in experience. Motivation is real; it is experienced. It would be as unreasonable to argue that happiness does not exist or that intellectual activity does not exist because these are psychic, not physical, as to argue that God does not exist because the object in question is psychic, not physical. The reluctance to accept the psychic as real is an anomaly of Western thought. In some Hindu thought one finds a complete reversal; only the psychic is real, the physical is illusion. There seems as little justification for one extreme as for the other.

Whatever may be said of the incompleteness of Dewey's point of view from a philosophical standpoint, it is entirely adequate for scientific investigation. Science does not concern itself with metaphysical inquiries about what may lie beyond sensory or motivational data. Such questions are irrelevant for science, however interesting they may be for philosophy. Science uses only data from experience and builds its analysis entirely upon

29 Macintosh, *The Problem of Religious Knowledge, op. cit.,* p. 73.
30 Jung, *op. cit.,* pp. 463–464.
31 John Dewey, *The Influence of Darwin on Philosophy,* Holt, 1910, p. 226–241.

these. To give a caricature of the irrelevance for science of what may exist between experiences or behind experiences, a cosmic caretaker may roll up the universe each night while people are asleep and roll it out in the morning before people are awake. All the scientist needs to know is that sensory or psychic data will be there when looked for under specified conditions. What happens in the interim is a problem for philosophy, not science.

The common-sense knowledge by which people live indicates that realities more enduring exist beyond sensory perception or inward experience. As Trueblood inquires, who would say the fire ceases burning when no one looks at it or that flowers halt their blooming when no one is there to enjoy them? The consumed remains later tell of the intervening process. Philosophers may defend or attack such common sense, but it suffices for the scientist and for people generally. In this respect, the data for the science of religion are as real as anything else in inward or outer experience, and it is unnecessary to resolve philosophical complexities in order for scientific investigation to proceed or for people in everyday life to depend upon the data of religion and to use them. The motivational system involved has a continuing existence in the functioning of personality whether one is aware of it or not. Philosophers may mystify themselves or others as to whether perceptual objects or motives or religious phenomena are real or nothing but reflections, but scientific research does not include these intellectual problems. Philosophical inquiry into realism beyond or beneath experience is an illuminating pursuit but is not included in practical steps of scientific procedure, steps which move from sensory or motivational data to conclusions about these data. Regardless of what philosophical hue of empiricism or realism one assumes, the same scientific problem remains of analyzing the data of religious experience to learn as much as possible about the psychological power in religion.

The intrusion into a scientific work of the distinctly philosophical question of what underlies experiential data is exceptional and would not occur in a work on religion were it not for the efforts of others to bring it into the ongoing process of scientific research. It has as little place in the study of religion as in studying any other aspect of culture. With the emancipation of each science from philosophy, it becomes necessary to explain why lingering philosophical questions are to be left to the parent discipline. As the scientific study of religion establishes itself as a field for empirical inquiry, a corrective action is needed against the intrusion of nonscientific questions into the scientific arena, in effect an action to separate the infant from the afterbirth. Psychology and sociology a century ago had to struggle to gain the same freedom, one which they enjoy today without interference in the research process by philosophical theorizing about realism. Of course the field for philosophers is unlimited. They have full right to examine anything they wish, but the reverse does not hold true. Scientists are not entitled as scientists to engage in philosophical speculation outside the scope of data. The point in digressing at all in saying anything here about subjectivism from a philosophical standpoint is simply to exclude a purely philosophical task from the procedure of scientific research, the scientific study of religion being no exception.

Subjectivism from a Psychological Standpoint

There still remains from a scientific standpoint the question of what reality God as a motivational system possesses in relation to facts of sensory perception or any other verifiable facts. Is motivation made up of thoughts? Psychology has long since taken it for granted that motivating drives are real. When religious phenomena are linked with motivation, the charge of subjectivism again makes its appearance among some religious psychologists.

Confusion arises in that the word *subjective* is an elastic generality which at a given moment may signify (1) a characteristic of a subject's personality, or (2) something in the experience of one subject not verified in the experience of other subjects, or (3) an idea held by the subject, which may or may not correspond to an object in experience, or (4) from a philosophical standpoint something in experience which has no underlying reality as its counterpart, or (5) in the sense of scientific method a bias of the scientific operator. In this fifth sense a person is subjective in his data collecting or analytical procedures if he is emotionally disregardful of demonstrable facts or obvious logic, that is, irrational and lacking in scientific objectivity.

Because of these shifting meanings, introduction of the term *subjective* has been largely avoided in the analysis undertaken here. If the term is to be retained in scientific work, its meaning as opposed to *objective* or *impartial* or *unprejudiced* seems the appropriate one to use. This does not mean that the first four meanings are not vital. They are, but alternative labels seem desirable, such as *personal, unverified, mental,* or *groundless.*

The term has, however, been introduced by critics of empiricist analysis, and the meanings they apparently assign to the term must be considered. The first meaning, that God is part of human personality, is considered in a moment. The fifth meaning is not at present an issue. The allegations in the second and fourth meanings were considered in previous sections. The third meaning of *subjective* remains, that of something which is merely an idea. The psychological criticism made by Pratt and others of the empiricist view of God is that God manifested in interior experience is simply an idea. The impression is given by this criticism that empiricists have been looking for the real thing, but all they found was an idea in men's minds. In the debate about empiricist analysis of religion, slogans have tended to displace objective consideration of the scientific issues. It is necessary to consider carefully what empiricists in the psychology of religion believe they find.

First, as to the impression conveyed that all which empiricists have found is that men have an idea of God, this is a mistaken impression. Such a finding would be trivial, since it is obvious that men have many ideas of God, supernatural concepts as well as experiential ones. Besides these ideas men have something else. According to empiricists they have found a motivational system which is the object to which much of men's ideas of God correspond and from which the ideas are derived. The connection of the ideas with their object is not a simple and obvious one, since the object is largely contained in the unconscious portions of experience from which the religious object is with difficulty differentiated through abstraction. If men act from unconscious motives, it is apparent that they are not aware of and may even deny the motives of which their ideas are psychic images.

Second, as to the object which empiricists find, this is an altruistic motivational system which has a physiological basis in the nerve structure of personality. It finds physical and social expression in behavior. The motivational system contains perceptions and responses as well as aims and ideas. Ideas, in the sense of thoughts of objects, are only a part of any motivational system, although indispensable to its functioning. The aims of the system cannot be pursued without ideas by means of which situations are comprehended and behavior organized to change situations. The system is effective when the ideas of action are real copies of the world within which the system functions. It is this kind of ideas which is involved in altruistic motivation.

False or unproved ideas have no place in it, since altruistic aims could not be realized with false premises or illusions.

The argument of the critics of empiricism shifts to an examination of the ideals which are the central force of the God-system. Are not ideals after all merely ideas? Then a God made up of ideals is nothing but thoughts in someone's mind. In facing this contention, it is to be noted that ideals are not ideas in the customary sense of thoughts by means of which situations are imagined or represented in an actor's mind. Rather, they are aims which have a compelling, insistent character and which stimulate the personality system to achieve their fulfillment. Ideals are driving forces of behavior. They are not to be discounted because of their psychic status shared by other kinds of ideas. Ideals of a better way of life are of priceless value to people impelled by them to seek something superior to what already exists. The objects to which ideals refer are objects in a process of becoming. Ideals are realistic when they are continuously being fulfilled by their possessor. As Dewey states, the motivational system designated as God consists of the process of actualizing ideals. In this process ideals are one component, although an important one.

In past generations, philosophers have employed arguments from psychology to prove that the world is nothing but dream or illusion or idea. People who read such arguments find in them an intellectual fascination which disappears when they find that the words *dream, illusion,* or *idea* have been used out of normal context, and that what has really been shown is that the world is nothing but experience. The argument that a motivational system is purely idea is of the same order. It is an argument which employs the term *idea* out of its normal context, that of a thought which is either imaginary or else a thin reflection of the real object. By the same argument one can "prove" that a human being, except for his body, is nothing but an idea to himself. One does not regard a friend as a mythical character because his inward existence is compounded out of ideas and impulses. As Jung points out, what is psychic or interior has real existence for us. In the flow of our ideas, drives, hopes, feelings, convictions, and ideals is found the real stuff of human personality. The personality system consists not only of external actions and physiological processes but also of habits of thought and motivation. A human being is alive and real because he thinks, wills, and feels. He is dead and nonexistent if he doesn't. God, as a motivational system, is a live God by consisting of thinking, willing, and feeling.

This kind of God possesses reality on a plane with the rest of personality within which the God-system functions.

The scientist of religion, whatever his conclusions, does not necessarily maintain that his concepts and principles afford a satisfactory set of ideas for the practicing religionist who is much more at home in his traditional religious ideas. The scientist is concerned to give an account of what goes on in human personality, especially its interior side, during the functioning of religion. It ordinarily is not necessary for a scientist to defend his views from a variety of counterclaims which involve him in semantics and philosophy. The empiricist analysis of religion impinges upon traditional ways of thinking which react with ingenuity. In the scientific study of religion it is therefore necessary to clarify a variety of issues not ordinarily arising in psychological or sociological inquiry.

By its reëxamination of established ways of religious thought, scientific analysis tends to interrupt the smooth functioning of religion while people catch a fresh look at their habits of thinking and desiring. Until these habits are realigned or at least renewed, the individual may develop a sense of isolation from the customary and familiar religious ways upon which he profoundly depends for peace and serenity of mind. It is possible to become so introspectively preoccupied that normal events in inward experience lose reality for a time. In any event, motivational systems, reaching as they do into the collective unconscious, are not easily recognized as firm realities by the individual. As he becomes familiar with their characteristics and incorporates them into his life activities, he discovers that his awareness of them increases and they gain keener reality for him. When he realizes that they continue to function in his experience whether he is conscious of them or not, he ceases to worry if they are there. In this way the religious individual gains a continuing sense of the presence of God as a psychological power in his life. As a social and psychological manifestation, God is as real as any other social or psychological object in experience.

RELATIONSHIP OF WORSHIPER TO GOD

The inclusion of both worshiper and God in the field of the personality system unquestionably comes as a difficult novelty to those schooled in traditional Christianity with its sharp separation between man and God. The idea that the supreme object of religious devotion is part of one system with human personality, or stated alternatively, the idea that human selves are part of a larger self, God, is a traditional one in Eastern religions. That the higher power of religion is within, not outside of, human life and experience is strongly asserted in Buddhism and Taoism, the former having arisen as a repudiation of supernatural gods. Primitive man was accustomed to thinking of his various psychic functions as residing outside of himself. The last of these to be reunited with his personality is the God of the universe. This unification effected by modern field theory in psychology may be rejected by some religionists who are unable to accept this analysis.

The viewpoint in Eastern religions that self and religious object are psychologically joined has sometimes been unfairly caricatured by the question: "How can anyone worship his own motivation?" This question calls forth a grotesque picture of superstitious human beings kneeling on the ground before their own psyche. Properly clarified, the question is of fundamental importance. However one answers the question, let it be kept in mind, first, that by worship in its highest sense is not meant begging at the feet of a capricious god for mercy, but rather meditation and communion, accompanied by reverence and respect which acknowledge the dignity of man and God alike. Second, as Jung pointed out, whatever is an overwhelming psychic factor is God to the individual. If its power is beneficent and indispensable, it commands thoughtful attention of human beings. If psychological attributes of benevolent power appropriate to a supreme being are identified, this being performs the role of God to the individual, wherever it might be located. Third, the circumstance that God is in man does not limit God to man. Incomparably more of this social and altruistic system is found outside the personality of any one individual than within it, including as it does all human beings. If one chooses to philosophize outside of experience, much more is included than altruistic motives of the human race. Fourth, the lines of the individual personality system have been extended in modern psychological field theory. It seems preferable to consider personality-in-its-environment as one continuum than to cut the lines of personality narrower than this. It can be reasoned that one's perceptual experience of the most distant stars is part of one's personality system, that is, the stars are an independently functioning system intersecting the personality system, including as it does the entire environment experienced by the individual. In modern physics both observer and observed are parts of the same functional continuum. The inclusion of God within personality means more an enlargement of the limits of personality than it does a diminution of God. The inclusion is an acknowledgment that man's highest aspirations are not isolated and inaccessible and that the domain of personality is not limited to self-seeking impulses. The motivation referred to by the question posed is not any motivation, but man's ethical ideals at their finest. These ideals include seeking for better ones. In this sense, the motivational system empirically identified as God includes man's spiritual efforts to seek for more of God.

Although to religious empiricists, ideal altruistic motivation seems entitled to be the object of a religious attitude, part of the question is whether human nature contains anything worthy of being considered God-like. Those whose view depreciates human nature in terms of the innate evil of man do not admit that it contains anything God-like. They argue that to merge God and man is either idolatrous or profane, that either man with his imperfection is exalted as divine or else God is pulled down in stature to the level of the human animal. Apart from the offense which such implications give to religious sensibilities, it is argued in a practical way, paraphrasing scripture, that devils cannot be driven out by Beelzebub, the prince of devils,[32] which is to say that man cannot lift himself by his bootstraps.

The confusion is dispelled if it is recognized that there are higher and lower traits in personality from the standpoint of social value. As the higher power has been analyzed, it is a system different from other motivational systems in personality, and exercises a transforming or socializing influence upon the rest of man's nature, especially when it is sought, found, and followed by the individual. The statement of A.A. members that they "Came to believe that a power greater than ourselves could restore us to sanity," can be understood in this sense. From the standpoint of scientific causation, it is necessary for the higher power of religion to be part of man or his immediate surroundings, presumably the group, if it is to have an effect upon human life, since science does not recognize effects found in experience uncaused by antecedent factors observable in experience. Unless supernaturalism of a kind opposed to science is accepted, the higher power must be part of personality or the group.

The risk of blurring the distinction between the higher power and the remainder of the personality system is so large that re-

[32] Matthew 12:22–28.

curringly in history man has placed God far off in the heavens where God ceased to be a functioning force in human affairs, merely being philosophized about or recollected from past legend but inaccessible except under extraordinary circumstances. The supernaturalization of God is one form of removal from man, for the channels of communication become uncertain except for the few whom God favors in ways beyond human comprehension. The periodic reaction to the divorce of God from man is a reinstallation of God in human life during a new religious movement. When God's covenant with Abraham came to afford too remote a tie, the revelation of God on Mount Sinai occurred. When a later Jewish sect felt that God had become inaccessible if their link with him was merely that of obedience to rules he had imposed, they rediscovered God incarnated in the person of their leader, Jesus. When submerged classes of people during the 1930's failed to find the reality of God in their traditional religious forms, they regained him in the person of Father Divine, a cult leader who at the peak of popularity may have had a million followers. At numerous times in history men have called themselves or others God or have insisted that their vocal utterances were the voice of God.

Buber and Jung

A chapter in the debate about the relationship of the worshiper to God consists of an exchange of views between Martin Buber, a distinguished theologian, and C. G. Jung. Buber grew up in a scholarly Jewish background and throughout his life played an active literary role in Judaism from both a social and a religious standpoint. In his classic little volume *I and Thou,* first published in 1923, he sets forth his profound faith in the existence of God outside of man. From a contrasting standpoint with conviction which became stronger through his years of research, Jung asserted the existence of God as a psychic category of human personality.

While lecturing at American universities in 1951 Buber presented his psychological objections to Jung's analysis of God as a psychic component of personality. The following year Buber's statements were published in a periodical with a reply by Jung and were also included in a volume of essays by Buber, *Eclipse of God.*[33] The exchange of views does not seem to resolve

[33] Martin Buber, *Eclipse of God,* Harper, 1957, pp. 78–92, 133–137; "Religion und Modernes Denken," *Merkur,* Februar, 1952, pp. 101–120; with C. G. Jung, "Chronik," *Merkur,* Mai, 1952, pp. 467–476.

the differences of viewpoint effectively, illustrating the difficulty with which minds meet on scientific issues central to religious empiricism. Most of the points raised refer to topics already discussed here. Consequently, a brief statement is given of each point which Buber makes and of Jung's reply. The replies are taken from Jung's writings in general as well as the exchange of views with Buber.

1. *Buber:* Jung fails to demonstrate an essentially personal relationship of man to a God who is experienced.
   Jung: The human psyche often generates archetypes of a personal deity, Jesus for example, to whom the individual experiences a personal relationship.
2. *Buber:* In asserting that religion is a living relation to psychic events which do not depend upon consciousness, Jung is making a statement outside the bounds of psychology as a science.
   Jung: The psychic events which do not depend upon consciousness are those which depend upon the unconscious side of personality, still a proposition within the scientific domain.
3. *Buber:* Although Jung acknowledges he can say nothing as a scientist about God outside of experience, he states that God does not exist independently of the human subject.
   Jung: Insofar as God has any existence which affects the individual subject, this existence is found in psychic experience, usually as an unconscious content of this experience.
4. *Buber:* Jung declares that metaphysical statements are expressions of the soul, which would deny philosophy the basis for truth independent of the individual's own psychological processes.
   Jung: Although philosophical beliefs are generated by the functioning of personality and answer personality needs, the origin of these beliefs in psychic functioning does not define the question of their truth or falsity.
5. *Buber:* Despite Jung's claim of sympathy toward religion approached by faith, he asserts that it is to psychic experience which the individual must turn for religious truth.
   Jung: People are to be encouraged to base their religious beliefs upon psychic facts, but this does not exclude the importance to the individual of faith held on other grounds. In Catholicism the dogmas of faith in the supernatural have a vital psychic role in making contact with systems in the unconscious side of personality.

6. *Buber:* Jung maintains that mystics experience God within themselves, when they experience instead the results of union of their selves with God.
   Jung: What mystics do or do not experience must be resolved by psychological analysis. This analysis indicates that mystics experience God as an archetypal system of motivation and ideation.
7. *Buber:* Jung concedes that people may have an experience of wholeness of personality, symbolized by the mandala, without a trace of divinity being found, which would make God an incidental psychological characteristic which might or might not be found in religious life.
   Jung: People develop an experience of God in various forms, and some do not develop an image of God at all, yet they may be profoundly influenced by ethical motivation. This outcome apparently depends upon variations in hereditary tendencies and opportunities for development.
8. *Buber:* Jung says that man is called by the inner voice of God to his vocation. How is this to be distinguished from the call to evil, a call which man avoids?
   Jung: Men answer calls from both good and evil motivation, as is evidenced by orgiastic cults or nationalism, in addition to higher forms of religion. Increasingly mankind identifies its psychic welfare with responding to spiritual motivation. Individuals who do not heed the spiritual call may succumb to nervous disorder, or groups which do not do so may undergo social disorder.
9. *Buber:* For Jung the goal of spiritual development is an integrated totality, the self. For religionists the goal of spiritual development is God.
   Jung: The whole self is the personality integrated with reference to spiritual motivation, typically the archetype of God.
10. *Buber:* Jung essentially puts man in place of God, identifying God with man.
    Jung: God is not identified with man, but God as experienced is identified with one function in personality.
11. *Buber:* Jung says that men make their own images of God.
    Jung: The human psyche generates imagery of God, but this does not mean mere ideas or copies. Rather the imagery is the concrete experience by which spiritual motivation expresses itself. This is an experience of motivation in oneself and in others.

12. *Buber:* Jung does not distinguish between psychic statements to which a superpsychic reality corresponds and those to which none corresponds.
Jung: Whether a superpsychic reality corresponds to man's metaphysical beliefs is a question outside of science. Where beliefs have a basis in psychic events, this basis is demonstrable by science.

The psychological principles at issue in the debate do not appear to be clear-cut, and their truth depends upon intuitive judgment of the data. It seems significant that the major empirical observations are not called into question, only whether the things to which they refer are to be called *God,* which in part is a verbal issue. Perhaps the weakest point in Jung's position is that no uniformly describable God is disclosed by his analysis. The God whom he finds does vary from culture to culture in accordance with data from comparative religion, although there are also universal characteristics. The variation appears to depend upon historical circumstances in the life of a society. Jung traces these substantially to hereditary determinants, a questionable interpretation. The relationship between the religious pattern of an individual or of a group and the causal factors which determine this pattern provides an important theme for research. This is a theme about which some answers are already accumulating and are considered in the section of this book on causation of religion. The conditions which bring about an optimum form of religious expression, including the most effective system of power in religion which is God, may sometime be much more fully comprehended than at present.

From the standpoint of science, the weakest part of Buber's argument is his implicit assumption of supernatural intervention by God in the natural processes of human life. This intervention is apparently in conflict with orderly scientific causation. In his rejoinder to Jung, Buber writes parenthetically.

(As a rule, I do not bring my own beliefs into the discussion but hold them in check for the sake of human conversation. But it must be mentioned here for the sake of full clarity that my own belief in revelation, which is not mixed up with any "orthodoxy," does not mean that I believe that finished statements about God were handed down from heaven to earth. Rather it means that the human substance is melted by the spiritual fire which visits it, and there now breaks forth from it a word, a statement, which is human in its meaning and form, human conception and human speech, and yet witnesses to Him who stimulated it and to His will. We are revealed to ourselves—and cannot express it otherwise than as something revealed.)[34]

On his part Jung would say that the human personality contains psychic functions adequate to produce the psychological effects believed by supernaturalists to be brought about by divine intervention. By itself, the statement that "human substance is melted by spiritual fire" would apply precisely to God as an autonomous complex functioning in the human psyche.

Further Questions About Empiricist Analysis

Those accustomed to traditional religious approaches offer additional objections to empiricist views of God. One of these is the question of where God was earlier in history before being found in human consciousness. The reply to this is relatively brief, that God existed in the collective unconscious of mankind. Prior to this the scientist cannot attempt an answer. The quest for the origin of human patterns rapidly dissolves into speculation as the social scientist moves backward in time. Nevertheless, research into the present continues unrestricted. The insistence that God be proved to exist prior to human experience stems from the anthropomorphic idea that God is a person who has always lived and always will live. Whether God merely undergoes development in history along with mankind, or whether there is an eternal God transcending history altogether seems a more suitable topic at our present state of data for philosophy than for science.

A question with more empirical basis is that of where are the other gods and spirits to whom man has prayed, sacrificed, or offered obeisance in the historical evolution of religion. Other psychic powers of man's existence besides altruistic motivation have been recognized by man as having some personlike characteristics. This readiness to acknowledge many spirit beings besides one God is a problem in religious causation to which a return will be made in a later chapter. At the moment a practical reason can be noted why these lack the personal recognition accorded to the higher ethical power of monotheistic religion. Verbal communion in religious worship has the effect of invoking or intensifying the manifestation of the motivational system involved. Those psychic powers which are harmful to man are not effectively controlled if a verbal appeal is made to them, as

[34] Buber, *Eclipse of God, op. cit.*, p. 135. Also see, for example, *The Writings of Martin Buber,* Will Herberg (ed.), Meridian, 1956, p. 165.

this intensifies instead of diminishing them. They become subordinated or assimilated by appealing to what is of greatest spiritual power in oneself to organize or displace them. Without basis for recognition in the verbal communion which is part of worship, the lesser deities and spirits cease to be recognized as personlike beings. Invalid to begin with, they die through disuse, and the one ethical God, the higher power of man's existence, remains supreme.

At the same time, a lesson can be learned from personification by primitive man of the malevolent powers confronting him. He did not hide these temperamental dispositions which prestige-conscious persons today try to overlook in themselves, lest they lose face with their peers. Primitive man gave these powers deliberate attention and took overt steps to control them through appealing to benevolent gods to help him keep them in subjection and through exorcising them by rituals effective in redirecting his personality patterns. Psychoanalysis has performed an invaluable service to mankind by bringing self-seeking and aggressive impulses into the open where they can be faced and understood, and then intelligently redirected or displaced by sounder motivations. If unrecognized or suppressed, these harmful impulsions provide the roots for nervous or social disorders which may erupt disastrously. While granting these psychic forces no personal status in worship, it is nevertheless important for man to keep aware of their existence and to come to terms with them realistically.

The role of religion in personality transformation leads to another question about God regarded as an altruistic power. The question arises of why religious-minded people often seem no more altruistic than the nonreligious-minded. Part of the answer is that altruism, in many persons only a dormant and undeveloped motivational system, is a psychological power to which people adjust with varying degrees of effectiveness. That people acknowledge the higher power of religion does not imply that they are successful in allowing this power to redirect their lives. Lip service to the principles of religion has long been a characteristic of many human beings, and it need hardly be expected that those whose acknowledgment of God is superficial or verbal will differ appreciably from those who ignore religion altogether. Furthermore, religious motivation in the personalities of misguided persons may provide the dynamic for much social damage. Those who act mistakenly are likely to be more persistent and more effective in their wrongdoing if motivated by religious purposes. Religion is essentially an affair of motivation, rather than intellection, and the energy which it liberates can have variable consequences. Especially the individual who is confident that his God speaks to him with infallible authority is capable of action whose effects are far from altruistic.

Another part of the answer to why undesirable traits may prevail among the religious-minded is that religious exercise is closely related to psychotherapy, and is a program to which the sick and the disturbed turn, besides the well and serene. Those who have deep temperamental difficulties may be those who acknowledge they have greater need of the psychological power in religion to help them. The net result, however, may mark them as less effective in their altruism than other human beings to whom altruism comes readily, as Cooley indicated, from the social experience of living in "primary groups" of family and friends.

Still another factor is that all human beings share much the same culture by living in it together. If religion is a constructive influence for some, it tends to "rub off" on others in social contact with religious-minded persons. At the same time, those whose personality traits are more egoistic tend to influence their associates, churchgoers or not, to become more self-seeking and disregardful of the good of the group. These features require more extended consideration and receive treatment in later chapters on the development of religion in the individual personality and in the culture of the group.

It is to be noted that empirical study of man's psychic life, whether of spiritual or self-seeking motivation, is characterized by formidable difficulties. Were the task a simpler one, the problems which have confronted man in his quest into religion would already have been solved. Nor would complex facets of the problems involved have required the extended consideration given here. Scientific study of religion, especially matters of empirical theology, will not soon lead to simple discoveries as when a chemical compound is found in the laboratory and a chain of related discoveries soon disclosed. On the contrary, investigation of the interior world will continue for a long time to be a difficult process for laymen and experts alike. Occasional backtracking while fresh mastery is gained will take place.

What is found and described serves as useful guide to the individual, a system of insights to be given more precise setting in terms of concrete life situations to which they are applied as the individual meets them. The individual must content himself with answers which are not complete or exact. In particular, it seems unlikely that the individual or the group will ever be able in the foreseeable future to declare with assurance that he or they know concretely and exactly the demands of God or the requirements of highest ideals. People can appropriately state and act upon their convictions, but knowledge in psychology and other social sciences is too approximate for specific predictions about individual lives to be declared with certainty. The empirical study of God as a social and psychological manifestation does not open the way for people to declare with more than probability what the details of the manifestation in their lives actually are. Claims of divine pronouncement or oracular revelation will become hardly more reliable in the future than they have in the past. The individual may with inner assurance and with substantial group consensus follow a dependable religious system. While this has a large measure of truth for him and for the group, neither he nor they are entitled to proclaim their views to others as having apodictic certainty.

In conclusion it must be recognized that neither empiricist or rationalist analysis of religious beliefs is sufficient by itself. Among man's religious needs is that for a faith which goes beyond experience and satisfactorily answers for him the profound questions of life after death and the reality of God extending beyond the compass of human experience. Such questions appropriately belong to philosophy. Empiricist analysis has no more to say concerning the truth or falsity of philosophical beliefs than does any other form of scientific analysis. On the other hand, philosophy draws upon facts of experience for a platform on which to raise its theories. Thus the religious philosopher may generalize as well as he can from experience to what may exist beyond experience. The trust which men have learned from experience to have in a personal God during their lifetime readily leads them to believe that the same God in a manner not now comprehended will take care of them in a continuation of life after death. Likewise, they generalize from what they know of God to be good to the eventual triumph of God's purposes for the human race beyond the achievements of the present generation. In this way empiricist analysis of religion provides important materials upon which religious philosophy can be built.

On the other hand, philosophizing which neglects empirical aspects of religion makes of it an other-worldly phenomenon divorced from the day to day struggles and victories of life. Such rationalistic philosophy can distort the religious perspective which empiricist analysis brings into focus. To quote the British anthropologist, R. R. Marett, "Rationalism can at most serve to temper a flame which it does not light and may easily extinguish."[35]

[35] R. R. Marett, *Faith, Hope, and Charity in Primitive Religion,* Macmillan, 1932, p. 20.

part IV Causation of Religion

TWO CASE STUDIES IN RELIGIOUS CAUSATION

Church of Jesus Christ of Latter-Day Saints

It was just a little more than one hundred years ago, July, 1847, that Brigham Young, leader of an indomitable company which had made an epic journey across the plains to escape religious persecution, let his eye range over the broad valley of Salt Lake and announced, "This is the place." Salt Lake City, built by the Mormons as their capital, remains today as the great Mormon center, but members of the faith, now more than three-quarters of a million [at present date of writing more than a million] in number, are found in many lands. Some 4,000 men and women, most of them young, are laboring through 34 missions in North and South America, Europe, Australia, New Zealand, and in the islands of the Pacific. This they do largely at their own expense, but aided by families and friends. Two years' missionary service from each member is the normal expectation, though this may not necessarily take them to distant fields. Many give a much longer period of service.

All this is a far cry from those early days in up-state New York, where young Joseph Smith, Junior, son of a not too prosperous farmer, announced the finding, under divine direction, of certain golden plates in Hill Cumorah, plates inscribed and left there centuries before by a prophet about to die. Written in an ancient hieroglyphic, they were deciphered by Smith with the aid of the Urim and Thummim, providentially found with the plates. Through these Joseph Smith, a very meagerly educated youth, was able to translate the meaning of the obscure characters into English. He is said to have sat on one side of a curtain and dictated to an amanuensis on the other side, who wrote it all down. Published finally, it was called the Book of Mormon, from which Mormonism gets its popular name, though the official church title is The Church of Jesus Christ of Latter-Day Saints.

The most commonly accepted explanation of the book's origin by non-Mormons is that it was based upon a historic novel written by a Presbyterian clergyman named Spaulding which he intended calling *The Manuscript Found in the Wilds of Mor-*

mon; or Unearthed Records of the Nephites. He offered it for publication to a printer in Pittsburgh, as yet without title. The printer agreed to publish it if the author would provide a title page and preface. Financial difficulties at this time caused Spaulding to move to Amity, Pennsylvania, leaving the manuscript in the hands of the printer. When he returned later with title and preface, the manuscript was missing. A young man, Sidney Rigdon, an employee of the establishment, was suspected of taking it. Sidney Rigdon was a primary figure in the beginnings of Mormonism. Arbaugh asserts boldly that Rigdon was the real founder of Mormonism, and that he used Joseph Smith as a ready tool in carrying out his purpose to found a new religion. The Spaulding story, it is asserted, reworked by Rigdon, and given to the world through the medium of Joseph Smith, became the Book of Mormon, and the basis of the new faith.

As Joseph Smith himself tells the story, as a boy of about fifteen he experienced something of a religious awakening. It was a time of revival in that section. He was troubled about the divisions in the church. Drawn to Methodism, he went one day into the woods to inquire of the Lord which church he should choose. Here he had a vision. A pillar of light appeared about him. He saw two figures. One of them, pointing to the other, said: "This is my beloved son; hear Him." When he asked which church he should join, he was told he must join none, since all of them were wrong and their creeds an abomination. He related the vision to a Methodist preacher who said it was of the devil, for there were no longer any revelations. He did not join a church, rather for a period of some three years fell into foolish ways "offensive in the sight of God"—not, he hastens to add, any great or malignant sins, for "a disposition to commit such was never in my nature"—but conduct "not consistent with that character which ought to be maintained by one who was called of God as I had been." Then in 1823 came another vision, thrice repeated, in which an apocalyptic figure revealed to him that he was to find the golden plates and the Urim and Thummim. Under divine direction he went to the spot indicated near the top of Hill Cumorah, near Manchester Village. He removed the stone covering of the box in which the plates were hidden and saw them, but was forbidden to remove them until the time for bringing them out had arrived. Every year for four years he returned to the site only to be told to wait. But in September 1827 they were delivered to him.

The countryside had been aroused by the story of Joseph's visions and when it was known that he had the golden plates "the most strenuous exertions were used to get them from him." He sought relief from this public pressure by moving to Harmony, Pennsylvania, the home of Emma Hale whom he had married that year. And here he set about translating the plates with the help of a former schoolteacher, Oliver Cowdery. In this he was occupied much of the time, through 1829, having moved once more to Fayette, New York. Martin Harris, a well-to-do farmer, financed the printing of the first edition of 5,000 copies by mortgaging his farm.

Thus, almost ten years passed between the first vision of Joseph Smith and the completion of the Book of Mormon. It was a time of training and preparation. But, says the *Short History of the Church,* "this did not give him a right to set up a church." This came one day while Joseph and Oliver were in prayer when "a messenger laid his hands upon us and ordained us, saying: 'Upon you, my fellow-servants, in the name of Messiah, I confer the priesthood of Aaron, which holds the keys of the ministering of angels, and of the gospel of repentance, and of baptism by immersion for the remission of sins,' " whereupon each baptized the other and were mutually ordained to the Aaronic priesthood. Some time later, they were ordained to the higher priesthood and given authority "to establish the church on earth, with all that belongs to it by way of gifts, ordinances and divine blessings."

On April 6, 1830, the first organization of the church was effected with six members, the oldest of them but thirty-one years of age. Smith and Cowdery were recognized as the spiritual head of the church. During the first service, Joseph received a revelation designating him as "a seer, a prophet, an apostle of Christ." Known at first simply as The Church of Christ, the name was changed four years later to The Church of Jesus Christ of Latter-Day Saints.

The newly formed church became at once an active aggressive group and quickly added to its numbers. It met serious opposition and persecution. Joseph Smith was twice arrested and imprisoned within the first year. Meanwhile, revelations continued to come to Joseph elaborating the simple organization of the church to meet the practical needs of the people until it assumed its present form, soon to be described. Once the principle of a living, continuing revelation was established, it was inevitable that revelations would be forthcoming as necessity arose. So grew the church in numbers and in complexity of form.

Intense missionary activity was carried on. Converts were made in many distant places: Canada, England, and in the Pacific Islands. Representation of Mormon interests was made to the national government in Washington. Talk of Joseph Smith for president of the United States was heard. He issued a pamphlet setting forth his platform which included purchase of all slaves by the U.S. Government for the purpose of freeing them, thus compensating their owners. An active propaganda in his behalf was carried on by friends all over the country.

But all was not peaceful. Several attempts were made to have Joseph and Hyrum Smith, his brother, returned to Missouri, where they had escaped from prison. Then internal enemies published certain statements regarded as libelous by the Mormon leaders. The city council acting, as they declared, under the city charter declared the paper a nuisance and ordered the mayor, Joseph Smith "to abate it." Smith issued an order to destroy the press and the libelous handbills. This was done by the city marshal. A little later, the mayor and council were charged with rioting and hailed before a justice of the peace in Carthage, Illinois. Fearing mob violence, they refused to go. Smith, it is asserted, wrote the governor inviting him to investigate the case in person in Nauvoo and offering to abide by his decision. The governor ordered them, however, to appear, adding, "I will guarantee the safety of all such persons as may be brought to this place either for trial or as witnesses for the accused."

The prophet, knowing that his life was in danger if he went, resolved to go west and make a home for his people. He even crossed the Mississippi into Iowa, but, besought by his wife to return and stand trial, he acquiesced and in company with his brother and others, went to Carthage for trial. Bound over by the judge to the next term of court on the charge of rioting, they were later charged with treason. An appeal to the governor having failed, they were thrown into the jail where on the 27th of June a mob shot Joseph Smith, his brother, and John Taylor to death. The prophet was martyred at the age of thirty-nine years. The Saints were without a leader. What would they do?

There was naturally great confusion at this unexpected turn of events. None had contemplated the necessity of determining a successor to the prophet. He was young—under forty—and active. The natural expectation that he would long continue to lead them left them with no plan for the future direction of the church. Sidney Rigdon presented himself as divinely appointed "guardian," and sought acceptance by the group before some of the more outstanding leaders who were away on various missions could return. They did return, however, before a meeting could be called and though Rigdon was given a chance to present his claim, the people did not respond favorably. On the other hand, when, at a later meeting the same day, Brigham Young spoke before them, they were quickly convinced that the movement needed no "guardian," but that control belonged properly to the "apostles" of whom Brigham was the president. Indeed, Mormon sources declare that when President Young rose to speak, "the people were astonished, for he stood transfigured before them and they beheld the Prophet Joseph Smith and heard his voice as naturally as ever they did when he was living. It was a manifestation to the Saints that they might recognize the correct authority." Thus, Brigham Young became the head of the church and to his organizing and administrative ability the church owes more than to any other man since the death of the prophet.

In early February 1846 the first of the Saints crossed the river into Iowa and began the epic journey to the west. This migration is too well known through books, articles, stories and moving pictures to need recounting here. Certain it is that there is no more thrilling story in the annals of the American frontier than this. For daring, patient acceptance of incredible hardships, and for dogged persistence on the part of a people seeking freedom to worship God according to the dictates of their own faith, it ranks among the great stories of all time. The necessity for the migration reflects little credit upon the American people of that day who were the descendants of an earlier generation which had fled their European homes in search of religious freedom, and had written into the fundamental law of the land a guarantee of religious liberty.

Thus, in 1847, they came to the valley of Salt Lake and began the building of their new home. But they had not yet come to the end of their hardships nor indeed of religious opposition. It was no easy task to convert a desert into a fabulously rich agricultural area. But wise planning, vigorous activity and an indomitable will to live, wrought the wellnigh impossible. A person today who motors through Utah, or goes by train, who visits Salt Lake City and other prosperous Utah cities, cannot fail to be impressed by the results of their labors. The two most familiar landmarks of Salt Lake City are the tabernacle, a building marvel for its time, and the great temple, the center of worldwide Mormonism. From here have gone forth literature and human representatives that have carried Mormonism around the world. There have been difficulties. At one time the United States sent armed forces against the Mormons. It was with difficulty that statehood was achieved. This came only after an agreement to abandon the practice of polygamy which was a primary source of opposition to the Mormons. Finally, in 1896, Utah became a sovereign state, and for more than half a century has taken its own part in the national life.[1]

Sharecropper Religion

The red sun hung low in a sultry sky when families of cotton workers drove in their rusty cars to the clearing beside the weather-beaten, one-room church. Beyond a few

[1] Abridged from Charles S. Braden, *These Also Believe,* Macmillan, 1949, pp. 421, 422, 424, 425–427, 429–431.

scrubby trees stretched row after row of cotton plants. Silhouetted against the horizon were shacks dotted here and there from which the cotton workers had come.

This particular night was the weekly revival meeting, held each Sunday. The people needed reviving after long hours of chopping weeds in the summer heat, working at a feverish pace to keep ahead of the dank growth fostered by days of rain. In debt to landlords and storekeepers, subsisting on a diet of sowbelly, corn meal, and molasses, and plagued by poor health, they sought release from the poverty which bound them. They loved to listen to stories of the kingdom of heaven where every man ate his fill, where the sick were made whole, and the dead reunited. At their revival meetings, a feeling of religious ecstasy settled over the crowd, a feeling costing nothing but the plateful of pennies and nickels collected for the revival leader.

He stood at the door with his gaunt face set while the people straggled in. Some he greeted with such words as, "The Lord is with us," or, "May the Holy Spirit have us." The sick ones he embraced with one arm while he repeated, "May the Lord help you, sister." His eyes watered with emotion.

The flock of a hundred persons assembled, he took his seat on the side of a slightly raised platform. For half an hour members of the congregation sang, or rather roared, hymns. There were neither songbooks nor musical accompaniment. When one round of verses was finished, someone would lead the lines of another hymn. People swayed and beat time as they sang. During the singing a tin plate was passed around and then up to the front.

The leader stood up and began a long prayer in a shrill voice, the prayer taken up by successive members of the congregation until a dozen had spoken. This was no quiet prayer but an exhortation of greatest intensity, "Oh Lord, Oh Lord, Oh Lord, have mercy on us. We have sinned, we are unworthy, we have been punished, our flesh is dead, give us the Holy Spirit." Toward the end, the prayer was for the leader, "May the Holy Spirit give him good words! May the Holy Spirit be a blessing to him."

By this time the crowd had worked itself into a fever of excitement and expectancy. The room was crowded and hot. People sat on window sills. Curious faces peered in the windows. Reports of miracles and strange orgies attracted almost as many outside as in.

"The jaws of Hell are open. But the Blood of the Lamb has saved us. Do you know what that means to you?" The leader began his sermon, if a repetitious torrent of words about a kingdom of plenty can be called that. He turned his piercing eyes from one to another. Some began to moan. Others shouted, "Oh Jesus, save us, save us!" A tall young girl rose from her seat and waltzed crazily down the aisle. "Now the Spirit's got her, Oh God, Oh God." A boy, apparently epileptic, slid from the bench in a convulsion. Several men rose and beat on the walls with their hands. Women jumped or rolled their heads or slapped themselves. The waltzing girl collapsed on the floor. A young man with muscles like steel bands pulled her to her feet and led her outside into the bushes. Other young couples, hugging each other, went out.

The excitement subsided somewhat as the voice of the leader gained control. "Now who will be saved?" Two girls came forward and knelt. The congregation shouted and prayed. Pails of creek water were poured over the two.

"Now who will be healed?" An old man hobbled forward on a crutch. "Pray for the Spirit," called the leader. The noise was deafening. The old man let his crutch fall to the ground. He stood alone. He took one step uneasily, then dragged his lame leg after. "The devil's licked. Keep it up." The man pushed forward, partly supported by persons beside him. "Let him alone. Don't give the devil a chance." With triumphant exertion, the cripple walked, first around the room, then straight out the door. The room broke into applause and more shouting.

The leader called on others chronically ill. "Still praying," one would say, or, "Still waiting for the Spirit," another would answer. No one else came forward to be cured. As if by prearrangement, the congregation launched into more singing. Some of the same hymns were sung a second time. People started to leave. The noise of autos being cranked signaled a general exodus.

Through each long week, people talked of the marvelous things done by the Holy Spirit at their previous revival meeting or daydreamed of miracles which the next revival meeting might bring.

The foregoing is a religious revival meeting among poor whites in the cotton country of Arkansas during the Great Depression of the 1930's, described by the present author from personal observation while working for a labor organization of sharecroppers. What does this type of religious expression have in common with that of the Mormons? The common element is that both religions are reactions to situations of dire economic hardship.

The Mormons reacted by building a fresh social order based upon their religious beliefs. At their hand the desert became luxurious farm land, and cities rose from waste land.

In contrast, the sharecroppers already found themselves living on the rich alluvial soil of the Mississippi and its tributaries. But the sharecroppers who engaged in weekly revival meetings were resigned to the economic fate which they faced. Living in poverty in a land of great potential abundance they failed to see the doorways of economic and political change which they could open by their own efforts. Instead of joining the union, whereby they could match the strength of their landlords, they released their emotional feelings in revival meetings conducted by churches which were allied with the landowners against them.

Their religion in their condition was born of frustration and desperation. Such religion has much in common with religious rites of primitive peoples similarly harried by hunger and disease. The conventional symbolism of Christianity is evident, but the spirit possession, the intermingling of sexual and religious feeling, and the emotional intensity of the escape through fantasy are exceptional features. The conclusion stands out that religion derives its character not only from its historical creed, but also from the social and economic circumstances in which people live. These circumstances push into prominence various ideological or emotional elements in the prevailing religious pattern.

Yet why did they not react constructively to meet adversity as did the Mormons? The answer to this type of question is a difficult and involved one. It illustrates the complexity of the task which confronts a student of religious causation. Several hypotheses, admittedly incomplete, can be suggested here as to the reasons for the differential reaction of Mormons and sharecroppers.

1. The Mormons beginning with their leaders rebuilt their religion and their patterns of economic and political life from the ground up. Although largely influenced by traditional Christian teachings, they saw these in a new light. Their revolution was essentially a religious one. They rejected existing religious institutions with their fetters of convention and conservatism. That they for a time espoused polygamy is evidence of the depth and thoroughness of their revolutionary thinking. In building a new life for themselves in desert lands, they labored under a keen sense of the common good. That their government and economic administration eventually became integrated with the competitive economic system of the rest of the United States should not mislead one concerning the extent to which community feeling dominated the early Mormons and still dominates them in considerable measure today.

2. Whatever was the spark which set off the new religious reaction leading to the Church of Jesus Christ of Latter-Day Saints, the Mormons with their intense missionary zeal at once encountered strong opposition from members of established Christian churches. The persecution to which they were subjected gave their church even greater vitality. The blood of martyrs was the seed of their church, as in the case of many other new religious movements. The sharecroppers were encouraged by landlords in their religion, which was considered a harmless escape, although their labor organization was ruthlessly attacked.

3. Learning was highly esteemed by the Mormons, as it very much is at the present time. They have constituted a cultural stream with a much higher educational level than the cultural stream to which the sharecroppers belonged. This intellectual attainment made possible a creative reconstruction of religious and social life for the Mormons. Lack of the same education handicapped the sharecroppers in gaining an understanding of the plantation system under which they lived.

4. The full causal explanation for the rise of the Church of Jesus Christ of Latter-Day Saints is enveloped in mystery which present-day scholarship cannot completely uncover. If the explanation is accepted that a fanciful novel provided the original spark of inspiration for the movement, its rise must depend to a considerable degree upon historical accident. Or did Sidney Rigdon already feel himself to be a religious prophet and then find that the manuscript sent to his printing shop provided an opening wedge to launch a new religion, much of whose ideas were already part of him?

5. The circumstances remain clear that there was sufficient discontent with religion of the time that large numbers of people welcomed a new religion offered by the Mormons. Likewise, the economic and religious condition of the sharecroppers predisposed them to turn energetically and enthusiastically to forms of religious expression which were available to them.

6. Also of basic significance is the circumstance that the religious system on which the Church of Jesus Christ of Latter-Day Saints grew and gained adherents was one which combined economic with religious ideas. In contrast the religious system available to sharecroppers as part of their culture contained a sharp cleavage between otherworldly religious ideas and the economic hazards of this world. Except for a few sharecroppers with greater insight than the rest, they failed to see in a labor union the opportunity for a religious crusade combining religious zeal with a drive for economic justice.

These two case studies help to give one a "feel" for scientific problems of religious causation. The scientific study of religion looks for cause-and-effect connections which account for the particular pattern which religion possesses in any locality. This study also seeks for causes in human heredity or in group life which explain why human beings in general are religion-building animals. How can we explain the prevalence of religion in the human species? Religion is found throughout history in every culture. It takes numerous forms and expressions. Not all persons in each culture accept or practice religion. Science asks the question "Why?" about these features of religion.

The primary task of all science is to discover cause-and-effect relationships. By means of these it is possible to predict future events or to control present ones. By means of science man becomes engineer of the present and previewer of the future. But science, especially the branches which study man, is not always successful in discovering laws of cause and effect. Then science must content itself with accurate observation and classification of facts to the end that facts of life become neatly systemized and catalogued. Since analysis of the causation of religion is in a highly developmental stage, many of the cause-and-effect relationships pointed to in the next two chapters are in the nature of intuitive theories. Whether proved to the hilt or not, men must live and continue to make decisions. What they understand of religion, as well as they understand it, affords the basis for making religious decisions. Still, the scientific consensus based upon psychic study of religion is growing and gaining more secure ground as scientific study unfolds. The student of religious causation will find much to which he is able to give firm assent in appraising religion and in pursuing patterns of religious development for the individual and for his culture.

chapter 11 Development of Religious Personality

Of the phenomena which the scientist seeks to explain by means of orderly cause-and-effect principles, religious behavior is one of the most profound. It is understandable that an animal organism periodically experiences physical deficiencies which impel it to act in search of food. When the metabolic balance is restored through ingestion of nourishment, activity subsides until the hunger need again asserts itself. But where is the chemical lack which motivates the spiritual quest? How do we explain Jesus' accepting the martyrdom which ended in a cross? How do we account for renunciation of wealth by Engels, the son of a well-to-do textile manufacturer who devoted his life to working for a socialistic society? This is a pattern of altruistic devotion repeated innumerable times by those today devoted to the goal of a coöperative economic world. No chemical imbalance has yet been found which provides the physiological basis for this unanimal-like behavior. The search for physical laws of cause and effect for altruistic and religious behavior comes up abruptly against a blank wall.

Experience the Key to Cause-and-Effect Analysis of Personality

Although the physical side of the mountain range of religion presents little except barren rocks and impenetrable forests, the psychic side of religious life is a green and sunny slope which invites scientific understanding. In the domain of interior experience are found characteristic features of desiring, believing, and feeling which differentiate religious from nonreligious activity. Here are found the psychic patterns of religious life. These patterns do not burst full-blown in the personality system. They grow by continuous degrees from rudiments present at birth or appearing in childhood, and they are continuously modified and augmented by the constant interplay of the experiences of group living. In the stream of experience can be found principles of cause and effect. Early experiences precourse later ones, and new experiences leave effects evident in the functioning of the personality system. The data of psychic experience provide the basis for a closed system of cause-and-effect processes, a dynamic system of which behavior is the expression or result. Not only religious activity, but the higher aspects of personality functioning in general yield more readily to study in terms of inward experience than they do in terms of analysis of the chemistry of the body.

To say this does not minimize the importance of connections of physical phenomena with psychic life. These connections are actual, and some aspects of personality absolutely require their consideration. The glandular basis for personality patterns has impressive scientific documentation in support of it. The point in respect to this causal connection of personality with physical variables is twofold. For one thing these variables are almost entirely inadequate to account for complex activities of human beings, such as religious behavior. For another, these variables only exercise an effect upon personality insofar as they evidence themselves in psychic experience. The person with a thyroid deficiency feels passive and depressed, while the person with a thyroid excess feels nervous and excitable. These physical factors are therefore experienced as absence or excess of tension in inward experience. Physical variables must be taken into account in analyzing the personality system, but only insofar as their effects are registered within the ongoing stream of experience. This stream is the royal highway upon which scientific investigation of personality proceeds. All other byways of causation affecting experience are no more than branches flowing from or springs feeding the main stream of causation.

Definition of Personality

It is customary in science to speak of a group of causally interrelated variables as a system. In this sense personality is a system. The enumeration of components of this system would include the behavior of the individual, what he says and does, and also the underlying substratum of physiological functioning which includes the chemical, physical, and biological processes of the body. Also included are the motivations and thought processes of the individual, his desires, beliefs, opinions, attitudes, and other patterns of psychic life. These patterns greatly color what is perceived in experiences of the external world. Perceptions also seem an intimate part of the personality system.

The individual's perceptions include other people and distant celestial objects. Are these all parts of the personality system? How shall the lines of this system be rigorously drawn? There seems no compelling reason for drawing a sharp line around the personality system and arbitrarily asserting what belongs inside the line and what falls outside. The simplest rule would be to declare that all things within the stream of the individual's experience, both perceptual and psychic, form the substance of his personality system. This would not exclude components of the personality system from belonging at the same time to other causal systems in the universe. Many objects are coördinate members of a number of systems at the same time.

The physiological details of his mind and body are not, except to a minor degree, perceived by the individual. Physiological variables are closely correlated with those of the stream of experience. It seems desirable to define the personality system as including not only the stream of experience of a person but those variables which stand in one-to-one correspondence with its movement and upon which the existence of experiences of any kind depends. Such variables include those of the physical processes of the brain and body of a human being.

Certain features of the personality system are of basic concern in religious study. Those features which define the individual's religious life, his experience of a higher power, and his adjustment to it are of basic importance. In a larger manner, religion is involved in the entire personality system. The goal of development of religious personality is for the entire system to function in a manner which fulfills religious goals to the maximum degree. In this way all of human personality is of concern in the study of religion.

Is the Human Will Free?

No sooner is it proposed in scientific study to treat personality as a causal system than some religionists protest that man's freedom of will is being jeopardized. If it is determined by laws of cause and effect what a man will do tomorrow, why should he make any effort to do anything at all? What he is going to do is predestined, and nothing he can strive to do will alter what will take place anyway. So the argument against determinism runs.

The scientist on his part would concede the absence of causal order with great reluctance, for this order is the heart of his goal of analysis. Beyond the scientific goal is the practical one of predicting behavior from laws or using laws to alter the course of personality development in socially desirable directions. If cause-and-effect processes do not determine religious development, how can proper means be followed for bringing human personality to its fullest spiritual attainment? Thus the answer of the scientist of religion is given. Of course what scientists or religionists may say about the functioning of human personality does not alter the functioning about which dispute goes on. People continue to choose and act, work and recreate, enjoy themselves or give of themselves to the common good. But one exception to what would otherwise happen does occur. If the pronouncements of scientists dishearten the individual from making any effort to develop himself, they do affect further personality development. If people think nothing they try to do will alter the level of their religious life, obviously their efforts will decline or disappear. Hence the concern of religionists about the presence or absence of freedom of will is of deep practical importance.

The answer to the dilemma is that it is one of point of view. To the individual within his own personality system, the future course of his behavior is not determined. He is in process of collecting information, thinking out consequences, and mapping his course of action. As long as no obstacles or restraints appear to what he would like to do, he feels free in the exercise of his will. From the standpoint of the data of experience, freedom of will is no more than an experience of thinking out and making choices without hindrance. So defined, freedom of will can hardly be denied.

As soon as the individual has decided what he will do, such as take a job in social work rather than advertising, then to him, as well as to others, his course of conduct is determined. Uncertainty of choice existed only so long as he was ignorant of which course to follow. When he has decided the course upon scientific grounds, he knows enough of his situation and his behavior to know, that is predict, what he will do. He no longer feels entirely free to select any alternative, but only that alternative which will most fully implement his desires and meet impediments in his situation. What the individual then knows of himself is similar to that which an outside observer may have known all along.

From the standpoint of an outside observer who can exhaustively record the numerous influences playing upon the individual's personality, the choice of job which he makes depends upon the hereditary capacities with which he was born and especially upon the learning experiences which have intervened. Was his family life one conducive to altruism or individualism? Did his student years inform him of the opportunities for service in social work or acquaint him with the shortcomings of advertising as often practiced? The answers to such questions, if completely known, would enable the scientist to predict with certainty what course the individual will choose. Predictions of behavior lack this precision at the present time, but the steady growth in their dependability strongly suggests that determinism is the rule in human behavior from the standpoint of an omniscient scientific observer outside the individual's personality system.

From within the system the psychic experience of freedom to choose prevails until the individual's mind is irrevocably made up. What the individual achieves depends upon the effort and concentration which he puts forth. Even these things depend upon past training. Possessing these abilities, the individual can make the effort required to achieve goals otherwise beyond his reach. Laws of cause and effect hardly absolve the individual from making the effort, but rather harness his desires to means necessary to bring about the goals which he seeks. In no other way except by reckoning with causes and consequences can the goals be achieved. The supposed conflict of freedom of will and determinism is a fiction in the minds of those who do not understand that freedom of will does not mean freedom from scientific laws, but rather freedom from particular obstacles or restraints. The individual is free to make up his mind and follow a chosen course of action even though an omniscient scientist could predict how he will act.

Such a scientist, if his prediction is to be valid, cannot inform the individual of the prediction, or else the knowledge of the prediction becomes an added circumstance altering the course of behavior, a circumstance omitted in making the prediction.

Constituents of Personality Development

The source from which the characteristics of religious life come is of more than casual scientific interest. Orthodox religionists have been accustomed to thinking of these characteristics as given by God through a supernatural act of grace. Psychologists and sociologists would like to trace the source of these to natural circumstances in heredity, group life, or culture. Such tracing does not diminish nor augment these religious qualities. They are what they are in the present, whatever their origin. Yet knowing the manner of their origin satisfies more than scientific curiosity. This knowledge makes possible fuller control over the processes of personality development.

HEREDITY

The individual starts life at birth with something going on. James shrewdly opines that what the infant encounters upon seeing the light of day is a "buzzing, blooming confusion." Psychoanalysis pushes back the dawn of life experience to the intrauterine environment, noting that this must be a blissful experience of floating on a sea of warmth and comfort. The desire for the environment of the womb is manifested long afterward in the need of the infant to be held, pressed, rocked, and cuddled. Emergence from the womb is a rude awakening to the hard circumstances of life, adjustment to which is a perpetual process.

Whatever constituents are present in personality at birth, or more strictly speaking, at the moment of conception in the oviduct, are given by heredity, that is by the parents and preceding ancestors. The characteristics given by heredity are not a copy of those of parents, nor those of any preceding individual, but represent a selection from a large reservoir of characteristics of which the parents are the carriers. This reservoir can be likened to a deck of cards, handed down from generation to generation. Each parent holds a deck of cards from which the child is dealt a hand. This compound selection of cards contains the characteristics received by the child from heredity. Not only does the child receive his own characteristics from the decks of the parents, but he in turn is given their two decks from which he, together with his future spouse, deal their children hands of cards. In summary, the child is given a set of characteristics by his heredity, but these are not a carbon copy of those of the parents, but rather are drawn from a storehouse of characteristics of which the parents are carriers.

Drives

The raw materials provided by heredity can be grouped under several headings. The materials which provide energy and movement are *drives*. When awake, a young infant is observed to be in continual motion, arms and legs thrashing, head turning from side to side. This motion is heightened when the infant is hungry. Gurgling gives place to crying. The head turns, the mouth opens, and sucking actions ensue in an obvious pattern of establishing contact with a nipple. The activity is the manifestation of the hunger drive.

A drive, then, can be defined as a tendency to act. This defines it in terms of behavior data. The drive is a force making for behavior. Using the word *force* summarizes changes which ensue, since force is evidenced by changes which occur. The heightening of activity marks the presence of a drive.

The psychic experience which a hungry infant undergoes can only be inferred. From the psychic side, a drive is an experience of discomfort. It is an experience of tension or need in the sense that one feels a force within oneself, impelling one involuntarily to look, think, and act. The term *drive* conveys this meaning of being driven or being pushed uncomfortably along. The principal drives given by heredity are hunger, thirst, sex, pain avoidance, play, and rest.

Responses

Besides these periodic forces producing activity, heredity of course gives each human being his bodily make-up, the instrumentality through which he acts. This can be thought of as consisting of a number of tiny units of behavior: *reflexes* or *responses* consisting of groups of reflexes functioning together. Some reflexes and responses are evoked by external stimuli and others by internal stimuli such as drives or other reflexes. Under the influence of a drive these units of behavior or response patterns are activated, and the activity continues until the experience satisfying the drive is obtained. Then the activity subsides for the time being.

A human being can be thought of as an experience-seeking organism. Periodically the infant's personality system is stimulated by drives whose operation continues until the infant's behavior has brought it the required experience satisfying the drive. Initially the behavior is largely random, although some reflexes are present in a few rudimentary patterns given by heredity. Turning the head is combined with sucking and swallowing in a sequence patterned for the successful ingestion of milk from the breast. Most of the responses of the body are initially amorphous and undefined. The frustration of hunger, for example, produces a chaotic display of activity in arms, legs, and vocal apparatus. Each time the activity appears under the influence of a drive, it becomes more specific and efficient. The child of two years at mealtime will clamber up his high chair, seat himself, throw the bib around his neck, and seize the spoon in his fist ready to eat. When the human being reaches adulthood he will be able to utter sounds in an intelligent talk about religion and is capable of the responses expected in taking Holy Communion.

The periodic flow and ebb of behavior under the influence of drives is a well-defined behavior cycle in young children and subhuman species. In the adult, a combination of drives usually function at any given time. In the crosscurrents of behavior, the typical pattern of increased activity, successful response, experience satisfying the drive, and repose is less clearly evident. In the human species alternatives are explored in the imagination rather than trial responses taking place. In a self-controlled adult overt behavior does not begin until the appropriate course of action is discerned.

Temperament

Conspicuous in human beings, as well as in other animals, is the characteristic manner in which the behavior cycle takes place. Such life qualities as quickness, slowness, energy, lethargy, and presence or lack of persistence are characteristics of the way in which the individual acts to fulfill his needs. In reacting to acute frustration of different kinds, behavior becomes emotional. The behavior manifests the uncontrollable surge of energy typifying anger, or the inhibition typical of fear. Emotional reactions are characteristics which may be called into play by circumstances of actual or threatened blocking of the behavior cycle. These various qualities of the behavior cycle can be loosely placed under one heading, *temperament*. Heredity gives each human being a particular temperament. While some modification of temperament is possible through learning, emotional aspects, at least, largely remain fixed quantities throughout life. The type of religious personality achieved in adulthood tends to conform to the basis for it in temperament. Rigid religious patterns are an outgrowth of a Philistine-like temperament. A religious pattern of revolt against orthodoxy is characteristic of a rebellious temperament which fights against conservative conditions. A passive religious outlook is colored by a submissive temperament. Strong religious convictions are strengthened by a durable temperament.

While emotional reactions of fear or anger have an obviously useful role in terms of simple survival of the organism in the face of danger, they provide a large impediment to social thinking and adjustment. The acquisition of their polar opposites of serenity and courage is prominent in most programs of religious development. The individual may learn to live with his emotions by choosing his circumstances and orienting his thinking so that fear and anger are not evoked. But given unexpected circumstances, temperamental reactions follow almost involuntarily. It is not surprising that the disruptive influence of emotions was recognized by prescientific religion in the guise of devils or evil spirits and that ritual means were devised of controlling them in human personality.

Religion helps to integrate the personalities of those prone to nervous breakdown. Hence hereditary tendencies toward fear, anxiety, anger, or sorrow may play a role in turning the developing personality toward religion. Research studies are not available to prove conclusively that this is the case. However, many persons who have wholeheartedly turned toward religion are those who acknowledge having done so in order to gain emotional stability. Christian Science with its emphasis on organizing one's life about the Divine principle of Love provides a doctrine especially valuable for one whose personality structure requires strengthening. It seems probable that many whose lives have been made whole by this doctrine were born with more than average emotional instability.

Capacities

The materials given by heredity so far reviewed seem to have only a moderate connection with religious motivation and behavior. It can be pointed out that speech reactions in worship utilize muscular reflexes given the body by heredity, or that emotional needs predispose the personality to find security in religion. But speech reactions can be used for many purposes, and emotional needs are resolved in various ways. What is distinctive about the religious side of personality is that such constituents become patterned in a unique way characterizing religious expression. That the raw material of heredity can be organized in complex patterns is a capacity for development which heredity also confers. There is little reason for believing that the intellectual capacity for absorbing and expressing a religious system in one's life differs markedly from the capacity for artistic, literary, or scientific achievements. However, this capacity is variable from individual to individual. Men like St. Francis of Assisi do not appear in history often. One of the determinants of religious development is the capacity for the organization of hereditary constituents into intricate habit systems of drives, responses, and temperament.

By definition, *capacity* means a situation which is capable of being changed by the operation of causes. The capacity given personality by heredity for the organization of its constituent materials may or may not be utilized, depending upon circumstances in the environment which hinder or facilitate this organization. It is apparent that religious growth does not proceed automatically as given by heredity but proceeds from circumstances of group living, such as family love, and from the religious patterns presented the individual by his culture. When we say that human personality has capacities given it for religious growth, all we are saying is that the human being is a system capable of being developed under the influence of environmental factors into a religious-minded being. Of course every capacity implies a limit of some sort. No cause operating upon personality can produce infinite changes in it. The capacities given by heredity are specified in terms of how much change particular factors in the environment are capable of bringing about. If necessary, these limits can be described in terms of mathematical formulas such as those used in the investigation of learning curves.

The organization of the constituents given by heredity is not a mechanical putting together of pieces of machinery. For one thing, the pieces undergo change as a result of biological maturation. The sex drive in adulthood is different in degree and kind from that apparent in childhood. For another, the materials given by heredity undergo change as a result of environmental influences. Hunger is universal, but the variety of foods craved by men is as great as the forms of nourishment yielded by the environment or taught by cultures in different parts of the earth. Sex is also universal, but the degree of its expression ranges from romantic patterns in sex-conscious Hollywood to the asceticism of Hindu holy men who marry, if at all, only to propagate children. Religious motivations, from whatever these stem, likewise seem greatly modifiable according to whether the cultural milieu is Catholic or Protestant, Communist or pacifist.

The modifiability of personality constituents is a second fundamental capacity bequeathed by heredity to each human being.

A third capacity, most important of all from the standpoint of religion, is the capacity to acquire additional constituents of personality. This is seen in an obvious way in the capacity of each personality to receive perceptual experiences from the environment. More important acquisitions than these are the ideas left by them in the personality system. When these ideas are in the form of knowledge and belief, they guide behavior realistically toward its objectives. When sound cause-and-effect principles are encompassed by religious ideas, religious activity proceeds effectively toward its goals.

A vital class of ideas are those which function as motives of behavior. The way in which ideas in the form of drives arise from experience is an important topic to which we turn in a moment. Such drives as those for possessions, companionship, social recognition, and altruism are conspicuous constituents of the personality system. Most of the motivations involved in religion are acquired by the personality system, rather than present as drives at birth. However, hereditary structure makes it possible for these motivations to be acquired. Other animals do not acquire them. Furthermore, such motivations, when once acquired, proceed toward more advanced levels of development of their own inward dynamic. Man is not only a value seeking animal; he tends to seek what he conceives to be of greatest value, which appears to be a tendency conferred by hereditary structure. But the casting of this tendency in social or religious patterns requires the experience of group living.

The ideas acquired from experience, whether beliefs or motives, are not necessarily concrete images or copies of experience. Most beliefs and aims result from the progressive differentiation of experience into components. Heredity gives a capacity for concepts to be distilled from experience in that a single characteristic or principle is incorporated into an idea. More than other aspects of life, religion is concerned with ideas which are differentiated from psychic experience with difficulty. The religious development of which a human being is capable depends in degree and form upon the individual's ability to think abstractly. His ability to make contact with the unconscious contents of experience and to sense the presence of God depends upon the facility with which the contents emerge from undifferentiated experiences of life. This is a capacity of which little is known from a physical standpoint, but the obvious variations from individual to individual indicate that hereditary variation in people, as well as learning opportunities, plays a prominent role in this capacity. However, the capacity seems, at least in part, to be a general one underlying various types of intellectual achievement.

Jung's Theory of the Hereditary Basis for Religious Development

How much does heredity have to do with religious traits of personality? Little research has been accomplished to answer this question in more than general terms. The research of Jung leads him to ascribe a large role to heredity make-up, which he believes is formed through the experiences of the human race in generation after generation. In keeping with the large role assigned heredity by psychoanalysis generally, Jung assigns a predominantly hereditary origin to religious traits of personality. The theory of hereditary origin of religion is part of his general theory of the hereditary basis for archetypes. According to Jung, archetypes are the ancient or traditional forms in which the ideas of every generation are cast. They represent a deposit of centuries of past experience built into the biological structure which each human being inherits at birth. Archetypes refer to both man's compelling religious beliefs and his religious drives. For instance, belief in a redeemer and in forgiveness, as well as drives for altruism and for religious development, are part of the system of archetypes of hereditary origin. At one place Jung describes archetypes as "self-portraits of instincts," meaning that they are psychic images with the dynamic force of instincts.

That religion is rooted in racial and individual heredity is perhaps the most controversial feature of Jung's religious psychology. Jung is led to this view of the role of heredity in religion from his observation that people recreate in their dreams the same symbolic images found in ancient and modern religious systems. These systems, together with mythology and alchemy, are similar in their imagery although widely separated in time and place. Because of the seriousness of the issue of hereditary determination of religious behavior, we consider some of his data and analysis. Discussing the dreams of one of his patients, he calls attention to the frequent use made of such symbols. In one of them destructive forces threatening personality are symbolized by a mercurial snake, the medieval solvent of gold, or the spiritual purity of life.

The dream of the golden serpent contains an anticipation of the patient's own development: she will be assimilated by the mercurial serpent, the totality of her own psyche. This obviously means that she will not overcome the unconscious psyche buried in the earth, but that the latter will devour her, thus producing a different being formed from the conjunction of her conscious and unconscious existence.[1]

The fact that spontaneous imagination makes such telling use of alchemistic symbolism is rather startling to anyone who has a knowledge of mediaeval alchemy. The patient's fantasy-pictures are just as if an ancient alchemist were at work—one of that number who have left us illustrated manuscripts, often consisting only of pictures, like the famous *Mutus Liber* of 1677. Those pictures try to express the seemingly inexhaustible mystery of transmutation by means of a symbolism that is only partly traditional. Often enough the expression is highly individual and closely resembles the pictures produced today by people who are presumably working under similar mental conditions.

Perhaps it is well to admit that there were naturally a great many alchemists who thought that they were learning no more than to make gold. But "making gold" was at the same time taken in an allegorical sense by the alchemistic philosophers; they understood it by a spiritual transmutation, or what we would today call a psychological transformation or readjustment. When he is faced with a transformation of this kind, man always unconsciously chooses such symbolism.[2]

There are peculiar parallels to alchemistic ideas in certain passages of the Gospel of St. John and in the baptismal rite. The same holds true of Taoist alchemy in China, and of certain philosophical systems in India called "The Quicksilver Systems." It is difficult to prove that these Eastern systems had any influence on the nearly contemporary philosophy of the West, and it is equally difficult to see how a modern person with the usual education in science could arrive at a correct use of alchemistic symbolism. If my woman patient were the only one who had produced such symbols, I should not be citing her case here. But I have seen numbers of similar cases. One could almost call the phenomenon a regular occurrence, though it is little known—and for obvious reasons.

The most sensible way of explaining such parallelism is by resorting to the hypothesis of the collective unconscious—of a universal similitude or identity of the basic structure of the human psyche. It seems likely that the collective unconscious contains a number of patterns, "archetypes," common to the whole of humanity. We must suppose that, under similar conditions, they function in the same way regardless of place and time, and that they produce the same ideas regardless of tradition. I assume, therefore, that my patients would

[1] C. G. Jung, *The Integration of the Personality,* tr. by S. M. Dell, Farrar and Rinehart, 1939, p. 47.

[2] *Ibid.,* p. 49.

have produced "alchemistic" symbolism even if alchemy had never existed.[3]

Jung makes it plain that ideas as such are not inherited, but rather the psychic mechanism which generates ideas.

As I have already pointed out, the connection of spontaneous modern symbolism with ancient theories and beliefs is not established by direct or indirect tradition, nor even by a secret tradition as has sometimes been surmised, though there are no tenable proofs of this. The most careful inquiry has never revealed any possibility of my patients' being acquainted with the relevant literature or having any other information about such ideas. It seems that their unconscious worked along the same line of thought which has manifested itself time and again in the last two thousand years. Such a continuity can only exist if we assume a certain unconscious condition as an inherited *a priori* factor. By this I naturally do not mean the inheritance of ideas, which would be difficult if not impossible to prove. I suppose, rather, the inherited quality to be something like the formal possibility of producing the same or similar ideas over and over again. I have called this possibility the "archetype." Accordingly, the archetype would be a structural quality or condition peculiar to a psyche that is somehow connected with the brain.[4]

Jung has shown by the data he cites that religious expression, whether group or individual, overt or subterranean via dreams, is a universal personality function. He has convincingly shown that religious motivation, whether suppressed or expressed, is a component of all personalities. It is a constituent of which account must be taken in personality development or this development is one-sided. The individual who says that religion is only for others who wish it ignores the spiritual impulsion within himself which gains mutilated expression in his dreams when it cannot find adequate opportunity for development.

The data cited by Jung concerning the universal expression of spiritual ideas and aims seem convincing refutation of the viewpoint of cultural relativism that the existence of religious traits in personality depends merely upon whether or not they are implanted by cultural patterns. Religious motivation would not make its appearance in dreams of nonchurchgoers unless the basis for such motivation was independent of secular culture. On the other hand, Jung recognizes that cultural teaching plays

[3] *Ibid.*, p. 50.

[4] C. G. Jung, *Psychology and Religion: West and East,* tr. by R. F. C. Hull. Bollingen Series XX, Bollingen Foundation, Inc. Pantheon, 1958, pp. 103–104.

a large role in the development of religious belief and behavior in personality. Religious systems of thought foster characteristic personality types, such as the ascetic personality of some Eastern religions, the pleasure-permissive patterns of traditional Mohammedanism or the businesslike expression of religion in Western Christianity. Of large consequence, the secular values in culture play considerable role in altering development of religious traits in personality.

Ferals and Isolates

Jung believes that he has disproved that religious motivation depends for its existence upon the variable cultural forms which may or may not give it opportunity for overt expression. But sociologists and anthropologists are equally convinced that they have disproved any immediate connection between the existence of religion and heredity. The notion that religion is an inborn function of human personality is strongly repudiated by them. Their case rests upon the analysis made by Durkheim, Cooley, and others of the social basis of religion and upon the remarkable data provided by feral children or socially isolated children.

A few instances are known to science of human infants lost in the wilderness shortly after birth who have managed to survive, sometimes through the aid of animals who adopt them. The case histories of such dramatic stories of human survival are of extreme scientific interest. The reason is that the nature of human personality when social factors are subtracted from development is shown. If religion or other personal traits are determined by heredity, they would be expected to make their appearance regardless of whether the experience of group living was present or not. Feral children provide a crucial test of whether or not heredity causes the appearance of such traits as altruism and religion.

One of the most complete scientific accounts of feral children has been given by a Christian missionary, the Rev. J. L. Singh, who operated an orphanage in India. In 1920 he discovered two children living in a den with wolves and endeavored, after removing them, to educate the children to civilized living. One of the children, aged two, died shortly after captivity. Key observations concerning the other, found at the age of eight years, are excerpted in the following account.

> Kamala's forehead was wrinkled but her face had a perpetually half-smiling expression, changing only when she was angry or afraid. When

approached, she would make faces and sometimes show her teeth. She disliked or ignored everything human and was as wolflike in her behavior as her human body would permit. She moved around on all fours, using her hands and knees when proceeding slowly. When running, she traveled on her hands and toes and was able to run "as fast as a squirrel.". . .

At first, Kamala ate her food like a dog, without any use of her hands. Milk was lapped with her tongue. She could smell meat at 70 yards, and the least smell of food, even a dead animal or bird, would bring her to the spot at once. Her appetite was ravenous and she was very possessive of her food. . . .

It was nine months before Kamala would trust Mrs. Singh enough to take food from her hand, and almost a year before Kamala showed any liking for her. Food, tender words, and massages given by Mrs. Singh finally brought her to this point. She seemed to have a "consciousness of kind" with the animal pets, making them her first companions. The dogs and a rooster that disliked the other children accepted Kamala. Only slowly did she learn to tolerate and eventually to like the children, the babies first and then the older children. . . .

Her only vocal expressions at first were growl-like sounds and howls. It was six years before she could understand most of what was said to her, and it was six years and three months before she formed a sentence: "Mama come." It was about this time that she first willingly wore a dress, or showed signs of modesty. She began to run simple errands. At the beginning of the seventh year, she became quite word conscious, repeating and humming them in a singsong way. At this time she also attempted to join in the singing of hymns, disturbing the service considerably with her irregular, shrill voice. She took on the chore of gathering the eggs. Her identification with the children became quite complete. At the end of this seventh year, one day, Kamala ". . . was standing at the dining table when the table was being laid for tea. Mrs. Singh, finding her there, gave her a biscuit. She ran to the children, and all the children flocked round the table, expecting to get a biscuit each. Mrs. Singh scolded them for thus coming in before the tea bell rang, and one by one they all left the dining room. Kamala, finding that they had gone away without a biscuit, put her biscuit on the table and went away. The biscuit lay there till the tea bell rang. After the bell, all the children congregated and were given two biscuits each. Kamala took only one biscuit from Mrs. Singh and picked up the one she had left on the table."[5]

Examining this account, we see that some of the important social traits which personality is expected to develop are lacking

[5] R. L. Sutherland, J. L. Woodward, and M. A. Maxwell, *Introductory Sociology,* Lippincott, 1956, pp. 98–99. Adapted from the diary of the Reverend J. A. L. Singh as published in J. A. L. Singh and R. M. Zingg, *Wolf-Children and Feral Man,* Harper, New York, 1942.

in the wolf-child until she began to live in a human group. The drive for human companionship, so strong in most people, is lacking, although Kamala had acquired an attachment to other animals while living with them. Gradually she learned to tolerate human company and then to desire it. That this required years shows that desire for human company is not a superficial habit taught by rote, but is deeply rooted in motivation which requires a long time for its growth.

The last paragraph quoted describes the emergence of ideas of right and wrong, combined with a desire for recognition and approval by others which heredity did not give Kamala. Of special interest is the manifestation of a desire to share food on an equal basis, even though Mrs. Singh, her teacher, offered her special privilege. The altruistic desire for others to have no less than she possessed made its appearance after the experience of living in the group.

The details cited from the case make little reference to religion other than her eventual inclination to join in hymn singing even though the others did not wish this. Although she lived to the age of approximately fifteen, religious motivation made no appearance until near the end of her experience of living with other human beings. No data are furnished of her dreams but it would be expected that the content of her dreams would have no religious significance, since the social experiences underlying religious behavior were lacking. Possibly the fear and wishful thinking which characterize magic and superstition might have been present, but not the type of religion which incorporates ethical power.

A tragic counterpart of human infants lost in the wilderness from peasant society is provided by a few instances in industrial society of illegitimate children hidden by their parents or grandparents from all human company. While such inhuman treatment of children is severely punished and deeply touches the sympathy of those who read of such children, their cases are of greatest interest from a scientific standpoint. If completely isolated by being shut in a room, their traits are also limited to what heredity brings into being without the aid of group living. A few details from the case of a social isolate, called by the pseudonym "Isabelle," discovered by the authorities in 1938 at the age of six and a half, show the poverty of traits connected with social living.

. . . she was an illegitimate child and had been kept in seclusion for that reason. Her mother was a deaf-mute, having become so at the age of two, and it appears that she and Isabelle had spent most of their time together in a dark room shut off from the rest of the mother's family. As a result Isabelle had no chance to develop speech; when she communicated with her mother it was by means of gestures. Lack of sunshine and inadequacy of diet had caused Isabelle to become rachitic. Her legs in particular were affected; they "were so bowed that as she stood erect the soles of her shoes came nearly flat together, and she got about with a skittering gait." Her behavior toward strangers, especially men, was almost that of a wild animal, manifesting much fear and hostility. In lieu of speech she made only a strange croaking sound. In many ways she acted like an infant. "She was apparently utterly unaware of relationships of any kind. . . ."

. . . the individuals in charge of Isabelle launched a systematic and skilful program of training. It seemed hopeless at first. The approach had to be through pantomime and dramatization, suitable to an infant. It required one week of intensive effort before she even made her first attempt at vocalization. Gradually she began to respond, however, and after the first hurdles had at last been overcome, a curious thing happened. She went through the usual stages of learning characteristic of the years from one to six not only in proper succession but far more rapidly than normal. . . .

When the writer saw Isabelle a year and a half after her discovery, she gave him the impression of being a very bright, cheerful, energetic little girl. She spoke well, walked and ran without trouble, and sang with gusto and accuracy. Today she is over fourteen years old and has passed the sixth grade in a public school. Her teachers say that she participates in all school activities as normally as other children.[6]

Owing to her superior intelligence, Isabelle learned more quickly than Kamala. In each case we see how heredity by itself could produce little or nothing of the social traits acquired through group living. Of key importance is means of communication, not simply to receive instruction, but to share sympathetically the experiences of others so that altruistic concern for the needs of others can grow in the personality system. The data on feral children and social isolates show rather convincingly, if indirectly, that basic religious traits of personality are not inborn constituents given by heredity. To the extent that religious traits depend for their existence upon prior development of social ones, they do not appear under conditions of isolation from other human beings.

GROUP EXPERIENCE

If religious traits are not developed primarily by either culture or heredity, what is their origin? The viewpoint of this text

[6] K. Davis, "Final Note on a Case of Extreme Isolation," *American Journal of Sociology,* March, 1947, pp. 436–437.

is that the experience of living in and interacting with members of the group provides an essential basis for developing religious motivation. The influence of culture is limited to the transmission of cultural patterns of thinking and acting, invented and accumulated by mankind. This is a type of influence on religious personality to be considered in detail in a later section. Group experience is fundamental in generating an important list of human drives, apart from whether cultural indoctrination occurs. We now turn our attention to the influence of group experience in the development of religious traits of personality.

The distinction between what is termed *group experience* and what is termed *culture* occasions some difficulty of understanding. In concrete life there is a single social environment, provided by living among other human beings. The social environment of an individual consists of people who are acting, thinking, talking, and feeling. These people provide the individual with his experiences of being helped, hindered, ignored, or sympathized with. They also transmit to him the cultural patterns of feeling, thinking, and acting which he gains. This distinction between group experience and culture refers to the type of effect produced by the social environment. If the effect is principally one of facilitating or thwarting personality growth, as when people coöperate or conflict with each other, encouraging or blocking each other's wants, the experience is designated as group experience. If the effect is one of transmitting patterns of behavior of the group to one of its members, the experience is referred to as cultural experience. In the first case it is human beings as objects or as affecting opportunities for learning culture who are experienced, and in the second case it is human beings as enactors of culture which is learned who are experienced.

Experience as a Source of Drives

Before considering the relationship of religious motives to group experience, it is necessary first to consider the way in which a drive for a particular experience arises from experience. The occurrence of a few biological drives, little related to religion, is immediately accompanied by pain, such as the drive experienced when one is acutely hungry or to avoid heat or cold. As soon as the pain is experienced, there is immediate tendency to act, even though no clear-cut goal of what experience will alleviate the drive is thought of by the individual. A hot radiator is touched by a child, who pulls energetically away without thinking of what his hand would feel like if it were not hot. After a time drives associated with pain are associated with idea-pictures of the experience which would relieve the discomfort. A newborn infant, thrashing and mouthing in search of his mother's nipple, has no concept of what the nursing experience will be like. After numerous feedings his pleasant smile of anticipation at the approach of the mother obviously suggests that the infant has a concrete desire for the nursing experience and is not motivated to act simply by the discomfort of hunger. The point with reference to these biological drives, however, is that they first go into action without any prior experience of what satisfies them.

It appears that most drives do not manifest themselves in the personality system without prior experience of the things which satisfy them. The drive for sexual experience, for example, is preceded by casual self-stimulation of the child's anatomy or by involuntary sensations which make their appearance, especially in the case of the male, at some point during childhood or adolescence. The drive for more such experience does not manifest itself until instances of such experience have occurred during life development.

While the hunger drive, if acutely blocked, has a pain aspect, most human beings in America eat their meals before serious privation of food has occurred. In this case the motivating drive experienced is not the pain in the stomach, but the pleasant anticipation of tasting, chewing, and swallowing nutritious food. It is a patent observation that the young child learns quite gradually to enjoy adult food. By letting him taste tiny portions for himself, he eventually acquires a drive for conventional eating experiences. As usually manifested, the adult hunger drive arises from experience. The sex drive and hunger drive are intensified by the experience of pleasurable feelings accompanying their satisfaction. The drive for any experience is augmented if a pleasant feeling tone accompanies the experience.

In the case of sex and hunger drives, the physiological mechanism given by heredity is largely responsible for producing the pleasurable experiences out of which a strong desire for more of the same emerges. The environment plays a less important role in the origin of these drives than is the case for most drives. Drives for possessions do not exist until the possessions have been perceived or at least thought about by vivid imagery or pictures. The drive to possess a camera is unknown except in a culture where cameras are used. The psychological principle involved has been given the name *adience*. The principle refers to the circumstance that the personality system seeks through its behavior to continue a stimulus once encountered.

In terms of what is psychically experienced in the acquiring of a drive for a camera, first the camera is seen, which leaves an idea of what was experienced. Initially this is simply an idea of a camera, something which can be thought about. After repetition, the idea of the camera acquires a more dominant character. It is linked in time and place with other experiences of the individual. When present, these other experiences recall the idea of a camera. When the idea has acquired a strong tendency to be recalled and is at the same time unfulfilled, it acquires the status of a desire. If its counterpart, picture taking, is absent, there is a conflict between the desire and the experience which leaves it unrealized. This conflict is accompanied by discomfort and restlessness until the individual's actions have been successful in securing the desired experience of a camera to take pictures. An idea which has gained the status of a desire, want, or wish, together with the underlying physiological mechanism, is usually designated as an acquired drive. What has been said of picture taking as a hobby applies to possessions generally. The desires for them are all acquired drives, not given by heredity. The most which heredity contributes is the physiological mechanism which makes perceptual experiences possible and which makes the acquisition of ideas and desires possible. But this mechanism does not prescribe what will be experienced, and consequently it does not specify what acquired drives make their appearance in the personality system.

These comments on principles of motivation may seem far removed from a consideration of religion. They are principles which have a direct application to religious drives and need to be fully understood if the acquisition of religious motivation is to be grasped. They are not only important in understanding the development of religious motives, but they are also important in understanding the type and degree of control which religion is capable of exercising over various motivations in personality, such as sexual desires or other desires involved in problems of social control.

Group Experience as a Source of Social Drives

We designate here as "social" those drives which are acquired from the experiences of living with others and interacting with them, excluding the specific patterns imposed upon personality by the cultural patterns of the group. Included among social drives are those for companionship, for social recognition and approval, and for altruistic living. While religious behavior has roots in many-sided motives, its fundamental manifestation in modern world religions is rooted in altruistic motivation. Religious motivation which has its basis in altruistic motivation is a social drive, and our major task of explanation is concerned with the relationship of this to the experiences of group living.

When companionship with people is sought as a form of possessiveness of others, to have the experience of seeing them, talking with them, and sharing their lives, the explanation for the drive is like that for other possessions. The basis for the drive for company is found in the experience which people have of each other as objects in their environment. The human infant is born into a world with people around him. Apart from what they do to minister to his needs, he soon acquires a desire for them to be present. By the age of one year, the average child is quite sensitive to whether he is left by himself, even momentarily. In early months before a child can communicate or imitate, he nevertheless gains an acute desire for company. This is a desire which is not initially learned by cultural indoctrination. While growing up, people become much affected by the emphasis which the culture of their group places upon winning friendships of others, and their desire for companionship thereby becomes reënforced by the example which others set. The enterprises of life are overwhelmingly group in nature. Throughout life most people are exposed to the company of others and in turn have a continuing drive for human companionship. The few misanthropes who crave isolation are found to be those whose experiences with others have been painful or who have grown up in situations of isolation.

Just as people experience each other as objects perceived in their environments, they experience each other's behavior expressing social recognition or social approval. These come to be especially desired because they are steps to larger opportunities and greater achievements. Rare is the human being who does not enjoy a few words of praise or acknowledgment of success, especially if sincerely given by a qualified person. The success ideology of Americans consists largely of an aim to be recognized by others for one's achievements in earning and spending money. People think they are successful if others think they are successful. The experience of what other people think is a breeding ground for a very powerful form of social motivation. The psychic environment which people's inner processes of thought and feeling provide for the individual is as important as, if not more than, the environment which people provide by being spatial objects for each other.

With this preliminary examination of the genesis of social drives, we next consider how it is that the drive to be altruistic is generated in the personality system. This is a drive acquired slowly. By a few psychopathic persons it is hardly acquired at all. It is rarely manifested in children before the age of 4 or 5 except in a superficial way. Youngsters may voluntarily share toys briefly at the age of 3. Usually not until the age of 10 or later is altruism expressed in a thoughtful, devoted manner, beyond a few friendly acts of politeness which call for little to be given up. Through preceding years the seeds of altruism are being planted and are slowly growing under normal social circumstances. Altruistic motivation was defined on pages 246–247.

C. H. Cooley: Primary-Group Experience

The theory that human personality is equipped by the experience of living in a group for altruistic participation in the group has a long history. Aristotle pointed out that man by nature is a social animal, although he offered little indication as to how man came to be that way. David Hume and Adam Smith developed insights concerning how man comes to sympathize with and act for his fellow men. In relatively recent times, C. H. Cooley, an American sociologist who worked first in economics, made great advances of clarification. In *Human Nature and the Social Order,* published in 1902, and *Social Organization,* published in 1909, he traced the genesis of altruistic sentiments to living in what he called *primary groups.* The most important of these is the family. The old rural neighborhood in which families cared for each other when in trouble is another. Play groups of children, friendship groups, and closely knit religious congregations also possess at least some qualities of primary groups. Cooley describes these qualities.

By primary groups I mean those characterized by intimate face-to-face association and cooperation. They are primary in several senses, but chiefly in that they are fundamental in forming the social nature and ideals of the individual. The result of intimate association, psychologically, is a certain fusion of individualities in a common whole, so that one's very self, for many purposes at least, is the common life and purpose of the group. Perhaps the simplest way of describing this wholeness is by saying that it is a "we"; it involves the sort of sympathy and mutual identification for which "we" is the natural expression. One lives in the feeling of the whole and finds the chief aims of his will in that feeling.

It is not to be supposed that the unity of the primary group is one of mere harmony and love. It is always a differentiated and usually a competitive unity, admitting of self-assertion and various appropriative passions; but these passions are socialized by sympathy, and come, or tend to come, under the discipline of a common spirit. The individual will be ambitious, but the chief object of his ambition will be some desired place in the thought of others, and he will feel allegiance to common standards of services and fair play. So the boy will dispute with his fellows a place on the team, but above such disputes will place the common glory of his class and school.[7]

Cooley defines human nature in terms of altruistic sentiments and other social drives. He points out that it can only arise from the experiences of living in a primary group.

By human nature, I suppose, we may understand those sentiments and impulses that are human in being superior to those of lower animals, and also in the sense that they belong to mankind at large, and not to any particular race or time. It means, particularly, sympathy and the innumerable sentiments into which sympathy enters, such as love, resentment, ambition, vanity, hero-worship, and the feeling of social right and wrong. . . .[8]

It is the nature which is developed and expressed in those simple, face-to-face groups that are somewhat alike in all societies; groups of the family, the playground, and the neighborhood. In the essential similarity of these is to be found the basis, in experience, for similar ideas and sentiments in the human mind. In these, everywhere, human nature comes into existence. Man does not have it at birth—he cannot acquire it except through fellowship, and it decays in isolation.[9]

The altruistic ideal is part of human nature and owes its origin particularly to family living where close association leads to imaginative sharing of each other's thoughts and feelings.

The ideal that grows up in familiar association may be said to be a part of human nature itself. In its most general form it is that of a moral whole or community wherein individual minds are merged and the higher capacities of the members find total and adequate expression. And it grows up because familiar association fills our minds with imaginations of the thought and feeling of other members of the group, and of the group as a whole, so that, for many purposes, we

[7] C. H. Cooley *et al., Social Organization,* Scribner, 1956, pp. 23–24.
[8] *Ibid.,* p. 28.
[9] *Ibid.,* p. 30.

really make them a part of ourselves and identify our self-feeling with them.[10]

A congenial family life is the immemorial type of moral unity, and source of many of the terms—such as brotherhood, kindness, and the like—which describe it. The members become merged by intimate association into a whole wherein each age and sex participates in its own way. Each lives in imaginative contact with the minds of the others, and finds in them the dwelling-place of his social self, of his affections, ambitions, resentments, and standards of right and wrong. Without uniformity, there is yet unity, a free, pleasant, wholesome, fruitful, common life.[11]

All mankind acknowledges kindness as the law of right intercourse within a social group. By communion minds are fused into a sympathetic whole, each part of which tends to share the life of all the rest, so that kindness is a common joy, and harshness a common pain. It is the simplest, most attractive, and most diffused of human ideals. The golden rule springs directly from human nature.[12]

Thoughts and feelings of others are shared by oneself since words and actions connected with these recall them to one's mind.

Thought and sentiment are from the first parts or aspects of highly complex and imaginative personal ideas, and of course may be reached by anything which recalls any part of those ideas. They are aroused by personal intercourse because in their origin they are connected with personal symbols. The sharing of a sentiment ordinarily comes to pass by our perceiving one of these symbols or traits of expression which has belonged with the sentiment in the past and now brings it back. And likewise with thought: it is communicated by words, and these are freighted with the net result of centuries of intercourse. Both spring from the general life of society and cannot be separated from that life, nor it from them.[13]

Cooley cautions against arbitrarily dividing actions into two classes, egoistic and altruistic, since all actions stem from a mixture of motives, never pure in quality.

The egoism-altruism way of speaking falsifies the facts at the most vital point possible by assuming that our impulses relating to persons are separable into two classes, the I impulses and the You impulses, in much the same way that physical persons are separable; whereas a primary fact throughout the range of sentiment is a fusion of persons, so that the impulse belongs not to one or the other, but precisely to the

[10] *Ibid.*, p. 33.
[11] *Ibid.*, p. 34.
[12] *Ibid.*, p. 40.
[13] C. H. Cooley, *Human Nature and the Social Order,* Free Press, 1956, p. 139.

common ground that both occupy, to their intercourse or mingling. Thus the sentiment of gratitude does not pertain to me as against you, nor to you as against me, but springs right from our union, and so with all personal sentiment. Special terms like egoism and altruism are presumably introduced into moral discussions for the more accurate naming of facts. But I cannot discover the facts for which these are supposed to be names.[14]

Cooley prefers not to use the term *altruism,* which for him has a categorical connotation he does not like. But it is apparent that the sentiments he describes are those placed here under the heading of altruistic motivation.

It is notable, however, that there are, after all, some ideas of right that are practically universal. Here, for example, are three things that all tribes, so far as I can discover, regard as obligatory:

1. Loyalty to the group. Dante's judgment that traitors belong in the lowest pit of Hell expresses a universal sentiment of mankind.
2. Kindness to members of the group.
3. Adherence to the customs of the tribe.

These are universal because they spring from universal conditions of social life. All men live in co-operating groups, and without loyalty and kindness they cannot co-operate successfully.[15]

Recapitulating features of the process by which Cooley states that altruistic sentiments arise from primary group life, the following may be stated: The words and actions of others in a primary group recall thoughts and sentiments with which these have become associated in one's own psychic experience and behavior. Coöperation requires the individual, in G. H. Mead's terms, "to take the role of the other" in his imagination. Through face-to-face coöperation, the individual repeatedly experiences the personalities of others. This recall of thoughts of others' feelings is the essential nature of the experience of sympathy. The result of sympathy is that the feelings, needs, and aspirations of the group become a part of one's own personality system. One acts altruistically toward the group to which one belongs. One's sense of right and wrong is an application of altruistic feelings toward members of the group.

Comments on Cooley's Views

As Cooley describes the process of formation of altruistic motivation, some additional details and qualifications may be noted.

[14] *Ibid.,* p. 128.
[15] *Ibid.,* p. 401.

1. If the behavior of others simply recalled psychic material with which this behavior was associated from one's own psychic experience, then the behavior of others would recall, not the needs of others, but one's own needs. While the latter undoubtedly occurs in children and is manifested by jealousy, the point apparently is that what is recalled by the behavior of others is an idea of their psychic experience, differentiated from one's own. The differentiation is a consequence of sympathetically experiencing the lives of others as well as one's own.

2. According to the principle of adience previously described, the result of the experience of sympathizing with others would be the acquiring of a desire for more experience of sympathizing with others. This is the essence of companionship. The desire for human company is not a desire simply to listen or look at someone, but is a desire to share the other's psychic world. However, altruistic desire is different from a desire for companionship. When altruism motivates the personality system one not only listens sympathetically to the troubles of others; one does something about them. How does the desire to sympathize become the desire to help?

At least two principles seem to be involved in the answer to this question. One of them is that the habit associations established between an awareness of one's own needs and doing something about them cause one who is aware of the needs of others to act involuntarily to help them. The older child who sees a small child wander toward a crowded boulevard reacts as he would to save his own life. He at once pulls the child away from danger. The experience of helping others in the primary group is almost inseparable from membership in it. Out of this experience, by the principle of adience, develops a desire to be helpful.

A second principle is one which is involved in the acquiring of desires for the means to things which are desired. Under the influence of drives, behavior proceeds in a manner which eliminates faulty responses which interfere with obtaining what satisfies the drive. The result is that the experience of successful responses prevails in place of the experience of unsuccessful responses. The drive is acquired for possessing an appropriate means, for example, money, while the experience of debt comes to be avoided. As was previously pointed out, the desire for recognition and approval by the group grows because these things are important means to one's own aims. Of great importance to satisfying one's own desires is the well-being of others. Individual welfare is inseparable from family welfare, and therefore family welfare becomes an aim of the growing individual. Moreover, the child soon learns that in society, as well as in the family, he receives benefits in return for the aid which he gives others. The child is immersed in a continuing experience of living for others from which the altruistic drive stems.

These refinements in Cooley's theory are principles which require study and documentation by factual studies. The relative importance of different principles in producing altruistic motivation can only be adequately assessed through specially designed studies of child development in which the effect of each generating variable is separately examined. Nevertheless, Cooley's main conclusion concerning the genesis of altruistic ideals in primary-group living seems soundly established.

An implication of this conclusion is that altruistic motivation is a universal characteristic, present throughout the human race, since everywhere people live in primary groups.

Writing fifty years ago, he indicated that this motivation is the criterion for judging social systems, and that it is the driving force of progress.

> Life in the primary groups gives rise to social ideals which, as they spring from similar experiences, have much in common throughout the human race. And these naturally become the motive and test of social progress. Under all systems men strive, however blindly, to realize objects suggested by the familiar experience of primary association.
>
> Where do we get our notions of love, freedom, justice and the like which we are ever applying to social institutions? Not from abstract philosophy, surely, but from the actual life of simple and widespread forms of society, like the family or the play-group. In these relations mankind realizes itself, gratifies its primary needs, in a fairly satisfactory manner, and from the experience forms standards of what it is to expect from more elaborate association. Since groups of this sort are never obliterated from human experience, but flourish more or less under all kinds of institutions, they remain an enduring criterion by which the latter are ultimately judged.[16]

Traditional religious leaders have objected both to the tracing of religious motivation to heredity and to ascribing it to group living. They would feel happier if the universality of religion were grounded in a supernatural God. Yet it seems immaterial whether the universality of the springs of religion is guaranteed by revelation or heredity or group life. The important thing is

[16] Cooley, *Social Organization, op. cit.,* p. 32.

not so much how religious traits come to be, but rather the fact that they exist in personality.

We have yet to analyze the progression in personality growth from altruism to religious behavior. This is less a question of motivating drives than it is one of beliefs about the nature of these drives and how they are to be cultivated by religious exercise. We leave the analysis of full religious growth to a later section and continue instead with an examination of factors which augment or diminish the growth of altruistic motivation.

Effects of Family Interaction on Altruistic Motivation

It is apparent that altruism does not equally manifest itself in all members of primary groups. Altruistic motivation is sometimes overshadowed by antisocial impulses, as in psychopathic criminals. Even these usually have loyalties to friends or gangs, which constitute primary groups of a kind. As Jung shows, such motivation may be dormant, gaining a place only in the dream life of the individual.

Perhaps the most obvious variable affecting altruistic growth is isolation from primary-group life. But this isolation is infrequently imposed by physical circumstance. Virtually all people are born into a family group and soon find play groups in the neighborhood. Institutional care of children born out of wedlock is now an uncommon and archaic practice, provision for adoption or foster-home placement having become standard procedure in social welfare. Yet membership in a family may be more illusory than real. If the child is rejected and mistreated, he grows up in a world of psychological isolation. Altruistic motivation grows out of the experience of sympathetic sharing of the lives of others. Where pain is encountered, the child is reluctant to think about the wants and satisfactions of others. Physical punishment, often relied upon by misinformed parents, instead of teaching altruistic behavior has the opposite effect of isolating the child from priceless qualities of sympathetic sharing of the lives of others necessary to altruistic growth. Arousing anger blocks use of imaginative ability to understand the other's point of view. Much more important than teaching politeness with a ruler is to practice the golden rule in the home so that the child has a normal opportunity to appreciate and to share the experiences of others by sympathetic imagination.

The traditional folklore of child rearing dies hard in a supposedly scientific age. Some of the data assembled by the renowned Swiss child psychologist, Jean Piaget, depict in children's own words the adverse effect of punishment on altruistic feeling. The data to be cited are part of a series of data tracing the growth of ethical responses assembled in *The Moral Judgment of the Child.* This research work is one of a number of studies by Piaget of the development of different traits during childhood. By asking children ingeniously contrived questions about hypothetical situations, the development of their altruistic attitudes is disclosed. A pair of stories used with children of different ages were as follows:

Story A. "A boy was playing in his room, while his daddy was working in town. After a little while the boy thought he would like to draw. But he had no paper. Then he remembered that there were some lovely white sheets of paper in one of the drawers of his father's desk. So he went quite quietly to look for them. He found them and took them away. When the father came home he found that his desk was untidy and finally discovered that someone had stolen his paper. He went straight into the boy's room, and there he saw the floor covered with sheets of paper that were all scribbled over with coloured chalk. Then the father was very angry and gave his boy a good whipping."

Story B. "Now I shall tell you a story that is nearly the same, but not quite (the story is repeated shortly, except for the last sentence). Only it ends up differently. The father did not punish him. He just explained to him that it wasn't right of him. He said, 'When you're not at home, when you've gone to school, if I were to go and take your toys, you wouldn't like it. So when I'm not there, you mustn't go and take my paper either. It is not nice for me. It isn't right to do that.

"Now a few days later these two boys were each of them playing in their garden. The boy who had been punished was in his garden, and the one who had not been punished was playing in his garden. And then each of them found a pencil. It was their fathers' pencil. Then each of them remembered that his father had said that he had lost his pencil in the street and that it was a pity because he wouldn't be able to find it again. So then they thought that if they were to steal the pencil, no one would ever know, and there would be no punishment.

"Well now, one of the boys kept the pencil for himself, and the other took it back to his father. Guess which one took it back—the one who had been well punished for having taken the paper or the one who was only talked to?"[17]

Children 7 and younger nearly always stated that the boy who was punished returned his father's pencil, while the majority of the children from 8 to 12 said the boy who was not pun-

[17] Jean Piaget, *The Moral Judgment of the Child,* tr. by Marjorie Gabain, Free Press, pp. 217–218.

ished wanted to return the pencil and did so. Excerpts from questions and replies for several of the older children are of interest in showing the desire to be helpful which is eventually acquired. The data particularly show the effect in the child's mind of punishment in inhibiting the growth of altruistic motivation.

Bric, aged 8: (Which one gave it back?) The one who had not been punished. (What did he say to himself?) That he ought to give it back because his father would be pleased. (And the other one?) He kept it. (Why?) Because he didn't want to please his father. (Which of the two fathers would you like to be?) The one who explains. (And which of the two children?) The one who was not punished. . . .

Schu, aged 8: The boy who gives back the pencil is the one who has not been punished. (Why did he give it back?) Because they explained to him [about the first theft]. (Why?) Because it's a better way to make him good. (Which of the two fathers is most of a sport?) The one who explained. (And which is fairest, explaining or punishing?) Explaining. (Why did the one who was punished begin again? . . . And if they had explained to him, would he have begun again?) No. (Why?) Because he would have understood. (And wouldn't he have understood that you mustn't steal if he had been punished?) He wouldn't have understood so well. (Now listen to me carefully. I am going to change the story round a little. Let us say that things have been properly explained to both boys. But one of them was also punished, and the other one was only talked to without being punished. Which of the two gave back the pencil later on?) The one who was not punished. (Why?) Because he had understood things better than the other one. (Why did the other one do it again?) Because he hadn't understood things quite so well. (Why not?) Because he was scolded and explained to at the same time. . . .

Cla, aged 9: (Which one gave it back?) The one that his father explained to. (And what did the other say to himself?) I may as well take it. Daddy won't see. (Which of the two fathers was fairest?) The one who didn't punish. (Which is fairest, to punish or not to punish?) Not to punish. (If you had been the boy what would you have done?) I'd have given it back. (And if you had been punished?) I'd have given it back all the same. (Which boy was nicest to his father?) The one who gave back the pencil. (But ordinarily, everyday, which one is nicest to his father, the one who is punished often, or the one who is not?) The one they explain things to. (Why?) Because you don't do it again. (Which is best, to explain and then punish, or to explain and then forgive?) To explain and then forgive.[18]

Concerning the teaching of rules of behavior which parents undertake, Piaget concludes: "Where, then, do these rules come

[18] *Ibid.*, pp. 222–223.

from? Even if adults never interfered, the social relations subsisting between children would perhaps be sufficient to create them. The play of sympathy and antipathy is a sufficient cause for practical reason to become conscious of reciprocity."[19]

What is overlooked by proponents of physical punishment of children is that altruistic behavior is not a matter of habits impressed upon the personality system by coercion, but results from creating the desire in the personality system to act altruistically or at least to act in a responsible manner with due regard for the welfare of the group. The opportunity for sympathetic sharing of experiences in the home is increased if parents act in a warm, kindly manner toward their children, seeking to exchange interests and enthusiasms with them. The relationship of love in the home to the child's capacity for the experience of sympathizing with others is described by Cooley.

We grow by influence, and where we feel the presence of an influence that is enlarging or uplifting, we begin to love. Love is the normal and usual accompaniment of the healthy expansion of human nature by communion; and in turn is the stimulus to more communion. It seems not to be a special emotion in quite the same way that anger, grief, fear, and the like are, but something more primary and general, the stream, perhaps, of which these and many other sentiments are special channels or eddies.

Love and sympathy, then, are two things which, though distinguishable, are very commonly found together, each being an instigator of the other; what we love we sympathize with, so far as our mental development permits.[20]

The best seller by Dr. Benjamin Spock, *Baby and Child Care,* reflects the findings of research in child development concerning the importance of sympathy and good will toward children if their personalities are to flourish.

A great deal of study has been given to the psychology of children in the past half-century by educators, psychoanalysts, child psychiatrists, psychologists, and pediatricians. Parents have been eager to read the results; newspapers and magazines have obliged by publishing them. We have learned a great deal bit by bit: that children need the love of good parents more than anything else; that they work hard, all by themselves, to be more grown-up and responsible; that many of the ones who get into the most trouble are suffering from lack of affection rather than from lack of punishment; that children are eager to learn if they are given school projects that are right for their age and

[19] *Ibid.,* p. 229.
[20] Cooley, *Human Nature and the Social Order, op. cit.,* pp. 158–159.

are taught by understanding teachers; that some jealous feelings toward brothers and sisters and occasional angry feelings toward parents are natural and that a child does not need to feel deeply ashamed of them; that a childish interest in the facts of life and in some aspects of sex is quite normal; that too harsh a repression of aggressive feelings and a sexual interest may lead to neurosis; that unconscious thoughts are as influential as conscious ones; that each child is an individual and should be allowed to be so.[21]

Nor is it proposed that children not be suitably restrained from harmful behavior.

A child needs to feel that his mother and father, however agreeable, have their own rights, know how to be firm, won't let him be unreasonable or rude. He likes them better that way. It trains him from the beginning to get along reasonably with other people. The spoiled child is not a happy creature even in his own home. And when he gets out into the world, whether it's at 2 or 4 or 6, he is in for a rude shock. He finds that nobody is willing to kowtow to him; in fact, everybody dislikes him for his selfishness. Either he must go through life being unpopular, or he must learn the hard way how to be agreeable.[22]

Removing from the scene of possible damage, calm explanation within the child's ability to understand, and withholding of privileges as a natural consequence of wrong action are advocated as means of imposing control. The major reliance is placed upon encouraging the child to desire to act with social concern toward others.

The main source of good discipline is growing up in a loving family—being loved and learning to love in return. We want to be kind and cooperative (most of the time) because we like people and want them to like us. (Habitual criminals are people who in childhood were never loved enough to make much difference to them, and many of them were abused, besides.) A child gradually lessens his grabbing and begins to share somewhere around the age of 3 years, not primarily because he is reminded by his mother (though that may help some) but because his feelings toward other children—of enjoyment and affection—have developed sufficiently.

Another vital element is the child's intense desire to be as much like the parent as possible. He works particularly hard at being polite and civilized and responsible in the 3-to-6-year-old period. This is the time when the boy acquires much of his desire to be cooperative with men, brave in danger, courteous to women, faithful to a job, just as his father is. This is the age when a girl is inspired to be helpful in the

[21] Benjamin Spock, *Baby and Child Care*. Copyright 1945, 1946, © 1957 by Benjamin Spock, M.D. Published by Pocket Books, Inc., New York, p. 323.

[22] *Ibid.*, p. 326.

home, devoted to babies (including dolls), tender to other members of the family, just as her mother is.[23]

Some children possess more antagonistic or rebellious temperaments than other children, nor are parents uniformly self-controlled in their emotional reactions. The consequence is that some children may experience more punishment than others. Although not directly transmitted from parent to child, the emotion of anger seems to have a strong basis in hereditary constitution. Since this anger is an impediment to harmonious relationships in the home, the achievement of sympathetic experience and the development of altruistic motivation dependent upon this are thereby connected with hereditary make-up. If patiently dealt with, the tendency of a child to anger easily may come under proper self-control and no serious impediment to altruistic growth occasioned. However, parents who are uninformed or lacking in self-control themselves can readily relay these traits to a child. Antisocial behavior is thereby induced, especially if other unfavorable factors operate in the child's situation.

The psychopathic component is essentially the polar opposite of altruism. A criminologist, P. W. Tappan, has described this motivational pattern and its genesis.

The psychopath has been interpreted as deficient in inhibition through the absence of an effective, coherent *super-ego*. He is a most unsocialized aggressive child—cruel, defiant, suspicious, egocentric, unfriendly, vindictive, primitive, and hypersexual (or sexually uncontrolled). In extreme manifestations, he shows an utter lack of capacity for sympathy; he is quite without compunction for his ruthless exploitations and injuries to others. Such a person usually comes from a home situation defective in affection and control. He is an unwanted child, unloved, consistently rejected; his response is uninhibited hostility and overt aggressions. Characteristically a deprived person, his most serious deprivations are emotional. Because of the seriousness of his misbehavior and his lack of identification with others, the psychopath is a difficult problem in treatment; the therapist requires infinite patience to provide him the consistent, close, and warm understanding that he needs. His history of rebellious responses to chronic rejection makes it almost impossible to come into touch with him. Usually committed to a disciplinary institution, the psychopath merely becomes more embittered and callous. Even if he receives therapeutic attention, the structure of his personality has ordinarily been too

[23] *Ibid.*, p. 332.

rigidly fixed from his earliest days to achieve much success with him.[24]

Since the growth of a substantial amount of altruistic motivation toward others is the normal experience of most persons, case studies illustrating this growth are not dramatic. The principles involved are much more conspicuously shown by case studies of the small fraction of persons who grow up to be lawbreakers. Study of lawbreakers is limited to those who are caught, and these tend to be those who do not have wealth and influence on their side. Nevertheless, case studies of criminality have much to demonstrate concerning what does or does not produce altruistic motivation in the personality system. The following case study concerns other principles besides those involved in the formation of an altruistic disposition, but the case illustrates the psychological isolation resulting from inhumane treatment by parents. The case also shows the reclamation which is possible when the delinquent boy finally found himself in sympathetic hands.

Isaac, a boy of fourteen and one-half, with high intelligence, was committed for stealing, truancy, vandalism, sexual perversions, and general incorrigibility. He was a handsome boy who always made a good impression until people got to know him; an only child whose mother died and whose father abandoned him when he was two years old. Reluctantly cared for by relatives, he was passed from one branch of the family to another, and finally to an orphan's home. From his very infancy he presented serious behavior disorders.

In the institution he had no regard for routine or discipline; he made the most unreasonable demands. He was bitter and antagonistic, even to two people whom he professed to like, the farmer and his social worker. His pleasure in farm work was encouraged even at the expense of formal schoolwork in which he had no interest. Both these people spent a great deal of time with him, remained consistently patient and sympathetic, and made no comment on his general misbehavior. His poor behavior was discussed with him when it was directed against these two people. They would stress their desire to continue to be his friends, but would point out that behavior such as this provoked others into disliking him. Continuous exposure to this kind of handling brought out a good deal of self-blame on his part, and some expression of doubts as to his worth-whileness. He clung to these two contacts and made conscious efforts to seek their advice and to follow their guidance. As he was able to achieve some success in adjusting, higher and higher standards were presented, and he was stimulated to meet them. The farmer and the social worker fre-

[24] P. W. Tappan, *Juvenile Delinquency,* McGraw-Hill, 1949, pp. 96–97.

quently shared experiences and ideas about him. These people became not only his ideals, but his conscience.

By the end of the second year he was able to do well, but his past reputation appeared to be against him. He was tried in a new cottage and told exactly why the change was made. Progress was then more rapid, the new cottage parents supplementing his two meaningful friendships.

The social worker then helped the boy reorient himself to his own past. By eliciting memories and piecing them together, the worker was able to help the boy understand that his misconduct was a consequence of his deprivations. He was told that while these explained his bad behavior, society did not excuse it on that account.

He then became concerned about planning for his future. Farming was his vocational choice. In order to earn admission to a farm school he turned to academic schoolwork with a new interest. He went to a farm school after three years in the institution and prepared himself there for a job.

He experienced some difficulties on parole but continued to maintain his friendship with the same social worker who helped stabilize him. He succeeded in being reasonably happy and self-supporting.[25]

It seems a reasonable inference that the family disorganization which fosters criminal traits in delinquent children is responsible in a less extreme way for reducing the altruistic and spiritual growth of numerous others. Furthermore, as shown by Freud and his followers, the emotional relationships of a child to his parents involve jealousies requiring sympathetic understanding, or else lifelong anxieties and hostilities may become established. Spock describes the difficulties which children experience in their early personal relationships. These problems mean more to children than most parents realize. At the time they arise children lack insight for understanding them.

Up to this age [3 to 6], a boy's love for his mother has been predominantly of a dependent kind, like that of a baby. But now it also becomes increasingly romantic, like his father's. By the time he is 4, he's apt to insist that he is going to marry his mother when he grows up. He isn't clear just what marriage consists of, but he's absolutely sure who is the most important and appealing woman in the world. The little girl who is growing normally in her mother's pattern develops the same kind of love for her father.

These strong romantic attachments help children to grow spiritually and to acquire wholesome feelings toward the opposite sex that will later guide them into good marriages. But there is another side to the

[25] A. L. Simon and Dorothy Dunaeff, "Differential Levels in the Institutional Treatment of the Juvenile Delinquent," *National Probation Association Yearbook,* 1942, pp. 154–155. Cited in P. W. Tappan, *op. cit.,* pp. 99–100.

picture that creates a little tension in most children at this age and a lot of tension in a few. When a human male, old or young, loves a woman very much, he can't help wanting her all to himself. He can't help feeling jealous of the love that exists between her and some other man. And so, of course, the boy of 3 and 4 and 5, as he becomes more aware of his possessive devotion to his mother, also becomes aware of how much she already belongs to his father. This irritates him underneath, no matter how much he loves and admires his father. At times he secretly wishes his father would get lost, and then he feels guilty about such disloyal feelings. Reasoning as a child does, he imagines that his father has the same jealous and resentful feelings toward him. He tries to push these scary thoughts out of his mind since his father, after all, is so much bigger and stronger, but they are apt to come to the surface in his dreams. We believe that these mixed feelings—of love, jealousy, and fear—toward the father are the main cause of the bad dreams that little boys of this age are so apt to have —of being chased by giants, robbers, gorillas, and other frightening figures.

The little girl, if she is developing normally, also becomes more possessive in her love for her father. She wishes at times that something would happen to her mother (whom she loves so much in other respects) so that she could have her father for herself. She may even say to her mother, "You can go away for a long trip, and I'll take good care of Daddy." But then she imagines that her mother is jealous of her, too, and subconsciously worries about this.[26]

Religious therapy is valuable in overcoming emotional instabilities derived from childhood or from hereditary tendency. The analysis of these involves a large area of personality study beyond the scope of an introductory chapter. Roots in childhood of emotional instability and corrective influences of religion have been analyzed with case studies in recent volumes by L. D. Weatherhead and by P. E. Johnson.[27]

We quote from one of Weatherhead's cases showing how deprivation of love in childhood took away capacity for love and led to making excessive demands on others.

The patient, a woman now in the fifties, was the first-born child of Mr. and Mrs. X. There was some disappointment that she was not a

[26] Spock, *op. cit.*, pp. 358–359.

[27] L. D. Weatherhead, *Psychology, Religion and Healing,* Abingdon, 1952; P. E. Johnson, *Personality and Religion,* Abingdon, 1957. An autobiographical account of mental disorder by one who has devoted himself to spiritual recovery of the mentally ill is given by A. T. Boisen in *The Exploration of the Inner World,* Harper, 1936. Also of interest is his *Religion in Crisis and Custom,* Harper, 1955. Of major importance in religion and psychotherapy is the work of C. G. Jung to which an introduction has been given in this text.

boy, and this the patient clearly apprehended from an early age. With her father she was a great favorite, but from the first she had very little belief in her mother's love. When the patient was six years of age, she was sent to boarding school and her parents went to China. Life at boarding school was hard. In those days canings were frequent. All letters were censored. The patient remembers having to rewrite her letters to China, so as to make her parents believe she was happy. The schoolmistress was neurotic and sadistic. At times—while the parents were on furlough in England, for instance—the patient was spoilt at school. But for long periods she was most harshly treated and caned unmercifully on the naked body for the most trivial faults.

By the time her parents returned to England to live, they had had a second child, a much desired son. Eagerly the patient awaited her parents coming to fetch her home to live with them. How desperately she longed for a mother! But when the great day came, the mother, who admittedly had lived without her first child for six years, said to her, "Why, I'd almost forgotten I'd got you." It was a fatal remark to make. And its implications were lived up to. It was always the son who was praised and she who was blamed. The former was "the light of his mother's eyes," and "Mummy's good little boy."

The patient still vividly remembers how her mother used to read to the two children on Sunday evenings. The mother always had her right arm around the younger child. With her left hand she held her book. The girl felt excluded, left out of the symbolized love relation of the embracing arm. So, in her own words, she "played up." The puzzled mother wondered why her son enjoyed Bible stories while her daughter hated them. But what the girl hated was the situation in which, rightly or wrongly, she *felt* deprived of love. Again, the younger child was invited to say his prayers at his mother's knee. The girl said hers alone. She still remembers a score of incidents in which she *felt* unloved. . . .

One of the patient's symptoms was a fierce jealousy. Jealousy is made up of two ingredients: the desire to be loved and the fear that love will be withheld. Often the measure of the jealousy is the measure both of the desire for love and the fear of its being withheld. People who have always been loved are not usually jealous because they are not afraid of losing love. The patient whose case I have given fully, because it so clearly illustrates this part of my argument, was jealous almost until her recent death, because the fear of the return of misery, consequent on thinking that she was not really loved, had so strongly implanted itself.

Secondly, she developed not only jealousy, but what might be called the "martyr complex." She really sought ways of being "miserable" because then, perchance, others would sympathize with, or pity her. And pity and sympathy are love-substitutes, but, of course, they have to be called out by misery. A happy, healthy person, with no hardships, calls out no pity or sympathy. Although wealthy, moderately healthy and without a need in the world, she could always recite some story of mishap, inconvenience, ill-health or grievance, which would draw pity from spectators.

Thirdly, she would develop a self-immolation to an almost unbelievable degree. She would work from morning till night, and though tired out would never rest. Rest calls forth no pity, overwork does. At all costs, she must get love or one of its many substitutes. Of course, she did not wistfully ask for love. Love had deceived her, so she would never try it or trust it again. But by fierce self-persecution, in martyrdom or immolations, she would seek its substitutes. People truly loved her. But she rarely believed them or that their love was genuine and for her own sake. She insisted that it was for some other reason! This is the genuine reaction-character-trait.[28]

In this case childhood experiences intensified the desire to receive love and obliterated the desire to give love. Whether a drive is intensified or eliminated depends upon whether it is strong or weak during deprivation and upon whether the frustration is partial or complete.

Still another phase of religious development is provided by the patterning of theological beliefs after experiences with parents. Freud has shown how God performs the role of a parental substitute after a child reaches maturity. The kind of a God in whom the person believes is modeled after the parents he has known in early life. A tyrannical father is replaced by an authoritarian, unforgiving God. A kind and loving father lays the basis for belief in a benevolent God. These brief references to development in psychoanalysis indicate the extensive connection of religious aims and beliefs with patterns of social interaction in the home during early childhood. The family as a primary group is the cradle in which the basic patterns of personality, including religious ones, are shaped. While a few good citizens come out of all homes, a warm, friendly home atmosphere seems of unquestionable value in encouraging the growth of altruistic ideals in each fresh generation of human beings.

Disorganization in the Social Order as an Impediment to Altruistic Growth

Social welfare workers seeking to improve the quality of American family living are impressed by the way in which family disorganization reflects the larger disorganization of society.

[28] From *Psychology, Religion and Healing,* by Leslie D. Weatherhead, pp. 345–347. Copyright 1951 by Pierce and Smith. By permission of Abingdon Press.

When race is set against race and hardly a major American city is immune from race riots, the effects upon families, both white and Negro, involved in the maelstrom of conflict cannot be other than unfavorable. When homes are broken temporarily by service overseas or permanently by casualties in war, the orphans who remain are deprived of their share of primary-group living. This applies much more to nations other than the United States who have borne the brunt of war.

What about economic disorganization? The recurring serious business depressions which agitated the American economy appeared for a time to have come to an end with the Great Depression of the 1930's. But as these lines are written, the American economy is again in the trough of a continuing depression. What if the jobless number only five million? Is this not five million families where economic catastrophe has struck? What of the many more millions for whom job insecurity is a gnawing threat? Is viable religious growth possible for those in such situations? While cases can be cited of those who have been spurred by adversity to greater religious growth, what of those who go down in spiritual defeat before the economic blows they experience? Can it be seriously advocated that a spiritually great society can be built upon an immoral social order?

In the years since World War II, a protest literature of best sellers has made its appearance on the American scene. These include: *The Lonely Crowd,* by David Riesman[29]; *The Organization Man,* by W. H. Whyte[30]; *The Hidden Persuaders* and *The Status Seekers,* by Vance Packard[31]; *White Collar* and *The Power Elite,* by C. W. Mills[32]; and *The Affluent Society,* by J. K. Galbraith.[33] Not since the stringent days of the Great Depression has such insistent and penetrating criticism been directed against the American economic way of life. The criticisms are not the traditional Marxian ones that the capitalist economy is doomed to end in a vast collapse at home or to exhaust itself in endless wars abroad. The federal government has through the years instituted a large measure of regulation and has demonstrated its ability to step in when required to keep the economic wheels revolving.

29 David Riesman, *The Lonely Crowd,* Doubleday, 1953.

30 W. H. Whyte, Jr., *The Organization Man,* Simon and Schuster, 1957.

31 Vance Packard, *The Hidden Persuaders,* Pocket Books, 1958; *The Status Seekers,* McKay, 1959.

32 C. W. Mills, *White Collar,* Oxford, 1956; *The Power Elite,* Oxford, 1957.

33 J. K. Galbraith, *The Affluent Society,* Houghton Mifflin, 1958.

Instead, the criticisms are directed at a commercial culture whose values and aims in life are sick, whose way of doing things is inhumane, and whose promotion exploits the minds of the children and the weak. The literature is a dynamic echo of the nineteenth-century criticisms of early industrial capitalism. Those criticisms were concerned with physical abuse of women and children in mines and factories. Today the criticisms are predominantly concerned with psychological damage to human personality in the worker and the consumer. These criticisms are of deepest concern to students of the religious scene in American culture.

The Lonely Crowd, by a leading sociologist, speaks of the mass of the lonely cogs lost in a vast social machine for whom economic meaning in life has become destroyed. *The Organization Man,* by an editor for the most prominent business publication in America, *Fortune,* tells of how corporations seeking greater profit demand of their employees behavior which goes counter to their conscientious feelings. *The Hidden Persuaders,* by an expert in marketing research, describes in detail how the minds of children and adults alike are misled and corrupted in the quest to sell more goods. *The Status Seekers* decries the futility of life spent on the treadmill of social climbing. In *White Collar* and *The Power Elite,* an influential sociologist at Columbia describes the deleterious influence of the dominant economic and political class over the way of life of Americans. In his writings, Mills articulates the mass stereotype of the "cheerful robot" who is satisfied to be another wheel in a purposeless machine. From a religious standpoint, this person is an aimles automaton whose mechanical grin masks the spiritual hunger within. *The Affluent Society,* by a distinguished professor of economics at Harvard, describes the predominant economic motivation of American men and women, a motivation which is opulent and wasteful. These things require thoroughgoing reappraisal of American economic organization.

Beyond this psychological damage is the mounting voice of those who decry the use of injurious insecticides and the adulteration of foods with harmful or questionable preservatives or flavorings. Their appeal has literally become, "All we want is to get our food before the insecticide sprayer, the chemist, or the food processor does." In the use of harmful food preservatives, they see the issue as one of "shelf life versus human life." Ridiculed as food faddists, such persons seek no more than the enactment of adequate laws which many nations already have to safeguard the consumer. While some improvement in federal action has occurred since 1958, inspection is still inadequate. America, with a standard of living higher than any country of the world, lags behind a half-dozen countries of Western Europe in the length of life of her citizens. Her higher death rates from cancer and heart disease are directly attributable by leading medical authorities to abuse of the human physique by noxious substances. Towering above all else is the world-wide disorganization induced by the recurring threat of atomic war and the continued poisoning of the atmosphere by radioactive dust.

To avoid mentioning these impediments to altruistic and religious growth in a textbook about religion would be either hypocritical or ostrichlike. Since the days of the ancient Jews, health and rules for eating have been of concern to religious societies. A New York clergyman, Rev. R. J. McCracken, declared in an address: "There is a creed of hygiene. There is a religion of sanitation. There is a morality of diet. It is a religious duty to maintain health. Eating and drinking, sleeping and waking and exercise are not outside the province of religion. They are as much a part of it as prayer and worship and daily work. They vitally effect temper and temperament and the way people look at the world. A healthy body makes for a healthy mind and a healthy soul. It is essential to the finest and fullest kind of life."[34]

As far as religious growth is concerned, the abuses described have their impact upon the quality of family living, and in turn affect the cultivation of primary-group ideals Cooley has analyzed. Besides this effect, the larger question arises of opportunity for expressing altruistic motivation. A basic principle of personality development is that motivation grows in the direction of opportunities for its expression. As a plant seeks the areas of nutritious soil and moisture, human personality is sensitive in its growth to areas of self-expression.

What happens to altruistic sentiments kindled in family living if these confront a social order where the means of livelihood unavoidably injures worker and consumer? As far as altruism in economic life is concerned, it seems obvious that it risks being extinguished. What residue is left can be expressed in family and friendship relationships. This is a tattered remnant of the motivational fabric which might find its full meaning in identification with a world-wide social order of brotherhood. This is of serious consequence to religion whose spiritual motivation

[34] Quoted in M. Shefferman, *Foods for Longer Living,* Whittier, 1956, p. 109.

is inseparable from altruistic motivation. The blocking of altruistic opportunity means a stifling of spiritual development.

Some personalities, like fighting salmon, swim upstream, hurtling the dams and by-passing contaminated rivers, until the fresh, cool waters of spiritual self-realization are achieved. This places large demands on the individual's personality. He aligns himself with social-action organizations. These organizations are ones which seek to build a social order in which racial discrimination, class strife, abuse of the consumer, psychological mistreatment of the employee, and the specter of atomic war finally become no more than frightening memories from the past. By swimming upstream, the altruistic motivation used becomes intensified through use. To fail to follow its leading is to invite decay in altruistic goals.

In pointing out the connections of religion with social malaise, this is not the place to examine in detail the causes and remedies for the difficulties which afflict an economically wealthy society. The interested reader is referred to books such as the seven previously cited or to more thorough study made possible by courses in economics, government, and sociology. The conclusion is unmistakable that the transformed society must be one which affords people the vital realization that they are working for each other and for the good of all, not against each other's life, liberty, and happiness.

This concludes our treatment of the ways in which the experiences of living in a primary group or world-wide society appear to channel the processes of personality growth. Another source of constituents for personality development remains to be reviewed. This source is cultural experience. In connection with this ground for personality growth, analysis of the effects of economic values and ideas is needed. The topic of cultural influences was introduced in citing literature about economic disorganization. We turn from the effects caused by interaction with economic society to those imprinted by the culture of this society upon personality.

CULTURAL EXPERIENCE

We have already pointed out that the social environment of the individual consists of people acting, thinking, talking, and feeling, and that this environment has two aspects, depending upon the kind of effect upon personality which is being considered. If the effect is to transmit the culture of the group directly, we call the experience of the social environment *cultural.* If the effect is to expand or restrict opportunities for learning what is in culture, the experience is called *group* to distinguish it from simple cultural influences upon personality.

Definition of Culture

The concept of culture is one which has occupied a conspicuous role in the social sciences since the work of E. B. Tylor in establishing the field of cultural anthropology almost a century ago. It is a concept of great importance. Culture is responsible for complex developments in personality growth which are learned from the group's own ways of thinking and acting. Culture includes the accumulated storehouse of ways of thinking and acting which have arduously been discovered, passed along, and added to by successive generations. It represents the prized possession of mankind which, if it were obliterated and forgotten, might require another million years for its re-creation. The earliest human beings or their predecessors in a subhuman species had no one to teach them how to read or write, for nothing was written. Writing itself had to be worked out by men who did not themselves know how to write. The slow transition from crude pictures to shorthand marks probably required many centuries. The accomplishment of written religious literature is an event only a few thousands years old. Early human beings literally came into a world without anyone to teach them, and what they learned was gained by a slow and intermittent process. Gradually bits of learning made their appearance and could be passed along by word of mouth to the coming generation. Without the possibilities which writing affords in storing information, the amount of culture which could be accumulated was limited. Especially where complex abstractions are involved, the amount of accumulation was severely restricted, possibly remaining at a static point for hundreds of thousands of years in nonmaterial matters such as religion. Toolmaking would fare better, since the visible evidence of tool improvements would endure for succeeding generations to build upon in making additional improvements.

These peculiarities of culture require being stressed if the overwhelming contribution of culture to the development of religious traits in personality is to be appreciated. Religion is an affair of extraordinary complexity. Were it not for its crystallization in culture, especially written culture, it seems doubtful whether the individual personality could undergo much development of latent religious motivations and capacities. While the roots of religion can be traced to heredity and group life, the particular form which it takes is almost entirely a cultural phenomenon. Of course culture has its limits. Cornstalks do not emerge from the roots of a radish. But whether either cornstalks or radish leaves make their appearance depends very largely upon the aid which culture gives in stimulating growth. The accumulated wisdom of religious culture is of paramount consequence for the full development of religious personality. But unaided by culture, overt religious development of the individual is almost nil, if its existence can be shown at all. As Jung has shown, those who reject religion still manifest embryonic seeds of religious development in their dream life. But nothing comes of these until culture intervenes to bring them to spiritual flower.

To put the matter more concretely, sex is a form of behavior in which individuals can experiment and learn without depending upon what their culture may teach them. Religion is a form of behavior in which individuals can gain little or nothing by their efforts alone, but must associate themselves with schools, teachers, or at least the writings of others who can aid individuals in their religious development. Marriage manuals facilitate the learning of sexual procedure, but many persons do without such manuals. It would be unthinkable to practice religion without depending upon religious literature or at least oral teaching as a source and guide for understanding. The contribution of culture to development of religious personality is very large. Altruism kindled by primary-group living alone falls as short of religious behavior as does maternal care differ from a prayer meeting. The difference in personality development is spelled out by culture.

It is well to have a concise definition of culture before us in order that its role in personality development can be fully seen. In a broad way, culture has sometimes been defined as the way of life of the group. This way of life refers to the totality of values, norms, modes of thinking, and ways of acting which are shared by members of the group. By a *group* is not meant simply a number of people, but rather those who participate in a common society or system of social organization. The beliefs, wants, and expectations which people have concerning each other define for them their system of social organization. Culture, therefore, is the basic setting in which organized activities of the group are grounded. The concept of culture includes the social structure of the group. The way of life of human beings has largely been accumulated from the past, but not entirely so. Actions which stem directly from hereditary stimulation often have very little cultural component. A more restricted definition of culture limits it to those features of the way of life of the group which have been accumulated from past generations. Limited in this way, the concept of culture is an abstraction from concrete human reality. Also to be included in culture are the additions which each individual or generation makes to what has been learned from preceding patterns.

It is important to realize that culture is not a set of unrelated discoveries passed along to the next generation. Animals discover answers to problems by trial and error, and offspring are often aided by imitating adult members of the species. The key which divides the way of life of animals from that of humans is that animals do not build on the discoveries of their forebears. Accordingly, the discoveries by animals are extremely simple and unelaborated. For that matter, animals reared in isolation can rediscover any of the things which they might learn by imitation. In contrast, the culture human beings now possess could not possibly be rediscovered by any individual in his lifetime. Human culture consists of discoveries built on discoveries, built on still other discoveries, and so on in a vast series of dependent innovations. The essence of culture is the side of human life which has been invented by numerous contributors and accumulated through enormous spans of time. Each generation is faced with the task, voluntarily or involuntarily assumed, of communicating this accumulated storehouse to the next generation. The problem of transmitting religious thinking and behavior to each succeeding generation is a very considerable one, and we find it necessary to give considerable attention to it.

Means of Transmitting Culture: Imitation

Imitation means quite simply that a pattern presented by the group is duplicated in one's own thinking, motivation, or behavior. This is an obviously basic means for transmitting cultural patterns. Persons reared in Judaism become Jews, those growing up in Catholicism become Catholics, and those living in Protestantism become Protestants. However, the different forms of imitation are fairly detailed and extensive treatises in psychology have been written about them. In order to discern the particular ways in which religion is imitatively acquired, we will note several common ways in which imitation takes place.

The simplest and earliest to affect personality development is involuntary imitation. A young child day after day sees his mother pick up a broom and sweep with it. Then one day the toddling child sees the broom in the corner, picks it up, and moves it back and forth in a sweeping motion. The child did not say to himself: "Now I am going to copy Mommy." Rather, his response is an impulsive, involuntary one. The establishment of the response can be traced as follows. First, he has come to associate the experience of seeing his own limbs in motion with the experience of muscular movement. Seeing another move in a particular way tends to evoke the same pattern of action in himself. Secondly, he associates seeing the broom with seeing his mother sweep with it. The result of these two links of association is that when he sees the broom on some new occasion, he recalls the mental picture of sweeping with it, and perhaps verbalizes this picture out loud. "Sweep, sweep." The mental picture in turn evokes his own activity of sweeping with the broom. In this elementary way innumerable bits of behavior, such as holding a hymnbook and appearing to sing from it, are learned by a small child.

At a more advanced stage of imitation, the child does not see the object and the action, such as putting out a fire with water. He hears others tell of fire and of dashing water on it. At a later time he sees leaves burning, and comes and pours water on them. In this type of imitation, the cultural pattern is presented by means of verbal symbols which evoke pictures in his mind, rather than by direct perception. How to behave in church is explained to the child before going. When he is in church, the pattern established by the verbal symbols is then evoked. If the verbal suggestion has been effective, he moves quietly to his place and sits still until the religious service is over.

Suggestions are planted by means of concrete actions, as well as by words. The cues presented by what others are doing guide the child's pattern of behavior. Not only his actions, but his thinking and his desires are directed by suggestions from others. Seeing cartoons and plays on television is a powerful stimulant of motives associated with what is seen. By witnessing such audiovisual material, the child's own motivation becomes deepened and developed in particular directions. If the material suggests antisocial motivation, that motivation is instilled. If, instead, socially approved motivation is inculcated, this motivation is the result. But the influence of television should not be overestimated. The kinds of programs which children like to watch are ones which represent motivations and feelings already coursing in the psychic life of children. If they secretly wish to circumvent authority, they can do so vicariously by watching "outlaws" gain victory over stupid law-enforcement officers. The implication for religious development is that watching religious scenes or growing up in a group which practices religion facilitates the development of religious motivation, but only to the extent that latent tendencies toward such motivation are already functioning in the child's personality.

As the child becomes older, goal-directed imitation plays a dominant role. In order to achieve the rewards and successes of adult living, the youngster reaching his teens becomes very conscious of whether his manners, dress, and speech are like those of others. When considered for inclusion in a peer group, he even tries to express the same political and religious attitudes and ideas. He wants very much to belong by being like others in every detail of his being.

The mechanism in voluntary imitation is more complicated. It involves, first of all, the goal of duplicating the pattern presented by others. Secondly, this goal or the motivations behind it call forth responses approximating the pattern. The responses continue by trial and error until the pattern achieved satisfactorily duplicates the pattern presented by the group. The altar boy who strives for the approval of his priest or his family practices the routine again and again until his part closely conforms to the part he is expected to play in the religious service.

The two forms of imitation so far described involve a rearrangement of response units already possessed by the individual. It is this prior possession which makes possible copying the pattern of behavior of others. The precise rearrangement needed to draw with a crayon or depress the keys on the piano requires practice to learn the combination of responses needed. Advanced levels of art are like religion in requiring deeper development. The processes of imitation so far described contribute little to an understanding of religious development of personality. The reason is that the most basic aspects of religious thinking and motivation cannot be acquired through simple forms of imitation. What to do on Jewish high holidays or how outwardly to deport oneself in church can be copied from others. But what to think and how to feel on these occasions are gained only after long study and religious exercise.

In the case of fundamental features of religious development of personality, new psychic experiences are gained. These do not consist simply in a rearrangement of psychic material which the individual already possesses. They consist rather in the acquiring of new content, as well as reorganization of old. Since the content is new in the individual's experience it cannot be represented by the group to the individual seeking to possess it. He must, with the aid of the group, discover it in his own psychic experience. The group, so to speak, induces its appearance in his own life. This way of transmitting culture leads to duplication of the thought and motivational patterns of others, but the duplication is more creative than mechanical. It makes possible sharing a common psychic life of the group.

This way of acquiring culture differs radically from what is ordinarily thought of as imitative behavior. Essentially what is involved is the differentiation of psychic experience into components of which the individual was not previously aware. This differentiation is the basis for a wide variety of types of personality growth. Most education consists in aiding the individual to move from one level of abstract thought to another, as in mathematics, physical science, or social science. This education begins in the earliest grades with the first manipulation of numbers and continues with increasing detail and complexity as long as one is able to learn. The skills employed in music, art, and literature also require the generation of abstract ideas. Not only ideas, as tools of thoughts, but ideas as compelling goals also evolve by processes of abstraction out of concrete social experiences. The motivations in religion, as well as the principles of belief, are gained by the individual undergoing growth in concepts from one level of psychic experience to another. By becoming associated with actions or symbols, latent and unconscious religious motives become differentiated and approach consciousness. Out of the raw experiences of altruism induced by primary-group living is developed an awareness of God or a higher power and of the qualities which this power possesses. What is done by the group is to teach the procedure whereby the new psychic material is to be gained. After applying the procedure the individual achieves psychic results similar to those of others.

Influence of Commercialized Culture

Different sectors of culture impose different effects on personality. Those expressing egoism, self-indulgence, and pleasure seeking bereft of social concern build up one side of personality.

Those which express the highest ideals and deepest altruistic sentiments of mankind build up another. However, the roots of each type of culture are found in social and biological experiences. The role which culture plays is to intensify or diminish motivations already present in the personality system.

The competition between motives supporting religion and those which undermine it is as old as history. The ancient Jews, among other forerunners of contemporary religion, personified motives inimical to spiritual attainment as "Adam" and as the devil. The priests of ancient times focused their religious efforts directly on deleterious motivation psychically experienced by the individual and much less on cultural patterns of others which might mislead the individual.

Of course the individual was warned against temptation by irreligious persons and told to avoid the cultural patterns of Sodom. The wife of Lot, who dared look back at that corrupt city, was turned into a pillar of salt. But stability of the personality system was jeopardized primarily from within, and it was within where religious salvation was worked out in an accommodation between man's spiritual and biological demands. Love was fulfilled, not in fornication or adultery, but in the lasting devotion of man and wife to each other.

With the rise of industrial civilization a new cultural phenomenon with profound implications for religious development has made its appearance. This is the use of mass media to sell goods. Advertising for mass consumption is scarcely a hundred years old. It was made possible, first, by the invention of printing and pictorial reproduction, and more recently by movies, radio, and television. Use of advertising is demanded by those who wish to sell more goods than their competitors. Whatever psychological appeal will persuade the consumer to buy is used. Rarely are religious or altruistic appeals used to sell goods. Almost entirely the appeals are to food, sex, smoking, drinking, luxury, conspicuous consumption, and material success. For the most part, these are shabby values to grace an affluent civilization which might have spiritual depth instead. We have today in advertising a widespread and unrelenting influence seeking to intensify motivations often hostile or at best neutral toward motivations cultivated by religion. This is done to make money whether the welfare of human personality is served or not. It is now possible, in a sense new in history, to speak of the influence of commercialized culture on personality. This is culture deliberately constructed and administered to motivate the consumer. Formerly the influence of culture was mostly limited to casual example. True, persons in the Middle Ages and in ancient times paid money to see plays, engendering commercial influences upon motivation. Before these, there were tribal raconteurs who sought to gain popularity by the stories with which they regaled their hearers. But the total effect of this influence on human nature seems inconsequential compared with the influences continually pouring out through the press and over the air waves into every American home. Nor are religious leaders the only ones who are concerned at the jeopardy in which their activity is placed. Intellectual leaders concerned for sound human values are raising their voices and moving their pens in increasing numbers. The protest literature of best sellers already referred to is an indictment of the influence of commercialized culture on human personality. To this literature may be added the recent novel by A. J. Cronin, *The Northern Light,* an indictment of the immorality of daily newspapers in England. A decade ago a Russian writer, Ilya Ehrenburg, wrote a commentary on his visit to America, published in *Izvestia* and translated in *Harper's Magazine.* Of the role of mass media in shaping personality, Ehrenburg writes:

> The press, radio, and cinema are in the hands of various reliable and unreliable firms. The editor of a large provincial newspaper said to me with a sigh: "Our independent paper depends entirely on advertisements. If we were to lose our advertising, we would not last a week." The wireless stations are owned by private firms and also depend upon advertising for their existence.
>
> I was reminded again of the book I wrote many years ago about the cinema "dream factory." The American's desire to forget and divert himself by day-dreaming in the evening has given birth to a vast industry; in Hollywood mass dreams are turned out just as skillfully and quickly as tinned meat in Chicago. However, the dream factory is more dangerous than the hash factory; film producers organize the spiritual world of the average American, inculcating him with portable morals and guiding his thoughts and feelings.[35]

The techniques of mass communication are not intrinsically harmful. The harm arises in the use to which these techniques are put. Intellectual leaders in America and elsewhere are becoming convinced that a rethinking of commercialized culture is needed, notwithstanding the ready optimism of its conserva-

[35] Ilya Ehrenburg, "Ilya Ehrenburg's America," *Harper's Magazine,* December, 1946, pp. 572–573.

tive defenders. Vance Packard writes of this problem of rethinking:

Perhaps the supporters of optimism-generation in both business and government can make an impressive case for the need to preserve public confidence if we are to have peace and prosperity. But where is it leading us? What happens, actually, to public confidence when the public becomes aware (as it gradually must) that the leaders of industry and government are resolutely committed to a confidence-inspiring viewpoint, come Hell or high water?

How can you know what to believe?

It is my feeling that a number of the practices and techniques I've cited here very definitely raise questions of a moral nature that should be faced by the persuaders and the public. For example:

What is the morality of the practice of encouraging housewives to be non-rational and impulsive in buying the family food?

What is the morality of playing upon hidden weaknesses and frailties—such as our anxieties, aggressive feelings, dread of nonconformity, and infantile hang-overs—to sell products? Specifically, what are the ethics of businesses that shape campaigns designed to thrive on these weaknesses they have diagnosed?

What is the morality of manipulating small children even before they reach the age where they are legally responsible for their actions?

What is the morality of treating voters like customers, and child-customers seeking father images at that?

What is the morality of exploiting our deepest sexual sensitivities and yearnings for commercial purposes?

What is the morality of appealing for our charity by playing upon our secret desires for self-enhancement?

What is the morality of developing in the public an attitude of wastefulness toward national resources by encouraging the "psychological obsolescence" of products already in use?

What is the morality of subordinating truth to cheerfulness in keeping the citizen posted on the state of his nation?[36]

The Christian Century editorializes in "How Long Shall We Indulge Television Brutality?" in the following vein.

Television's insipid dramas are, with rare exceptions, merely thin frameworks on which to hang beatings, kickings, stabbings, shootings, bombings and every other form of violence. The slimmest pretext is used to occasion a knock-out punch, crack on the skull or kick in the groin—even by the "good guys." Television portrays violence as man's legitimate response to any situation which irks him. The rationality of this response is seldom called into question. The effect of all this on our young people has been described by the Senate subcom-

[36] Packard, *The Hidden Persuaders, op. cit.*, pp. 221–222.

> mittee to investigate juvenile delinquency. "The predominance of brutality in television is making our nation's youth insensitive to human suffering. They are becoming so accustomed to an overwhelming amount of crime and violence that death and pain are becoming meaningless," it reports. How long shall we continue to countenance the relentless indoctrination of a value system which runs counter to all we believe about the dignity of man and the sacredness of life? The time is overdue for the churches to make some massive attack on the unwillingness of television producers to observe the canons of decency or good taste. The broadcasting and film division of the National Council of Churches should lead the attack.[37]

It is possible to overestimate the psychological harm of TV and for people to overreact to its effects, especially those on children. Many programs are excellent or at least harmless. The need for control is provided by those programs which encourage poor dietary habits, invite disrespect for parental or civic authority, undermine decency and honesty, intensify race prejudice, and generally debase children's personalities. On the positive side, TV and other mass media enlarge the child's world of experience and thereby stimulate social growth. But in a neighborhood of TV sets it is difficult to deny children the opportunities to watch inferior programs, although some control can be exercised by parents over how much time their children spend before the television screen.

A powerful psychological mechanism exploited by commercial molders of personality in the quest for markets or mass audiences is the appeal to conform, to be like others, to be approved of by them. That the standards of success of others may be worse than one's own is immaterial. What counts in the conventional success story is to be regarded as a success by others. The individual succeeds if others think he succeeds. They think he succeeds if he has a longer car, a smoother lawn, more expensive delicacies on his table or more lavish clothing and furniture for display. He succeeds in the matrimonial market if he gains the most highly coveted sexual object. He succeeds in the friendship market if he has more friends and more influential friends than anyone else. The list of those who send Christmas cards is an annual audit of his friendship assets. The frequency of dinner invitations given or received is a sensitive barometer of social standing in the community. The individual whose actions are governed by what others think of him is called by Riesman

[37] "How Long Shall We Indulge Television Brutality?" *Christian Century,* May 27, 1959, p. 637.

"other-directed." The outcome of his actions is that he becomes lost in a "lonely crowd" of conformists, his life deprived of meaning and moral purpose.

These cultural observations strike at the heart of the way of life of American business. They are not to be lightly made or lightly disregarded nor is the commercialization limited to people as consumers. It is found also in the psychological control exercised by corporations over their employees. This is epitomized in the life of the "organization man," the functionary in the business corporation whose life is surrendered to its purposes in return for his livelihood. W. H. Whyte writes of the social ethic which the corporation imposes on its employees:

My charge against the Social Ethic, then, is on precisely the grounds of contemporary usefulness it so venerates. It is not, I submit, suited to the needs of "modern man," but is instead reinforcing precisely that which least needs to be emphasized, and at the expense of that which does. Here is my bill of particulars.

It is redundant. In some societies individualism has been carried to such extremes as to endanger the society itself, and there exist today examples of individualism corrupted into a narrow egoism which prevents effective co-operation. This is a danger, there is no question of that. But is it today as pressing a danger as the obverse—a climate which inhibits individual initiative and imagination, and the courage to exercise it against group opinion? Society is itself an education in the extrovert values, and I think it can be rightfully argued that rarely has there been a society which has preached them so hard. No man is an island unto himself, but how John Donne would writhe to hear how often, and for what reasons the thought is so tiresomely repeated. . . .

Held up as the end-all of organization leadership, the skills of human relations easily tempt the new administrator into the practice of a tyranny more subtle and more pervasive than that which he means to supplant. No one wants to see the old authoritarian return, but at least it could be said of him that what he wanted primarily from you was your sweat. The new man wants your soul. . . .

It is self-destructive. The quest for normalcy as we have seen in suburbia, is one of the great breeders of neuroses, and the Social Ethic only serves to exacerbate them. What is normalcy? We practice a great mutual deception. Everyone knows that they themselves are different —that they are shy in company, perhaps, or dislike many things most people seem to like—but they are not sure that other people are different too. Like the norms of personality testing, they see about them the sum of efforts of people like themselves to seem as normal as others and possibly a little more so. It is hard enough to learn to live with our inadequacies, and we need not make ourselves more miserable by a spurious ideal of middle-class adjustment. Adjustment to what? Nobody really knows—and the tragedy is that they don't realize that the so-confident-seeming other people don't know either.[38]

What is the Social Ethic which corporations follow? While some business leaders are scrupulously honest and require their associates to be equally exemplary, the larger the corporation, the more easily is a sense of personal responsibility lost. The individual becomes governed by what the business group demands of him. Much which goes on is innocuous for personality development. Illegal practices and those which violate principles of decency or fair play are the corrupting influence. The fixing of TV quiz shows and "payola" are symptomatic of the dishonest rigging of economic rewards which permeates much, if not most, of the business world. In food, steel, transportation, and almost every large area of consumer service, serious law violations have occurred in which the employee is expected to acquiesce if he wishes to hold his job. The late E. H. Sutherland, one of the nation's foremost criminologists, made an extensive study of crime in big business, published as *White-Collar Crime* in 1949. Reviewing his work, H. E. Barnes and N. K. Teeters state:

> Professor Sutherland has explored persistently the area of white-collar criminality. In his recent book *White-Collar Crime,* he carefully examines the depredations of seventy large corporations. He found that the courts had declared a total of 980 legal decisions against these giant combines. The charges included: violations in restraint of trade; misrepresentations in advertising; infringements against patents, copyrights, and trademarks; "unfair labor practices"; rebates; financial fraud and violation of trust; violations of war regulations; and other miscellaneous offenses. Although only 158, or 16 percent of the decisions listed against the seventy corporations were made in criminal court, 60 percent of the corporations had an average of 4 criminal convictions and could therefore be classed as "habitual criminals" according to the laws governing a traditional criminal.[39]

Barnes and Teeters underscore the effects of crime in business on ethical development.

> There have always been crooks and unethical men in business, the professions, and in public life. We have neglected to denounce such persons in schools, churches, homes, and other places where the public is being trained for citizenship. As a result, a large part of the population believes that illegal activity can be carried on with impunity and

[38] Whyte, *op. cit.,* pp. 439–441.

[39] H. E. Barnes and N. K. Teeters, *New Horizons in Criminology,* Prentice-Hall, 1954, pp. 10–11.

without loss of caste or prestige. But we are beginning to see that when we speak of crime and criminals this group can no longer be considered unmentionable or untouchable.

A man's most precious asset is his integrity. When those who operate a business or are in the professions lose this attribute, that loss reacts harmfully upon society as a whole. The public becomes cynical and distrustful of those they have traditionally relied upon and trusted.

This condition is a threat to our moral code. These violations of trust are undermining the faith and respect that we all have acquired in school, home, and church. Such a trend does not augur well for a democracy.

White-collar crime flows from a competitive economy and a philosophy that reveres success based almost exclusively on money and material consumption. The job of the schools, courts of justice, legislators, and a regenerated public is to wipe out this insidious philosophy.[40]

One of the spiritually demoralizing qualities of much industrial production is the preparation for waging war, not building peace. The Senate investigation of the munitions manufacturers two decades ago disclosed how their agents fomented war between rival nations in South America and even meddled in international peace conferences to block agreement to disarm.

As the Geneva conference in 1927 drew near, Mr. Shearer was prepared for it. He had already performed some publicity work in connection with an earlier conference and his views on the danger of naval armament reduction and the menace of the British Navy were pronounced. These patriotic views seemed to interest three American gentlemen—Mr. Bardo, president of the New York Shipbuilding Company, Mr. Wakeman of the Bethlehem Steel Company, and Mr. Palen, vice-president of the Newport News Shipbuilding Company. After some preliminaries Mr. Shearer was hired by these men to go to Geneva; according to his own story, to see that the United States should "get out their side of the story," at the conference, to obtain a treaty of parity, if possible, but failing that—no treaty at all.

The consideration was $25,000 a year and with some of this money Mr. Shearer went to the capital of the League of Nations, took an apartment in the exclusive Champal quarter and set to work. He betrayed a most unusual modesty about the identity of his backers and referred only to the Daughters of the American Revolution and other patriotic organizations. The New York *Times* correspondent present, Mr. Wyeth Williams, said, "He was silent as to his sources of revenue." But his credentials must have carried no little prestige, for according to Mr. Williams, "The first day of the conference when the proposals of the

[40] *Ibid.*, pp. 21–22.

three powers were first submitted for public consideration, Mr. Shearer managed to obtain a seat in the famous glass room of the League secretariat where the meeting was held—no mean feat—where he was able to make copious notes of the session."

He lost no time in fraternizing with the most gregarious of creatures, the American newspaperman. Technical data on gun elevations or diameters were naturally rather difficult for these scribes to understand. Mr. Shearer was able to provide "handouts" for the press on these questions and few of the correspondents were inclined to refuse to consult these papers which clarified matters thoroughly. According to Mr. Williams, he prepared a "tremendous amount of elaborate data," and he also prepared and gave to correspondents weekly brochures under his own signature which were, Mr. Williams said, "violently and tactlessly anti-British."

It was no wonder that Mr. Shearer was better informed about such details than the inexpert members of the Fourth Estate. According to his own statement, he had secured from the U.S. Navy Department, under official frank, a more or less confidential document dealing with navy statistics. He conversed, he claimed, with about a dozen admirals, as many captains and every commander and lieutenant commander in the Navy Department before he went over to Geneva. . . .

The world knows now that the conference of that year was a failure. The armament interests had a worthy agent. Shearer was indeed the lion of the conference. He was known among European journalists as "the man who broke up the conference," and when a newspaper item painted him in these flattering colors, he took the trouble to clip it and sent it home to his backers.[41]

The world would like to know more of what armament hucksters are doing now in the postwar period to disrupt efforts to achieve disarmament and banning of atomic weapons. That these pressures continue to thwart arms reduction is indicated by the following report appearing in the *Atlantic Monthly.*

Early this spring a number of top congressional leaders attended an important White House meeting on the military program. They were startled to hear the President, who was opposing talk of beefing up the missile and other "hardware" programs, say with some bitterness that the "munitions makers" were behind such pressures, that if they had their way they would want national mobilization. Similar talk had been heard elsewhere in the Administration, apparently reflecting similar presidential remarks to his own Cabinet family, but not until after the White House meeting did the remarks gain general circulation.

Several weeks later a reporter asked the President about the remark during a press conference. Eisenhower quite obviously was annoyed

[41] H. C. Engelbrecht and F. C. Hanighen, *Merchants of Death,* Dodd, Mead, 1934, pp. 207–209.

at what he considered a breach of a confidence, but he did not flatly deny the remark. Almost at the same hour, by chance, the House came within one vote of barring defense industries from hiring retired generals or admirals. Only the promise of a House committee inquiry of such practices and of what is called the "munitions lobby" kept the provision out of the defense appropriation bill.[42]

Scientists and engineers have undergone inward torment over the exploitation of their skills in constructing and testing atomic bombs. Many have resigned from their jobs rather than accept the consequences of such work, and numerous men probably would also leave their industrial posts if the livelihood of themselves and their families did not depend upon their work. How great can be their demoralization if they remain where they must acquiesce in continued explosion of atomic bombs is shown by the language used by Norman Cousins, editor of the *Saturday Review* of literature, to describe the inventor of the hydrogen bomb.

Edward Teller, who invented the hydrogen bomb in the United States, has been attempting to raise a campaign to convince the American people that he has invented something which in the course of testing does no harm and is necessary. He has gone to see the President of the United States; he has been brought there by the A.E.C.

I would like to say some things about Edward Teller. I was brought up always to use polite language; I was taught never to question the good faith of another person. But a few months ago I became an angry man, and I tell you that I believe that Edward Teller is a liar and a murderer. He is a liar because it has been demonstrated that what he has said is not true; he is a murderer because a policy has been based on what he has said, and people are being hurt by it, people have died because of that policy.[43]

Another feature of the clash between spiritual values and economic behavior should be emphasized. A disturbing feature of present employment methods is job insecurity. Few persons, outside of teachers and civil-service employees, have tenure. At the convenience of the employer they can be cast aside in favor of others. The competition among job seekers would not be harmful if economic society could guarantee a man employment in a situation for which he is best fitted. This, with few exceptions, neither government nor business is willing to do. Permeating present economic life is the philosophy of letting the best man

[42] "Report on Washington," *The Atlantic Monthly,* August, 1959, p. 10.

[43] Norman Cousins, "The War Against Man," *Friends Journal,* August 9, 1958, p. 466.

win, no matter what happens to the loser. Profits are made at the expense of competitors, employees, and consumers. It is difficult to imagine how altruistic or religious impulses can become firm traits of personality through an economic example where man is set against man. While competition among qualified persons for economic rewards serves the best interests of all, no orderly means at present exist to make reasonable provision for the loser. He may possess a lifetime of experience and unique skills, but if others find it more convenient to hire or to upgrade their friends than to give him a job, his future may be ruined. A treatise in religion is not the place to examine particular economic remedies to problems such as those raised here. This is left to the economist. However, the responsibility is inescapable to point out things in the present economic system which thwart the true spiritual purposes of religion. To require human beings to do lifelong economic injury to each other seems as outmoded in a scientifically enlightened society as the gladiatorial contests of ancient Rome, and as incompatible with Christian ideals.

Influence of Religious Culture

What does religious culture provide to oppose the influences of commercialized culture? The altruistic sentiments and ideas generated by primary-group experience become structured into religious motives and beliefs through the influence of culture. ". . . it is the prime task of all education (of adults) to convey the archetype of the God-image, or its emanations and effects, to the conscious mind. . . ."[44] The key principle here is that religious motives and ideas are components derived from concrete social experience. The process of their development is difficult and requires the aid of guidance by culture. No one can think out theology unaided by verbal symbols which incorporate the collective efforts of many generations.

Religious motives and ideas are capable of great variety of development and expression. "Every archetype is capable of infinite development and differentiation."[45] Innumerable levels and combinations of abstraction are possible from among the motivating drives and ideas in the personality system. Since culture guides the development, the particular pattern which the personality takes in its religious development is largely determined by culture. Universal components of power, religious

[44] C. G. Jung, *Psychology and Alchemy,* Pantheon, 1953, p. 12.
[45] *Ibid.,* p. 11.

search, and experience of salvation are involved in this development, but the details are culturally determined in the individual. One has only to compare the diverse religious development of the Indian youth in quest of a guardian spirit, the Jewish boy experiencing family ritual or studying the Torah, and the Christian child at family prayers or learning the catechism to realize the diverse cultural forms into which the religious material of personality can be poured. A rereading of materials quoted in Chapters 5 and 6 provides useful illustration of the variability of personality development in different cultures. The influence of religion on personality is as variable as the patterns of religious practice and belief possessed by human beings. Two cases from the author's materials illustrate various principles of religious growth and development.

Beatrice was born in an upper-middle-class home. Her father was mild-mannered and owed his success in the business world more to his honesty and industry than to his aggressiveness. Her mother was active in social service and church work. Of the three children, Beatrice was the youngest and the most easygoing by temperament. She toddled after her brother and sister at play, sharing their toys, if they allowed her, otherwise playing with her own. Her school years were uneventful ones. Her intellectual ability permitted her to get good grades. She felt secure in school and at home. Since her parents felt little of the social striving which drives many American families, she was content with a few companions from nearby homes. In adolescence, she rarely went to parties. High-school dances did not especially appeal to her since the boys seemed loud and awkward in their manners, but she attended because of her parents' encouragement. Her personal beauty was only average, but she was kindhearted in her manner and boys occasionally dated her.

Going to college, she majored in religion. The "fast" life of her college sisters dismayed her. They good-naturedly listened to her warnings. The courses she took in economic problems disillusioned her about the business world. None of the men she met while in college appealed to her. She went on to graduate school to study social work. There she met a thin-voiced man who was studying theology. His temperament was similar to that of her father, and he became her husband. He lacked the social skills of the Rotarian type of minister which his first church appointment required of him. He became disillusioned with the ministry and took a modest job as a copy editor in a trade publishing house. They settled in a small town. Her husband's income was never adequate, but Beatrice's parents aided them liberally. Besides devoting herself to her children, Beatrice became active in church affairs in the town. Although her marriage was not a success according to moneymaking standards, she felt quite happy in her personal ministry to others. She spent much of her time organizing worship groups in homes of neighbors.

The foregoing case is perhaps exceptional, but illustrates how altruistic sentiments develop in the personality of a girl who was mild in disposition and whose parents provided a warm, happy home life. A psychologist might remark that Beatrice was not sufficiently encouraged to be aggressive and to seek aggressiveness in others for her own abilities to receive full opportunity. Nor did she direct her humanitarian concern into channels of social action. On the other hand, case studies of religious leaders in history often disclose a stubborn, rebellious nature in youth which, when properly disciplined, becomes an effective driving force in the leadership of social movements.

In the next case, the subject also gained strong altruistic and religious ideals from his family, but carried them to the level of political action.

Charles was born the youngest of three children, two boys and a girl. He grew up in a home strongly marked by parental love and ethical ideas. His mother was acknowledged by all who knew her to be a person of extraordinary gentleness and understanding. Her strongest admonitions to her three children consisted of letting them know her feelings were hurt, at which they would perhaps also cry. His father was a man with high intellectual attainments in a physical-science vocation and with a marked tendency toward convictions of righteousness. The parents were regular church attenders, but felt that the expression of religious purposes in daily living was more important than theology or ceremonial. During his college years, Charles endeavored to think out the most useful vocation he could follow. He came to the conclusion that the ministry afforded the best opportunity and he attended a prominent and liberal theological school. He took up his ministry in a modernist church. During a political campaign, he came to feel, like his father, that it was more important to live religion than to talk about it. Having a background in the social sciences, he turned to larger goals of social engineering than those which appealed to his father. Despite family opposition he enrolled in a radical political party and married a girl who shared his enthusiasm. He used his church pulpit as an opportunity to advance his political cause and eventually lost his post. He continued to follow a career in the labor movement which combined religious and political ideals.

Using such criteria as church attendance and surveys of religious belief, it is found that women in western culture are somewhat more religious than men. The statistics show that religious behavior and beliefs are approximately 25 percent more prevalent among women than men.[46] Of course if the statistical criteria of religious interest are drawn broadly enough, such as professing a belief in God, almost 100 percent of both men and women profess such a belief. On the other hand, if the criteria of religious interest are rigidly drawn, such as weekly church attendance or daily prayer, the percentages fall to 10 to 40 percent in various studies, with higher levels of prevalence among women than among men. These data suggest that hereditary sex differences play a substantial role in religious behavior. However, recognition that in other cultures religious activity may be primarily a characteristic of men weakens, if it does not entirely destroy, the hypothesis of hereditary sexual determination of religious characteristics. What seems much more plausible is that the roles and opportunities assigned in a particular culture to men and to women encourage religious expression by one more than by the other.

While a comparative study of religious cultures discloses great variability in personality patterns, it is the thesis of this text that some patterns of religious culture and personality are superior to others in accomplishing functions of group welfare, personality integration and individual satisfaction. It is possible that psychological science may be able to demonstrate an optimum pattern of religious motivation. Several features of such a pattern have been suggested in preceding pages. (1) The altruistic motivation of the individual is the best of which he is capable under normal conditions of development and assistance from the group. (2) His motivation is realistic. Motivational energy is not wasted upon efforts to achieve what is impossible. This involves appreciation of the ways in which altruistic goals are achievable, not only through material accomplishments, but through psychological effects upon the motivation of others. (3) The motivation is conceptualized as a higher power performing the role of God. (4) The belief is present that the higher power can be cultivated and sustained through religious activity. These features distinguish religious motivation from simple altruistic motivation. Their development involves intricate differentiation of ideas and motives in the developing life of the individual.

Hereditary tendencies, group experiences, and cultural influences jointly play their part in the development of religious motivation which goes beyond simple altruism. In part, Jung seems

[46] Michael Argyle, *Religious Behavior,* Free Press, 1959, pp. 71–79.

correct in that the structure of human personality induces growth beyond limited altruistic motivation to a larger and more idealistic social goal. Given the opportunities in group experience, man grows up to be a social value seeking animal. He is drawn by an inner dynamic to seek for the highest which he can know. Evidence for this is seen in the spontaneous growth which individuals undergo in relative isolation or relative independence of the group. But culture in general plays an almost indispensable role in facilitating this spiritual unfolding.

All of the mechanisms of imitation described in a preceding section are involved in the development of religious patterns in the individual personality. The influence of family ideals and convictions on children, especially through example, can hardly be overestimated. Outside of the family the individual can in part choose the cultural stream he wishes to absorb by selecting friends with whom he will associate. Of particular importance are religious education and religious exercises. The first of these is the principal means for developing religious motivation from one level of differentiation to another. The second is a replicative means for intensifying or periodically reviving the ideas or motivations which religious education has developed. Through worship and prayer the individual can deliberately develop the kind of personality he wishes to achieve within his potentialities. Because of the importance of these procedures for acquiring and retaining religious traits of personality we examine them in some detail.

Religious Education

According to a line of psychological theory, the differentiation of psychic experience into its components takes place when one of the components is experienced more often than the other components. This variation may occur during the natural life experiences of the individual or the variation may be caused deliberately in turning a psychic problem over in one's mind. The result is to give one component a greater tendency to appear in experience than the other components. Eventually it becomes associated with characteristic verbal symbols or actions and functions by itself in the personality system. For example, altruism as a goal is present in truthfulness, coöperation, aid, loyalty, sincerity, and love. By turning these over in one's mind, the common factor of altruism becomes apparent. For the individual to do this without the guidance of verbal symbols is a long and difficult task. Communication with others as well as opportunity for thinking in isolation play distinctive parts in the intellectual growth of concepts. Written and spoken instruction is of great assistance to the mind in formulating its concepts. Appropriate preliminary experiences are presented to the mind by verbal symbols for the mind to reflect upon. The aid of any related characteristics or constituent elements may be enlisted by verbal instruction to assist the mind to form a new concept. At the same time, the new and undefined word for the concept becomes associated with it in its various contexts. By means of the verbal symbol with which it is associated the new concept can then be recalled by itself when needed, differentiated from the amorphous experiences from which it was distilled.

It is to be kept in mind that the components into which experiences can be broken may be either concrete or abstract. When, for example, the Christ child is thought about apart from the entire Nativity scene, this is a concrete fragment separated from the total experience. On the other hand the qualities in the character of the personality of Jesus Christ are thought about as abstractions. To repeat an example from the tale of *Alice in Wonderland,* the grin of the Cheshire Cat which supposedly remains after the cat disappears is an abstraction. That is to say, many qualities and structural elements in experience are not physically separable from the experiences of which they are a part. In either case verbal symbols can become associated with a particular component so that the verbal symbol can be used to recall the component to mind. In general, spiritual experiences are not concretely divisible into parts which can be distinguished from each other. Rather, the constituents in the amorphous experience become evident through their association with particular words or acts. Beyond this, the individual is simply aware of spiritual experience going on. Because components of this experience become uniquely associated with external actions, it is concluded that these components exist as different realities even though the individual is not directly aware of them as different realities.

While these principles of differentiation of concrete and abstract ideas apply to all forms of education, the task of religious education is to differentiate religious realities within psychic experience and to connect these with ritual acts, dogmas, or other verbal symbols so that they can be readily controlled or evoked when needed. The concept of God, whether personal or impersonal, is difficult for the individual to grasp. Many years of religious education from childhood onward are needed to build toward the requisite meaning so that the word *God* stands for something in the individual's psychic experience. Superior methods of teaching and inspiration by example play important parts in the cultivation of spiritual motivation in others. Eventually the individual becomes aware of God because of the profound differences which God makes in his life.

Since the task of education in general and of religious education in particular is a slow one, there is a strong tendency by teachers to hurry it up more than is psychologically feasible. Abstractions become differentiated and associated with words at a relatively fixed rate for each individual. If the learning process is hurried, the individual acquires the new vocabulary without the corresponding meanings. He becomes a parrot in his proficiency for memorizing phrases which might make others think he has religious insight. In religion especially, the frequent discouragement of independent thought causes the process of religious education to be one of memory work. A self-constituted dogmatic authority seeks to declare what is the truth and to compel the individual to learn it. The result is the individual acquires words which by themselves are little more than trash, while the real treasure, the genuine religious insights, are never attained by him.

Moreover, the failure of teachers to find valid religious experiences in their own lives not infrequently leads them to declare to the student that he cannot expect to find in psychic experience a fundamental religious reality, God. Strong authority can be found in religious tradition for attaining such experience. Martin Luther wrote: "No man can rightly know God, or understand the word of God, unless he immediately receive it from the Holy Spirit; neither can anyone receive it from the Holy Spirit, except he find it by experience in himself; and in this experience the Holy Ghost teacheth, as in his proper school, out of which school nothing is taught but mere talk."[47] The difficulty with which religious insight corresponding to verbal symbols is gained causes people to mistake verbal symbols, ritual acts, and other outward forms for the actual religious realities. Of the tendency to substitute outward forms for inward realities, Jung has strong words to say.

> The demand made by the *imitatio Christi*—that we should follow the ideal and seek to become like it—ought logically to have the result of developing and exalting the inner man. In actual fact, however,

[47] Quoted in Robert Barclay, *An Apology for the True Christian Divinity*, Friends' Book Store, 1908, p. 30.

the ideal has been turned by superficial and formalistically-minded believers into an external object of worship, and it is precisely this veneration for the object that prevents it from reaching down into the depths of the soul and transforming it into a wholeness in keeping with the ideal.[48]

Yes, everything is to be found outside—in image and in word, in Church and Bible—but never inside. Inside reign the archaic gods, supreme as of old; that is to say the inner correspondence with the outer God-image is undeveloped for lack of psychological culture and has therefore got stuck in heathenism. Christian education has done all that is humanly possible, but it has not been enough. Too few people have experienced the divine image as the innermost possession of their own souls. Christ only meets them from without, never from within the soul; that is why dark paganism still reigns there, a paganism which, now in a form so blatant that it can no longer be denied and now in all too threadbare disguise, is swamping the world of so-called Christian culture.

With the methods employed hitherto we have not succeeded in Christianizing the soul to the point where even the most elementary demands of Christian ethics can exert any decisive influence on the main concerns of the Christian European. The Christian missionary may preach the gospel to the poor naked heathen, but the spiritual heathen who populate Europe have as yet heard nothing of Christianity. Christianity must indeed begin again from the very beginning if it is to meet its high educative task. So long as religion is only faith and outward form, and the religious function is not experienced in our own souls, nothing of any importance has happened. It has yet to be understood that the *mysterium magnum* is not only an actuality but is first and foremost rooted in the human psyche. The man who does not know this from his own experience may be a most learned theologian, but he has no idea of religion and still less of education.[49]

Besides the importance of effective teaching and person-to-person inspiration the part played by individual study and meditation should be emphasized. The subtle process of differentiation of psychic components of religion is stimulated in part by teaching and example from without, but also depends profoundly upon the individual's undergoing a prolonged and earnest inner quest. This is to say that the individual must consciously direct his attention to the raw materials of religious experience as he initially is aware of these and turn them over in his mind. By facing life's problems and thinking them through he comes into possession of higher levels of insight. To declare these principles of religious education is not to enunciate new psychological doc-

[48] Jung, *op. cit.*, p. 7.
[49] *Ibid.*, p. 12.

trines, but merely to reaffirm what ancient seers in Judaism, Hinduism, or other mature world religions have declared as strongly as they were able. Ultimately, the individual must come face to face with the God reality rooted in the ground of his own soul.

When the educational skills of guiding each generation of young people to rediscover religious realities are lost, a break in the ongoing stream of religious culture occurs. Until rediscovered the religious insights remain buried in the psychic experiences of human beings. Until these realities are rediscovered the religious life of people continues barren and spiritually impoverished. Yet the social process is self-correcting. At intervals in history, a few self-taught individuals with a minimum of aid or interference from the culture of the group undergo a program of psychic seeking which enables them to rediscover great spiritual truths. If we ask what conditions the development of this religious originality, one answer is that the religious genius possesses the rare capacity by heredity to undergo spontaneous differentiation of religious realities from his psyche. In examining the lives of great religious personalities, it seems apparent that a second important factor is considerable isolation from the rest of the group. This isolation in childhood and during formative years is valuable in two respects. (1) Empty rituals or words do not have the usual opportunity to cloud and confuse the religious seeker's mind. (2) At the same time the individual, being cut off from time-consuming activities and responsibilities shared by the group, has time to think. Case histories of religious leaders frequently report the expenditure of very long periods of time meditating in solitude.

Religious Exercises

After the individual has gained religious meanings in the form of new ideas and motivations, religious exercises such as worship and prayer perform the role of intensifying these and organizing personality material about them. At the risk of overgeneralizing, it may be said that religious education performs the task of analysis into parts, while religious exercises accomplish the task of synthesis of parts into a reconstructed personality system. Of course part of the function of religious education is to give understanding into how personality reorganization takes place and to provide the blueprint for the reorganization. The function played by religious exercises requires close examination, especially since the psychological efficacy of prayer and worship in altering the organization of personality is questioned by some.

It will be recalled from Chapter 9 on influencing the power in religion that prayer is understood empirically to be a verbal appeal addressed to a higher part of the personality system. When the words are read or uttered, corresponding impulses and ideas are revived in psychic experience. Through this revival they are placed in association with whatever is present in psychic experience at the same time. In the words "God grant me courage," the higher power of religion is recalled in the specific context of courage and this is associated with "me" or the rest of the personality system. In this way, prayer fastens on new elements in the organization of personality. When the same prayer is repeated from time to time, the bonds connecting the new element are strengthened and the element becomes intensified in the personality system. Prayer may also intensify religious study.

By the self-administration of verbal symbols, personality is affected in the same way as if the words were voiced by the group. The individual in this way becomes a transmitter to himself of cultural patterns of the group. As contended in Chapter 9, the personal form of address and address in the imperative mood of exhortation constitute a more compelling stimulus than other verbal statements. While research demonstrating the superiority of individual prayer or group worship in personality reorganization has not yet been assembled to a scientifically adequate degree, the widespread testimony of religious devotees who are able to reconstruct their lives is noteworthy. Especially convincing are the reports by members of Alcoholics Anonymous that praying to God as a higher power enables them to withstand alcoholic drink. What can be accomplished by prayer to rebuild the personality system against alcohol can also be accomplished in reorganizing personality to withstand other disruptive forces, as fear, anger, or wanton pleasure seeking.

Since egoistic forces in the personality system are renewed by biological stimulation, by environmental pressures, and by indoctrination of commercialized culture, periodic strengthening of the personality system by religious exercises is required. Religious exercises provide human beings with a means for matching the natural tendency of disruptive forces to grow in the personality system. These can be dispelled or channeled in harmless or even useful directions, or sufficient strength to withstand or overcome them can be gained. Spiritual traits which transform personal relationships into ones of love and beauty and which give energy and vision for socially creative living can be found through prayer and worship. P. E. Johnson describes a case illustrating the way in which these results occur.

> I seemed always to be able to pray more effectively when out of doors. When my life is troubled with great problems and issues, communion is sweeter in some quiet spot in nature. Such an experience was a little difficult since I was living on a main thoroughfare in a busy city; but returning to my apartment, I opened wide one of the windows and, kneeling where I could see the stars and feel the night breeze, I talked with God. With my confession came the realization that I was failing in the very thing God wanted me to do in life; i.e., in loving people, understanding them, feeling with them, counseling them. True, I was doing plenty of counseling in my work, but I was conscience-stricken over my impatience, my mental categorizing of people into the worthy and unworthy, the manner in which I had used particular instances to satisfy my own ego, my self-pity because of an unhappy childhood. Insight regarding self was developing, and with it a new understanding of the love of God. The fullness of life can be realized only by responding to his great love. Whatever means I used in life to earn a living would be secondary to the primary goal of being available to those who wished counsel and help.[50]

The phenomenon of religious conversion was once much more conspicuous than it now is. This phenomenon was one of the things which initially attracted psychologists to a scientific study of religion. The classic pattern of religious conversion is that of an adolescent or a young adult suddenly abandoning his former self-seeking and pleasure-loving ways of existence and professing a new loyalty to Christ or God. Such conversion frequently took place during mass religious meetings in which the influence of crowd psychology on the individual's decision was prominent. Studies of religious conversion beginning with those of E. D. Starbuck down to observations of those who have become converted through the efforts of the revival leader, Billy Graham, show that only a minor fraction of those who are converted undergo a substantial change in personality orientation. For the remainder the conversion is primarily a matter of temporary enthusiasm for religion and of verbal acknowledgment of having been "saved" by the power in religion. The superficial character of such religious conversions tends to bring into disrepute the role which constructive forms of religion can play in human life.

[50] P. E. Johnson, *Personality and Religion,* Abingdon, 1957, pp. 98–99.

In an analysis of the influence of religion on personality development, it is necessary to explain the phenomenon of religious conversion and to account for the superficiality of the results which take place. The dynamics of religious conversion were clearly outlined by the work of William James in *The Varieties of Religious Experience,* and W. H. Clark has recently contributed a detailed and illuminating chapter reviewing what is known about the processes of religious conversion.[51] The typical route by which most persons undergo religious development is a slow one in which spiritual beliefs and motives gradually take root and achieve expression in the individual's life as he grows toward adulthood. The process is one of gradual ascendance of spiritual motives and progressive control or subordination of non-spiritual tendencies. In the average religious adult an equilibrium is reached in which self-seeking tendencies are modererated and channeled in constructive directions but not eliminated.

In individuals who undergo the experience of religious conversion, there is a sudden overbalancing of non-religious motivation by religious motivation. In James's terminology, the higher self, whose presence has been latent, at once turns the scales and replaces the dominant control which had been exercised by the lower self. The individual abruptly gives up his former ways of living, and at least at a verbal level professes new interests and convictions. Psychoanalytic study shows that the spiritual motivation involved was actually growing in latent form in the unconscious world over a long period of time. When it has gained sufficient strength it suddenly erupts and produces more or less change in the individual's visible behavior.

The more dependable route of religious development is that in which the individual from year to year systematically seeks to deepen his religious understanding and to strengthen his religious motivation. Nevertheless, abrupt religious conversion continues to play an important part in the lives of individuals who have neglected usual means for religious growth. They then reach a crisis in their lives when they gain new and vivid religious understanding of themselves. This has been the avenue of growth for members of Alcoholics Anonymous. In the case of these members, their prompt and complete sobriety is graphic evidence of the reorientation of their personality systems. In the case of those who are converted under the influence of crowd psychology at revival meetings, the depth and duration of the

[51] W. H. Clark, *The Psychology of Religion,* Macmillan, 1958, pp. 188–217.

personality changes are, for the majority of converts, much less in evidence.

The question arises not only in the case of religious conversion but in the case of many whose religious development is gradual, of why so much discrepancy exists between profession of religion and practice of altruism. It can always be pointed out that their lives might be far worse without the influence of religion in the functioning of their personalities, but such questions of "if" have not been and may never be satisfactorily settled from a research standpoint. What does seem quite evident is that an interest in religion, even regularly practiced, often fails to reach the point of positive results in altruistic living. The biting criticism of religion by some, expressed in such stereotypes as "He follows the cross on Sundays and the double cross on weekdays," or "He prays to God on Sundays, and on his neighbors the rest of the week," has a good deal of foundation in fact. Pillars of the church are sometimes the predators of society, to the dismay and disgust of those whose interest in religion achieves expression in altruistic living. Data are cited in later chapters indicating the lack of concern on the part of many church people for economic fair play in the business world.

The personality needs which bring people to religion frequently fall short of what is necessary to produce deep and durable spiritual growth. This is not a condition peculiar to religious motivation. In the area of physical health, for example, people frequently talk of how much they do to get well, but recurringly eat or live unwisely. The personality needs which bring human beings to the doorway of religion provide no assurance that the individual will actually cross the threshold and move into a world of spiritual opportunity. Instead, the individual talks about his loyalty to religious requirements but does little about them. He is the type of individual who professes having been saved by Christ but does nothing to express the spirit of Christ in building a better society. Life goes on in the same narrow, selfish routines as formerly. The failure by religious motivation or any other kind of motivation to accomplish the reorientation in the personality system needed for a maximum experience of fulfillment in no way diminishes the positive and far reaching gains in personality transformation accomplished by other people more receptive to the opportunities for growth.

Determining the Influence of Religious Culture on Personality

A topic of much interest and importance is that of how much influence religious education and worship activities have on human personality. Whether or not religion is a necessary or desirable institution in its claim upon human time and attention depends upon the outcome of this question. Formidable difficulties of research procedure stand in the way of gaining satisfactory answers. The results which have so far been accumulated through research are fragmentary and sometimes inconclusive. The general impression, however, is that religious education and religious exercises have a constructive effect on the growth of personality characteristics which are desirable from the standpoint of group welfare or individual well-being. We now review the research problems, research procedures, and research results in some detail.

The answer to how large the influence of religious culture is upon human personality is one which is given, at least as an aim, in terms of the mathematical relationship existing between the causal variables determining personality and those which describe its resulting characteristics. The question can be cast in such practical terms as, "How much personality change is produced by how much cultural influence?" Or the question is set in mathematical terminology by computing the partial derivatives of the mathematical function describing personality development. The larger is the partial derivative of the personality variables with respect to the cultural variables, the larger is the influence of culture. Again, from a practical standpoint, human beings are interested in variables over which they have control. It might be shown, although in our present knowledge it seems unlikely, that tremendous variation in religious personality results from hereditary factors. Since human beings are unwilling or lack the knowledge to practice a systematic program of controlling behavior through selective mating, the demonstration of hereditary influence is of little practical value. But if it can be shown that suitable circumstances of primary-group living and appropriate aid from culture through religious education or religious exercises possess considerable control over personality development, this kind of mathematical relationship is of great interest and practical value to religious or educational leaders.

Since psychology has barely succeeded in defining and measuring a few qualitative variables of personality development, comprehensive investigation of the mathematical functions involved is largely in the future. The problem is complicated by the enormous number of personality variables which are simultaneously involved. The type of studies which have been performed to date have been piecemeal ones which select one pair of variables at a time and report the way in which one of these variables changes when the other does. Sometimes the relationship simply refers to the presence or absence of factors rather than to a full series of degrees of change. Examples of two-variable study are the effect of Sunday School attendance upon honesty, or the effect of religious affiliation upon the divorce rate. Such studies assume that all of the other variables which might affect the situation remain constant on the average and can be ignored. This is a very risky assumption. For example, religious affiliation might seem to reflect the influence of religious culture, but it may in reality stem from a temperamental tendency to seek religion. Do studies of the effect of religious affiliation actually show the effect of religious culture, or do they show instead the effect of a temperamental disposition toward affiliating with a church? With these introductory comments upon methodological difficulties we consider some of the studies which have been made of the effects of religious culture upon personality development.

A detailed review of statistical studies of religious behavior has been made by Argyle.[52] The journals, *Religious Education* and *Review of Religious Research,* publish reports of research. Two principal series of statistical studies of the effects of religion upon personality have been made in America. One of these took place a generation ago on the initiative of the Institute of Social and Religious Research. The chief investigators were Hugh Hartshorne and Mark A. May. Their work was published in three volumes and covered a long list of formative influences in such personality traits as honesty, service, coöperation, self-control, and moral knowledge. Batteries of ingenious tests and questionnaires were used to determine the presence or absence of these traits. Among the factors considered were the religious affiliation, Sunday School enrollment, and frequency of Sunday School attendance. The findings which relate to the effects of religion are appropriately summarized in the authors' own words.

> Those enrolled in Protestant Sunday schools cheat less than those not enrolled. There is no relation, however, between Sunday school attendance and deception. Children who attend regularly cheat in day school about the same as those who rarely or never attend.[53]
>
> Those who have at any time been enrolled in Sunday School are more coöperative than those who have not been, but the difference is

[52] Argyle, *op. cit.*

[53] H. Hartshorne and M. A. May, *Studies in Deceit,* Macmillan, 1928, p. 411.

very slight. Those regular in attendance are more coöperative than those who attend only occasionally. There is a small correlation (.10) between length of attendance and service. . . .[54]

Regularity of attendance shows no constant relation to self-control.[55]

Where our records are unambiguous, it is clear that regularity of attendance is definitely associated with ability to score on the moral knowledge tests.[56]

The conclusions of Hartshorne and May are supported by copious statistics which were obtained by them from groups of school children. The differences in personality traits between those with religious factors present in their background and those lacking these factors are generally small, and sometimes were not found at all. The failure to find a functional relationship by statistical analysis does not mean that such a relationship does not exist, but merely that the research procedure used failed to detect whether the relationship exists or not. Research procedures for showing the influence of variables have improved since the work of Hartshorne and May. In particular, more adequate measures of religiosity than membership or attendance are needed.[57]

The other major series of statistical studies are those which have been conducted since 1935 by the Character Research Project at Union College under the leadership of E. M. Ligon.[58] These studies are especially concerned with discovering more effective means of religious education. They show that religious attitudes are effectively modified by such devices as direct instruction in character training, home participation in religious training, and building the religious-education program on pupil interest. Again, the differences disclosed between experimental and control groups are usually not large, often amounting to a few percent, but point to the effectiveness of religious culture in inculcating socially desirable traits of character.

Another type of studies are those which investigate causal factors in criminal behavior. It is usually found that a higher proportion of delinquents and criminals report religious affili-

[54] H. Hartshorne and M. A. May, *Studies in Service and Self-Control,* Macmillan, 1929, p. 268.

[55] *Ibid.,* p. 449.

[56] H. Hartshorne and M. A. May, *Studies in the Organization of Character,* Macmillan, 1930, p. 132.

[57] C. Y. Glock, *Towards a Typology of Religious Orientation,* Bureau of Applied Social Research, Columbia University, 1954.

[58] *Union College Studies in Character Research,* Character Research Project, Union College, Schenectady, issued periodically; E. M. Ligon, *Dimensions of Character,* Macmillan, 1956.

ation or activity than the rest of the population. This result is not surprising when it is realized that those in trouble in court claim influences in their lives which may entitle them to more lenient treatment. Some years ago in a study of 85,000 convicts, F. Steiner found that less than 10 percent gave no religious affiliation and that less than two-tenths of 1 percent declared themselves to be atheists.[59] It is obvious that little can be learned about the role of religion in personality development from such casual findings. P. R. Hightower found "no relationship of any consequence between Biblical information and [dishonesty or delinquency]." Concerning the implications of his study he says: ". . . it does not show in the least that the Bible or a knowledge of it is valueless in character building. It does indicate, however, very definitely that mere knowledge is not of itself sufficient to insure proper character growth."[60]

When small differences are found between personality traits of Sunday School attenders and nonattenders, it is to be kept in mind that persons living in the same community share a common culture. If religious education and exercise are beneficial to character development, the influence is likely to be transmitted through churchgoers to nonchurchgoers with whom they associate. Similarly, the traits of nonchurchgoers tend to rub off on the churchgoers. It is not surprising that the differences found between the two groups are small, especially when a single factor out of many factors influencing personality growth is examined by itself.

Another aspect which complicates the investigation of the influence of religious culture is that those whose personalities are less adequately integrated may tend to seek the aid of religion in larger proportion than the general population does so. Jesus remarked: "Those who are well have no need of a physician, but those who are sick . . . for I came not to call the righteous, but sinners."[61] In considering the personality traits of those who seek the aid of a psychiatrist, it would be grossly in error to attribute their deficiencies to the practice of psychiatry, and for the same reason, the shortcomings of religious-minded persons cannot be attributed to religion in general. This is not to say that either psychiatry or religion is always soundly practiced and may not fail to improve the patient.

Freud strongly criticized the type of rigid religious culture

[59] F. Steiner, *Religion and Roguery,* The Truth Seeker, 1924.

[60] P. R. Hightower, *Biblical Information in Relation to Character and Conduct,* University of Iowa, 1930, pp. 33–34.

[61] Matthew 9:12–13.

which sets up intolerable strain in personality and does not permit flexibility of adjustment. Likewise, both Freud and Adler were critical of religious ideas which afford a wishful means via supernatural imagery of escaping conflicts of life which should be faced honestly and intelligently. For example, the religious doctrine that God makes everything come out right in the next life which was wrong in this life encourages fleeing, not facing, life problems. It is beyond the scope of this text to deal in detail with pathological forms of religious expression. On the other hand, the constructive role which altruism plays is referred to by Adler:

> The most important task imposed by religion has always been, "Love thy neighbor." Here again, in another form, we have the same striving to increase interest in our fellow men. It is interesting, too, that now from a scientific standpoint we can confirm the value of this striving. It is the individual who is not interested in his fellow men who has the greatest difficulties in life and provides the greatest injury to others. It is from such individuals that all human failures spring. There are many religions and confessions which try in their own way to increase cooperation; and I, for my own part, would agree with every human effort which recognized cooperation as the final goal. There is no need to fight, criticise and undervalue. We are not blessed with the possession of the absolute truth and there are several ways leading towards the final goal of cooperation.[62]

Another way of examining the effectiveness of religion and personality development is to determine whether the life achieved is characterized by a feeling of fulfillment. Religion teaches the individual to restrict his goals to what is attainable and to work realistically within life as it is. He is encouraged to pursue altruistic goals which express his deep social longings. This type of motivation provides a central power about which personality can be integrated and emotional insecurity overcome. Furthermore, the individual may be taught a philosophy of immortality and divine reality beyond experience, which makes misfortune and death easier to accept in the larger scheme of things.

Studies of marital adjustment show that married couples are, on the average, happier if they have religious interests and activities.[63] It has also been shown that persons reaching old age

[62] Alfred Adler, *What Life Should Mean to You,* Little, Brown, 1931, p. 253.

[63] E. W. Burgess and L. S. Cottrell, Jr., *Predicting Success or Failure in Marriage,* Prentice-Hall, 1939, pp. 122–126; H. J. Locke, *Predicting Adjustment in Marriage,* Holt, 1951, pp. 236–243; P. H. Benson, "Familism and Marital Success," *Social Forces,* March, 1955, pp. 277–280.

are happier and make a better adjustment to the frustrations and difficulties of advancing years if they participate in religion.[64] The interpretation which Burgess and Cottrell make of the role of religion is that it is not religious affiliation as such which is conducive to marital happiness, but rather the circumstance that the sentiments underlying religious behavior are favorable for happy marriages. This interpretation receives support from the findings of D. O. Moberg which show that it is religious activity and not religious affiliation which is associated with happiness during old age.[65]

Experience as a Criterion of the Influence of Religion on Personality

While statistics describe what happens on the average to a series of cases, individual case histories show in detail what happens in the life of a single individual. They represent the relationship between combinations of conditions. Properly analyzed, case studies provide convincing scientific material. Those introduced in chapters on the functioning of religion, such as those of members of Alcoholics Anonymous, demonstrate the effect which the higher power of religion has upon personality development. It follows as a conclusion that religious culture which is effective in facilitating the growth of this psychic power has beneficial effects upon personality integration. If religious activity is understood to be cultivation of altruistic motivation, such activity leads necessarily to the acquisition or intensification of altruistic traits.

One's own life provides the case study most intimately known to the individual. Because of the tendency of wishful thinking to get in the way of clear understanding, study of one's own psychic experience is more vulnerable to error, but intelligently conducted such study provides much illumination concerning the role of religion. One of the primary ways of assessing the validity of cause-and-effect principles is to examine their operation in one's own psychic experience. An Old Testament psalmist wrote: "O taste and see that the Lord is good! Happy is the man who takes refuge in him!"[66] George Fox, the founder of the Re-

[64] For a bibliography of studies demonstrating this relationship, see D. O. Moberg, "The Christan Religion and Adjustment in Old Age," *American Sociological Review,* February, 1953, p. 87.

[65] *Ibid.,* pp. 87–90.

[66] Psalms 34:8.

ligious Society of Friends, wrote of his discovery that God lifted him from spiritual depression and gave him spiritual peace: "And this I knew experimentally."[67] Fox knew what life was like before and after he found God in inward experience.

The testimony of members of Alcoholics Anonymous that the higher power of religion is a matter of life or death to them can be duplicated from other situations of human life. Those who have discovered that they can overcome the corrosive influences of commercialized culture by religious practices are glad for their change in outlook. Those who find that religion transforms their personal relationships with others from those of antagonism and frustration into ones of joy and beauty are convinced of the effectiveness of religious motivation. Those whose family life was crumbling or whose vocation was deteriorating and who felt the experience of being rescued and sustained by a higher psychological power know the effect of religion from experience. The circumstance that meticulous scientists have not gained all of the proof which scientific rigor requires does not matter to them. Having found love and peace in their relationships with others, they are not to be dissuaded from their religion because scientists have not achieved unanimity concerning its role. For them religion does not mean perfection, only that life is better than it otherwise would be.

In analyzing the effects of religion on personal experience, we are operating in an area with shifting and unstable psychological categories. A Jewish thinker, Rabbi J. L. Liebman, wrote a book entitled *Peace of Mind,* and a little later a Catholic priest, Bishop F. J. Sheen, wrote a book in which he declared the experiential achievement to be *Peace of Soul.* However these viewpoints may differ, they are united in recognizing that religion has an experiential function greatly transcending the ritual behavior of religion and permeating all of the activities and adjustments of life.

An essential feature of meaningful experience is wish fulfillment in the widest sense of the concept. *Wish* is used in the sense of a fundamental craving, more diffuse than *desire,* which is specific. We know psychologically that man is an animal with wishes, and that he acts to achieve what he wishes, his activity continuing until his wishes are fulfilled. If they are fulfilled he experiences a pleasant feeling tone of satisfaction and achievement. Life which is satisfying to the individual has more than a neutral

[67] J. L. Nickalls, *The Journal of George Fox,* Cambridge University Press, 1952, p. 11.

quality; it is pervaded by a feeling tone of enjoyment. This may be very mild, almost unnoticeable, but most human beings prefer it to endure steadily, even if mildly, rather than to have infrequent intervals of strong euphoria divided by long intermissions of worry and anxiety.

If we inquire how religion aids in wish fulfillment, it is evident that one of the ways in which this is accomplished is by teaching the individual to restrict his goals to what is attainable, accepting and working within life as it is. This restriction is not simply negative. Examination of the scriptures of religion discloses that positive social goals to live for are taught, but the distinctive feature of these is that they are usually within reach of the individual. The homely satisfactions of love, friendship, loyalty, service, while not always followed, are frequent starting points in religious teaching. The values of success, competition, and individual rivalry are conspicuously lacking. One might quote in this connection part of the Sermon on the Mount, a keystone of Christian teaching:

> Blessed are the poor in spirit, for theirs is the kingdom of heaven.
> Blessed are those who mourn, for they shall be comforted.
> Blessed are the meek, for they shall inherit the earth.
> Blessed are those who hunger and thirst for righteousness, for they shall be satisfied.
> Blessed are the merciful, for they shall obtain mercy.
> Blessed are the pure in heart, for they shall see God.
> Blessed are the peacemakers, for they shall be called sons of God.
> Blessed are those who are persecuted for righteousness' sake, for theirs is the kingdom of heaven.
> Blessed are you when men revile you and persecute you and utter all kinds of evil against you falsely on my account. Rejoice and be glad, for your reward is great in heaven, for so men persecuted the prophets who were before you.[68]

Or, quoting from the Old Testament: "He has showed you, O man, what is good; and what does the Lord require of you but to do justice, and to love kindness, and to walk humbly with your God?"[69]

Such values, frequently translated by religion into family behavior and experience, are found to be ones associated with happy marriage. Home, love, and children as motivations for marriage are all found to be favorably associated with happiness

[68] Matthew 5:3–12.
[69] Micah 6:8.

in marriage, while such individualistic interests as success, money, and commercial entertainment, for example, are unfavorably associated with marital happiness.[70]

Another way in which religion may aid wish fulfillment is by giving the individual psychological aid in the pursuit of his goals. This aid may take the form of encouragement, of development of qualities of character and persistence, or of shaping of social traits of friendliness and coöperation which facilitate achievement. It is vital for psychic health to *do* something about compelling social goals. To fail to follow their inner leading is to stifle centers of energy which give personality its strength and structure.

A third way in which there seems to be agreement that religion fosters wish fulfillment is in the answers it gives to life's questions. No human being wishes to die. Religion strenuously affirms that neither he nor his loved ones will die. The desire for immortality becomes satisfied. The realization is anticipatory, not actual, but such anticipation constitutes a large part of the wish fulfillment of human beings, even when anticipation is not immediately followed by actualization. To become convinced that one will not only live forever, but live in endless bliss, brings with it vast emotional relief and boundless anticipation.

It is this form of wish fulfillment by imaginative or philosophical exercise which leads Howells to declare that religion is "the normal psychological adjustment by which human societies build a barrier of fantasy against fear."[71] This thesis is demonstrated by Howells' analysis of religious rituals of dozens of primitive tribes reported in anthropological research, and he points out ways in which the same fear-dispelling function is found in the religion of contemporary culture. In discussing the role of the funeral service in affirming immortality, Howells says: "The idea of an immortal soul fulfills our wishes, and there is no society, anywhere, that dares to disbelieve it."[72]

Many case studies of persons who have undergone religious conversion are reported and analyzed by James, and these help to illuminate the role of cause and effect. In these case studies, from which a couple of excerpts are given here, we see that the individual reports his religious orientation to be the primary causative agent in the sequence of experience which he describes.

[70] Burgess and Cottrell, *op. cit.,* pp. 254–255, 258–261; Locke, *op. cit.,* pp. 97–100; Benson, *op. cit.*

[71] W. Howells, *The Heathens,* Doubleday, 1948, p. 22.

[72] *Ibid.,* p. 153.

"The near presence of God's spirit," says a German writer, "may be experienced in its reality—indeed *only* experienced. And the mark by which the spirit's existence and nearness are made irrefutably clear to those who have ever had the experience is the utterly incomparable *feeling of happiness. . . .*"[73]

In the following we note how the individual gained a sense of increased at-homeness in his universe after conversion.

After this my sense of divine things gradually increased, and became more and more lively, and had more of that inward sweetness. The appearance of everything was altered; there seemed to be, as it were, a calm, sweet cast, or appearance of divine glory, in almost everything. God's excellency, his wisdom, his purity and love, seemed to appear in everything; in the sun, moon, and stars; in the clouds and blue sky; in the grass, flowers, and trees; in the water and all nature; which used greatly to fix my mind. And scarce anything, among all the works of nature, was so sweet to me as thunder and lightning; formerly nothing had been so terrible to me. Before, I used to be uncommonly terrified with thunder, and to be struck with terror when I saw a thunderstorm rising; but now, on the contrary, it rejoices me.[74]

The role of religion in providing answers to questions which are vital to the emotional security of the individual, such as those of death, destiny, and divinity, is described in the observations of a Catholic writer. Speaking of the results of religious conversion in the broader sense of fundamental growth, F. J. Sheen states:

Before conversion, life is a confused and unintelligible blur, like the figures on a flattened Japanese lantern; afterward, it resembles that same lantern opened to its full height, with a candle inside to reveal the unity of pattern and design. Faith not only puts the candle into the lantern of life—it also lights it. A highly educated person before conversion may have had a vast knowledge of history, literature, science, anthropology, and philosophy, but these branches of his knowledge were divided into watertight compartments with no live correlation of one to the others; they were only isolated tidbits of information, a vast hors d'oeuvre of detail. After conversion the same facts are gathered into a unity, ordered in a hierarchy of knowledge which reveals an overwhelming evidence of Providence in history and also confers a new unity on one's personal life. What was before information, has now become wisdom.

[73] William James, *The Varieties of Religious Experience,* Modern Library, 1936, p. 78. Permission to reprint granted by Paul R. Reynolds & Son, 599 Fifth Avenue, New York, N.Y.

[74] *Ibid.,* p. 243.

The unconverted soul was often exhausted, fatigued from having used up all its energies trying to find a purpose in life. It was tired in its mind and then tired in its body. A mind that cannot decide where it is going next soon exhausts itself by indecisiveness. Anxieties and fears possess the mind and fritter away the strength of the body. But once the goal of life is discovered, one does not need to waste his energy trying to discover it; the energy can now be spent in making the journey. The travel circulars are thrown away as one plunges into the joy of a voyage of discovery.

Many a young student in college is confused because he is without a philosophy of life or a pattern of existence. His education is but a substitution of this theory for that, a jettisoning of one relative point of view for another. The statistics he studied in his senior year are obsolete the year after graduation. His professors, who used the philosophy of Spencer as their inspiration twenty years ago, are now using Marx or Freud—within another ten years they will have found another substitute. Education has become little more than the mechanical replacing of one point of view by another, as the automobile displaced the horse and buggy. The mind is constantly solicited by contrary and contradictory points of view; it becomes more harrassed than a body in constant oscillation between chill and fever. With conversion, education becomes an orderly progression from one truth which need never be discarded to the next. The student is given reasons and motives of credibility for an ordered philosophy of life; his education is now a growing penetration into a central mystery, a sounding of new depths of truth. His knowledge and understanding accrue, as life expands from cell to cell in the development of every living body.[75]

The writer also points out that the individual becomes reconciled to the difficulties and frustrations of life.

Conversion brings the soul out of either chaos or this false peace of mind to true peace of soul. "Peace I leave with you, my peace I give unto you: not as the world giveth, do I give unto you. Let not your heart be troubled, nor let it be afraid" (John 14:27). This true peace is born of the tranquility of order, wherein the senses are subject to the reason, the reason to faith, and the whole personality to the Will of God. The true peace that follows conversion is deepened, not disturbed, by the crosses, checks, and disquietudes of the world, for they are all welcomed as coming from the hands of the Loving Father. This true peace can never come from adjustment to the world, for if the world is wicked, adjustments to wickedness make us worse. It comes only from identification of one's own will with the Will of God. . . .

Regret, remorse, fears, and the anxieties that flowed from sin now

[75] With permission of McGraw-Hill Book Co., Inc., from *Peace of Soul* by Fulton J. Sheen, Ph.D., D.D., pp. 274–276. Copyright 1949 by Fulton J. Sheen.

completely vanish in repentance. The convert no longer regrets what he might have been; the Holy Spirit fills his soul with a constant presentiment of what he can become through grace.

. . . it [conversion] roots out anger, resentments, and hate by overcoming sin; it gives the convert faith in other people, whom he now sees as potential sons of God; it improves his health by curing the ills that sprang from a disordered, unhappy, and restless mind; for trials and difficulties, it gives him the aid of Divine powers; it brings him at all times a sense of harmony with the universe. . . .[76]

[76] *Ibid.,* pp. 287–289.

chapter 12 Development of Religious Culture

Comparison of Personality Development and Culture Development

We turn from the religious development of the individual to the religious development of the human race. Unlike personality development, which lasts less than a century and is repeated countless times, the cultural development of the human race has required something like a million years. When human beings first began to accumulate a culture, that is to build their way of life further upon what was learned from the preceding generation, is not known. If one reasons from the size of brain case and the degree of differentiation of brain structure presumed necessary for the ability to build culture, the initial date may be several million years ago. If dating is established from the first stone tools to show evidence of progressive improvement in fabrication and use, the beginning of culture may have been no more than a few hundred thousand years ago, depending upon the dating assigned to the implements. Accurate dating of materials by radioactive carbon does not at present extend beyond a hundred thousand years, although improvements in technique may eventually afford a definite fixing of the early epochs when particular techniques of stone processing were in use. It cannot be assumed that stone was the principal or even a prevalent material used by prehistoric peoples. Its present recovery from junk heaps of primitive man depends upon its ability to endure to the present, while other materials, such as clay, wood, or skin have long since disintegrated.

Cultural development has not followed a linear path. Study of civilizations in recorded history shows that considerable cyclical movement is evident. Civilizations have their birth, rise to a peak of achievement, and then sink into obscurity, known only to archeologists who dig for their remains. Analogous to the vacillating tendency of children and some adults to retrogress as well as to progress, the cultural development of the human race has not been steady, but up and down. The linear trend is more evident in the case of toolmaking and use than in other features of culture. Innovations which build upon previous innovations can be traced, and the growth in length of human life and the higher standard of living is apparent.

What has happened in the development of religious culture is much less known since religion, an affair of feeling and belief, leaves no traces except for inferences which can be drawn from burial of the dead or from places of sacrifice or from material achievements of a civilization. One thing seems obvious: other species besides man do not have a religion. On the assumption that human beings evolved from other species, the human race or its forebears progressed from a stage without religion to one in which religion exists. Linearity is evident in that respect. Whether the spiritual achievements of present-day Christians equal or excel those of Christians in the Roman Empire is a highly speculative question. However, more adequate data nearer the present permit some inferences to be drawn about trends in the past few generations.

The study of personality development takes an individual at infancy and traces his psychic and social growth from year to year or stage to stage. In a given culture the individuals at a particular age in years tend to be somewhat alike. They have similar roles for their age, depending upon sex and status, and similar expectations are placed upon them. These norms of behavior can be summarized statistically and provide a description of the culture of the people. Culture refers to thought, motivation, and behavior patterns of a mass of people; personality refers to patterns of a single individual. While patterns of the individual may change fairly rapidly from one year of his life to the next, patterns of culture change much more slowly. Until the era of modern science and industry, cultural change was frequently so slow that significant variations might not occur over thousands of years.

In a sense the individual recapitulates in his own lifetime the progressive achievements of the human race over thousands of years. He begins life in a purely animal state and eventually becomes a highly cultured being. The difference between his development and the cultural development of the human race is that from birth onward he is immersed in culture, surrounded by people who are voluntarily or involuntarily aiding him to become like themselves and to share with them the same way of life. No analogous aid was offered to the human race in its upward climb, which accounts, of course, for the extremely slow rate of progress as the mind of man slowly unraveled the intricacies of his own behavior and that of the universe around him. Nevertheless, the analogy between personality and cultural evolution is closer than might appear. Insofar as the key ideas of civilization must be rediscovered by the individual, not taken by rote from others, he must in his development emulate the tedious path of human race through thousands of years. Much the same psychological laws of development are at work in both processes. The difference is that the individual's peers can tell him the successive experiences or ideas to think about, train him in the ability to be a scientific seeker, and maintain him a third or half of his life during the seeking process. In prehistoric times, the individual beginning in childhood had to work for food and shelter. He learned how to think by the uncertain process of trial and error. He had little guidance concerning what were and were not productive problems for him to think about. If he discovered something new, he also faced the obstacle of persuading his uninformed tribesmen to accept it. That an individual in his lifetime can encapsulate the intellectual history of thousands of years is due to modern opportunities and methods of education. Still, the student specializes, and thus relives only a segment of this past history, relying upon others in a vast system of division of labor to reconstruct other necessary portions.

MATERIALS FOR DEVELOPMENT OF RELIGIOUS CULTURE

The Quest for Culture Origins

The young child sooner or later asks his mother: "Where did I come from?" In adult terms the scientist asks: "Where did the human race come from? How did its institutions begin?" The curiosity concerning human origins is overwhelming. When satisfactory explanations could not be found they have been invented, if only to give some answer, any answer to the insistent question of "from where?" The story of the creation of the earth and of Adam and Eve in the Book of Genesis is one of the early attempts within the span of those who first recorded history. This account, fanciful in its details, displays primitive ingenuity in its astronomical description. The story of the Garden of Eden, in which food and leisure prevailed in abundance, may have some basis in historical fact. Half-starved Stone Age tribes wandering into the rich valleys of the Tigris and Euphrates Rivers might well have believed that they had found paradise. Their failure to achieve peace and happiness set moral problems of self- and social control which have perplexed social thinkers ever since. In the past two centuries of the industrial revolution the human race has stumbled into a fresh valley of unbelievable abundance. The human race is still struggling to achieve the degree of social organization and moral maturity to enjoy the fruits of this industrial valley without destroying itself through internecine conflict as Cain slew Abel in mythology.

A story of human origin, with some plausibility in its account of the role of psychic factors in religion, is that given by the Potawatomi Indians. Knowledge and leadership are attributed to their Great Spirit, although the cosmogony leaves much to be desired.

The Potawatomi people came from above, and were placed on the earth by the Great Spirit. The first person whom they encountered after their arrival was a man whom they found sitting beside a fire. He spoke to them, saying: "Hau, my friends, my brothers! Sit here and warm yourselves."

The Potawatomi gathered around the fire and talked to him. They told him that the Great Spirit placed them on this island, the earth, but he said that he was the one who had called them there. He said that he had made the earth and all that they could see there growing was his creation. He said that he was glad that they had come, and that, in order to live, they must hunt and kill game. For this purpose he told them that they must have bows and arrows, and he showed them how these were made and used.

This being who seemed human was Wisaka. He was the first person that the Potawatomi met on earth. In those days deer were gentle and one could make himself a bow and arrow, shoot down, skin, and butcher a deer while the rest of the herd looked on without fleeing. . . .

After they had lived at their place of arrival on earth for some time, Wisaka left them, promising to return. When the time was up, he did indeed come back. He told them that it was plain that they were doing well, but that now they needed a chief.

"Not so," they replied. "We have one already, and that is the Great Spirit."

Wisaka laughed, "Don't you think I am the Great Spirit?" he asked. "Where is your Great Spirit? I can do anything. I want you to be noted in the world, so you must have a chief to rule you."

On this account the Potawatomi appointed a man from the Fish Clan to be chief. Wisaka told him how to give orders, and helped him. After a while Wisaka again went to the people and said: "You are going to have troubles with other nations from time to time, so I am going to give you a pextcigosan or sacred bundle to help you. You will worship and rely on it and call on it for help when you are in danger."[1]

The foregoing account is significant in its crude recognition of the role of psychic forces in the evolution in human institutions, and in acknowledging the need for stable social organization in the hands of functionaries acting under the influence of religion. Cultural anthropologists under the stimulus of scientific achievements in tracing biological evolution during the nineteenth century undertook explanations for the origin of religious and other human institutions. Their principal handicap was lack of suitable data. The remains of prehistoric cultures yield evidence of a very fragmentary nature which are mostly concerned with only one small facet of culture, techniques in fabricating and using stone tools. Data pertaining to religion may go back at most fifty thousand years. What the sacrifice of human beings at altars or burial of the dead in uniform ways or with possessions signify can only be inferred by devious steps of speculation. Thwarted in the quest for prehistoric data, cultural anthropologists turned to the data provided by the life of contemporary primitive peoples. They at first erroneously assumed that the cultures of these peoples represented an early stage of human development, when actually these peoples were neolithic in their institutions, which corresponded to those institutions of people who lived five to ten thousand years ago. Far from representing human institutions in their original state, these contemporary preliterate cultures were in a relatively advanced stage of development, considering the half million or more years of cultural evolution which preceded them.

Exaggerated, one-sided, and conflicting claims were made about the origin of religious institutions by anthropologists during the late 1800's and early 1900's. The result was that the quest for origins was largely repudiated as incapable of scientific ac-

[1] A. Skinner, "The Mascoutens or Prairie Potawatomi Indians," *Bulletin of The Public Museum of the City of Milwaukee,* January 22, 1927, pp. 334–335. Quoted in R. L. Sutherland and J. L. Woodward, *Introductory Sociology,* Lippincott, 1948, pp. 42–43.

complishment, and anthropologists turned their attention to more fruitful, if less grandiose, problems. The net conclusion of anthropologists from these initial efforts seems irrefutable with the present state of data: the actual origin of human institutions, either as to their pattern or their time, cannot be proved with scientific dependability. On the other hand, it appears that a legitimate field for application of scientific deduction to the problem of origins remains. As long as it is acknowledged that conclusions are inferential and approximate, it seems to be as legitimate a use of present-day social and psychological knowledge to predict backward to the past as it is to predict forward to the future.

The essential problem of the anterior deduction concerning origins is the question of what kind of life do human beings with their present hereditary tendencies and capacities build, starting in the absence of culture. The problem is complicated by the circumstance that culture may already have become manifested in some areas, such as family and economic life, before it developed in religion. What these interacting effects may have been cannot be known. The question of dating is virtually unanswerable in the deductions which can be drawn of what happens if human beings live without a preceding culture. Were it not for the demands of human decency, an extremely interesting scientific experiment could be performed by placing small children on a distant island to find out, as they grew up and reproduced from generation to generation, what institutions they developed and the form in which these institutions appeared. Such an experiment would reveal a great deal about the natural course of human events in the absence of cultural traditions.

The theories of anthropologists and others concerning the origins of religion are useful in calling attention to psychic and social forces upon which the appearance of religious institutions depends. Without attempting exact delineation of the genesis of religion, we may still discuss the causes which have been operating through human evolution and which may be presumed to have produced religion as their resultant. As Pratt states the scientific question: "Why do people continue to believe in God, and what are the psychological factors that influence or determine the meaning of that term?"[2] More concretely, the question is: "Why is man a religion-building animal?" Other species do not exhibit a religion. What is there about human beings which

[2] J. B. Pratt, *The Religious Consciousness,* Macmillan, 1920, p. 200.

causes them to manifest religion? The traditional religionist considers the question quite simple. Human beings believe in God because there is a God who has revealed himself to mankind and who enables human beings to believe in him. At first glance this answer seems naïve. Yet this answer, as a surface explanation, is the thesis of religious empiricists. Human beings believe in God because of a psychic factor they discover within themselves which they call "God." The analysis of the functioning of religion discloses, from the data and reasoning given, that a higher psychic power operates within the personality system. Those who have made contact with this power are not under an illusion in their belief concerning its existence, although their philosophical elaboration of a theology and a cosmogony is speculative. The more fundamental question, of course, is to explain the causal basis for the experience of a psychic power.

Of course, no one-factor explanation for the existence of religion in its extraordinary variety of forms is tenable. The roots of religion are multifarious and complex. Their disentanglement and detailing provide a task for generations of scholars. Our approach and conclusions here must be modest. We simply review theories given of the causal basis for religion and attempt to construct an eclectic view of why man is a religion-building animal. The theory distinctive with religious empiricists such as Durkheim and Jung, that man believes in God because he finds God in his experience, requires supplementation in terms of other psychic factors to which they and other scientific students of religion have called attention. These factors are as easily reviewed in historical perspective as by any other approach. We largely by-pass the description attempted of how religion emerged, such as whether polytheism or animism was the original religious condition. We turn instead to explanations of why religious traits made their appearance in culture. In essence the question is one of what are the materials out of which religious culture is built, a question examined without trying to show when or how religion originated.

Types of Causal Factors in Religious Culture

Before proceeding further it is relevant to set in mind the kinds of causal factors out of which cultural development takes place. What are the ingredients of the way of life of human beings? These include much the same things as those out of which individual personality is formed, but with differences in emphasis. Personality is regarded as a product of heredity, group life, and culture. A factor which figures more conspicuously in the development of the life of the group than the development of the individual is the geographic environment. As this influences the individual, it is usually mediated through culture, which incorporates attitudes and adjustments toward the geographic environment which the individual then makes a part of his personality. A rare individual may strike oil in his back yard and have his personality considerably changed by this experience, and an occasional individual in a rural region may be affected by unusual fertility of land or inadequacy of moisture and sunshine. But the net effect of geography apart from cultural patterns shaped by geographic factors is of slight consequence for an understanding of the development of personality. The situation is quite different for the group. Its culture is affected by geographic conditions and opportunities in numerous ways. The technology it follows, the standard of living it enjoys, and the social organization it builds all have obvious connections with geographic factors.

In explaining the genesis of cultural patterns, culture is not one of the original ingredients. These include only the physiological make-up of man given by heredity, people living in a group, and the geographic environment in which the group lives. A common form of redundant explanation is to explain culture in terms of itself. For example, to explain that some people are monotheists because they are Christians, or to say that they are worldly in outlook because they pursue material gain does no more than offer further synonyms for the particular cultural trait or pattern whose scientific explanation is sought. On the other hand, culture is a useful explanatory principle of itself, if we use culture at one stage to explain what culture is like at a later stage. This type of explanation is not only scientifically legitimate, but entirely necessary unless the ultimate origins of cultural phenomena in remote times are traced. The customary pattern of causal explanation is to take one stage of culture and then to indicate how, under the play of forces in heredity, group life, and the geographic environment, this stage developed into something new. The latter three factors are primary ones and have been continuously operating to produce culture since its beginning. Some aspects of these factors are almost unchanging circumstances, such as the human physique, or geographic circumstances such as air, water, and weather. Others undergo change from time to time, owing either to the processes of physical evolution or to the interaction of culture upon the environment.

We may distinguish levels of causal explanation. Culture can be explained at any given time in terms of the causal conditions immediately proceeding, or these may be traced back to earlier stages of development. In either case, a causally sufficient explanation may be found, since, in theory at least, each set of causes at one time is itself a product of an earlier set of causes. An explanation of culture in terms of the earliest set of causes which predate the beginning of culture itself is equivalent to the task of determining cultural origins, a task which we have seen is one which cannot be approached in terms of precise dates or events. We can, however, examine it with reference to kinds of causes known to be operative and consider how the effects of these eventuate in religious patterns. At first sight the hereditary make-up of human beings, their living together in a group, and their geographic environment seem bereft of religious causation. Yet somehow, if the development of religious culture is to be causally accounted for, the causes must be located in these three types of factors.

Content of Religious Culture to Be Explained

Religion was defined in Chapter 5 as a system of beliefs in an unseen order of higher power, of activities to influence this power to meet human needs, and of experiences accompanying these things. The elements in this definition refer primarily to religious motivation. Activities are impelled by drives and beliefs as to how drives can be fulfilled. Religious practices are a direct consequence of the motives and ideas which people hold. The religious experiences which people have depend upon the practices, overt or psychic, which they follow to satisfy their needs. The term *need* emphasizes the form of motivation into which a drive develops in personality after being shaped by prevailing culture and connected with means for satisfying the drive. *Need* then refers to the desire for means necessary to satisfaction of drives as well as to the drives themselves. *Need* further implies the circumstances which must be achieved to avoid jeopardizing normal fulfillment of drives. The characterization of what are the religious needs which people experience is a topic of controversy, as is also the explanation of the causal origin of these needs.

The higher power of religion is a part of religious culture if it consists of a motivational system in the personality and in the group. If the power or powers in religion are outside the domain of empirical investigation, the beliefs in this power, but not the power, are within the demonstrable culture of the group. In the series of chapters on the functioning of religion, the thesis of religious empiricists was given, that the higher power which men regard as God in contemporary monotheistic religion is a motivational system with altruistic, social, and unconscious components. The task of causally explaining the presence of this system in culture is one of tracing the roots of the system in heredity, group life, and the geographic environment.

At the same time this motivational system is frequently fused with and sometimes almost replaced by supernatural beliefs and practices. One of the difficult tasks of scientific explanation in religious study is to account for the range and peculiarities in the religious beliefs held by mankind at various times and places. Beliefs which stem from experience afford less of a problem since they are composed of ideas which are copies of or abstracted from the events experienced. Beliefs which refer to a world outside of experience, or which refer to supernatural intervention in the world of experience, contrary to what impartial analysis would disclose, present the greatest difficulty. Essentially, the scientist of religion must explain the causal processes that produce thinking which is unsupported by experience or which goes contrary to experience as a scientist today observes and analyzes it.

The student will recall from the series of chapters on the functioning of religion that the scientific explanations of religious beliefs fall into two main classes. These are empiricist and rationalist, which are not mutually exclusive types of explanation. The empiricist traces the connection, often obscure, between religious beliefs and experiences from which these beliefs arise. The empiricist assumes that the major religious beliefs in contemporary culture are based upon psychic experience. On the other hand the rationalist is less convinced that religious beliefs in general are a reflection of inward experience. The rationalist seeks to find explanations for why people believe what is unproved by experience or which contradicts experience as the scientist knows it. Since people frequently hold both supernatural and natural beliefs in their systems of religious ideas, both empiricist and rationalist explanations perform essential scientific roles.

Causal Factors Affecting the Higher Power in Religion

The central feature of religious motivation in contemporary monotheism is a psychic power functioning in the life of the individual and of the group. This power, articulated by people in a wide variety of theological and ethical forms is, in the empiricist view, essentially a system of altruistic motivation. The task of explaining the existence of this system is twofold. The causal sources out of which the system emerges must be described. The successive stages of emergence which occur through cultural evolution must be explained. In this section we are concerned with the first problem and with the second only to the extent of indicating why, in general, successive stages of differentiation of motivation from psychic experience occur.

Turning to the latter question, we note that religion involves subtle differentiation of psychic experience into complex components. The refined differentiation of motivation requires a physiological counterpart in a highly differentiated brain and nervous system. No other species besides the human species possesses the brain capacity to develop religious motivation. Moreover, species other than the human lack the ability to develop altruistic motivation as understood here or the closely related phenomenon, sympathy. Possessiveness toward objects in the environment, including such objects as other members of the same species, is a trait of many animals, but this does not develop further into sympathetic understanding of motivation or into altruistic drives based upon sympathetic sharing of experience, or more difficult still, into spiritual motivation or theological compulsion. Animals react to behavior cues in a manner which simulates sympathy, but awareness of the psychic experience of others is lacking, as far as any evidence can be found from scientific efforts to observe, teach, learn from, or communicate with trained animals. Indispensable to the development of religious sentiments in culture is the large, physically differentiated brain which human beings possess, a piece of equipment representing the precipitate in hereditary structure of millions of years of biological evolution in the survival of the fittest.

Animals lack a culture, that is, a way of life accumulated and transmitted from generation to generation. This lack is readily shown by allowing offspring to grow up in isolation. When they grow up isolated from older individuals of the species from whom they would learn culture if one existed, they still recreate the same way of life as that possessed by parents. This way of life may involve complex adjustments to the environment in coping with food-finding problems, but these are adjustments learned by trial and error or by the limited insight of which animals are capable. Animals are able to learn a little from parents by imitation, but they are unable to build much further from what they imitate nor to pass along results of their more advanced learning for culture accumulation. The abstractions of which animals are capable are of a very simple order, while culture is mostly composed of abstractions referred to by symbols.

The intellectual capacity of human beings can be developed in many diverse directions. Its existence hardly predetermines that religion will develop. The circumstance that feral children and isolates do not display any moral or altruistic behavior, much less religious ideas or activity, is convincing evidence that hereditary capacity by itself does not generate religion. On this particular point it is necessary to part company with the eminent scientific scholar of religion today, C. G. Jung. He attributes growth of religion in the individual and in the race to the hereditary capacity to generate the God-archetype. To paraphrase Jung, man is an archetype-producing animal, containing the psychic mechanism to generate a wide variety of archetypal ideas and motivations, including religious ones. Jung reasons from the universality of religious imagery in dreams, artistic productions, and myths created by human minds in all places and times that this imagery is due to the hereditary make-up of the human race. The prevalence of mandalas, which are circular or symmetrical geometric figures in religion, is an important type of evidence to which Jung calls attention. He does not contend that archetypal images are inherited, but rather the psychic mechanism for producing them is inherited. This line of thinking was examined in the preceding chapter on personality development. Similar problems of causal explanation arise in the study of cultural development.

The hereditary structure which produces religious archetypes is attributed by Jung to many centuries of group experience which have left their imprints upon this structure. This involves Jung in problems of biological mutation which he does not satisfactorily explain. Ira Progoff in his exposition of Jung's psychology stresses the group origin of religious archetypes, but does not maintain that heredity is the means whereby group experience centuries old influences religion today.

The fact that Jung starts with an inherently social definition of man—rather than a biological or epistemological one—has two main roots in his thought. One is the nature of his conception of the psyche. He derives the deeper levels of the unconscious not from individual experience, but from the great communal experiences of mankind, and he thus places social factors at the origin of the psyche. The second root lies in his intellectual sources. On this question of the social nature of man, Jung has not at all been influenced by psychological writers, but has rather worked out his basic conceptions in the spirit of Durkheimian sociology. That is to say, he begins with the view that society is the primary reality, and therefore the primary datum in the study of man. Because he starts this way, the logical order for thinking of the problem is: first society, and then the individual. If he took the other point of view, that is, if he took the individual as his starting point the problem would be reversed, and he would have to turn his analysis to the question of how it is that society emerges from the concourse of individuals. But Jung assumes society, and he assumes that the nature of man is inherently social. Society, therefore, is not his problem for study, but it only serves to provide a foundation for the interpretation of individual human beings. He is thus accepting a sociological point of view and adding to it the extra dimension of his analysis of the unconscious.[3]

From a sociological standpoint, the only tenable explanation is that the group experience in which the individual member of society grows up provides material for growth of his religious motivation. However, if the detail of hereditary transmission of social characters is abandoned and attention focused upon immediate, rather than historical, group experience, then Jung's preoccupation with collective experience is a sound one. The fact that the psychic mechanism of human beings does generate religious motivation is not the point at issue. Rather, the point is that it does not do so exclusively or primarily because of features built into that mechanism by heredity.

The social genesis of religion is contained in the sociological theories of Cooley and Durkheim. Durkheim's analysis of religious causation does not succeed in going further than to affirm that society is God and that the roots of religious ideas and practices are in the reality of group life, a line of analysis introduced in Chapter 7. His demonstration consists of showing the correspondence between religious phenomena and such collective aspects of group life as tribal assemblies and ceremonials, permeated by crowd psychology. In Durkheim's analysis the factor of heredity does not intrude except as it gives man organic urges in opposition to religious motivations. Prior to Durkheim, Robertson Smith showed that the theological ideas of the ancient Semites reflected their prevailing political organization,

[3] I. Progoff, *Jung's Psychology and Its Social Meaning,* Grove Press, 1953, pp. 161–162.

God being a king among tribes with monarchic organization.[4]

Later, E. S. Ames pointed out that in democratic society God becomes liberal and equalitarian toward all men, equivalent to ideals of justice and brotherhood.[5] If heredity plays a decisive part in this relationship between religion and society, it is not disclosed in the study of religious variables by these men.

In the quest for religious origins, Durkheim attempts to show that totemism is the initial stage of religion, and he displaces other one-factor explanations for the primal stage. In Durkheim's simply giving still another one-factor explanation, his analysis has been strongly criticized by A. A. Goldenweiser and other anthropologists.[6] But their criticisms seem to leave intact the substance of his conclusion that basically religion is social and its origin found in group life. Imogen Seger has published a monograph analyzing the criticisms brought against Durkheim, showing that these criticisms do not dislodge his main conclusion about the social reality and social genesis of religion.[7]

Cooley, as we have seen in the development of religious personality, placed large stress upon the role of the primary group as a formative influence in moral sentiments, and at least by suggestion, in religious sentiments as well. Cooley does not pursue implications of this line of analysis into the problem of religious origins or the causal factors out of which religion appears. But the implications are readily drawn. It is the fact of living in groups which provides the experience out of which sympathy, altruism, idealism, and an ethical God emerge. This conclusion is as effectively supported by the data of ferals and isolates in the case of religious culture as in the case of religious personality. In either situation heredity fails to provide an adequate explanation for the generation of religious motives and ideas.

Causal Factors in Religious Needs

So strong a dynamic in the life of people as altruistic motivation, crystallized in religious expression and development,

[4] W. Robertson Smith, *The Religion of the Semites,* Meridian, 1957, pp. 28–83.

[5] E. S. Ames, *The Psychology of Religious Experience,* Harper, 1910, p. 312.

[6] A. A. Goldenweiser, *History, Psychology, and Culture,* Knopf, 1933, pp. 361–373.

[7] I. Seger, *Durkheim and His Critics on the Sociology of Religion,* Bureau of Applied Social Research, Columbia University, 1957.

imposes strong demands upon their personality systems. One of these is the need which people experience for altruistic growth. The idea occurs in the cultural development of religion that man can more fully realize his ethical ideas if altruistic motivation or the will of God becomes stronger in his life and if competing drives for pleasure or material success are subordinated in favor of spiritual ones. The need is experienced to bring biological motivations and emotions under organized control. When in opposition to altruistic motivation, these motivating forces curtail its expression. In the analysis of James, the conflict of the divided self ceases when the higher self gains control of personality and organizes its constituents according to ethical ideals.

The need for ethical growth is an immediate consequence of the existence of ethical motivation. This motivation seeks wider achievement, and in so doing seeks to have more power to gain its aims. Many religious practices are intended to establish and maintain dominance of religious power over the rest of personality. The need experienced for personal growth arises ultimately from the same social conditions as those which generate the original motivation.

So strongly are the requirements of religious and ethical ideals sometimes felt that the human personality suffers acute conflict if failure to achieve these ideals is experienced. Especially if intrusion of self-seeking drives or emotions blocks ideals, the religious-minded individual experiences a deep sense of guilt or despair. We can speak, therefore, of the need in religion to control feelings of guilt and remorse. Freud and Reik regard a primary root of religion to be the assuaging of guilt feelings in the tension between the superego and the id. Certainly much of the ritual of the Catholic Church and other groups in the Christian tradition is directed toward confessing sins and achieving forgiveness. Because of the demands which God places upon man, he must somehow reconcile the conflicting drives within his personality system. This is a need whose genesis is partly biological and partly social.

Apart from altruistic considerations, human beings experience a need for personality integration. This is simply an assertion that the personality system of human beings is vulnerable to disorganization. It is unnecessary to point in detail to the long list and wide variety of neuroses, psychoses, and other disorders of which statistics today are accumulating. Short of medically diagnosed illness are the lesser breakdowns and letdowns of life which bring tears, fear, or anger. Over all these things human beings would like to maintain serenity and control. By many procedures, secular as well as religious, human beings seek to achieve stable, energetic personalities. The almost unanimous conclusion of religious psychologists is that religion, properly viewed and practiced, affords an effective and often indispensable means for meeting this need. The role of the higher power of religion is conspicuous in the theories of personality integration given by James and Jung. The causal genesis of this need seems to be primarily biological. The hereditary structure of human beings does not provide an optimum basis for personality growth for civilized living. Vulnerable to emotional upset, worries, anxieties, hostilities, aggressiveness, fear, and addiction to self-indulgence, the personality material given by heredity is not well suited to personality stability. These biological forces apparently served an important function in early epochs of the human species when being quick to react to danger insured life rather than death.

At the same time, heredity confers spiritual characteristics in the irreconcilability of pleasure-seeking and peace of mind, and in the thirst which the individual experiences for deeper meaning and greater worth. While physical data for these spiritual characteristics have not yet been found, the characteristics are not primarily caused by group or cultural factors. The residual explanation is that these spiritual conditions are built into the physical structure of mind and body, although a number of years of development may be required for their full effects to be felt by the individual.

Closely related to the need for personality integration is the need for integration of society, or as often referred to, the need for social control. When emotional forces in the personality system erupt outward in behavior which destroys coöperation or wages aggressive conflict, the need for social control is paramount. The functional role of religious ideas and practices in maintaining orderly social control in primitive society was acknowledged by Durkheim and analyzed extensively by Malinowski. The need is one which is met by educational and political institutions as well as religious. The problems of social control in modern society have gained world-wide dimensions with the invention of the nuclear bombs now at the beck of warring nationalisms. The need finds its way into contemporary culture through both heredity and group life. Obviously, if human beings lived a solitary existence, the need for social control would not appear, nor would the need arise if human beings were fully suited from a biological standpoint for group participation. Other religious needs involve personality demands or compulsions to believe. The explanation for the existence of these is considered in connection with beliefs.

Experiential Religious Beliefs

We turn next to a question closely related to explaining the existence of social power in religion, namely the existence of beliefs that such a power or God exists. This type of belief is experiential if its origin is acknowledged to be experience, even though the basis in experience for the belief is unconscious most of the time. In examining the psychic basis for religious beliefs, scientific opinions do not necessarily agree as to what is disclosed, since the psychic life of mankind is difficult to differentiate into precise components. The topic of what can be discerned through introspective or sympathetic study of religious experience was dealt with at length in the series of chapters on the functioning of religion. To the extent that religious beliefs are a crystallization of man's knowledge about his psychic life, the immediate explanation for the beliefs is that they are given by inward experience. They are not given in an obvious, direct way, as are beliefs from perceptual experience. Rather they represent a slow and arduous differentiation from vague and evanescent ideas and impulses which circulate largely in the unconscious side of life. In considering the causal factors which produce experiential religious beliefs, the wider task of explanation is to trace the roots in causation responsible for the psychic experience in which religion has an empirical basis, a task already undertaken.

The lines between religious beliefs which are alternative reflections of varying social conditions, beliefs which are erroneous, and those which are supernatural are not easily drawn. The psychic life of human beings is susceptible to great variety of differentiation, and the variability in religion is abundant evidence of this. The differentiation is slowly and laboriously performed by human thinkers with many opportunities for errors. It is hardly surprising that religious thinking abounds in errors, especially since religious leaders often arrogate to themselves apodictic certainty and will not countenance correction or change. Moreover, errors arise easily when thinking is governed by emotional needs. Errors committed in the deliberate pursuit of empirical understanding of religious realities are not the same thing as supernatural thinking. The latter is characterized by at least the suggestion that the supernatural events are somehow exceptions to or reversals of orderly everyday principles of cause and effect. Primitive man, lacking a concept of science, lacks the sharp dichotomy which social scientists draw between supernatural and natural beliefs. Supernatural beliefs shade into errors in natural beliefs. These are polar concepts, useful for theorizing, but often unworkable when the attempt is made to diagnose and classify the religious thinking of human beings. Let the reader ask himself whether he is a supernaturalist or not. If his priest or rabbi has instilled in him the notion that religion is an affair of the supernatural, he will probably say yes. Then let him ask himself in what respects his thinking is supernatural, and he may be taxed, even with the aid of the conceptual lines laid down in this text, to answer his question. The point is that the primitive religionist is likewise not a self-conscious definer of supernatural and natural categories. He has a vague idea of events which are somehow remarkable or extraordinary, and which excite his fascination because he does not understand them. The problem of the social taxonomist is that classifications of beliefs are undertaken when the believers themselves have developed imperfectly differentiated and often contradictory patterns of religious beliefs. Much that some anthropologists or psychoanalysts would regard as supernatural thinking, such as the belief in the resurrection of Jesus, would be viewed by others, such as Jung, as picturesque imagery depicting the survival of spiritual power beyond the body of Jesus in the hearts of succeeding generations. The image of Jesus ascending into heaven may portray to the believer a profound psychological generalization. The belief, if rigidly rather than allegorically held, is supernatural in some respects, but the content may be a naturalistic expression of abstract principles otherwise grasped by the believer with intellectual difficulty. In turning to the topic of why man thinks in supernatural terms, we must recognize that we are trying to explain a phenomenon which is not always sharply divorced from realistic thinking.

Factors in Philosophical Religious Beliefs

When men consciously focus their intellectual abilities on the problem of what exists outside the span of human experience, we have a form of supernatural thinking which is usually clear-cut. Philosophizing about immortality, divinity, and destiny beyond the present life of people figures in large dimensions in religious beliefs. It is appropriate from the standpoint of scientific inquiry to ask why, from the standpoint of causal explanation for religious patterns, man bothers himself so extensively with events beyond his reach. It is hardly necessary at this point to mention again the role which man's brain capacity plays. He is a philosophy-building animal at least in part because his brain can perform this activity. Primitive man, although handicapped by lack of writing, is no exception.

At this point an hereditary intellectual component of religion may be noted, a component to which E. B. Tylor called attention.[8] This is the insatiable need to find answers to puzzling questions, a need which predisposes human beings to invent explanations as part of religious systems. According to Tylor, primitive man is faced by baffling psychic phenomena. When he dreams, he goes fighting or hunting, which leads him to the view that his soul can be detached from his body and go traveling. When a human being dies, something seems to go out of his body, his soul. The capricious behavior of natural objects is explained by their being inhabited by spirits of their own. Thus animism as a form of religion arises as an attempt to explain otherwise incomprehensible events. This system in turn places demands upon the individual for propitiation of hostile spirits. So religion is traced to men's intellectual need to understand himself and life around him. While Tylor failed to prove that animism is the earliest form of religion, he exhaustively analyzed a component of religion which dominates much philosophical speculation in religion today. Man's need to find answers drives him to elaborate his systems of religious beliefs. These in turn place demands upon him in religious behavior directed towards a supernatural realm.

Other investigators have shifted attention away from intellectual motivation to desire and emotion. With reference to the emotional thinking involved, Malinowski writes:

> Let us realize once more the type of situation in which we find magic. Man, engaged in a series of practical activities, comes to a gap; the hunter is disappointed by his quarry, the sailor misses propitious winds, the canoe builder has to deal with some material of which he is never certain that it will stand the strain, or the healthy person suddenly feels his strength failing. What does man do naturally under such conditions, setting aside all magic, belief and ritual? Forsaken by

[8] E. B. Tylor, *Religion in Primitive Culture,* Harper, 1958.

his knowledge, baffled by his past experience and by his technical skill, he realizes his impotence. Yet his desire grips him only the more strongly; his anxiety, his fears and hopes, induce a tension in his organism which drives him to some sort of activity. Whether he be savage or civilized, whether in possession of magic or entirely ignorant of its existence, passive in action, the only thing dictated by reason, is the last thing in which he can acquiesce. His nervous system and his whole organism drive him to some substitute activity. Obsessed by the idea of the desired end, he sees it and feels it. His organism reproduces the acts suggested by the anticipations of hope, dictated by the emotion of passion so strongly felt. . . .

These reactions to overwhelming emotion or obsessive desire are natural responses of man to such a situation, based on a universal psycho-physiological mechanism.[9]

In accounting for the belief in immortality, Pratt dwells at length upon man's desire to keep on living. He cites questionnaire studies which his students and others performed showing that the large majority believe in immortality and a small minority, only 10 percent, admit they do not wish to live after death.[10] A Gallup poll in the United States in 1948 disclosed that 68 percent of the people questioned believed in life after death, 13 percent did not, and 19 percent were undecided. Howells analyzed the wishes which underlie beliefs in immortality and in supernatural beings, assembling anthropological results.[11] Freud contends that people, because of their attachment to a human father during childhood, believe in a loving father who helps them through life and whom they join after death.[12] Jung on a more positive note concludes that such concepts of religious philosophy as those of God as judge or God as redeemer stem from archetypal tendencies in the personality system to articulate such concepts. The beliefs involved may have a compulsive nature.[13]

Does this mean that the profound thinking of religious philosophers is to be discounted as wishful fantasy? Whether the religious thinking of laymen is compulsive does not decide its validity. It is possible for the philosopher, seeking to apply scientific discipline insofar as conditions permit, to ask himself what

[9] Bronislaw Malinowski, *Magic, Science and Religion and Other Essays,* Free Press, 1948, pp. 59–60.

[10] J. B. Pratt, *The Religious Consciousness,* Macmillan, 1920, pp. 232–233.

[11] William Howells, *The Heathens,* Doubleday, 1948.

[12] Sigmund Freud, *The Future of an Illusion,* tr. by W. D. Robson-Scott Liveright, 1949, p. 42.

[13] C. G. Jung, *Psychology and Alchemy,* tr. by R. F. C. Hull, Pantheon, 1953, pp. 17–26.

is the most reasonable view of the cosmos which can be taken on the basis of the fragments of information disclosed within human experience. During this weighing of incomplete evidence, the speculative conclusion may be reached that God exists beyond human experience and that life exists beyond death. One line of moral argument proceeds that since the piece of life experienced by man demonstrates its inherent goodness under the influence of spiritual motives, therefore the rest which is outside experience is likewise benevolent to man. This type of philosophy generalizes from the fulfillment of human desire here and now to a larger fulfillment elsewhere. Desire fulfillment plays an important part in such philosophizing, not as distorter of intellectual analysis, but as an important type of data.

Insofar as desire, either as wishful thinking or as the basis for philosophizing about eternal values, functions in philosophy, the explanation for why man philosophizes is found in the causes of his desires, social and biological. Man philosophizes because the personality he acquires from heredity and group living impels him to philosophize.

Factors in Myths and Magic

The literature analyzing the causation of why myths appear in religious culture and the functions which they serve is long and impressive. We can do little more than call attention to some of the salient observations which have been made by some of the more eminent thinkers. The pioneer work of J. G. Frazer and especially of B. Malinowski in analyzing mythology is conspicuous in anthropology. Malinowski modestly writes of the relation of his own work to that of Frazer.

> *The Golden Bough* contains the theory of the ritual and sociological functions of myth, to which I have been able to make but a small contribution, in that I could test, prove, and document in my field work. This theory is implied in Frazer's treatment of magic; in his masterly exposition of the great importance of agricultural rites; in the central place which the cults of vegetation and fertility occupy in the volumes of *Adonis, Attis, Osiris,* and in those on the *Spirits of the Corn and of the Wild.* In these works, as in so many of his other writings, Sir James Frazer has established the intimate relation between the word and the deed in primitive faith; he has shown that the words of the story and of the spell, and the acts of ritual and ceremony are the two aspects of primitive belief.[14]

[14] Malinowski, *op. cit.,* p. 123.

Thus myths and rituals interact. Myths justify rituals, but rituals reënact and bring myths to life. Malinowski is critical of attempts to account for myths as intellectual efforts to explain puzzling origins, such as Andrew Lang's theory of myths as primitive science. Rather, myths stem directly, if unconsciously, from the feelings and desires of people to make over life as they wish it to be or as they believe it should be. Thus myths on the one hand justify life as it is, whether the conditions are physical or social, and on the other hand enable people to engage in an imaginative fulfillment of desires blocked by immediate circumstances. A rationalization for accepting death is given in the following myth.

The parallel between primeval and spiritual existence can be drawn even further. The ghosts of the deceased move after death to the island of Tuma. There they enter the earth through a special hole—a sort of reversed proceeding to the original emergence. Even more important is the fact that after a span of spiritual existence in Tuma, the nether world, an individual grows old, grey, and wrinkled; and that then he has to rejuvenate by sloughing his skin. Even so did human beings in the old primeval times, when they lived underground. When they first came to the surface they had not yet lost this ability; men and women could live eternally young.

They lost the faculty, however, by an apparently trivial, yet important and fateful event. Once upon a time there lived in the village of Bwadela an old woman who dwelt with her daughter and grand-daughter; three generations of genuine matrilineal descent. The grandmother and grand-daughter went out one day to bathe in the tidal creek. The girl remained on the shore, while the old woman went away some distance out of sight. She took off her skin, which carried by the tidal current, floated along the creek until it stuck on a bush. Transformed into a young girl, she came back to her grand-daughter. The latter did not recognize her; she was afraid of her, and bade her begone. The old woman, mortified and angry, went back to her bathing place, searched for her old skin, put it on again, and returned to her grand-daughter. This time she was recognized and thus greeted: "A young girl came here; I was afraid; I chased her away." Said the grand-mother: "No, you didn't want to recognize me. Well, you will become old—I shall die." They went home to where the daughter was preparing the meal. The old woman spoke to her daughter: "I went to bathe; the tide carried my skin away; your daughter did not recognize me; she chased me away. I shall not slough my skin. We shall all become old. We shall all die."[15]

Malinowski concludes from his study of primitive myths:

[15] *Ibid.*, pp. 103–104.

Myth fulfills in primitive culture an indispensable function: it expresses, enhances, and codifies belief; it safeguards and enforces morality; it vouches for the efficiency of ritual and contains practical rules for the guidance of man. Myth is thus a vital ingredient of human civilization; it is not an idle tale, but a hard-worked active force; it is not an intellectual explanation or an artistic imagery, but a pragmatic charter of primitive faith and moral wisdom.[16]

It is clear, then, that the myth conveys much more to the native than is contained in the mere story; that the story gives only the really relevant concrete local differences; that the real meaning, in fact the full account, is contained in the traditional foundations of social organization; and that this the native learns, not by listening to the fragmentary mythical stories, but by living within the social texture of his tribe. In other words, it is the context of social life, it is the gradual realization by the native of how everything which he is told to do has its precedent and pattern in bygone times, which brings home to him the full account and the full meaning of his myths of origin.[17]

The historical consideration of myth is interesting, therefore, in that it shows that myth, taken as a whole, can not be sober dispassionate history, since it is always made *ad hoc* to fulfill a certain sociological function, to glorify a certain group, or to justify an anomalous status. These considerations show us also that to the native mind immediate history, semi-historic legend, and unmixed myth flow into one another, form a continuous sequence, and fulfill really the same sociological function.

And this brings us once more to our original contention that the really important thing about the myth is its character of a retrospective, ever-present, live actuality. It is to a native neither a fictitious story, nor an account of a dead past; it is a statement of a bigger reality still partially alive. It is alive in that its precedent, its law, its moral, still rule the social life of the natives. It is clear that myth functions especially where there is a sociological strain, such as in matters of great difference in rank and power, matters of precedence and subordination, and unquestionably where profound historical changes have taken place. So much can be asserted as a fact, though it must always remain doubtful how far we can carry out historical reconstruction from the myth.[18]

In the foregoing lines from Malinowski's writings, the functional role performed by myth in integrating culture and maintaining social organization is emphasized. What is functional in fulfilling the needs or desires of one group in society may or may not be functional from the standpoint of another group. One man's function may be another man's dysfunction. Paul Radin

[16] *Ibid.,* p. 79.
[17] *Ibid.,* p. 93.
[18] *Ibid.,* pp. 102–103.

has analyzed primitive myth as an instrument by which the ruling clique exploits tribe members.

The most striking feature of Yokuts culture from the religious viewpoint is the fear inspired by the shamans. This is not due to any unusual power that they possess, for they have little, but to the alliance between them and the chief of the tribe. The latter controls, or at least, once controlled all the sources of income. These were, relatively speaking, fairly extensive considering the simple nature of the wealth-producing agencies. He had a monopoly on the trade of certain coveted objects, such as eagle-down, and the control of the rituals; he shared in the payments received by the local shamans and received money gifts from all visiting practitioners.

To understand fully the power of the shamans we should remember that all the organizational gifts they possessed went into the elaboration of the relations between them and the chief of the tribe. These two worked hand in glove, the chief increasing his sources of wealth by his alliance with the shamans and the latter gaining the protection of the chief, a protection sorely needed, for great risks attended the exercise of their profession.

How the two, the chief and the shaman, worked together, is admirably described by a native:

If a man, especially a rich one, did not join in a dance, the chief and his doctors would plan to make this man or some member of his family sick. . . . The doctor then sees to it that he is called in to make the cure. He makes several successive attempts to cure his victim, each time being paid for his services. He withholds his cure until he has financially broken the man and got him in debt. If he then cures the patient, he sucks the shot out and shows it to the bystanders, saying that the nigot [spirit] or a spring [spirit] has made him ill. On the other hand he may let the person die, in which case the family must perforce join in the mourning ceremony.

The money which the shaman has collected as fees in the case, he divides with the chief. Should the victim's relatives seek vengeance, for which they must obtain the chief's permission, the chief refuses his sanction on the ground of insufficient evidence. Has not the doctor shown that the nigot [spirit] had caused the illness?

Thus the dread of the shaman hangs over the ordinary individual. That this dread is the outcome of the alliance between the chief and the shamans the example quoted above clearly demonstrates.[19]

While it seems too narrow a scientific view to regard myths simply as conscious attempts by man to explain himself and the universe, the part played by the intellectual processes in the formation of myths indicated by Tylor should not be overlooked. The tension man experiences until disordered facts become ar-

[19] P. Radin, *Primitive Religion,* Dover, 1957, pp. 42–43.

ranged in an orderly manner seems a universal force in psychic structure of personality. The earnestness with which man, both ancient and modern, applies himself to the task of explaining puzzling phenomena of life is ample evidence of this tension. More adequately than Lang, Levy-Bruhl and Jung have examined the relationship of myth-making to intellectual processes. Levy-Bruhl, a French sociologist, calls attention to the logic of primitive mentality. The primitive believes his soul participates in external events outside his body. This psychic projection is what Levy-Bruhl called *participation mystique*. By it primitive man personally participates in natural objects which he infuses with his own social and psychological characteristics. Jung cites an instance of this. "A white man shoots a crocodile. At once a crowd of people come running from the nearest village and excitedly demand compensation. They explain that the crocodile was a certain old woman in their village who had died at the moment when the shot was fired. The crocodile was obviously her bush-soul. Another man shot a leopard that was lying in wait for his cattle. Just then a woman died in a neighboring village. She and the leopard were one and the same."[20]

As we have seen in the previous examination of Jung's views concerning myths, he does not regard their essential meaning as supernatural or fictitious but as profoundly revelatory of psychic contents. They provide the concrete vehicle by means of which psychic contents in the unconscious mind gain conscious existence as motives and ideas in the personality system. Much of what is alleged to be supernatural consists of imperfectly understood but natural impulsions of personality. It is true that these impulsions are frequently surrounded by supernatural trappings, but for Jung these are inconsequential details.

The key to the relation between myths and intellectual processes is found in the concept of differentiation. With the ongoing life of the individual, the unconscious contents of his personality system gradually become differentiated into articulate components. This differentiation in part takes place because of the individual's deliberate desire for answers to what he does not understand. But to a greater extent, it takes place spontaneously. While taking place it does not necessarily follow lines of scientific logic. The principles of psychic life by which ideas become differentiated do not necessarily yield a correct picture of the cause-and-effect connection between things. Thus the primi-

[20] C. G. Jung, *Modern Man in Search of a Soul,* tr. by W. S. Dell and C. F. Baynes, Kegan Paul, Trench, Trubner, 1933, p. 162.

tive may believe his soul is in the crocodile. The evolution of scientific techniques for differentiating concepts according to cause-and-effect realities is a latter-day development in culture. A major part in erroneous differentiation is played by wishful thinking. The process of differentiation is weak and shifting. The way in which it unfolds readily conforms to what men desire. Their beliefs become extracted, not from cause-and-effect considerations, but from the perspective which their desires impose upon their psychic experience. The errors and the fabrication in religion are a consequence of inadequate differentiation of psychic experience into its components. Moreover, the error in imputing supernatural qualities to religious rituals stems from the difficulty of abstract analysis of unconscious motivation and from the thin, indistinguishable character of the resulting psychic components.

When we turn to a consideration of the beliefs surrounding magic, the thesis that inadequate differentiation of ideas is the major root of supernatural thinking about things experienced receives added confirmation. Frazer analyzed in detail the ideas of misplaced causation involved in the practice of magic. W. Howells has summarized Frazer's ideas with examples of magic. We quote from Howells' fascinating presentation.

> Frazer devoted the first part of *The Golden Bough* to an analysis of magic, with a great many examples, and little can be added to this. One general law, he found, determined most magical formulas, the Law of Sympathy. That is to say, magic depends on the apparent association or agreement between things, and is firmly founded on two great misapprehensions: that things which are alike are the same, and that things which were once in contact continue to be connected. These two principles he called the Law of Similarity and the Law of Contagion. This takes in most of magic except for one more stout fallacy, that of "post hoc, ergo propter hoc," which is the belief that since *B* happens after *A, B* was therefore caused by *A*. The finest magic you could have, of course, would be based on all three of these delusions.
>
> The Law of Similarity gives rise to homeopathic magic, of which the most familiar kind is image magic or, as it is known in the trade, envoutement. This is the business of making an image to represent a living person, who can then be killed or injured by the sorcerer via the image. It is best if you make as good a likeness as possible (modern science enables you to paste a photograph over the face, a technique employed by Pennsylvania hexers) and formally name it after the person who is to undergo treatment. You may then stab it, or burn it, or shoot it, or chop it up, or bury it to rot slowly, as your pleasure dictates. There is no need to be precipitate, of course; you may be-

gin by rubbing pepper all over it, and end by roasting it very slowly. It is not necessary to kill the victim at all. You can hold the effect down to shooting pains if you prefer. But there is the method; it is up to you.[21]

Contagious magic, from the Law of Contagion, is equally popular. An example from Codrington shows the idea: if a Melanesian (island not stated) has been hit in battle by an arrow, his friends will bind up the wound and put a cool poultice on it, to keep the fever down and make him comfortable. And they will also put a poultice on the arrow which they have taken out of the wound, because it was connected with the wound, and this, too, will help the cure. The enemy who fired the arrow and saw it hit has other ideas, however; back in his camp he keeps the bow near the fire, and twangs the string from time to time, because the bow fired the arrow that made the wound, and through this connection he can send twinges of pain, and tetanus. Throwing in a little homeopathic magic, he increases the inflammation by drinking hot, spicy drinks himself.[22]

To homeopathic, contagious, and repetitive magic has been added a fourth classification, will magic, based upon confusion between the thought and the event. In will magic, results are accomplished by sheer act of will. That the roots of this and other forms of magic are deep in contemporary culture is evident from their prevalence. The student who opens the sheet with his grades, determined not to let himself think he might have gotten an *F,* for fear that his thinking can make the *F* a reality, is using will magic. Will magic is to be distinguished from the type of faith healing which has sound basis in psychotherapy. The determination not to let oneself think of being sick may aid in getting or keeping well, if only because worry and anxiety, which are deleterious to health, are avoided.

Will magic more than any other form illustrates the corrupting role played by desire in the reasoning process. If we inquire why so much erroneous or even absurd beliefs are held in magic and religion, one answer is that heredity, while it gives the human species superior brain capacity, does not provide a perfect thinking machine. Mistakes readily arise, which require centuries of painstaking scientific inquiry for their elimination. The other major factor is provided by drives and emotions which human beings possess. Following Frazer, Malinowski, and others, Howells states this thesis of the causation of religion and magic, but emphasizes the aspect of fear.

[21] From *The Heathens,* by William Howells, pp. 50–51. Copyright 1948 by William Howells. Reprinted by permission of Doubleday & Company, Inc.
[22] *Ibid.,* p. 53.

If I were to try a definition here, I should say that a religion is a set of earnest policies which a group of people adopts under an unconscious compulsion in order to tidy up their distraught relationships with one another and with the universe as they perceive it, without the aid of science. In man's own eyes, perhaps, religion is a diplomatic conspiracy against the invisible, and since he keeps the score himself he usually manages to be satisfied with the results. But I would go completely around behind him and define it still again, as the normal psychological adjustment by which human societies build a barrier of fantasy against fear. And since, like any psychological adjustment, it is born in stress, it is therefore a source of emotion.[23]

Since the wishes which religion rationalizes touch every aspect of life, the causal determinants of the rationalist aspect of religion include the causal determinants of desires in general. These determining factors are social as well as biological. Religion from this standpoint is an outgrowth of man's imperfect capacity to think, distorted by the various drives which motivate him. Only man is able to think well enough, yet poorly enough to develop supernatural ideas which go counter to the facts of his experience.

A further comment may be made concerning the roots of magic in man and his environment. Practices of magic nearly always pertain to situations where chance reigns. "It is most significant that in the Lagoon fishing, where man can rely completely upon his knowledge and skill, magic does not exist, while in the open-sea fishing, full of danger and uncertainty, there is extensive magic ritual to secure safety and good results. Again, in warfare the natives know that strength, courage, and agility play a decisive part. Yet here also they practice magic to master the elements of chance and luck."[24] From the uninformed standpoint of primitive man, sickness is an unfortunate accident. Having no idea what causes disease, he has no idea when or whom it will strike. Weather variations which cause crop failures conform to the principles of probability. Where man lacks knowledge, or where laws of chance prevail, it is difficult for him to think soundly. If he does not have data of causation, he cannot deduce laws of causation. He readily projects his own desires in reaching false principles of cause and effect. Areas of uncertainty are the breeding ground of magical and other supernatural ideas. An important causal root of magic is found in those circumstances of man's environment which

[23] *Ibid.*, p. 22.
[24] Malinowski, *op. cit.*, p. 14.

confront him with happenings of chance. The geographic influence upon magic is thereby evident in the greater prominence which magic has in those areas where life is more hazardous and uncertain, and especially in economic pursuits characterized by unexpected danger.

Our conclusion concerning the causal factors responsible for the development of religion in culture is an eclectic one. The fundamental basis is found in group life, which fosters altruistic ideals in which God is discerned. But religion has many manifestations apart from ethical content. It has been permeated by magical thinking as have other fields of human enterprise, and probably more than other fields. The presence in religion of supernatural ideas contradictory of experience is caused by the same factors which have from time to time permeated medicine and other branches of knowledge with magical beliefs and practices. These are factors producing the form of motivation and the degree of intellectual equipment which human beings bring to the cultural development of their religion.

PRINCIPLES OF DEVELOPMENT OF RELIGIOUS CULTURE

It is now our purpose to examine the processes whereby religious characteristics of culture develop. Many of the same principles of psychology are involved as were considered in the development of religious characteristics of personality. But the role which the principles play is somewhat different. In life study of the individual, the focus is upon how the raw material of personality given by heredity and group experience changes under the impact of culture into personality patterns already shared by others in the group. In life study of civilization, the focus is upon how the raw material given by heredity and environment grows slowly into something else, not by the aid of others, but through the instrumentality of human discovery. Whatever is added to culture in life development is tortuously discovered or devised by the human mind trying to solve ways of meeting pressing needs in a more adequate manner. No local schools with kindhearted teachers as convenient sources of information exist. The only school of the human race is that of experience.

On the other hand, whatever is added to the life development of the individual is primarily given to him by the personal assistance of others who already have the cultural patterns which he is to acquire. They give him these patterns either by indoctrinating him or by leading him along paths of inward psychological development which the group knows can be followed. In individual development the emphasis is upon communicating what the group knows but which the individual does not know. The emphasis is upon helping him to retrace a route of discovery which the group has already designated.

In cultural development the key act of learning is the original act of discovery or invention. Also of importance is the process whereby the innovator communicates to others the ideas or behavior patterns discovered or invented. If an invention cannot be or is not learned by others, it does not become a part of cultural heritage. If a generation of human beings lose the ability to relearn past discoveries in religion, these religious patterns vanish. The psychology of discovery and the psychology of acceptance of discovery are the two primary foci in the study of the development of religious culture.

Innovation and Diffusion

All growth in the content of culture takes place by innovation and by diffusion. One fundamental form of cultural growth is provided by the accumulation of knowledge about the physical universe and about the social and psychological nature of man. Based upon new knowledge, man devises new ways of doing things. These innovations in practice are a second form of cultural accumulation. In a sense they are discoveries, since new patterns of acting or thinking are found, but it is convenient to distinguish new practices as inventions from new knowledge as discoveries. Part of the accumulation of religious culture is provided by man's discoveries about his psychic nature, and part of the accumulation is given by the new patterns of religious activity, religious beliefs, or spiritual development which he has created and used.

Diffusion means that a new piece of knowledge or a new practice is accepted by others. The new piece of knowledge discovered is incorporated into the knowledge systems of others as, for example, when others accept the discovery of the ancient Jews that the God of separate tribes is one and the same God. Or, a new pattern of religious exercise, such as repeating the Twenty-third Psalm, is taken up by non-Jews or non-Christians.

The principles under which cultural change takes place are essentially the principles under which discovery, invention, and diffusion occur. These principles have been given extensive attention by anthropologists, and to some extent by sociologists. However, the heart of discovery and diffusion is the process of psychic differentiation, a concept given conspicuous importance in psychology and cultural history by Jung. In this process, as we have noted in analyzing personality development, psychic experience becomes separated into component elements or combinations of elements. These become discovered in the sense that the individual becomes aware of them when he did not previously know of their existence. Inventions, except of the trivial kind, represent differentiation of one type of combination of elements from another grouping of elements during the interplay of thought and experience. Those who imitate the original discoverer or inventor must replicate the process of differentiation within themselves if they are to possess the new knowledge or master the new invention in an understandable way. The analysis of when or whether cultural change takes place depends on an analysis of the principles of the process of differentiation. These principles have been formulated by cultural anthropologists, although the fully articulated concept of differentiation is the work of psychologists.

Principles of Innovation

Principles of invention and diffusion, or of cultural differentiation, can most readily be grasped in terms of the culture base. This refers to the culture already in existence upon which innovations are built. Whatever is new can only come from what has already appeared. In this sense cultural evolution moves by progressive stages of differentiation of elements or differentiation of configurations from one pattern to another. What has already come into being through invention and diffusion forms the base on which succeeding culture traits or patterns are built. This is most easily seen in the succession of improvements in the fabrication and use of stone implements recovered from prehistoric times.

A classic series of successive religious innovations has been described by Shailer Mathews in *The Growth of the Idea of God.*[25] He traces the sequence of theological ideas in the Judeo-Christian tradition from early polytheism through henotheism to monotheism, and at the same time traces the growth in the moral attributes ascribed to God from a God of vengeance to one

[25] Shailer Mathews, *The Growth of the Idea of God,* Macmillan, 1931.

of love and from a God who is indifferent to man's weakness to one who is a helping power. These developments in theological conception are evident in the successive additions to scripture in the Bible. They continue in refinement down to the present time. A number of principles of cultural change govern these developments in religious culture.

1. Discoveries and inventions can only come out of existing materials. Obviously, scientific discoveries are limited to what exists in the universe, previously unknown and which becomes known. Similarly, discoveries about religious forces or factors in personality or society are restricted to the possibilities which these contain. With respect to inventions, it has long been a truism of cultural study that an invention cannot be made except from materials available. Carpentry requires workable wood, pottery requires clay, and so forth. Where new patterns of thinking or acting are synthesized, these patterns are limited to the social or psychic materials out of which the patterns can be formed. The materials from which technological inventions are formed are those provided by the geographic environment. The materials from which religious discoveries are obtained or out of which religious inventions are made are those of heredity and group living.

The series of inventions in religious thought and practice which have appeared in recorded history represent a structuring of latent psychic material pertaining to religious motives or development. In this material religious patterns have endless possibilities for variation. It is helpful in analyzing empirical religious patterns to remember that these can only come out of psychic materials which are the same today in the human personality system as they were in the dawn of religion. By keeping their social and psychic basis in mind, their outlines and composition can more reliably be determined from fragmentary evidences in religious writing. For example, the religious episode reported as the experience of Moses on Mount Sinai might at first consideration be regarded entirely as a fanciful product of imagination. In considering more carefully its basis in psychic forces operative then as now, its empirically meaningful components are more readily discerned. That Moses was able to read the will of God in the commandments given derives from the presence of moral and religious ideas in his own psyche which he was able through earnest contemplation and seeking to differentiate from amorphous psychic experience.

2. Discoveries and inventions tend to follow a sequence of

step-by-step logic. This is readily seen in terms of such mechanical inventions as the automobile and the radio. The automobile could not be perfected until the carriage, pneumatic tires, the internal-combustion engine, and good roads had been accomplished. The radio depended upon electrical circuits, batteries or dynamos, wireless telegraphy, and telephones. It is quite unlikely, although remotely possible, that the order of these inventions and their necessary components might have been reversed. In a few instances, the logical order of the unfolding inventions or scientific discoveries has been reversed, but generally these follow the logical order imposed by the way in which concepts proceed from each other. The way in which the human mind unravels problems in the universe depends upon their logical relationship to each other, simple problems being solved before the more complex ones are mastered.

The series of developments in the idea of God described by Mathews follow in general a logical order. The conclusion that the God of each tribal nation is actually one God over all nations is a logical generalization made by the human mind after it experiences the God of other tribes. The generalization of monotheism from polytheism is less obviously a one-way deduction, and some anthropologists, such as Andrew Lang and Wilhelm Schmidt, have reasoned that polytheism is a regression from earlier monotheism. However, the ascribing of progressively refined moral ideas to God as he is conceived clearly follows a logical sequence. The earlier discoveries were more or less crude, and the later ones represent moral improvements. God as judge and punisher reflects the mores of primitive society, which enforces rules by quick vengeance. God as forgiver and savior depends upon human beings' discovering psychological subtleties of social control in which help and sympathy accomplish more for the wrongdoer than retributive punishment. These subtleties are much less obvious to the human mind confronted by problems of social control than the crude fact that superior force in the short run subdues opposition.

The logical sequence in cultural developments refers not only to the direction in which innovations occur, but also to the necessary involvement of intervening steps. This is most clearly seen in the cultural development of mathematical ideas. The same, however, applies to religion. Rarely does the human mind proceed to a totally new answer without covering intervening steps, and such discovery is more a matter of chance than logical reasoning. The discovery that penicillin destroys harmful bacteria was not preceded by detailed analysis of the therapeutic properties of various molds, but was a chance happening, although it also depended upon the mental alertness of the research worker who could visualize a problem and its solution. The slow and painstaking growth in moral and religious ideas seems to manifest the necessity of intervening intellectual steps as fully as discoveries in physical science. The concept of a God of love, which seems so superior to theologians today to a God of vengeance, was not at all obvious to primitive tribesmen, whose lives depended upon quickness to strike back and kill. The evolutionary dependence of religion upon fundamental social and cultural changes is closely knit from a logical standpoint.

An important aspect for religion of the dependence of a particular stage of culture upon preceding cultural patterns may be noted. Various parts of the cultural fabric tend to move towards consistency with each other. For example, the prevailing pattern of civil government tends to be reflected in the type of ecclesiastical organization which prevails. Democratic societies foster democratic types of religious organization, while political dictatorships tend to accompany autocratic patterns of religious organization. The interaction is mutual in that prevailing patterns of church structure also tend to bring political patterns into harmony with them. This strain toward consistency may stem in part from the desire of human beings for uniformity in their cultural patterns. More basically, the consistency probably results because the same set of basic human needs and beliefs express themselves in various parts of the total social organization. Thus those who believe that dictatorship is more effective than democracy will express this authoritarian philosophy in all of the institutions of their society, whether political, religious, family, economic or educational.

3. When alternative lines of discovery or invention are possible, those which are pursued are ones which conform to the prevailing pattern of group needs found in the culture. That necessity is the mother of invention is the rule, although illegitimate births of inventions occasionally occur unrelated to need. Since much time and effort are required to unearth discoveries or formulate inventions, human beings do not expend such time unless pressed by need to do so. The concept of research as an end in itself is a very late development in human history, and even this concept is justified by the belief that pure research will in the long run be of greater practical benefit than research pursued to solve immediate, day-to-day problems. Even discoveries

or inventions which occur by luck would not be comprehended if apparent needs did not sensitize the innovator to the implications, nor would others incorporate the innovation in their own lives unless they derived practical satisfaction from doing so.

The relationship of human motivation to discovery and invention is a complex one in which a single need, straightforward in effect, rarely operates. What needs, can we theorize, stimulated ancient Jews in their religious innovations? Spiritual impoverishment plus occasional glimpses of a better quality of life perhaps stimulated Jewish prophets to seek for the right view of and the right relationship to God. At the same time, the role of established religious values is always strong. Those priests whose vocation depended upon animal or human sacrifice would repress innovations in a different direction. Since their own status would be threatened, they would not seek such innovations themselves, nor would they want others to do so. Resistances to cultural change, analyzed by T. K. Noss,[26] play a very large role. Noss shows that those who resist social inventions do so because they feel their dominant interests are threatened.

In the realm of religion extraordinary conservatism prevails. This is understandable since a group, having once developed a workable religious system, is reluctant to permit it to be tampered with at the risk of detrimental innovations. Furthermore, each generation in attempting to justify what is inherently difficult to prove tends to assert that doctrines are divinely infallible and admit of no change or rejection in whole or in part. The desire of man to convince himself that he has been successful in finding eternal salvation scarcely encourages him to look further afield for improved religious knowledge. If we inquire why religious culture, and other sections of culture dominated by religion, may remain static for hundreds of years, we find that conservatism has put blinders upon men so they travel in the same grooves generation after generation. The relatively static quality of Christian culture following the innovations in the ancient world, and the relative rigidity of Hindu culture in past centuries, can both be attributed to needs in conservatism effectively suppressing tendencies toward innovation.

Even today religious authority jealously feels itself threatened by the newer and more flexible insights of modern social and psychological science and seeks to dissociate itself from them,

[26] T. K. Noss, *Resistance to Social Innovations, as Found in the Literature Regarding Innovations which Have Proved Successful,* published Ph.D. dissertation, University of Chicago, 1944.

although the time has now passed when intellectual control could be imposed by the churches to thwart such innovations. At the same time, the doctrines of Marxians, when rigidly embraced as a religious system by millions of people in organized hierarchies of power, pose a fresh impediment to freedom of the human mind to pursue threads of truth in unlimited directions. With enlightened government this does not have to occur. The doctrine that man may be allowed to seek truth as long as he does not end in error is exceedingly hazardous since the minds of censors have on innumerable occasions been proved guilty of wrong judgment concerning where error lies and truth rests.

In a more indirect way, a culture dominated by sensate values affords a discouraging milieu for spiritual development to take place. God, as one of the most intangible differentiations from psychic experience of which the human mind is capable, readily slips from the intellectual grip of human beings, especially if materialistic concepts overshadow the scene. Not until these run their course of satiation and human beings can stomach them no longer is the need to turn again to religious development experienced. Moreover, the intellectual obsession with behavioristic psychology for several decades strongly discouraged scientific study of man's psychic existence. There is no scientific need to introspect when it is believed that social science can succeed by limiting itself to the spatially perceived data of the physical world. However, such intellectual currents run their course and reach their limit. If the single road of behaviorism is a dead-end street, sooner or later the human mind finds the path blocked and seeks new avenues of truth.

One of the peculiarities of cultural development of religion is the tendency of religious needs to function in an episodic manner, producing cultural cycles. Religious development, unlike technological change, does not progress uniformly. Rather, mankind seems prone to forget lessons already learned and to rediscover again and again essential truths of human existence. The resulting cultural cycles of growth and decline are not simple to explain. We return to this topic for more detailed treatment in a subsequent section of this chapter.

4. Discovery and invention require time. The intellectual process of differentiation of more advanced ideas from those which are less elaborate takes place slowly, as students in the quest of such ideas can readily testify. Only a culture based upon living conditions which permit ample leisure for reflection can enable growth of new traits or patterns. Probably the reason

why cultural growth was so slow for a million years prior to the present is that the human mind lacked sufficient leisure to progress above the solution of the simplest problems of technology and social organization. It is understandable that fertile river valleys have been cradles of civilization, especially if easily defended from hostile tribes as is the Nile Valley, flanked by desert, in contrast to the Mississippi Valley, which is accessible to warring tribes. The growth of philosophical speculation among sheepherders in the ancient Semitic world is an understandable accompaniment of the free time to exercise the mind which watching flocks permits. Leisure depends upon favorable geographic circumstances, but it depends more immediately upon a sufficient standard of living to permit time to be taken for improvement in technology or in psychic or social existence. Yet a high standard of living is not of itself assurance that leisure prevails. Recurring threat of war may divert wealth into feverish preparation for war while leisure for scientific study or reflection is curtailed.

Even where peace and prosperity prevail, if the personal goals of people are simply in the direction of greater accumulation or conspicuous expenditure of wealth, leisure does not appear. The human mind tends to abhor the vacuum of inactivity. The present leisure time of urban, suburban, and rural dwellers is filled with civic demands, friendship obligations, and social pressures to perfect the appearance of property and care of personal possessions. The concept of leisure has become an anachronism in contemporary culture. Few indeed are the persons capable of resisting the appeal of a larger home, finer car, expensive entertainment of friends, and similar cultural advantages for children in favor of a life of simplicity and contemplation. Although the original sixty-hour work week of preindustrial agrarian culture has almost been cut in half, most persons succumb to social pressures and expend their leisure in exhausting, rather than creative, activities.

In some respects the slave-supported cultures of past history afforded more encouragement to the growth of arts, literature, religion, and science. Where great disparity of wealth exists, those few who control the wealth are not governed by cultural pressures imposed by the mass of people. They can, without distressing their neighbors, reduce their waste of wealth and expend more time upon nonmaterial pursuits. Or they can liberate their employees for vocations of creativity in arts or letters, without these employees feeling a compulsion to spend their time instead in "keeping up with the Joneses." A landowner of ancient Athens or a protégé of a medieval prince frequently enjoyed more leisure for creativity than can be found today. Furthermore, the high degree of division of labor now found in scientific research often necessitates that the individual creator conform to the interests of the research team. Thus the creative individual may not be free to choose his problems or methods, but must give up his individuality under pressure from the business group to which he belongs. These circumstances indicate that wealth, by itself, is not assurance that time is available for creative growth in culture, especially growth not immediately connected with day-to-day economic rewards. There is much to be said in favor of the type of society which deliberately liberates its best minds from routine tasks to pursue creative projects. On the other hand, a religious establishment which believes itself in possession of final and immutable truth will not liberate its personnel to work at creative tasks of religion, but at most will permit them time to work within the confines of existing doctrines.

5. Discovery and invention require intellectual capacity on the part of the innovator. It seems obvious to point out that inventions cannot occur without inventors, yet the principle points up the necessity for an inventive mind. Individuals of great imagination and creativity are infrequently found among the human population. The distribution of characteristics of intelligence by the law of probability means that large variations in ability can occur, although the chances of extremes become increasingly small the larger the extreme. Men of the intellectual keenness of Moses or Jesus are rare.

While heredity is a major determinant of reflective or inventive ability, it is to be remembered that the law of averages means that gifted minds are born occasionally in all times and places. No culture can plead that its lack of accomplishment is due to lack of hereditary material. What is of decisive importance in the appearance of intellectual ability is the opportunity for training afforded by the culture. The concept that one-third of the normal lifetime is to be expended in training the minds of the mass of people is a new one in human history. It is made possible by the much improved standard of living, and it is required by the complex system of specialization in modern economic life. However, the opportunity for education is hardly a guarantee that suitable methods of training will prevail. Where education is geared to the mediocre majority or where teachers are prodded and in turn prod their students to increase the accomplishment on memory tests, creative abilities are abused or neglected. With reference to religion, if the methods of instruction require memorizing infallible truth, the capacity for religious innovation is wasted.

While the five foregoing principles involve component factors in heredity, group life, and the geographic environment, they all involve the culture base upon which innovation is built. The occurrence of religious innovation depends directly upon the type of religious structure already in existence. If this structure is impervious to growth, innovation cannot occur. If the structure is conducive to intellectual creativity, then religious innovation is not only possible, but can be expected.

Principles of Diffusion

The principles under which discovery or invention occur are also the ones under which diffusion of the innovation takes place. Diffusion means that the discovery is accepted as knowledge by others or that the invention is duplicated in the practices of others. If other persons are to do this, they must possess a frame of mind similar to that of the original innovator. His contribution is simply that he was the first to do what others following him repeat. Whether they think or act according to the pattern brought to their consideration depends upon whether they possess the requisite culture-building materials, whether they have moved sufficiently in preceding stages, whether their needs as they experience them are served, whether they have time to consider the innovation, and whether they have the intellectual equipment to appreciate its nature.

The followers of the innovation are aided in replicating it in their minds by having its existence as an accomplished fact called to their attention. However, seeing is not believing. It may be recalled that in so obvious a matter as the achievement of heavier-than-air flight, the Wright brothers were considered by the ignorant public as impostors who deceptively flew their kite on a concealed wire. More than this, eminent men of science published articles proving that heavier-than-air flight was physically impossible. These bits of history about the problems in diffusion of something new are important in understanding the much greater difficulty with which innovations in religion, an unseen affair, are accepted by others.

Innovations which involve highly differentiated abstractions from psychic experience can hardly be communicated to others without the aid of writing. Religion does not become a sophisticated and growing institution until its principles can be recorded in writing. Prior to this its content is a kaleidoscope of shifting myths whose enduring qualities, to the extent that such qualities exist, depend upon enduring social and geographic conditions rather than upon stability of communication. The unique importance of writing is that the description of the thoughts and psychic experiences of others can be held available for study and reflection by others. The assistance of word of mouth lasts only so long as the speaker is talking, while the written record can be reëxamined whenever desired. The building of the world's great religions could not have occurred prior to the mastery of written communication.

A second condition besides writing of fundamental importance in diffusion must be noted, for without it, religious principles diffuse ineffectually or disappear after their innovation. This condition is the presence in the culture of adequate techniques for aiding others in the rediscovery of the religious principles in their own psychic experience. This rediscovery depends, for most persons, upon a carefully guided process of differentiation from one level of concepts to another. This begins with the raw experience of group living, proceeds through sympathetic sharing of the experience of others, continues with the gradual emergence of altruistic motivation, and leads to religious concepts of God and worship. In different religious systems, the terminal concepts vary, and the modes of transmitting religious knowledge to the coming generation also differ from culture to culture. The American Indian youth induced visions by self-torture in quest of his guardian spirit. It has been advocated in some cults of mysticism, as in the East, that the individual spend his lifetime in contemplation, in the expectation thereby of eventually arriving at the sought-for religious insights. Some religious systems, such as Christianity, have stressed the role of prayer as a means of striving for growth in religious understanding. Others have stressed oral instruction combined with reading, or independent study and reading. What is important in any of these systems of religious education is that the learner realize that he must find religious truth for himself and that he be given help in the psychic processes through which he grows to religious understanding.

If, instead, the novice is pressed to learn by rote the wording by which religious ideas are expressed, his understanding is thwarted. One of the primary reasons why great religious systems suffer decline and are forgotten is that their spokesmen failed in the task of communicating what had been discovered. Generation by generation the hold upon psychic reality became increasingly lost. Finally with few or none having the understanding, aid to others in recapturing the psychic truths in their own experience is impossible. Until fresh individuals driven by spiritual impoverishment rediscover religious ideas by their own efforts, and construct a new movement, religion remains verbal, superficial, and dormant. The periodic rise of inspiration in Judaism, the growth of early Christianity, the Golden Age of the Catholic Church in the time of Thomas Aquinas, and the successive waves of spiritual revival in the Protestant Reformation illustrate this rediscovery. The subsequent waning in the wake of each movement indicates how religious understanding recedes through failure to inspire it in succeeding generations. Religious innovations, more than those in any other area of human culture, are vulnerable to evanescence. Obsolescence means that traits are discarded in favor of something of more functional usefulness. This, too, occurs in religion. But evanescence, through insights being lost although people would like to find them, is a marked quality of religious traits and patterns.

CULTURAL CYCLES

The tendency of the cultural development of religion to proceed by ups and downs has already provided occasion for comment. We now turn to this problem. We begin our consideration by reviewing the work of several analysts of cultural change: Oswald Spengler, P. A. Sorokin, and Arnold Toynbee. Each of these men has developed his own interpretation of why cycles of religious development occur.

Spengler and Sorokin

Spengler argues by analogy from the biological life cycle. Each of the great civilizations of the world is born, grows, declines, and dies. A culture is born when human beings acquire social and religious ideas for better possibilities of life. Civilization acquires a new "soul." Under the expanding impetus of fresh ideas, a civilization is built. When the apparent possibilities of these ideas have run their course, their appeal recedes and the civilization declines. In the grip of downward movement, people become pessimistic and then despairing. They live for immediate pleasures. Finally the soul of the civilization dies. Human life continues only on a level of biological survival. Spengler's conclusion is one of pessimism in that present-day civilization is in a phase of decline.

Sorokin sees history as a fluctuation between two types of culture, ideational and sensate. Ideational culture is dominated by intellectual and spiritual concepts. Sensate culture is characterized by pleasure-seeking and material satisfactions. He documents his theory of cultural cycles with extensive statistical materials from different fields of culture, such as literature, art, science, and religion. Whether or not one agrees with Sorokin's explanation of the reason for cultural cycles, he has conclusively demonstrated the cyclical nature of culture. He attributes the rise in sensate culture, a form now dominating the Western world, to the false notion that reality is given by sensory observation. The alternate phase of ideational culture is brought about by realization that supersensory experience, what has been described here as psychic experience, is the true source of reality. Sorokin does not explain why the alternation of orientation to reality occurs, except that it results from an intrinsic dynamic in which each form of culture must run its course and be replaced by its polar opposite.

Let us trace the course of the revolution in some detail. As has been pointed out in earlier chapters, at the close of the sensate periods of the past the formerly magnificent edifice began to totter. Material pleasures and comforts, utility, security, safety, and freedom progressively declined. War and other forms of strife, brutality, bloodshed, and destruction became endemic. Efforts to patch up the crumbling system invariably miscarried. Under such circumstances people could not fail to perceive eventually the hollowness of sensate culture, the hopelessness of further allegiance to sensate values, and the impossibility of attempting to preserve an orderly way of life on so rotten a foundation. This realization, in turn, led to a defection from the banner of sensate culture and values and to a transfer of allegiance to ideational or idealistic values which appeared to be eternal, indestructible, and independent of anything material and external. Through this fiery ordeal was the catharsis, or purification, of society from its sensate sins and vices finally achieved.

With this catharsis accomplished, there ensued the next phase—that of grace, or charisma. The destructive phase was followed by one that was constructive. The "atomization" of values was replaced by their universalization and "absolutization"; expediency, pleasure, and utility, by duty; licentious freedom, by the sanctity of norms and justice; coercion and egoistic contract, if not by all-embracing, all-bestowing, and all-forgiving love, at least by more familistic and altruistic relationships. Religion, ethics, and law overcame the unbridled sway of force and fraud. God took the place of materialism; spiritual values, that of sensate values. In brief, all the essential sensate values were replaced by less sensate values, either ideational or idealistic.

Purified and ennobled, society proceeded to erect a new house based on the Absolute, God, love, duty, sacrifice, grace, and justice. The poison of decadent sensate culture eliminated, strife and bloodshed diminished, security and safety of life returned, stable order was re-established, and fresh creative forces were released. Society and individuals were once more at peace with themselves, with their fellow men, with the world, and with God. Thus was ushered in the phase of resurrection, with its long perspective of new creative life.

Such was the invariable course of the great crises of the past. Such is the way out of our own crisis. There is no other possibility.[27]

In Sorokin's analysis, as well as in that of Spengler, the question largely remains unanswered of why the cyclical effects occur. Why do civilizations rise? Why does sensate culture recur when the ideational phase obviously offers a superior mode of existence? To attribute such changes to the ebb and flow of ideational versus sensate views of reality does not explain why this cognitive fluctuation occurs. Contemporary psychology has shown that what people perceive or contemplate is conditioned by what their desires are which sensitize them to different aspects of life. The more fundamental question is why shifts in human motivation from ideational to sensate occur in the ebb and flow of cultural cycles.

Toynbee: Upward Cycles

A more adequate answer to the explanation of cultural cycles of religious development and decline is furnished by Arnold Toynbee. He regards the role of religion to be central in human history. His views of this role, fully developed in the ten-volume work *A Study of History,* are given briefly and concisely in *An Historian's Approach to Religion.* In recent years many historians have avoided the quest for laws of cultural history and have criticized Toynbee for his preoccupations and conclusions concerning these. The controversy serves to show that the interpretation of cultural development is not a clear-cut scientific

[27] P. A. Sorokin, *The Crisis of Our Age,* Dutton, 1957, pp. 323–324.

demonstration, but requires an imaginative reconstruction of the psychic variables which operate in history. All of the methodological problems of case-study analysis of a single individual are replicated on a vast scale when the history of civilizations or of the entire span of the cultural development of the human race is made the topic for a case study.

Toynbee's view of cultural development is not that of either cultural cycles or linear development, but a combination of the two patterns. He describes the progress of civilization as the path described by a point on a chariot wheel moving up a slope. The long-run trend is upward, but the short-run trend is cyclical. However, the explanation which Toynbee gives of why the pattern of development occurs is an ambitious advance over that of Spengler and Sorokin. Like Sorokin, he cites voluminous data in *A Study of History* from civilizations past and present. These data, however, are case-study data, rather than statistical, and they refer in a particularistic way to individual people, their actions, writings, beliefs, and purposes. These data are mobilized to demonstrate and interpret the thesis that religious motivation is the prime mover of history. The resulting movement has been periodic, but upward.

Higher religion, according to Toynbee, arises in human history as a reaction to suffering. It is a reaction consisting of love for others, rather than an exercise of physical power over them.

> The converted soul abandons an unconverted Human Nature's effort to escape Suffering for oneself by the acquisition and exercise of some kind of Power—whether collective and physical or individual and psychic. It adopts, instead, the opposite attitude of accepting Suffering for oneself and trying to turn one's own suffering to positive account by acting, at the cost of suffering, on one's feelings of Pity and Love for one's fellow-creatures. This change of heart in Man opens his eyes to a new vision of God. It gives him a glimpse of a God who is Love as well as Power, and who is not a deification either of Human or of Non-Human Nature, but is the deliverer of these and all His creatures from the evil of self-centeredness to which every creature is prone. The new religions in which this change of heart expresses itself may be called "higher religions," because they rise above Man-worship as well as above Nature-worship.[28]

The religious movement which arises, whether Eastern or Western, encounters obstacles which make its progress uneven and may serve temporarily to defeat its spiritual purposes. The

[28] From *An Historian's Approach to Religion,* by Arnold J. Toynbee, p. 78.

first of these obstacles is the initial encounter with political empires. When the religious inspiration first manifests itself and gains adherents, these are typically intransigent men whose purposes cannot be withdrawn in the face of a hostile political regime. They are persecuted and become martyrs for the religion. In Toynbee's analysis, religion succeeds in this initial encounter with the state, but succumbs to other obstacles.

Of all the challenges that are encountered by the sower of the seed, the challenge of persecution is the one to which the followers of the higher religions have succeeded in responding with the greatest measure of success. Though, in all persecutions, there are, no doubt, always many weaker vessels who do not fail to stand the ordeal, the followers of the higher religions have been conspicuous, on the whole, for their steadfastness and courage when put to the test.[29]

The question what the higher religion's relation to the old order is to be remains simple and easy so long as the old order is proscribing and persecuting them; it becomes complicated and difficult if and when the old order offers to come to terms. "Blessed are ye when men shall hate you and when they shall separate you from their company and shall reproach you and cast out your name as evil for the Son of Man's sake. . . . Woe unto you when all men shall speak well of you! For so did their fathers to the false prophets." So long as a Church is proscribed and is exposed to the peril of being persecuted at any moment, its membership is likely to be limited to a spiritual elite who are both disinterested and courageous. As soon as it is taken into partnership by the powers that be, its moral quality is likely to be diluted through mass conversions of the time-servers eager to jump on to the victor's band-wagon. So long as a church is proscribed, it can build up a new society at its own peril without being implicated in the old society's weaknesses and sins. When it has been taken into partnership with the old society, it will be involved in its failures and be led astray into serving its purposes instead of continuing to serve its own incompatible purpose single-mindedly. Therefore the negotiation of a concordat with any of the institutions embodying the old order is likely to blunt a church's edge for the execution of its own spiritual mission, and even to divert it from this mission into the old order's service. Yet since a church's mission is to preach the gospel to every creature, a church would be acting at variance with its own purpose if it were to rebuff offers of reconciliation proposed by former opponents, even if these offers are suspect of being insincere and of being inspired, at least subconsciously, by an intention to carry the old struggle on by means of a new, more subtle, and more effective strategy.

Conversely, the old order stands to gain by proposing terms for a concordat. It is losing nothing further by making a public acknowl-

[29] *Ibid.,* p. 92.

edgment that it has tried and failed to suppress the preachers of the new gospel by physical force. It is merely acknowledging an already patent fact; and, in making this concession, it is purchasing cheaply for itself a chance of carrying on the struggle by a new strategy. It can now try to defeat its adversary by mobilizing, for its own purposes, the strength which has enabled this adversary to withstand victoriously all forcible attempts to suppress him. This strength resides in two elements: the new gospel's spiritual appeal to human souls in virtue of its truth and rightness; and the new institution—the church—which the preachers of the new gospel will have had to build up as a necessary means for carrying out their spiritual aim. The construction of a church is unavoidable, since institutions of some sort—Devil's work though all institutions may be—are the only instruments that Mankind has yet devised for giving human relations a wider range than can be obtained through direct personal intercourse. Cannot the hold which the Church has secured over people's minds and hearts by disseminating a new gospel with a strong appeal be turned to account for the benefit of the old order? The answer is that the Church can be captured and converted into an instrument for the furtherance of the old order's interests if the maneuver is not advertised or avowed.[30]

Besides the dilution of a religious movement by its encounter with the prevailing social order, another obstacle to which religions of the world succumb in part is intellectualization of their spiritual message. The intellectually elite whose support is sought put in arbitrary words the vision of religion. Thus love gives way to talking about love, and genuine religious life is replaced by theological exercise.

The Church could not afford to rebuff an overture for an intellectual rapprochement with the philosophically educated upper-class, any more than it could afford to reject an offer for a political rapprochement with the Imperial Government—and this for the same reason: the Church's mission was to convert the World, not to hide her light under a bushel. So, at her peril, the Church must embrace any opportunities for conversion that might offer themselves; and the conversion of the professional philosophers called for special efforts, because these were the most difficult of all elements in the Graeco-Roman Society for the Christian Church to win. Unlike the rest of the pagan majority of the population of the Roman Empire, the philosophers were too proud to jump onto the Church's band-wagon just because the Emperor Constantine I had patronized Christianity and because the Emperor Theodosius I had penalized Paganism. The philosophers' ideal was self-sufficiency, intellectual as well as moral; they had worked out an intellectual as well as a moral system of their own, and

[30] *Ibid.*, pp. 108–110.

they believed that they could live by it. If Christianity was to have any prospect of converting the professors at the universities of Athens and Alexandria or the magnates of the senatorial aristocracy at Rome, the Church must be prepared to come on to the philosophers' intellectual ground by translating her gospel into their terms.[31]

Thus the attempt to translate Prophetic Vision, expressed in the language of poetic truth, into a metaphysical blueprint, expressed in the language of scientific truth, has two untoward effects. It forces us to direct our attention from what is essential and momentous in the poetic truth of Prophetic Vision to the trivial and intrinsically insoluble question of its relation to scientific truth; and it substitutes a provisional report for a timeless intuition. Even if we could succeed in translating poetic truth into scientific truth at the risk of robbing it of its meaning and value, our scientific formula would no sooner have been drafted than it would be already obsolete.

This is what has happened to Christianity and Islam as a consequence of the attempts to translate them into terms of Hellenic metaphysics. This intellectual "processing" took the life out of them even for the small minority of philosophically educated people in the Graeco-Roman World who thought in the particular terms of Hellenic metaphysics; and these Hellenic terms have become a greater and greater stumbling block as the progress of Science has traveled farther and farther away from the local and temporary formulation of scientific truth in the blueprint of Hellenic metaphysics.[32]

The final obstacle described by Toynbee is the tendency to idolize religious institutions, which begins with idolization of founders and sacred writings. This opens the way to degeneration which men are powerless to combat because of their veneration of the prevailing institution.

In any living creature, the worst of all sins is the idolization of itself or of its own handiwork. This sin is the worst of all because it is the greatest moral and intellectual rebellion that a creature can make against its true state of subordination to God the Absolute Reality, and also because it opens the door to all other sins. This arch-sin is committed by the followers of a higher religion when they idolize their own religious institution; and self-idolizing claims to uniqueness and finality have been made, in authoritarian terms that forbid dissent and even discussion, by all the higher religions, and particularly by those of Israelite origin.[33]

For, whether the founder of a higher religion is or is not deemed to be God Himself, he is credited with a superhuman authority; and this authority is deemed to have been bequeathed and transmitted by him,

[31] *Ibid.*, pp. 120–121.
[32] *Ibid.*, pp. 128–129.
[33] *Ibid.*, p. 131.

after his departure from This World, to some perennial depository of his legacy.

This perennial authority may be invested in a living corporation or in a canonical holy scripture; and, if in a living corporation, in one of this or that alternative type. It may be an unorganized body like the doctors of the Jewish and Islamic Law, who are recruited by apprenticeship and co-option, or like the Brahmans, who are qualified by birth for the efficacious performance of religious rites. Or it may be an organized priesthood, like the hereditary Israelite priests and the Levites and the hereditary Median magi who took possession of Zarathustra's religious heritage. These two types of living corporation may also be combined, as they are in the Roman Catholic Christian Church, in which the priesthood, like the Jewish and the Zoroastrian priesthood, is an organized hierarchy (though it differs from them both in being non-hereditary), while the highest source of authority is the head of the hierarchy acting in unison with an oecumenical council of fathers whose powers correspond to those of the Jewish and Islamic doctors.

The alternative is for the perennial authority to be invested in a canonical holy scripture. All the higher religions made their epiphany in literate societies; all of them have therefore had sacred books purporting to be authentic records of their founder's words and acts; and so, when the adherents of a higher religion have revolted against the authority of a living corporation, they have been apt to appeal to the authority of Holy Scripture as an alternative depository of the founder's legacy. They have taken the line that Holy Scripture, not the priesthood or the doctors, is the ultimate perennial authority representing the founder, and that each individual member of the Church has a right, at his peril, to interpret this written oracle for himself. Protestant Western Christianity is perhaps, among all the higher religions, the one in which the attribution of authority to a book instead of to a priesthood has been the most conscious and deliberate. Sikhism—in which the Granth is virtually deified—is perhaps the religion in which the idolization of a book has been carried to the farthest lengths.

There is no higher religion in which both the alternative depositories of authority are not to be found side by side, though their relative importance has varied greatly as between one religion and another.[34]

The persistent survival of a number of competing claimants to the privilege of being the recipients and vehicles of a unique and final revelation is a challenge to all the competing claims alike; for the privilege, if it has ever been granted, is necessarily exclusive. Only one of these absolute claims can be valid if there is any validity in anyone of them. The rest of them must be false in any case when made in these absolute terms.[35]

[34] *Ibid.*, pp. 133–134.
[35] *Ibid.*, pp. 138–139.

Toynbee acknowledges that he draws the rudiments of his principles of cultural change in religion from the parable of the sower. "And he told them many things in parables, saying: 'A sower went out to sow. And as he sowed, some seeds fell along the path, and the birds came and devoured them. Other seeds fell on rocky ground, where they had not much soil, and immediately they sprang up, since they had no depth of soil, but when the sun rose they were scorched; and since they had no root they withered away. Other seeds fell upon thorns, and the thorns grew up and choked them. Other seeds fell on good soil and brought forth grain, some a hundredfold, some sixty, some thirty.' "[36]

The interplay of spiritual forces and secular obstacles accounts for the rise and relative decline of religious cultures. Each fresh growth begins at a higher point and moves further than preceding cultures in spiritual achievement. The formulation of succeeding ideas and ideals becomes clearer and more profound. Toynbee concludes his analysis on a note of cautious optimism, that all of the world's religions contribute to human progress, that they are continually being tested by events, and that the simple homely virtues of love and charity will prove supreme in history after the present idolization of technology has receded.

Meanwhile, all the living religions are going to be put to a searching practical test. "By their fruits ye shall know them." The practical test of a religion, always and everywhere, is its success or failure in helping human souls to respond to the challenges of Suffering and Sin. In the chapter of the World's history on which we are now entering, it looks as if the continuing progress of Technology were going to make our sufferings more acute than ever before, and our sins more devastating in their practical consequences. This is going to be a testing time, and, if we are wise, we shall await its verdict.

If we do not feel that we can afford to wait for Time to do its discriminating work, we are confessing to a lack of faith in the truth and value of the religion that happens to be ours. On the other hand, if we do have faith in it, we shall have no fear that it will fail to play its full part in helping human souls to enter into communion with the presence behind the phenomena and to bring themselves into harmony with this Absolute Reality. The missions of the higher religions are not competitive; they are complimentary. We can believe in our own religion without having to feel that it is the sole repository of truth. We can love it without having to feel that it is the sole means of salvation. We can take Symmachus's words to heart without being disloyal to Christianity. We cannot harden our hearts against Symmachus

[36] Matthew 13:3–8.

without hardening them against Christ. For what Symmachus is preaching is Christian charity. "Charity never faileth; but, whether there be prophecies, they shall fail; whether there be tongues, they shall cease; whether there be knowledge, it shall vanish away."[37]

The flow and ebb of religious inspiration is evident in the fluctuating fortunes of the ancient Jews as recorded in their Bible, the long-run trend being toward fuller inspiration. The rise of Christianity was followed by a decline as it came to terms with the Roman Empire, intellectualized its spiritual content, and idolized its institutional expression. Occasional revivals are evident during the dominance of the Catholic Church in the Middle Ages, but these upswings were neither universal nor enduring. In Toynbee's view, Christianity has followed a generally downward path since its initial growth in the ancient world. He minimizes the revival in spiritual culture during the Protestant Reformation in the sixteenth, seventeenth, and eighteenth centuries. He strongly scores the religious persecutions and wars which characterized this period, one so unlike the period of original Christianity.

> The nemesis of the Reformation was the bout of Western wars of religion, and these fratricidal wars . . . exhibited Catholics and Protestants in France, the Netherlands, Germany, and Ireland, and rival sects of Protestants in England and Scotland, in the brutal act of trying to suppress one another by force of arms. It was a still more lamentable spectacle to see Religion being used as a tool for the furtherance of mundane military and political purposes, and to recognize that this was a consequence of Religion's own unprincipled attempt to use War and Politics as weapons in ecclesiastical struggles for supremacy.[38]

Since the Protestant Reformation, Christianity has fallen into moral and intellectual discredit in the West's own estimation, according to Toynbee.

In the present author's opinion, Toynbee fails to appreciate the moral regeneration which occurred with the rise of Protestant churches, and in particular the pacifism which characterized Quakers, Anabaptists, and others. Martin Luther, John Calvin, Menno Simons, George Fox, and John Wesley were architects of the Reformation. They possessed powerful inward convictions and much tenacity of purpose and gave themselves without limit to bringing men to the spiritual reality of God. Nor can the con-

[37] Toynbee, *op. cit.,* pp. 298–299.
[38] *Ibid.,* pp. 171–172.

tributions of Protestants to the growth of civil liberties, to prison reform, and to expansion of economic productivity and improved standard of living be overlooked. Secular though these enterprises are, their religious roots are strong. That the Protestant ethic is no longer the spirit of capitalism is, of course, true. The present decay of culture to which Spengler, Sorokin, and Toynbee point seems irrefutable. But the decline seems of shorter duration than Toynbee indicates.

Forces Producing Religious Cycles

The three principles which Toynbee concludes bring about reversal in the forward movement of religious culture seem to cover the three main aspects of religious decline: compromise with the existing social order, intellectual formulation in meaningless words, and assumption of infallibility or at least idolization of words and deeds of religious leaders and of the institutions involving them.

These principles, especially the first and second, seem to require fuller statement and more precise conceptualization of the forces which they represent. To point to compromise with the existing social order merely describes the decreasing saltiness of religion. "Salt is good; but if salt has lost its taste, how shall its saltness be restored?"[39] The question is one of why the original forcefulness becomes diluted.

A basic principle of the cultural development of religion is that religious movements arise because of deeply felt desires, such as for the reintegration of personality and for intensification of altruistic motivation. Bearing in mind that religion is essentially a system of practices which reconstruct motivation, the intensity with which these practices are pursued is obviously related to the degree with which needs are felt. When a reformed institution gains momentum, the need which it serves is less acutely experienced. Consequently, the social structure of behavior provoked by the need recedes with recession in the immediate need. Numerous instances can be found of waves of reform activities which arise when need becomes severe and then disappear until members of a group are rearoused by a recurrence of their feeling of distress. Only if human beings have rational foresight do they pay continuous attention to maintaining their institutions in good social health. This foresight depends upon an understanding of the cyclical forces involved, an

[39] Luke 14:34.

understanding not likely to arise until the cyclical effects have been both experienced and scientifically analyzed.

In line with the general principle of institutional fluctuation in response to need, we conclude that religious activity also fluctuates in response to the needs for it. Because of the general obscurity of religious activity in relation to the needs which stimulate it, it follows that the fluctuations in religious development are likely to be more marked than for any other human institution which might be the focus of efforts at reform. Nor can any novelty be claimed for pointing to the tendency of human beings to forget religion after they have regained emotional security or economic success. Martin Luther and John Wesley noted the tendency of religious consecration to give way to economic wealth and the disregard of religion. A contemporary novelist, Theodore Dreiser, wrote a book, *The Bulwark,* describing the experiences of several generations of a Quaker family from religion to riches to ruin. It is quite understandable, as Max Weber points out in *The Protestant Ethic and the Spirit of Capitalism,* that religious dedication should bring worldly success, since such dedication encourages careful stewardship of God's talents and wealth, hard work, thrift, help to others, and honesty. These qualities of character attract trade from customers seeking dependable service. The tendency of people to live in the present, forgetting the past and being blind to the future, keeps them from seeing the needs in a previous generation which their religion rose to meet. Motivation for economic life today is not religious, but secular. Success in the eyes of others and lavish consumption are central motives for vocational life. Not until the cultural assets of religion accumulated from previous generations are exhausted do people again turn to the help of religion. Then altruistic forces reassert themselves anew.

Toynbee's second principle also touches a critical area. But it must be explained why the intellectual formulation of religion by philosophers in past history has robbed religion of its meaning. An answer is initiated by Jung. When people substitute empty forms and phrases for religious meaning, they have lost the ability to make contact with essential psychic components in their unconscious. Specifically, we may say the fault rests with the methods whereby proponents of religion endeavor to instruct others. The fault is not necessarily in their technical vocabulary, which may serve essential purposes of precision and clarity. The fault lies in teaching people to memorize words instead of equipping them with the techniques of study whereby they can gain genuine psychic truth for themselves. It need surprise no one that the intellectualization of religion has in the past strangled its spiritual vitality. The purveyors of the intellectual formulations have sought to push them sideways into people's heads instead of guiding and allowing the formulations to grow from the depths of the mind through introspective seeking.

Related to the second principle is the tendency of religionists to claim divine sanction for their institution and its pronouncements and activities. The institution is an expression of motivation *felt* to be the will of God. The fault arises when it is claimed that the institution *is* the will of God. Especially when this will is considered infallible and unchangeable, such a claim freezes any further development or refinement in the institutional pattern. The claim of infallibility for the institution, or at least of infallibility for its religious scriptures, arises from wishful thinking that absolute salvation has been found, from fear that any innovation will worsen, rather than ameliorate the religious system, and from efforts to convince others of adequate authority for scriptural truth. The insistence upon infallibility discourages individual inquiry into psychic experience. In the present cultural context this orthodoxy combats science as a method of gaining religious truth. The insistence upon adhering to orthodoxy combines with defective methods of religious instruction to destroy the possibility of renewing the religious patterns when these succumb to dilution by the rest of the cultural situation. The initial rise of new religious forms, under these conditions of idolization of the institution, is inevitably followed by a downswing in the religious patterns which were built up by previous effort and sacrifice.

The implication of these three principles is that cyclical fluctuations in religious culture are not a necessary development. If human beings are aware of the tendencies counter to religious growth and exercise foresight in meeting them, steady development of religious culture seems possible.

TRENDS IN CONTEMPORARY RELIGIOUS CULTURE

The long-run trend in America has apparently been away from religion, as far as intensity of religious observance is concerned. At the same time numerical church membership and per capita church giving have increased, especially since the years of World War II, although a leveling off or possible recession in these figures is perhaps indicated. The net impression is one of a decline of religion in America, a long-run trend undergoing some reversal in the decade following World War II. The concept of "decline" may mean no more than that a quantitative or statistical recession takes place in the amount or extent of a particular form of culture. It can also imply that there is a reduction in human achievement or human welfare. Data to document how well religion serves human welfare today compared with formerly are difficult to obtain. Within the past three decades, considerable research has been done in assessing levels of happiness and personal adjustment in such areas as marriage and vocation, but numerical measures of religious satisfaction or overall adequacy of culture have not been undertaken. No psychometric data in any form are available from past centuries. If an evaluation is sought, it is necessary to draw inferences from indications in writing, thinking, and acting associated with individual and group well-being. In discussing the decline in contemporary religious culture, our attention is principally upon the change in the relative extent of religious aspects compared with other aspects of culture. In this section we consider contemporary trends and some additional reasons for the trends besides the factors examined under cyclical effects. We start with the long-run trend of the past hundred years.

Data of Decline in Religious Culture

In sections of colonial America solid religious communities were established, while in other places religion was forgotten in the rush for land and easy wealth. W. E. Garrison states that less than 10 percent of the U.S. population were church members in 1800.[40] Membership statistics leave little doubt of the numerical growth of church membership.[41] The crude statistical increase is impressive. By decades beginning with 1850 the percentages of the total population who are church members are 16, 23, 18, 20, 22, 36, 43, 43, 47, and 49 in 1940. In adjusting these figures to show the percentage of the population aged 13 and over who are members, Argyle finds a decline in percentages from 55 in 1916 to 51 in 1940, with a rise to 64 in 1950. Much of the earlier

[40] W. E. Garrison, "Characteristics of American Organized Religion," *The Annals of the American Academy of Political and Social Science,* March, 1948, p. 20.

[41] *Yearbook of American Churches,* National Council of the Churches of Christ in the U.S.A., 1960, p. 279. M. Argyle, *Religious Behavior,* Free Press, 1959, pp. 28–29.

growth is explained by relaxation in qualifications for church membership and by the former practice of listing heads of households as members. But also adding to the growth are the effectiveness of Protestant evangelism in reaching the unchurched and the immigration to the United States of Roman Catholics with nearly inclusive church membership. The zeal of "circuit rider" preachers on the frontier, the popularity of "camp meetings" for wholesale conversion, and the organizational efficiency of the Catholic Church swelled church membership from a small minority to a large majority of the population. At the present time about three-fifths of the population has been persuaded or pressed into church membership by the efforts of organized religion. The word *pressed* is used advisedly. There seems little question that many persons belong to church through a desire to conform. Such membership is due to what Riesman calls "other-directedness" or social pressure from without, rather than spiritual incentive from within. Will Herberg, a discerning analyst of contemporary religious trends, elaborates this idea.

> In particular, it is not difficult to see the current turn to religion and the church as, in part at least, a reflection of the growing other-directedness of our middle-class culture. The people in the suburbs want to feel psychologically secure, adjusted, at home in their environment; the very character structure that makes this so urgent a necessity for them also operates to meet the need. Being religious and joining a church is, under contemporary American conditions, a fundamental way of "adjusting" and "belonging"; through the built-in radar apparatus of other-direction it becomes almost automatic as an obvious social requirement, like entertaining or culture. The vogue of Van Gogh and Renoir reproductions in the suburban home and the rising church affiliation of the suburban community may not be totally unconnected; both may, without disparagement, be interpreted, in part at least, as the consequence of the craving for adjustment and conformity involved in other-direction. The right kind of art reproductions testify to one's being adjusted to the culture of one's "peer-group"; belonging to the church is experienced as the most satisfactory form of social "belonging." The trend toward religious identification and church affiliation may thus to an extent be a reflection of the growing need for conformity and sociability that the drift to other-direction brings with it.[42]

Offsetting the change in numbers of members is a pronounced decline in the extent to which religion is observed in life activi-

[42] From *Protestant-Catholic-Jew,* by Will Herberg, pp. 72–73. Copyright © 1955 by Will Herberg. Reprinted by permission of Doubleday & Company, Inc.

ties. In the early days of the republic, it was common for church members to be expelled for moral or religious deviation. Membership implied a serious obligation to fulfill religious requirements. Going to church for long services on Sunday and attendance at mid-week prayer meeting was expected. At the present time, the Sunday service is conveniently packaged in a one-hour administration. If the minister "talks overtime" members become restless and look at their watches. Wednesday evening prayer meeting is almost a thing of the past, very few churches continuing it, and those which do finding scarcely a handful of attenders. From 1906 to 1936 the U.S. Census returns show that the number of Sunday School pupils per 1,000 church members dropped from 418 to 329.[43] A comparison of literature today with that of a century or two ago indicates that religious-minded people speak more reticently about God than formerly. For the social conversation in the 1920's and 30's to turn enthusiastically to God was rare. "Religion and the churches were in retreat, faith was taken as a sign of intellectual backwardness or imbecility, and the initiative had passed to the 'emancipated' debunkers of the superstitions of the 'Babbitts' and the 'Bible Belt.' "[44]

One of the striking pieces of evidence of the decline in religious thinking in the twentieth century was assembled by H. Hart in *Recent Social Trends.* He and his research staff tabulated the changes in magazine circulation of religious and scientific periodicals. In 1900 the magazines devoted to religious subjects formed 5 percent of the total circulation of all magazines, and in 1930 this had fallen to 1 percent. Meanwhile, the circulation of scientific periodicals rose from 1 percent to 4 percent.[45] The trend through the decade following 1930 is shown by Hart by a tabulation of entries for religious articles in the *Readers' Guide.* This shows a drop from .8 percent of the total entries in 1930 to .5 percent in 1941.[46]

That church membership became a relatively minor incident in the lives of the majority is shown by an opinion poll in the *Ladies' Home Journal* in 1948. Herberg describes this poll:

> But perhaps the most significant discrepancy in the assertions Americans make about their religious views is to be found in another area.

[43] H. Hart, "Religion," *American Journal of Sociology,* May, 1942, p. 892.

[44] Herberg, *op. cit.,* p. 66.

[45] H. Hart, "Changing Social Attitudes and Interests," *Recent Social Trends,* McGraw-Hill, 1933, p. 391.

[46] H. Hart, "Religion," *American Journal of Sociology,* May, 1942, p. 889.

When asked, "Would you say your religious beliefs have any effect on your ideas of politics and business?" a majority of the same Americans who had testified that they regarded religion as something "very important" answered that their religious beliefs had no real effect on their ideas or conduct in these decisive areas of everyday life; specifically, 54 percent said no, 39 percent said yes, 7 percent refused to reply or didn't know.[47]

The shallowness and hypocrisy in contemporary religion have been documented in a shocking study by Schneider and Dornbusch of the content of religious best sellers.[48] Even allowing for their apparent lack of appreciation of some essential features of religion, their conclusions are still a stinging rebuke which is acknowledged by the managing editor of the *Christian Century*.[49]

Turning to broader social indices, the trends in divorce, sexual activity, and crime are illuminating when considered in relation to the opposing numerical trend in church membership. Until the latter third of the nineteenth century, the number of marriages in the United States terminating in divorce did not exceed 3 percent. According to reports of the Bureau of Census, in 1900 the number had risen to 9 percent and by 1940, 21 percent. The peak in 1945 immediately following World War II was 33 percent. Since 1950 the rate has been about 22 percent. These figures are based upon the marriage rate during the preceding ten years. In view of the powerful role which religion has traditionally played in sanctioning stable marriage, the declining influence of religion is evident. Religion has not been able to resist more powerful cultural forces making for more prevalent divorce.

Chastity before marriage and fidelity within marriage bonds are deeply ingrained in traditional religious culture. Accurate statistics concerning sexual behavior have been difficult to obtain. Not until Kinsey and his associates conducted their large-scale studies was the American public receptive to such inquiries. Despite the criticisms made of the research methods of Kinsey, the consensus of scientific opinion is that he and his workers have assembled the most complete and dependable statistics available. By interrogating respondents of different ages, a method introduced by L. M. Terman, it is possible to gain knowledge of the sexual behavior of people in somewhat different

[47] Herberg, *op. cit.*, p. 86.

[48] Louis Schneider and S. M. Dornbusch, *Popular Religion*, University of Chicago Press, 1958.

[49] T. A. Gill, "Best-Seller Religion," *Christian Century*, October 8, 1958, pp. 1144–1145.

cultural stages. For men, Kinsey finds little change between those born in different decades, except that the more recent men become premaritally active younger.[50] For those with grade school, high school, and college education, the cumulative incidences of premarital coitus for men are 98, 85, and 68 percent, and for extramarital coitus the cumulative incidence for all males is approximately 50 percent. For women a definite cultural trend is evident. For those women born before 1900, the incidence of premarital coitus is 14 percent and for those born after it is about 37 percent. The incidence of extramarital coitus is 22 percent for the earlier generation of women and 30 percent for the later.[51] Studies by Terman and Locke comparing different birth-date groups show similar results, except that the trend of increasing nonmarital coitus with reference to men as well as women is well marked, the incidence approximately doubling between earlier and later groups. The increase found by Terman may be due to the higher education of the male in his samples, a group sexually less active outside of marriage and in which opportunity for a rising trend more clearly exists.[52]

Crime rates are significant in showing the extent of behavior opposite to altruism taught by religion. Criminal statistics reflect changing standards of conduct, as well as the conduct itself, since the number of laws has increased markedly with the years, and higher expectations are placed on juvenile behavior than formerly. Statistics of crime are also peculiarly vulnerable to waves of enforcement by police who are alternately lax and severe, depending upon changing political conditions. Nevertheless, the rise in the amount of crime is a conspicuous feature of American life. From 1900 to 1930, shown by arrests analyzed by E. H. Sutherland and C. E. Gehlke, the crime rates for all offenses rose twofold, and the homicide rate for five cities rose fourfold.[53] Since 1931, according to *Uniform Crime Reports,* compiled by the Federal Bureau of Investigation, homicide rates have fallen somewhat, to 5 per 100,000 population, and rates for all offenses by 1958 had increased about 10 percent to 2 per 100 population.

[50] A. C. Kinsey, W. B. Pomeroy, and C. E. Martin, *Sexual Behavior in the Human Male,* Saunders, 1948, p. 411.

[51] A. C. Kinsey, W. B. Pomeroy, C. E. Martin, and P. H. Gebhart, *Sexual Behavior in the Human Female,* Saunders, 1953, pp. 330, 331, 437.

[52] L. M. Terman, *Psychological Factors in Marital Happiness,* McGraw-Hill, 1938, p. 321; H. J. Locke, *Predicting Adjustment in Marriage,* Holt, 1951, p. 136.

[53] E. H. Sutherland and C. E. Gehlke, "Crime and Punishment," *Recent Social Trends,* McGraw-Hill, 1933, pp. 1125, 1127.

Before turning to the upward trend in religious interest and activity since World War II, we will examine reasons for the long-run decline, one which Toynbee believes has gone on since the initial centuries of Christianity and one which seems at least to have proceeded since the spiritual revival during successive waves of the Protestant Reformation in the sixteenth, seventeenth, and eighteenth centuries. It is difficult to evaluate the religiosity in former times, but journals and letters disclose that intense religious feeling and devotion to God gripped such groups as Quakers and Methodists during their inception. In the view of Max Weber, the Protestant ethic, with its ideals of hard work, frugality, honesty, and stewardship to God played a dominant role in the rise of capitalist enterprise, and prior to that, in medieval economic life, Catholic ethics were influential. In contrast, the values which motivate contemporary economic life today are, relatively speaking, those of monetary success, conspicuous consumption, and individual pleasure. Besides the cyclical influences previously referred to, large cultural developments, such as urbanism, capitalism, and scientific thought have played important roles in the long-range decline in religious culture. These cultural developments are intertwined with a series of inventions which are the heart of the industrial revolution. We now examine these in relation to long-run changes in religion.

Urbanism

Urbanism refers to the concentration of population in large communities and to the way of life connected with this concentration. The growth of cities is much older than the industrial revolution, but at no previous time in history did more than a small part of the population live in cities, which were of small size. Peasant subsistence on agriculture was the prevailing pattern. U.S. census figures indicate that in the time of the American Revolution nine out of ten families lived on farms and grew food for themselves and only one other family in cities or villages. In 1959 the rural farm population had declined to 11.5 percent of the total. Through vastly improved technology this farm population grew enough food for the nation and large blocks of population outside of it.

The revolution in the efficiency with which food can be grown and life sustained, compared to the way in which the human race previously survived for thousands of years, stems from a series of inventions. These include: (1) mechanical power, such as steam, electric, internal combustion, and now atomic energy; (2) labor-replacing machines, ranging from weaving of textiles to fabrication of automobiles, buildings, and highways; (3) fast, efficient transportation, including the conveyor belt of the assembly line; (4) instantaneous communication; (5) automation and computing devices which substitute for human thinking wherever memory or repetition is involved; and (6) scientific organization of human beings, machines, and resources for effective use of the preceding five inventions. Concentration of population is essential to taking advantage of these inventions. *Urbanism* has come to mean in a broader sense the way of life in cities resulting from inventions in the industrial revolution.

The connections of urbanism with development of religious culture can be seen after detailing some of the features of the urban way of life. One of these is the growth in division of labor and specialization. The inventions referred to, especially transportation and the assembly line, make possible specialization, since goods can be moved from person to person, that is from specialist to specialist. Inventions such as power plants, factories, space travel, communication, automation, and social engineering require a high degree of specialization if the human mind is to master the tasks of design and operation. Despite the specialization, a third of a lifetime or more may be required to train the human mind to perform its tasks. The division of labor has been characterized by a large growth in the amount of time expended simply in education and training. The division of labor is also characterized by a growth in such types of work as problem solving to design and manage machines, and in a decline in clerical and manual labor.

One consequence of these changes is that people must live more in the psychic world than ever before. No longer following wandering herds or the plow, they gain their livelihood more through intellectual ingenuity and less through physical strength. They largely live in an abstract world known to them only by communicating with others in terms of abstract symbols. The problems of living are much more complex. A larger burden is placed upon religious and educational agencies to create psychic equipment adequate for this changed way of life. This is a burden which might be expected to stimulate interest in the church as well as in the school.

Of more immediate consequence for religion is that its agencies, too, have become more specialized. The variety of functions undertaken in industrial society has multiplied. No longer simply an affair of ministering to families living on farms or facilitating aid for the needy, religious institutions now engage in operation of schools, vocational counseling, social service agencies, recreational facilities, building programs, and social planning to solve a wide variety of social problems. Failure to permit sufficient specialization in these tasks or to avoid them altogether has diverted religious leaders away from their original religious tasks and has sapped the spiritual vitality of the church. Religious institutions have become interwoven with the rest of the industrial fabric, instead of being an independent force within it.

Attendant upon perfecting the intricate division of labor has been the occasion for widespread mobility of the population. People have found it necessary to move from the country where new farm technology has displaced them to the city where the assembly lines in factories and offices are awaiting them. This uprooting of the population from traditional social moorings has created problems of cultural shock and adjustment to new surroundings, perennially repeated with each wave of migrants or immigrants. The relaxing of ties with European churches is one factor in the unchurching or nominal churching of the immigrant population. After reaching the city, frequent movement from residence to residence, as the family size and family fortunes rise or fall, prevents effective integration of people's lives with the culture surrounding them. Of immediate consequence for the outreach of religion is the difficulty with which organized religion maintains contact with its adherents. Other problems are the obsolescence of one-room churches in the country and the downtown churches in city centers, and the mushrooming of population in suburban areas for whom new church programs must be launched. The difficulties of church work in the large city have been analyzed in detail by M. H. Leiffer, F. A. Shippey, and R. W. Sanderson.[54]

A more fundamental implication for religion is the decline of primary groups. These are groups knitted together by relatively permanent, face-to-face ties. The old neighborhood as a rural institution, in which mutual aid to the sick or suffering prevailed, has disappeared from the American scene. While it is true that patterns of kindliness continue to prevail among friends, those

[54] M. H. Leiffer, *The Effective City Church,* Abingdon, 1949; F. A. Shippey, *Church Work in the City,* Abingdon, 1952; R. W. Sanderson, *The Church Serves the Changing City,* Harper, 1955.

who are unknown or unwanted ail and die alone except for public charity, a circumstance unthinkable in the primary-group rural neighborhood. The family is less of a primary group than formerly. Children are out of the home in school or at play, and the father and often the mother are away at work or absorbed in civic pursuits. The pattern in which parents and children together faced problems of survival and developed close-knit dependence upon and loyalty to each other is not typical of the casual, come-and-go ways in urban living. These primary groups have been called the cradle of civilization because of the formation of altruistic and religious sentiments which they foster. How far they have declined in their effectiveness to generate these psychic dispositions is difficult to determine. Certainly people have more leisure to turn their thinking to each other and thereby to develop deeper sympathy and sharing of each other's experiences. It seems doubtful whether this opportunity is generally utilized when even the time in the home is spent upon manufactured entertainment.

A more specific function of primary groups in the past was the counsel and encouragement which neighbors were ready to provide each other in times of stress or misfortune. This borders upon religious ministry. In the case of religious communities this was a distinctly spiritual function. Survival of this pattern of mutual religious aid is still found among some Mennonite communities which have been largely able to withstand disruption in their ways of living by urban conditions. It is a pattern of interpersonal religious inspiration which organized religion today substantially lacks.

At the same time, a prominent feature of urbanism is the system of values which motivate workers, consumers, and family members today. Here again, it is difficult to obtain precise indications of the fundamental shifts in motivation. Yet it is apparent that the motivation in economic life is no longer the Protestant ethic analyzed by Max Weber. In place of the mutual struggle for survival, the battle for individual success is uppermost in people's minds. Success is appraised by whether other people think you are a success, and what they think is largely in terms of money and conspicuous consumption. Instead of producing for the greater glory of God, men produce only in order that they may consume, insatiably and incessantly. The pressures of other-directedness described by Riesman are the stronger for their subtlety. Consider the embarrassment people feel today if their lawns are not trimmed to putting-green smoothness, or if company arrives to find nothing tasty in the kitchen, or if the youngsters must face their friends in the same old family wagon. Possessions of all kinds are cast aside when they lose their luster, long before their utility is gone. Hardly two generations ago people were glad to have their friends visit in homes with bare board floors and faded walls. If dirt, toys, and confusion covered the floor, the neighbors jokingly pitched in and helped set things in order. If there was nothing ready to eat, the women went into the back yard, picked vegetables, and lent a hand in the kitchen to get the meal ready. Now typical suburbanites knock themselves out in a day of polishing the home to perfection and in preparing the most elegant delicacies, and then stagger exhausted to greet their guests. If this is the reality of life, then life has become an absurdity, and it is slight wonder that a flooding tide of protest literature swirls from indignant critics of contemporary urban living.

What has been said with reference to the development of religious personality applies with equal force to the longer development of religious culture. Erich Fromm's analysis *The Sane Society* is a hard-hitting, keen-cutting disclosure of the soft spots in contemporary culture. In his chapter, "Man in Capitalistic Society," he paraphrases the modern urban dweller:

> *I am—a system of desires and satisfactions;* I have to work in order to fulfill my desires—and these very desires are constantly stimulated and directed by the economic machine. Most of these appetites are synthetic; even sexual appetite is by far not as "natural" as it is made out to be. It is to some extent stimulated artificially and it needs to be if we want to have people as the contemporary system needs them—people who feel "happy," who have no doubts, who have no conflicts, who are guided without the use of force.
>
> Having fun consists mainly in the satisfaction of consuming and "taking in"; commodities, sights, food, drinks, cigarettes, people, lectures, books, movies—all are consumed, swallowed. The world is one great object for our appetite, a big apple, a big bottle, a big breast; we are the sucklers, the eternally expectant ones, the hopeful ones—and the eternally disappointed ones. How can we help being disappointed if our birth stops at the breast of the mother, if we are never weaned, if we remain overgrown babes, if we never go beyond the receptive orientation?[55]

Nor is the motivation of the urbanite as worker in the capitalistic system less deleterious than his motivation as consumer. Fromm goes on to say:

[55] Erich Fromm, *The Sane Society,* Rinehart, 1955, pp. 165–166.

Modern man does not know what to do with himself, how to spend his lifetime meaningfully, and he is driven to work in order to avoid an unbearable boredom. But work has ceased to be a moral and religious obligation in the sense of the middle-class attitude of the eighteenth and nineteenth centuries. Something new has emerged. Ever-increasing production, the drive to make bigger and better things, have become aims in themselves, new ideals. Work has become alienated from the working person.

What happens to the industrial worker? He spends his best energy for seven or eight hours a day in producing "something." He needs his work in order to make a living, but his role is essentially a passive one. He fulfills a small isolated function in a complicated and highly organized process of production, and is never confronted with "his" product as a whole, at least not as a producer, but only as a consumer, provided he has the money to buy "his" product in a store. He is concerned neither with the whole product in its physical aspects nor with its wider economic and social aspects. He is put in a certain place, has to carry out a certain task, but does not participate in the organization or management of the work. He is not interested, nor does he know why one produces this, instead of another commodity—what relation it has to the needs of society as a whole. The shoes, the cars, the electric bulbs, are produced by "the enterprise" using the machines. He is a part of the machine, rather than its master as an active agent. The machine, instead of being in his service to do work for him which once had to be performed by sheer physical energy, has become his master. Instead of the machine being the substitute for human energy, man has become a substitute for the machine. *His work can be defined as the performance of acts which cannot yet be performed by machines.*[56]

It is apparent that the industrial revolution has instilled aims of material success and conspicuous consumption through giving human beings an experience of success and consumption never before known. As far as religion is concerned, the values of success and wasteful consumption induced by the present industrial way of life are antithetical to those encouraged by religion. As recorded in scripture, religion seeks for humility and simple living, not lavish display or waste of wealth. Religion wishes production for the good of others, not irrational indulgence in the whims of self, irrespective of the welfare of society. Religion strives for spiritual achievement, not monetary success or absorption in pleasure. The foundation of religious values is altruism, which gives all else its purpose and meaning.

The clash between the values fostered by the industrial revolution and those of religion has resulted in a diminution of the

[56] *Ibid.*, pp. 179–180.

latter. Compromises with the demands of industrial culture have secularized and weakened the influence of religion. Reflecting changes in religious values are changes in the roles expected of ministers and in the program of their churches. These centers for religious development have become not much more than social clubs for fellowship. The spiritual depth which characterized the lives of early Protestants is replaced by spiritual indifference. Evidence of this is seen in the recession of religious debate and controversy which were once marked features of American life. These and other changes in religious culture are a major theme in recent analyses of American denominational life, such as those of J. H. Fichter, Will Herberg, and Marshall Sklare.[57] Some of these shifts in values, outlook, and practices of church members and their clergy are described further in remaining chapters.

Abuses of Capitalism

The motives in opposition to those of religious culture are not merely incidents of the industrial revolution. The crisis for religious leaders is that sensual cravings are stimulated with unceasing effort by those seeking to sell goods. The present organization of the industrial mechanism is alien to the interests of religious institutions. Much of the decline in religious culture can be attributed to this pattern of organization, or rather disorganization. A momentous consequence of the industrial revolution is that few men, if any, can work for themselves. As long as they are dependent as workers or consumers upon others, their lives are subject to control by others. This dependence occasionally existed prior to the industrial revolution, but was moderated by neighborhood controls of primary-group living which fostered sentiments of loyalty and fairness toward face-to-face work associates. How the conflict between religious and capitalistic culture will eventuate remains to be seen. Prospect of curtailment of abuses in advertising and mass entertainment in the United States is revealed by the achievements in some other countries. While most democratic-minded citizens feel that Russia has not yet achieved some of the freedoms to which they are accustomed in the United States, it seems prob-

[57] J. H. Fichter, *Dynamics of a City Church,* University of Chicago Press, 1951; *Social Relations in the Urban Parish,* University of Chicago Press, 1954; Will Herberg, *Protestant-Catholic-Jew,* Doubleday, 1956; Marshall Sklare, *Conservative Judaism,* Free Press, 1955; (ed.), *The Jews: Social Patterns of an American Group,* Free Press, 1958.

able that these citizens at home will come to covet the freedom which Russians and others have from abuse by mass media in the hands of commercial interests, as well as their job security and experiencing of social purpose. Nor does it seem necessary to copy any given economic system in order to correct shortcomings in our own. It is the function of textbooks in politics and economics, rather than in religion, to determine the ways in which these shortcomings are to be regulated or removed. But it is the responsibility in analysis of religion to identify the cultural forces hostile to it, as well as those which are friendly.

In view of the extensive treatment given in the chapter on development of religious personality, it is unnecessary to elaborate again the ways in which capitalist culture is harmful to the development of either religious personality or religious culture. What thwarts individual growth also curtails cultural growth, since culture is the way of life of a group of individuals. We may note briefly (1) the aggressiveness fostered by excessive economic competition, (2) the defeat to people's altruistic impulses from their being required to do harm to consumers and employees in the quest for higher profits, (3) the shock administered by waste of natural resources to ideas of stewardship of wealth entrusted by God, and (4) the offense to spiritual orderliness of living caused by lack of economic planning and dependence upon the hackneyed assumption of nineteenth-century capitalism that if each seeks his own money, the economic good of all will be served. These things are an affront to the spiritual life sought by religion. The condemnation of capitalist culture voiced by world-famous theologians such as Karl Barth, Martin Buber, and Paul Tillich is strongly reminiscent of the revulsion of Old Testament prophets against malpractices of their time. These religious leaders and many other religious-minded persons believe that the shortcomings of contemporary culture are not necessary. The decline in religious culture wrought by these defects can be arrested.

Rise of Science

A cultural movement of major magnitude with mixed effects upon religious culture is afforded by the rise of modern science. Reliance upon systematic observation and logical analysis has roots extending into philosophies of the ancient world. The perfection of these techniques and their undisputed sway as arbiters of truth about the world of experience are achievements of the past few hundred years, culminating in the present century of overtowering dominance of the rest of culture by scientific ways of thought. The rise of modern science is in part a generating cause of inventions in the industrial revolution. In part, scientific research has been intensely stimulated by problems of this developing revolution. Corporations and government yearly spend billions of dollars in research not only in the physical sciences but in the social ones also. Science is thus a basic factor in religious culture because of the industrial revolution which, as we have seen, has occasioned much of the decline in religious culture.

Science has profoundly affected religion from a more immediate standpoint. The authority which the method of science possesses as a way of the individual's gaining truth means that religion has been subjected to rethinking in a manner without historical parallel. The authority of religion in all fields of knowledge was once virtually uncontested. First, in physical science the sixteenth-century discoveries by Copernicus and Galileo displaced the dicta of theologians about the universe. This initial retreat by religion was orderly. By agreement religion and physical science held sovereignty over different domains. God and the stars traveled their separate courses. As time moved on the two met in the minds of men. When doctrines of evolution in the nineteenth century pushed back the frontiers of knowledge to the dawn of history, no God was found. The suspicion that, if God could not be found in the universe he created, he did not exist, crept into man's pessimistic imagination. As the achievements of physics and biology became more spectacular the opinion grew that physical science alone could bring men to the truth about life. The philosophy of matter in motion became king of a secular civilization. The work of Bertrand Russell and more recently the work of W. T. Stace and W. A. Kaufmann in philosophy portray such philosophy in various nuances.

Simultaneous with the rise of physical science another movement of scientific thought has taken place. The past century of critical scholarship has shown that our sacred scriptures are subject to continual revision in translation. The particular symbols and ideas by means of which we translate the manuscripts of antiquity are categories of contemporary thinking. Viewing the scriptures through the prisms of our knowledge and our vocabulary, we find they do not possess the certainty of God's speaking to man in his own tongue. The tide of history has carried human beings far out from the Christian rock of salvation established by Jesus and Paul.

New Extension of Science

The sovereignty of physical science has come to dominate social and psychological thinking as well. In America this dominance over social science reached its apex in the behaviorism of the 1920's. This was a phase during which human beings lost contact with the psychic realm, except in its surface aspects. Social and psychological scientists have increasingly moved into the area left by the shrinking dominion of religion over men's minds. Some of them have tried to wean human beings from what they consider ghost worship and the dependence upon a father illusion which only the wistful imagination of childhood or the credulity of the primitive could accept. These men have imposed a wide influence through contemporary writers and teachers who have studied their works and who pass their ideas along, often in distorted form. Students who feel they must choose between science and religion give up their religion, especially if instructors or classmates deride them for being unscientific.

This last assault is of greater moment for religion than is generally realized. Little did it matter if the currents of physical science swirled through the visual world of animals and minerals. Religion then held to a separate domain of thought, feeling, and inspiration where the grossness of space did not enter. The heart of religion remained as warm and vital as before the advent of modern science. The new onslaught in social and psychological science is not just another excursion into the world of spatial objects. Rather, these disciplines invade the inward territory where religion had been unchallenged. They seek to apply the accepted scientific canons of observation, analysis, discovery of laws, and verification to the dim and insubstantial realm of internal experience.

Many do not know that modern social and psychological science does not stop with the study of man's behavior but steps by introspection, case studies, and personal interrogation into this inner realm. Thoughts, feelings, ideas, values, satisfactions, and emotional securities are as commonplace in the vocabulary of the social scientist as in the writings of the religionist. The wall built by medieval-minded theologians to keep empirical science from getting at religion has blown away as a hill of sand before the wind. For seventy-five years scientific ideas have been pouring through the breach in unprecedented volume. Science not only studies what can be seen and touched, but it studies religion in its experienceable features.

In the melee, orthodox religionists have retreated into the abstract heights of philosophy, failing to give battle on the plain of science. Not least among these have been well-intentioned physical scientists who, knowing little of the outreach of social science, continue to think of science as dealing only with what can be seen or touched, and of religion as outside the area of science altogether. This retreat pushes religion out of the realm of experience into speculative philosophy. God must exist because it is reasonable to believe that he exists. Christ must exist because the Christian plan of salvation is the most acceptable answer found by man's philosophizing. But a God outside human experience cannot love man in any way which they know with their sensibilities. They are as sheep who hear only the rebounding echo and feel no shepherd near to guide them along the tortuous pathways of life.

Under the impact of modern science, divorced from religion, it is not surprising that religious culture in the Christian world has suffered decline, whether the high-water mark is taken to be the springtime of Christianity in the ancient world, the Golden Age of the Catholic Church during the Middle Ages, or the Protestant Reformation. Nor is the crumbling of religious tradition all that has taken place. Of incomparable consequence, physical science has placed in the trembling hand of man the vast forces of the atom. What theologians would say God alone once controlled has been unloosed by human ingenuity. Never has the need been greater for man to submit to the ideally conceived will of God. Yet rarely has there been a time in two thousand years when God seemed more remote from the minds of so many. Science has created incredible fury to be harnessed and at the same time has ripped loose the spiritual reins by which religious tradition has guided mankind.

Future of Religious Culture

The scientific study of religious phenomena cannot be expected to make its largest achievements in the early stages of this study. The overturning of traditional authority and its replacement by the method of science is an enormous upheaval which leaves an extensive problem of reorganizing religious systems of thought with reference to scientific findings concerning the psychic realm. During the change of intellectual wind, it is inevitable that the ship of religion must experience lost motion. When its course is set on the opposite tack and its sails are trimmed to a fresher and stronger wind, it seems reasonable to believe that the lost motion will be replaced and former motion exceeded. Whatever is inherently true about religion from an empirical standpoint will more and more gain scientific status. Human beings will then be guided by the most scientifically dependable view of the situation. Whatever the future course of religion, it will not be hampered by past errors which science can eliminate, but will have full sails of truth for its propulsion. What takes place ahead may be expected to be superior to the course of religion in the past.

Fresh growth in religious culture may be anticipated for other reasons than the fuller illumination which scientific study gives religious belief and practice. Problems created by the industrial revolution, principally those of eliminating commercialized culture and restoring primary-group life, can be overcome by human ingenuity. The *kibbutz* in Palestine and the Bruderhof in America are examples of planned communal living. Ideals which characterize these colonies are being pursued on a vast scale in large areas of the world outside the United States. The cyclical forces responsible for the downward course of religion will run to depletion, as they have periodically done in the past. Men, having found religion, tend to forget the basis for their improved life. But as unmet religious needs reassert themselves, the upward phase of the cycle, which is rediscovery of religious approaches to problems, takes place. The existence of altruistic forces in human motivation seeking for fuller development through religious activity is the strongest assurance of the inevitability of spiritual progress. If humanity can get across the threshold of world peace, wide avenues for growth are open. Although difficulties in communicating religious insights from generation to generation have reduced the reservoir of religious insights gained by previous generations, eventually, as past surges of religious history show, widespread rediscovery of religious insights occurs. With improved knowledge of how religious motivation can be cultivated in each new generation, the tendency of religion to endure and to grow increases. With the realization that security of truth is not found by idolizing past religious pronouncements or institutional forms as infallible and immutable, but rather through perennial demonstration and achievement of new knowledge, religion is freed from the heavy baggage of tradition which held it down. Those who ask why Christianity has declined from its original achievements might appropriately ask how it could grow while frozen in an institutional structure from which scientific seeking was largely excluded.

Some beginnings of the recovery of religious culture are evident from a statistical standpoint. Church membership according to official reports has increased from 49 percent of the population in 1940 to 57 percent in 1950 and 63 percent in 1958.[58] The proportion who consider themselves church members is larger, approximately 75 percent, as shown by public-opinion polls. This growth in church membership might merely be a surface indication were it not for indices of increased participation and larger financial giving to churches. The percentage of adults attending church rose from 37 percent in 1940 to 49 percent in 1958.[59] The percentage of the population attending Sunday School reached a low point of 14.3 in 1936 and has since risen to 22.8 in 1957. The value of construction of new church buildings was $59 million in 1940, $409 million in 1950 and $863 million in 1958. Protestant and Eastern Orthodox church contributions in 1957 totaled $2207 million compared with $326 million in 1940.[60] However, Michael Argyle has shown that per capita giving to a group of Protestant Churches relative to available income is substantially lower at the present time than it was three decades ago, although it has increased since 1943.[61] During the past five years the statistics of interest and participation from the *Yearbook of American Churches* have tended to level off.

Following World War II a questionnaire study was made by G. W. Allport, J. M. Gillespie, and J. Young of 414 Harvard undergraduates and 86 Radcliffe undergraduates. Allport summarizes findings from this college study as follows.

> May we sum up by saying that (1) most students feel the need of including a religious sentiment somewhere within their maturing personalities; (2) for the most part they believe in a God, though their view is not usually of the traditional theistic variety; (3) a bare quarter are in essential matters orthodox and historically faithful to theological dogma; (4) the majority maintain some of the forms of traditional religious practices including prayer; (5) but the majority are

58 *Yearbook of American Churches, op. cit.*, p. 279.
59 *Ibid.*, p. 282.
60 *Ibid.*, pp. 275, 284.
61 Argyle, *op. cit.*, pp. 29–31.

clearly dissatisfied with institutional religion as it exists, so much so that 40 percent of those who feel a religious need yet repudiate the church in which they were reared. If we take the entire student population who have had a religious upbringing, including those who feel no religious need and those who do, we find that 56 percent reject the church in which they were trained.[62]

Of interest in relation to the study by Allport, Gillespie, and Young is a poll a decade later of 319 Harvard and Radcliffe students reported by *The Harvard Crimson.*[63] While the questions are not directly comparable, they indicate similar findings with little change evident in religious interest. (1) Two-thirds subscribe to the statement: "On the whole, the Church stands for the best in human life, although certain minor errors and shortcomings are necessarily apparent in it, as in all human institutions." A little more than two-thirds say that they would like to raise their children in their own religious tradition. One-third say they are "equally concerned with both" religion and politics, one-third are "more concerned with religion," and one-third are "more concerned with politics." (2) Two-thirds believe in God in one form or another. (3) About one-quarter subscribe to orthodox theological beliefs. (4) One-third attend religious services once a month or oftener, and one-third attend several times a year. (5) Two-thirds report "a period in which" they "reacted either partially or wholly against the religious tradition" in which they were raised.

S. Rettig and B. Pasamanick have recently contributed some interesting data concerning trends in moral values by 10 year intervals from 1929–1958. A questionnaire previously used by P. Crissman with groups of several hundred college students was administered by Rettig and Pasamanick to another group of students in 1958. The students were asked to mark the degrees of "rightness" or "wrongness" of 50 different actions on a scale from 1 to 10. Items were then ranked from 1 to 50 according to the average severity of the moral judgment. Three items dealt with religious behavior. "Disbelieving in God" increased in rank from 11 to 23 over the thirty year period, "Not giving to support religion when able" increased from 9 to 19, and "Seeking amusement on Sunday instead of going to church" increased from 5 to 11. Since 50 represents the highest rank it can be seen that

[62] G. W. Allport, *The Individual and His Religion,* Macmillan, 1950, p. 44.

[63] *The Harvard Crimson,* June 11, 1959; reprinted in Parker Rossman, J. R. Adler, C. S. Maier, and D. L. Farnsworth, "Religious Values at Harvard," *Religious Education,* January–February, 1960, pp. 24–42.

religious actions have not yet risen beyond the halfway mark on the scale of moral concern.[64]

As further indication of the continuing interest of youth in religion, the findings by M. G. Ross are relevant. A study was conducted among 1700 subjects through the YMCA. Forty-two percent stated that they prayed at least once daily. Less than 15 percent did not pray at all. When asked the question "Why do you pray?" the reasons given were: "God listens and answers your prayers," 33 percent; "It helps you in time of stress and crisis," 27 percent; "You feel relieved and better after prayer," 18 percent; "Prayer reminds you of your obligations to man and society," 11 percent; and 11 percent gave other replies.[65]

Billy Graham has been leading the nation in a series of mass religious revivals involving a larger proportion of the population than ever before in U.S. history. Television brings men such as Graham and Bishop F. J. Sheen to audiences in the tens of millions. Yet how deep are the religious beliefs of Americans? Herberg has summarized data on this point.

> What do Americans believe? Most emphatically, they "believe in God": 97 percent according to one survey, 96 percent according to another, 95 percent according to a third. About 75 percent of them, as we have seen, regard themselves as member of churches, and a sizeable proportion attend divine services with some frequency and regularity. They believe in prayer: about 90 percent say they pray on various occasions. They believe in life after death, even in Heaven and Hell. They think well of the church and of ministers. They hold the Bible to be an inspired book, the "word of God." By a large majority, they think children should be given religious instruction and raised as church members. By a large majority, too, they hold religion to be of very great importance. In all of these respects their attitudes are as religious as those of any people today, or, for that matter, as those of any Western people in recent history.
>
> Yet these indications are after all relatively superficial; they tell us what Americans say (and no doubt believe) about themselves and their religious views; they do not tell us what in actuality these religious views are. Nowhere are surface appearances more deceptive, nowhere is it more necessary to try to penetrate beyond mere assertions of belief than in such ultimate matters as religion.[66]

Whether the present upturn is in the nature of a temporary enthusiasm or whether it reflects a permanent reversal of a

[64] S. Rettig and B. Pasamanick, "Changes in Moral Values over Three Decades, 1929–1958," *Social Problems,* Spring, 1959, pp. 320–328.

[65] M. G. Ross, *Religious Beliefs of Youth,* Association Press, 1950, p. 63.

[66] Herberg, *op. cit.,* p. 85.

downward trend centuries old, is not shown by the data available. However, it is noteworthy that America has undergone a series of religious revivals since the founding of the republic which have produced little results except for superficial religious conversions and increases in nominal church membership. In what is a penetrating cultural analysis of religious development in American history, W. G. McLoughlin has described these successive waves of religious revival.[67] These revivals have been much more preoccupied with peace of mind than peace of society or peace of the world. The most recent wave of religious revival is no exception. The "peace of mind cult" dominates the content of both religious writing and preaching in the present revival movement. For an analysis of literary aspects of popular religion, the work of L. Schneider and S. M. Dornbusch is illuminating, if sobering, in laying the shallowness of the religious heart of America bare.[68]

The current revival does not reflect any new reasons for expecting sustained religious progress. The hostility of contemporary commercial culture to the real spirit of religion is not yet checked. Prerequisite changes in the thinking of most people towards religion have not yet taken place.

The author asked why certain long-time acquaintances of his who were irreligious in the 1930's were now returning to church. They replied with such words as "It feels good to be back in church again." Asked if they had reconciled the conflict between science and religion which previously kept them from accepting religion, they replied that they no longer cared whether the conflict was reconciled or not. How widespread is this attitude of returning to religion despite the supposed irreconcilability of science and religion would require detailed study. As leaves in the wind, the scattered viewpoints expressed do not show that scientific study of religion is a widespread reason for revived interest in the church. In a 1954 poll, by the American Institute of Public Opinion, the reason most often given for increased churchgoing is "fear, unrest, and uncertainty of future." The next of the reasons given is "renewed faith in God as Supreme Being," and the third is "post-war reaction, effect of religion on military personnel." These reasons indicate the re-

[67] W. G. McLoughlin, *Modern Revivalism,* Ronald, 1959. See also A. R. Eckardt, *The Surge of Piety in America,* Association, 1958; "The Rise and Fall of a Popular Religion," *Religion in Life,* Autumn, 1959, pp. 587–594.

[68] Schneider and Dornbusch, *op. cit.*

assertion of religious needs in the face of the crisis in international affairs. Herberg comments incisively on this crisis.

The contemporary crisis of Western civilization, which has brought a sense of total insecurity to men everywhere, is surely one of the most significant of these [forces]. The utter predicament of human existence is no longer simply a philosophical or theological proposition; it is the most patent of everyday facts. The hydrogen bomb, on which our survival depends, yet which threatens us with destruction, is the sinister symbol of our plight. Confronted with the demonic threat of Communist totalitarianism, we are driven to look beyond the routine ideas and attitudes that may have served in easier times. On every side insecurity assails us, and yet security is becoming more and more the urgent need of our time.[69]

Herberg points to revived interest in family living as a sign of return to basic human values.

On another, more personal, or rather more domestic, level, too, religion has been found to serve the need for security. On this level the turn to religion is to be linked, many think, with the sensational reversal of long-time population trends and the sudden rise of birth rates among college graduates and professional people in the United States. Since 1946 these rates have been increasing every year, and in 1954 married graduates of the class of 1944, ten years out of college, already averaged more children than the class of 1921 when it had been out 25 years in 1946, the year the study we are citing was initiated. This demographical fact would seem to confirm the impression many observers have had in recent years that, amid the mounting insecurities of our time, increasing numbers of younger people are turning to the security to be found in the enduring, elemental ways in institutions of mankind; in the family, they feel, they can find the permanence and stability, the meaning and the value they crave amid a world falling into chaos. Religion, like the family, is one of the enduring, elemental institutions of mankind; indeed, the two have been closely linked from the very earliest times. The search for meaning and security in what is basic and unchanging, rather than in the fluctuating fortunes of social or political activity, is one of the major factors in the upswing of religion among the American people today.[70]

That the stresses of industrial culture play a compelling role in the return to religion is also the opinion of Herberg.

Confronted with the depersonalizing pressures of contemporary life, modern man experiences a profound exigency to preserve some rem-

[69] Herberg, *op. cit.,* p. 73.
[70] *Ibid.,* pp. 74–75.

nant of personality and inwardness against the erosions of a mass culture. Increasingly, he turns to religion to provide him an inexpugnable citadel for the self in a world in which personal authenticity is threatened on every side; indeed, the quest for personal authenticity is itself substantially a religious quest. Reflecting, as it does, the crisis of our time, it also points to its deeper meaning. For ultimately, the crisis of our time is a crisis of faith. The secular faiths of our culture have ignominiously collapsed under the shattering impact of the events of our time. Many of the "truths" by which "modern-minded" men lived in earlier decades have revealed themselves to be little more than vain and fatuous illusions. We can no longer look to science, to "progress," to economics, or to politics for salvation; we recognize that these things have their value, but we also know that they are not gods bringing redemption from the confusions and perils of existence. An age intoxicated with utopian dreams about the boundless possibilities of "scientific progress" and "social reconstruction" has been succeeded by an age more sober, more realistic—some would say too much so. But one cannot live by sober, limited, pragmatic programs for restricted ends; these soon lose whatever meaning they have unless they are imbedded in a transcendent, actuality-defined vision. Man needs faith, a total all-embracing faith, for living. The faiths by which men live in a secular age "base the meaning of existence upon some assumed stability of human virtue or reason [or power], some pattern of history or societal security"; when these are swept away by the great upheavals of history, the way is opened for a better appreciation of the power and relevance of the historic faiths. How far turning to these faiths at a time of crisis represents "escapism" in the bad sense of the term, and how far it reflects a deeper searching for the realities of existence, no one can tell for another, perhaps not even for himself; we may safely assume that something of each is present, compounded with the other. But that it is not simply irresponsibility or a "failure of nerve," that it may indeed help to nerve one for greater endurance and unyielding resistance to evil and unreason, is surely sufficiently attested by the events of our time. At its deepest level the turn to religion we are witnessing owes much of its force to the search for a new and more viable "philosophy" of existence amid the spiritual chaos of our age.[71]

On the other hand, Herberg recognizes that the return to religion is accelerated by a desire to be like others. In the 1954 poll cited, of the reasons for more churchgoing the next in frequency is "church programming, publicity better." This shows that organizational efficiency in controlling public opinion is an important factor. The high-pressure public-relations procedures of Billy Graham have been criticized by the *Christian*

[71] *Ibid.*, pp. 76–77.

Century.[72] That the return to religion may not be lasting is evidenced by failure of the Graham revival meetings to produce more than a handful of converts or to produce visible changes in most of the participants. To say this does not overlook the subtle regeneration of spiritual feeling and purpose fostered by Graham as a religious leader. But measured in terms of changes in institutional structure of society, the effects of his revivals seem to have been minor. The *Christian Century* has commented editorially on the meager results gleaned from the Graham crusade.[73] The upswing in religion on the wider scene is not appreciably reflected in changed living. While divorce and crime rates show indications that they may level off, they continue at rates which are among the highest in the world and their long-run trend has unquestionably been upward. If the heart of religion is altruistic power, the evidence of this power in rebuilt individuals and in a rebuilt society is absent. The current revival seems no more than a surface poultice on the deep-seated wounds in the human psyche. It may mark the beginning of long-range development of religious culture, but it seems from the immediate perspective to be a temporary oscillation, rather than a permanent upswing.

Martin E. Marty, as well as Will Herberg, has dwelled upon the lack of spiritual substance in American religion today. What currently prevails is a watered-down system of religion in which genuine differences of conviction among Jews, Catholics, and Protestants have become minimal because the convictions themselves have weakened or disappeared. The religion which remains is a religion of democratic values or friendly sentiments, a type of religion which differs little from Pollyannish conversation and bits of do-gooding by luncheon clubs. In this religion God-the-father remains a conventional image to be invoked on special occasions but of little depth. The answer which Marty gives to America's spiritual need is a new culture ethic to replace that of decadent economic life. He considers the emergence of this ethic as necessary to a revitalization of religion. "As this ethic is forged in seminaries and universities, in conference

[72] "Whose Billy Graham," *Christian Century,* November 21, 1956, pp. 1351–1352.

[73] "Mass Conversions," *Christian Century,* May 29, 1957, pp. 677–679; "A Tale of Two Cities," June 12, 1957, pp. 725–727; "Needed: Evangelism in Depth," June 26, 1957, pp. 282–283; "The Long Anticlimax," August 7, 1957, pp. 933–934; "Protestants on Broadway," September 18, 1957, pp. 1095–1096. Also see Graham's statement, "What Ten Years Have Taught Me," *Christian Century,* February 17, 1960, pp. 186–189.

rooms and local churches and private closets, it will make its way inspired by confidence and urgency."[74] However, America's spiritual problem is multi-sided.

In the author's opinion, until the adjustments in the scientific status of religion have been realized by the majority of church-goers, renewed impoverishment of religion by a false rejection of it on scientific grounds is a perennial threat. The conflict has not been between science and religion, but between a scientific view of religion and a dogmatic view of religion. Now that science has broken the bonds of tradition which confined it and has at last gained its full access to the subject matter of religion, greater spiritual growth may be expected in the future. The remaining debris of the wall between science and religion is still to be cleared away. For too long that barrier has kept men from the arsenal of scientific weapons by means of which they might advance and deepen their religious principles. In the new turn of events, psychology is not just a peripheral aid to religion in personal counseling or the cure of mental disorder, but rather becomes a major cutting instrument in the discovery and demonstration of religious truth.

Indications of scientific growth of religion are shown by the increasing popularity of the writings of Jung. Short of the theism which his writings support, numerous members in Unitarian churches and in liberal wings of other churches accept a religion which is largely psychological, based upon the writings of men such as Erich Fromm, who advocate self-realization through altruistic living. This scientific interest in religion seems likely to continue until the full picture of empirical religious reality is disclosed. Herberg, whose approach to religious truth has been more philosophical than psychological, writes:

> Particularly significant as reflecting a reversal of trend is the new intellectual prestige of religion on all levels of cultural life. . . . The renewed interest in religion in the academic community, and among intellectuals generally, is indeed a noteworthy sign of the times. The extraordinary expansion of departments of religion and programs of religious instruction is only one aspect; perhaps even more important is the widening interest that transcends the academic and goes beyond instructional programs. There is, many observers have noted in recent years, a genuine "stirring" on the campuses of the nation, particularly among the intellectual elite.[75]

[74] M. E. Marty, *The New Shape of American Religion,* Harper, 1959, p. 168.

[75] Herberg, *op. cit.,* pp. 66–67.

How far can the development of religious culture conceivably be expected to continue? Limits of growth seem to be imposed by several things: (1) the hereditary capacity of human beings in each generation to acquire insights from the preceding generation, (2) the hereditary capacity for fresh innovation, and (3) the hereditary forces of self-seeking which are in opposition to religious motivation. If a biological limit exists, it seems likely that it would not be approached for many centuries, and that the approach would be gradual. Furthermore, man may become master of his own biological material. Through controlled eugenics he may develop hereditary material more favorable for social and religious living. There seems no substantial reason for believing that human progress cannot continue indefinitely if the current crises in world affairs are resolved without the destruction of all mankind. The altruistic forces generated by living together seem destined to gain dominance as motivations over all of culture when scientific means for their fulfillment are adequately recognized. The Marxian view of economic development may be extended to religion as well: human progress is inevitable, although each individual may hasten it by his own decisions and actions.

part V Religion and Society

RELIGIOUS WAYS OF LIFE

New Year and Passover

The Jewish new year begins in the early fall. Its observances are far removed in spirit from the celebrations surrounding January 1, for it ushers in a ten-day period of penitence culminating in the fast of Yom Kippur. The new year is regarded not as the occasion for carousing but for spiritual stock-taking. What is man? What is our life? What will be our fate?

There is, in this holy day period, a very solemn approach to the facts of our frail human existence. No attempt is made to gloss over the evils of life. God's ways may be inscrutable but ultimately they are accepted as just. Therefore, the fear of the Lord is the beginning of wisdom. Judaism offers no easy way to God. No son has been sent down to take us by the hand and lead us to Him. No mediator intercedes for us. No priest dispenses God's grace. In the final accounting, there is a purely personal relationship between the individual and his God. This is an awesome responsibility. Need we wonder then that this penitential period is known as The Days of Awe? Even the blowing of the shofar, the ram's horn, which from Biblical times has announced the new year, penetrates into the heart of the modern Jew and causes it to tremble.

The climax is reached on Yom Kippur. Like all Jewish holidays it begins at sundown, for Jews follow the biblical pattern of creation—"There was evening and there was morning, one day." The service opens with the Kol Nidre chant. This is the most stirring, the most haunting melody in the entire religious experience of Jews.

After the evening service, some Jews remain in the synagogue all night and stay on until the services conclude at sundown the next day. Most American Jews, however, go back to their homes after the evening prayers and return the next morning to remain for the entire day. They fast for twenty-four hours, fulfilling an ancient injunction. This reminds them of their human frailty and of their dependence on God. It establishes the necessary mood of self-discipline and of self-sacrifice.

The spiritual concern of Yom Kippur is with our human sinfulness, but what is sin?

In its Hebrew origin the most commonly used word for sin actually means "missing the mark." It is the denial of the heritage, the repudiation of God's commandments. There are, it must be added, various formulations of God's requirements. The Torah, the basic law contained in the Pentateuch, lists six hundred and thirteen commands ranging from dietary specifications to right motivations. ("Thou shalt not covet.") Micah reduced them to three, "To do justly, to love mercy and to walk humbly before God." How do we walk in God's ways? The answer is given in the climactic moment of the Yom Kippur morning service when the rabbi stands before the open ark about to remove the sacred scrolls. He prays in the words proclaimed of old to Moses, "God, merciful, gracious, long-suffering, abundant in goodness and ever true." Such are God's ways; such must be ours.

If a poll were to be taken among Jews, Passover would be chosen the most popular festival. For, gladsome as is Purim, radiant as is Chanukah, charming as is Succos, inspiring as are the holy days, none has that combination of ceremonial loveliness, treasured family associations, springtime exuberance, hallowed national memories and hopes which are contained in Passover.

The holiday probably originated in antiquity as a festival of spring. When the winter months are over and passed, spring bursts into bloom in Palestine. There is none of the slow unfolding of Northern climes. Suddenly the hillsides are covered with red anemones. The fruit trees are in blossom. The sweet fragrance of the acacia stirs the blood of the young and the memories of the old. From the hills of Nazareth, the valley of Jezreel looks like a vast oriental rug woven of fields of golden grain, blossoming almonds, figs and olives and flowers bursting with color from the caresses of the hot sun. The moon has a special brilliance and feeling of closeness. One can read by its light on a spring night in Palestine. Understandably the ancient Israelites who loved their earth and sky could cry out, "The Heavens declare the glory of God; the earth showeth forth the work of His hands."

This exultation found expression in a springtime festival. But the moral genius of the Hebrews was not content with a holiday that had no ethical or historical significance. They transformed this nature festival into a memorial of freedom. According to the account in Genesis, Joseph's brothers and father followed him into Egypt. His forgiveness and his bounty provided for their needs in a time of famine. Then Joseph died, and all that generation. In the course of time, a new Pharaoh arose who "knew not Joseph." He enslaved the Israelites and ordered the destruction of their male babies. One child was hidden in the bulrushes, was found there by Pharaoh's daughter, then was raised in her home as a prince. This youth, Moses, could not endure the oppression of his brethen. After some trials and preparation, he came before Pharaoh to demand his people's freedom. In the name of the stern God he had found in the wilderness he cried, "Let My people go that they may serve Me." After ten dreadful plagues, described vividly in the Book of Exodus, Pharaoh relented. The Israelites fled in haste. There was no time for the leavening of their bread; so it was baked unleavened. Jewish tradition selected this incident for special significance. Jews were required to remove all leaven (*chometz*) from their homes for seven days, and to eat matzos, the unleavened bread of affliction. Passover probably derives its name from the Avenging Angel's passing over the houses of the Israelites when the Egyptian firstborn were stricken; although it has some connection also with the Paschal lamb.

Through the ages, Passover has meant many things to the Jews. Its most enduring meaning is suggested by the first of the Ten Commandments—"I am the Lord Thy God . . ." Here is the supreme announcement of all history. But what follows? ". . . who created the heaven and the earth"? No. ". . . who brought forth man, and food to sustain him"? No. The great proclamation of God's being is followed by the words, ". . . who brought thee out of the land of Egypt, out of the house of bondage." From the very beginning, the Jew saw God's hand in history. He owed his very existence as a people to Divine intervention. The Passover ritual relates, "Few in numbers with but seventy souls went thy fathers down into Egypt and now thy God has made thee as numerous as the stars . . . not one only sought to destroy us, but men in all generations; and the Holy One, Blessed be He, saves us from their hands." Note the present tense "saves." Jews may continue to be persecuted, but the Guardian of Israel slumbers not. He will not permit His beloved people to be destroyed.

When the Jews were exiled from Palestine, when their holy Temple was destroyed, they adapted their institutions to new conditions. This adaptability made survival possible. The agricultural aspects of Passover were de-emphasized; the Temple observances were transferred symbolically to the home. Thus the Seder came into being. The word "seder" literally means order. Actually it means the arrangement of ceremonies on Passover eve. This is a home observance as so many Jewish holidays are, principally. In this way Jewish home life was beautified; family ties were strengthened. Thus divorce, desertion, drunkenness, crimes of violence were little known among the Jews. The sweetness of devoted family life compensated for the world's mistreatment.

Because of its association with the home, the Passover Seder exercised a very strong appeal among the Jews. For this observance the families gather from near and far. Even the prodigal, the cynic, the skeptic returns. The atmosphere is festive; the service includes ancient gay songs and games for the children. The symbols of the first Passover are displayed—the lamb's shankbone, recalling the marks on the Israelites' houses which the Angel of Death passed over; the bitter herbs, a reminder of the bitter hardships of Egyptian bondage; the unleavened bread as a remembrance of the hasty flight to freedom. At a dramatic moment of the service, the door of the house is thrown open for the return of Elijah, the prophet, to bring word of the coming of the Messiah.[1]

The Amish

Amish religion, unlike that of most Protestant denominations, is highly integrated with everyday life, affecting economic organization, family life, education, recreation, even dress and speech. Since the Amish believe that the cardinal virtue is obedience to the will of God, they follow literally certain teachings of the Bible, particularly the New Testament, as interpreted by the church leaders. One important rule of Scripture to which they subscribe is, "Be not conformed to the world." (Rom. 12:2.) In the eyes of the Amish, this means the renunciation of modern inventions and innovations, for they are worldly and, therefore, evil. Tabooed are such things as automobiles, radios, telephones, electric lights, central heating, bathrooms, even curtains, carpets, and pic-

[1] Abridged from *What the Jews Believe*, copyright 1950 by Philip S. Bernstein, pp. 25–29, 57–59, 61–62. Used by permission of the publishers, Farrar, Straus and Cudahy, Inc.

tures, so that the houses seem quite bare. Another teaching to which they adhere is, "Be ye not unequally yoked together with unbelievers." (II Cor. 6:14.) This is given as the reason for not taking out fire and life insurance, and for not sending the children to consolidated schools. This teaching also underlies their refusal to take oath, bear arms, or participate in civic duties, since they believe the state is unchristian. In support of their pacifism and conscientious objection they cite additional passages from Scripture; for example, "Thou shalt not kill," and, "If a man hate his brother, he is a murderer." (I John 3:15.)

The Amish attitude toward sex is surprisingly liberal. A person whom we of other conventions might consider had bad sex habits is seldom regarded as any worse, in the Amish home, than one with any other fault. In any case the Amish do not emphasize it as an outstanding moral wrong, as we do. Chastity is expected until marriage and extra-marital relations are frowned upon, but those who stray from these customs do not become moral outcasts.

At the wedding, which is the most important social event in Amish experience, as many as one hundred to three hundred guests may be invited, since the Amish live in self-contained little communities and are surrounded by relatives and friends. Later the newly-weds pay visits to all the guests, and it is at this time that they receive their wedding presents. Since they may spend several weeks visiting, staying a night or several nights here and there as the honored guests of their hosts, the trip is virtually a honeymoon.

The Amish people are exceptionally good farmers, and take great delight in working their fields which are usually extensive. On the place is a huge barn with a wooden floor, sometimes used for dancing or for church services, and a large stable. The houses are of plain wood with big cool cellars and enormous kitchens. The living-rooms, or parlors, are seldom used except for special company. The partitions on the lower floor of the house are all movable, so that the main floor may be made into one large room. This is done so that there will be room for everyone when it is time to have "preaching" in the home. The Amish have no churches, but they take turns in having services. When the house is built, wooden benches are made to be used during "preaching." Amish women are superlative housekeepers and are noted for keeping their homes immaculately clean. The absence of carpets, curtains, pictures, and other decorations would seem to simplify the problem of housekeeping.

The building of a home and of farm units is a collective enterprise in which neighbors participate, on the theory that if they lend a helping hand they themselves will be helped when they are in need. The homogeneity of the group and their relative isolation from outsiders helps to promote this policy of mutual aid, for the Amish disdain help proffered by unbelievers.

As indicated, religion plays the central role in the life of the Amish. Children are taken to "preaching" from the time they are infants, although they do not join the church until they are about twelve years old. There is no meeting house or church, services being conducted in the members' homes.

The people gather in the "parlor" or barn, wherever the benches have been placed. Men sit on one side of the room, women on the other. They sing songs while the ministers meet in another room and plan the day's service. When the ministers return, one of them reads an entire chapter in the Bible which is followed by silent prayer. The sermon is long and unprepared. It is followed by an audible prayer. After that the other ministers may talk. This is followed by testimonies from the congregation, which may be as long as an ordinary sermon. After announcements and a hymn, lunch is served. The men then smoke and chat while the women clean up and wash the dishes. A supper is also served for those who stay that long, and in the evening there is a "singing" for the young people.

Ministers are not trained, they are chosen from the congregation by lot. Each church has at least two ministers and a bishop. When the time comes to select a new minister, nominations are made by the members of the church. As many Bibles as there are candidates are placed on a table. Each candidate selects a Bible. In one is a slip of paper reading, "And they gave forth their lots, and the lot fell upon Matthias; and he was numbered with the eleven apostles." (Acts I:26–28.) The man who receives this Bible becomes the minister.

The church governs behavior through its sanction of the virtues, sobriety, industry, and piety. A member of the church may be ex-communicated for committing a crime. When this happens he is cut off from the church, his friends, and his family for the period of seven weeks. No one may have any contact with him until he is again received into the church. Thus the church, through its power to regulate behavior, has enormous influence over the Amish.

The play of the Amish is like that of other rural groups, in that much of it is useful, and there is an emphasis on group and family fun rather than on individual activity. Where there are no separate recreational institutions, play activities are tied in very closely with economic and religious functions. A distinctive aspect of Amish play is its rigid avoidance of all forms of commercialized recreation, excepting one or two like the circus, although even at the circus the Amishman is supposed to see only the animals and not the main show. Movies, dancing, and cards are frowned upon. The Amish get together and have a good social time while accomplishing necessary work. Examples of such practical play are chestnut parties and corn huskings, which permit much visiting and laughing by the young people, and there is always the eager hope of finding a red ear of corn, since this entitles the boy to kiss his partner.

Singing is in much favor, perhaps because it is a part of the church activity. A regular occasion of recreation is the Sunday night singing, which provides an opportunity to learn the hymns of the church and do a little visiting or courting on the side. Since no musical instruments are tolerated by the Amish, the singing is "a capella." The Amish have also various competitive sports, such as ball and wrestling. In the former, one side takes up positions at corners and then tries to hit one of the two opposition players who stand in the middle and try to dodge the ball when it is thrown at them. These active, simple games are in interesting contrast to our commercialized sports with their emphasis on watching rather than participating.

It may be observed further that when a culture provides few entertainments, people look to one another for recreation, and visiting is often highly developed. This is true among the Amish. The fortnightly church services provide good opportunity for visiting, since the church-goers may arrive before nine o'clock in the morning and remain until after dinner has been served. On the Sundays without church services, there is even more time for visiting. Near kinsmen feel an obligation to visit each other as often as possible. Parents and grandparents visit their children and grandchildren several times a year, and since families are large most people are usually behind the visiting schedule. Winter is the time for lengthy visits, sometimes to distant places, where there are likely to be relatives and friends.

The Amish family, then, is a highly integrated unit with many bonds—religious, economic, recreational, and protective—tying the members firmly together. In its economic functions it resembles our rural American family, except that these functions are more numerous and varied for the Amish. The religious functions are clearly more prominent in the Amish family than in American farm families generally, since every Amish home is a part-time church and every Amishman is a potential minister.[2]

The foregoing are examples of ways in which religion exerts influences on society. At the same time religion is shaped by the society of which it is a part. By religion is meant not only a system of thought impinging on the individual, but religion as an institution. By institution is meant an organized group with relatively permanent membership whose ways of desiring, thinking, acting, and experiencing are transmitted from generation to generation with little change. The five basic institutions of society are usually considered to be the family, religion, economic system, government, and school.

In the chapter on the development of religious culture, some of the causal factors responsible for the shaping of religion were examined. This inquiry is extended in the next series of chapters to include ways in which religion causally affects other institutions and ways by which it is affected by them. The first chapter in Part V analyzes the internal structure and functioning of religious institutions. The ways in which religious ideas and motives express themselves in the social organization of church and synagogue are described. The next chapter following examines the connection between religion and the social order. This involves consideration of the ways in which the economic order, government, and the school system affect religion and of the ways in which religion affects these institutions. In the final chapters the relationship between religion and small intimate groups such as those of friendship and family is analyzed. Involved in personal relationships of people to each other is the phenomenon of social class based on attitudes of acceptance or rejection of people by each other. Religion is deeply involved, sometimes dysfunctionally, in processes of social stratification as well as in the economic, political, and educational organization of society. The principal contribution of religion to society is considered by proponents to be the upbuilding of family life. Here are found its keenest institutional interest and its most frequent social teaching. These brief comments suggest the large and intricate dimensions of the problems for inquiry undertaken in the concluding section of chapters of this book.

[2] Abridged from Meyer F. Nimkoff, *Marriage and the Family*, Houghton Mifflin, 1947, pp. 241–242, 245–253.

chapter 13 Religious Organization

The organization of an institution is an overall term referring to the things of which it is composed and the way in which these things go together. Religious organization consists of thinking and activities which are effective in bringing about satisfaction of the religious needs and desires of participants. These things are structured in such a way that the activities are effective in satisfying the desires. If the activities are not effective in producing satisfaction the institution may be said to be disorganized. Implied by the concept of disorganization is the possibility, in the minds of participants, of achieving a condition of organization of their behavior in relation to their needs so that the latter are met.

Study of church structure helps answer the question of what kind of structure is most effective in the accomplishment of religious purposes. The term *structure* has special meaning in the study of social organization. Structure in the mathematical sense refers to the loci or points of location of the parts of a geometric figure. In much the same sense the structure of a social institution refers to where its elements are located in space and in time. The location of an institution within particular individuals provides more important aspects than any of the trivial spatial details pertaining to an institution. Where a family lives or which direction of the compass the house faces is much less significant than the personal interrelationships of members of the family to each other. Similarly the key features of the structure of the church as an institution refer to the relationships of religious participants to each other and to their leaders rather than to the incidental spatial loci of religious activities. The structure, then, of an institution refers to the location of its component parts in time, place, and people. The fact of location is always described in relation to something else whose location is known. Therefore the structure of an institution can be designated as the pattern of relationships in time, space, and people which component elements of the institution have to each other. The structure of an institution is a system of interrelationships.

A vital part of social structure is internalized in the minds of participants. We are here concerned with the ideas and aims which people have concerning their institution and their attitudes towards each other. The structure of this psychic material is the most important feature of the structure of an institution. The structures of the personalities of participants in a social institution are building blocks in the total structure of the institution.

The series of chapters on the functioning of religion have described in part the behavior and motivation involved in religious organization. However, the description was primarily of actions of individuals. We are now concerned with the larger pattern of participation in religion by the group. This more extensive topic might be approached by detailing the parts out of which a religious institution is composed and the structural features in accordance with which the component parts are combined into an entire institution. However, the nature of religious organization can be better understood if the historical reasons for its particular development are kept in mind. It is impractical if not impossible to go back to the earliest beginnings of religious institutions in cultural evolution. However, religious evolution tends to repeat itself in a series of recurring cycles. Religious institutions have their inception again and again in religious movements. In these movements religious organization takes progressive shape as the movement unfolds. We start our analysis of religious organization by examining the nature of religious movements out of which religious institutions from time to time develop anew.

ORGANIZATION OF RELIGIOUS MOVEMENTS

Dawson and Gettys' Theory of Social Movements

Within the past generation the most important work done in defining concepts and principles for the analysis of social movements has been done by Carl A. Dawson and Warner E. Gettys, and by Herbert G. Blumer. Blumer gives a concise and convenient sketch of the nature of a social movement.

Social movements can be viewed as collective enterprises to establish a new order of life. They have their inception in a condition of unrest, and derive their motive power on one hand from dissatisfaction with the current form of life, and on the other hand, from wishes and hopes for a new scheme or system of living. The career of a social movement depicts the emergence of a new order of life. In its beginning, a social movement is amorphous, poorly organized, and without form; the collective behavior is on the primitive level that we have already discussed, and the mechanisms of interaction are the elementary, spontaneous mechanisms of which we have spoken. As a social movement develops, it takes on the character of a society. It acquires organization and form, a body of customs and traditions, established leadership, an enduring division of labor, social rules and social values —in short, a culture, a social organization, and a new scheme of life.[1]

The primitive level to which Blumer refers is that of behavior which takes place when people lack rules, norms, or ideas from past experience concerning how to meet a new and critical situation. The mechanisms of interaction are those of milling.

One gets a clue to the nature of elementary collective behavior by recognizing the form of social interaction that has been called *circular reaction.* This refers to a type of interstimulation wherein the response of one individual reproduces the stimulation that has come from another individual and in being reflected back to this individual reinforces the stimulation. Thus the interstimulation assumes a circular form in which individuals reflect one another's states of feeling and in so doing intensify this feeling. It is well evidenced in the transmission of feelings and moods among people who are in a state of excitement. One sees the process clearly amidst cattle in a state of alarm. The expression of fear through bellowing, breathing, and movements of the body, induces the same feeling in the case of other cattle who, as they in turn express their alarm, intensify this emotional state in one another. It is through such a process of circular reaction that there arises among cattle a general condition of intense fear and excitement, as in the case of a stampede. . . .

The basic type of such elementary forms is that of *milling*. Milling can be thought of as a pure instance of circular reaction. In milling, individuals move around amongst one another in an aimless and random fashion, such as in the interweaving of cattle and sheep who are in a state of excitement. The primary effect of milling is to make the individuals more sensitive and responsive to one another, so that they become increasingly preoccupied with one another and decreasingly responsive to ordinary objects of stimulation. It is such a condition to which the term *rapport* refers.[2]

[1] H. Blumer, "Social Movements," in A. M. Lee (ed.), *Principles of Sociology,* Barnes and Noble, 1951, p. 199.

[2] H. Blumer, "Elementary Collective Behavior," in Lee, *op. cit.,* pp. 170, 174.

Dawson and Gettys have defined four distinct stages of development through which a social movement goes. To illustrate these four stages, they cite the development of the Methodist movement. The first stage of a social movement is one of social unrest. This is a situation in which people have fundamental wants and needs which are blocked by the existing state of affairs. They would like to act to do something about their dissatisfaction but are frustrated in doing so. Their experience is much like that of a mass neurosis in which discomfort, anxiety, insecurity, and unhappiness and irritation are experienced. Because of these disturbed feelings people feel an urge to act but can only do so in aimless, restless ways. The dissatisfaction and unrest communicate themselves from person to person by the circular milling process referred to.

The presence of social unrest indicates that the traditional order is breaking down. It indicates that people no longer find the traditional ways of acting and thinking to be adequate for fulfillment of their desires in life. Applied to religion, social unrest arises when people have lost the means of controlling and expressing their deep-seated religious longings. In theological terms they have lost touch with their God. In the previous chapter the reasons why entire societies retrogress in their religious life were analyzed. When this decline has taken place, before an upward trend occurs, people are in an acute state of social unrest. Blumer writes: "Social unrest may be regarded as the crucible out of which emerge new forms of organized activity—such as social movements, reforms, revolutions, religious cults, spiritual awakenings, and new moral orders."[3]

The moral and spiritual decay which preceded the rise of the Methodist movement is described by Abel Stevens as follows:

> The vigor of its (Puritanism's) Commonwealth has illustrated the name of England in the history of the world; but its reaction under the Restoration spread over the country greater demoralization than had preceded it under the Papal reigns. The court became a royal brothel. The play-house became the temple of England. The drama of the day could not now be exhibited, nor even privately read without blushes. Many of the most learned and devoted clergymen, whose writings are imperishable in our religious literature, were either silenced or displaced. The ministrations of the Church grew formal and ineffective. The Puritan churches themselves at last fell into general decay, while the masses of people sunk into incredible vice and brutality.
>
> Natural religion was the favorite study of the clergy, and of the learned generally, and included most of their theology. . . . The de-

[3] *Ibid.*, p. 173.

cayed state of the English Church, in which Methodism was about to have its birth, was, in fine, the cause, direct or indirect, of most of the infidelity of the age, both at home and abroad. . . . The higher classes laughed at piety, and prided themselves on being above what they called its fanaticism; the lower classes were grossly ignorant, and abandoned to vice, while the Church, enervated by a universal decline, was unable longer to give countenance to the downfall and cause of truth.[4]

Each stage in the development of a social movement is characterized by a particular pattern of leadership. A leader is not necessarily one to whom authority has been delegated by his followers. A leader in the sociological sense is simply an individual who responds first to a situation and who by his example or by what he says induces others to respond in a similar way. When leadership has not yet crystallized in terms of an organized procedure for determining who is to be recognized as the leader, many individuals may stand out as performing roles of leadership. In the first stage, that of social unrest, the individuals who first react with acute discontent and restlessness are unnamed and largely unnoticed until the situation of others in proximity is sufficiently acute to predispose them to experience similar discontent and to act with similar restlessness. At any given moment of time there are always at least some individuals who are discontented with the status quo. When they are able to infect others in a contagious manner with their mood and reactions, then a social movement begins.

At successive stages of a social movement, characteristic types of leadership are in evidence. In the first stage of a social movement the leaders are agitators.

As the term suggests, agitation operates to arouse people and so make them possible recruits for the movement. It is essentially a means of exciting people and of awakening within them new impulses and ideas which make them restless and dissatisfied. Consequently, it acts to loosen the hold on them of their previous attachments, and to break down their previous ways of thinking and acting. For a movement to begin and gain impetus, it is necessary for people to be jarred loose from their customary ways of thinking and believing, and to have aroused within them new impulses and wishes. This is what agitation seeks to do. To be successful, it must first gain the attention of people; second, it must excite them, and arouse feelings and impulses; and

[4] Abel Stevens, *The History of the Religious Movement of the 18th Century Called Methodism,* 1858, vol. I, pp. 26–27, quoted in C. A. Dawson and W. E. Gettys, *An Introduction to Sociology,* Ronald, 1948, p. 691.

third, it must give some direction to these impulses and feelings through ideas, suggestions, criticisms, and promises.[5]

One type of agitator is aggressive and emotional. The religious leader who storms, weeps, and shouts to arouse a deeper reaction against sin in the minds of his hearers is of such a type. Such an agitator functions more successfully if his hearers are already in a somewhat emotionally disturbed condition or are at least prone to develop the same type of response as he displays.

A second type of agitator is calm and restrained. "He is likely to be a man sparing in his words, but capable of saying very caustic, incisive, and biting things—things which get 'under the skin' of people and force them to view things in a new light."[6] A religious leader of this type is one who continually reminds people of moral and spiritual conflicts which they have. He brings troubles which are latent and unconscious in peoples' minds to the surface. He compels them by his verbal skill to confront their moral and spiritual shortcomings face to face. He does not let people forget the overwhelming importance of abandoning their old, demoralized ways of living. The function of agitation is to deepen the discontent and restlessness of people so that they are ready to find and to accept a new way of life.

The second stage in the development of a social or religious movement is one of popular excitement. The reason for the excitement is that at this stage people have discovered a new way which they believe will solve their troubles. In a religious movement this is a stage when a new system of religious insights is discovered which people realize will rebuild their lives and enable them to gain a sense of spiritual fulfillment. The greater has been the spiritual hunger of people for something worth-while and meaningful to supplant their personal and social disorder, the keener is their joy and excitement when they realize that life can be beautiful and satisfying to them.

At this second stage the characteristic type of leader is a prophet. He is one who has either discovered the new system of religious insights or else who has been stirred to action by the discovery of another. Frequently the individual who is capable of the intense psychological search necessary for the discovery and organization of a new religious system is not one who possesses much talent for persuading others to follow him. He may be a quiet, introspective, even cold and taciturn individual. If the discoverer is lacking in vocal talents for influencing others,

[5] Blumer, "Social Movements," *op. cit.*, pp. 203–204.
[6] *Ibid.*, pp. 204–205.

his discoveries would pass unnoticed were it not for an individual of the stature of a prophet who can bring others to a realization of the new religious insights. The leaders of religions of the world, such as Moses, Buddha, Jesus, and Mohammed, have typically been individuals who combined great talent for psychological insight and discovery with the ability to communicate their discoveries and to influence large numbers of people to embrace a new way of life. They possessed an irresistible, almost magical, appeal which Max Weber refers to as *charisma*. Originally meaning *spiritual gift,* this term is extended by Weber to designate extraordinary qualities of leadership.

The stage of popular excitement is more sharply marked by the circular reaction of milling than any of the other stages of development of a social movement. People experience an intense emotion of joy when their disordered or deficient outlook on life is replaced by something noble in which they can believe and to which they can give allegiance readily. This emotion readily communicates itself from person to person when people have become sensitized by prolonged social unrest and are already seeking hopefully for something better for themselves. We read in scriptural history that the spirit which Moses experienced fell upon the elders of the tribe.[7] Scripture also records how the Holy Spirit descended upon the early Christians at Pentecost.[8] The successive emergence of different Protestant sects from the Reformation was marked by waves of acute excitement. George Fox, the founder of the Quakers, stirred intense feeling wherever he went and spoke to people who were spiritually disposed to accept the ideas he described. Dawson and Gettys cite material illustrating the influence of George Whitefield, a leader with the Wesley brothers of the Methodist movement.

At a time when he was himself excluded from the pulpits of Bristol, and was thus deprived of the chief normal means of exercising his talents, his attention was called to the condition of the colliers of Kingswood. He was filled with horror and compassion at finding in the heart of a Christian country, and in the immediate neighborhood of a great city, a population of many thousands, sunk in the most brutal ignorance and vice, and entirely excluded from the ordinances of religion. Moved by such feelings, he resolved to address the colliers in their own haunts. The resolution was a bold one, for field-preaching was then utterly unknown in England, and it needed no common courage to brave all the obloquy and derision it must provoke, and to commence the ex-

[7] Numbers 11:24–25.
[8] Acts 2:1–4.

periment in the center of a half-savage population. Whitefield, however, had a just confidence in his cause and in his powers. Standing himself upon a hillside, he took for his text the first words of the sermon which was spoken from the Mount, and he addressed with his accustomed fire an astonished audience of some 200 men. The fame of his eloquence spread far and wide. On successive occasions, five, ten, fifteen, even twenty thousand were present. It was February, but the winter sun shone clear and bright. The lanes were filled with the carriages of the more wealthy citizens, whom curiosity had drawn from Bristol. The trees and hedges were crowded with humbler listeners, and the fields were darkened by the compact mass. The voice of the great preacher pealed with a thrilling power to the very outskirts of that mighty throng. The picturesque novelty of the occasion and of the scene, the contagious emotion of so great a multitude, a deep sense of the condition of his hearers and of the momentous importance of the step he was taking, gave an additional solemnity to his eloquence. His rude auditors were electrified. They stood for a time in rapt and motionless attention. Soon tears might be seen forming white gutters down cheeks blackened from the coal-mine. Then sobs and groans told how hard hearts were melting at his words. A Fire was kindled among the outcasts of Kingswood, which burnt long and fiercely, and was destined in a few years to overspread the land.[9]

A social or religious movement cannot long survive on enthusiasm and excitement alone. It must become organized in order to accomplish its objectives, in order to defend itself against opposition, and in order to perpetuate itself as a stable institution. A social movement, whether religious or not, must develop a clear-cut ideology which serves as a basis of common understanding of the aims, ideas, and assumptions of the movement. It must also develop a practical program of step-by-step procedures for bringing its objectives about. It must develop a system of division of labor among its participants, including delegation of or recognition of authority of its leaders. There must be rules and regulations developed for the orderly control of the membership. These rules frequently provide for qualifications for membership or leadership. As part of the system of social control in the movement, procedures are developed for educating or indoctrinating followers or prospective members.

In addition to these things, a religious movement is distinctive in its development of procedures for worship and for cultivation of spiritual growth by members. These things involve psychic processes which take place largely within the individual's

[9] W. E. H. Lecky, *A History of England in the Eighteenth Century,* 1878–1890, vol. II, pp. 561–562, cited in Dawson and Gettys, *op. cit.,* pp. 697–698.

thinking and experience, in contrast to the comprehensive and highly organized procedures of an economic or a political movement. Religion is much more an affair of individual participation in that the individual himself comes to terms with the ultimate purposes and values rooted in his own personality system. At the same time these purposes and values are ones shared by others in the group. Religion is nearly always a group undertaking, even if the behavior of the group is largely expressive of feeling and not necessarily involved in the practical problems of living with which the group copes. Typically, and especially in its highest and most socially useful form, religion is much more than ceremonial or worship, permeating all phases of human existence. In this sense religion is more a preparation for life and a fulfillment of life than it is an incidental or extracurricular activity.

Leadership plays an important role in the third stage, as also in the second. Leaders in this stage of organization can be called statesmen. By this is meant that the leaders are capable of combining the vision and enthusiasm of a prophet with the practical skills of one capable of bringing about reorganization of people according to a new way of life. A simple prototype of the effective leader in the third stage of a social movement is the labor organizer for a new trade union. He is one who combines imagination and enthusiasm for a new social pattern with the practical skills for persuading people to act together in an orderly and united way. He must be a good judge of character so that he can place his weight in support of other likely leaders. He must know to what extent practical concessions in the ultimate purposes of the movement are necessary in order to achieve results today.

The responsibilities which rest upon a religious statesman for a new movement are large ones. As is said in Scripture, "If salt has lost its taste, how shall its saltness be restored?"[10] If religious ideals are appreciably compromised they lose their power in inducing people to achieve a new way of life. Typically, the greatest religious leaders have been those of stubborn and unyielding convictions who would not tolerate dilution of their principles in order to meet practical exigencies. Dawson and Gettys cite material indicating the importance which leaders play in the process of organization.

> The colonial work devolved chiefly on Whitefield, who, in as many expeditions to Georgia, revived something of the old spirit of the Pilgrim fathers. He made, however, no attempts to form a separate community,

[10] Matthew 5:13.

and the first Methodist Society in America was created at New York in 1776, by some Irish emigrants, under a local preacher named Embury. America Whitefield regarded with a peculiar fondness; he became a fervent advocate of its independence, and he at last left his bones in its soil. The clergy in the colony were far more favorable to Evangelical preaching than those in England; but in the perhaps somewhat partial judgment of Wesley, the impression made upon the people was more transient. This judgment, however, was not justified by the event. Methodism in America grew and flourished beyond all its rivals.[11]

Most religious movements have as one of their cardinal aims the bringing of a new way of life to those who are not yet converted. It is typical of social movements in general that they must seek many new adherents in order to achieve a constituency large enough for the accomplishment of objectives. In the case of religion, there is a strong altruistic dynamic which, whether intelligently expressed or not, seeks to help others by sharing with them the opportunities and benefits of a new way of life. Missionary activity has, at various times in history, commanded major attention among the followers of some world religions.

In the stage of organization Blumer has pointed out that the development of esprit de corps and morale are important features which the movement must acquire. Esprit de corps refers to organization of the feelings and sentiments of members of the movement so that they feel intimately identified with it and identified with each other. The presence of esprit de corps means that the members consider themselves to be closely linked together in a working relationship. Esprit de corps is fostered by recreational activities which build up bonds of mutual acceptance and encouragement. Esprit de corps is also fostered through ceremonial behavior and ritual. By worshiping together, the participants of a religious movement come to feel part of the same great spiritual undertaking.

Morale refers to persistence of the group in pursuit of its purposes. Morale is extremely important in holding members in the face of adversity. Most social movements encounter more or less opposition. If it were not for tenacity of purpose people would lose heart and fall away from the movement. How is high morale achieved? Blumer describes the essential ingredients of morale.

Morale seems to be based on, and yielded by, a set of convictions. In the case of a social movement these seem to be of three kinds. First is a conviction of the rectitude of the purpose of the movement. This is

[11] Lecky, *op. cit.,* p. 601, cited in Dawson and Gettys, *op. cit.,* p. 704. Whether Methodism in America began in New York is subject to question.

accompanied by the belief that the attainment of the objectives of the movement will usher in something approaching a millennial state. What is evil, unjust, improper, and wrong will be eradicated with the success of the movement. In this sense, the goal is always overvalued. Yet these beliefs yield to the members of the movement a marked confidence in themselves. A second conviction closely identified with these beliefs is a faith in the ultimate attainment, by the movement, of its goal. There is believed to be a certain inevitability about this. Since the movement is felt to be a necessary agent for the regeneration of the world, it is regarded as being in line with the higher moral values of the universe, and in this sense as divinely favored. Hence, there arises the belief that success is inevitable, even though it be only after a hard struggle. Finally, as part of this complex of convictions, there is the belief that the movement is charged with a sacred mission. Together, these convictions serve to give an enduring and unchangeable character to the goal of a movement and a tenacity to its effort. Obstructions, checks, and reversals are occasions for renewed effort instead of for disheartenment and despair, since they do not seriously impair the faith in the rectitude of the movement nor in the inevitability of its success.[12]

In the case of a religious movement the conviction of the rightness of the purposes of the movement is directly implied by working for a superior way of life. However, difficulty arises in convincing people that a new religious program is actually superior to modes of existence with which they are already familiar. The benefits which are experienced by the followers of a new religion come only after a lengthy program of religious exercise and development. Once a movement gains root the enthusiasm and example of its followers greatly facilitate the conversion of the new members. Moreover once the movement is making substantial progress, members are influenced by the enthusiasm and example of each other. Having tasted the benefits of the new way of life their conviction in the rightness of the movement's purposes and program is much more readily maintained. While it is true of some social movements that its goals are overvalued, it seems unwise for the followers of a religious movement to be oversold on its purposes, or disappointment and disillusionment are likely to occur which can be very damaging to the morale of the movement.

Traditionally, faith in the ultimate achievement by a religious movement of its objectives was sustained in part by supernaturally based beliefs that God had intervened in the course of human events and assured his children that his purposes would

[12] Blumer, *op. cit.*, pp. 208–209.

ultimately triumph. In the contemporary scientific era this type of faith is no longer readily maintained. Instead, it is necessary to show that the forces built into the reality of history inevitably will bring about the triumph of the movement. Morale in Communism is sustained by conviction that the economic forces of history will ultimately bring about a socialistic way of life. What this means is that despite temporary setbacks or even serious defeat, the followers of Communism are thoroughly convinced that their way of life will ultimately triumph. This gives to the Communist movement a tenacity of purpose far exceeding that of conventional political parties.

In the case of a new religious movement today, if it is to make lasting headway, the conviction in its eventual success must likewise be established by an analysis of the forces working within history. The guarantee is provided by the discovery of psychic forces slumbering in the unconscious side of human personality which impel the human race toward a higher way of life. When the proof is accepted on scientific grounds that human beings find their greatest fulfillment in living for others through the spirit of God, then it follows logically that human beings will seek this way of life. When it has been shown that the strongest and most lasting motivation in human life is altruistic, and that this motivation is capable of unending development, then people realize that spiritual forces in history will triumph in bringing about a way of life in the future superior to that now found by human beings.

The third belief in the complex of convictions referred to by Blumer is that the movement is charged with a sacred mission. This means that people believe that they are on the side of God and that he has laid upon men an obligation to aid the movement toward its success from which they cannot turn aside. In a religious movement these three convictions in high morale are summarized by the simple and direct faith that when people in the movement go forward God is their immediate companion. The most famous example in history of the achievement of this morale is given by the life-long journey of the ancient Jews from bondage in Egypt to a new homeland. So strongly did they believe that God walked with them every foot of the way in the long and hazardous journey which they undertook that they recorded how God showed them the way. "And the Lord went before them by day in a pillar of cloud to lead them along the way, and by night in a pillar of fire to give them light, that they might travel by day and by night; the pillar of cloud by day and the pillar of fire by night did not depart from before the people."[13] In the same way today, if participants in a religious movement gain the conviction that God himself walks with them every foot of the way in the long and complex journey of life, this is productive of morale of great tenacity.

We now come to the fourth and concluding stage of a social movement, the one in which it has become part of the prevailing social order. The social movement from its inception constitutes a new institution in embryo. This embryo progressively grows from amorphous germ plasm into a new section of society. At each stage of the social movement the new institution can be seen to be progressively taking shape. An example of the historical continuity of an institution with its earliest stirrings of life is provided by the growth of Communism from its earliest stage of deep social unrest through the stage of popular excitement when Marx proclaimed a new way of life to enthusiastic bands of followers, through the stage of formal organization, especially as this occurred in the first quarter of the twentieth century in Russia, into its concluding stage of social and economic institutionalization in Russia at the present time. Social movements do not necessarily progress evenly from one stage to the next. At different places and in the minds of different people various stages of the social movement may be taking place. At the present time the situation in Russia is largely one of a political and economic movement which has become the existing social order, while in some other areas Communism is in one of the first three stages.

The outcome of a religious movement is the establishment of a church as one of the five major institutions of society. Such a church can be traced from its earliest beginnings in the vague, undefined unrest which people experience because their old religious and moral ways have broken down, through a stage of enthusiasm and excitement when new religious insights presage a higher way of life, through a stage of formal organization in which a church is built, to the concluding stage where the church functions as one of the ongoing institutions of society. Describing this outcome of the Methodist movement, Dawson and Gettys cite Lecky.

> He [Wesley] lived to see the sect which he founded numbering more than 70,000 souls upon British soil, and about 300 itinerant and 1,000 local preachers raised up from his own people. . . . They [the Meth-

[13] Exodus 13:21–22.

odists] have already far outnumbered every other Nonconformist body in England and every other religious body in the United States, and they are probably destined largely to increase, while the influence of the movement transformed for a time the whole spirit of the Established Church, and has been more or less felt in every Protestant community speaking the English language.[14]

At the present time many churches in contemporary America are primarily in the fourth and last stage, that of institutionalization. At this stage there is little or no drive left for further growth. This is not to say that occasional members may not hunger for something better and may even engage in sporadic efforts to bring something better about. The dynamic, however, is weak, if nonexistent, since the majority of people go their customary ways accepting whatever benefits contemporary religious institutions seem capable of offering. The typical leader in the institutional stage of a social movement is an administrator. His job is one of keeping the wheels of the institution moving smoothly. He is certainly not an agitator, for that would be upsetting to the prevailing order. He lacks the vision of a prophet, and has little or no insight or concept of how a superior way of life can be brought about. He is not an organizer of a movement, for there is nothing incipient left for him to organize. He is a functionary, a useful wheel in a social machine. The administrators in some denominational organizations are religious leaders of this type. Others are leaders of social change.

The successive stages in the evolution of a social movement are largely irreversible. From a practical standpoint what this means is that when a social movement has reached its final stage of institutionalization it is extremely difficult to breathe into that structure the new life characteristic of earlier stages. What is necessary is to begin again by working with individuals and building by progressive stages a new social order with their participation. Examples of new religious growth at the grass-roots level of religious participation are furnished by Alcoholics Anonymous and social action liberals whose programs have evangelical fervor. Also exhibiting some characteristics of new social movements are the waves of religious revival which periodically sweep America. As in previous waves of revival, the large-scale meetings led by Billy Graham have drawn participation from members of traditional churches. What Billy Graham's revivalistic crusade does show is that people continue to hunger at the present time for something more spiritually meaningful,

[14] Lecky, *op. cit.*, pp. 631–632, cited in Dawson and Gettys, *op. cit.*, p. 708.

and that they are readily aroused to a pitch of popular excitement by someone who can promise them something better. They are in a new stage of unrest.

The reasons are readily seen why the stages of a religious movement are almost irreversible. When in the second stage, that of popular excitement, people have found an improved scheme of life, they can hardly be diverted into something else. When the stage of active organization is reached, the movement has gained dynamic in the fulfillment of particular purposes. An alternative set of purposes almost entirely lacks the dynamic necessary to divert the social movement in a new direction. When the final stage of the social movement is reached, people have lost the capacity for developing ideas which are fundamentally new. Their institutions are in the hands of leaders who have a strong stake in the existing order. Typical administrators lack the temperament to be agitators; they are almost totally lacking in the depth of insight necessary to be prophets, they are not organizers, for there is little or nothing of their institution which is not yet largely developed; and hence they are not a normal vehicle for the forwarding of a new social movement.

The soundness of the Dawson and Gettys four-stage theory of the development of social movements can be recognized in terms of simple principles of motivation and action. The phenomenon of drive-motivated activity begins first with a condition of frustration and blocking of the wants and needs of the individual. Next there is imaginative awareness of responses that can be made to end the frustration and achieve fulfillment. Third, there is the stage of action in which the responses are made to bring about satisfaction of wants. Finally there is a stage of habitual action in which people almost unthinkingly act to fulfill their wants and achieve a condition of stability and continuity in the functioning of their personality system.

This analysis of the evolution of religious movements describes the way in which the upturn of a cycle of religious culture proceeds. This does not mean that religious institutions cannot achieve a steady stage of growth combined with institutional stability. If the participants and leaders are sensitive to what is necessary for periodic rejuvenation of their institutions, growth can conceivably take place without going through the labor pains of rebirth in a pattern of cultural cycles. However, when prevailing religious institutions have outlived their usefulness, a stage of social unrest is spontaneously induced which provides the birth setting for a new religious movement.

Besides the development which it undergoes through the life cycle of religious movements, religious organization undergoes change in its details from time to time as does any other part of the social structure. These developments of lesser scope are attributable to the effects of deep-seated cultural currents such as the rise of science or the evolution of industrial technology. These more gradual changes in religious organization may improve its functioning or may cause its functioning to deteriorate. The major evolution of contemporary world religions appears to have come about through the life cycle of social movements.

Religious Typology

Religion is so complex and variable in its manifestations that the problem of establishing a classification of types of religious organization has been a keen challenge to sociologists studying religion. The quest for a simple uniform scheme of classification of different types of religious organization has proved incapable of fulfillment. As many different ways of classifying religious organization can be found as there are variables with respect to which religious organization undergoes variation. Three important dimensions of variation in religious organization are provided by type of government of the religious institution, type of worship, and type of educational methods used to familiarize members with the content of ritual and belief. These three dimensions of variation in religious organization are later topics in this chapter.

Two other dimensions of basic importance in a typology of religious institutions are contained in the analysis which has been given of the development of religious institutions through social movements. These are (1) the stage of development reached by the religious organization and (2) the degree of cleavage of the religious institution from the cultural patterns of the majority of people. Not all religious movements reach the concluding stage of institutionalization. If they are short-lived they might not even reach a temporary stage of formal organization, but exist only in the second phase of enthusiasm and temporary appeal. Or the movement may develop a loose form of organization with leadership and division of labor sufficient to keep the religious activity going for a number of years but not enough to ensure its continuity and perpetuation from generation to generation.

To religious movements which command passing enthusiasm of devotees, often oriented about a leader who has charismatic appeal for them, is given the designation of *cult*. Usually a cult has not endured long enough nor gained a sufficient number of adherents to challenge seriously the existing social order. The cult is looked upon by others as curious or mysterious, or at least as an odd form of religious expression. Cults are as perennial as the plants which grow in the spring, being plentifully sprinkled through human history. We read of numerous cults among the Egyptians, Jews, Greeks, and Romans of the ancient world. These run the entire gamut of religious expression from orgiastic cults in which bucolic or sexual rites are mingled with elements of religious worship, to cults whose devotees practice extreme asceticism or even self-flagellation. Cults tend primarily to be expressive of the feelings and moods which people in any particular cultural stream or at any given time of history happen to experience. It can usually be assumed that transient cults are not successful in answering the deep-seated spiritual longings of people, or they would not, by their nature, so readily pass out of the social picture. In contemporary America the "I Am" movement, which achieved great popularity during the years of the Great Depression and then ended in collapse when its leaders underwent criminal prosecution for fraud, was such a cult. It remains to be seen whether the Peace Mission movement of Father Divine will eventually pass out of existence with the death of its leader or whether it will gain enduring institutional form. Likewise, it is not yet clear whether the Oxford Group movement will survive its cultlike phase. These cults and related sectarian groups, such as Jehovah's Witnesses and the Mormons, have been painstakingly and interestingly described and analyzed by Charles S. Braden,[15] and by Marcus Bach.[16]

Cults are of special interest in the scientific study of religion as a commentary upon religious needs which traditional religious organizations fail to meet. Thus, in the years of the economic depression of the 1930's, Father Divine's Peace Mission movement gained as many as a million adherents, principally among underprivileged Negroes in urban areas of the North. These were persons who were economically destitute and found in the cooperative living colonies of Father Divine a means of livelihood as well as fellowship. One of the slogans of the followers of Father Divine has been "We live in our churches." Also, the failure of established churches to provide religious experience with real

[15] Charles S. Braden, *These Also Believe,* Macmillan, 1949.
[16] Marcus Bach, *They Have Found a Faith,* Bobbs-Merrill, 1946.

social significance was a dynamic factor in the popularity of Father Divine's teachings.

With the progressive development of a religious movement it may reach the concluding stage of institutionalization without, however, gaining the support and participation of the majority of people. In this case it becomes an institutional island surrounded by a sea of culture from which it is differentiated to a greater or lesser degree. The followers of a religious movement may succeed in gaining a new way of life for themselves without persuading or influencing the majority of people to join with them in their religious scheme. In this case the religious group is known as a *sect*. By definition a religious sect is a group which consists of a small minority of people who follow a way of life which protests against that of the majority. Important examples of sects in American religious history are Christian Scientists, Jehovah's Witnesses, and the Mormons. As these groups become increasingly merged in their thinking, activities, and values with the culture of the majority, they cease to be sects. During the Reformation the successive rise of groups such as Baptists, Presbyterians, Quakers, and Methodists brought into being sectlike groups. These, with the possible exception of some Quakers, have long since ceased to have a sectlike character and have become integrated into the social order. Current examples of sectlike groups are organizations of pacifists or Communists.

Since a sect by definition is made up of a piece of social organization sharply differentiated from the way of life of the majority, it almost invariably clashes with the social organization of the majority. As in the case of the Christian Scientists in their earlier development and as in the case of the Jehovah's Witnesses even at the present time, a vigorous struggle for existence against the hostility of the majority is necessary. A sect, therefore, is typically a religious group which is at war with the existing social order. Where religious values are at stake, human beings are readily drawn into overt conflict for the supremacy of one religious system against another. Hence, it has been the exception, rather than the rule, in religious history for sects to survive peaceably without interference by others. The missionary zeal of the followers of many sects has, of course, intensified the reaction of opposition shown by the majority. The disfavor with which sects are usually regarded by others results in loss of social status for sect members in the society of the majority. At the same time, those of lower social status may turn to sectlike religion as a means of self-expression and protest against those in power. R. R. Dynes found in Columbus, Ohio, that churchness is strongly associated with high socio-economic status and sectness with low economic status.[17]

Standing in contrast with either cult or sect is what sociologists of religion designate as the church or denomination. This represents the final stage of a religious movement in which either the social order has been transformed or, what more commonly happens, the religious movement has greatly modified its aims and demands and reached compromises with the existing order so that it effectively becomes integrated with it. Ernst Troeltsch extensively analyzed the contrasting concepts of sect and church and stimulated a line of inquiry which has been intensively pursued by sociologists of religion down to the present time. The factors which determine the appearance, survival, or absorption of religious movements into the existing social order are complex cultural variables. The separate morphologies of sects and denominations have been studied by Ernst Troeltsch, Max Weber, H. R. Niebuhr, Joachim Wach, Marshall Sklare, and J. M. Yinger.[18]

PATTERNS OF WORSHIP

The heart of religious organization is found in the activity of worship. While worship to the outsider may appear to be couched in apparently inconsequential forms, the manner in which worship is performed according to the convictions and aspirations of the participants profoundly affects the entire structure of the church. The principal link of members to their religious organization is through the activity of worship. The term *worship* refers to group ways of communicating with or influencing God or the higher power of religion. Worship is a recurring activity to maintain and renew a heightened state of spiritual motivation. Much of the character of religious organization stems from the

[17] R. R. Dynes, "Church-Sect Typology and Socio-Economic Status," *American Sociological Review,* October, 1955, pp. 555–560.

[18] Ernst Troeltsch, *The Social Teaching of the Christian Churches,* tr. by Olive Wyon, 2 vols., Macmillan, 1931; Max Weber, *The Protestant Ethic and the Spirit of Capitalism,* tr. by Talcott Parsons, Scribner's, 1948; H. R. Niebuhr, *The Social Sources of Denominationalism,* Holt, 1929; J. Wach, *Sociology of Religion,* University of Chicago Press, 1944; Marshall Sklare, *Conservative Judaism: An American Religious Movement,* Free Press, 1955; J. M. Yinger, *Religion in the Struggle for Power,* Duke University Press, 1946. Also see L. Von Wiese and H. Becker, *Systematic Sociology,* Wiley, 1932, chap. 44; F. A. Shippey, "Sociological Forms of Religious Expression in Western Christianity," *Religion in Life,* Spring, 1958, pp. 172–184.

characteristics in the pattern of worship. We proceed next to consider the ways in which worship can be classified according to its several dimensions.

Divinely Sanctioned Worship

The prescribed rituals in worship which is divinely sanctioned are ones which the participants believe have been authorized directly by God. They can only be performed in the prescribed manner, and participation in them is considered to be an absolutely necessary condition of religious salvation in this life and in the next. Together with the divine sanction for the service of worship is usually the conferring of God-given authority to the priesthood who officiate at the religious services.

The Catholic view is that the Catholic Church was founded by Jesus, who gave his disciple Peter authority to be its ruler. At the same time Jesus gave Peter supernatural power for the performance of religious rites. This authority and this power are ones which have been transmitted, in the Catholic view, in a line of succession from Peter down to the present pope.[19]

The significance of this divine sanction is that there is placed in the hands of men a priceless religious possession, namely the performance of rituals which are considered to be the gift of God, while alternative rituals are assumed to be inferior and not God-given. There is thus given to a group of men a degree of religious power over the lives of others which is immense in magnitude. As might be expected, the type of church government premised upon this type of worship is not democratically controlled but is administered by a self-perpetuating group of leaders. This far-reaching power over the lives of men who accept it carries with it temptations for abuse of the power. The remarkable thing is not that at some times and places those in the Catholic hierarchy have succumbed to the temptations of power, but rather that the religious functionaries have maintained as high a degree of purity of religious motive as they have. Whether one agrees with the type of leadership which the Catholic Church offers to the world, informed persons are bound to recognize that the popes in the modern era are deeply consecrated men of great ability despite their advancing years and who are intensely devoted to the welfare of the human race. At the same time, there are indications that some of the rigidity of Catholic claims to exclusiveness is being tempered by the realities of coexistent religions with much ethical and religious merit.

[19] Matthew 16:17–19; 28:19–20; John 14:16–17; 16:13–15.

Sacramental Worship

Closely related to and sometimes identical with worship forms which are divinely sanctioned are those which are in the nature of sacraments which must be performed by the faithful. While the Catholic claim that the system of seven sacraments of Eucharist (Holy Communion), Baptism, Confirmation, Penance, Holy Orders, Matrimony, and Extreme Unction are considered to be the necessary means of salvation for people as functioning members of the Church of Christ, there is recognition among Catholic theologians that God may, if he chooses, grant salvation in exceptional circumstances in other ways. Thus it is not assumed that all outside of the active membership of the Catholic Church are inevitably condemned to eternal punishment. However, to the extent that the Catholic religion or any other religion prescribes sacraments which must be performed or accepted by the faithful, this confers upon particular religious forms great value in the minds of participants. Hence, as in the case of divine or supernatural sanction, instruments of great social power are placed in the hands of religious functionaries.

Priestly Worship

Overlapping the two worship categories already described is priestly worship. A priest is usually thought of as one who is acknowledged to have particular duties to perform in religious ceremonies. Those in the Catholic Church authorized to carry out religious work under the direction of bishops are generally known as "priests." Those who officiate in most Protestant denominations are usually referred to as "ministers." Their appointments are institutionally controlled, but their duties may be more flexibly defined. It is apparent, however, that ministers carry out duties in religious ceremonies which are officially assigned to them, and in this sense they also are priests.

Priestly worship stands in contrast to that worship in which what is said and done is carried out by nonpriests or laymen. Most systems of religious worship provide for more or less lay participation, but usually reserve for officially designated functionaries the utterance of key phrases or the administration of sacraments. The significance of priestly worship is that, again, unusual power reposes in the hands of religious leaders and that hence the system of social organization for the maintenance of religious services is polarized by this possession of power.

Lay worship as opposed to priestly worship characterizes what was once a prominent feature of Protestant church life, Wednesday evening prayer meeting. This is an informal worship service in which individuals take the initiative for starting the singing of favorite hymns and in which members offer prayers or testimonials in rotation. Among contemporary religious groups Quakers are conspicuous for the lay character of their worship services. Anyone attending a Quaker Meeting for worship may rise to his feet to communicate a few words of inspiration or to offer a prayer. However, it is recognized that some members of Quaker Meetings have superior gifts for religious ministry, and they are encouraged by their fellow members, while those who are lacking in spiritual gifts are encouraged to speak rarely, if at all. Some Quaker Meetings manifest their recognition of those whose capacity for inspiration is greater by appointing them to a list of recorded ministers. Many Quakers outside of the eastern United States have adopted the conventional pastoral form of worship in which a single individual serves as minister, as in other Protestant congregations.

In Jewish congregations the principal post is that of rabbi. He is regarded primarily as a learned teacher in religious doctrine. There are no roles in Jewish religious worship which cannot be performed by laymen. While there is some tendency in contemporary Jewish congregations for a rabbi to assume some of the functions performed by ministers in Protestant congregations, he is not a minister or a priest in the sense of performing duties in religious worship different from those which can be performed by other members of the congregation. Rabbis were formerly much more influential in the regard held of their authority by their congregations.

One of the characteristics usually associated with priestly religion is that the priest pursues his activities as a vocation. The word vocation originally meant one who was spiritually called by the voice of God. Vocation now means an economic livelihood. Priests in contemporary religion may be those who are maintained at a level of economic subsistence by their constituents and who in that sense do not engage in religion as if it were a commercial activity for sale. Catholic priests give unstintingly of themselves in the service of Christ. J. P. Williams summarizes this life of devotion to spiritual purposes.

> The priest's life is arduous and full of cares. Like a physician he is constantly on call to give succor to the sick and the dying. Yet early each morning he is up preparing to celebrate the Mass, in order that the members of his parish on their way to work may visit their Lord

and partake of His Blessed Body. This ministry accomplished, the priest's day is full of activities: he comforts the sorrowful, hears confessions, visits the sick, buries the dead, solicits funds, distributes alms, administers schools, directs clubs, consults his superiors. And every day he must spend about an hour in personal prayer, devotion and reading of the Breviary; and regularly he must himself go to confession.

Every priest takes the vow of absolute obedience; he must conduct his life exactly as his superiors require in all matters over which they have legitimate jurisdiction. Every priest also takes a vow of chastity. The taking of this vow is not believed to be a divine requirement. Chastity is simply a rule of discipline; it has been imposed only since the fourth century. The Church asks her leaders to remain single in order that she may be strong, in order that she may have from her priests service that knows no stint. An unmarried priest has fewer obligations than a minister with a wife and family. An unmarried clergy also costs less to maintain.[20]

Thorough analysis of the parish life of a Catholic Church has been made by J. H. Fichter.[21] Examination of this work indicates that the principal motivation of Catholic priests is spiritual as opposed to economic. On the other hand, there is a tendency, at least historically, for those in positions of high authority in an organized group of priests to live in economic circumstances which are beyond a level of subsistence. The Catholic Church throughout much of its history has been a group which collectively possesses great wealth and economic power even though this is inadequate to meet its numerous purposes. One of the things against which Protestant sects during the Reformation rebelled was the traffic in religious sacraments as if these were commercial articles. The sale of indulgences was one of the cardinal points of attack by Martin Luther. This was a source of rich financial support for the church to replenish its treasury.

Among the Protestant sects, the Quakers went further than most in rejecting any religious activity performed as an economic pursuit. Quakers of the traditional variety have no paid ministers, only individuals who give of their time voluntarily.

It is apparent to any who have been concerned with the employment of ministers for congregations in Protestant denominations that the salaries which they earn are largely determined

[20] J. P. Williams, *What Americans Believe and How They Worship*, Harper, 1952, p. 60.

[21] J. H. Fichter, *Dynamics of a City Church*, University of Chicago Press, 1951; *Social Relations in the Urban Parish*, University of Chicago Press, 1954.

by the laws of supply and demand. Since for some years capable ministers have been in short supply, it is now common for some of them to enjoy salaries about equal to those paid in other professions such as law, engineering, or selling. Yet the average salaries of all ministers are scarcely better in terms of purchasing power than they were twenty years ago. The effort is made by religious leaders to discourage commercialization of ministerial activity. However, it is hardly to be expected that some who are capable of earning a high salary in their ministerial capacity will reject the money offered to obtain their services. If nothing else, it can be reasoned on ethical grounds that human beings are entrusted as stewards with the wealth and opportunities which their Creator makes available to them. Nevertheless, it is clear that the salaries, high or low, paid ministers in many church congregations are a temptation to modify what they preach or do in order to hold their employment. Quakers argue that the only sure guarantee of eliminating commercialization from religion is found by avoiding any payment of those engaged in religious work. Rather, this work is left to those who feel the religious concern to undertake it and to minister to their fellowmen.

Problems of the Professional Ministry

Various critics besides Quakers have pointed to the circumstance that the minister of a large Protestant congregation has now become an "organization man." This means that he is not only subject to the requirements of his congregation in doing things the way they want them done, but he is extensively involved in a long list of secular activities which detract from the distinctively spiritual ministry which he might perform. Also, he is subject to demands by his superiors and governed by pressures of community groups and their leaders.

The excessive demands which congregations, often in ignorance, place upon their ministers has drawn criticism because of the destruction of their spiritual vitality and the mental breakdown which occurs among them. The Rev. Wesley Shrader, a teacher at Yale Divinity School, drew wide attention to the predicament of ministers with an article entitled "Why Ministers Are Breaking Down." In this article he describes a typical working day of an urban minister with whom he is acquainted. This minister described his work on the previous day.

I arose at 6:30, my usual hour. Had morning devotions and breakfast with my wife and arrived at the church at 8. I had planned two hours of intensive study and preparation of two sermons for Sunday, a noon address to the Rotary Club on Monday, and five early morning radio talks next week. Thus far during the week I had been unable to give any time to these speaking commitments, so I needed those two hours. However, when I arrived at the church my secretary reminded me that I had agreed to write a brief article for the Sunday church bulletin which was due to go to press at noon that day. She also reminded me that I was to make three important telephone calls, one of which involved a 20-minute conversation with the chairman of our finance committee (we are in the midst of our annual fund-raising campaign).

After writing the promised article and making the necessary telephone calls, I began the preparation for next week's radio talks. At 10 A.M. I was scheduled to attend the meeting of the program committee of the Ministerial Association, of which I am chairman. I had exactly 30 minutes to work on the radio talks—at least I thought I had 30 minutes. Just as I got started, my secretary informed me that the mother of the president of the Women's Auxiliary had passed away and I was wanted at once. I went to the home of my member who lived 5 miles from the church. I offered a prayer, spoke words of comfort and reassurance to the bereaved and helped make plans for the funeral. I will conduct the funeral Saturday afternoon at 3 P.M. I had promised my wife and children that we would go on a picnic Saturday afternoon, but as you know, death takes precedence over everything else that is on a minister's schedule.

I missed the meeting of the program committee of the Ministerial Association, but at 12:30 I attended a luncheon meeting of the Women's Auxiliary, after which I spoke briefly to a mission study class.

At 2 I performed a wedding ceremony. It was a small, informal wedding and it was held in my study. I regret that I did not have time to counsel with the young couple before the wedding. I keep telling myself that a minister should give more time to the young people whose wedding ceremony he performs. Perhaps I will get myself better organized in the future and be able to do this.

At 3 P.M. I began the rounds of the hospitals. The hospitals are located in different sections of the city, so it takes considerable time to get from one to another. However, I made the rounds and visited all the patients before 6 P.M. I did not get home for dinner but went from the hospital directly to church. A supper meeting of the Men's Bible Class was being held and I had been requested to give the invocation. The class meeting was over at 7:30. At 8 an important meeting of the Every Member Canvass Committee (pledge raising) was held. I was on hand to make suggestions and boost the committee's morale. The meeting did not last long. I was home by 9:30.[22]

Statistics concerning the extent of mental breakdown among ministers relative to the general population do not appear to be

[22] W. Shrader, "Why Ministers Are Breaking Down," *Life,* August 20, 1956, pp. 98–102.

available. The article by Wesley Shrader was answered by another by William H. Hudnut, Jr., in "Are Ministers Cracking Up?" in the *Christian Century*.[23] In Hudnut's opinion the overwhelming majority of ministers are in good spiritual health.

That the picture of a minister's day just described is not overdrawn is indicated by extensive data collected by a sociologist, Samuel W. Blizzard. In a study of 690 representative Protestant clergymen, Blizzard finds that the average workday in a seven-day week is just about ten hours. Blizzard summarizes the findings in the survey of how ministers spend their time.

> Considering all ministerial informants, almost two-fifths of their total work day was spent as administrator. Slightly more than one-fourth was devoted to the pastor role. Preaching and priestly activities took up almost one-fifth of the work day. Organizing consumed more than one-tenth of the work day. The residual time (about one-twentieth) was devoted to teaching. This order of priority from most time to least time (administrator, pastor, preacher and priest, organizer, teacher) was the same for both urban and rural parish ministers.
>
> An incidental but revealing item of intelligence is the time parish ministers devote to sermon preparation and to stenographic work each day. The average time devoted to sermon preparation is 34 minutes for rural men, 38 minutes for urban clergymen. The time taken up by stenographic tasks is one hour and 4 minutes for both country and city men.[24]

The time spent on these roles is in approximately reverse order to what the clergymen report as the most important. In order of importance they list these as follows: preacher, pastor, priest, teacher, organizer, administrator. It is obvious that not only are ministers called upon to perform a large multiplicity of roles but there is also serious conflict between what the minister believes he should do in his ministry and what his congregation requires him to do.

Another writer, James B. Moore, in "Why Young Ministers Are Leaving the Church," in *Harper's Magazine,* calls attention to other pressures to which ministers are subjected. The more recently trained ones with more liberal ideas come into conflict with older fellow ministers who demand literal subscription to such dogmas as the Virgin Birth, the Physical Resurrection of Jesus, the Deity (rather than the divinity) of Jesus, and the Bible as the *actual words* of God. Moore states, "To put it bluntly, they [the more recently trained ministers] no longer believe

[23] W. H. Hudnut, Jr., "Are Ministers Cracking Up?" *Christian Century,* November 7, 1956, pp. 1288–1289.

[24] S. W. Blizzard, "The Minister's Dilemma," *Christian Century,* April 25, 1956, p. 509.

in the Gospel *as they are expected to preach it,* and no longer believe in the denomination they are expected to support."[25] Moore also directs attention to the highly artificial standards of behavior to which ministers and their families are held, in contrast to the freer and easier ways of living which members of congregations follow. Thus the minister is subjected to intense criticism for following patterns of life with which he and his family are indoctrinated by the culture which they share with members of their congregation. "The coercive influence of the church and the society of which the minister's wife is a part is no less damaging to her own individuality than to her husband's. She is always expected to say 'the right thing' and to do 'the nice thing'—if it kills her. And it often does kill her—the real self God gave her."[26] Also of serious consequence is the role of politician which the minister must play in order to get ahead. Moore goes on to say: "Probably the most serious charge which the young minister would make is that he is forced into playing the role of a politician if he is going to get ahead in his profession. . . . It is no wonder that Theodore M. Greene, a distinguished Christian philosopher, in a widely discussed article published in *Motive* magazine a few years ago, remarked that the one greatest trouble with our age was the absence of spirituality among our spiritual leaders."[27]

Ministers appear to be victims of cultural conflict, that is, the clash of two different cultural streams which impinge upon their personality systems. On the one hand are the high spiritual values which have drawn men into religious work. On the other hand are the crass commercial values held by many, if not most, Americans, among them members of religious congregations. The conflict between spiritual and material values is intensified by the employment relationship in which ministers are expected by their congregations "to deliver the goods" as if their parishioners were buying commodities at a store. But the parishioners all too often want from their ministers the evidence of superficial success symbols, such as a larger church membership, greater church wealth, a church which is higher up in the social class system, and in addition a minister whose silver tones from the pulpit are impeccable and whose remarks never offend anyone but make everyone happy, just as a TV entertainer, a new

[25] James B. Moore, "Why Young Ministers Are Leaving the Church," *Harper's Magazine,* July, 1957, p. 67.
[26] *Ibid.,* p. 68.
[27] *Ibid.*

toothpaste, or cigarette smoke are expected to do. Confronted by this spiritual decadence, the wonder is not that ministers are cracking up, but that the churches themselves do not disintegrate after becoming completely secular pieces of the social structure. Historically, ministers have played an inestimable role in kindling the religious vitality of their congregations. This function, by whomever performed, should be upheld above all other churchly considerations. The building up of the religious life of others strengthens one's own as well.

Programed Worship

The religious services of most groups are clearly defined by tradition and from week to week are repeated with much the same identical ritual. When religious activities are divinely sanctioned, they are considered to be sacraments which the faithful must observe; and when they are administered by an organized priesthood, it follows that these activities assume the character of a liturgy which is performed again and again according to the same specifications. In contrast to an established liturgy is the practice once much more common in Protestantism of holding informal prayer meetings or testimonial meetings in which participation is informal and unplanned. On many occasions the use of the synagogue by Jews has assumed the same informal, unprogramed character. On some holy days, Jews move about their place of worship and offer prayers according to spiritual inclination. A religious group which has traditionally stressed worship activities which are not programed in advance are the Quakers. Howard H. Brinton, a Quaker leader, describes their way of worship in one of many pamphlets which Quakers publish and circulate among their members and among associates.

> To believe that there is in man that which is more than himself, through which he is lifted up beyond himself, is by no means peculiar to Quakerism or even to Christianity. What is peculiar is the type of religious worship based entirely on this experience, yet not divorced from Christian concepts. Such worship is not sermon-centered as in Protestantism, nor altar-centered as in Catholicism; but centered in the Divine Life flowing into and through human hearts whereby we commune with God.
>
> The meeting quietly assembles at the appointed hour. Members should gather without conversation. Late-comers are sources of disturbance. The "service" begins when the worshiper begins to serve. Each one sits in expectant silence, his soul reaching upwards. The Society of Friends has never issued specific instructions regarding what the wor-

shiper should do during the silence, believing that such instruction would limit the freedom of the Spirit which, like the wind, "bloweth where it listeth." Sufficient for many is the admonition so often heard in Quaker meetings: "Heed the intimations within." The way of true worship can eventually be found though it may sometimes require devout and patient search.

Friends do not use visible Sacraments of Baptism and Communion because they endeavor to seek directly the inward Reality of which these are outward symbols. To those who hold that the sacraments have more than a symbolic value, Friends reply that outward observances cannot carry more of Divine grace than is found in the inward baptism of the Spirit and inner communion with God. Any event in life is sacramental if it is truly an outward evidence of inward grace.

For similar reasons, Friends do not sing hymns nor recite prayers in their meetings for worship, because, when this is done, words are uttered for which there may be no corresponding personal experience. Words, whether sung or spoken, should, in this most important of all exercises, be the spontaneous outward expression of an immediate inner condition. This is seldom the case when the form of words is prescribed in advance.[28]

The spiritual exercises of the meeting may include spoken words. No one should go to a Friends' meeting with the definite expectation either of speaking or of not speaking. Each attender should be open to dealing appropriately with whatever may be laid upon him by the Spirit of Truth and Life.

It is no light matter to break the living silence. This should be done only with a sense of humility. Spoken words should not come as an interruption of the silence but rather as a component part of it. The tone of voice and manner of the speaker must harmonize with the character of the meeting.

As the worshiper sits in silence some message may arise out of the depth of his soul which he recognizes by its nature to be intended not simply for himself but for the gathering as a whole. If he does not express it, he finds himself burdened with a sense of omission, but if he faithfully utters it there follows a sense of clearness and relief.

This peculiar sense of urgency is usually the sign of divine requirement. There is no sure, no single test of guidance. A sensitive person learns to recognize the call as clearly as he recognizes the voice of his friend. He knows his friend's voice even though he may be quite unable to describe its quality. A clear conviction that the need of the meeting or of some persons in it or even that one's own need requires that words be uttered is often the only assurance when there is doubt. Though a message may seem intellectually fitting it should not be given unless it glows with life.[29]

[28] Howard H. Brinton, *Guide to Quaker Practice,* Pendle Hill Pamphlet, Wallingford, Pa., 1959, pp. 11–12.

[29] *Ibid.,* pp. 17–18.

While what is said during a Quaker meeting for worship often lacks the polished elegance of sermons preached by professional ministers, Quakers believe that what is said possesses higher fidelity to spiritual insight and spiritual experience if it is voiced without previous rehearsal. By not programing their religious service and by not paying for the participation of religious leadership, Quakers are convinced there is greater assurance that what is said in a meeting for worship will flow more genuinely from the spiritual feelings of people. They gain more from hearing plain people express their actual spiritual feelings than from listening to a polished speaker give a rehearsed address.

At the same time it is kept in mind that the programing of a religious service is a matter of degree. Even the most rigidly defined of liturgies not only allows for but expects voluntary participation of worshipers within suitably defined forms and limits. Nor is it the case that a Quaker meeting for worship lacks entirely a programed character. By common consent some spiritual messages are considered appropriate in a Quaker meeting while others are not. While the rules are flexible and are intended to unfetter rather than to restrict spiritual expression, they are still defined by tradition.

Artistic Expression in Worship

Quaker meeting houses are plain and unadorned. The overt part of worship activity which the traditional variety of Quakers perform consists of verbal communication. Organ music and singing, so typical of the worship services of most Christian groups, are absent from Quaker worship.

At the opposite pole from the Quaker mode of worship is the rich pageantry of liturgy of the Roman Catholic Church. In this pattern of worship arts of painting, architecture, music, and drama are brought to the highest possible perfection. One who has not yet attended Catholic Mass and seen the gold chalice raised by the priest with rays of sunlight streaming upon it through stained-glass windows has missed a stirring aesthetic experience as well as one which is deeply moving from a religious standpoint. The drama of the Nativity, performed on Christmas Eve, is a theatrical production with profound effects upon the worshiper at Christmas time.

Religious ritual is not only a means of producing religious feelings, but these in turn are a force productive of ritual behavior. The feelings of participants, whether based on socially or supernaturally conceived powers, give rise to expression in religious acts. The activity is a direct and spontaneous outgrowth of feeling because of its fundamental connection with feeling. A Catholic writer describes this expressive tendency in religious ceremony.

Now when a man is very convinced of anything, he always wants to *do* something about it. If he is a simple person, he probably does it at once, and rather noisily. With education, he may behave with greater restraint: but if he never tends to *express* himself, as we say, he is probably a languid and colorless person. If children are pleased, they jump and dance. When a man feels in good form, he sings in his bath. When he is in love, he wants to kiss the girl he loves; and, in short, he wishes to do something exterior to give vent to the interior state of his feelings. So when men have been convinced of the existence of God, they have always done and said things to reveal the fact. They feel how small they are compared to him—they fall flat on the ground, or kneel. They feel he is good and great and takes care of them—they sing hymns or gesticulate or even dance. . . . They will also feel the need of expressing outwardly what they think in their minds and picture with their imaginations, and so they make images, and surround these images with signs symbolical of the homage they want to pay to the invisible God. They will do all the things that occur to them; and everything that their senses or imagination can suggest does occur to them. They will burn sweet spices: they will light bright fires: they will sing and dance, and they will collect colored flowers or stones or anything else that strikes them. And above all, since man is "social" and lives together in groups, of which he feels the unity very acutely, men will tend to do all these things in common, and make social acts of them.[30]

This expressiveness of religious feeling is prominent in the art with which Catholic churches are adorned.

. . . connected with the Mass we have the wonderful churches of every century of the Christian era, from Sancta Sophia in the sixth century to the cathedral of Westminster in our own. The painting and sculpture of the greatest artists have adorned these churches with the theme of the Incarnation, and the perpetuation of the Incarnation in the Eucharist. The greatest musicians have delighted to write Masses.[31]

Protestant churches vary in the degree to which religious feeling is given expression in artistic form. Most Protestant church services contain music, typically that of the organ, whose tremendous tones seem appropriate to express the depths and

[30] C. C. Martindale, "The Sacramental System," in G. D. Smith, ed., *The Teaching of the Catholic Church,* Macmillan, 1949, Vol. II, pp. 734–735.

[31] L. Finkelstein, J. E. Ross, and W. A. Brown, *The Religions of Democracy,* Devin-Adair, 1941, pp. 152–153.

heights of religious feeling, and singing of hymns by the congregation or anthems by the choir or soloist. The verbal participation of Protestants through audible praying or reading in unison is more conspicuous than in Catholic worship. Expressive behavior of an extreme type is found in the unrestrained emotion of some Fundamentalist congregations, who at their revival meetings vociferously shout, pray, sing, or engage in other physical motion.

Expressive behavior for Orthodox and Conservative Jews excludes painting or sculpture of the human form or any artistic representation of God. Chanting takes place, but organ music is not permitted except in the services of Reform Jews. Praying is usually performed according to established procedures but among the Orthodox it may take place as informal expressive behavior which each member carries on audibly by himself.

Found in Jewish as well as in Christian worship are ceremonial actions which are considered to have at least symbolic value, if not supernatural. Prescribed ritual behavior takes place prior to and after reading from the Torah. Overt actions are more characteristic of Christian religious services. The taking of Holy Communion is a worship procedure during which the individual kneels, swallows a wafer, and is given a taste of wine, thereby receiving the body and blood of Jesus Christ. For Catholics this reception is a supernatural phenomenon, while for most Protestants the procedure is merely symbolic. By supernatural is meant that the worshiper believes he actually receives the body and blood of Christ. By symbolic is meant that the wafer and wine symbolize the body and blood of Jesus Christ. These symbols call forth in the worshipers' inward experience a sense of the presence of God, an awareness of the Spirit of Christ. In contrast Quakers believe that words alone are useful symbols, and that for liturgy to be effective the worshiper first must be verbally instructed, anyway, to understand the meaning of the actions. While at times in history the communion service of Christians has had intense meaning, casual observation at the present time indicates that for many the practice of communion is a ceremony which does not stir their feelings appreciably and which they would rather not have performed in their church services except at infrequent times through the year.

Crowdlike Worship

Expressive behavior not only expresses feelings, but in turn performs the function of intensifying the feelings of participants. We recognize in this a fundamental mechanism of crowd psychology. The feelings of each individual stimulate the feelings of other worshipers, whose feelings when expressed reinforce the feelings of the former. Where hundreds are responding to the ritual the behavior of each tends to heighten the feelings of the rest. In this way the state of excitement becomes built up considerably in excess of the effect which the ritual would have produced upon a single individual in isolation. The phenomenon of spirit possession may arise in such crowd excitement. The individual feels himself to be carried away by an impulsion, not part of his individual nature, which comes into being during the conditions of crowd excitement. In the case of some revival meetings, the emotional intensity exceeds any limits of restraint other than the psychological capacity of the participants.

In Catholic ceremony and in most Protestant services definite limits are placed upon the extent to which random expressive behavior may take place, and the circular process of crowd psychology does not go beyond a general feeling of spiritual well-being communicated in imperceptible ways from member to member. Yet it is typical in the Protestant service for the minister to act as the primary catalyst in fostering religious feeling. He is employed as the chief inspirer of the congregation. His sermon, if effective, must be inspiring to his hearers. If feeling seems to lag, then when he announces the next hymn he may fairly shout: "Now everybody sing of the joy in his heart." The emotion may hardly be felt, if at all, to start with, but it makes its appearance as a result of the exhortation and noise in a circular psychological pattern. The minister may in turn depend on the response of his congregation before he can get fully warmed up himself.

The conclusion of those who reject the instrumentality of crowd psychology in their religious services is that the feeling produced is temporary, and scarcely outlasts the duration of the religious service. We have so far spoken only of the feelings of worshipers during their religious ceremonies, but the secondary effects in the life and outlook of worshipers between times of ceremony are considered by many to be the most important. The worshipers then seek for a change in their state of mind and feeling through the week. Their religious observances become adapted to that function, rather than to temporary satisfaction during the service itself. For them the trial and torment the individual may undergo in wrestling with the conflicts of life during worship are features of religious activity which may be unpleasant, but which are a necessary preparation for an inward state of equanimity and harmony during the active portions of one's life. Although they feel that achieving peace of mind should be a natural accompaniment of religious worship, they do not believe that degree of enjoyment should be made the criterion of the desirability of the worship service to the participants.

At the same time the function of crowd excitement in breaking up old personality patterns and creating a fluid condition during which new personality patterns can be formed should not be overlooked. Almost without exception the different Protestant sects which emerged during the Reformation, including the Quakers, engaged in religious worship or fostered preaching which were intensely emotional in nature. We read of the spiritual revival in the rise of the Methodist movement.

In the intense religious enthusiasm that was generated, many of the ties of life were snapped in twain. Children treated with contempt the commands of their parents, students the rules of their colleges, clergymen the discipline of their church. The whole structure of society, and almost all the amusements of life, appeared criminal. The fairs, the mountebanks, the public rejoicings of the people, were all Satanic. It was sinful for a woman to wear any gold ornament or any brilliant dress. It was even sinful for a man to exercise the common prudence of laying by a certain portion of his income. When Whitefield proposed to a lady to marry him, he thought it necessary to say, "I bless God, if I know anything of my own heart, I am free from that foolish passion which the world calls love." "I trust I love you only for God, and desire to be joined to you only by His commands, and for His sake." It is perhaps not very surprising that Whitefield's marriage, like that of Wesley, proved very unhappy. Theaters and the reading of plays were absolutely condemned, and the Methodists employed all their influence with the authorities to prevent the erection of the former. It seems to have been regarded as a Divine judgment that once, when "Macbeth" was being acted in Drury Lane a real thunderstorm mingled with the mimic thunder in the witch scene. Dancing was, if possible, even worse than the theater. "Dances," said Whitefield, "please the devil at every step"; and it was said that his visit to a town usually put "a stop to the dancing-school, the assemblies, and every pleasant thing." He made it his mission to "bear testimony against the detestable diversions of this generation"; and he declared that "no recreations, considered as such, can be innocent." A poor Kingswood collier was noted for his skill in playing the violin. He passed under Methodist influence, and at once consigned his instrument to the flames.[32]

[32] Lecky, *op. cit.,* pp. 589–590, quoted in Dawson and Gettys, *op. cit.,* pp. 699–700.

The crowd excitement in religious revival meetings at the present time is sometimes a prelude to personality reconstruction. However, too often the religious excitement becomes an end in itself and personality transformation is forgotten. The large and popular revival meetings of Charles Finney, Dwight Moody, Billy Sunday, and Billy Graham, occurring at various times over more than a century, have been described by William G. McLoughlin in what amounts to a social history of Protestantism in America.[33] The waves of revival have been subjected to criticism by Christian leaders because of their failure to produce more than a few religious conversions and the failure of those who have been converted to undergo any obvious change in the direction of reconstructing their personal, family, or community relationships. As is unfortunately characteristic of much religious feeling, that fostered by crowd excitement frequently falls far short of inducing the individual to work for the construction of a better economic and political world order. The injunction of Jesus that to love God and to love man are one and the same commandment is forgotten if the cultivation of religious feeling through crowd excitement becomes an end in itself. At the same time, these revival movements have generated some renewed enthusiasm among church members and have played a part historically in augmenting church membership in the U.S.

In evaluating religious forms from the standpoint of their spiritual effectiveness, it is necessary to keep firmly in view the immediate religious needs of participants and the patterns of worship to which they are accustomed. It is possible to consider in theory how the traditional roles of a church minister might be redefined in the future. The possibilities of more or less lay participation, or of more or less liturgy, are intriguing. Yet the circumstance remains that present-day patterns with which communicants are familiar are vital to the satisfaction of their spiritual needs as they now understand them. Proposed changes require slow and cautious introduction. What seems of more immediate concern is a revitalization of people's religious ideas, rather than an alteration in the religious structure in which they participate.

Charismatic Worship

In the view of Max Weber, charismatic worship is that in which the spiritual influence of unusual personalities performs an indispensable role. The religious services of Billy Graham are an example. A college major in anthropology, Graham was sur-

[33] William G. McLoughlin, *Modern Revivalism,* Ronald, 1959.

prised to discover the spiritual gifts he possessed and was almost overwhelmed by demands for his ministry. He has led revival meetings around the world which have drawn the largest crowds in history. That those who have been attracted have not been visibly moved to build a more acceptable kingdom for their Lord or as an economic and political expression of their Lord's spirit is incidental to the categorization of Graham's religious services as infused by charisma. In other respects they are like conventional worship.

However, these services have been a one-man act. In the broader and traditional sense of charisma, any religious service in which spiritual gifts of the congregation play an essential part is charismatic. In this situation, religious initiative is not limited to an outstanding personality but is widely shared by all.

What characterizes the personality of people in charismatic worship? The rise of religious sects during the Protestant Reformation whose worship was charismatic on a large scale reveals two important factors. (1) Religious feeling was emphatically expressed in family and community living. To speak much of God and make little mention of man makes religious expression a fiction. Whatever enthusiasm is briefly kindled is soon burned out unless it is given fuel of personal and social living. In the agrarian society of early Protestants the tasks energetically faced were those of neighborly aid in sickness, old age, fire, or famine. In industrial society the tasks to be taken up are those of social planning and orderly performance to overcome worldwide insecurity and to end the erosion of the human spirit by rampant commercialism.

(2) The early Protestant and his Bible were inseparable companions, that is to say, religious study was a daily concern. In Jungian terms, these Protestants, like those in any charismatic religion, made effective contact with the spiritual impulsion in their collective unconscious. What is necessary now, as then, is to establish bonds of association between spiritual contents in the collective unconscious and images, words, and rituals by which religious feeling is expressed. Charismatic worship presupposes intense study and meditation through which man makes contact with God within himself.

RELIGIOUS EDUCATION

Religious education and religious worship are both conceived by church leaders as means of bringing individuals into closer awareness of and dominance by God. These two phases of the programs of churches and synagogues perform different roles in the achievement of this function. Religious education is the means whereby the individual, especially during his formative years, comes into possession of insights and understandings concerning himself and his deity. These insights and understandings pertain chiefly to motivations in the personality system. In the cultivation of insights, the principal contribution of education is to stimulate and guide the psychological process whereby experience becomes differentiated into its components. While differentiation of inward experience into its spiritual components frequently occurs during worship activity, this is not the principal purpose of worship. The principal function of worship, as discussed earlier in this text, is to revive again and again, to intensify, and to perpetuate the presence of the spirit of God in the worshiper's life. This involves an endless cycle of subordinating and redirecting nonspiritual motivation in the personality system, at the same time as spiritual motivation is induced to become dominant. This is a description of religious worship and of religious education with reference to the special functions which they can be discerned to perform from a psychological standpoint.

It is apparent that large numbers of people following one or another of the world's religions also see other important, if not more important, functions which they believe their religious activities accomplish for them. Insofar as these functions have a supernatural reference, analysis of them by social and psychological science is limited to a description of what people believe, say, and do of an observable character and to cause-and-effect inquiry concerning the reasons for what they believe, say, and do. Furthermore from a strictly educational standpoint, the function of religious education is here stated much more as an aim than as an accomplishment, and as an aim which many teaching Sunday School classes appreciate very little, if at all. In the past several decades those responsible for Sunday School programs are becoming increasingly aware of the educational philosophy of John Dewey and others allied with his point of view. But traditionally religious education has been primarily a method of conversion or a means for religious leaders to preach their precepts to the young in a juvenile setting. To understand the divergence between traditional Sunday School or parochial-school work of churches and modern educational methods, it must be recalled that Christianity almost from its beginnings has been deeply dyed with supernaturalism. Just as parents have conceived of their religious principles as supernaturally revealed to the human race by God, their religious education of their offspring has been primarily a process of communicating supernaturally revealed dogmas. While much progress has been made in recent years in the reconstruction of religious-education programs on a sounder basis, the full reconstruction is likely to be delayed until there is full appreciation of the extent to which religious principles, like other principles of motivation and behavior, are grounded in experience except for their distinctively philosophical aspects.

No adequate survey has been performed to disclose the extent to which different educational methods are used in Sunday School and parochial-school programs of religious education. Scattered observations, however, readily disclose that religious groups in America may be placed on a continuum according to the relative emphasis placed upon indoctrination as a method of education and upon thinking for oneself as a method of education. Those religious groups whose principles consist of dogmas supernaturally revealed to them rely strongly upon implanting these dogmas in the minds of students without encouraging critical reflection on their part. At the opposite extreme are religious groups which rely almost exclusively upon encouraging students to develop and formulate religious principles by their own intellectual efforts.

While generalization is difficult and it is apparent that all religious groups in America are yielding at least somewhat to the liberalizing influence of the educational approach identified with the work of John Dewey, it is characteristic of the Roman Catholic Church and of Fundamentalist Protestant churches that they rely primarily upon indoctrination of their precepts as a means of laying an intellectual groundwork of belief in the minds of growing children. Unitarians, Universalists, Quakers on the eastern seaboard, and Reform Jews rely considerably upon modern literature and educational methods. In between are the great majority of Protestant churches, whose religious-education programs are in a state of change and development with traditional doctrines coming under the impact not only of new educational methods but new ideas about religion furnished by the psychological and social sciences. It should be added that the religious education of even Orthodox Jews as well as Conservative Jews has stressed the importance of building individual understanding and assent even though the religious doctrines which are communicated are considered to be immutable principles divinely revealed.

These general comments concerning the limitations of religious education as carried on by religious groups in America should not be permitted to detract from the very large positive contribution of their programs in transmitting and deepening religious convictions and purposes from generation to generation. The Catholic parochial-school system is an immense program serving about one-half of the Catholic children. Catholic parents pay for this schooling, a heavy financial burden imposed because of the conscientious conviction that secular education is inadequate. The Catholic view of religious education is that of educating the *whole* person from a religious standpoint. Most subjects taught possess a religious aspect, whether philosophical, historical, or practical, which is introduced along with the regular subject matter. The religious orientation of the subject matter is, of course, defined by Catholic teaching authority, ultimately the pope as head of the Church.

Particularly in the case of Protestant churches, the Sunday School program has provided for many the heart of the spiritual vitality of congregations. These highly organized affairs claim more time on the part of church members, young and old, than other features of church life. They provide a program into which large numbers of members enter with determination and enthusiasm, if not the most scientific of concepts. The program of Sunday School classes gives individual church members opportunities for self-expression and participation in the religious life of the group which formal liturgies in the hands of priests, ministers, choirs, and musicians do not otherwise provide. In Sunday School classes church members mutually share their convictions and deepen their understandings, building up and strengthening the religious life of all.

While in theory the lines between worship and religious education can be drawn, in practice much of the attitudes of worship are expressed in the Sunday School program. The breadth covered by religious education is indicated by the following set of objectives adopted by the International Council of Religious Education in 1930, having been formulated by Paul H. Vieth.

1. To foster in growing persons a consciousness of God as a reality in human experience, and a sense of personal relationship to him.
2. To develop in growing persons such an understanding and appreciation of the personality, life and teachings of Jesus as will lead to experience of him as Saviour and Lord, loyalty to him and his cause, and manifest itself in daily life and conduct.
3. To foster in growing persons a progressive and continuous development of Christlike character.

4. To develop in growing persons the ability and disposition to participate in and contribute constructively to the building of a social order throughout the world, embodying the ideal of the Fatherhood of God and the brotherhood of man.
5. To develop in growing persons the ability and disposition to participate in the organized society of Christians—the Church.
6. To develop in growing persons an appreciation of the meaning and importance of the Christian family, and the ability and disposition to participate in and contribute constructively to the life of this primary social group.
7. To lead growing persons into a Christian interpretation of life and the universe; the ability to see in it God's purpose and plan; a life philosophy built on this interpretation.
8. To effect in growing persons the assimilation of the best religious experience of the race, preëminently that recorded in the Bible, as effective guidance to present experience.

From this statement of objectives it is evident that religious education is concerned with more than the cultivation of insight and understanding and is directed also to the development of desires in the individual to make use of worship techniques as a means of gaining and maintaining a close relationship to God.

Organization of Religious Education

Among primitive groups religious beliefs are transmitted from one generation to the next along with folklore and techniques considered important to children growing up into adulthood. Religious education in the sense of propagation of beliefs and practices seems then as old as religion itself. Within recorded history we have descriptions of religious education among the ancient Jews. Study of the Law and of teachings of the prophets was considered of much importance. Classes for instruction and study were organized as part of synagogue life. Religious services contained teaching. Primary responsibility for religious instruction of children was taken by the family. Interwoven with oral instruction was the observance of religious rituals as part of family living. The rituals included recitation of scripture.

The missionary activities of early Christians necessitated extensive instruction of those who were not yet informed of the cardinal points in the Christian gospel. Religious instruction together with literary, scientific, and philosophical inquiry found an important place in academies of the Greek and Roman worlds. During the Middle Ages monasteries were places of study for those preparing for the priesthood. The study of theology was a major pursuit in universities of medieval Europe. With the invention of printing and the availability of the Bible to large numbers of people, religious study gained new impetus. This impetus expressed itself in a breaking away from the established church by large groups of people during the Reformation. For Protestants the written record in the Bible became the principal source of authority rather than pronouncements by a religious head. With the Bible gaining a fundamental role in religious life, extensive reading and study of it became common. In the religious meetings of Protestant groups there was frequently no sharp distinction between worship practices and religious instruction. Down to the present time sermons preached by Protestant ministers during the worship service contain much by way of instruction as well as exhortation and inspiration.

In the American colonies colleges were first founded for the education of ministers, who in turn assumed responsibility for maintaining a clear understanding of the principles of Christian faith among members of their congregations. Concern for religious instruction of children was expressed by John Wesley. "Wherever there are ten children in a Society, spend at least one hour with them twice a week. And do this, not in a dull, dry, formal manner, but in earnest, with your might. 'But I have no gift for this.' Gift or no gift, do it, else you are not called to be a Methodist preacher. Do it as you can, til you can do it as you would. Pray earnestly for the gift and use the means for it, particularly study the children's tracts."[34]

The regular practice of providing instruction for children on Sundays was begun by Robert Raikes in 1780, who sought to replace the idleness of underprivileged children with useful religious instruction. Sunday Schools steadily gained popularity, and societies were formed to further the movement for Sunday Schools. In 1824 the American Sunday School Union was founded, representing over seven hundred schools in seventeen states. Within a decade the number of Sunday Schools increased tenfold. Although divided by theological schisms and rivalries between denominations, the Sunday School movement continued to grow. Practically every church congregation came to have a large and active Sunday School. With the turn of the twentieth century, innovations in Biblical scholarship as well as insights into religion contributed by psychology, sociology, and anthropology altered the theological orientation of many church

[34] *Minutes of the Methodist Conferences, 1744–1798,* Vol. I, pp. 63–69, cited in R. C. Miller, *Education for Christian Living,* Prentice-Hall, 1956, p. v.

members and their leaders. The religious-education movement has been a major avenue for introducing church members to the contributions of scientific scholarship, even though these contributions have been strongly resisted by those holding to fundamentalist and orthodox views of the Bible.

Religious educators from different Protestant denominations joined together in 1922 to form the International Council of Religious Education. In 1950 this organization to promote religious education was constituted as the Division of Christian Education of the National Council of the Churches of Christ in the U.S.A. This group of workers in religious education derived its origin in part from the reaction in the previous century of Horace Bushnell and others against what they felt to be the morbid ideas of sin and guilt which had been taught to children. By the end of the nineteenth century, uniform lesson materials had been developed for use in the Sunday Schools of different denominations. The preparation of sets of Sunday School materials has been a continuing responsibility of Departments of Christian Education in the National Council of Churches and its component denominations.

How is a Sunday School in a typical church congregation organized? Organization is much more than the performance of tasks by church leaders, teachers, and pupils. The organization of any institution refers to the structure of thinking and motivation as well as the structure of behavior. Especially when education is considered, the structure of the internal processes which go on occupies an important role. From superficial observation two Sunday Schools may look much alike as far as the presence of teachers and learners is concerned. The inward processes whereby education goes on may diverge considerably from one Sunday School situation to another. To the nature of the educational processes which go on we will return in a moment. We shall consider first the external organization of the Sunday School, its classes, and its leaders and teachers.

Throughout the history of the Sunday School movement, lay members of congregations have assumed extensive responsibility for the operation of classes. Depending upon the type of church government, whether by a self-appointed group of church leaders or by members of the religious congregations, control and direction of Sunday School programs has been authoritarian or democratic. Even those Protestant churches which have been under the administration of a hierarchy of clergymen have increasingly given laymen a large share of responsibility and control of their Sunday School programs. Among Catholics the church-school program, like that of their parochial schools, is firmly controlled by priests acting under the direction of their bishops. Usually classes are held during a weekday hour for children not able to attend Catholic parochial schools. In Jewish congregations the religious-education program is under the supervision of the Hebrew school principal selected by the congregation and with whose members he coöperates closely in the religious-education program. In the program of a large congregation there are usually other trained persons employed to assist him.

In Protestant churches a Sunday School superintendent and often a director of religious education are appointed by the denominational leadership controlling the church, or more commonly by a local governing body or religious-education committee of the members of the congregation. It is the responsibility of this superintendent or director to organize and administer the program of classes within the framework of policies and decisions adopted by his superiors or by the governing body of the congregation. He is usually responsible for selecting teachers and for seeing that they gain whatever instruction or training is available. These teachers are nearly always unpaid members of the congregation. In larger churches the post of superintendent or director of religious education may be a paid one. This permits the employment of persons trained in religious education, strengthening the quality of the Sunday School program.

The lesson materials used in the Sunday Schools of Protestant denominations are usually uniform ones which are adjusted to the age group or which undergo a cycle of lessons over a period of years. These are usually lesson materials standardized and approved by the denomination in question, and the same materials may be used by different denominations working together in the preparation of their materials. In some cases the local congregation may select the lesson materials used from among the published options available. In a few cases a church congregation may formulate its own individual program and either draft its own lesson material or leave the selection of material to the individual teacher, who draws upon whatever books or periodicals he feels are suited to the needs and interests of his pupils. Those churches which are more liberal in theology tend to be those which are more flexible and informal in selecting content for their Sunday School programs. The Sunday School program of a church is typically an enterprise which members support loyally with their time and interest. The ongoing success of their Sunday School program is usually of major concern to them, if the church congregation to which they belong is active and effective at all.

The inclination of Quakers to avoid any paid personnel in the administration of the programs of their congregations has usually meant that well-trained and properly compensated teachers have not been employed in the First-Day school program of religious education. Quakers have relied upon lay resources for teaching as well as for ministry. It appears to the author that the teaching and counseling role performed by a trained rabbi in a Jewish congregation is a role which needs filling in Quaker congregations. Quakers place the conduct of their religious-education program in the hands of a committee which, often without training, devises its own lesson material rather than use materials made available either by a central body of Quakers or by other denominations. In contrast to Quakers who have traditionally frowned upon university-trained clergy, Protestant churches in general, through the teaching ministry provided by sermons during worship services and through a strong Sunday School program, have carried out a vigorous program of religious education. In Catholic churches the part-time classes, as well as the parochial schools, are under the efficient administration of priests and their bishops. Catholic priests are careful to see to it that both young and old are properly instructed in religious matters. Considerable time is spent by them in informal teaching and counseling as well as in more formal opportunities for instruction through school programs.

Methods of Religious Education

In no other field besides religion is it more important to review carefully the different ways in which education can be carried on and to consider carefully what pattern of education is most desirable from the standpoint of what is accomplished. The distinction was drawn in Chapter 3 between gaining ideas by thinking for oneself and acquiring ideas through indoctrination by others. When ideas are gained by the individual's own efforts, the psychological process of differentiation of experience into its component elements and structures is the source of the individual's ideas. These ideas are genuine insights, since they are derived directly from experience or from relatively concrete ideas which in turn came from experience. In indoctrination ideas are implanted by the spoken or written words of an instructor. Frequently the ideas obtained through indoctrination are merely verbal, rather than meaningful. They are then ideas of words rather than ideas obtained by differentiation of experience. It is also possible for meaningful ideas to be obtained by the individual through being indoctrinated if the process of indoctrination attempts to follow at least the outline of the psychological process of differentiation. That is, the sequence of ideas aroused by the words of the instructor may be that by which differentiation takes place. However, in this situation the listener is a passive respondent in the hands of the instructor, and he simply lets the flow of thinking in his mind follow that of the instructor word for word.

When the individual gains ideas by his own efforts, he frequently needs some guidance from an instructor who (1) helps him to understand how the process of differentiation of ideas occurs, (2) sets the stage in the student's mind for differentiation to occur by seeing to it that appropriate experiences or ideas are presented to him for him to think about and turn over in his mind, and (3) motivates him by encouraging him and by giving him interesting materials to stimulate his thought processes. In self-directed differentiation the individual carries responsibility himself for fixing his mind upon appropriate data or subsidiary ideas, for turning them over in his mind and looking at them from various standpoints, and for continuing the process of reflection until the component variables and relationships have emerged in his conscious mind.

From this review it appears that at least four kinds of educational process can be discerned: (1) verbal indoctrination, (2) meaningful indoctrination, (3) guided differentiation, and (4) self-directed differentiation. Verbal indoctrination is of little use to anyone except as a means of getting quick cues for making responses, as if one were a wheel in a machine or particles of electricity in an automatic computer. Verbal indoctrination finds application in those social situations where it is desired that the individual function only as an automaton. Such situations arise in military strategy where it is more important for the individual to know immediately what he is to do than it is for him to understand fully why he is to do it, or even what he is doing. Those political systems in which a dictator seeks to control the population by telling them what to do and discouraging independence of judgment likewise find ready use for verbal indoctrination, or sometimes meaningful indoctrination when it is clear that people must understand something about their tasks if they are to perform them efficiently.

What is designated here as meaningful indoctrination also finds an important place in transmitting traditions in a democracy. The reason is that the individual manifestly has far too little time to think out everything which he needs to know by himself. Therefore much of what he learns is gained from listening to or reading the words of others. If, however, education consists solely of indoctrination, then the individual's own ability to think for himself fails to develop. He is helpless then to direct his own life or to play an intelligent part in the decisions made by the group under a democracy.

Until the individual gains facility after long effort and experience, he is unable to make much use of self-directed differentiation. He gains a gradual introduction to how the process operates by its being performed in his own mind under the guidance of an instructor who selects the experiences or concrete images for him to think about and even indicates verbally the general nature of the ideas whose emergence in the student's mind is expected. An important skill of an instructor who seeks to teach students how to think rather than what to think consists in turning their attention to key problems by means of concrete experiences or specific conditions and then according them maximum opportunity to complete the process of differentiation by themselves. When the individual has gained understanding of scientific methods of analysis by being guided through them, he is then in a position to proceed as a self-directed scientific thinker in assembling his own materials and in thinking out his own conclusions. This should not be considered an ability exclusively of the scientifically elite. The ability to direct one's own thought processes in gaining a meaningful understanding of problems is necessary to a considerable extent for the business of living of everyone. It is quite impossible for any individual to be instructed by mechanical routines what he shall do every day of his life. In order to exercise intelligent judgment, it is necessary for him to be capable of self-directed differentiation in at least the simpler problems of living. The greater is his skill in this direction, the more highly qualified he is to participate in difficult decisions of the group and to evaluate for himself how well democratic ideals are maintained. The type of technological society which is evolving at the present time requires large numbers of people who are capable of thinking out new problems creatively and setting up the routines which are followed by computing machines or the lines of procedure in the social machinery of which we are all a part.

When it comes to the use which the individual makes of religious ideas, it is apparent that ideas which are merely verbal echoes of words heard or read are of almost no use to the individual at all. If the individual is to go through a meaningful experience of worship it is necessary that he have religious insights into himself and into the object of his worship. The internal conversation which goes on in the personality system during prayer or worship cannot take place in any intelligible way unless the component psychological systems involved have become differentiated during a long program of religious study.

What we have called meaningful indoctrination can be an effective source of the religious insights needed by the individual. However, this type of education fails to give the individual the ability to make religious decisions and solve religious problems for himself. Unless we envisage a situation in which the individual's religious thinking is all done for him by his church leaders, religious education must equip him with the ability to think out religious problems by himself. In religion, as in government, if the individual surrenders control over his life, the way is opened for leaders without scruples to use religion or government as instruments parasitically to exploit the individual. Furthermore, if religious ideas, like other human ideas, are to grow and develop as the history of the human race moves forward, it is absolutely necessary that there be widespread encouragement of individuals to gain the ability to do their own religious thinking.

Although the cultivation of religious understanding is of paramount importance in religious education, it is nevertheless necessary, if religious principles are valid, for them to be followed by the individual to the best of his ability prior to the attainment of full understanding. The process of differentiation which is the heart of genuine religious education or of any other field of education, is a slow, tedious, and painstaking process. It is a process which requires many years for its fruition. Indeed, the process of religious education is one which does not end for the individual until the end of his life, since there always remains more for him to differentiate from the rest of his ideas and experiences. C. G. Jung has pointed out that the present practice of drawing a line between childhood and adulthood at approximately twenty-one years lacks foundation in educational reality. Not until people reach their forties do they approximate those levels of insight and self-control usually associated with adulthood. For a span of twenty years after reaching physical maturity they are literally grown-up children. The onset of sexual maturity in the early teen years brings with it the necessity for orderly direction and control of the sexual side of living. The valid teachings of religion concerning boy-girl relationships are therefore to be observed during years considerably prior to the attainment of deep religious understanding. Hence there is a considerable span of years during which the individual may order his life according to religious precepts which he does not fully understand. The expectation, however, is that he learn as much as he can through gaining meaningful understandings. To the fullest extent of his abilities, he should be expected to learn religious principles in terms of insight rather than indoctrination. It is not possible to impose a rigid requirement concerning how much indoctrination in religious education is permissible as opposed to differentiation in religious education. For one thing this line will differ for different types of people. For another, extensive empirical research is needed to define where and how the line is to be drawn.

One of the earliest attempts in recorded history to draw the line between indoctrination and allowing the individual to think for himself about right and wrong is contained in the myth of Adam and Eve. It will be recalled that in this story they were forbidden by God to eat the fruit of the tree of knowledge of good and evil.[35] This fanciful tale has a ring of reality in its recognition of a basic problem of religious education, that of how much individuals can properly decide on their own responsibility and reflection, and how much they should be expected to follow their religious leaders' guidance. However, the line between taking religious precepts on someone else's say-so and thinking them out for oneself is too narrowly drawn in the story of Adam and Eve. Certainly not all mature adults should be expected to take religious teachings on the say-so of their leaders or their scriptures. They may be expected to think them out anew after reaching a sufficiently high level of intellectual ability. But the admonition not to eat of the fruit of good and evil until reaching an age of discretion seems sound.

This discussion of religious education is primarily concerned with intellectual aspects, since these are the aspects of contemporary religious education most in need of attention. On the

[35] Genesis 3.

other hand large strides have been made by the International Council of Religious Education, now the Division of Christian Education of the National Council of the Churches of Christ in the U.S.A. A study by the Division of Christian Education, *A Guide for Curriculum in Christian Education,* places considerable stress upon experience and insight as materials for education.[36] A current text for training workers in Christian education, by Randolph C. Miller, builds extensively upon the work of John Dewey.[37] The present leadership at the higher levels of Protestant denominational organization in religious education is giving effective support to improved methods of religious education, although among Fundamentalist and Orthodox groups religious education still consists of indoctrination, a practice stemming historically from the supernatural dogma and priestly power in the Catholic Church.

Where patterns of religious education seem especially strong is in the recognition of the importance of providing children with adequate motivation for their Sunday School activity. In a chapter on "Principles of Good Curriculum" the Division of Christian Education lists such important motivational factors as "Sense of Security," "Sense of Belonging," "Clear Moral Guidance," "Christian Motivation," and "Experience in Christian Action." A large section is devoted to religious education which "takes into account the laws of growth." Here it is recognized that not all young people grow at the same rate and that religious instruction should be oriented to each individual rather than to the mass as if all were alike.[38] The importance is also stressed of religious education covering such topics as "Social Problems," "World Relations," and "Service and Christian Leadership," as well as "Personal Experiences in Christian Living," "Christian Family" and "Church Life and Outreach."

For children, there is mounting concern for learning by doing, seeing and talking. Study content is selected which is oriented to participation in the family and the community. Group projects and visual aid materials stimulate children's discussion. While Catholic spokesmen repudiate John Dewey, both as psychologist and philosopher, the educational movement which he represents is increasingly affecting Catholic educational methods as well as

[36] *A Guide for Curriculum in Christian Education,* National Council of the Churches of Christ in the U.S.A., 1955.

[37] R. C. Miller, *op. cit.* A current review of religious education is given by M. J. Taylor, ed., *Religious Education: A Comprehensive Survey,* Abingdon, 1960.

[38] *A Guide for Curriculum in Christian Education,* chap. 2.

those of Protestant churches. The following news item is indicative of this trend.

> Nun's soft-sell teaching produces student champs. Her youthful scientists seize national awards.
>
> A teacher who wants to get the most out of his students should never drive them, one of the nation's most successful high school instructors said today.
>
> "To drive is to kill," said the teacher, Sister Mary Lauretta, science instructor at Columbus High School, Marshfield, Wis.
>
> Since 1955 Sister Mary Lauretta has produced a national winner every year in the highly regarded Westinghouse Science Talent Search competition.[39]

An important part of the content of religious principles consists of philosophical ideas. These refer to things which cannot be proved directly by experience. Such questions as those of what happens to people after death and whether there is a God outside of human experience are ones approached through philosophical inquiry. While the answers cannot be proved by the data of experience, this does not mean that education must proceed by indoctrination. A dominant view in philosophy today is that its subject matter is to be studied by scientific method. What this means is that the principles of scientific method are to be applied to problems for which data are partly lacking or insufficient for reasons beyond the control of the investigator. What is then done is to develop orderly reasoning on the basis of what facts are available. This involves generalization from those sectors of reality within experience to what may plausibly be expected to prevail outside of experience. To take a simple illustration, it can be argued that because life within the span of human experience conforms to a moral order we assume that an extension of this moral order applies after death. Or it can be maintained that the forces working for good in the universe are not limited to those which come within the compass of human experience, since what has been found by human beings often proves to be only a part of what is later found. Whether these philosophical lines of reasoning are sound or not is outside the study of religion as a psychic or social science. The point here is that the subject matter of philosophy can be approached by scientific methods even though adequate data are lacking. What is done is to proceed as logically as possible from the limited data which are available and to reach conclusions couched in terms of what

[39] Sheila Gallagher, "Nun's Soft-sell Teaching," *New York World-Telegram,* August 3, 1959.

seems probable. Because the data upon which philosophy builds are frequently fragmentary and diverse, statistical principles of probability apply poorly. There is room for wide difference of opinion as to the particular otherworldly construction to be placed upon events occurring within human observation.

Since the content of philosophy can be approached by scientific inquiry or at least by whatever pieces of scientific inquiry are applicable, it follows that religious education can be based upon differentiation rather than indoctrination when philosophical questions are taken up. The ideas involved require the same differentiation from those portions of reality within the experience of the individual. Nor need philosophical topics be reserved for later grades in a program of religious education. Children are almost as much stimulated by the sense of mystery concerning the baffling questions of life after death and God as creator and sustainer of the universe as are adults. What is important is that children not be given philosophical answers by indoctrination as if they were proved dogmas. Rather, it is important to the critical faculties of children for them to know that the philosophical answers given by religious proponents represent what are considered to be intelligent guesses rather than assured facts.

CHURCH GOVERNMENT

In order to provide for worship services, own property in which services take place, provide for admission to membership, conduct a religious-education program, and perpetuate religious doctrines from generation to generation, it is necessary for a religious group to have some form of administrative organization. As in the case of civil government and many other institutions, the administrative direction may be democratically controlled by church members or it may be given by a self-perpetuating set of leaders. The religious counterpart of a dictatorship in civil government is found in the form of religious organization which has come to be known as episcopal. The designation of this type of church government is not to be confused with the Episcopal Church, which historically was governed by a monarchical episcopacy but which has since incorporated features of representative government. When members of church congregations select representatives to a regional body which has control over the affairs of local congregations, this representative pattern of government is known as presbyterian. When a religious congregation is governed either by a meeting of the entire membership of the congregation or through a council selected by the entire membership of the congregation, the pattern of government is known as congregational. These three types of church government, two of them democratic in structure, are ideal types to which the various religious denominations in America conform in varying degrees. It is also to be kept in mind that church government is characterized by somewhat more informality in practice than is rigidly set forth in written doctrines or than is found in civil government of the nation, state, and local municipalities. On the other hand, when critical issues about which there is sharp difference of opinion confront the governing institutions of religious denominations, these can on occasion become highly legalistic, and in some cases their differences or quarrels may be brought into court in the civil system of government for judicial settlement.

Episcopal

Catholics believe that the authority of their priesthood is derived through an unbroken line of succession from Jesus Christ, that is, from God. Therefore the selection of those who are leaders in authority is not left to popular vote. Supreme control of the Church is vested in the pope. When he dies, his successor is chosen by the College of Cardinals. Members of this group are appointed by the pope. Many of the cardinals hold important administrative posts concerned with diplomacy, doctrinal problems, education, finance, and direction of bishops. While the pope is the ruler, in practice he must depend considerably upon decisions made by those under him. Each territorial unit of the Roman Catholic Church is a diocese ruled by a bishop who has extensive power in the administration of church affairs. Under the bishops are the pastors in charge of the local parishes of the church. The dioceses are combined into larger territorial units called provinces. The head of a province is an archbishop who gives spiritual and intellectual leadership, but in most matters the bishops within the province are governed directly by the pope and his administrators in Rome. An archbishop has the same authority over his own diocese, known as an archdiocese, as any other bishop. The vast properties belonging to the Catholic Church and necessary to its system of worship and education belong to members of the hierarchy who hold nominal title under the pope as head of the Church.

While this pyramid of priestly power might seem to exclude laymen from any say-so, in practice the church exists for the good of its laymen as well as priesthood, and therefore their needs and wishes receive close consideration if their spiritual welfare appears thereby to be benefited. While members of the Catholic hierarchy frequently seek the advice of laymen they are under no obligation to divulge church affairs to them nor are they answerable to them in any way. The Catholic Church is a religious organization which the individual is free to accept or reject, although to reject it would be tantamount to repudiating the source of his religious salvation. As an active member of the Roman Catholic Church he is obliged to accept the religious direction given by the Catholic hierarchy, which is governed at the top by a self-perpetuating group of cardinals and the pope. On the other hand, lay organizations, such as the National Council of Catholic Men and the National Council of Catholic Women, are encouraged by the Catholic hierarchy.

The contention of most Protestants is that the spiritual welfare of people is better served if they have a larger share in the self-determination of their religious affairs. The problem of how to keep the door of a religious institution open to new truths at the same time as it is kept closed against new errors is not easily answered. While in the short run in history individuals gain greater religious security by depending upon an episcopally organized church, in the long run succeeding generations in such a tradition cut themselves off from the advent of new religious truth. If it is asked why Christianity has made so little progress in the two thousand years of its existence, the answer can well be given that its doctrines have been anchored in a rigid institutional system in which the birth of new ideas is extremely difficult. This is not to say that the Catholic Church does not grow in religious insight with history. Obviously it does with the appearance in each new generation of priests and their superiors of new minds who have been exposed to or who have evolved fresh ideas. The doctrine that the pope in his teaching authority has supernatural power to define and interpret what has been revealed in the lives of the early apostles, including what has been recorded outside of scripture, admits of some evolution and change even if these are slow to develop. While the Catholic Church has great inertia, the door of religious truth is open for the establishment of any fresh ideas which can grow by differentiation out of the experiences and concepts of the first Christians. While the practical route to innovation of the Catholic system of faith and practice is slow and halting, the church has considerable latitude in a long span of history to change its character. Even past pronouncements which appear to be rigid because of their supposed infallible character can be interwoven with fresh interpretations which alter little by little the original meaning of these pronouncements.

Modified Episcopalian

The Catholic Church has failed at times to make sufficient adjustments to the new needs and ideas of those affiliated with it. The result has been a series of schisms. One of these culminated in the separation of the Eastern Orthodox Churches in the eleventh century. A series of breaks occurred during the Protestant Reformation. The Lutherans, Episcopalians, and from the latter the Methodists, represent branchings from the original body of Catholicism. Initially these groups retained a clear-cut episcopal pattern in which the leadership consisted of a self-perpetuating group whose authority in religious affairs was accepted by members. The major Christian denominations migrating to America gave up their strict episcopal polity in various degrees, with the exception of the Roman Catholic and Eastern Orthodox churches. The episcopal form of polity has sometimes been used as a means of compelling all inhabitants to accept regimentation by the rulings of the state church. This authoritarian approach to demanding religious conformity occasioned much persecution and religious warfare until it was given up. When Calvin's ideas spread to England, the Church of England imposed his ideas through the instrumentality of the Catholic Church structure which it retained. Such indigenous groups as Baptists, Puritans, and Quakers suffered persecution until enactment of the Toleration Act in England in 1689.

Two of the social forces responsible for dissolution of the rigid episcopal system were the democratic climate in America and the intellectual realization that divine authority did not repose in the hands of any self-appointed group of religious leaders. The Episcopal Church can now be characterized as a constitutional democracy. Its bishops are chosen by a legislative body composed of clergymen and elected lay representatives. The bishops are administrative officials who carry out policies which have been democratically determined. Local parishes select their own pastors, called rectors, but must secure approval by the bishop for their selection. Once installed, the rector has tenure for life, which gives him much independence of the opinions of members of the parish. The clergymen in this system of government are regarded by Episcopalians as being in the apostolic succession.

In European countries, churches largely retain the original episcopal pattern of government, while in the United States they have often become presbyterian or congregational in church organization. Methodism arose as a movement within the Church of England and retained the episcopal structure after establishing a new home for itself outside the Church of England. The Methodist Church, like the Episcopal Church, has moved considerably in the direction of democratic control of church affairs. The local church is controlled by a self-perpetuating committee which usually follows the recommendations of the minister. The churches in each local geographic area are under the nominal direction of a district superintendent, whose authority is more advisory than actual. A hierarchy of district conferences, annual conferences, jurisdictional conferences, and a general conference contains representatives from both ministers and laymen. The official at the level of the annual conference is a bishop. In this system of government laymen exercise no say-so in the ordination and supervision of ministers or in the selection of bishops. While formerly the power to appoint was solely that of the bishop, now laymen in many church congregations insist upon deciding who shall be their minister, the bishop's appointment becoming a mere formality. Both Episcopalians and Methodists tend to be flexible in maintaining their theological doctrines, such as that general acknowledgment of Christian ideas of salvation suffices for church membership. On the other hand, Lutherans tend to be more exacting in the religious doctrines to which they expect their laymen and especially their clergy to subscribe. The Lutheran Churches are more of a stronghold of orthodoxy than are the Episcopalian or Methodist Churches.

Presbyterian

The Presbyterian Church is distinctive for the pattern of representative government whose name it bears. The Presbyterians developed their religious organization outside of the Church of England and in doing so built into it democratic control. The Presbyterian churches in America are not all united into one religious organization. Each local church is governed by the minister and a small group of elders elected by members of the church. The churches in a local geographic area are organized into a presbytery consisting of ministers and one elder from each church. This body has power to approve the local church's choice of minister or decision to replace him. The presbytery has authority to organize, unite, or divide local churches. The presbyteries are organized into larger governing units of which the highest is the general assembly, in which both laymen and clergymen are represented. The principal feature which distinguishes the church government of Presbyterians is the higher control over religious affairs of local congregations. While this control is exercised with discretion, this is not a type of control found in the congregational pattern of church government.

Congregational

In the religious ferment in England following the breaking off of the Church of England from the Catholic Church, the Congregationalists, Baptists, and Quakers moved furthest in their insistence upon the autonomous right of each local congregation to manage its own religious affairs. Added to these are the Disciples, a religious denomination originating in the United States, and the Unitarians, a denomination which represents a division from the Congregationalists. In the congregational pattern of government the local congregation acts through an assembly of its members or in some cases through committees made up of representatives selected by the local congregation. Those churches with the congregational pattern of church government are loosely organized into larger groupings by membership of the congregation in an association with other congregations. The officers of such an association function in an advisory role. Associations possess no power over local congregations other than to admit or reject their membership in the association. Those Protestant groups with a congregational pattern reject the special authority claimed by any priests or ministers to perform sacraments. If the original sacraments remain as part of the worship pattern, they do so without having the significance attached to them by those related to the Catholic viewpoint.

Those following the congregational pattern of church government have usually been more liberal in their theological views, with the exception of Baptists. The latter have been characterized by more literal adherence to scripture as the word of God.

In the struggles for religious liberty from the Protestant Reformation onward, those having a congregational pattern of government have typically been those most insistent upon the protection of religious liberties. Since they were dissenters from episcopally organized churches, they frequently endured much persecution before gaining freedom for themselves. It should not be assumed that the episcopal pattern of church government implies lack of toleration for unbelievers. But the social instrumentality is obviously present for suppression or discouragement of individualists if this is desired by the church leadership. The Catholic Church on the American scene enjoys considerable tolerance for itself and accords similar tolerance toward others. Elsewhere in the world are places where Protestants find freedom of worship and especially freedom to propagate their ideas to be curtailed. There are also some Protestant areas in which Catholics are restricted.

Nor can it be assumed that the presbyterian pattern of church government or even the congregational is free from the potentiality for suppressing individual religious liberty. Calvinism in Geneva strictly regulated individual freedom. J. Paul Williams, who has given an analysis of the theoretical and practical aspects of church government in different denominations, describes the situation which prevailed in Geneva.

> Moreover, Calvin considered it the duty of ministers to point the road toward purity, and when necessary to force travel along that road. Consequently, the citizens of Geneva were punished not only for such sins as dishonesty, violence and lewdness, but also for dancing, staying away from church, criticizing ministers and speaking well of the Pope. One man received a three-months' banishment for observing when he heard an ass bray, "He chants a fine Psalm." This stern view of morals had subsequently a pronounced influence on the moral ideals of the Puritans, both in England and in America, as we shall see.[40]

Protestant groups in early America typically imposed rigid controls over persons living in their communities and especially upon members of their own congregations. The democratic pattern of congregational government was one in which the majority imposed its will upon the minority. This it did through such primary-group controls as social ostracism and economic boycotts, as well as political control. Frequently such religious groups succeeded in enacting into law their religious prescriptions for behavior. The present code of laws regulating sexual behavior in most states survives from this time of severe repression of individual behavior.

Religious organization in Judaism consists of a simple congregational polity. Each congregation is autonomous. Members

[40] Williams, *op. cit.*, p. 188.

of the congregation select their own committees for administrative purposes. All males have equal say-so in the affairs of the local congregation. The rabbi is a teacher and counselor employed by the congregation. Rabbis are members of rabbinical associations, of which there are principally four, corresponding to Orthodox Judaism, Conservative Judaism, Reform Judaism, and Reconstructionist Judaism. These associations adopt formulations of policies and clarify doctrines, but they have no control over local synagogues. The authority which rabbis possess is that of teachers whose words depend for their acceptance upon their appeal to truths in the individual's mind. In their teachings Orthodox rabbis follow closely Jewish scriptures and writings and commentaries based upon these. Conservative rabbis are less rigid in their adherence to orthodox principles and are inclined to overlook or ignore traditional prescriptions having no evident relevance to contemporary times. Reform Rabbis give flexible interpretations of traditional Jewish ideas and, like liberals in Christianity, turn freely to contributions made by psychologists and philosophers outside their main historical stream of religious culture. Reconstructionist rabbis seek to maintain the cultural identity of Judaism without literal insistence upon religious teachings which are not relevant or which cannot be adequately supported by contemporary scholarship. Reconstructionist rabbis hold that those traditional forms which have no valid meaning for the present need to be modified or replaced by others, but such changes should not be imposed by group pressure on those not convinced of the need for them.

Nation-wide Religious Bodies

While the individual authority of rabbis in their congregations has receded somewhat in contemporary times, the nation-wide associations of Orthodox, Conservative, Reform, and Reconstructionist rabbis and their central body, the Synagogue Council of America, have played an influential role in formulating and implementing constructive public policies to meet present social and economic problems. The coördinated support which Jewish leaders give to such programs as interracial and interfaith harmony is outstanding in American history. The rabbinical associations are, of course, principally concerned with social and religious needs confronting their own constituents. In addition two nation-wide bodies, one representing Catholics and the other Protestants, occupy important roles in the American scene.

The National Council of the Churches of Christ in the U.S.A.

was formed in 1950 as the successor to the Federal Council of Churches and seven other interdenominational bodies. The Federal Council of Churches came into being in 1908 by joint action of major Protestant denominations which desired a means of working together in areas of common interest. The interdenominational bodies combining with the Federal Council of Churches represented Protestant activity in such fields as home and foreign missions, religious education, world service, laymen's organizations, broadcasting, and films. These became divisions and departments in the National Council. Neither the Federal Council nor its successor the National Council can be regarded as a church analogous to the Catholic Church. The separate denominations retain autonomy of religious life. They work together where they have common purposes. This Protestant organization should be regarded as a body for mutual consultation by representatives of Protestant denominations rather than as an organization with authority to govern the affairs of its members. The objectives of the Federal Council were stated as follows: "The objects of said corporation shall be, to promote the spirit of fellowship, service and coöperation among the Churches of Christ in America, to secure larger efficiency in their work, to endeavor to prevent their duplication of effort and expenditure and to increase their influence by united action in every department of their operations, at home and abroad."[41] A major impetus to the formation of the Federal Council was the social-reform attitude of Protestant leaders who wished to awaken churches to their responsibility for improving the political and social conditions of American life.[42]

The National Council of Churches is now an interdenominational organization of twenty-six Protestant and seven Eastern Orthodox denominations, representing approximately three-fifths of all Protestant church members. The National Council has four major divisions responsible for broad areas of interdenominational coöperation. These are: Christian Education, Christian Life and Work, Home Missions, and Foreign Missions. There are also central departments concerned with public relations, research and survey, broadcasting and films, publication, and finance. There are joint departments where two or more divisions intersect, such as Family Life, Evangelism, and Stew-

[41] Federal Council of Churches of Christ in America, *Annual Report,* 1949, p. 219. In its constitution the National Council of Churches lists similar objectives in more detail.

[42] A. P. Stokes, *Church and State in the United States,* Vol. III, Harper, p. 4.

ardship and Benevolence. Encouragement of lay participation in the National Council is provided by two general departments of United ChurchWomen and United Church Men. Paralleling interdenominational coöperation at the nation-wide level are nearly a thousand city and county councils of churches and about two thousand local ministers' associations. These groups provide for interdenominational coöperation at a local level.

One of the major features of contemporary religious life is called the ecumenical movement. Basically this is a movement toward Christian unity, and it finds expression in two directions. One is church union, and there have been a number of denominational mergers within recent years. Theoretically, at least, this wing of the ecumenical movement hopes for the ultimate union of all churches. The other direction, and the more popular of the two, is the emphasis upon spiritual unity. This is largely theological and finds expression in discussion and study groups. The Oberlin conference in 1957 on "The Nature of the Unity We Seek" was an important expression of this latter direction.

The National Council of Churches is definitely an ecumenical organization, as are the local and state councils. However, the National Council is actually a council of denominations and provides an opportunity for mutual study and coöperative programs. The separate Protestant churches arose primarily within different nations and at various times in history. Since the historical context of reasons for their separate existence differs from denomination to denomination, they have well-recognized differences in beliefs, practices, and church government. It does not seem likely that ecumenical union will be achieved in the near future.

The National Catholic Welfare Conference performs much the same role among Catholic religious leaders as does the National Council of Churches among Protestants. The National Catholic Welfare Conference derives its origin from World War I when a group of Catholic clergymen and laymen came together in a conference to consider how to promote the spiritual welfare of men in the armed forces and to coördinate Catholic activities incidental to the war. As a result of this conference the archbishops of the United States formed the National Catholic War Council. Following the war, in 1919 the pope announced that he wished the bishops to meet annually to take common counsel on matters of general importance and to establish definite departments under their supervision and direction to carry out work assigned. In 1923 the organization was named the National Catholic Welfare Conference.

The administration of the conference is performed by a board of members elected by bishops of the United States. According to the *Official Catholic Directory* the conference "has for its objects the unifying, coordinating and organizing of the Catholic people of the United States in works of education, social welfare, immigrant aid, civil education and other activities." The work of the conference is performed by eight departments: executive, legal, press, lay organizations, social action, education, youth, and Catholic action study. The conference has its headquarters in Washington, D.C., with a staff of several hundred persons. According to A. P. Stokes, the National Catholic Welfare Conference "has won the respect of all thoughtful groups, Protestant, Catholic and Jewish."[43]

In connection with references made to religious denominations, the following membership figures reported for 1958[44] are of interest:

Adventist	338,603	Latter Day Saints	1,546,751
Baptist	20,493,381	Lutheran	7,791,248
Brethren	256,845	Mennonite	156,230
Churches of Christ, Disciples of Christ	3,943,599	Methodist	12,213,097
Churches of God	409,458	Pentecostal	391,099
Congregational	1,381,124	Presbyterian	4,126,583
Eastern Orthodox	2,545,318	Reformed	459,869
Episcopalian	3,042,286	Roman Catholic	39,509,508
Evangelical	1,673,539	Spiritualist	175,158
Friends (Quaker)	120,766	All other	3,483,279
Jews	5,500,000	Total membership reported	109,557,741

[43] *Ibid.,* p. 11.

[44] *Yearbook of American Churches,* National Council of the Churches of Christ in the U.S.A., 1960, pp. 253–258, 272–273.

chapter 14 Religion and the Social Order

In small tribal societies economic, political, and educational institutions are relatively minor features of social organization apart from the family. The family economy often provides for most of the wants of members, trade taking place on a modest scale. Some primitive societies lack government in the sense of either assumed or delegated political control. Those societies which are composed of sparsely settled or wandering families may experience no need for governmental action to make or enforce rules of behavior. This does not mean that rules are nonexistent, but rather that consensus concerning right and wrong grows spontaneously out of the feelings and opinions of tribal members. If these mores are infringed, reaction takes the form of reprisals by relatives or joint action by the tribe. No school system, much less one operated by government authority, may be found. Nor does this mean education is absent, but its functions fall primarily to the family and to adults of the tribe whose influence and authority are exercised by informal association with the younger generation. The family is the original social institution. The other four—church, economic order, government, and school system—making up the social order have today become large and dominant systems of social organization. This is a latter-day development attributed to changing economic technology as well as to religious motivation seeking superior ways of living.

With improved technology and growth in division of labor extending outside the family, the economic order makes its appearance and assumes the functions of food, clothing, and shelter which were once the exclusive responsibility of the family. With the appearance of agriculture, crops and stored food must be protected, occasioning need first for defense and policing, then for the judicial function of defining rules, and finally for group planning to construct new social organization to employ industrial technology more effectively. The school system has largely arisen in the past century so that the immense task of equipping human beings for their part in the industrial order can be adequately performed. Ecclesiastical organization, as far as can be determined from recorded history, makes its appearance in alliance with tribal government. Today it functions on a scale of organization matching in size the social order which it seeks to influence. The purpose of the chapter before us is to examine the interaction between religious organization and the rest of the social order of which it is a functioning component. We begin by considering the interrelationships of government and religion.

POLITICAL ORDER

Concept of Government

The interaction between political and religious institutions is complex, and the task of grasping its details is simplified if the principal features of governmental activities are first placed in mind. It is then possible to see the ways in which government affects religion and the roles which religion plays in influencing government.

Government is a system of group behavior through which all of the people inhabiting a common territory do things for themselves together instead of acting individually. It is a system relying upon coercion if necessary and exercises force superior to that of any other group. Also inseparable from the concept of government is the function of defending the liberties of people, although not all governments succeed equally well in maintaining the freedom of all persons. This maintenance requires the definition of rules of acting such that the individual enjoys maximum freedom without thereby infringing the freedom of his neighbors. One man's rights end where another man's rights begin. Lawmaking and judging the application of laws to individual cases are indispensable features of the function of defending the individual from harm by another member of the group.

Governments have moved on from their initial task of mutual protection to assume added functions which can apparently be done more readily by the entire group acting together than separate individuals can do by themselves. The postal service is such a function. In many countries all or most forms of distance communication are operated by the government. Transportation and public utilities are functions of many city governments in America and are functions on a nation-wide scale of most European governments. Social security is a function assumed by the federal government in 1935 on a large scale. Most European countries have moved in various degrees toward the operation of basic industries, such as banking and steel, by the government. Although the United States remains aloof as the citadel of capitalism, the number of laws restricting the scope of entrepreneurs in favor of equalizing the rights of consumers and workers has increased in the past few decades. Mounting government regulation, if carried far enough, can reduce the status of large owners of industries from that of full-fledged stockholders in private enterprise with personal control to that of bondholders whose money is invested in public enterprise without personal control. By one route or another people through their government find it useful to perform economic tasks for themselves which self-selected individuals previously performed. In the United States the proportion of all tasks, measured in cost, which people do through their government is now about one-fourth of the total. To this extent economic and political institutions have become merged as a socialistic society. On the other hand, not only is three-fourths of the economy, measured in cost, not socialistic, but the entire social and political system is dominated by a power elite. While people freely exercise the right to vote in national and local elections, they appear to use their franchise in a perfunctory manner. Little real choice is offered to voters confronted by the Republican and Democratic parties. The President and his administrative hierarchy have become increasingly removed from control by either Congress or the people. Decisions of momentous consequence are assumed by self-appointed cliques in government, the Army and in corporations. While C. Wright Mills possibly overstates the argument in his analysis of the American political and economic system, his writings leave much food for thought.

The power elite is composed of men whose positions enable them to transcend the ordinary environments of ordinary men and women; they are in positions to make decisions having major consequences. Whether they do or do not make such decisions is less important than the fact that they do occupy such pivotal positions: their failure to act, their failure to make decisions, is itself an act that is often of greater consequence than the decisions they do make. For they are in command of the major hierarchies and organizations of modern society. They rule the big corporations. They run the machinery of the state and claim its prerogatives. They direct the military establishment. They occupy the strategic command posts of the social structure, in which are now centered the effective means of the power and the wealth and the celebrity which they enjoy.[1]

The spirit of religion is closely involved in the ways in which men get their daily bread. Hence religion takes a large interest in the functioning of economic life. What government does or fails to do in this respect is a concern of religion in seeking to improve the quality of human existence.

One of the lesser functions of government in the United States from the standpoint of financial outlay but one of the greatest in human importance is the operation of public schools by local communities and the operation of universities through the machinery of city and state governments. Because the practice of religion is deeply involved in education as preparation for religious living, churches have taken a great deal of interest in the opportunity or lack of opportunity in public schools for teaching in religion or about religion.

A number of leading governments of the world assume the function of operating religious institutions. This is alien to the present principles of separation of church and state in America, but stands as a potential function which many persons, especially Catholics, would like to see their government assume, at least to the extent of using tax support for subsidizing existing religious enterprises.

Types of Interaction Between Religion and Government

With this view of governmental activities before us, we can enumerate the points of contact between religion and government. In subsequent sections the interrelationships will be examined in detail.

1. Religious persons look to government for protection of their right to engage in religious activities without interference or persecution by others. It may seem strange that so innocuous a form of behavior as religion can incur the antagonism of others. The principal source of interference comes from those who hold different religious beliefs and follow different practices. If they are convinced that theirs are superior and that those of others are defective or destructive of their own religious ideals, they

[1] C. Wright Mills, *The Power Elite,* Oxford University Press, 1957, pp. 3–4.

may seek to suppress or curtail the religious activities of others. Especially in countries where one major religion is imposed by the state, as in some Catholic domains, those who, as Protestants or Jews, are regarded as not practicing the true religion are prevented from propagating their beliefs and perhaps also from practicing them.

2. Furthermore, if a religious group in power believes that forcible conversion to the one true faith is preferable to living in ignorance or infidelity, then those regarded as heretical are in severe jeopardy. A second protective function by government with respect to religion is to maintain the freedom of people from forcible conversion by a dominant religious group or from other disabilities owing to their nonbeliefs. While the terrors of the Inquisition have receded into history, the discrimination practiced in American society against those who do not hold the beliefs of the majority is a serious problem of democracy, and occasional outbreaks of violence have occurred against Jews or Catholics.

Part of the protection of people from religion relates to the protection of citizens from crimes committed in the pursuit of religion. Perhaps *crime* is too strong a word. However, religious cultists believing in handling poisonous snakes as part of their ritual have been held accountable for injury to others. In some instances, the children of Christian Scientists have been required to submit to vaccination in the interest of public health. But generally laws provide for those who follow spiritual methods of healing to be exempt from medical treatment not of their own choosing. Conscientious objectors opposed to war have been required to perform civilian or noncombatant services for their government in lieu of military conscription. It is apparent from these instances that religious rights are not unlimited, but like all other rights are limited when their exercise is believed to impose demonstrable injury upon others.

3. The closest relationship between religion and government occurs when a government establishes and operates a church for its people. While this does not currently exist in America to any considerable degree, vestiges of it remain in such patterns as exemption of church properties from taxation, exemption of ministers, priests, and rabbis from military draft and the extensive chaplaincy service. Nor should it be assumed that a state-operated religion, as in England or Scandinavian countries, necessarily means curtailment of the religious freedom of dissenters, although risk of this exists. For example, dissenters in

public schools are excused from participation in worship contrary to their beliefs, nor are any citizens required to attend church, although they pay taxes in support of the state religion with everyone else. In theory it is as practicable for the state to assume religious functions without encroaching upon the freedom of those not desiring those functions for themselves as it is for the state to undertake any other service in behalf of its people without forcing them to consume that service whether they want it or not.

4. While in the United States the government in general maintains a "hands off" policy as far as religious groups are concerned, this policy is a one-way street. Religious groups can and do exercise considerable influence, along with other citizens, upon the workings of their government. Through social action committees and lobbies, churches take an interest in social problems, such as those of mental health, alcoholism, drug addiction, gambling, vice, and crime. Their interest is not always well informed nor enlightened in its aims and assumptions. Yet the interest is there, nonetheless. Consider the imposition of the prohibition of alcoholic beverages after World War I until 1933, or in the recurring efforts to suppress prostitution or gambling. A major social problem which has claimed the interest of church leaders is that of war.

5. Religion affects government in an inconspicuous but far-reaching way in its stimulus of altruistic motivation. Its general effectiveness in this regard appears to have declined in the past few generations. However, its specific efforts in political activity are obvious in the exhortation by ministers, priests, and rabbis of their constituents toward the achievement of greater civic virtues and in the publicizing of social policies by denominational bodies. In a more fundamental way, religion as a formative influence during childhood eventually affects the responsibility and integrity of citizens and their leaders in government.

6. The relationship of religious motivation to political motivation is one of interaction, as is the case for religious and economic motivation. Especially during time of impending or actual war, nationalism tends to displace the higher ideals taught by religion. In place of peace as an aim, violence becomes the rule. In place of the sacredness of life is taught the necessity to kill. In place of loyalty to God, loyalty to the state becomes supreme. The ways in which political motivation affects religious motivation include the suppression of religious growth and develop-

ment by curtailment of religious freedom during periods of harsh government insensitive to the importance of religion.

With this overview of ways in which religious and political institutions interact, we now proceed to consider some of the topics more fully. The plan of treatment is first to take up points 1, 2, and 3 with reference to the historical development of church and state in the United States. Next, the application of the principles of the church and state in the U.S. to the pressing question of religion in the public schools is considered. Then the role of religion in solving social problems is examined. Problems raised by nationalism and war for religion are next reviewed. In the latter portion of the chapter, the ways in which religion influences economic functions of governments are taken up in conjunction with the more general topic of the relationship between religious and economic institutions.

Historical Development of Church and State in the United States

The extent to which religious liberties are protected and the degree to which government participates in religious activities have constituted a developing pattern of church-and-state relationships. Four stages may be distinguished. (1) The pattern of church and state relationships has Old World roots in those religious liberties gained by some groups during the Protestant Reformation. (2) The pattern underwent growth after colonists holding different religious ideas migrated to America and found it necessary to work out accommodation to each others' ideas and practices. (3) During the drafting of the U.S. Constitution and the Bill of Rights, political leaders wrestled further with problems of what should be the church-state pattern. (4) Finally, the ways in which the written constitution has been interpreted by the Supreme Court and the changing needs of religious denominations have brought about further developments in the church-state pattern.

A. P. Stokes of Yale University has performed the most comprehensive examination of church and state relationships in the United States.[2] No other study approaches his massive three-volume work for thoroughness, and few equal its clarity of organization and presentation. His work, apart from church-state implications, is an extensive historical study in the sociology of religion. His analysis goes behind legal patterns to the motivat-

[2] A. P. Stokes, *Church and State in the United States,* 3 vols., Harper, 1950.

ing social forces which are responsible. The analysis presented here draws substantially upon his work.

Concerning the Old World origins, it is to be emphasized that the revolt of Protestants against the Catholic Church was primarily in opposition to some of its religious beliefs and practices, not in most situations to the concept of religion imposed by government. In the cultural background of the Protestant Reformation was the earlier pattern of government as a partner of the church in maintaining religion, and especially there was the practice of suppressing heresy and converting people to Christianity by force in order to save their souls from damnation. The futility of force in religious conversion was recognized slowly and haltingly. The Anabaptists and similar sects making up the left wing of the Reformation played the most prominent role in advocating freedom of religious belief. The widespread persecution of Quakers in England during the seventeenth century eventuated in the Toleration Act which granted wide exercise of religious liberty without molestation by the state. Luther argued for the autonomy of the church from the state and, to some degree, recognized the rights of conscience within broad limits of Christian faith, thus permitting Protestants and Catholics to exist in the same nation. He became hostile to Jews and advocated persecution against them. Calvin, especially, desired to substitute his theocratic society (government by religious leaders) for that of Rome, and to use government to support worship of God and exact compliance with religious tenets. At the same time, the church was to be independent of control by the government.

Those who settled in America beginning in the seventeenth century were as advanced or as backward in their concepts of religious freedom as the cultural situations from which they came. Roger Williams in Rhode Island and his followers, and William Penn and the Quakers of Philadelphia were liberal. Others had come seeking freedom for themselves, but as in New England, they wished to establish a bibliocracy (government by rigidly defined religious principles) of their own design. In 1647 the Reverend Nathaniel Ward wrote:

> I dare take upon me, to be the Herald of New England so far, as to proclaim to the world, in the name of our Colony that all Familists, Antinomians, Anabaptists and other Enthusiasts shall have free liberty to keep away from us, and such as will come to be gone as fast as they can, the sooner the better. . . . He that is willing to tolerate any religion . . . either doubts of his own, or is not sincere in it. . . .

That state that will give liberty of conscience in matters of religion, must give liberty of conscience and conversation in their moral laws, or else, the fiddle will be out of tune, and some of the strings cracked. . . . Experience will teach churches and Christians, that it is far better to live in a state united, though a little corrupt, than in a state, whereof some part is incorrupt and all the rest divided.[3]

C. H. Moehlman comments on this as follows: "What the New England Puritans aimed at was a bibliocracy, for democracy was without scriptural support. They meant to found Zion in the American wilderness, requiring attendance upon church, vesting the choice of candidates for membership as well as the founding of new churches in the elders and magistrates, and controlling heresy by general synods. The ministers' salaries were raised by public taxation."[4]

In other colonies, the scope of religious freedom varied, with Catholics and Jews generally under disability. Not until the political upheaval of the American Revolution with its reaction against the Church of England and its desire for support by Catholics in Canada was freedom of religious worship without restriction a general practice. At the same time, state operation of religious institutions and religious control over marriage regulations and over education was gradually surrendered. Marriage was previously an ordinance of the church but came under civil authority. Schools were originally for the training of ministers, but eventually gained a status separate from ecclesiastical organization. Apart from the political and economic factors, such as growing wealth, which led to the supremacy of the individual over the church, a genuine development in humanitarian understanding took place. This independent development in spiritual tolerance is reflected in the ideas of Locke and other English philosophers, as well as in the deliberations of the leaders of the American Revolution. In 1772 Samuel Adams prepared a statement of the natural rights of colonists, reflecting Locke's views which entertain restrictions upon Catholics.

As neither reason requires nor religion permits the contrary, every man living in or out of a state of civil society has a right peaceably and quietly to worship God according to the dictates of his conscience.

"Just and true liberty, equal and impartial liberty," in matters spiritual and temporal, is a thing that all men are clearly entitled to by the eternal and immutable laws of God and nature, as well as by the law

[3] C. H. Moehlman, *School and Church: The American Way,* Harper, 1944, p. 7.

[4] *Ibid.,* p. 8.

of nations and all well-grounded municipal laws, which must have their foundation in the former.

In regard to religion, mutual toleration in the different professions thereof is what all good and candid minds of all ages have ever practiced and, both by precept and example, inculcated on mankind. And it is now generally agreed among Christians that this spirit of toleration, in the fullest extent consistent with the being of civil society, is the chief characteristical mark of the true Church. Insomuch that Mr. Locke has asserted and proved, beyond the possibility of contradiction on any solid ground, that such toleration ought to be extended to all whose doctrines are not subversive of society. The only sects which he thinks ought to be, and which by all wise laws are excluded from such toleration, are those who teach doctrines subversive of the civil government under which they live. The Roman Catholics or Papists are excluded by reason of such doctrines as these, that princes excommunicated may be deposed, and those that they call heretics may be destroyed without mercy; besides their recognizing the Pope in so absolute a manner, in subversion of government, by introducing, as far as possible into the states under whose protection they enjoy life, liberty, and property, that solecism in politics *imperium in imperio,* leading directly to the worst anarchy and confusion, civil discord, war, and bloodshed.[5]

Although these views of Samuel Adams are an advance in liberality, the concluding sentence sounds much like the arguments used to justify the persecution of those with Communist beliefs in the present day if "Moscow" is substituted for "Rome." However, the framers of the Constitution went further than Adams and sanctioned freedom of belief for all persons. Several of the colonies at the time of the Revolution had already widened their concept of freedom of worship. The Constitution put in operation in 1789 provided at the end of Article VI that "no religious test shall ever be required as a qualification to any office of public trust under the United States." This effectively put an end to theocratic government imposed by leaders of a particular church.

The Bill of Rights adopted in 1791 included as its first amendment: "Congress shall make no law respecting an establishment of religion, or prohibiting the free exercise thereof; or abridging the freedom of speech, or of the press; or the right of the people peaceably to assemble, and to petition the government for a redress of grievances." In 1871 in *Watson* v. *Jones,* a case involving disputed control of church property, the U.S. Supreme Court declared in emphatic language: "The full and free right to en-

[5] A. P. Stokes, *op. cit.,* Vol. I, pp. 146–147.

tertain any religious belief, to practice any religious principle and to teach any religious doctrine which does not violate the laws of morality and property, and which does not infringe personal rights, is conceded to all. The law knows no heresy, and is committed to the support of no dogma, the establishment of no sect."[6] By means of the Fourteenth Amendment following the Civil War, the scope of the First Amendment was extended to state legislatures, but it was not until 1940 that the Supreme Court decided to bring the states under the religious provision of the First Amendment. In 1940 the Supreme Court unanimously held in *Cantwell et al.* v. *State of Connecticut,* a case where Jehovah's Witnesses had been restricted in the sale of religious literature, that governments of states are bound equally with Congress in conforming to the First Amendment. The First Amendment is the foundation of church-state relations in the United States. The reasons for its adoption, together with its meaning to those who framed it and its meaning to the courts which have interpreted it, merit close consideration.

The establishment of a state church, comparable to the Church of England, or subsidies or privileges for one denomination, as for Catholics in Quebec, was out of the question, owing to the multiplicity of American religious groups. It likewise became clear that for the government to intervene in behalf of one religious group against another would promote sharp civil discord. It was apparent that the state must keep its hands off religious controversy. The long history of religious persecution suffered by Protestant groups which sought refuge in America predisposed them to articulate generous concepts of freedom of religious belief and practice.

At the same time, deep in the background of those who sought religious refuge in America was the conviction that political or any other kind of force is futile for converting minds or maintaining religious beliefs or practices. Those in New England found their church life fell into disrepair, despite the support which it received from civil government. The spirit of religion could not be captured by coercion, but would only grow spontaneously through the power of spiritual appeal. Risk of imposing error by legislative authority and the importance of allowing free play for reason and conscience were recognized. More than this, forcible conversion worked great suffering upon those stubborn in faith who would not accept conversion. Where dissenters possessed sufficient political power, civil war was the out-

[6] *Ibid.,* Vol. III, p. 452.

come in European countries of using the state as an instrument of religious proselytizing. Torn by Old World struggles between Catholics and Protestants and by conflicts among different branches of Protestantism, the colonists were receptive to ideas of separation of church and state. Their experiences of living together in the colonies steadily disposed them to articulate concepts of separation of church and state wider than those which prevailed in the countries from which they came, countries which usually had one predominant denomination with a state-supported church.

That the government could not engage in the business of operating a church did not necessarily mean that all religious expression was barred from its activities. The amendment is explicit concerning "an establishment of religion," and does not appear to be aimed at religion in general. However, a few legal proponents have held the view that the state under the Constitution cannot further in any way religion in general. They have advocated that suits be brought to halt tax exemption of church properties and to eliminate all teaching or acknowledgment of religious beliefs in public school education, such as Christmas stories and festivals.

Three distinct ways exist by which governmental institutions in the United States have continued to participate in religion in general, without becoming involved in "an establishment of religion."

1. In various forms government gives general support to religious purposes. The most obvious way is through tax exemption of church properties. Churches are considered in a class with philanthropic and educational institutions, being regarded as beneficial to the common welfare, and do not pay property taxes. Another form of support to religious activity is through exemption of clergymen from the military draft. This support extends to those who live within religious orders, such as Catholic brothers, but has not accommodated the Jehovah's Witnesses, who claim ministerial status in their door-to-door proselytizing.

2. Active participation of government in religion is provided by the institution of the chaplaincy in prisons and for the armed services. Religious denominations have little voice in the selection of their representatives, but the costs are paid by the government. The military program is one in which the government has sought to grant participation in rough proportion to the number of religious constituents of each group involved.

3. A third way in which governmental functioning overlaps religious functioning in the United States is in public religious observances. The opening of sessions of Congress with prayer and the existence of worship at commencement exercises for graduating students are instances of this. In essence what is involved is not the propagation of religion by the government, but rather the feeling by participants that they wish to express their religion in political as well as in other phases of their lives. This expression is not one in which others must compulsorily be involved since they can remain silent, stand aside, or absent themselves altogether. Another way in which government cooperates in religious observance is in the designation of religious holidays. The United States, being predominantly a Christian nation, recognizes Christmas as a holiday. Thanksgiving in a vague way is a religious holiday for giving thanks to the Creator. It can be validly maintained that, in deference to the widespread contribution of Jewish culture to American life, the Jewish New Year should also be designated a national holiday. School children affected are already excused on Jewish holidays.

The attitude of the U.S. government toward religion has been characterized by Stokes as one of "sympathy." Beyond very general tenets, religious ideas are not defined or fostered by the government. Doubtless this attitude of sympathy for religion in general does not satisfy atheists or other small philosophical groups. The result of the attitude of sympathy is to give general support to religion without coercing anyone into religious belief although, as in other legislative matters, groups of taxpayers sometimes help to pay for programs not of their choosing. The government in the United States is not completely beyond the end of the continuum of religious activity which includes state-supported religions, but it does exist at a far end where there is little involvement in the operation of religious institutions.

The lengths to which the courts are willing to go in protecting citizens from compulsory religious services of any hue are shown in the celebrated Gobitis case. In 1943 the U.S. Supreme Court reversed the decision it had made three years before in *Minersville School District* v. *Gobitis* and decided by a 6 to 3 vote that participation in the flag ceremony in public schools must not be compulsory. The case was brought by parents who as Jehovah's Witnesses were willing for their children to "stand in respectful silence" while others saluted the flag, but not to "bow down before a graven image." Justice Jackson wrote in the majority opinion: "If there is any fixed star in our constitutional constellation, it is that no official, high or petty, can prescribe what shall be orthodox in politics, nationalism, religion, or other matters of opinion or force citizens to confess by word or act their faith therein."[7]

The guarantee of freedom of worship without interference by governmental authority stems historically from the deep concern of early Americans that religion is one of man's priceless possessions, part of the basic fulfillment of life, never to be taken away from man by an arbitrary or despotic government. In the interpretation given by courts this freedom of religious activity is limited only when it is reasonable for public order and safety to keep persons from proceeding in the name of religion to perform injurious acts which all persons, religious or not, are prohibited from doing. Several such examples of limitation of religious freedom may be cited. In 1878, in *Reynolds* v. *U.S.* a federal statute prohibiting polygamy, directed against Mormons, was held constitutional on the ground that polygamy is damaging to human society. At the same time, "celestial marriages for eternity," a form of spiritual marriage of Mormons without cohabitation were not restricted. Judicial opinion stated that the government concerns itself with actions and does not limit religious thinking about the natural or the supernatural world. On the other hand Roman Catholics have been allowed to conduct gambling games for fund raising. Priests are immune from testifying what is said in confessional. Christian Scientists have generally been permitted by public health laws to follow their religious beliefs concerning the psychic cure of disease. But in Texas in 1918 the courts held in *New Braunfels* v. *Waldschmidt* that the requirement to submit to vaccination in the public schools is a reasonable health regulation. The courts have also upheld the authority of Congress to draft for civilian or noncombatant service conscientious objectors to war or conscription.

Religion and the Public Schools

The Gobitis case involved children attending a public school, but it concerned religious practices rather than whether or how instruction in or about religion is to be introduced in the curricula of public schools. This problem is an acute one for American parents. On the one hand, many of them are anxious for their children to grow up in an educational situation where some religious appreciation or religious atmosphere prevails. On the other

[7] *Ibid.,* Vol. II, p. 615.

hand, there exists the stubborn restriction of the Constitution which does not permit the enactment of local or national laws furthering the purposes of a particular religious group. The situation is one in which citizens cannot have both freedom from religion inimical to them and freedom in public schools to teach doctrines of a religion amiable to them. The working out of the compromise between presence or absence of religion in the public schools is an important instance of church-state principles. Instruction of public school children in the beliefs of a particular denomination is excluded, but the general support which government gives religion in other areas, extends into the programs of many schools through nondenominational religious exercises, Bible reading, and celebration of religious holidays. We will briefly trace prevailing patterns in their historical, legal, and practical contexts.

Before the adoption of the Bill of Rights, one prevailing pattern of school instruction was that of schools maintained by religious denominations, often for the training of their own ministers. As originally settled by a farm population which remained located mostly in one place, many American communities contained a large majority belonging to one denomination in a given locality, so that people of a particular faith found it convenient to work together in their tax supported, religiously based school. After the adoption of the Bill of Rights, with the increased mobility and the large mingling of Americans from different localities, and with the large growth in the public school system, it became apparent that religious instruction or religious exercises could not legally be imposed by denominational groups in public schools against the will of substantial minorities. The initial impetus through the efforts by figures such as Horace Mann was to make religious instruction nonsectarian rather than to eliminate it from public schools altogether. The more recent tendency, under the influence of some Christian and non-Christian groups has been to eliminate religious instruction altogether from public schools, besides sectarian forms of such instruction. The response of churches has either been to withhold participation and establish their own system of schools, as in the case of Catholics and some Protestants, or else to acquiesce in the absence of denominational teaching of their children in public schools. Despite urgent efforts by Protestants during the nineteenth century, their parochial schools never gained wide support. The 1936 religious census lists an enrollment for them of only 275,643, two-thirds of these pupils being in Lutheran schools. Enrollment in Catholic parochial schools has approached one-half of all Catholic pupils. A study reported in 1959 disclosed that there were 358,739 pupils in Protestant church-related day schools and 4,090,200 in Catholic elementary and secondary schools.[8]

The secularization of the public school system, while welcomed by many, including religious-minded persons, has occasioned considerable restlessness on the part of church people who would like their children to have the benefits of religious instruction as part of the regular school program. The most popular answer has been the Sunday School program and similar programs by Jews and by some Catholics, described in Chapter 13. Another answer to the secularization of public schools has been to secure the release of children from classes at an appointed time each week for separate classes in religion given by representatives of particular denominations. An aim of this program has been to reach nonattenders in Sunday Schools. The released-time program was begun in the United States in 1914 in the schools of Gary, Indiana, and spread to communities in most other states, although some school boards decline to sanction the program. A survey by the National Education Association in 1949 disclosed that 27 percent of the school systems reporting provided some degree of formal religious instruction. Of these 68 percent released students to attend classes away from school, with 15 percent attending classes in public school buildings during school hours. Eighty-six percent of students covered by the survey participated in none of the released-time provisions of public schools. Even in schools with released-time programs, the number of students coöperating frequently does not exceed one-fourth.[9]

The released-time program received a legal setback in 1948 when the Supreme Court ruled in *McCollum* v. *State of Illinois* that use of public school buildings in a released-time program is illegal. The case was one in which the wife of a college professor, Vashti McCollum, protested that her son was under social pressure to accept some form of religious instruction as part of the school program since he was given alternative tasks and exposed to ostracism by playmates for failing to participate in a released-time class held in the school building. The Supreme Court in an 8 to 1 decision reversed the lower court and reaffirmed its doctrine of a year before in the case of *Everson* v. *Board of Educa-*

[8] *Information Service,* National Council of Churches, January 3, 1959.
[9] Stokes, *op. cit.,* Vol. II, p. 529.

tion. The Everson-McCollum doctrine is a policy declaration of fundamental importance for church-state relations which gives new meaning to the First Amendment. In the Everson case, a New Jersey statute passed in 1941 provided for free bus travel for students. A taxpayer challenged the provision of bus transportation for parochial school students. In its 5–4 decision, the majority of the Supreme Court said:

> The "establishment of religion" clause of the First Amendment means at least this: neither a state nor the Federal Government can set up a church. Neither can pass laws which aid one religion, aid all religions, or prefer one religion over another. Neither can force nor influence a person to go to or to remain away from church against his will or force him to profess a belief or disbelief in any religion. No person can be punished for entertaining or professing religious beliefs or disbeliefs, for church attendance or non-attendance. No tax in any amount, large or small, can be levied to support any religious activities or institutions, whatever they may be called, or whatever form they may adopt to teach or practice religion. Neither a state nor the Federal Government can, openly or secretly, participate in the affairs of any religious organizations or groups and *vice versa.* In the words of Jefferson, the clause against establishment of religion by law was intended to erect "a wall of separation between Church and State."[10]

The court went on to declare that providing bus travel as a public welfare service from which no religious group should be excluded does not constitute support of religious education, since it merely helps parents, regardless of religion, to get their children to school. The minority of the court dissented from this factual conclusion. The factual controversy is secondary in importance to the court's declaration that laws which aid all religions are contrary to the First Amendment. According to such authorities as E. S. Corwin and A. P. Stokes, this would appear to open the way for a suit to be brought against tax exemption of religious institutions and to eliminate chaplaincies to the armed services. In the McCollum case the lone dissenter, Justice Stanley Reed, citing Madison and Jefferson, contended that the framers of the constitution did not intend such wide separation of church and state and that the First Amendment sought to outlaw governmental favoritism toward one religion and any compulsion in religion while envisaging friendly coöperation between church and state.

The decision in the McCollum case left in doubt the question of whether children might be released during school hours to attend

[10] *Ibid.,* Vol. II, p. 704.

classes in religious instruction off the school grounds. In the case of *Zorach* v. *Clauson,* decided in 1952, the Supreme Court, still striving for an answer, took a more moderate line. In this case suit was brought because of released-time classes held away from school property. The decision upheld this practice. According to F. E. Johnson, Chairman of the Committee on Religion and Education of the American Council on Education, the opinion given by the court conforms more nearly to the realities of American practice.[11] The court declared: "When the state encourages religious instruction or coöperates with religious authorities by adjusting the schedule of public events to sectarian needs, it follows the best of our traditions. For it then respects the religious nature of our people and accommodates the public service to their spiritual needs."

The judicial picture is still not fully clarified from the standpoint of whether tax exemption of church property is an appropriate form of legislative aid to religion in general, as educational and philanthropic purposes are similarly aided by government. In view of the Zorach case it appears unlikely that the extreme view in the Everson and McCollum cases of complete government aloofness from religious purposes will prevail as the continuing policy of the Supreme Court. The legal difficulty is that the First Amendment taken literally goes beyond what its authors intended. What is required to suit the feelings and needs of the majority of religious-minded persons is a realistic construction, rather than a literal construction of "Congress shall make no law respecting an establishment of religion, or prohibiting the free exercise thereof." A reasonable view, following Justice Reed, is that government shall not coerce any individual in his religious or nonreligious practices, nor shall it, beyond self-expression by participants in government, engage in any religious enterprise. However, impartial aid in coöperating with existing religious establishments is legally and practically feasible. While this interpretation does not satisfy atheists or some members of religious minorities, it is to be kept in mind that the extent of the injury to them is payment in taxes for purposes with which they do not agree but in which they are not themselves the worshiping participants. For them to pay trifling sums for the religious behavior of others is in harmony with the legal view that citizens are not exclusively taxed according to the

[11] F. E. Johnson, "Summary of Policies and Recommendations of the American Council on Education Committee on Religion and Education," *Religious Education,* July-August 1957, p. 251.

particular benefits which each receives. In the give and take of civic life, people frequently pay in part for benefits which others receive from government.

There remains the practical question of whether released-time programs are a suitable means of religious education. In the opinion of the author, this depends upon local circumstances. Such programs are regarded as an administrative burden by school administrators. The programs benefit only a fraction of the student population. Furthermore, there is question as to whether the indoctrination and regimentation methods used by some religious teachers should be tolerated in an educational program administered by a government seeking to train its future citizens to think for themselves. On the other hand, many religious leaders feel there are real gains in a released-time program of religious education classes for public school pupils. R. C. Miller summarizes these gains.

> The most important result of this program is that it brings religion into weekday life and identifies it with the developing attitudes toward life that are the goals of the public school. Home, church, and school cooperate at this level. A second result is the surprising number of unchurched children who attend the weekday classes—in many systems one-third of the pupils have no church connection. The investment in terms of missionary work alone justifies the expense. Third, in over half of the situations, professionally trained teachers and supervisors bring to the learners a proficiency that is absent in many Sunday church schools. Fourth, it provides for unity in terms of church cooperation and racial and economic crossing of lines, for the Protestant class meets at a place near the school and is open to all Protestant children.[12]

A program which has gained considerable impetus among public school administrators is that of teaching moral and spiritual values without introducing theological or sectarian considerations. Values on which it is assumed that American people agree are: the worth of human personality, moral responsibility, institutions as the servants of men, common consent, devotion to truth, respect for excellence, moral equality, brotherhood, pursuit of happiness, and spiritual enrichment. This list was compiled by the Educational Policies Commission of the National Education Association of the United States and the American Association of School Administrators and published in 1951.[13]

12 R. C. Miller, *Education for Christian Living,* Prentice-Hall, 1956, p. 113.

13 Educational Policies Commission, *Moral and Spiritual Values in the Public Schools,* National Education Association, 1951.

These are values which are readily introduced during the teaching of history, social studies, and English. They can also be made an informal part of the classroom experience in other courses. The limitation of the approach as far as religion is concerned is that a specific core of religious beliefs central to personality integration is not encompassed by a general list of what are called moral and spiritual values. In particular, the desire of many parents for their children to experience a more distinctive religious background as part of their public school education is not met if there is simply recurring reference to social values on which Americans agree.

As to non-sectarian worship exercises, if a local community overwhelmingly desires that these have some place in the school program, it does not seem that a minority should bar these for the majority. In many school districts they are now permitted. The test, both practical and legal, is whether deep-seated religious controversy is aroused to which the school board becomes a party. Those who would exclude all acknowledgment of religion in public school programs seek an impossible purpose, since religion touches numerous aspects of human life which require treatment in public education. Furthermore, the development of motivation is one of the responsibilities shared by the schools. When this development is furthered by periodic class exercises or by inspiration of a teacher, the activity is religious within Durkheim's meaning of the term. The issue is not one of eliminating religion but of seeing that treatment of it is based upon the common denominator of a consensus of parents, with protection of the rights of dissenters. If necessary, dissenting children in American public schools can remain silent or stand aside while others perform their religious observances, even as children in English public schools and in the schools of other democratic nations are excused from overt participation if they or their parents so desire.

What of government aid to parochial schools? Besides bus transportation, the closest to which the Supreme Court has come to approving such aid was in the Louisiana textbook case, *Cochran* v. *Louisiana State Board of Education.* In this opinion, given in 1930, it was held that for the state to pay for the same secular textbooks, whether used by public or parochial school children, in no way involved support of religious education. If this principle were extended, the state might appropriate funds to pay private teachers in secular subjects or for the construction of school buildings. It is this author's opinion that such aid to private, as well as public schools, is socially desirable, provided at the same time proper control over educational standards is maintained. Furthermore, it should be provided that in no community too small for proper support of multiple school installations shall such aid to private schools be given. As long as no convincing reason can be adduced why a community of parents cannot educate their children in the religious atmosphere they desire, they seem entitled to the benefit of governmental aid in secular aspects of their program. For them to be penalized for their beliefs by shouldering the staggering burdens of modern education continuing through fifteen or twenty years of a growing person's life, seems unreasonable and unnecessary.

A question of critical importance is that of state supervision of educational standards in order to insure that children in parochial, as well as public, schools shall grow in healthful conditions and that their minds and motivations shall have the benefit of the best training possible. Indoctrination stultifies, rather than stimulates, intellectual keenness. To teach children that their race or their religious group is superior to that of others is contrary to democratic principles. The most effective answer to these problems of religious instruction is given if children are taught about religion, rather than simply indoctrinated in religion. Teaching about religion is the type of religious instruction advocated by the Committee on Religion and Education of the American Council on Education.[14] In its survey published in 1953 the Committee found lack of uniform practice concerning religious education or exercises in public schools, but discovered "a high degree of receptivity toward the general position which the Committee had formulated on the part of educational leaders and a corresponding readiness for experimentation designed to test its practicality." The movement for pupils in public schools, especially at the secondary-school level, to receive instruction about religious ideas and practices is growing. The Educational Policies Commission in its report in 1951 recommended objective study of religion as empirical cultural fact. The future pattern in both grade schools and universities seems likely to be one of treating religion in social studies courses along with other basic human institutions. Such treatment includes factual acquaintance with existing religions in the community and introduction to findings of scientific scholars of religion. The requirement is not that the student give assent to what he finds, but that he gain familiarity with and insight into what he finds. Undue memory

[14] Johnson, *op. cit.,* pp. 247–255.

work has no more place in teaching about religion than it does in any other branch of instruction.

Interest in religious education at the university level appears to be minor but growing. Especially when religion is considered from the standpoint of firm scientific inquiry does it command more enthusiastic consideration by students. However, the religious effect of the college experience upon the values of students is considered by Philip E. Jacob to be slight, with few exceptions. He made an exhaustive study of research reports which assess the changes which students' values undergo, and his negative findings have gained wide attention among educators. He writes: "The impact of the college experience is rather to *socialize* the individual, to refine, polish, or "shape up" his values so that he can fit comfortably into the ranks of American college alumni. . . . He is more concerned with status, achievement and prestige [than the rest of society]."[15]

Role of Religion in Solving Social Problems

Closely allied with the questions of religion in public education are those of religion in relation to behavior standards of the public. The declared purpose of religion is usually to improve the quality of human life. In historical perspective it should be recalled that church leaders in America have generally taken an active part in ameliorating social conditions where substantial consensus and support were forthcoming. Church leaders played a part in fomenting the American Revolution, in the antislavery crusade which culminated in the Civil War, and in the Prohibition movement and the era of the "noble experiment." In various instances, religious leaders have been active in jail and prison reforms and in improving conditions in mental hospitals. Sunday "blue laws" against baseball and periodic drives against the "red-light district" have been an animus of Protestant clergymen. The Catholic Church has functioned with organized effectiveness in combating certain practices in birth control and childbearing to which it is opposed.[16] The wisdom of these efforts by religious groups to remake culture or society is open to question. One of the questions at issue is that of how specifically it is appropriate

[15] P. E. Jacob, *Changing Values in College,* Harper, 1957, p. 4. The Jacob report is discussed in R. C. Gilman, "Postscript to the Jacob Study," *Religious Education,* January–February, 1960, pp. 15–23. Another recent study is that by E. D. Eddy, Jr., *The College Influence on Student Character,* American Council on Education, 1959.

[16] K. W. Underwood analyzes an episode of this kind in *Protestant and Catholic,* Beacon, 1957.

for religion to spell out the standards or requirements of a better society. A second question arises of the extent to which it is proper for the church to intervene in politics or exercise other types of pressure to bring about desired social conditions.

These questions converge in the sharp issue of whether the church by force should exact obedience to moral norms. The churches have typically opposed sexual behavior outside of marriage, but the laws they have helped enact in order to restrict such behavior are at strong variance with occasional acts of large numbers of Americans, as disclosed by the Kinsey reports and similar surveys. In contrast it may be noted that European governments typically do not try to regiment conformity to sexual norms, and that even the Catholic Church does not exact of its clergy the temperance standards which Protestant churches sought through Prohibition to impose upon all the American people. However, in the United States the Catholic Church has reflected the Puritan environment and imposes censorship on movies and books which would be tolerated in Catholic countries abroad. This censorship is imposed through the power of the Catholic Church to boycott and hurt persons responsible. This suppression is regarded by many non-Catholics as an abridgment of a basic civil liberty, freedom of expression.

It is worthwhile noting that most criminologists and mental hygienists regard the present laws making sexual promiscuity a crime as both harmful to the individual and weakening of respect for those laws which should be enforced. It is further pointed out that the attempt through legislation to control gambling, prostitution, and drug addiction provide organized crime in America with its major hold on American life. Encouragement of illegal traffic pays the overhead for the business operations of criminals, who in turn have a well-established base of operations from which to launch their predatory activities upon other phases of American life. So strongly engrained is this Protestant tradition of trying to create good behavior by legislating it that almost every new generation in American history finds some new legislative panacea foisted upon the people.

Detailed aspects of the social problems involve cause and effect analysis of considerable complexity. But general questions of political action and compulsion arise in most of them. The courts have usually upheld the constitutionality of laws regulating moral behavior. They have done so even if it is merely a belief by the legislature that injury or benefit is involved and that legal control is sound. If sufficiently repugnant, the act prohibited in public may merely be an affront to the feelings of some religious participants. The questions now confronting Americans seem largely ones of social, rather than judicial, policy.

A century or more ago, churches frequently exacted high standards of moral behavior of their members, expelling those who engaged in sexual affairs outside of matrimony, or even those who performed any of a long list of actions believed to be pleasure seeking or luxury seeking. The effect of this strict regulation was to force many members out of their congregations. Churches have now come to the view in most instances that they have a responsibility to "sinners" as well as "saints," and that to exert their influence in behalf of higher ideals, they must maintain association with their members, as long as their waywardness is not too flagrant. In general, the principle now seems accepted that arbitrary imposition of social or political doctrines is divisive of church congregations, and except where there is substantial consensus such doctrines are not imposed. "Let the church be the church" is the aim, followers being urged to live righteous lives but according to their own social and political views. Religious leaders offer guidance and inspiration for specific ways of living, but these ways are not usually obligatory upon members.

Realization appears to be growing that enforced morality is a pseudo morality in which the value system of the individual is not favorably affected. It is possible that actions by being forbidden under penalty become more alluring because of their forbidden character. When correct behavior is exacted under duress, the underlying motivations required for mature, self-controlled living remain unbuilt. These motivations are acquired by subtle processes of social, cultural, and intellectual experience. The myth that force can be used to reform has plagued the treatment of criminals for generations and is fortunately disappearing somewhat from the public mind. Thinking still lags in dealing with problems of drug addiction and prostitution, in which resort to law rather than therapy causes organized crime to flourish and to support and even stimulate demand.

The mood in character education in both churches and public schools seems increasingly to be one of giving young people intellectual resources for self-understanding and then encouraging them to take responsibility for making their own life decisions. The values and convictions of teachers are part of the educational atmosphere, but these are offered by way of example and inspiration, not by way of coercion. However, where the behavior of a few, such as drunkenness or open sexual promiscuity, is obviously offensive to the moral standards or ideals sought by the majority, schools and colleges, as well as local communities, maintain at least a semblance of proper standards by rules and regulations.

In the realm of political action, many religious groups are directly or indirectly involved in lobbying to secure the passage of legislation which is favorable to their own religious programs or which achieves broader social-welfare objectives pronounced by church leaders. The relationship of these lobbies, whose visible constituencies are often slight or uninformed, to the parent church bodies is often like that of the "tail which wags the dog." Enthusiasm for world-peace programs and for antidiscrimination laws often bubbles merrily in the upper echelons of ecclesiastical hierarchies while the laity are uninformed and uninvolved. Legislators undoubtedly gauge the degree of effective political support when they listen to the recommendations of church representatives in the nation's capital. The National Catholic Welfare Conference, composed of Catholic bishops, is an effective organization which commands closer attention by legislators than do smaller segments of religious institutions. At the same time, some of the representatives of church or synagogue groups become highly respected for their technical competence in legislative problems. Their views are then sought, not so much because of their constituency, as for their level of insight. Luke Ebersole concludes his story of church lobbying with the summary:

> The place of the churches among the interest groups to be reckoned with in the enactment of Federal legislation is well established. There are no signs that the churches are withdrawing from the ranks of political protagonists; on the contrary, their participation is increasing, and cautiously, but with assurance, they are learning to play new roles.
>
> Diffuse and sporadic campaigns of propaganda and pressure, which have been characteristic of many of the political activities of the churches in the past, still continue. By passing resolutions, appointing delegations, calling mass meetings, and sending letters and telegrams, religious groups across the country pressure and protest, approve and disapprove legislative measures.
>
> Also continuing are the operations of church-related special cause lobbies which have performed in Washington for many years. For half a century, the temperance forces have attempted to control from the capital the drinking habits of the nation. Next to the temperance groups, peace lobbies have had the longest and most active life. Lesser varieties of lobbies have come and gone. While the strength of some of

the older special cause lobbies has waned, others with new vigor have been organized in recent years.

But the churches have moved far beyond mere opposition to "liquor, war, and sin." They are not relying upon impulsive campaigns and special cause lobbies for representation before government. The trend is to form agencies which have the assigned function of representing their respective denominational and interdenominational church bodies before the Federal Government. These agencies are establishing offices in Washington. The Catholic Church has had offices in Washington since the second decade of the century. Almost all of the Protestant denominational lobbies have located in Washington since the end of World War II.

In the main, the methods of church lobbies are unspectacular and involve few political threats. Church lobbies are organized to perform two chief functions: to inform, advise, and persuade legislators and administrators; and to channelize information concerning legislation and governmental actions to the church public. The lobbies vary in their willingness to apply political pressure, in their willingness to admit the use of political pressure, and in their ability to use political pressure. . . .

The interests of church lobbies are legion. Traditional opposition to liquor and war is still in evidence. The most recent battle in the long but less forceful war against alcohol was waged against liquor advertising. Church lobbies have maintained their record for opposition to war and militarism by opposing compulsory military training, military aid to Greece and Turkey, and military aid under the North Atlantic Treaty.

The strong humanitarian motivation of the churches is demonstrated by interest in civil rights, health, housing, European recovery, displaced persons, and social security.[17]

The latter concerns appear to be commendable expressions of religious values and convictions. As long as social policies adopted and promulgated through legislation do not split church congregations, nor interfere with the freedom of individuals to work out their own life decisions, they have an acknowledged place in contemporary religious living. The shortcoming which many thoughtful persons would note, is not that churches intervene in political life, but that their net influence, potentially large, is pathetically weak in behalf of human progress. This weakness is especially discernible with reference to problems of nationalism and industrial capitalism, and to these problems we next turn.

[17] L. Ebersole, *Church Lobbying in the Nation's Capital,* Macmillan, 1951, pp. 176–177, 178.

Religion and Nationalism

One of the fundamental ways in which religion interacts with governmental activity is through nationalism and war. Nationalism, especially in wartime, frequently curtails freedoms, including religious ones. As a pseudo religion, nationalism competes with the deeper spiritual values of monotheistic religion. Furthermore, in wartime, nationalism demands of its citizens homicidal behavior at strong variance with religious teachings of kindly and peaceable living. Following every war, a backwash of demoralization is evident in family breakdown, juvenile delinquency, and other augmented social ills. For these reasons, religious groups have often pressed their peace teachings in an effort to establish harmony and coöperation among peoples of the world. These peace teachings are, of course, unpopular in a nation in which the majority is united in prosecuting a war.

To see the interaction between religion and nationalism, it is important to fix in mind the concept of what nationalism is. Various definitions have been given which bring out its different causes or effects. Since nationalism is often involved in warlike behavior, we will here delineate its nature in terms of the psychology of war. This psychology has been aptly summarized by General Douglas MacArthur in a speech to the American Legion in 1955. He said present tensions are "kept alive by two great illusions. The one, a complete belief on the part of the Soviet world that the capitalist powers are preparing to attack it; that sooner or later we intend to strike. And the other, a complete belief on the part of the capitalist countries that the Soviets are preparing to attack us. Both are wrong. Each side, so far as the masses are concerned, is equally desirous of peace. For either side, war with the other would mean nothing but disaster. Both equally dread it. But the constant acceleration of preparation may well, without specific intent, ultimately produce a spontaneous combustion."[18]

Jerome D. Frank, a psychiatrist, points out the failure of negotiations under these conditions of mutual fear. "The mutual expectancy of Russia and the United States that the other plans to attack leads each to negotiate to gain a supposed advantage, intensifying the mutual distrust. Russia wanted to ban atomic weapons when we alone had them; we want to ban outer space as an area of conflict now that Russia seems to be ahead in this

[18] J. D. Frank, "The Great Antagonism," *The Atlantic,* November, 1958, p. 60.

field. We ring Russia with bomber and missile bases, she treacherously crushes Hungary and develops ICBM's, each thereby strengthening the other's fear of attack and increasing the probability that it will occur."[19]

Nationalism can be defined as the policy of using force to place the interests of one's own nation over the interests of other nations. A nation is a group maintaining authority by force over a definite territory. In a broader sense, a nation also refers to a subjugated group of people bound by cultural or historical ties, who would like to exercise independent authority if they could. A nation is differentiated from political subdivisions exercising lesser control by its superior authority and its use of the power instruments of war against other nations. Nationalism is rooted in a war psychosis of fear of other nations, a state of mind often incited by those whose business depends upon war preparations. The psychosis is one of grossly misunderstanding the motivation of other nations. It is intensified by mutually opposing preparations for war and by the emotional virulence of crowd psychology. The psychosis periodically boils over into military conflict.

Also at root is the clash of economic interests, especially between capitalists and communists who want the state to take over land and factories to operate them for the welfare of all people. The relative importance of the psychological and economic roots of war has been, and continues to be, a topic of fundamental debate among social scientists. Upon the relative importance of these factors depend details of the strategy required to forestall the threat of further war.

Recurring voices have been raised in churches against nationalism because it is a force provoking the outbreak of war. These voices range from those of absolute pacifists who refuse to bear arms, whatever the extremity of their nation, to those who, like MacArthur, deplore the psychological tendencies which make for war, but are always ready to participate in their nation's defense when war has arisen. Others are outspoken in their assertion that nationalism is a force manipulated by business groups for their own interests, as German industrialists used Hitler to maintain their economic power over the masses. Pacifists who abstain from war even after it has arisen argue that each additional blow struck augments the emotional bitterness which thwarts lasting peace.

Most persons concerned about eliminating war believe in the importance of establishing orderly political machinery whereby

[19] *Ibid.*

opposing groups can negotiate their differences and accept decisions reached by voting procedures. Some place great reliance upon superior power being wielded by a world government. Pacifists contend that such superior power beyond policing individuals induces the same war psychosis in a recalcitrant nation as that which inflames nations against each other today. They point out that the threat of superior political power has not prevented civil wars in the past, nor does it seem likely by itself to prevent world civil war if sufficiently keen differences arise among peoples of the world. Pacifists who reject the military role of a superstate emphasize the importance of peoples working out their differences voluntarily. They theorize that when people are not threatened by opposing military force, they are much less misguided by irrational fear and are much more receptive to ideas of justice and mutuality. Some pacifists base their philosophy on the supernatural assumption that God will right the scales of justice Himself. "Vengeance is mine," says the Lord in the Bible.[20] Other pacifists put their faith in "that of God" in human beings, which if appealed to, brings out the better side of men's natures. They derive scriptural justification from Jesus' Sermon on the Mount, in which men are counseled: "You have heard that it was said, 'An eye for an eye and a tooth for a tooth.' But I say to you, Do not resist one who is evil. But if any one strikes you on the right cheek, turn to him the other also; and if any one would sue you and take your coat, let him have your cloak as well; and if any one forces you to go one mile, go with him two miles. Give to him who begs from you, and do not refuse him who would borrow from you."[21]

Pacifists derive practical support from the effectiveness of the Hindu leader Mahatma Gandhi, who relied upon spiritual power in political activity. Gandhi organized "nonviolent resistance" against the British, boycotting British goods and refusing to pay taxes. This strategy, known as *satyagraha* or loyalty to truth, involves meekly accepting whatever punishment or mistreatment is imposed as a result of holding fast to ethical principles in one's conduct. The theory is that by refusing to strike back, the opponent's hostility is disarmed, and at the same time the appeal through suffering causes the opponent to reflect upon the morality of his own course of action. While it is a matter of historical fact that the Hindus gained their independence of the British through nonviolent noncoöperation, the majority of churchgoers

[20] Deuteronomy 32:35.
[21] Matthew 5:38–45.

doubt the effectiveness of Gandhian techniques against the Nazis, and many also question whether these techniques are an appropriate answer to Communist expansion in the world today. Pacifists point out that while Nazi conquest of France imposed severe restrictions upon the people their lives did not suffer the dire consequences which had been feared. Pacifists recall that early Christians worked within the authoritarian political regime of Rome but eventually succeeded in achieving conversion of its rulers to Christianity.

With this review of the range of attitudes of church people, especially religious pacifists, toward nationalism and war, we turn to an analysis of the ebb and flow of peace-mindedness among religious groups, particularly in the period between World Wars I and II and in the post-World War II years. The most extensive review of the role of religion in America in relation to nationalism and war has been given by J. M. Yinger in *Religion in the Struggle for Power.* A detailed account of pacifists during wartime is that given by M. Sibley and P. Jacob in *Conscription of Conscience.*

Following the extremely costly Civil War, sentiment for peace grew in churches in the United States. With a watchful eye on the European powder keg, members of peace societies advocated arbitration as a means of settling differences between nations. The hope that war had become a thing of the past was rudely shattered by the outbreak of World War I. Feeling in the United States was at first neutral, and pacifist opposition to war was outspoken. Linguistic and financial ties with England swung the balance toward U.S. intervention on the side of the allies. War fever seized the country after submarine warfare took American lives. Church leaders joined their fellow Americans in their crusade to put the "Hun" in his place and to "make the world safe for democracy." This abdication of religious principles has been detailed by Ray H. Abrams in *Preachers Present Arms.* Yinger describes the mobilization of religious feelings in behalf of making war.

That most of the churches were thoroughly behind the government in its prosecution of the war is a matter of record. They acted as recruiting stations, urging the men to support the government and to defend Christianity. They sold liberty bonds aided by nationally prepared sermon topics, and advertised them in their papers. The *Christian Work* wrote: "Kill the Hun, Kill his Hope.—Buy Bonds." In the food-saving campaign the churches led the war, for here was an activity in which self-sacrifice, generosity, and thrift—virtues highly esteemed by the churches—could aid in the war. The churches contributed to the war excitement, for many of them were most energetic in telling atrocity stories; in many cases they drew brutal pictures of the Kaiser and the German people. We need not give a cynical explanation of this fact, however, when we realize the *raison d'être* of atrocity stories: they are an attempt to offset the inhibitions against hate and killing that have been established by Christianity and democracy.[22]

Members of certain religious groups, known as the "Historic Peace Churches," which include the Mennonites, Brethren, and Quakers, have had an intransigent and long-standing tradition of nonparticipation in war dating back to the inception of these churches during the Reformation. The right of exemption from war on grounds of religious conscience was generally respected in early American wars, such as that of the American Revolution and the War of 1812. During the Civil War, conscription created some difficulties, especially for pacifists in the South. After U.S. entry in World War I, on the side of the Western Allies, pacifists who clung to their views became very unpopular. The conscription law enacted made provision only for those conscientious objectors willing to serve in uniform in a noncombatant capacity. This status was eventually accepted by about 1,300 men.[23] After special review of their cases, others were furloughed out of the Army into farm work or humanitarian relief work. Five hundred were court-martialed and sent to prison; of this number 17 were sentenced to death and 142 to life imprisonment. These severe sentences were later modified, but not until 1933 were the last of those sentenced pardoned by President Roosevelt.

Out of the experiences of World War I emerged the formation of pacifist groups such as the War Resisters League, the Fellowship of Reconciliation, and the American Friends Service Committee. Members of these groups played an active role in intensifying support for world-peace measures, such as disarmament, and the League of Nations. Enlightened Americans became aroused by disclosures such as those in *The Genesis of the World War,* by H. E. Barnes, which showed that both Germany and the Allies desired peace but followed policies of ultimatum which drove their armies toward war. Yinger describes the postwar swing to pacifism.

After the war came the reaction. Preachers by the hundreds renounced their earlier war position; resolutions denouncing war were passed by all the major denominations. Reinhold Niebuhr wrote: "Ev-

[22] J. M. Yinger, *Religion in the Struggle for Power,* Duke University Press, 1946, p. 181.

[23] M. Q. Sibley and P. E. Jacob, *Conscription of Conscience,* Cornell University Press, 1952, p. 14.

ery soldier fighting for his country in simplicity of heart without asking many questions, was superior to those of us who served no better purpose than to increase or perpetuate the moral obfuscation of nations. . . . I am done with this business." Harry Emerson Fosdick declared: "I do not propose to bless war again, or support it, or expect from it any valuable thing." Stephen S. Wise pledged his word to his congregation never again to favor war. Charles Clayton Morrison, editor of the *Christian Century,* has for years been calling upon the churches to renounce war forever. Leavenworth will have to be enlarged for the new apostolic succession, he wrote, in event of another war. The *World Tomorrow,* canvassing 53,000 clergymen, found that (out of 19,372 replies) 54 per cent of the ministers stated it to be their present purpose to sanction no future war. More than ever before, pacifism became the creed of American churches; prosperity and isolationism made it quite acceptable to the layman as the Sermon on the Mount made it acceptable to the religious.[24]

Notwithstanding the deepening shadow of Hitler's Germany over Europe, pacifism continued strong among American church leaders. One of the pacifist strongholds was the *Christian Century,* unofficial spokesman for American Protestantism. Another factor was the reluctance of the American Catholics to side with Russia. An abrupt shift in sentiment resulted when Hitler marched into Poland and the second world-wide conflict broke out. For a second time, the pacifist pronouncements of church leaders washed away in the torrent of war feeling. This time the acceptance of the war was much less idealistic than in World War I. The *Christian Century* editorialized: "We, too, must accept the war. We see no other way at the moment but the bloody way of slaughter and immeasurable sacrifice. Our government has taken a stand. It is *our* government. . . . The nation has chosen the hard way. It is the way of unimaginable cost and of doubtful morality."[25]

This time the core of pacifists who clung to their ideals was larger and stronger than during World War I. The problem of conscientious objectors for a nation at war was a much larger one numerically. The handling of the problem was an improvement over World War I but left much to be desired. The Selective Service law provided for both noncombatant military service, accepted by approximately 25,000 draftees, and "Civilian Public Service" outside of the army, administered jointly by Selective Service and the churches, and accepted by 12,000 draftees.[26] Pro-

[24] Yinger, *op. cit.,* pp. 187–188.
[25] *Christian Century,* December 17, 1941, p. 1565.
[26] Sibley and Jacob, *op. cit.,* p. 124.

vision was not made, as in England, for those whose conscientious objection would not allow acceptance of conscription in any form. Six thousand men, about three-fourths of them Jehovah's Witnesses, were prosecuted for refusing the draft, most of them receiving prison sentences. The objection of Jehovah's Witnesses was that conscription failed to acknowledge their claim for exemption as ministers. Their ministry was one to which they were called by God, a call higher than that of the state. The protest of the remainder is illustrated by the following excerpt from the federal trial of one of them.

Counsel for Richards. Fred's deliberate and voluntary return to the United States from Mexico, when he did not have to do so, for the specific purpose of making a maximum protest against what he considers the greatest of all evils, war and conscription, called to mind the story of the journey and protest of another man in history.

In the year A.D. 404, the custom was to hold gladiatorial fights for public amusement in Rome—A Christian monk, Telemachus, reached the conviction that it was his duty to make an open protest. Leaving Syria, he made the journey all the way to Rome for the specific purpose of protesting against the gladiatorial fights. In the midst of such a fight he ran into the arena, calling upon the Emperor to stop the cruel performance. When his purpose was realized, he was stoned to death before the watching multitude. Losing his life, Telemachus apparently failed to accomplish his purpose. In reality, however, his vicarious sacrifice succeeded, for that gladiatorial fight was the last one ever held in Rome.[27]

The backbone of the Civilian Public Service system was a chain of labor camps in which men were compelled to work without pay, often at tasks which were "busy work." Toward the end of the war, dissatisfaction in these labor camps mounted and strikes occurred. Two hundred and thirty-three men were sent to prison for refusing to work or for leaving the labor camps. One of them, Corbett Bishop, went on hunger strikes for 426 days, during which time he was kept alive in prison hospitals by forced feeding. Most men in Civilian Public Service continued faithfully at their tasks of soil conservation, reforestation, and hospital work. Since World War II the conscription provisions relating to conscientious objectors have been relaxed to permit

[27] *Ibid.,* p. 342. Pacifist aims and methods are described in detail in R. B. Gregg, *The Power of Nonviolence,* Fellowship Publications, 1959. Sources for pacifism in Christian doctrine are given in G. H. C. Macgregor, *The New Testament Basis of Pacifism* and *The Relevance of an Impossible Ideal,* Fellowship Publications, 1960.

draftees to take individual assignments with constructive use of skills at normal rates of compensation.

What of the thinking and activities of churches concerning peace in the post-World War II era? Throughout the war years church leaders were active in building public opinion favorable to some form of world organization. The founding of the United Nations received strong support from religious groups through the Commission to Study the Bases of a Just and Durable Peace of the Federal Council of Churches. The "Six Pillars of Peace" publicized by the Commission are world government, economic coöperation among nations, provision for changing international agreements, freedom for colonial peoples, provision for international military control, and world-wide religious freedom. The statement of these pillars was regarded by the *Christian Century* as watered down compared with the need for forgiveness of opponents and abandonment of nationalistic policies by the United States in favor of full coöperation with peoples of the world. The Synagogue Council of America and the Social Action Department of the National Catholic Welfare Conference have also been active in behalf of world peace. The influence of organized religious groups on public opinion is through their publications and especially through speeches and sermons given by ministers, priests, and rabbis. In this postwar peace interest, religious pacifism has receded in influence, possibly because of the seeming ineffectuality of passive resistance against war in a world overshadowed by intercontinental ballistic missiles with atomic warheads. Currents of pacifism have become channeled into efforts to build a durable world organization. At the same time, individuals such as Milton Mayer refuse to pay taxes which are used in preparation for war, and an occasional scientist declines to work upon atomic bomb or military missile projects. The effect of the peace testimony of these persons is not widespread, but neither is it negligible. The official pronouncements of churches concerning the conflict between East and West tend to be unprovocative and equivocal. Cautious tolerance of the Communist way of life and advocacy of recognition of Communist China are exhibited in a recent declaration by the Fifth World Order Conference called by the National Council of Churches in 1958.[28]

In summary, the pacifist convictions of churches have waxed and waned with the rise and fall of the emotions of nationalism and war. In a world of current tension, the voice of religious

[28] *Christian Century,* December 10, 1958, p. 1426.

pacifism in the United States is far weaker than in England, Germany, or Japan. The philosophy of Gandhi finds its most immediate expression in race relations through the work of Martin Luther King and other religious leaders associated with his point of view. To this phase of religious pacifism we return in a succeeding chapter.

ECONOMIC ORDER

Rise of Capitalism: Max Weber

The rise of the modern industrial order in the past three hundred years is a social phenomenon of immense magnitude. This revolutionary development in man's economic existence poses tough problems of scientific explanation. At first sight the unfolding of improved technology by mechanical inventions presents an appealing explanation for the rise of the present industrial way of life. But the problem remains of explaining why other culture areas besides the West possessing similar inventions did much less with them or did so much later. Capitalism, or the pursuit of economic activity for a profit upon capital invested in land or tools, a system in which the means of production are owned by a few and worked upon by many, is at least several thousand years old. What characterizes industrial capitalism is the extraordinary growth in division of labor and in the amounts of capital invested in machines. The first of these, division of labor, if it is launched with little institutional precedent, requires that human beings be motivated to accept new and often monotonous tasks. The second, investment of capital, requires accumulating large amounts of money instead of spending them in consumption. While higher wages or interest paid on capital provide incentives of self-interest, there is question of whether self-seeking appeal alone accounts for the rapidity with which industrial capitalism grew in cities of western Europe among Protestants and Jews and not in other culture areas to the same extent or with the same rapidity. To leave farm and home is an economic wrench requiring persuasive motivation and is not quickly undertaken purely for self-interest. The capitalist, at least in the early stages of economic development, gained less physical enjoyment from life by saving his capital together with the interest than if he followed the prevailing pattern of using his income for more luxurious consumption, not bothering to deny himself by saving so that others would have a larger income to spend after his death.

The first major analyst of the rise of modern capitalism was Karl Marx, who attributed its rise to the self-interest of those who appropriated and organized the means of production whereby others must work to survive. Except for originality of invention, all culture was considered by him to be a function of two economic determinants, self-interest and technology. Religion was a pawn in economic conflict, being used by capitalists to drug factory workers into insensibly accepting their miserable conditions. By promising "pie in the sky by and by," religion was the opiate of the people. In the classical Marxian view, religion is a pale reflection of powerful economic forces. That economic motives corrupt religion is a general principle which can be shown by numerous data from primitive and modern cultures, some of which are introduced here. But the problem is one of not overstating the case and of recognizing the independent contribution which religion makes to economic life.

A German sociologist of world eminence, Max Weber, placed the issue of religion in economic life in bold relief in his epochal study, *The Protestant Ethic and the Spirit of Capitalism,* first published in 1904–05. In this study he answers the Marxian view of the rise of capitalism. Max Weber argued for the indigenous influence which the Protestant religion imposed upon the rise of modern capitalism. Analyzing the religious ideas of Lutherans, Calvinists, Pietists, Baptists, Quakers, and Methodists, Weber points out how their ideas gave the rise of capitalism a dynamic which self-interest alone did not give it in Catholic or Eastern cultures where economic conditions and technological advances necessary for the development of capitalism were equally favorable. To give full demonstration of the decisive role of Protestantism, Weber undertook comparative studies of Eastern cultures to show that industrial capitalism did not arise where the Protestant ethic was absent.[29] Weber's work and the commentaries upon it illuminate the interaction between religion and economic institutions.

Weber begins his essay on the Protestant ethic by pointing out that capitalist enterprises in European cities are largely in the hands of Protestants rather than Catholics. He gives figures for Baden in 1895 which show that taxable capital per individual is nearly twice as large for Protestants as for Catholics, but four

[29] Max Weber, *The Religion of China,* tr. by H. H. Gerth, Free Press, 1951; *The Religion of India,* tr. by H. H. Gerth and D. Martindale, Free Press, 1958. Also see Reinhard Bendix, *Max Weber: An Intellectual Portrait,* Doubleday, 1960.

times larger for Jews than for Protestants. T. F. Hoult in a current work in the sociology of religion summarizes additional data showing the same relationship between Protestantism and capitalism.[30] He also calls attention to Isidor Thorner's study showing rates of invention in the industrial revolution to have been ten or more times larger in Protestant countries than in Catholic.[31]

Weber's explanation of the connection between Protestantism and capitalism, also accepted by Ernst Troeltsch, is that the spiritual motivation generated during the Reformation impelled men into the acquisition of capital and the acceptance of factory division of labor. With reference to Martin Luther's teaching, Weber notes:

> The monastic life is not only quite devoid of value as a means of justification before God, but he also looks upon its renunciation of the duties of this world as the product of selfishness, withdrawing from temporal obligations. In contrast, labor in a calling appears to him as the outward expression of brotherly love. This he proves by the observation that the division of labor forces every individual to work for others. . . . there remains, more and more strongly emphasized, the statement that the fulfillment of worldly duties is under all circumstances the only way to live acceptably to God. It and it alone is the will of God, and hence every legitimate calling has exactly the same worth in the sight of God.
>
> That this moral justification of worldly activity was one of the most important results of the Reformation, especially of Luther's part in it, is beyond doubt, and may even be considered a platitude.[32]

The impetus given to the rise of capitalism by Luther's idea of work as a calling was moderated by his rejection of accepting interest on capital or accumulating capital beyond personal needs, which Catholics had rejected before him. Although Luther preached ascetic self-denial, it remained for other Protestant reformers to evolve the ideas that the accumulation of wealth was a stewardship entrusted by God for service to others through this wealth and that the obligation of the Christian is to organize the economic life of the community for the glory of God.

> It seems at first a mystery how the undoubted superiority of Calvinism in social organization can be connected with this tendency to tear the individual away from the closed ties with which he is bound to

[30] T. F. Hoult, *The Sociology of Religion,* Dryden, 1958, pp. 256–257.

[31] *Ibid.,* p. 371.

[32] Weber, *The Protestant Ethic and the Spirit of Capitalism,* tr. by Talcott Parsons, Scribner (George Allen & Unwin Ltd., outside U.S.), 1948, p. 81.

this world. But, however strange it may seem, it follows from the peculiar form which the Christian brotherly love was forced to take under the pressure of the inner isolation of the individual through the Calvinistic faith. In the first place it follows dogmatically. The world exists to serve the glorification of God and for that purpose alone. The elected Christian is in the world only to increase this glory of God by fulfilling His commandments to the best of his ability. But God requires social achievement of the Christian because He wills that social life shall be organized according to His commandments, in accordance with that purpose. The social activity of the Christian in the world is solely activity *in majorem gloriam Dei.* This character is hence shared by labour in a calling which serves the mundane life of the community. Even in Luther we found specialized labour in callings justified in terms of brotherly love. But what for him remained an uncertain, purely intellectual suggestion became for the Calvinists a characteristic element in their ethical system. Brotherly love, since it may only be practiced for the glory of God and not in the service of the flesh, is expressed in the first place in the fulfillment of the daily tasks given by the *lex naturae;* and in the process this fulfillment assumes a peculiarly objective and impersonal character, that of service in the interest of the rational organization of our social environment.[33]

It is true that the usefulness of a calling, and thus its favour in the sight of God, is measured primarily in moral terms, and thus in terms of the importance of the goods produced in it for the community. But a further, and, above all, in practice the most important, criterion is found in private profitableness. For if that God, whose hand the Puritan sees in all the occurrences of life, shows one of His elect a chance of profit, he must do it with a purpose. Hence the faithful Christian must follow the call by taking advantage of the opportunity. "If God show you a way in which you may lawfully get more than in another way (without wrong to your soul or to any other), if you refuse this, and choose the less gainful way, you cross one of the ends of your calling, and you refuse to be God's steward, and to accept His gifts and use them for Him when He requireth it: you may labour to be rich for God, though not for the flesh and sin." [Quoted from Richard Baxter]

Wealth is thus bad ethically only insofar as it is a temptation to idleness and sinful enjoyment of life, and its acquisition is bad only when it is with the purpose of later living merrily and without care. But as a performance of duty in a calling it is not only morally permissible, but actually enjoined. The parable of the servant who was rejected because he did not increase the talent which was entrusted to him seemed to say so directly.[34]

When the limitation of consumption is combined with this release of acquisitive activity, the inevitable practical result is obvious: accumulation of capital through ascetic compulsion to save. The restraints

[33] *Ibid.,* pp. 108–109.
[34] *Ibid.,* pp. 162–163.

which were imposed upon the consumption of wealth naturally served to increase it by making possible the productive investment of capital. How strong this influence was is not, unfortunately, susceptible of exact statistical demonstration. In New England the connection is so evident that it did not escape the eye of so discerning a historian as Doyle. But also in Holland, which was really only dominated by strict Calvinism for seven years, the greater simplicity of life in the more seriously religious circles, in combination with great wealth, led to an excessive propensity to accumulation.[35]

We may hence quote here a passage from John Wesley himself which might well serve as a motto for everything which has been said above. For it shows that the leaders of these ascetic movements understood the seemingly paradoxical relationships which we have here analyzed perfectly well, and in the same sense that we have given them. He wrote:

"I fear, wherever riches have increased, the essence of religion has decreased in the same proportion. Therefore I do not see how it is possible, in the nature of things, for any revival of true religion to continue long. For religion must necessarily produce both industry and frugality, and these cannot but produce riches. But as riches increase, so will pride, anger, and love of the world in all its branches. How then is it possible that Methodism, that is, a religion of the heart, though it flourishes now as a green bay tree, should continue in this state? For the Methodists in every place grow diligent and frugal; consequently they increase in goods. Hence they proportionately increase in pride, in anger, in the desire of the flesh, the desire of the eyes, and the pride of life. So, although the form of religion remains, the spirit is swiftly vanishing away. Is there no way to prevent this—this continual decay of pure religion? We ought not to prevent people from being diligent and frugal; *we must exhort all Christians to gain all they can, and to save all they can; that is, in effect, to grow rich."*

There follows the advice that those who gain all they can and save all they can should also give all they can, so that they will grow in grace and lay up a treasure in heaven. It is clear that Wesley here expresses, even in detail, just what we have been trying to point out.

As Wesley here says, the full economic effect of those great religious movements, whose significance for economic development lay above all in their ascetic educative influence, generally came only after the peak of the purely religious enthusiasm was passed. Then the intensity of the search for the Kingdom of God commenced gradually to pass over into sober economic virtue; the religious roots died out slowly, giving way to utilitarian worldliness.[36]

The last paragraph quoted from Weber indicates that the motivation and the acquisition of capital were far from purely

[35] *Ibid.,* pp. 172–173.
[36] *Ibid.,* pp. 175–176.

spiritual, but were a mixture of selfish and spiritual motives. In view of the rampant exploitation and unbridled indulgence in luxury to which the rise of capitalism has led, it may seem grotesque to regard the original spiritual strand of motivation as altruistic. Yet so it appears from Weber's analysis. In a somewhat similar way in the present era, ethical motivation plays a part in the building of power machines to accomplish social reform, power machines which later not infrequently come to be motivated by acquisitiveness and self-indulgence, rather than a concern for the common good. The tendency of wealth to corrupt was noted by Weber in his quotation from John Wesley.

While there are exceptions, such as the life of T. J. Watson, who founded the empire of International Business Machines on religious principles, the Protestant ethic is no longer the spirit of capitalism. There may be a few who see in the administration of corporations an opportunity to be of service to fellow men, or who humbly accept their place on the assembly line as a chance to serve the consumer. But for the most part the religious light has gone out of capitalism. The practices which its system of organization forces upon human beings are too incongruous with religious ideals for people to feel that God has called them to their task in capitalist industry.

> Since asceticism undertook to remodel the world and to work out its ideals in the world, material goods have gained an increasing and finally an inexorable power over the lives of men as at no previous period in history. Today the spirit of religious asceticism—whether finally, who knows?—has escaped from the cage. But victorious capitalism, since it rests on mechanical foundations, needs its support no longer. The rosy blush of its laughing heir, the Enlightenment, seems also to be irretrievably fading, and the idea of duty in one's calling prowls about in our lives like the ghost of dead religious beliefs. Where the fulfillment of the calling cannot directly be related to the highest spiritual and cultural values, or when, on the other hand, it need not be felt simply as economic compulsion, the individual generally abandons the attempt to justify it at all. In the field of its highest development, in the United States, the pursuit of wealth, stripped of its religious and ethical meaning, tends to become associated with purely mundane passions, which often actually give it the character of sport.[37]

Weber's thesis that the Protestant ethic gave initial impetus to modern capitalism has encountered criticism by religionists who deny that religion played a part in the rise of the capitalistic system, by scientists who reject a religious interpretation of his-

[37] *Ibid.,* pp. 181–182.

tory in favor of an economic one, and by others who make constructive qualifications in his statement of the thesis. Among writers in the English-speaking world, R. H. Tawney has been at pains to point out that Protestantism did not merely influence the rise of capitalism, but that capitalism also influenced the growth of Protestantism. This is a qualification which Weber would accept.[38] Tawney conceded that Protestantism influenced the rise of capitalism, but not quite as Weber described it.

> "The capitalist spirit" is as old as history, and was not, as has sometimes been said, the offspring of Puritanism. But it found in certain aspects of later Puritanism a tonic which braced its energies and fortified its already vigorous temper.[39]

> Puritanism had its own standards of social conduct, derived partly from the obvious interests of the commercial classes, partly from its conception of the nature of God and the destiny of man. These standards were in sharp antithesis, both to the considerable surviving elements of feudalism in English society, and to the policy of the authoritarian State, with its ideal of an ordered and graded society, whose different members were to be maintained in their traditional status by the pressure and protection of a paternal monarchy. Sapping the former by its influence and overthrowing the latter by direct attack, Puritanism became a potent force in preparing the way for the commercial civilization which finally triumphed at the Revolution.[40]

Tawney's thesis is that capitalism, during its rise in the industrial revolution, continuously interacted with and modified religion. Calvin's ideas gained popularity because they were congenial to the rising capitalist class.

> Such teaching, whatever its theological merits or defects, was admirably designed to liberate economic energies, and to weld into a disciplined social force the rising *bourgeoisie,* conscious of the contrast between its own standards and those of a laxer world, proud of its vocation as the standard-bearer of the economic virtues, and determined to vindicate an open road for its own way of life by the use of every weapon, including political revolution and war, because the issue which was at stake was not merely convenience or self-interest, but the will of God. Calvinism stood, in short, not only for a new doctrine of theol-

[38] Max Weber, "The Protestant Sects and the Spirit of Capitalism," *From Max Weber: Essays in Sociology,* tr. and ed. by H. H. Gerth and C. W. Mills, Oxford University Press, 1958, pp. 302–322.

[39] From *Religion and the Rise of Capitalism* by R. H. Tawney, copyright 1926, by Harcourt, Brace; renewed 1953, by R. H. Tawney. Used by permission of Harcourt, Brace and John Murray Ltd. Also see R. Niebuhr, *The Social Sources of Denominationalism,* Holt, 1929.

[40] Tawney, *op. cit.,* pp. 192–193.

ogy and ecclesiastical government, but for a new scale of moral values and a new ideal of social conduct. . . .

It is not wholly fanciful to say that, on a narrower stage but with not less formidable weapons, Calvin did for the *bourgeoisie* of the 16th century what Marx did for the proletariat of the 19th, or that the doctrine of predestination satisfied the same hunger for an assurance that the forces for the universe are on the side of the elect as was to be assuaged in a different age by the theory of historical materialism. He set their virtues at their best in sharp antithesis with the vices of the established order at its worst, taught them to feel that they were a chosen people, made them conscious of their great destiny in the Providential plan and resolute to realize it.[41]

Not until Protestantism had been substantially corrupted by economic motivations was the full impetus of religion given to capitalist enterprise.

What in Calvin had been a qualified concession to practical exigencies appeared in some of his later followers as a frank idealization of the life of the traitor, as the service of God and the training-ground of the soul. Discarding the suspicion of economic motives, which had been as characteristic of the reformers as of medieval theologians, Puritanism in its later phases added a halo of ethical sanctification to the appeal of economic expediency, and offered a moral creed, in which the duties of religion and the calls of business ended their long estrangement in an unanticipated reconciliation. Its spokesmen pointed out, it is true, the peril to the soul involved in a single-minded concentration on economic interests. The enemy, however, was not riches, but the bad habits sometimes associated with them, and its warnings against an excessive preoccupation with the pursuit of gain wore more and more the air of after-thoughts, appended to teaching the main tendency and emphasis of which were little affected by these incidental qualifications. It insisted, in short, that moneymaking, if not free from spiritual dangers, was not a danger and nothing else, but that it could be, and ought to be, carried on for the greater glory of God.[42]

As the development of capitalism proceeded, religion came to sanction even its obvious abuses.

In a famous passage of the *Communist Manifesto,* Marx observes that "the *bourgeoisie,* wherever it got the upper hand, put an end to all feudal, patriarchal, idyllic relations, pitilessly tore asunder the motley feudal ties that bound man to his 'natural superiors,' and left remaining no other bond between man and man than naked self-interest and callous cash payment." An interesting illustration of his thesis might be found in the discussions of the economics of employment by English

[41] *Ibid.,* pp. 98–99.
[42] *Ibid.,* p. 199.

writers of the period between 1660 and 1760. Their characteristic was an attitude towards the new industrial proletariat noticeably harsher than that general in the first half of the 17th century, and which has no modern parallel except in the behavior of the less reputable of white colonists towards colored labor. The denunciations of the "luxury, pride and sloth" of the English wage-earners of the 17th and 18th centuries are, indeed, almost exactly identical with those directed against African natives today. It is complained that, compared with the Dutch, they are self-indulgent and idle; that they want no more than a bare subsistence, and will cease work the moment they obtain it; that, the higher their wages, the more—"so licentious are they"—they spend upon drink; that high prices, therefore, are not a misfortune, but a blessing, since they compel the wage-earner to be more industrious; and that high wages are not a blessing, but a misfortune, since they merely conduce to "weekly debauches."

When such doctrines were general, it was natural that the rigors of economic exploitation should be preached as a public duty, and, with a few exceptions, the writers of the period differed only as to the methods by which severity could most advantageously be organized. Pollexfen and Walter Harris thought that salvation might be found by reducing the number of days kept as holidays. Bishop Berkeley, with the conditions of Ireland before his eyes, suggested that "sturdy beggars should . . . be seized and made slaves to the public for a certain term of years." Thomas Alcock, who was shocked at the workman's taste for snuff, tea and ribbons, proposed the revival of sumptuary legislation. The writers who advanced schemes for reformed workhouses, which should be places at once of punishment and of training, were innumerable. All were agreed that, on moral no less than on economic grounds, it was vital that wages should be reduced. The doctrine afterwards expressed by Arthur Young, when he wrote, "Everyone but an idiot knows that the lower classes must be kept poor, or they will never be industrious," was the tritest commonplace of Restoration economists. It was not argued; it was accepted as self-evident.[43]

Tawney's modifications do not appear to vitiate the basic thesis that indigenous religious development encouraged the rise of modern capitalism, although he obviously takes a much more reduced view of the role of these developments than do Weber and Troeltsch. However, some scholars following Tawney's work have narrowed his views to exclude any independent role of religion in the rise of modern capitalism in a way which the quotations given here show that he did not intend. R. M. MacIver is quoted by Hoult.

But it might easily be claimed that the rise of the Protestant ethic itself, with its stirring individualism, its "worldly asceticism," and

[43] *Ibid.*, pp. 223–224.

its doctrine of Stewardship, was the expression in the religious sphere of a pervasive change of social attitudes corresponding to and causally interdependent with the changing socio-economic order. Unless this claim can be refuted—and I do not see how a claim of this sort admits of definite refutation—we cannot establish the fundamental role in the process of social change attributed by Weber to the Protestant sects.[44]

Hoult goes on to conclude:

Weber's critics are, in one sense, advancing a "political-economic interpretation of the Reformation." They tend to explain the latter in terms of the former. The present writer feels that this view is probably the most valid. Weber's insights have been tremendously significant and his work has certainly done a lot to correct the view, often accepted unthinkingly by social scientists, that religion has no really significant impact on complex human groups. But at the same time it must be admitted that in a complex culture religion is only one of many aspects of life. It would be unrealistic to assert that under such conditions religion originates more than it accepts.[45]

This view entertains afresh the Marxian thesis that religion is a passive function of economic life. While religious ideas are often used for propaganda purposes to facilitate economic exploitation of the underprivileged or to justify the status quo, it does not seem plausible that these ideas would be effective unless they appeal to indigenous religious sentiments. Nor does it seem plausible that the tremendous religious enthusiasm generated during the Protestant Reformation could merely have been an economic by-product.

Leaning toward Tawney rather than Weber is J. M. Yinger, who has given an incisive analysis of the controversy concerning the relative roles of religious and economic developments in the rise of modern capitalism. In *Religion in the Struggle for Power,* Yinger asks the question of how the religious dynamic of Protestantism originated and the question of why some of the elements and not others survived from the teachings of Luther and Calvin. These penetrating and perplexing questions were only partly answered by Weber, with scattered references to the role of prophecy and charismatic leadership and to the dependence of religious culture upon social conditions. Lacking good answers, the student is led to an economic interpretation of the Protestant Reformation, that the Reformation resulted from economic and political causes primarily.

Somewhat like Hegel's view of the independent role of ideas

[44] Hoult, *op. cit.,* pp. 258–259.
[45] *Ibid.,* p. 259.

in history, the view of men such as Jung and, to some extent, Toynbee is that the Reformation resulted because deep-seated psychic forces in the unconscious, which had been ignored or repressed, ultimately gained overt expression. Their emergence takes place according to principles of the development of religious culture described in Chapters 12 and 13. They appear when existing religious patterns of belief and behavior no longer fulfill man's religious needs for personality integration, social control, and above all for achievement of worth and meaning in his life. The tracing of the spiritual genesis of the Protestant Reformation is a vast task of scholarship lying beyond our present scope. But it may be pointed out that numerous scholars, even Catholic ones, are agreed that the times preceding the Protestant Reformation were ones of religious impoverishment and corruption. Out of such cultural soil, a fresh cycle of religious rebirth takes place.

The views of Jung and Weber receive support from the inability of economic determinists to account for why the Protestant Reformation or industrial capitalism appeared in Western Europe. The contention of Weber that industrial capitalism arose most readily where religious conditions were congenial seems the only available hypothesis to account for the uniqueness of its rise. In turn, the appearance of the Protestant ethic points to prior processes of religious evolution. At the same time, it seems apparent that industrial capitalism of the modern variety would have arisen eventually through the operation of economic motives, although it could not have arisen anywhere until the sequence of mechanical inventions upon which it depended for its factory system and efficient transportation had been unearthed by the ingenuity of human beings. The development of these inventions is intertwined with financial resources from overseas discoveries of wealth, with the rise of modern science, and with a breaking of the authority imposed by Catholic religious culture during the Middle Ages.

Contemporary Capitalism

As the work of Tawney and others indicates, the religious impetus given capitalism eventually became a sanction for its shortcomings. To examine these shortcomings and the involvement of religion in them does not lessen the importance of the positive gains in higher standard of living nor the industrial expansion accomplished by the capitalistic economy. But our thesis is that a needed function of religion is to improve conditions of life, not to adulate present accomplishments, an adulation which dulls ethical sensibilities and leads to social stagnation. If there are ways of improving the level of living still further, of expanding industrial facilities for meeting human needs, of creating a social order with fuller justice and mutuality for all persons, of enabling people to work with rather than against each other, and of generating a more spiritual culture, then the function of religion in this regard merits close examination. Is religion causing altruism to be expressed in rebuilding the social order? If it is not doing this, why not?

The record of the churches is readily charted against the background of economic changes which have taken place during the past hundred years. One of the earliest means at hand which workers found for matching the economic power of employers over their lives was trade-union organization. By this instrument, now a far-reaching component of the contemporary economy, workers bargain collectively so that their power more nearly matches that of employers. They may be able to get as fair conditions as is the employer. Trade-union organization made a few minor starts during the nineteenth century, but not until the American Federation of Labor with its practical "business" principles displaced the visionary "uplift" ideas of the Knights of Labor in the 1880's did organized labor become a real force in American life. How did the churches view the struggling bands of workers trying to gain a foothold in the economic system? C. H. Hopkins, J. M. Yinger, H. F. May, and R. M. Miller have reviewed the part played by Protestant churches in industrial America.[46] During the nineteenth century churches generally shared the attitude of the public that the rising trade unions were enemies of society. Use of troops was advocated from the pulpit to smash them. Workers were encouraged to be content with their wages and to let God take care of their salvation. Organized groups in the churches expressed concern over labor problems but the pronouncements which they made were ineffectual generalities about social justice, not support of organized labor.

Gradually, as the labor movement became a reality and as economic evils multiplied more rapidly than they could be solved

[46] C. H. Hopkins, *The Rise of the Social Gospel in American Protestantism, 1865–1915,* Yale University Press, 1940; J. M. Yinger, *Religion in the Struggle for Power,* Duke University Press, 1946; H. F. May, *Protestant Churches and Industrial America,* Harper, 1949; R. M. Miller, *American Protestantism and Social Issues, 1919–1939,* University of North Carolina Press, 1958.

by improved wages or by piecemeal legislation curbing factory accidents and sweatshops for women and children, a few voices for economic reform were heard in the churches, principally through book writers such as Josiah Strong and C. M. Sheldon. What was called the "social gospel" crystallized around the figure of the most influential of these writers, Walter Rauschenbusch. When he published his first work, *Christianity and the Social Crisis,* in 1907, he left the country for a year while the storm he feared had time to blow over. He miscalculated the degree to which he spoke to a slumbering movement in Protestantism. His writings came to receive wide acclaim and provided the inspiration for different denominations to initiate social-action departments. His basic theme was that one cannot be a Christian at peace with God while ignoring the poverty and demoralization of human beings caused by an unjust economic order. Jesus' Sermon on the Mount, taken literally, forbade passive acceptance of these conditions. The coming of the Kingdom of God demanded reformation of the economic order.

At no time until the Great Depression of the 1930's did more than a vocal minority of Protestant clergy align itself with principles of the social gospel. In an advisory capacity, the Federal Council of Churches, now the National Council of Churches, adopted economic platforms commencing with its founding in 1908. That year it adopted almost verbatim the Methodist social creed formulated the year prior, which read:

The Methodist Episcopal church stands:

For equal rights, and complete justice for all men in all stations of life.

For the principle of conciliation and arbitration in industrial dissensions.

For the protection of the worker from dangerous machinery, occupational diseases, injuries, and mortality.

For the abolition of child labor.

For such regulation of the condition of labor for women as shall safeguard the physical and moral health of the community.

For the suppression of the "sweating system."

For the gradual and reasonable reduction of the hours of labor to the lowest practical point, with work for all; and for that degree of leisure for all which is the condition of the highest human life.

For a release from employment one day in seven.

For a living wage in every industry.

For the highest wage that each industry can afford, and for the most equitable division of the products of industry that can ultimately be devised.

For the recognition of the Golden Rule and the mind of Christ as the supreme law of society and the sure remedy for all social ills.[47]

But the record of pronouncements by the Federal Council of Churches shows that support for remedial legislation in labor relations and social insurance materialized scarcely before the passage of such laws by legislators. Not until the 1930's were resolutions in support of social insurance adopted. However, a study by M. L. Trott and R. W. Sanderson during this time showed ministers of Baltimore to be somewhat ahead of their congregations in social and economic thinking.[48] In 1954, 46 years after its founding as the Federal Council of Churches, the National Council of Churches issued a pronouncement on economic problems which included the following principles.

All the resources of the earth—such as land and water and mineral deposits, which under the laws of man become private or public property—are gifts of God, and every form of ownership or use of such property should be kept under such scrutiny that it may not distort the purpose of God's creation. God is the only absolute owner. Every Christian particularly should look upon all of his possessions, as well as his talents, as a trustee, and should use them in the light of his understanding of God's purpose for him. "The earth is the Lord's, and the fullness thereof.". . .

Men were made to love one another, and to live as members of a community that transcends all barriers of race or nation or class. All economic institutions and practices that tend to divide men because they enhance false pride, covetousness, and bitterness, or encourage laziness or the selfish use of power, stand under Christian moral judgment. The Church should seek to influence the development of economic life in such a way that economic institutions, policies, and practices are favorable to right relations between people. "You shall love your neighbor as yourself.". . .

In some situations Christians have had the misconception that the one sure road to economic justice is the socialization of all the major means of production. During periods of exploitation of large classes of the population, and also in times of depression and unemployment, it was understandable that some Christians and others concerned about the welfare of the victims of the situation should regard every move toward increasing social control as an advance. Today we have enough knowledge of what happens under a thoroughgoing collectivism to realize that uncritical recourse to the state to remedy every evil creates its own evils. It may easily become a threat to freedom as well as to ef-

47 Yinger, *op. cit.*, pp. 140–141.

48 M. L. Trott and R. W. Sanderson, *What Church People Think About Social and Economic Issues,* Association Press, 1938, p. 42, cited in Yinger, *op. cit.*, p. 157.

ficiency. The union of political and economic power is a dangerous road, whether it leads toward complete state control of economic life or toward control of the state by private centers of economic power. A wide distribution of centers of power and decision is important to the preservation of democratic freedom. . . .

In recent generations there have been great movements of protest against unjust inherited privileges and institutional relationships. Christians may properly welcome the rise of such protests, as distinct from some of the methods used or the outcomes of many such movements. Sometimes movements of social protest have rejected the Church and the Christian faith and have developed ideologies, often based on illusory hopes, that have become for millions of people inadequate substitutes for religion. The Christian Church should do all that it can to disclose the illusions in these ideologies and to confront the world with the Gospel in its fullness; but at the same time it should in humility not forget that it has often obscured the radical ethical demands of the Gospel and that it shares responsibility for the resulting spiritual confusion.[49]

In 1946 after carefully reviewing economic policies of the Protestant churches Yinger wrote:

Thus Protestantism adjusted to the contemporary world. A few leaders actively challenged the basic social arrangements; and though they had very little direct influence, they goaded the main church bodies into keeping fairly well abreast of social changes, at least in their official pronouncements. There seems to be very little evidence for an interpretation of the "social gospel" as a product simply of the inherently radical qualities of the Christian doctrine. It seems, rather, to be, at least on the part of the larger religious groups, a response to a changed environment in which new material powers and new ideologies were challenging the power of the churches.[50]

The Roman Catholic Church represents more of a working-class population than do the Protestant churches. Dating back to the papal encyclical on labor in 1891, the Catholic Church has criticized abuses in capitalism well in advance of Protestant churches, yet has consistently rejected socialistic ideas. The most progressive record is shown by Jews, who, starting in 1885 through a conference of rabbis in Pittsburgh, called for an economic order founded upon justice. The circumstance that Jews reside almost entirely in cities, where they experienced industrial society at first hand, is a factor in their pronouncements.

[49] *Christian Principles and Assumptions for Economic Life,* Statement adopted by the General Board of the National Council of the Churches of Christ in the U.S.A., September 15, 1954.

[50] Yinger, *op. cit.,* p. 142.

Although ahead of Protestants, Catholic and Jewish religious leaders have not pioneered in an organized way for a new social order. On the other hand, stringent criticism is mounting, as reflected in organized opposition of church leaders to commercialized culture. In a recent article in *Fortune* magazine, Rabbi Finkelstein excoriates the demoralization of the business community by the quest for larger profits.[51]

The most exhaustive study in America of the relationship between economic interests and churches is that made by Liston Pope.[52] In *Millhands and Preachers* he describes the roles played by mill owners and churches in the Loray textile strike of 1929 in Gastonia, North Carolina, led by a Communist-sponsored union. Although the objectives of the strike were better wages and abolition of sweatshop conditions, the town soon became polarized along the lines of capitalism and Marxism. What Pope showed to be significant about the role of the churches in Gastonia was not their opposition to Marxism, which they did not understand anyway, but the degree of control which the mill owners exercised over the churches and the church coöperation in suppression of the civil liberties of the strikers, many if not most of whom were not Communists.

At the outset of the strike a new departure appeared imminent: when a preacher mounted a box at one of the first strike meetings and implored the strikers to do nothing hasty or violent, he was forcibly pulled down and ejected—a novel method of treatment for a preacher in the reverent South. But the strikers held their own religious service, led by a lay preacher who had joined them, on the first Sunday after the strike began. They brought their religious convictions with them into the strike and pronounced it right in the eyes of God. Many of the lay strike speeches were religious in tone, and "Praise the Lord!" was a characteristic exclamation of approval from workers at strike meetings. Though the strikers learned to sing "Solidarity Forever," they continued also to use spirituals and hymns at strike meetings.[53]

Evidence that practically all the ministers were opposed to the strike in personal views is so abundant and unchallenged as to represent, beyond question, the real fact of the case. Representatives of all the conflicting forces in the struggle agree on this one point. A sample of ministerial reaction was observed by Dr. James Myers, industrial secretary of the Federal Council of Churches, who attended a meeting of the Gastonia Ministers' Association on April 11, at which about a dozen ministers were present. Dr. Myers asked for information on the strike situa-

[51] Louis Finkelstein, "The Businessman's Moral Failure," *Fortune,* September, 1958, pp. 116–117, 194.

[52] L. Pope, *Millhands and Preachers,* Yale University Press, 1942.

[53] *Ibid.,* pp. 262–263.

tion. He writes as follows of the response: "The attitudes revealed were defensive, cold, unresponsive to a degree I have never met before in a group of ministers. Evidently they had not yet thought of any connection between the mind of Christ and low wages or night work for women or child labor. A number of mill village ministers were present. They especially felt called on to defend the system."[54]

The failure of the ministers to condemn mob terrorism and police brutality against the strikers is more significant of their reaction than the positive steps they themselves took against the Communists. Several ministers recall pleasantly stories such as the one of a Baptist minister who was accused, jokingly, of leading a tar party during the strike; he replied that he did not lead it but had said "Amen."[55]

Concerning the type of control over the churches which mill owners imposed, Pope points out that the control was more that of a major culture over a minority culture than that of direct administrative control.

The philanthropic mood has not prevented judicious discrimination by mill owners between the type of church to be supported and the type to be ignored. Direct subsidies have been allocated by the particular mill owner, almost without exception, to the churches attended by his own workers, whether or not these churches needed his help more than others in the vicinity.[56]

At its meeting in October, 1929, the Western North Carolina Annual Conference of the Methodist Episcopal Church, South, openly acknowledged the system of mill supplements to some of its churches, and urged the extension of the system, recommending that manufacturers "should bear at least one-half the burden of maintaining religious worship in mill communities." The chairman of the committee which brought this recommendation to the conference was the presiding elder of Methodist churches in the Gastonia district, and another member of the committee became the new presiding elder of that district for the following year. When reminded a decade later of this overt appeal to mill owners for heavier subsidies, the chairman said: "Amen! I've always believed that mill churches serve the mill as much as they serve the folks; let the mill pay for the service. Churches help the mills to have a steadier and more intelligent supply of labor. Let the mills give more than they do, and let it all be perfectly above board. It's worth something to the mills to have churches work among their people. Why Mr.—— [one of the largest textile manufacturers in North Carolina], a Jew, helps the preachers, and the first thing he does when a strike threatens is to call them up—and the strikers can't win with the preachers against them so let Mr.—— pay."

[54] *Ibid.*, p. 279.
[55] *Ibid.*, p. 283.
[56] *Ibid.*, p. 147.

The Methodist appeal drew vigorous criticism from various sources. A correspondent wrote to the Raleigh *News and Observer:* "Pastors are very human. . . . they cannot bite the hand that feeds them. . . . In times of stress the employers and the employed clash. . . . What is a subsidized pastor and a subsidized church to do? . . . As a matter of fact they can do nothing. . . . Better have no church at all than to have one that is subsidized. . . ."[57]

The reasons for the dilatory attitude of churches toward problems of the economic system which their ethics originally helped to build are not difficult to find.

1. A church is an integral part of culture. If it is to retain its functional ties, it cannot be much in the vanguard. Its spokesmen must reflect prevailing ideas and practices if they are to build improvements upon these ideas.

2. Religion functions within a context of needs experienced by persons living under the existing order. As long as their stake is in the existing order, they are unwilling to tolerate preaching against it. Since Protestantism has been more of an upper-class and middle-class phenomenon in American history, sermons against higher profits or in favor of sharing the wealth or aiding organized labor are against the economic interests of persons in these classes.

3. Professional ministers are dependent upon others for their financing. As long as church adherents esteem fine buildings, large and prosperous congregations, and polished ministers to soothe, rather than upset, their parishioners, they cannot expect their religious leaders to lead the way against the established order which pays for these things. A study by Jerome Davis of American Protestant Churches shows that 55 percent of the board members are proprietors, managers, or professional persons, with merchants most numerous on church boards in towns over 5000 population and bankers most often elected chairmen in proportion to their numbers.[58] Yinger contends that advocacy of the social gospel did not occur until the church was faced with loss of members with whom excessive conservatism is unpopular.

This phase of the development of "social Christianity" was an about-face for a great many churchmen and churches. For the most part it represents, not the triumph of radical Christian doctrine forcing society to justice, but the emergence of a new power to which the churches had to adjust—as they adjusted to the *bourgeoisie* in the

[57] *Ibid.,* pp. 149–150.

[58] J. Davis, "A Study of Protestant Church Boards of Control," *American Journal of Sociology,* November, 1932, pp. 418–431.

17th century—if they were not to lose what influence they yet maintained over a large group of people.[59]

Evidence for Yinger's thesis is found in the ebb and flow of the advocacy of economic reform with alternation of depression and prosperity. A peak of popularity of socialism occurred in the 1930's when 31 percent of ministers who replied to a poll conducted by *The World Tomorrow* voted for "socialism," and 57 percent for "drastically reformed capitalism."[60] These opinions disappeared with the return of prosperity and the coming of World War II.

4. Operators of the economic order not infrequently look to churches for aid in maintaining the present system against those who seek to disturb it. Through their financial control of churches these operators curb progressive pronouncements and require propagation of conservative ideas.

5. In its motivation, religion expresses an equilibrium between altruistic and egoistic drives. During the past several hundred years, as Sorokin and Toynbee have pointed out, religion, together with the rest of Western culture, has been in a decline. If the altruistic drive is weak or lacking, owing to enfeebled religion, it is unrealistic to expect religion to crusade for the remaking of economic life. Not until religion undergoes deep regeneration of its own and the pendulum of religious progress swings upward again, can religion be expected to become revolutionary in seeking a new way of life. That there have been prophetic voices such as those of Norman Thomas and Harry Emerson Fosdick, who have advocated fundamental reconstruction of the economic order, is a contrasting sign of the times.

6. Finally, the question may be asked: Is it the function of the church to formulate specific pronouncements about economic problems? Is it not sufficient for religion to foster altruistic motivation and to encourage people to make an effort to think and to follow their own conscience in the correction of social evils? For the church to set itself up as an economic authority is to invite more schisms among adherents who do not agree. It is argued by church spokesmen: let active leadership in economic reform movements come from outside of church organization. Let the church stay out of politics and "let the church be the church" in its task of ministering to spiritual needs. Whether one agrees fully with this point of view, it is at least understandable that for

[59] Yinger, *op. cit.,* p. 138.
[60] H. Hart, "Religion," *American Journal of Sociology,* May, 1942, p. 895.

the church to be too much ahead of its constituents in economic pronouncements may be disruptive within church ranks.

The indirect connection between churches and economic changes attributable to altruistic motivation should not be overlooked. Sherwood Eddy, Harry Emerson Fosdick, John Haynes Holmes, and Kirby Page are among religious leaders whose altruism has been directed into working for socialism. In America, the Socialist leader Norman Thomas was previously a Presbyterian minister. In Russia, Stalin studied four years for the priesthood in a theological seminary before being expelled for political activities. A long list of lesser Socialist and Communist leaders and masses of followers are spiritual offspring of churches and synagogues. While they have often reacted against the economic conservatism of church organizations, they express in their lives altruistic motivation fostered by religious development. Even if churches do not succeed in teaching constructive expression of altruistic motivation, their role in kindling the necessary dynamic for social movements is a basic one. Finally, the altruistic teachings of churches soften to some degree the economic antagonism of people towards each other. Any economic system functions more equitably when the effort is made to practice kindliness in human relationships. This is a contribution of churches to capitalist life.

Philanthropy

The most direct way in which the altruism of church members can be expressed is by means of giving to charitable projects through their churches. In 1957 this amounted to $12.88 per member in Protestant and Eastern Orthodox churches. Roman Catholic churches do not report their finances to the National Council of Churches. Included in the figure for benevolences are amounts for home and foreign missions, but these increasingly take the character of educational and social service projects instead of preaching to the unconverted. The amount contributed to the churches referred to for all purposes, including administration and maintenance was $63.27 per person in 1957.[61]

While figures for Catholic giving are not published, it seems likely that organized methods of collection result in larger per member giving, considering church operation and benevolences, than per member giving by Protestants. Parochial schools place a heavy financial burden upon Catholics. But Catholic charities

[61] *Yearbook of American Churches,* National Council of the Churches of Christ in the U.S.A., 1960, p. 275.

are quite extensive in the amount and quality of services which they provide. The largest giving to benevolences among the members of any large religious group apparently occurs among Jews. Their contributions to aid their own people overseas for a period of years following World War II approximated $50 per capita, and they also give generously to non-Jewish projects. The words *Jewish philanthropist* have become one word in American history because of the many libraries and hospitals founded by Jewish donors. This giving is part of the Jewish belief that gentiles are to be turned to God, not through missionary activity, but through example.

The history of social-service organizations in the United States discloses that these have generally been started under religious auspices. In the preindustrial era, charity was primarily a preoccupation of religious bodies. The Salvation Army is a well-recognized religious body whose work is to aid the destitute, the downhearted, the sick, and the alcoholic, and through this work bring the dispossessed to Christ.[62] Since the depression of the 1930's it has become plain that privately financed organizations are incapable of assuming the public burdens of relief to unemployed or destitute persons, especially during economic crises when the need is great and the funds low. The traditional mutual-aid pattern whereby religious groups cared for the sick and aged has largely given way to governmentally organized and financed social security. In 1957 private philanthropy in all forms amounted to $1.8 billion, while $4.6 billion was paid by taxes for public assistance and public welfare. These figures are only two percent of the total personal income of $305 billion. Amounts spent on assistance abroad by the U.S. government have averaged $5 billion a year in recent years. Americans are philanthropically inclined, but not deeply so, and the proportion of the national income contributed to philanthropy through church giving has been diminishing.

While accurate statistics are not available, there is evidence that church people in recent decades increasingly give financial support to social-action organizations which seek to end causes of personal or economic distress, rather than to alleviate them through philanthropy distributed among victims. Among the organizations which have substantial support from funds contributed by church members are organizations working for world peace, organizations seeking to improve Negro-white relationships, and organizations seeking to improve or to change

[62] H. A. Wisbey, *Soldiers Without Swords,* Macmillan, 1955.

the present economic and political system. Two important groups found among church memberships, in some ways as a church within a church, are pacifists and Communists. Both of these groups also are organized in agencies outside of the churches. While pacifists, whose ideas and practices were described earlier in this chapter, are basically individualistic and might be said to pursue almost as many different programs as there are pacifists, Communists through the four decades of their existence in the United States have functioned as a tightly organized and highly disciplined force in American life.

Religion and Communism

From the time of Marx's declaration that religion is the opiate of the people, the Communist movement has generally been regarded as antireligious or at least unreligious. On the other hand, the persecution of Christians in Russia appears to have declined in recent years and the pronouncements against religion have softened. One factor in the changing policy has been the cessation of opposition by the churches to Communism. Another factor has been the discovery that religion was important in building morale during the Nazi invasion of Russia in World War II, a struggle in which a staggering price in human life was paid by Russians for victory. It is possible that Russian leaders are discovering that Christianity fosters altruistic ideals in Communism.

The entire topic of Communism is so much charged with partisan emotion that it is extremely difficult in America to view the topic with any degree of objectivity. A scholar who takes his pen in hand and seeks to sketch the role of Communism in American life is almost certain to be criticized by those who feel he is "soft" or "apologetic" on the subject of Communism. A casual survey of contemporary textbooks in social science discloses a shrinking of authors away from a topic which they feel they would rather not deal with at all, if they cannot do so with objectivity and frankness. It is easy to rationalize that the number of Communists in America, estimated by the Federal Bureau of Investigation in 1957 to be around eight thousand, is small and that therefore the topic is undeserving of attention, especially in a study of religion in which the connection with Communism is not at once apparent. It is vital, therefore, to keep in mind why the topic cannot be by-passed, however unpopular is discussion of it. These reasons appear as our examination of the nature of Communism unfolds. In the past few years the nature of Communism in America has been subjected to thorough and repeated study by scholars such as Gabriel Almond, Morris L. Ernst, David Loth, Ralph Lord Roy, Irving Howe, Lewis Coser, Max Kampelman, and R. W. Iversen.[63] Books by former Communist writers such as Howard Fast and John Gates also provide useful documentary material.[64] The account given here of Communism in America is drawn from these accounts by Communists and non-Communists. We begin by reviewing the religious aspects.

1. Communism in America has demonstrated a dynamic tenacity which is not to be underestimated. The movement which has gained the enthusiastic support of large masses of human beings abroad, as well as much opposition, inevitably has a binary component within the frontiers of the United States, for similar reasons. This component is less inspired from Moscow than it is generated by the response of human beings in America to the economic system they live under and dislike. There are John Browns in every generation who are a militant vanguard of social change. Over half a million Americans have been members of the Communist party since its inception forty years ago, in 1919. Although the movement has resembled more of a procession than a permanent membership, it has perennial appeal for new ranks of followers. The splintering in 1957 which deeply cut back the membership left in control the faction apparently allied with the Communist party in Russia. Following the 1957 crisis, Howe and Coser wrote: "American Communism as an organized movement had reached the end of the road. The political fate of the Gates group—expulsion, quitting the C.P. or, most likely, a slow disintegration—might be of interest to those few people still concerned with Communist politics, but not a matter of public import. For all intents and purposes, as these lines are being written in late 1957, the American Communist party is dead."[65]

Since its beginning the Communist party has repeatedly undergone splits and defections. It has often been heralded as "dead" but has always rebounded with new vitality. As a whirlwind sheds its rain and moves on, the Communist vortex con-

[63] Gabriel Almond, *The Appeals of Communism,* Princeton University Press, 1954; M. L. Ernst and David Loth, *Report on the American Communist,* Holt, 1952; R. L. Roy, *Apostles of Discord,* Beacon, 1953; Irving Howe and Lewis Coser, *The American Communist Party,* Beacon, 1957; Max Kampelman, *The Communist Party vs. the C.I.O.,* Praeger, 1957; R. W. Iversen, *The Communists and the Schools,* Harcourt, Brace, 1959.

[64] Howard Fast, *The Naked God,* Praeger, 1957; John Gates, *The Story of an American Communist,* Nelson, 1958.

[65] Howe and Coser, *op. cit.,* p. 498.

tinues to draw more people into its activities for a greater or shorter time. The *New York Times*'s expert on Communist affairs, Harry Schwartz, writes: "There is still public controversy, for example, as to whether what remains of that party is an impotent sect having no importance or is a more dangerous and subtle threat to the republic than ever before."[66] The same forces of discontent which sustained the movement for four decades are operating in contemporary society with unabated, if not increased, intensity. That no one starves in America is beside the point. Inequality in the distribution of the goods and finer things of life rankles just as deeply in the feelings of people whether their expected length of life is 27 or 87. Moreover, "man does not live by bread alone" but seeks to identify himself with a larger whole which has meaning and purpose for him. To say these things makes more intelligible a movement which is much misunderstood if it is thought of purely in terms of recruits from the ranks of those who are out of work. The question is less that of whether one has work to perform than it is a question of whether that work has social significance and is compensated by suitable psychic as well as monetary rewards. Nor should the motivation generated by the heavy storm clouds of war be overlooked. The vistas of the promised land look all the more glowing when projected against the background of a dark and threatening sky.

That Communists are peculiar people who do not exist because they cannot be seen or that they are typically foreign agents or military spies or saboteurs is an illusion. One notes that eminently respected people such as an editor of *Time* and a high official in the State Department have been active in behalf of Communism. Our thinking concerning Communists in America shifts into a more realistic plane of reference if they are thought of as a kind of religious denomination, not readily distinguishable from other Americans at work and play unless they choose to share their ideas. This they no longer do in a public way. The historical prototype of the Communist party is found in the secret religious and political orders of the Middle Ages which sought to change the existing religion or government. Such movements endure underground for generations owing to their virile core of altruistic motivation and their implacable rejection of evils in the existing order. The Communist party in the United States is an organization less for the "down-and-outer"

[66] Harry Schwartz, "The Party's Public Face," *New York Times Book Review*, June 22, 1958, p. 6.

than the "up-and-outer" in economic life who is denied a climb above a second-rate managerial or engineering post. The Communist party is the alter ego of Madison Avenue, New York, having much the same lack of honesty in the pursuit of its own power objectives.

2. Communism is a social movement which has a substantial strand of altruistic motivation generated by religious institutions. It is a child of these institutions, even if an unacknowledged and unwanted one. In his study of 221 former Communists, Almond found that of the 150 reporting, for 63 percent their parents were "pious" or "observant" toward religion. He concludes, "These findings may suggest that the popular stereotype to the effect that Communists are recruited from irreligious homes is on the whole incorrect. If these data reflect the general pattern, it would appear that more often than not Communists grew up in settings in which religious tradition was observed."[67] Howard Fast, a sharp critic of Communism, writes from personal experience:

> We who in our youth and hope and pride had pledged ourselves, our lives and passions, to justice and brotherhood made no wedding with wickedness. Intimately, I know only the Communist Party of the United States; yet of this tiny organization I can say, honestly and forthrightly and under oath if need be, that never in so small a group have I seen so many pure souls, so many gentle and good people, so many men and women of utter integrity.
>
> And unless you are ready to accept this as the truth, coming from a man who has broken with them and cannot call them comrades again, you will not even begin to understand the most complex and incredible situation of our time—and perhaps of any time in all human history.[68]

How it is possible for religious institutions to foster an ethical dynamic which then becomes directed against the religious aims of these institutions poses a serious task of scientific explanation. Just as religion has played a conspicuous role in the rise of capitalism, in various ways it is involved in the generation of Communism. Examination of the interaction between religion, on the one hand, and economic and political institutions, on the other, requires consideration of the relationship of religion and Communism.

3. Of basic importance, the Communist movement has substantial characteristics of a religion. It is not theologically oriented, but neither are other basic ethical systems which gained

[67] Almond, *op. cit.,* p. 211.
[68] Fast, *op. cit.,* p. 39.

the status of religions, such as Confucianism or Buddhism. In Communism the higher power of religion is not clearly defined. Some turn to Christianity for their religion and to Communism for the fulfillment of religious teachings. For them religious worship is distinct from Communism and is needed to create altruistic motivation for Communism to succeed. For some the higher power of religion is the party to which they belong, for others the way of life which the party seeks to establish, and for still others the ideals which motivate the party. For the latter groups, Communism more nearly approximates a religion. Nor should the presence of opportunists who seek only self-aggrandizement mislead the observer as to the religious character of Communism. Throughout history, religious institutions have had a fluctuating share of leaders who sought power, profit, and pleasure from the opportunities for exploitation presented when catering to or manipulating the spiritual needs of human beings. Communism addresses itself to the deep spiritual hunger of people for a better way of life. It employs altruistic motivation as one of its cardinal assets. In such circumstances, it is possible for corruptible leaders to gain positions of control for their own gain, just as Christian churches have at times been led by opportunists.

The power in Communism serves some of the same psychic needs as does God in conventional religion. It gives its followers the basis for personality integration. Their lives become reorganized about the purposes of the party. The psychic power in Communism gives energy and direction for living. It enables members, as long as they accept the principles of Communism, to experience ethical fulfillment, probably the strongest satisfaction for which human beings consciously or unconsciously hunger. This is not to say that Communism provides an enduring basis for religious experience. Somewhat like the periodic revivals of nineteenth-century and twentieth-century Protestantism in America, Communism "burns over" the ground of incipient religious feelings, and then moves on to fresh conversions.

While religious exercises for continuous self-development are conspicuous by their absence from Communism, much of its ritual and education fall within the category of reviving or intensifying motivation for Communism. In November, 1958, the Communist party in Russia announced a campaign to promote loyalty, dedication, and discipline.[69] On the American scene, end-

[69] E. J. Simmons, "Russia in Transition," *Atlantic Monthly*, May, 1959, p. 72.

less attendance at class sessions in which the goals and programs of Communism are considered and reconsidered are one feature of the religious function of periodic renewal of motivation to which Durkheim referred. Covert assemblies in which members of a cell group gather again and again for fellowship and encouragement, and those infrequent occasions when larger groups assemble as a self-demonstration of their own existence, are both opportunities for a thrill of religious feeling. Outside exists the bleak, hostile world, but within the Communist fellowship is experienced the paradise of anticipating the coming of ultimate victory.

If Communism is regarded as a religion, then what of other political movements, such as the Socialist, Democratic, or Republican parties? The answer to this question from the standpoint of the scientific study of religion is that most adherents of the major political parties do not regard these parties or their platforms as the supreme psychic power of their own lives. They look to church or conscience as above political pursuits, or else they are secular and acknowledge no superior power which they seek to influence and adjust to. With reference to Communism, one recalls Jung's statement that whatever is the overwhelming psychic factor in one's life performs the role of God. While the Communist party, like other radical groups, has had stimulating educational consequences in agitating people to seek economic reforms by practical routes or inducing them to influence foreign policy, it can point to almost no achievement in its immediate program of seizing power for collectivization. It continues at present, as it has in the past, to be an isolated political sect in American life.

The spiritual aspect of Communism is acknowledged by Toynbee in saying:

> It looks as if, in the encounter between Russia and the West, the spiritual initiative, though not the technological lead, has now passed, at any rate for the moment, from the Western to the Russian side. We Westerners cannot afford to resign ourselves to this, because this Western heresy—Communism—which the Russians have taken up, seems to the great majority of people in the West to be a perverse, misguided, and disastrous doctrine and way of life. A theologian might put it that our great modern Western heresiarch Karl Marx has made what is a heretic's characteristic intellectual mistake and moral aberration. In putting his finger on one point in orthodox practice in which there has been a crying need for reform, he has lost sight of all

other considerations and therefore has produced a remedy that is worse than the disease.[70]

Yinger in his text on the sociology of religion describes the religious aspects of Communism.

Religious Aspects of Communism. The search for an "overwhelmingly strong power" on which to rely may lead one person to give himself to God while another may give himself to "the party." It is a mistake to disregard the differences which these choices indicate, but equally a mistake to overlook important personality similarities. There is ample evidence that some of the recruits to the Communist Party have been highly sensitive people, bewildered by the confusions of modern society, idealistic, and needing a clear cut program that claimed to be able to solve the problems they felt so deeply. They found in the authoritative program of Communism and in its seeming dedication to justice an "escape from freedom" that gave them both a sense of belonging and a sense of power. They were no longer the alienated; they had a "home" and a program. For many of them, of course, Communism became "the God that failed," able to give them a sense of identity with an exciting movement, but scarcely able to satisfy their idealism. As they became disenchanted with Communism, they turned to other programs, propelled by the same burning needs for a way to struggle with their bewilderment and sense of powerlessness. Some turned to vigorous anti-Communism, investing it with the same energy and dedication they had formerly shown for Communism. Others turned to classical religion, in several celebrated cases to Roman Catholicism. Such a dramatic change doubtless indicates a strong reaction against Communism; but it also shows some personality continuity, for the Catholic Church, more than any other in Christianity today furnishes its members a fixed dogma, definitive rites, and an unchallenged structure of power that can bring a sense of certainty to those torn by doubt—something of the same appeal that Communism had for some.[71]

Aims and Methods of Communism in America

The isolation of the Communist movement from the majority culture does not mean that it fails to touch it at important and influential points. After the crisis in its policies in 1957 following Khrushchev's revelation of Stalin's misdeeds, the Communist party in the United States abandoned all pretense of seeking to operate in the public view. The faction led by John Gates, editor of the *Daily Worker,* was defeated and Gates resigned. Now the party operates entirely in secret, sometimes behind

[70] Arnold Toynbee, *The World and the West,* Meridian, 1958, pp. 244–245.

[71] J. M. Yinger, *Religion, Society and the Individual,* Macmillan, 1957, pp. 120–121.

carefully designed and manipulated "front organizations." This stands in contrast with the somewhat greater openness with which the party functioned in the 1930's. However, party membership for many if not most has always been a secret affair. The march underground has been forced on Communists by the repressive policies of the American people in their government ever since the inception of the Communist party. The repression has become more severe since World War II, especially during the McCarthy hysteria and the Korean War, which resulted in jail sentences for leaders and expulsion of persons from jobs for merely being suspected of Communist affiliation. What this emotional reaction has done is to induce Communists to perfect their apparatus of operating in secret and to remove them entirely from the public view so that it is now extremely difficult to know reliably what is going on. Analysis of Communism in America must be based principally on the chapter of its history which came to an end in 1957. Whether dormant now or not, Communism in America provides interesting data for the analysis of religious or quasi-religious movements.

The Communist party can be regarded as a church of intellectuals. While containing many disillusioned by religion, it ministers to their psychic needs as does conventional religion to the large unthinking mass of people. Because its appeal is intellectual, it takes root in educational, professional, and scientific occupations. It seems a fair estimate to say that the Communist party has pervaded the intellectual world to somewhat the same degree as did the Socialist party during its peak in the 1930's.

Because the appeal of Communism is altruistic, it also takes root in religious, philanthropic, social-service, and labor undertakings. A million dollars was raised from philanthropic individuals during the Scottsboro case of nine Negroes falsely charged with raping two white women on a freight train. Diverting money from its specified purposes is rationalized by the Communist party in the fulfillment of larger objectives.

One of the most frequent charges made against the small party, both by its political opponents and by many of its ex-members, is that it cavalierly used funds collected for the Scottsboro boys to finance a variety of Communist institutions and causes. While such charges are extremely difficult to prove in specific instances, we have the word of no less an authority than T. Gussev, for a time the Comintern "rep" to the American party, that the "shortcomings of inner-party democracy stand out with increasing prominence in the attitude taken toward mass organizations. They are looked on and treated as a source of money. . . . The mass organizations have repeatedly protested against the free way in which the party organizations deal with their money."[72]

Earl Browder excused the misappropriation of funds in the Scottsboro case by saying:

"Quite early in the defense, when its only funds were those contributed by the Communist party, I engaged in a discussion with a group of lawyers. . . . The issue discussed . . . was the relative importance of spending what money was available for a mass appeal to the moral and intellectual conscience of America or of spending it for high-priced lawyers. I took the position that conceding that the best lawyers possible must be secured at whatever fee current practice dictated, this alone would get the defense nowhere without previously arousing the nation's conscience."[73]

The platform of Communism in America is characterized primarily by its drive for power. The party seeks by whatever means it can find to outmaneuver the capitalists who now hold power. Lacking vote-getting ability of its own, the Communist party seeks to operate behind a façade of existing parties and movements and to supplement political activity with strategic gains in economic power. Conventional agencies are "captured" in a policy of "rule or ruin." Ultimately the Communist party seeks to establish the same type of coöperative commonwealth as that prevailing in the Soviet Union, in which goods in general are produced for the common good, not for private profit. But the Russian political-economic system diverges from the classless, stateless society envisaged by Marx and Engels. For one expedient or another the ideals of Communism conflict with its practices in gaining and holding power. A new aristocracy, the priesthood of Communism, has arisen in Russia, such as that described by Milovan Djilas in *The New Class*.

Above all else in Communist ideology is the necessity for the party to grow and defend itself as an institution. Power is no longer thought of primarily in terms of allegiance of the masses. Rather, the intricate system of division of labor and specialization in modern society is most easily captured by a strategy adapted to the nature of this division of labor. This strategy involves gaining members, but especially the placement of these in key posts in industry and government. Posts are sought which are important in recruiting or protecting sympathetic or affiliated employees. Communism grows principally by

72 Howe and Coser, *op. cit.,* pp. 215–216.
73 *Ibid.,* p. 216.

individual conversion. This proselytizing requires that missionaries be protected against exposure or loss of employment. A feature of the party strategy is to use the system of division of labor as a means of inducing those whose jobs and lives depend upon coöperation from others into accepting Communism. In this system of division of labor, each position gained provides leverage for further penetration. After he has joined, the individual's livelihood depends upon his performance for the Party. An oblique tactic is openly to develop public opinion toward a rejection of existing institutions without actually in public proposing Communism as an alternative. This latter proposal is introduced during private proselytizing.

The actual step of conversion may be accomplished in a subtle manner. The proselyte is surrounded by friends who curry his favor. He is invited to homes where the evening discussion turns tactfully to economic questions. Prospects are carefully screened. When the prospect has been sufficiently enlightened, his friends encourage him to make contact with a key individual who is reputed to be a Communist. If at any point the prospect reacts unfavorably, all concerned deny their complicity. If the prospect becomes objectionable in charging Communism, he may be threatened with libel, made the target of vilification, or forced out of his job. The intricate system of division of labor in modern society makes it possible for personal economic power to be used to gain adherents, or at least to neutralize opposition from those who might be unsympathetic. Thus has the cutting edge of Communism penetrated the system of capitalism.

It would be a serious error to regard these incidents of strategy as the deciding influence. The moral enthusiasm of the Communist organizer is comparable to that of John Brown in his abortive crusade against slavery. The convert becomes persuaded by his moral sentiments into accepting a program which has strong appeal for him and about which he may only later come to have any intellectual misgivings. Arthur Koestler has described the religious appeal which Communism held for him before his break with it.

By the time I had finished with *Feuerbach* and *State and Revolution,* something had clicked in my brain which shook me like a mental explosion. To say that one had 'seen the light' is a poor description of the mental rapture which only the convert knows (regardless with what faith he has been converted to). The new light seems to pour from all directions across the skull; the whole universe falls into pattern like the stray pieces of a jigsaw puzzle assembled by magic at one stroke. There is now an answer to every question, doubts and conflicts are a matter of the tortured past—a past already remote, when one had lived in dismal ignorance in the tasteless, colorless world of those who *don't know*.[74]

A typical route whereby a student is drawn into Communist activity is described by Almond from his study of former Communists.

A young intellectually interested student, seeking a meaningful interpretation of the world and his mission in it, busily sloughing off the layers of parental or clerical admonition and rapidly absorbing magnificent and sweeping ideas, was readily attracted to the "Socialist Club" or the "Student Union," where he found spirits who shared his confusion and his interest in finding a gratifying intellectual and moral order. Most of these students who came into the party via anti-Fascist student societies of one kind or another left it when they left the university or soon thereafter, when the enchantments and transports of student life fell afoul of the requirements of career and family and of more mature views of what prospects the world held open. It is technically correct to describe these students as alienated from their families and their communities and unsure of their values, but it would be incorrect to view them as permanently alienated, as being capable only of "mass behavior." For, in actual fact, like the immigrants and children of immigrants who found in the party a momentary stopping place in the difficult and painful process of cultural adjustment, so also many of the university students who joined the party were engaged in a process of self-discovery and reality testing in which this experience was but an incident.[75]

Discussion of Communism in America

Having noted these details concerning the "Communist Church" in America, many Americans react with excessive emotional aversion. This is unfortunate, whether they reject Communism or not, since it blinds them to intelligent thinking about Communism. To set the activities of Communists in better perspective, several things should be noted.

1. Secrecy and deception are dictated by the persecution to which Communists are subjected. They regard themselves, not incorrectly, as at war with those presently in power. They see visible evidence of a war against them in prison sentences meted out or in summary dismissal from jobs. According to J. Edgar Hoover, 109 individuals had been convicted under the Smith Act

[74] Arthur Koestler, in Richard Crossman (ed.), *The God that Failed*, Harper, 1950, p. 23, quoted in J. M. Yinger, *op. cit.*, p. 121.

[75] Almond, *op. cit.*, pp. 215–216.

by the end of 1959. The convictions of two-thirds of these persons were set aside by courts of appeal. The remaining third were sentenced to serve a total of 143 years and to pay fines of $187,500. These sentences do not include prosecutions under state sedition laws or of those found in contempt of court for refusing to become informers. For party members deception is only one of a number of weapons to be used in defending and advancing their principles in a hostile situation. If necessary, they direct their tactics against those who are indifferent as well as against those who oppose them. Whether their subterranean war is an appropriate way to gain the objectives of a coöperative society is a separate question. The initial point to be grasped if Communist tactics are to be understood is that these tactics are rooted in a situation of sharp and intense social conflict.

2. The tactics of Communists are to be judged by the same criteria as other features in contemporary culture. That Communists advance their own members up the economic or professional ladder is not different from Jews, Catholics, Protestants or families owning corporations doing the same. It is an unfortunate feature of American society that various groups show favoritism in employment of others.

3. Stimulation of public opinion about the shortcomings of the present capitalistic culture, and in particular, about its inherent disharmony to the spiritual ideals of religion, seems a constructive activity. The activity is constructive in that it prepares people to discover better ways of living, whether these are isolated reforms or fundamental changes in society. It is not the function of this text to argue economic aspects of solutions to problems encountered by religion. It is left to the economist and the political scientist to determine whether minor or major reforms or revolutions are needed to terminate the shortcomings in culture which have been examined here. It is certainly unnecessary to agree with the Communist program in order to acknowledge the usefulness of criticism by Communists and other radical agitators in American history. This role, unpopular though it may be, is analogous to that of intemperate opponents of slavery before the Civil War, whose propaganda was violent and who operated underground railways for helping slaves to gain their freedom.

4. The legal question of whether the Communist party is actually a conspiracy has not been satisfactorily resolved. Some authorities in constitutional law maintain that the Communist party, as long as it does not take physical steps forcibly to seize

political power, should be tolerated on the American scene. If it engages in malpractices in employment situations, it should be subjected to the controls of fair employment practices legislation. At the same time, the practice of discriminating in employment against those holding Communist ideas is a species of persecution which has no place in a democratic society. As for keeping the Communist party underground, it has already become a difficult and baffling phenomenon with which to deal. It will probably be decades before the mischief caused by the late Senator McCarthy has been undone. The appropriate course for a democratic society, as in England and Scandinavia, is to give free status to the "Communist Church" but to intervene when wrongful practices are demonstrated in specific situations. At the same time, if the Communist party is tolerated, it or its successors may undergo evolution and come to play a more satisfactory role on the political scene. Since the ascendance of Khrushchev in Russia, more moderate policies are in evidence. Defections remove those less effective in working for Communism. The American Socialist party, which championed the cause of democratic socialism for several decades, is now virtually defunct. It or something like it requires reviving if the altruistic sentiments of Americans, as expressed in social organization, are to measure up to the standards which proponents of ideal religion, such as Sherwood Eddy, Harry Emerson Fosdick, John Haynes Holmes, E. Stanley Jones, and Kirby Page have urged upon their fellow citizens.

5. The basic issue posed by Communism in America is one of whether a party structure polarized by intense conflict and geared to fighting for its survival provides the appropriate plant out of which the flower of a superior society can grow. The proponents of Communist power tell themselves and others that they will use that power for a good end. Pacifists claim Communists fail to see that the presence of power in their hands invites counterattack from others. Once the opposition has reacted forcibly, as it is already doing in America, the initiative passes from the original leadership. It then becomes led by the logic of conflict to do what is necessary to win. If the upward climb has been a pattern of defending the Communist party by any means, the tendency is to continue the same means of secrecy, deception, espionage and devaluation of the individual in endeavoring to impose the framework of a new society. In any event, the risk of resurgence of the opposition may necessitate the continuance of a dictatorial regime for an indefinite time. The degree of

dishonesty or force used in the revolution or in the continued repression of opposition is a function of the extent of disbelief in and opposition to Communism among others. This lack of sympathy is widespread in western democracies.

Socialist critics say that the corrupting role which power plays in the personalities of those who wield it must be kept squarely in view. Political or economic power is no better than the motivation of those who wield it. That social system is soundest which takes full account of the self-seeking and self-indulgence which are aspects of the motivation of all human beings. Only control by the masses through free elections of candidates of their choice is an effective check upon the abuses of power centralized in the hands of a few leaders. While American voters may seem now to be apathetic in the exercise of their voting franchise, at least they retain the opportunity of voting out of power any group whose tyranny might become excessive. Just as the capitalists who gained economic power through the impetus of the Protestant Reformation came to be corrupted by their economic power, so also the "new class" in Russia according to Djilas is losing its moral idealism and is succumbing to temptations of luxury and privilege. When liberties have been surrendered to or seized by this class, the basis for fresh exploitation of the large mass of people is renewed. Djilas speaks for lovers of freedom in pointing out that what has appeared in Russia is a new theocracy comparable to that prevailing during Calvin's dominance in Geneva.[76]

Experience with Communism in Russia and Asia shows that many millions of people have risen against indescribable conditions of squalor and disease to achieve a new level of decency and health and a new sense of participation in human society. Others who have disagreed with Communist methods have found their freedom of speech curtailed and concentration camps to be the fate of those who persist in anti-Communist agitation. The political concepts of Russian and Asian Communism have had little appeal for those accustomed to much broader civil liberties in the democracies of western Europe and America. While rule of personal lives by the economic power of gigantic corporations is becoming increasingly odious to many, they are reluctant to exchange this type of curtailment of individual freedom for an alternative loss of liberty. Critics contend that "democratic centralism" is not a doctrine of real freedom even for those

[76] Milovan Djilas, *The New Class,* Praeger, 1958, p. 130.

within the Party, since the healthy growth of competing factions is discouraged and the individual is expected to comply in accepting group decisions which regulate most details of his conduct. The problems which arise when a power machine is built to impose a new way of life upon people are one of the principal reasons why the spell cast by Communism elsewhere does not captivate many Americans. These problems explain why enthusiastic joiners sometimes become disillusioned when they see the consequences of the power machine of which they are a part.

Communists, for their part, contend that these difficulties are mere incidents along a path to a collectivist society. Those who have been faithful through the years to the Party and its principles are little perturbed by defections among the squeamish or the inability of the great majority of Americans to understand what the program and practices of Communism are all about. They believe that America is a sick patient, and that a sick patient requires strong medicine.

Communists argue that capitalists in power can only be dislodged by bringing superior power to bear. They point out that many societies in the past, among them that of colonial Americans, have gained freedom from economic or political shackles through revolution. During such a time, semi-military organization is needed, in their view. Some Communists in America today are animated, in their own particular way, by the "spirit of 1776." There the issue is joined. On the other hand, there is a fundamental difference in the consequences of a revolution by a minority against the majority who are disinterested or opposed, and a revolution by the overwhelming majority against a small minority of alien rulers. Also, there is a difference between fighting to destroy an enemy and fighting to impose a way of life. Furthermore, there is serious question whether most revolutions do not produce more harm in the process than the good which is their purpose.

It is the conclusion of many social scientists that the present power alignment at least requires vigorous political action if it is to be changed. C. W. Mills believes that it is realistic to appeal to thinking people but not to those in power.

To *appeal* to the powerful, on the basis of any knowledge we now have, is utopian in the foolish sense of that term. Our relations with them are more likely to be only such relations as they find useful, which is to say that we become technicians accepting their problems and aims, or ideologists promoting their prestige and authority. To be more than that, so far as our political role is concerned, we must first of all re-consider the nature of our collective endeavor as social scientists. It is not at all utopian for one social scientist to appeal to his colleagues to undertake such a re-consideration. Any social scientist who is aware of what he is about must confront the major moral dilemma I have implied in this chapter—the difference between what men are interested in and what is to men's interest.[77]

Others, such as Toynbee, are led by their studies to the conviction that a new way of life cannot be effectively imposed by political force wielded by one group against the rest. Forcible political conversion seems no more effective than forcible religious conversion, especially when a political faith, rightly or wrongly, is advocated as if it were a religion. The human animal must not be made a puppet at the end of a string of political power, capitalist or Communist. He is a creature with hopes, feelings, aspirations and ideals. He must be appealed to voluntarily if a real revolution is to take place in his heart. The revolution of Christianity in ancient times gained its place in civilization by the power of spiritual appeal. More recently many economic reforms have been accomplished in American capitalism by legislative curtailment of the power elite. What has been done before can be done again. It seems possible to overcome undesired consequences of the capitalist way of life and at the same time to retain the spiritually positive freedoms which have traditionally been associated with capitalism. Complete parliamentary democracy and full civil liberties can be retained at the same time as abuses of economic privilege are curtailed.

From the standpoint of social science, concluding comments on the reason why Communism appears in American culture in the form in which it does are called for.

1. A tie with the world-wide Communist movement exists, but this can be overemphasized. This tie sets the pattern about which the movement is built in America, but the tie does not explain why the movement gained support in America. More than the political connection is the encouragement given by the achievements of socialism in Russia.

2. Major generating factors are the insecurity fostered by the threat of atomic war, the increasing spiritual impoverishment of people by capitalist culture, and the growing concentration of economic power as documented by C. W. Mills in *The Power Elite*. Job insecurity in corporations makes the Communist party a secret labor organization to find and to protect

[77] C. Wright Mills, *The Sociological Imagination,* Oxford University Press, 1959, p. 193.

jobs for the professional and managerial class of persons who belong to it. While there are many possible plans of action, only the Communist party has come forward with a concrete plan for dealing with unsolved problems of capitalist enterprise. The Socialist party and other economic reform movements active in earlier decades have largely receded into the background. The world today desperately needs planning and organization to meet its problems. Year by year, economic life in America becomes more wasteful. Despite unprecedented productivity due to scientific invention, technological and human resources are dissipated by disorderly management of the economy. Following the prolonged steel strike of 1959, in which it was shown that the steel industry exercises a monopoly in setting prices and securing a 16 percent profit on net worth for its stockholders, Senator Estes Kefauver wrote: "The question of how to bring about an equitable distribution of the technological gains in non-competitive industries is thus essentially a new problem. It is a problem for which there is no existing public policy. It is a problem which the whole Congress must face up to in the not too distant future.[78]

3. The two-party system in the United States frustrates the efforts of parliamentary reformists, since it is almost impossible for them to make their influence felt except by slow education of the two existing parties, which are much alike. A two-party system is not an any-party system. Without question many reform-minded individuals feel that it is as necessary to build a revolutionary movement in America as it would be under a one-party system, a conviction intensified by the McCarthy persecution.

4. The history of religious movements shows that those with authoritarian organization are best adapted for survival as institutions in the short run, even if they fail in their long-range objectives of bringing the benefits of spiritual freedom. The Socialist party in the United States was largely a debating society, and when the leadership of Norman Thomas ended it fell into oblivion, although there is no inherent reason why it was necessary for it to do so.

5. The resort to force advocated by Communists is no novelty in American history. America was born in revolution and nurtured in a succession of wars, averaging one each generation.

[78] Estes Kefauver, "The New Economic Crisis," *The Progressive,* January, 1960, p. 17. Among the popular treatments analyzing ethical aspects of economic disorganization are: Marquis Childs and Douglass Cater, *Ethics in a Business Society,* Harper, 1954; and K. E. Boulding, *The Organizational Revolution,* Harper, 1958.

The readiness to resort to governmental force to reform life has been recurringly shown by such adventures as the Prohibition attempt. The Communist party in this respect retains cultural continuity with American Protestantism. Furthermore, its program of economic aims is an expression of religious motivation.

6. By and large, the churches have abdicated from their responsibility of suggesting, let alone demanding, that altruistic motivation be expressed in the context of modern economic life. When the Communist party comes forward with altruistic motivation and this demand, it tends to the extent of its outreach to displace or infiltrate religious institutions.

7. Perhaps of most importance of all, the Communist party undergoes mutation into a religion because of the failure of contemporary religions to give their members a God of love whom they can experience. These religions offer instead no more than a pale philosophical fiction whom followers can imagine. The last act in the millennial conflict between religion and science is the last of a long chain of consequences stemming from the rejection of religious experience as having any but supernatural validity. Human beings have rediscovered in crude form the empirical power of God in their secularized lives. According to Jung's view, when religious impulses first well up from the collective unconscious, they do so in terms of earlier levels of development.[79] The worship of the group described by Durkheim reasserts itself, especially in a crisis of survival. Not until painful lessons of history have been endured, does psychic differentiation refine the religious concepts of men and move them forward to more idealistic conceptions of the higher power in religion. A child repeats in his own development the spiritual heritage of the race, moving from allegiance to the group to allegiance to God. Likewise when the human race must re-create its spiritual heritage, its pattern of development resembles the life of the child in his encounter with God. The rise of Communism around the world is consequently symptomatic of preliminary stages of spiritual rebirth. The process of full rebirth can be facilitated by recognition of what it is for which men unconsciously hunger. It can be aided by giving them, to use a figure of William James, a real spiritual meal, not merely a bill of fare describing food in a nonexperiential realm, which is the bill of fare offered by some prevailing philosophies of religion.

The noted pacifist Milton Mayer summarizes the problem

[79] C. G. Jung, *Psychology and Religion: West and East,* tr. by R. F. C. Hull, Pantheon, 1958, p. 28.

which denial of God poses for Communists who disavow theistic religion, a problem which leads to revival of religion.

> The Communists, too, pursue a durable balance between liberty and equality. But they believe that life and society are human experiments and that there is no God. But what if there is one? What if Jefferson was right? Then the revolution—at least the Communist revolution—will fail for want of the superhuman means proportionate to the superhuman end of conceiving a nation in liberty and dedicating it to the proposition that all men are created equal.[80]

An instance from American history more than a century ago which illustrates the importance of religion to the success of a social system is provided by the experience of a communistic settlement at New Harmony, Indiana. The Rappites, a devout sect of German peasants, established a religious community on a thirty thousand acre tract of land on the Wabash River. Owning their land and tools in common and motivated by Christian love for each other, they created a community which prospered. Robert Owen was a pioneer socialist who desired to establish a coöperative community for those dedicated to socialist ideals. In 1825, hearing of the success of the Rappite community, he purchased their land, equipment, and livestock, and opened his social experiment, named New Harmony, to all persons interested in establishing Utopia. Idealists, intellectuals, and opportunists flocked in considerable numbers. This band of socialist pioneers lacked what the Rappites possessed—a religious foundation for their socialism. Begun with high hopes, the community rapidly decayed into a condition of social disorder. Shirking of work, greed, quarreling, and bickering became rampant. To the disillusionment of Robert Owen and his fellow idealists, their experiment in socialist living failed. The remnants of the project were taken over by survivors who reverted to the capitalist pattern of their neighbors. With discipline rooted in a religious way of life, the communism of the Rappites succeeded. Without religion and without discipline, the communism of the intellectuals failed. The testimony of history, according to Arnold Toynbee, is that higher religious convictions and religious ideals are the foundation of a society of people who work together sacrificially for the good of the individual.[81]

[80] Milton Mayer, "The American Spirit," *The Progressive,* January, 1959, p. 65.

[81] A. Toynbee, *An Historian's Approach to Religion,* Oxford University Press, 1956, pp. 77–91.

chapter 15 Religion and Personal Relationships

Face-to-face associations are of the greatest importance to people in the fulfillment of their life purposes. People find their deepest and most lasting satisfactions in family living and in their experiences with those whom they think of as friends. In these personal relationships are found the principal opportunities for living for other people. In these relationships are the principal opportunities for sharing interests, counseling, encouraging, sympathizing with others, and giving and receiving mutual aid.

The study of personal relationships is the study of social organization, or, more briefly, society, at the level of contacts between individuals. In the study of the social order, the emphasis is on the structure of social organization involving large numbers of people. The relationships between people who are linked by face-to-face association occupy only a small part of the total social structure. On the other hand, in the investigation of personal relationships between friends and in family living, attention focuses primarily on the intricate involvement of the personalities of two or three or a relatively few people with each other.

C. H. Cooley has given the designation of primary groups to those groupings of people which are both face to face and relatively permanent in duration. The family is a primary group in this sense. Sometimes friendship groupings, as those in the traditional rural neighborhood, are those of primary groups. Often friendship relationships of people in contemporary urban culture are impermanent because of the frequency with which people change their residential and social locations. As discussed in Chapter 11, primary groups play an important part in the generation of altruistic motivation because of the superior opportunities which exist in permanent groups for people to gain complete understanding of each other's personalities and through this sympathetic experience to develop strong motivations of affection and loyalty.

The organization of people in friendship groupings and in families constitute an extensive and important sector of any human society. Face-to-face relationships of those standing in varying degrees of friendships and those linked by family ties also reach into the economic, political, educational, and religious institutions which make up the rest of the social structure. The orientation of people as friends or as nonfriends has much to do with the organization of people's economic life. People like to work with those who are their friends. They feel responsible for giving members of their immediate families a better break in filling jobs or making promotions. This means that whom one knows rather than what one can do may play a deciding part in the job which one can get. The connection of face-to-face relationships of friends and members of families with economic life is one of determining or at least influencing whether one is allowed or denied a particular job opportunity. This is a statement of fact, not a statement of what is most desirable from the standpoint of maximum freedom of economic opportunity for all.

The friendship and family loyalties which may seem of little net consequence for each two or three people involved add up in totality to a gigantic social class system. The barriers which separate people from the opportunities they would like to enjoy run throughout the social class system. What seems in the individual case to be a harmless desire of an uncle to give his nephew a job or of a school chum to help someone from the same alma mater turns out when systematically pursued as a policy by all to set up harsh barriers of exclusiveness which deny many human beings the right to live and enjoy the fruits of life.

Interaction of Religion with Personal Relationships

Religion, like any part of society, interacts with all other parts. The involvement of religion in the personal relationships of people is larger than in other aspects of society. The primary teachings of religion about group living are directed at how people live as members of their families and how they treat those whom they meet in face-to-face association as neighbors or on the job. Religion seeks to help people find fulfillment in living for others. It is much concerned with the purposes and performance of people in neighborly and family living since these are the most concrete and the most prevalent opportunities for altruism.

At the same time, ugly dysfunctions of religion in personal relationships are glaringly evident. Because of their religion, people often shun those who follow a different religious faith. Because religion in a subtle manner makes people think they are better if they profess affiliation than if they do not, and because the pursuit of religion often fosters economic prosperity, religious stigmata mark those at the top of a social class system and are used by them as a means of differentiating insiders from outsiders.

Besides being at the root of religious discrimination and social exclusiveness, religion or at least those who profess it thrust into the life of congregations the antidemocratic lines of a racial caste system by keeping out Negroes.

Nevertheless, the picture of interaction is a mixed one. Many religious leaders and laymen labor energetically and persistently to tear down religious exclusions, social class barriers, and the social inequalities of Negroes and whites. The infusion of religion, primarily a beneficial one, into the life stream of personal relationships in face-to-face and family pursuits claims our attention in the two concluding chapters.

RELIGIOUS DISCRIMINATION

Significance of the Problem

Leaders of religious groups widely and sincerely repudiate the discriminatory attitudes and practices of members of different religious groups toward those in other religious groups. In America, Protestants are in the majority among those with religious affiliation. Those who have felt the effects of religious discrimination in varying degrees have been Catholics and Jews. But more recently, as shown by K. W. Underwood in *Protestant and Catholic,* Protestants may suffer community pressure at the hands of Catholics, whose organized power is increasing. Anti-Catholic sentiment has receded in the past three decades and Catholics have more nearly been accepted as members of one more of the Christian denominations in America, notwithstanding their unique ties with a church leadership which centers in Rome. It seems possible now for a Catholic to become elected President of the United States, while for the century up to and including the Presidential contest in 1928 with Alfred E. Smith as a Catholic candidate religious issues played an acute part. In the past sharp anti-Catholic sentiment has been spearheaded by a noisy minority of misguided Protestant spokesmen apprehensive about growth in Catholic power and political opportunists capitalizing on religious feeling. This antagonism has erupted at times into mob violence against Catholics which serves as a grim historical reminder of how near the surface Protestant feeling against Catholics slumbers.

Anti-Catholic feeling was sporadic or latent in colonial times and during the early days of the Republic, owing to the relatively small numbers of Catholics in isolated groups. Protestant migrants to the American colonies brought with them bitter and painful recollections of persecution and suppression in European localities where they had been under or menaced by the power of the Catholic Church. Early state constitutions or the laws passed under them sometimes discriminated against Roman Catholics. The Alien and Sedition Acts of 1798 were directed in part against Catholic immigrants and were intended to assist the early American government to secure the respect and cooperation of dissident groups of citizens. It was generally realized that these acts went too far in restricting freedom of thought and expression. As President, Jefferson pardoned those who were fined and imprisoned under the Sedition Act. His attitude is expressed in the words carved on the Jefferson Memorial in Washington: "I have sworn upon the altar of God eternal hostility against every form of tyranny over the mind of man." However, Jefferson did not speak for the leadership of Protestant churches of the time. He was vigorously opposed as a free thinker who did not properly conserve the orthodox principles of Protestantism.

In the decade following 1825 mounting debate took place on such questions as whether Roman Catholic religion is inimical to civil or religious liberty. In 1834 false and groundless tales of mistreatment of nuns in convent life were circulated in Boston and led to the burning of a convent by a mob of men. Other serious instances of anti-Catholic violence occurred. In 1844 there were riots in Philadelphia, and Catholics fought back.

A series of anti-Catholic organizations and societies culminated in the Know-Nothings, who were a nationally organized secret political organization. They gained their name because of their typical answer to outsiders trying to uncover details of their secret organization, "I don't know." In the decade prior to the Civil War the Know-Nothings succeeded in electing candidates in many states. For a time it appeared that a new political party based on religious prejudice had arisen to rival the existing Whigs, Democrats, and Republicans. Inspired by the Know-Nothings, mobs engaged in such depredations as tarring and feathering a priest and wrecking Catholic chapels. Riots occurred when Catholics retaliated in Brooklyn and in Kentucky. These things occurred despite the statements of responsible men in public office who condemned Know-Nothingism. In 1855 Lincoln wrote: "I am not a Know-Nothing; that is certain. How could I be? How can any one who abhors the oppression of Negroes be in favor of degrading classes of white people? Our progress in degeneracy appears to me to be pretty rapid. As a nation we began by declaring that 'all men are created equal.' We now practically read it 'all men are created equal, except Negroes.' When the Know-Nothings get control, it will read 'all men are created equal, except Negroes, foreigners and Catholics.' "[1]

Following the Reconstructionist era, the Ku Klux Klan, founded at first to restore white supremacy in the South, shifted its attention and became an anti-Catholic movement in various sections of the country. The Klan became anti-Semitic as well. The principal effect of Klan activity was to stir up religious prejudice on a large scale through its scurrilous verbal attacks on Catholics. In 1915 several persons were indicted but later acquitted for sending "obscene, lewd, lascivious, filthy and indecent matter in the mail." Reaching a peak enrollment in the 1920's of more than four million members, who stressed supremacy of native white Protestantism as their doctrine, the Klan played an influential role in Presidential elections. It is to the credit of the growing maturity of the American people that the agitation in the 1928 election was peaceable and that since that year anti-Catholicism has subsided on the American scene. Paul Blanshard argues that the Catholic Church in the United States would suppress religious freedoms of non-Catholics, especially the right to proselytize, if the Catholic Church became the church of the majority.[2] This suppression has recently occurred in some Catholic areas in other portions of the world.

[1] A. P. Stokes, *Church and State in the United States,* Harper, 1950, Vol. I, p. 836.

[2] Paul Blanshard, *American Freedom and Catholic Power,* Beacon, 1958; *Communism, Democracy and Catholic Power,* Beacon, 1951. Also consult K. W. Underwood, *Protestant and Catholic,* Beacon, 1957; J. J. Kane, *Catholic-Protestant Tensions in America,* Regnery, 1955; J. O'Neill, *Catholicism and American Freedom,* Harper, 1952; D. J. Hager, C. Y. Glock, and I. Chein, eds., "Religious Conflict in the United States," *Journal of Social Issues,* Vol. XII, No. 3, 1956.

Most non-Catholics do not seem apprehensive about this possibility, although some Protestant leaders keep a watchful eye on Catholic power. The proportion of Catholics to Protestants in the United States has not been growing significantly. A measure of anti-Catholic prejudice is still evident in the social relationships of many Americans. This prejudice is evident in favoritism practiced in the business world towards those who are Protestant in background or at least non-Catholic and non-Jewish. Prejudice appears in the tendency of both Catholics and Protestants to move in separate social worlds as far as their leisure-time associations are concerned. Prejudice takes root in the strong discouragement by religious leaders on both sides of intermarriage. These walls of social isolation are becoming thinner. J. L. Thomas estimates that approximately one-fourth of all Catholics now marry someone outside of their church.

Considering the religious conflict between Christians and Jews, the student of cultural history is forcibly impressed by the almost two-thousand-year duration of this conflict. That a pathological and injurious pattern of behavior could endure for so long a time without the natural processes of human enlightenment effecting a sensible reconciliation is a difficult phenomenon to explain. In the modern era the Nazis exterminated six million Jews among their own and neighboring populations. Regardless of how remotely connected with this mass genocide responsible Christians may be, the stark fact remains that these six million were singled out and killed as Jews. Contemporary world leaders in Protestantism and the pope in Rome are well known for their humanitarian, constructive, and compassionate policies toward non-Christians, yet there has been poor carry-over of public pronouncements into the actions and attitudes of laymen and those who have drifted away from ties with churches while continuing to share a common cultural world with Christians.

The picture of more immediate concern is that of Jewish-Christian relationships in American culture. Here we find conditions superior to those prevailing in many European areas. Furthermore, it is a picture of smoldering embers of anti-Semitism dying out. Yet much remains to be achieved before full social acceptance and mutuality of Jews and Christians toward each other are achieved.

The first Jews came to Colonial America in small numbers with advanced social status. Jews found a common bond with enlightened Christian leaders, predominantly Protestant, who were anxious to establish and maintain conditions of full religious freedom. Although numerically small, Jews played an energetic and inspiring role in the founding of the American Republic. More than this, Columbus' voyage was largely financed by a Jewish merchant, Luis de Santangel. In 1790 Washington visited a Hebrew congregation in Newport and in an exchange of letters afterward wrote: "May the children of the stock of Abraham, who dwell in this land, continue to merit and enjoy the good will of other inhabitants, while everyone shall sit in safety under his own vine and fig-tree and there shall be none to make him afraid. May the Father of all mercies scatter light and not darkness in our paths and make us all in our several vocations useful here and, in His own due time and way, everlastingly happy."[3] After the adoption of the Constitution and Bill of Rights the states, a few of them belatedly, proceeded to adopt constitutions which granted Jews full political liberty as citizens, rejecting the disqualification that a citizen or officeholder must subscribe to the New as well as the Old Testament. The debate which took place in Maryland before that state incorporated Jewish equality in its laws in 1826 was of prolonged public importance in crystallizing the thinking of Americans in general. A devout Presbyterian serving as delegate to the Maryland Assembly, Thomas Kennedy, earned a place beside other builders of American freedom because of his vigorous and inspiring political efforts to end the discrimination against Jews which limited officeholding to Christians.

In the first century of the American Republic it was possible for Jews and Christians to lead a relatively amicable existence which did not provide occasion for close association in employment or leisure-time pursuits. Near the turn of the twentieth century Jewish immigration increased, especially from the lower income levels of the segregated communities of Central Europe. As a consequence, class and immigrant prejudice became part of religious prejudice against Jews. At the same time rapid industrialization of the economy brought Jews and Christians close together in a vast and interdependent system of division of labor. The results of these things were that Christians came into much more frequent cultural contact with Jews, and for Jews social and economic discrimination became much more serious because of their common dependence with other Americans upon the same system of division of labor for their livelihood. Anti-Semitism in the form of an organized movement came to a head in the years of reaction which followed World War I. This was

[3] Stokes, *op. cit.,* p. 862.

the time of the new mushrooming of the Ku Klux Klan, the persecution of Communists and other radicals, and repression in the trade-union movement. It is difficult to account for the wave of religious intolerance which flared at this time. A student of cultural history might observe that it was a time when feelings of religious orthodoxy made a final attempt to dominate American culture against evolutionism, radicalism, religious dissent, and religious unbelief. At any rate, the historical facts are clear that the decade of the 1920's was one of religious reaction, although obviously a reaction by unthinking and irresponsible persons censured by the respected and statesmanlike leadership representing the overwhelming majority of Protestant churches.

One of the shocking episodes of this time was circulation of the so-called "Protocols of the Elders of Zion," which were forgeries of documents purporting to prove a plan by Jews for domination of the world. That these were later realized to be vicious impostures upon public credulity did not undo the harm which these documents caused in the hands of gullible persons, among them Henry Ford. He gave them much publicity in the paper he personally sponsored, *The Dearborn Independent*. Henry Ford later retracted and apologized for his publicizing of the protocols. The years of the Depression of the 1930's were ones of economic insecurity which helped to popularize the appeal of Fascist organizations such as the Silver Shirts of America, and other groups through which such demogogues as the late Huey Long, Father Charles Coughlin, the Rev. Gerald L. K. Smith, and the Rev. Gerald B. Winrod exerted their influence. These clergymen were eventually if not immediately repudiated by the responsible church organizations with which they had a connection, but not before they had gained much publicity in inflaming religious hatred.

The decade during and following World War II was one of large gains in both religious and racial tolerance as Americans became more closely welded together in their common efforts to build a more democratic world. A series of fair employment practices laws, brought about by the devoted efforts of Protestant, Catholic, and Jewish leaders as well as of other concerned persons, more nearly established equality of economic opportunity, especially for those in mass occupations, such as clerical, service, and manual types of employment. Also significant has been the growing success of educational leaders in ending quota restrictions on minority-group members seeking that important avenue to economic success, a college education.

Taking detailed stock of the present situation of minority-group members in the full range of situations in which residual discrimination is still practiced would be a statistical task well beyond the scope of this book. Current texts analyzing problems of majority-minority group relations, such as that of G. E. Simpson and J. M. Yinger,[4] bring together large numbers of relevant studies detailing the extent and causation of racial and religious prejudice in America. The picture is, by and large, an encouraging one, even if slow and halting. The circumstance that such a large number of studies have been carried on is itself evidence of a deep and widespread concern on the part of many groups of Americans for rooting out what remains of religious, as well as racial, intolerance.

Nevertheless, it is important to observe here that the social, educational, and economic disabilities under which Jews labor in America are still substantial and necessitate much growth in public understanding if they are to be fully effaced. That Jews are able to equal or surpass Catholics and Protestants in securing a college education and in finding productive economic opportunities for themselves should not mislead us as to the full depth of the situation. Jewish students find that there are fewer colleges to which admission is readily available for those well qualified, as indicated by the concentrations of Jewish students in state and municipal universities and the relatively small numbers enrolled in exclusive, prestige colleges and universities.

Success in the business world is largely conditioned upon friendship relationships. Where competitors for business are much alike in the economic services which they are able to provide, which one of them gets the business depends very considerably upon slight swings in the balancing of decisions by friendship loyalties. There is nothing wrong with the desire to help those whom we would like to help because we sympathize with and share their experiences and needs. What is wrong is for such a policy to become one of favoring friends in granting economic opportunities at our disposal and thereby systematically excluding deserving persons all along the lines of the system of division of labor, especially at those points where opportunities are more specialized, more valuable, and more highly sought after. As long as Christians do not mix readily with non-Christians in their friendship relationships, there is bound to be more or less carry-over of discriminatory practices in eco-

[4] G. E. Simpson and J. M. Yinger, *Racial and Cultural Minorities: An Analysis of Prejudice and Discrimination,* Harper, 1958.

nomic decisions which affect the economic livelihood of others. At the point of mutuality in leisure-time and friendship relationships, the facts are unmistakable that generally neither Christians nor Jews seek to make friends with others irrespective of their religious background. The sharpest evidence of social discrimination against Jews is found in the refusal of a few gentiles to permit them to live in the same residential neighborhoods. A study by Elmo Roper of prejudice expressed by college seniors disclosed that 10 percent stated they would prefer not to have Jews move into the neighborhood where they live. The corresponding percentage rejecting Catholics in a neighborhood relationship is zero, and those rejecting Negroes 45 percent.[5] This study was carried out a decade ago, and judging by the contemporary trend the amount of prejudice expressed against Jews or Negroes would now be less. This fractional amount of residual aversion on the part of those of Christian background is seized upon by real-estate operators as excuse for their solid walls of resistance against renting homes to minority-group members whom they imagine might be unpopular with their neighbors. This discrimination in housing opportunities is of deadly consequence because of the barriers which it places in the path of mutual friendships. The number of laws curbing discrimination in housing is growing. As these laws increasingly set the standard by which a minority of reactionary-minded persons are curbed, equality of residential opportunity and with it equality for forming friendships seem destined to prevail. University students rebel with increasing frequency against the edicts of alumni who endeavor to prohibit membership of Jewish students in fraternities which the alumni control.

The controversy over public school integration in the South has stimulated the existence of irate and intolerant groups of citizens seeking to block the social mixing of Negroes and whites. This anti-Negro sentiment has in a few instances reawakened latent anti-Semitism at the same time. Bombings and threats of bombings of Jewish synagogues are a humiliating reminder to the overwhelming majority of right-minded people in the United States of the slowness with which the disease of religious, as well as racial, prejudice disappears. When these instances of anti-Semitic violence have occurred, the readiness with which responsible citizens have reacted in condemning this vandalism speaks favorably for the lessening of religious conflict and religious prejudice in the future.

[5] Arnold Forster, *A Measure of Freedom,* Doubleday, 1950, p. 150.

The expression of such optimism for the future can be questioned on some grounds. The trends of improvement are not long enough nor deep enough in duration to find much security in them. In particular, risk exists that a modest amount of improvement will lull people who would otherwise be concerned into insensibility to the need for much further growth in human relationships.

The phenomenon of anti-Semitism is of serious consequence for religion, its institutions, its leaders, and its followers. Social scientists who are critical of religion, especially as it is practiced by Christians in America, are quick to point out that a system of belief and behavior which makes the attainment of brotherhood one of its cardinal ideals seems unable to extend this brotherhood to those who come out of much the same religious tradition, such as Catholics and especially Jews. Such critics set for social and psychological scientists the problem of explaining how it is that an ideology which aims at brotherhood all too often ends in fratricide. A thesis of this text is that religious ideas and institutions are an upbuilding force, making for superior qualities of living for the human race. If this thesis is accepted, it is necessary to show how it happens that internecine conflict prevails between followers of different world religions. The recurring phenomenon of religious warfare or genocide against those of differing religious affiliation is, of course, spiritually disheartening to those who try to find in religion the basis for creative altruism. It is of greatest importance from both a practical and scientific standpoint to undertake a systematic explanation of why religion which preaches brotherhood so often eventuates in the practice of injury. Through an understanding of causal factors which operate, it becomes more nearly possible to control these and to eliminate religious conflict and prejudice from the American as well as the world scene.

Causal Analysis of Religious Prejudice

The tendency of those with religious motivation to resort to unscrupulous means to combat what they consider to be false doctrine clearly belies the spiritual power to influence people which they claim to possess. How can it be that what begins in love and lofty idealism can end in tragedy and mutual destructiveness? Data sufficient to answer this question are meager and susceptible to shifting interpretations. We shall undertake an imaginative reconstruction of the psychic processes which operate behind the data. As Sherlock Holmes chafed against lack of data and remarked that the mind cannot work without data, so also the earnest student of religion is frustrated by the lack of readily observable data with which to work and the degree to which he must rely upon examination of the inward processes of religion. In the psychic realm there is much room for differences in interpretation, yet here is where the vital processes of religion have their existence.

Any cultural phenomenon, such as religious prejudice, is a product of both historical and continuing causes. Any cultural pattern is a product of the preceding cultural pattern and the continuing forces with which that pattern has been in interplay. The easiest point at which to begin an explanation for contemporary religious prejudice is given by a review of the history of preceding manifestations of prejudice, whose cultural momentum goes far to fix the development of contemporary events. Following a review of historical processes, we will then attempt the more difficult task of seeing and assessing the continuing psychic forces which occasion renewed flare-ups of religious antagonism and discrimination.

The historical background of religious prejudice in America has been traced by a review of manifestations of religious prejudice during the years of the American Republic down to the present time. What took place during these years is a carry-over of patterns of religious culture in Europe which colonists brought with them. These in turn are a continuation of events during the Reformation, medieval times, and ancient history. As far as the religious conflict between Christians and Jews is concerned, evidence is ample that this conflict assumed an immediate and intense form as soon as Jesus began his preaching. There is some evidence that the Christian sect did not appear full-fledged with the teachings of Jesus but had at least a forerunner in a sect of Jews whose religious practices were so unpopular that they withdrew from centers of population in order to practice communal living in isolated colonies. The teachings of Jesus therefore touched areas of emotional antagonism already in existence. Jesus attracted large crowds of people as he traveled from place to place in ancient Palestine. His teachings had extraordinary effectiveness, according to scriptural record, in helping people to find a new and meaningful way of life in the midst of the political disorders and moral corruption of the time. It is difficult at the present point of time to assess how much of the antagonism to Jesus' ministry was shared by Roman officials who governed Palestine and how much was shared by Jewish leaders. It was Pontius Pilate who ordered Jesus' crucifixion, whatever pretext he may have taken for this order. Jesus is reported in scripture to have said some vituperative things about orthodox Jewish leaders. Whether these are words put into his mouth by later writers of scripture, we cannot be certain. What he is reported to have said seems in stark contrast with his Sermon on the Mount, in which he went to unprecedented lengths in advocating peace, gentleness, and humility toward all people. While individual Jews, such as Paul, participated in the persecution of Christians after Jesus' death, evidence is lacking that this persecution was caused by organized Jewish leadership. The persecution, at least at first, seems to have taken more of the pattern of mob reaction by those intolerant of the early Christians than suppression by responsible Jewish leaders. However the religious conflict started, it rapidly assumed widespread and violent expression.

It seems likely that details in the story of Judas Iscariot betraying Jesus were generated as propaganda during the highly emotional rivalry between early Christians and other groups which did not agree with them. That the story of Judas Iscariot is in part mythical is evidenced by the conflicting testimony in the Synoptic Gospels. For example in one account Iscariot is reported to have betrayed Jesus with a kiss and in another it is stated that Jesus identified himself. As to what Iscariot did with the thirty pieces of silver, one account says that the priests took the money and bought a burying ground and another says that Iscariot bought a piece of ground himself. As to the manner of Iscariot's death, one account says that he hanged himself and another account says that he fell headlong and ruptured his bowels. More than this it might be noted that among the twelve disciples there were two men with the name of Judas. The faithful one might well have been called "Judas" and the unfaithful one "Iscariot." Actually Iscariot was no more a Jew than the other members of the Christian sect. The presentation of him as a representative of those faithful to Judaism is a grotesque stereotype. The circumstance that Jesus went openly to Jerusalem, anticipating death as a result of his public stand, indicates the unlikelihood that secret betrayal could have occurred. One piece of incontrovertible evidence that Jesus was executed by the Roman government under suspicion of treason is the inscription placed on his cross, "This is Jesus, the King of the Jews." This statement expressed the true reason why the Roman ruler had Jesus put to death. Conrad H. Moehlman has described and analyzed data of religious history with the motive of repairing the historical wrong done the Jews by Christians.[6] These details, which might seem to have a minor place in a scientific treatment of contemporary religion, are illuminating in showing how folklore can weave a tissue of fabrication out of the emotional hostilities which people feel. These details further show the wisdom of revising scripture to eliminate anti-Semitic echoes which have no relevance for our time, or at least to revise scriptural materials read by children who lack the objectivity of scholarship to place the details in their proper cultural setting.

In century after century reverberations of the Christian-Jewish conflict, Jews received a minority status after Christianity gained the ascendancy. Corresponding echoes of hostile propaganda can be found in Jewish writings directed against gentiles. The Jews were accorded a ghetto status in European countries, ostracized and cut off from social intercourse with Christians. Occasional outbreaks of violence against Jews occurred in countries where the Catholic Church was dominant, but the most severe persecutions have occurred in areas predominantly Protestant. The contribution of Martin Luther to anti-Semitism, influenced by his belief in the infallibility of scripture, is a sorry episode in the Protestant Reformation. Moehlman writes: "Martin Luther in 1523 published a tract entitled *That Jesus Christ Was Born a Jew* in which he mercilessly criticised the medieval Christian treatment of the Jew. But when Judaism failed to embrace Lutheranism, the Wittenberg Colossus reversed himself in two tracts of 1543 *Regarding Shem Hamphoras* and *Concerning the Jews and their Lies,* recommending their persecution and suppression."[7]

The way in which this religious antagonism can reverberate is illustrated by the following quotation from Adolf Hitler, whose words inflamed a sufficient number of his henchmen, not Christians but living in a Christian culture, to destroy the Jews.

> I say: my feeling as a Christian points me to my Lord and Saviour as a fighter. It points me to the man who once in loneliness, surrounded only by a few followers, recognized these Jews for what they were and summoned men to the fight against them and who, God's truth! was greatest not as sufferer but as fighter. In boundless love as a Christian and as a man I read through the passage which tells us how the Lord at last rose in His might and seized the scourge to drive out of the Temple the brood of vipers and adders. How terrific was His

[6] Conrad H. Moehlman, *The Christian-Jewish Tragedy,* Hart, 1933.
[7] *Ibid.,* p. 175.

fight for the world against the Jewish poison. Today, after two thousand years, with deepest emotion I recognize more profoundly than ever before the fact that it was for this that He had to shed His blood upon the Cross. As a Christian I have no duty to allow myself to be cheated, but I have the duty to be a fighter for truth and justice. And as a man I have the duty to see to it that human society does not suffer the same catastrophic collapse as did the civilization of the ancient world some two thousand years ago—a civilization which was driven to its ruin through this same Jewish people.[8]

It is earnestly to be hoped that such documentary references as these will forever be past history. It is not fitting to revive them, except to point to the potentiality of their recurrence. Anti-Semitism and anti-Catholicism both seem on the wane. Anti-Catholicism stems from the religious wars between Catholics and Protestants in which conduct on each side was harsh toward the opposition. The history of Catholicism in America has been one of somewhat decreasing rigidity toward Protestant heresy, and at the same time Protestants evidence steadily increasing willingness to accept Catholics as a sister denomination in the society of Christianity, although power struggles between Catholics and non-Catholics for control of schools and communities continues.

Furthermore, as enthusiasm for religious orthodoxy wanes, less occasion arises for competing orthodoxies to come into conflict. The decline in religious prejudice in the modern era seems as much a function of the weakening of religious doctrines on the minds of men as it is growth in the ability of religious-minded people to get along with each other. Also, with improved opportunities for communication and cultural exchange, mutual appreciation and respect for the views of those from different religious backgrounds have grown. The scientific study of religion helps people to see beyond the symbols in which a particular religion envelops itself to the universal psychic forces common in all religion, of which Durkheim spoke.

Having recounted past history of Christian-Jewish relationships in painful detail, the sour adage should be added: "The only thing we learn from history is that we do not learn from history." This is a cynical comment if taken literally. It serves to place concerned people on a perpetual alert to avoid any new recrudescence of religious warfare.

As it happens, a fresh devil's brew has reached a boil since the social analyses and prophecies of Karl Marx. A new religious

[8] Adolf Hitler, *My New Order,* Reynal & Hitchcock, 1941, p. 26.

war has taken shape and has already manifested itself on the European scene in wholesale destruction of non-Communists by Communists and in similar destruction of noncapitalists by capitalists, especially by the Fascists. The previous chapter referred to the persecution of Communists by other Americans, and also indicated that Communists would like, if they could, through their secret organization to take control of American life and impose upon it their own economic and ethical tenets. As long as each side is stubborn and inflexible toward the other, the fuel is laid for the fires of religious warfare to soar anew. Likewise, the way in which untruthful propaganda fans the flames of emotional hysteria is convincingly shown by the Christian-Jewish tragedy. The Hindu leader Gandhi spoke from actual experience when he observed that loyalty to truth is of greater consequence for the welfare of society than any other principle of thought or behavior.

We turn now to an examination of the continuing forces which keep religious conflict and prejudice alive, once these have gained historical basis. The student of these forces can discover applications to the continuing conflict between Communism and capitalism.

The causal explanation for the phenomenon of religious conflict involves the circumstance that religions differ. While it is obvious to point out that conflict between the followers of different religions would not take place unless there were different religions, the reasons why religions manifest so many points of difference are of causal relevance. The connection of the geographic environment with fundamental aspects of religion is a slender one. Environmental circumstances explain to some extent the content of religious teachings. But the ideas which are central in a religious system consist of psychic material differentiated from concrete social experience. This differentiation can take place in different ways according to the various possibilities for combination of psychic components. The particular way in which this intellectual process of differentiation unfolds in the history of a people apparently depends a good deal upon chance circumstances. This reference to chance is another way of acknowledging scientific ignorance concerning the precise sequence of causation. Differences in degrees of cultural development, as well as the role played by cultural retrogression when earlier advances in thought are lost, are involved in this variation in the content of a religious system. Geographic relationships involved in war and nationalism indirectly influence the content of religious systems. Also evident is the role played by historical personalities. These are involved because their lives provide an effective vehicle for communicating the content of a religious system from one generation to the next. Thus the key personages and religious prophets differ from religion to religion. Since the historical circumstances of their lives are not the same, variations in religious ideas dramatized by their lives also differ.

Whatever the particular reasons why religious systems diverge from cultural area to cultural area, to the extent that human beings can move toward religious ideas shared in common or at least those which are substantially similar from place to place, the occasion for religious conflict and prejudice is removed. The scientific study of religion tends to bring human beings closer to a realization of the common factors in all religions and also helps people to understand differences in religions not their own.

Religious institutions are not the only ones which differ from people to people. Variations occur with reference to economic, political, educational, and family institutions as well. Yet the differences in these institutions, much as people do disagree concerning them, do not engender as much emotional feeling and conflict as do differences in religious institutions. We must recognize that religion, if it means anything to people, means a great deal to them. Religion encompasses those values which are supreme to its followers. Because religion means so much to people, anything which jeopardizes or appears to threaten the effective functioning of the religion is a matter of great consequence to people. The emotions of people tend to be involved in whatever is of great importance to them. Anything which might harm the role played by a religious system in the life of a people is the target for defensive action.

Competing religious ideas, experienced when followers of different cultural streams of religion come into contact, are a threat in the sense that any proposed innovations in a religious system are a potential threat to the stability and continuance of that system. Innovations are readily accepted in economic technology when these visibly demonstrate their worth. Innovations in religion are not only difficult to see, but the experience of people frequently tells them that novelties do more harm to religion than good. A perennial form of novelty is provided by those who urge relaxation of the principles of their religion in favor of more casual enjoyment of life. So the cultural complex is forged within a religious system that the system must be maintained pure and intact. Moreover, religion depends for its effectiveness upon a considerable measure of group consensus. If it is to be effectively practiced by the group, the group must unite in their support of it. It sometimes seems of lesser importance what particular religious system a group follows than that the group agree upon the system which they do follow. From this line of reasoning, a line which may be followed unconsciously by a religious group, a religious system gains great rigidity in the minds of people. Innovations are frowned upon, such as those presented to people by an alternative religious system.

When people believe that their ways of thinking are best as they are, they tend to develop rationalizations for this belief. Especially do the advocates of a new religion exaggerate its doctrines in advancing them. These rationalizations lie close at hand and come forward of their own accord, anyway. Since a religious system of thought consists of ideas about God, the source of these ideas is readily attributed to revelation by their object, God. In a sense, the ideas are God-given in that they are generated through the operation of what men conceive to be the Divine Spirit in their lives. The line between God-given doctrines and God-perfect doctrines is a fine one and easily lost in the energetic defense which men develop for their religion. What is God-given becomes divinely authorized, and because divinely authorized therefore infallible. How could God be so disposed as to give human beings erroneous ideas to follow? When a religion has reached the stage of being considered divinely revealed and infallible, it comes into inevitable and profound conflict with any other religious system which differs from it.

Still, men usually must recognize that others follow religions which are for them divinely authorized and infallible. Hence some religious systems, such as Judaism and Hinduism, incorporate the broad-minded realization that God also speaks to followers of other religions and in different ways and with different commands. Such religious systems are better able to live in accommodation with contrary ones than can the Roman Catholic or Protestant Fundamentalist forms of Christianity which, in orthodox theory, presuppose that their doctrines are the only true religion, or at least much superior to any other system of religious doctrines.

Coupled with the belief that one's own religion is superior to that of others is the belief that those who follow an inferior religion are thereby in some respects, at least, inferior to oneself. The logic is loose which leads people to prejudge a person on the basis of his religious affiliation. Yet stereotyped images are readily engendered by loose thinking about religion, with the consequence that immoral and antisocial traits are attributed to those who hold a different religious faith. Stereotyped pictures of Jews, Catholics, and Protestants held by each other readily circulate and provide the basis for rejection of people from social and economic relationships. When prejudiced persons think in terms of stereotypes instead of individuals, refusal to grant employment or friendship is an automatic reflex of their nervous system.

Prejudice means the prejudgment of people before the facts concerning their qualifications are considered. The prejudgments which people entertain of minority-group members following a different religion become a "self-fulfilling prophecy."[9] Minority-group members who suffer discrimination may react defensively in order to gain their share of what is denied them. Some individuals may develop traits of aggressiveness and possessiveness which serve to embroider the false stereotype which others hold of them. Traits of aggressiveness and defensiveness are a function of a conflict situation, such as might exist in a university which followed a restricted-quota policy of admissions. If the conflict situation is removed the traits disappear.

Involved in the phenomenon of religious conflict and prejudice are the cultural forces of ethnocentrism and nationalism. Ethnocentrism is a culture complex whereby members of a group believe themselves superior to outsiders. They make their own ethnic characteristics the standard or center of judgment for evaluating the characteristics of others. Ethnocentrism is fostered by the isolation of groups from each other. Lacking acquaintance with and an understanding of each other's ways, members of such groups have no standard of reference except that of their group. When ethnocentric groups come into contact they tend at the same time to come into conflict. Rather than work together in harmony born of understanding, they seek to obstruct others of whom they are suspicious and whom they think of as aliens. Such conflict readily proceeds from the level of cultural disagreement to antagonistic behavior and then to warfare to drive the cultural outsiders away. Since anger is an emotion readily aroused by differences between people, and since fighting those who are regarded as vicious or depraved is a common reaction, ethnocentrism intermittently expresses itself in

[9] R. M. MacIver, *The More Perfect Union,* Macmillan, 1948, pp. 52–81; R. K. Merton, *Social Theory and Social Structure,* Free Press, 1957, chap. 11.

war. In killing and being killed, people readily harbor stereotypes injurious to the character of their opponents. Realizing this, it becomes more understandable that the religious wars between Catholics and Protestants deeply implanted vicious stereotypes held by each other.

Closely allied with the phenomenon of ethnocentrism is that of nationalism. In nationalism the group toward which the individual is ethnocentric is his nation. When war breaks out between nations the manufactured stories of atrocities soon incorporate religious differences if these exist. Much of the roots of religious prejudices arising in Europe and other parts of the world and transplanted to the United States can be attributed to wars between nations in which differences in religion were incidental circumstances. Not only does nationalism enmesh with the vicious circle of religious prejudice toward outsiders, it also plays a large role in prejudice directed toward minority-group members within the nation itself. A nation at war or approaching a state of war becomes preoccupied with the task of destroying the enemy. Sometimes its enemy has a visible, if remote, counterpart among the people of that nation. For example, irrational as it was, during World War II Americans penned up those of Japanese ancestry in concentration camps while those of German ancestry lived and traveled freely. From the standpoint of the danger of espionage, a disloyal person of German extraction, looking like most other Americans, could much more readily act as a spy than could one of Japanese ancestry, whose facial features served to identify him wherever he went. Nevertheless, loyal U.S. citizens of Japanese ancestry were singled out for imprisonment, not citizens of German ancestry. How could this occur? The answer is that those of Japanese ancestry bore a visible resemblance to one of the enemy groups. In the emotional hysteria permeating the prosecution of war, American people readily turned against those who might be, however tenuous the connection, their enemies on the domestic scene.

The disgraceful chapter in American history of the imprisonment of Americans of Japanese ancestry illuminates the immeasurably greater tragedy which occurred when Nazi leaders caused the wholesale destruction of those of Jewish faith. Hitler was probably convinced in his belief that Jews were enemies of the rest of the German people. He saw in the diplomats of other nations and in the representatives of the League of Nations the presence of Jews. Except for the circumstance that Jews are an international-minded people, statistics readily disprove such a fiction to reasonable minds, but not to the minds unbalanced by the psychosis of war. In nation after nation whatever minority group happens to be more unpopular suffers during wartime. Because of anti-Semitism lingering from past centuries, the Jews were an unpopular minority in Germany, at least in the minds of those who held power. Thus the virulent passions of nationalism tipped the balance of latent religious conflict to produce a result which would otherwise defy explanation.

When religious conflict places a lid of repression upon those with opposing religious views or when religious conflict boils over into war, these things occur because of the false belief by the adherents of a religion that they can maintain their own ideas or change those of others by physical force. The religious wars in Europe between Mohammedans and Christians and between Catholics and Protestants, and the persecution of Jews and other religious minorities stemmed in part from the futile and entirely fallacious belief that religious conversion can be accomplished by force. Torture of Jews was considered successful if they could be made to die acknowledging Jesus Christ as their Saviour. Fantastic as such practices may now appear, they were duplicated only a few short years ago in the practices of both Nazis and Communists, who sought to thwart the expressed convictions of men by the rubber truncheon. With less brutality but in a no less real way fanatical nationalists in the United States have persecuted and suppressed Communists. The religious or ethical scenery shifts, but the blind fanaticism of reliance upon force to change tenaciously held religious and social beliefs endures as a cultural pattern.

In analyzing the continuing forces which keep religious or racial prejudice alive there is also much to be said for the Marxian view that religious and other ethnic differences are inflamed by excessive economic competition. When employment is scarce, as in a business depression, prejudice against Catholics, Jews, and Negroes who get jobs increases. Emotional feelings about loss of employment flood the system of stereotypes by which insiders view those whom they regard as outsiders. Moreover, those who hold economic or political power find it to their advantage to stir up conflict between ethnic groups in order to direct hostility away from themselves. Thus the plantation or factory owner who employs mixed labor sets one ethnic group against another. Similarly, Hitler found it useful to direct the antagonism of German people away from his government to those whom he could designate as enemies. The involvement of religious persecution in international, as well as economic, anarchy is deep-rooted.

RELIGION, CLASS, AND CASTE

So far we have considered the religious conflict and discrimination which divides those who hold different religious views. We now consider the way in which religion is a divisive influence between those who have more religion and those who have less or between those who have a religion and others who have none. In this and in other ways religion is involved in the separation of people into social classes.

Concept of Social Class

When social classes exist those within a preferred social class restrict economic and social opportunities to themselves. At the same time they keep out members from a less preferred social class and exclude them from economic, political, friendship, and matrimonial opportunities. When it is impossible for an individual to change the social class location into which he is born by family affiliation, the social class is then known as a caste. The distinction between class and caste is one of degree. Most individuals in American society are able to change their class location somewhat through a combination of superior intelligence, personal qualifications, hard work, and luck. Thus individuals move from a working-class situation to a middle-class one, or from a lower-middle-class location to an upper-middle-class location. As one approaches the higher levels of the social class system, this upward mobility becomes more and more difficult. At the top one finds opportunities largely controlled by a few families who hold their position of power on an hereditary basis. It should also be noted that while Jews attain a complete range of class locations of wealth and social position within their own religious group, they have usually been excluded more systematically from upper social levels in the gentile world. This phenomenon of parallel systems of social stratification divided by caste barriers is much more evident in the case of Negroes. Among these are millionaires, writers, artists, and statesmen of world renown, as well as many in positions of less desirable social and economic status. While caste barriers have been weakening somewhat in the decade since World War II, Negroes are still largely excluded from class membership in white society, especially in the southern part of the United States.

The barriers which divide social classes or social castes are not visible walls as in ancient or feudal times. Rather the barriers are socioeconomic intangibles, but just as real and painful nonetheless. The middle-class white youth attending a leading university may succeed in dating the daughter of a family listed in the *Social Register*. When she politely declines to continue their association he will feel humiliated and will feel angry that his opportunities for personal association should be regulated by rules of class and caste. Or, having gained an engineering degree and graduated with a Phi Beta Kappa key, he goes to work in a large corporation expecting that his superior abilities and self-confidence will bring him to the top in a reasonable course of time. Then it dawns on him with a shock when junior vice-presidencies are awarded that he is not included. Rather, he finds that incompetent or indolent sons of wealthy families or relatives of the owners, whose work he has been doing, receive the credit and get the promotions. He realizes that he has unwittingly dashed his head against social class walls. After unhappy reappraisal of his opportunities he becomes resigned to his inferior status or else gives himself to group efforts to establish a classless society.

The phenomenon of class and caste is rooted in the psychological disposition of people to choose their associations in employment, residence, leisure time, friendship, and marriage, not by criteria of the greatest good of all, but on the basis of individual idiosyncrasies of like and dislike. Some qualities are much sought after in associates, such as those characterizing an attractive personality cultivated through leisure rather than the urgencies of hard work. Those with more wealth and social power are especially esteemed because of the capacities for achievement which these things suggest. Since religion is, in general, an indication of higher achievement and superior qualities of living, the practice and profession of religious beliefs and aims become attributes sought by people in their associates.

These personality characteristics represent only the beginning of the bases for choice of associates in a social class system. Very important is the desire of people to identify themselves with others who are recognized as having a higher social class affiliation. In social class ideology people believe that they succeed if they associate with those who are thought to be successful. But more than this, the opportunities for wealth and power mushroom for the few who attain the higher social levels. In order to gain these coveted opportunities, people governed by a social class ideology struggle desperately to move upward in the social class system. They become hyperconscious of the qualities of those with whom they associate. They draw sharp lines between those whose association they accept in human relationships and those whose association they reject. Their struggle to climb is dictated by the structure of the pyramid of power to whose sides they precariously cling.

In applying their social class ideology, people tend to agree in their judgments of the desirability or lack of desirability of associating with given individuals. Groups of people are viewed similarly by others as to how desirable or undesirable it is to associate with them. People become pegged in the common understanding of members of a social class as to whether they belong or don't belong. A vast and intense competition goes on among human beings for the different locations which the social class system assigns to people and which gives them different economic rewards and opportunities. Impressing others through achievements identified with social class position is a means whereby one gains acceptance by others with a higher social status. Thus the average American, should he possess only a twenty-foot plot for a front yard, will waste his time and his sustenance trying to make the grass in this plot simulate the surface of a billiard table. Or, at the expense of his own educational or religious development, he will mortgage his future to live in a ranch house with a larger picture window or one which has a larger built-in television screen. Of serious consequence, he will widen social class cleavage by refusing to associate with those whose status he thinks would be damaging to his own. To make these comments about the American social class system is hardly a novelty. These observations have been studied and documented by a long list of eminent students of social class and caste, not necessarily in full agreement, such as John Dollard, Milton M. Gordon, August B. Hollingshead, Floyd Hunter, C. Wright Mills, Thorstein Veblen, W. Lloyd Warner, and Max Weber.[10]

[10] J. Dollard, *Caste and Class in a Southern Town,* Yale University Press, 1937; M. M. Gordon, *Social Class in American Sociology,* Duke University Press, 1958; A. B. Hollingshead, *Elmtown's Youth,* Wiley, 1949; F. Hunter, *Community Power Structure,* University of North Carolina Press, 1953; F. Hunter, *Top Leadership, U.S.A.,* University of North Carolina Press, 1959; C. W. Mills, *White Collar,* Oxford University Press, 1951; C. W. Mills, *The Power Elite,* Oxford University Press, 1956; Thorstein Veblen, *The Theory of the Leisure Class,* Modern Library, 1934; W. L. Warner *et al., Yankee City Series,* 5 vols., Yale University Press, 1941–1959; Max Weber, *From Max Weber: Essays in Sociology,* ed. and tr. by H. H. Gerth and C. W. Mills, Oxford University Press, 1946. See also the collection of readings by R. Bendix and S. M. Lipset, *Class, Status and Power,* Free Press, 1953.

Of course, social competition is an inevitable fact of life. To some extent it is desirable. People ought to be rewarded according to their social usefulness. What gives the present social class ideology its feverish temper is the power structure of which it is a function. Social class ideology is part of the sickness of contemporary capitalistic culture. The inimicality of this culture for religion was examined at some length in previous chapters. Concern in this chapter is with the part played by religion in a system of class and caste which distributes the opportunities and rewards of life arbitrarily and unequally.

In defining the phenomenon of social class several further ideas require presentation. One of these is that what is called a social class does not exist apart from the consciousness which people have of possessing a preferred or rejected social status. This is a status from which they exclude those whom they regard as inferior or ineligible. Thus the sheer achievement of wealth, scientific discovery, artistic creation, or religious development does not of itself imply the existence of social classes. It is only when people on the basis of these achievements set themselves apart from others and seek to exclude others from performing the same achievements or by making unequal the opportunities for such achievements that the sociological phenomenon of social classes exists.

It should also be noted that social class levels are not drawn in clear-cut ways in the thinking of people. Sometimes people have an approximate view of three major social class groupings: upper, middle, and working class. Within these major divisions are further subdivisions at least evident to those whose social location is close to the subdivisions involved. In this way evidence can be developed for the existence of a six-class system or a nine-class system, according to the number of levels into which each of the three major classes is divided. Actually we are closer to a correct view of the social class system if we acknowledge it to be composed of a continuum of statuses with almost imperceptible gradations from one status to another. It can be argued that each individual in the social class system is conscious only of three social classes: the class consisting of those whom he accepts and who accept him, the social class consisting of those with whom he would like to associate but who do not accept him, and the class consisting of those who would like to associate with him but whom he does not accept. As for the numerous other groupings who vie for social position beyond the range of his social contacts he may dimly perceive their existence if at all. It should also be noted that people have different patterns of association, depending upon whether the institutional area is family, school, church, employment, or government. As was previously noted, the continuum of statuses is not a one-dimensional one, separate classes existing in the societies of minority groups who in turn are divided from the society of the majority by more or less castelike barriers.

Class distinctions become diffuse and flexible as one descends the social pyramid. At the apex the social class system comes to a sharp and clearly visible head. At the top are a relatively few wealthy families who are not only conscious of themselves as being the uppermost class but who have developed internal organization for the consolidation and perpetuation of their power. Their power depends upon their ownership of means of production and opportunities upon which the lives of most other people depend. At the top these persons work hand in glove, if somewhat uncoördinatedly, to retain and extend their personal and pecuniary opportunities. Their organization lacks the systematic leadership characteristic of a feudal caste system. Yet the emergence of such leadership, as in Fascist epochs in Europe, Asia, South America, and Africa, is an ever-present possibility in the United States.[11]

Those in lower economic brackets in America enjoy material things for themselves which far exceed those possessed by even the emperor cliques in ancient nations. The point is that such opportunities as spiritual freedom, leisure for educational, cultural, and religious pursuits, long life, and the maintenance of health and decency from childhood through old age are just as important, if not more so, to those dispossessed of these today as was bread to starving populations in other historical eras. To call attention to these things is to stress the large unfinished business in American democracy.

Role of Religion in Social Stratification

Studies of social class composition of religious groups indicate that the percentages of Episcopalians, Congregationalists, Presbyterians, and Jews in upper income levels in business and professional occupations and having college degrees are approximately two or three times the proportions having these upper-class characteristics among Methodists, Lutherans, Baptists, and Catholics.[12] These data are very approximate and regional

[11] For statistical documentation of the nature and extent of power exercised by the uppermost class in American life, see Mills, *The Power Elite.*

[12] Liston Pope, "Religion and the Class Structure," *Annals of the American Academy of Political and Social Science,* March, 1948, pp. 84–91.

variations are large. Church affiliation diminishes but still remains substantial among lower income levels. In interpreting such data as these it is necessary to show (1) why those with religious affiliation and attendance are found disproportionately at upper-class levels, (2) why substantial religious affiliation and attendance is found also at lower-class levels, and (3) why some religious denominations have a much higher proportion of members in upper-class levels than other denominations.

As analyzed in the preceding chapter, the two polar explanations for the association between religion and social class are those given by Karl Marx and Max Weber. These men contended respectively that religion is an instrument of economic exploitation and that religion is an influence generating economic success. Intermediate views have been given by R. H. Tawney, H. R. Niebuhr, J. M. Yinger, and other sociologists.

The sincere practice of religion cultivates habits of character, such as honesty, service, and frugality, which facilitate success in business relationships with others. The precise extent to which this influence is responsible for the past economic success of Protestant groups compared with Catholics is an important research question but one on which it is difficult to obtain carefully controlled data. Max Weber's data document the process whereby fresh religious motivation in the Protestant Reformation encouraged rapid economic success in the capitalist class in the initial stages of the industrial revolution. Depending upon the relative economic opportunities with which the individual begins, not all religious exercise eventuates in economic success. Those less economically successful also experience religious needs, with the result that religious affiliation and attendance more or less permeate all social and economic levels.

Data such as those of Trott and Sanderson disclose a high proportion of bankers and business executives on boards of control in Protestant churches. The effort to control churches as agencies of public opinion is unquestionably a factor in this control, as shown by such studies as Liston Pope's *Millhands and Preachers*. On the other hand, churches are among the less immediately effective instruments for influencing public opinion compared with such agencies as newspapers and magazines. Another motivation which prevails, especially in smaller communities, is that of businessmen seeking to establish themselves in the public view as morally upright and honest. Where church affiliation and attendance is made an informal test in primary-group society of habits of character, regular church attendance is a necessity for a small-town businessman.

The particular circumstances which caused three Protestant denominations and Jews to stand, relatively speaking, above other religious groups in social class attainment include the following.

1. The religious revival during the Protestant Reformation primarily affected Protestants rather than Catholics.

2. When religion gravitates toward upper-class levels, new religious movements arise to meet the needs of lower-income persons. Examples of such movements are provided by those of Methodists and Baptists, and more recently Fundamentalist and Holiness groups among low-income groups. It also seems apparent that the Baptist congregational polity would have less appeal for ambitious capitalists than the Presbyterian and Episcopalian forms of church organization and more appeal for low-income groups desiring to control their own affairs.

3. In the successive migrations of Europeans to America, those who arrived earlier, such as the Congregationalists, were "on the ground floor" of economic opportunity. Methodists, Lutherans, and Catholics appeared later.

4. Also important in explaining the social class picture of American denominations is the foreign-language prejudice shown by those of English ancestry. The discrimination against foreign-language-speaking church people, such as German Lutherans and Italian Catholics, reduces the proportions of upper-class persons among these groups.

5. The relatively high economic position of Jews is not easy to explain. In part the explanation is that Jews are predominantly an urban people, and economic success of urban dwellers exceeds that of those whose background is rural. Another factor is that the religious ethic of Jews, like that of Protestants, is conducive to those habits of business efficiency which foster economic success. Furthermore, Jews have a long history of successful experience in mercantile pursuits.

6. Approximately two-thirds of Negroes with religious affiliation are Baptists, and ranking next is their membership in Methodist and Catholic churches. The social and economic discrimination which forces Negroes into lower-income levels is a factor in the average economic status characterizing these three denominations.

Religion as a Conservative Influence in Class and Race Prejudices

One of the ways in which churches accede to social wrongs contrary to the religious ideals professed is provided by complying with the class and race prejudices of people. Religious institutions, like other institutions, are geared to the prevailing purposes of people, whether these are commendable or not. Administrators of these institutions tend to cater to prejudiced attitudes of others in order to gain their support.

A theological student reported to the author that when serving as an assistant in an upper class suburban church he was advised by a minister to discourage applications for membership from those with lesser social status. He was told to do this by advising the applicant that he and his family would be happier joining a church where they had friends or where they could find people with whom they could share things in common. If this discouragement failed, then the assistant was told to inform the applicant that he probably could not afford the amount customarily expected from members to defray church expenses. If none of these things worked then the assistant was to tell the applicant that there was a waiting list and that it would be a year or more before sufficient vacancies would occur for him and his family to be admitted. The minister said to his assistant, "We have a nice congenial fellowship, and we wish to keep it that way." In this case the discrimination was directed against white persons lacking an Ivy League education and sufficient income to merit membership in the socially exclusive church. This blatant instance may be exceptional. Data concerning ways in which upper-class churches retain their upper-class constituencies are not readily available. However, it is apparent that many ministers are more interested in building up a wealthy upper-class congregation worshiping in expensive buildings surrounded by smoothly tailored grounds than they are in carrying Jesus' ministry to the socially unfortunate at a sacrifice in material rewards to themselves.

The instance just described refers to discrimination practiced by white persons against others of the same skin color. The same experience of discrimination in much sharper and less disguised form is generally encountered by Negroes should they be so indiscreet as to seek membership in a white church. Most Negro Protestants belong to segregated denominations, that is, ones with either all-Negro congregations or all-white congregations. One of the exceptions to this prejudiced situation is provided by treatment of Negroes by the Roman Catholic Church. The policy of the Catholic Church is for all faithful Catholics, regardless of skin color, to share in the same communion services. This policy varies in its effectiveness in the South, but the weight of the Catholic hierarchy is brought to bear from time to time in order to diminish the islands of segregation which remain in the Catholic Church. Membership in Catholic as well as Protestant churches is still governed considerably by lines of residential segregation.

The leadership in Protestant denominations has since World War II been vitally concerned with eliminating segregated churches, but progress toward mixed congregations has been slight, owing to the lethargy or opposition on the part of members of all-white congregations. Protestant churches are much less able to impose policies by administrative order, since their churches are for the most part democratically controlled. The principal opportunity which Protestant churches have for integrating their congregations arises when population movement makes their neighborhoods mixed. The following account describes how a church confronted by racial mixing in its neighborhood became a genuine Christian fellowship.

Twelve years ago First Baptist, on Chicago's south side, was an all-white church in an all-white, aging neighborhood. But it was staggering under the pressures wrought by the departure of long-active families for the suburbs, by the influx of new residents uninterested in its—or any church's—program. It still had 500 names on the rolls, but on Sunday no more than 75 people were to be found in the pews. Meanwhile, into the near-by apartment house area and beyond the square mile of magnificent homes set in wide lawns that constitutes the once-elite Kenwood area, were moving dozens of Japanese-Americans, relocated from the western concentration camps where a war-frightened nation had blindly thrust them. Passing up a suggestion that it provide separate churches for these newcomers, the Chicago Baptist Missionary Society recommended that they be welcomed into existing congregations. Soon large numbers of Nisei, particularly young people, were taking advantage of First Baptist's hospitality. Before 1944 was out, modest, dedicated Jitsuo Morikawa had been called to serve as assistant minister. Two and a half years later, when the second of two ministers with whom he had served left for other fields, Dr. Morikawa was invited to take his place. He is still there, fulfilling a ministry that has enriched not only the handsome brownstone church on 50th Street but all Chicago Protestantism as well.

Rapid industrial growth after World War II brought a great wave of Negro migration from the south to Chicago, and in 1948 the Supreme Court decreed an end to restrictive residence covenants. As a result, First Baptist soon began to have Negro neighbors. Seeing a church whose name was familiar, a few of them made their way into the sanctuary on Sunday mornings. One day in 1950, a Negro who had been attending regularly signed a card indicating he would like to join the church. Through normal procedure, he was called on by a representative of the board of deacons, whose duty it is to recommend congregational action on candidates for membership. The twelve members of the board pondered the course before them. Should they treat this as a crisis, call a congregational meeting? For a week they thought about the matter, prayed about it. At the end of that time they met again—calm and confident that only one course was possible.

It is implicit in the Christian faith, the deacons agreed, that the church, not a private club but the channel through which that faith operates, is by its very nature open to all who wish to become a part of it and are willing to fulfill the responsibility membership entails. To treat an application for membership as "different" because it was signed by a black instead of a white hand would be to admit that First Baptist was something less than God's own instrument. So on the next "membership" day the chairman of the board of deacons—a young veteran of World War II, product of a strong Baptist upbringing—forthrightly read off the list of proposed members, the Negro's along with the rest. The congregation assented—and that was all there was to it.

Today, First Baptist is flourishing. Of the active members about half are Negro, 40 per cent white, the rest Oriental. The change in racial complexion did lead some white members to transfer out—but except for a few these were "fringe" members; the "salt" remained. And through the experience of the past few years a deeper sense of Baptist churchmanship, a new realization of what the Christian faith means, has developed. Says a member through 70 years: "Never before have I had such a sense of the church as a spiritual community." One elderly man who entered First Baptist a half-century ago but who for 20 years had not attended its services, has returned to full-time participation. "We have now a depth of meaning and fellowship I never found before," he says. For the first time, First Baptist is attracting members, white and Negro alike, from the academic University of Chicago community a mile to the south.[13]

Those living outside of the United States who decry the persistence of race prejudice in American culture sometimes fail to appreciate how deeply rooted the pattern is in American history. The transformation of culture by people working from within can be likened to the clearing of water in a lake by pouring in fresh water from its source. If the lake could be emptied and refilled, the clearing process could be carried out much more quickly. But culture cannot be emptied and replaced without eliminating the human beings who are its carriers. The alternative is a slow process of introducing new ideas and ideals in the minds and personalities of each new generation of children who

[13] Margaret Frakes, "Two Churches Unafraid," *Christian Century,* April 11, 1956, pp. 450–451.

are born. Since these children largely receive their views of Negro-white relationships from their parents and older associates, the inpouring of a fresh stream of culture mixes with and gradually displaces the undesired discoloration in people's thinking, feeling, and acting. Furthermore, a series of circular mechanisms or self-fulfilling prophecies operate against the achievement of sound perspectives. One of these vicious circles is that the beliefs which people have concerning the inferior ability of Negroes are caused by the denial of educational and economic opportunity to Negroes, who then cannot show what their abilities actually are. Another vicious circle is that provided by the ongoing economic conflict between Negroes and whites. When Negroes are unfairly treated they quite naturally react with actions which are aggressive but which are taken by whites as necessitating the repression of aggressive behavior. Similarly, the oppression by whites is taken by Negroes as necessitating aggressive action on their part. Economic competition for jobs and homes accelerates these vicious circles.

An understanding of vicious circles which forestall progress permits them to be broken and constructive steps to be taken toward the achievement of mutual respect and equality of treatment of all people by each other. In the achievement of mutual understanding the avoidance of stereotyped or loaded words is to be avoided. Even the term *race* is not in good scientific repute because of the false connotations which are sometimes read into it. Some scientific students go so far as to maintain that so-called racial characteristics are largely if not entirely the product of social selection during mating in early centuries of human evolution.[14] If this theory is valid, this means that racial characteristics are actually a form of cultural baggage accumulated from past cultural patterns and lack foundation in permanent biological determinism.

If the term *race* is to be used in a scientific sense, it refers to a group of people who possess similar external physical characteristics and who are conscious of these characteristics as a basis for their behavior towards others. So defined, the concept of race would dwindle in importance when discriminatory behavior becomes past history.

It is hoped by democratic-minded persons that the present situation of largely all-Negro churches is a temporary phase and that eventually people will be no more conscious of differences in skin color than they now are of differences in eye or hair color

[14] M. F. Ashley Montagu, *Man's Most Dangerous Myth,* Harper, 1952.

in the free association of blondes and brunettes. In the present phase of the religious life of Negroes, their churches provide an opportunity for self-determination and pursuit of personal interests without interference by whites. Negro churches play a more important role in the community life of Negroes than is the case of white churches in the lives of whites. Ministers are influential leaders among Negroes, frequently rising to political as well as religious prominence.

Religious Answers to Class and Race Prejudice

Since religious institutions ostensibly seek to improve the quality of human life, they may be expected to play a useful role in the ongoing programs of American people to eliminate social class and race prejudice. These programs are developed and pursued by many different agencies in different parts of the country but they include three major prongs or lines of attack. One of these is scientific research. This research is necessary to find out the social, psychological, and economic dynamics of prejudiced behavior. By accurately determining the causal factors involved and assessing their relative importance, it becomes possible to develop a realistic program to eliminate prejudice from people's thinking and behavior. Research is necessary to determine the extent and severity of prejudice of different kinds in different localities. By seeing situations in accurate factual perspective, programs can be realistically and efficiently carried out in order to reduce prejudice. It then becomes possible to work with existing social resources insofar as possible and to combat antisocial forces in the most strategic manner. To determine the needs for education and legislation and to evaluate their effectiveness, scientific research plays an indispensable role in meeting all social problems, including those of class and race prejudice.

Another prong is education. This is a pleasant-sounding word, waved like a wand in connection with many social problems. In order for education to go forward, it is necessary to consider in detail through what institutional channels and by whom the education is to be carried on. Schools and universities play the principal role in introducing growing human beings to new ideas which enable better and more democratic ways of living to come about. This in turn implies the necessity for those engaged in teaching to receive the type of training which acquaints them thoroughly with the ideas they are expected to arouse in the minds of their students. Generally speaking, teacher-training colleges are doing an effective job in informing prospective teachers with findings from scientific research concerning the mechanisms of class and race prejudice.

For those who have left school, education reaches them principally through adult programs. It is here that churches and synagogues in their educational programs can introduce adults as well as children to scientific ideas about prejudice and discrimination which were missed as part of regular schooling. If denominational groups lay upon their memberships responsibility for learning as a means to altruistic living, the opportunity is readily available for introducing sound scientific content in Sunday School programs as a means of combating ignorance and misinformation about minority groups. Beyond Sunday School programs, churches along with other civic groups frequently conduct or sponsor forums or institutes to give people fuller preparation for participation in contemporary world affairs. These educational activities now draw in no more than a small fraction of people, principally those who are already converted.

If churches are to fulfill their present-day responsibilities, it is necessary for them effectively to arouse concern for the continuous educational growth of their members as part of the ethical obligations of modern life. If people are to be brought into a meaningful relationship with the ultimate purposes of their religions, they need to have strongly brought home to them the importance of creative citizenship. By this is meant that in place of the dissipation of time in idle pursuits such as watching television or engaging in superficial conversation, intellectual energies instead are focused upon learning about and performing those things which create a better world for people today and for posterity. There seems no reason why such education under the sponsorship of churches cannot assume the dimensions of past crusades, such as the abolitionist movement, the women's rights movement, and the temperance movement.

Not least in importance in any educational program is that carried on by word of mouth from one person to another. The most influential form of education is that in which people in face-to-face relationships influence each other to think more understandingly. Word-of-mouth education is a form for which responsibility falls squarely upon each individual. Along with other ethical obligations placed upon the individual by his church is, or at least should be, the obligation to build up human life through what one says and does.

Legislation as a means of social change is usually viewed by scientific proponents as a means of securing concerted action after sufficient enlightenment and support for such action has grown in the minds of those who are to be regulated by the legislation. This does not mean that fair employment practices laws should be delayed until there is unanimity, but rather that such laws to be effective are to be passed after education has reduced opposition to a minority of prejudiced persons. Americans have long had a flair for attempting to solve social problems by passing laws about them. Unfortunately, experience shows that the force of law has serious limitations. Prohibition produced an unfavorable reaction. Present efforts to control drug addiction, prostitution, and gambling by passing ill-considered laws have been largely ineffective. For much the same reasons, legislation cannot be expected to accomplish results among those not adequately prepared by education. The present policy of the U.S. Supreme Court in ending segregation in public schools is not to force integration of all schools at once, but rather to require that school districts at present segregated move steadily and deliberately toward a condition of integration. However, compliance by local communities has been slow or nonexistent, and obstructive tactics numerous.

In many states and cities fair employment practices legislation is acknowledged by most concerned persons to have made large progress in equalizing economic opportunities for majority and minority group members. At the same time, such legislation has shown its limitations in that it cannot go much beyond advances in public opinion concerning equal employment opportunities. The principal achievements of such laws have been in equalizing mass employment opportunities for unskilled, semiskilled, or skilled workers. Such legislation has not been effective in equalizing employment opportunities at higher levels of training and income. As far as social class prejudice is concerned, such laws have not attempted to deal with discrimination practiced on the basis of family or friendship connections. One of the needs which must be met before effective legislation against social class prejudice can be enacted is for psychological research to define more accurately job specifications and the qualifications of people in situations where specialized training and abilities are required.

Differences of opinion exist as to the role which religious groups should play in advocating the enactment of legislation to solve problems of society. It is argued by some that the function of the church should be to encourage thoughtful fulfillment of altruistic sentiments without specifying in detail the political steps to be taken. Church members are then to be encouraged to think out and to carry out their civic responsibilities, but the actual thinking out and carrying out are left to individuals. It is argued that for the churches to take decisive political stands causes alienation of church members who do not agree. They are then left outside of the influence of churches altogether. It is also argued that, judging by past history, ecclesiastical organizations frequently make serious mistakes. For them to set themselves up as authorities in political matters invites the enactment of unwise laws which, if left to individual initiative of citizens, might not be passed. The principal objection, however, is to the church's being built into an instrument of far-reaching political power by encouraging it to take active part in political affairs. Having painfully learned the importance of separation of church and state, many would be reluctant to see their churches use their organization as a political machine. It seems sufficient for denominational bodies to function, as they now primarily do, in an advisory capacity. In this capacity they or their committees recommend the passage of social legislation, but they do not require that their constituents as a condition of church membership support such laws. An opposing view holds that churches should take a more vigorous part in mobilizing their memberships in support of political action.

From the foregoing review of research, education, and legislation as means of eliminating prejudice, it becomes apparent that the principal contribution of religious institutions is found in creating motivation for change. The broader function of these institutions is the intensification of altruistic ideals. If there is success in arousing and strengthening these ideals, people of their own accord will seek superior social and economic conditions with little direction or prompting. If churches fail in this task of making altruism live, no amount of paper programs spelled out in endless detail will produce a better society. While self-interest is an inevitable factor in the working out of any social problem, unless there is a sufficient amount of altruistic interest, human beings are unable to work together to solve their problems. It is difficult to discern any important movements in history which produced constructive changes through the working out of self-interest alone. On the other hand, many instances can be cited of movements for change which were successful because of the heroic or at least devoted altruistic motivation of their proponents. Much the same can be said concerning the elimination of social class and race prejudice. Until altruistic concern is aroused for the attainment of mutuality and equality of opportunity for all human beings, progress toward this goal is slow and halting.

While it seems impractical for a religious institution to turn itself into a political instrument, there is no reason why participants in a political organization need not be religiously motivated. A dramatic example of this in modern times is provided by the movement of the Indian nationalists for independence from Great Britain. Gandhi and his associates viewed their activities as much more than boycotts, noncoöperation, and disobedience of British laws. They realized that what they did would bring severe punishment, as in the massacre of hundreds of Hindus at Amritsar in the early stage of the nonviolent movement for independence. Hundreds of thousands suffered imprisonment and physical privation as a result of rejecting British rule. In this suffering Gandhi saw a means of reaching the conscience of the British. By accepting suffering with humility and good will toward their persecutors, the Hindus succeeded in making a moral appeal to the British. Gandhi argued that if instead the Indian nationalists had engaged in violent revolution, the British would have retained the upper hand and the movement for independence would have been crushed. According to Gandhi, the strategic value of nonviolent direct action is that it is the only effective weapon against superior military force.

The Gandhian movement is significant in that it involved brown men against white. The prejudice of the British was a color prejudice as well as a desire for dominion and economic exploitation. Inspired by Gandhi's achievements, Martin Luther King, a Negro leader in Montgomery, Alabama, persuaded his fellow citizens, Negro and a few white, to end discrimination in bus transportation.[15] A committee largely made up of religious leadership was formed, called the Montgomery Improvement Association. This committee succeeded in organizing a 100 percent boycott of city buses by Negro citizens. It raised financial support and organized auto transportation for those dependent upon bus travel. During the bus boycott, Martin Luther King and his associates maintained good will and equanimity in the face of violence and threats of violence. Despite bombing and gunfire, the Montgomery Improvement Association persisted in its boycott. The city and the bus company capitulated after the U.S. Supreme Court ruled bus segregation illegal in Montgomery, but

[15] M. L. King, Jr., *Stride Toward Freedom,* Harper, 1958.

not before the Negroes had demonstrated the effectiveness of their boycott. Nonviolent direct action has been taken up by numerous students engaging in sit-in strikes or prayer marches, regardless of danger, to end segregated treatment of Negroes.

The Fellowship of Reconciliation, an organization of religious pacifists, has played an active role in advocating the application of Gandhian techniques to solving problems of discrimination and injustice. Its members have taken part in the Congress of Racial Equality, which has upon numerous occasions succeeded in ending discrimination against Negroes in restaurants. The usual procedure of CORE is for a mixed group of white and Negro patrons to seat themselves in a restaurant and wait for all to be served before they begin to eat. Prior to this procedure conciliatory efforts are made to secure the coöperation of the management in ending its discrimination. Throughout the campaign, members of CORE are careful to maintain good will and friendliness toward those whose policies they are seeking to change. The Fellowship of Reconciliation has formulated in detail the procedure to be followed in ending racial injustice through nonviolent resistance. In a pamphlet, *How to Practice Nonviolence,* the following statement is given.

Nonviolence is a way of overcoming injustice, not of retaliating for it. Basically it is rooted in the recognition that your opponent is human. Being human, he will probably react with fear if you threaten him, but in the long run he is likely to respond with good will if you go out of your way to encourage it. Don't expect immediate results. Your opponent's first reaction may be surprise that you have not answered injustice with injustice. He may then become exasperated that you are not "talking his language," and he may try to provoke you further, try to incite you to violence.

He will probably be very suspicious and think that you are planning to trick him in some secret way, or he may think that your nonviolence stems from weakness, and try to take advantage of you. But gradually, if you hold fast to your nonviolent program, your opponent will gain respect for you. If your campaign succeeds, it will not be by defeating him but by removing his hostility. You will not only have attained your objective but will have given it a firm foundation in good will to make it permanent. In the following, it is assumed that the campaign is conducted by a group rather than an individual.

Four basic ground rules: 1. Define your objective. There is much injustice around you. A single nonviolent campaign will not remove it all. Focus sharply on the immediate injustice: it must be fairly simple and easy to discuss in clear-cut terms. Other matters may be drawn into the struggle later, and other major objectives will call for a major campaign later on.

2. Be honest. Part of your goal is to win your opponent's respect. Conduct yourself in a way to encourage it; let him know by your own scrupulous care for truth and justice that you merit his respect. This may mean giving more than you get, but you will find that it is worth it in the long run. Remember, too, that you are not without guilt yourself. You may benefit greatly by examining your present and past conduct.

3. Love your enemy. This sounds like a paradox, but it works. You are not up against a deep-dyed villain but only a man who has done wrong. Even though you are striving to undo that wrong, show good will to him no matter what he does. Do not vilify, ridicule or humiliate him at any time, in any way. Let him know at all times that you are out to establish justice, not to defeat him.

4. Give your opponent a way out. By using nonviolence, you are showing a kind of strength that shows up the weakness of injustice. Don't lord it over your opponent. Recognize his weakness and his embarrassment. Find a way to let him participate in your victory when it comes.

Five strategic steps: 1. Investigate. Get the facts. Clear up any possible misunderstandings right at the start. If you are sure that an injustice has been done, be equally sure who is to blame for it. A nonviolent campaign based on false or shaky assumptions is licked before it starts.

2. Negotiate. Go to your opponent and put the case to him. Maybe a solution can be worked out at this point. Maybe your opponent has a grievance that you didn't know about. Now is the time to find out. If no solution is possible, let your opponent know that you intend to stand firm to restore justice, and let him know that you are always ready to negotiate further.

3. Educate. Keep your group well-informed of the issues, and spread the word to the public. This may involve issuing mimeographed handbills, printed leaflets or a number of pamphlets. It may also call for door-to-door personal visits, telephone calls, public speeches, press releases. Talk to the editor of the local newspaper and explain your position. Organize a letters-to-the-editor campaign and a similar campaign of letters to government officials. Always stick to the facts, avoid exaggeration, be brief and show good will.

4. Demonstrate. Picketing, poster-walking, mass meetings and the handing out of leaflets on the street are called for at this stage. All of these must be conducted in an orderly manner. The people who are demonstrating should be neat, well-informed and calm, able to endure possible heckling and to withstand possible violence without panic, and without resorting to violence in return. It is most important to maintain discipline at this stage and "keep cool under fire."

5. Resist. Nonviolent resistance is the final step, to be added to the other four as a last resort. This means a boycott, a strike, the defiance of an unjust law, or other forms of civil disobedience. Discipline must be firm to avoid making your resistance violent; every provocation must be answered with continuing good will, and you must be ready for self-sacrifice that will leave no doubt as to your integrity and courage. But remember that suffering is to be endured, never inflicted—in this is the moral victory from which your struggle can be won.[16]

It is easy for the individual, enthusiastic about eliminating class and race prejudice, to become enamored of large programs of educational or political action while overlooking the vital opportunities for eliminating prejudice in day-to-day relationships with others. Churches can without risk of political compromise strongly lay upon each individual the responsibility for democratic conduct in accepting his associates. Since vocational opportunities depend so much upon friendship relationships, it is of paramount importance that there be avoidance of discrimination in forming friendship relationships. This means going well beyond casual acquaintanceship with members of other ethnic groups. It means insisting upon the admission of those from other ethnic groups into the organized friendship groups to which one belongs. Social or fraternal organizations which practice exclusion of minority-group members do not have an ethically legitimate claim for the membership of anyone. Here is a situation where individual direct action can be followed either to procure the admission of all on an equal basis or else to sever one's own relationship to the organization practicing discrimination. In place of the prevailing practice of granting economic opportunities to those who are our friends the opposite rule of friendship should be followed of developing friendships among those with whom we are vocationally associated. Instead of choosing employment associates on a basis of friendship, friends should be chosen on the basis of association in employment. Instead of the capricious basis upon which people consent to share experience and mutual aid in friendship relationships, a sounder social policy is to give these things on the basis of vocational or residential propinquity. Instead of keeping people out of our residential neighborhoods because they are not our friends, we should let them live next to us and then because they are our neighbors make them our friends.

A thoughtless aspect of the well-meant efforts of some who

[16] *How to Practice Nonviolence,* pamphlet issued by the Fellowship of Reconciliation, Nyack, New York.

think they are serving the cause of democratic race relationships is that they say: "Of course, Negroes should be allowed to own homes wherever they wish, as long as they don't live on our block." When this attitude is systematically followed block by block, the inevitable consequence is that Negroes remain penned up in their urban ghettos or rural slums, denied the educational and cultural advantages of living in attractive residential surroundings. These comments have direct application to members of religious congregations. Congregations are organized on the basis of residential neighborhoods. They, more than any other institutions, have primary responsibility for dissolving the ethnic barriers which keep human beings from living where their economic means and desire for congenial neighbors would otherwise lead them to live. A religious congregation which seeks to grow by accepting members who want to keep out those from another class or race is engaging in a palpably unethical practice. Ministers or religious leaders have the responsibility to coöperate with their congregations in the formulation of well-defined policies of open membership. Nor is it sufficient for the "welcome" sign to be hung in front of a church. Well-meaning white church members are sometimes distressed because Negroes do not respond to encouragement to join all-white or nearly all-white congregations. Such white persons fail to realize that a church is much more than a place of worship. It is a social center for fellowship of those who are intimate friends. To invite a Negro to join a white church congregation and then to deny him this fellowship which is the religious reality of congregational life is hypocritical. The only sound basis for integrating church congregations is for this integration to extend throughout the range of friendship relationships in the congregation. If there is failure at this point, Negroes naturally prefer their own churches, where they receive a warm reception.

Discrimination in economic relationships is woven of one piece with discrimination in friendship relationships. It is precisely because prejudiced people are disposed to reject those of a different ethnic group from leisure-time relationships that they seek to do the same in economic association. Moreover, economic relationships reach directly out into leisure-time associations, since people set the basis for economic coöperation while meeting as friends over the luncheon table or evenings in their homes. This interdependence of human relationships reaches inescapably into another area of human association, that of marriage. If we inquire as to the principal reason why parents mold the associations of their children to avoid play with members of minority groups, we find that courtship and matrimonial opportunities are uppermost in parent's minds. Parents wish to avoid romantic entanglements between their children and individuals in a different ethnic group. So they seek to keep the two groups apart, and thereby they pass along their prejudices to their children. Looking at the connection between friendship and marriage from another standpoint, parents are concerned that their sons and daughters not lose social status by associating with those whose status they consider to be inferior. Thus, dating a Negro is frowned upon. Likewise association with that nice boy or nice girl from the other side of town is discouraged because of fear of loss of social status. We are forced to the conclusion that discrimination in employment and in friendship relationships is interwoven in the same social fabric with discrimination in mate selection. The only thorough-going answer to prejudice and discrimination is for persons to intermarry freely.

A strong statement supporting the divinely given rights of persons of different races to marry was published in the newspaper of Vatican City in opposition to antimiscegenation laws imposed by the Italian fascist government in 1938. "When two Catholics of diverse races have decided to contract marriage and present themselves to her, free from any canonical impediments, the Church cannot, just by reason of the diversity of race, deny her [official] assistance. This is demanded by her sanctifying mission and by those rights which God has given and the Church recognizes for all her children without distinction. Thus, on this point, a general and absolute prohibition of marriage is in opposition to the doctrine and laws of the Church."[17]

Intermarriage as an answer may pose dilemmas. Many persons lack the unusual personality qualifications required to make a success of interracial marriage. Nor can they lightly bring into the world children who face discrimination practiced against them by members of the ethnic groups of both parents. Furthermore, to encourage or even allow miscegenation is provocation to mob violence or at least violates the laws in some states. Those with a fuller vision of the level of brotherhood which different branches of the human family may eventually achieve look forward to the time when all impediments to intermarriage are removed. Short of that time it is still of vital importance to recog-

[17] *L'Osservatore Romano,* November 14–15, 1938, number 265. Quoted in J. F. Doherty, *Moral Problems of Interracial Marriage,* Catholic University of America Press, 1949, p. 34.

nize the manner in which discrimination in friendship and in employment rests upon discrimination in marriage. Through this recognition it becomes possible to steer a line of friendship relationships closer to social acceptance of members of other ethnic groups, even if this association cannot practically eventuate in intermarriage. Also, from a religious standpoint it remains questionable whether those whose religious faiths are fundamentally different can achieve a workable marriage, as we shall consider in the next chapter. Yet the necessity remains of extending sympathetic assistance and sharing of experience, which are the substance of friendship, to other human beings on the basis of their need for these.

chapter 16 Religion and Family Life

Altruistic Opportunity

For most people the deepest and most lasting satisfactions of human existence are found through living as members of a family. The experience of family life is like a satisfying food which can readily go sour if improperly cared for but which under appropriate conditions gives a keen and zestful flavor to all of one's life. The enjoyments of family living shift from one age level to another. This makes accurate anticipation of what lies ahead for the individual vaguely defined until each new level of participation is reached. In a well-adjusted family, the child's earliest memories of family joys are afforded by his close emotional attachment to his parents, first of all his mother. He probably recalls listening to stories while seated on his mother's lap, eating favorite meals at the family table, or the warm reassurance felt after running to Mommy when hurt or threatened by harm. The child will also recall the long-awaited moment when Daddy returns from work to romp and play with his children. Of course the family is a means of discipline and direction of the child's personality, which imposes limitations and frustrations, just as adults experience these at the hands of the larger society which helps as well as hampers them.

As young people grow toward adulthood they are expected to assume more and more responsibilities in the operation of the family household. Until their goals and values have grown to the stage where they easily and willingly identify themselves with family purposes, household duties seem irksome. Not until they have married and formed new families of their own can they fully appreciate the happy experiences which come from ministering to their children and to each other through household activities and expression of affection. As parents, together with their children, grow older they come to feel greater competence and at-homeness in fulfilling family functions. They become capable counselors to their youngsters, who eventually leave to form their own families. Then in the serenity of later years they continue to look out upon the social world of their making and to lend a hand where it best seems needed. Finally, as they approach the twilight of life they depend increasingly upon their grown children for advice and aid and perhaps physical care. When they leave this life for whatever life is beyond, they do so surrounded by loving and affectionate children and grandchildren. Whatever trust they have gained during their lifetime that life is good and has spiritual significance beyond death is fortified at the final moment of parting. Whether life is lived in this way largely depends upon the inspiration breathed into it by religion.

Family living with its care of the helpless young and the care of a man and woman for each other provides life's largest opportunity for altruistic fulfillment. The bearing and rearing of children create something of greatest value. Participation in the larger society outside the family likewise brings altruistic fulfillment to those who are working for the common good. But living in a family gives the individual an immediate and first-hand experience of achievement which he can see and feel. Furthermore, those who live for the good of their society do so ultimately for the individuals whose families are part of the society. At the same time, the family can be a reciprocal instrument for the upbuilding of the social order and the religious life of others through its offspring and through what husband and wife do as partners in enterprises outside the home. Those individuals who by circumstance or choice form no new families of their own can still identify themselves with families of relatives or friends, or, in living for a social cause, feel their ultimate purpose is the enrichment of individual and family living.

Interest of Religion in Family Living

What has just been said is by way of underlining the interest of religion in family living. Since religion, whether as a system of ideas or as a set of institutional practices, seeks to arouse and achieve altruistic purposes, it follows that religion has interested itself more in the family as an institution than it has interested itself in other institutions which compose society. Most of the world religions today have much to say concerning what the appropriate goals for family living are and how these goals can best be fulfilled. Nowhere in the network of institutions making up society do the teachings and inspiration of churches and synagogues touch these institutions more closely and continuously than they do the family.

It is of course true that many organized religious groups endeavor to make their members see a long-range significance which extends far beyond the span of life for the contemporary generation. Sometimes this significance is supernatural in that a church is anxious to survive, or better still to multiply, in order, as it thinks, to serve the purposes of a heaven beyond this life. This involves a keen interest in the birth rate of families whose souls are future candidates for salvation in the next world. At the same time, religious groups primarily concerned with life on this earth feel a larger sense of achievement if they can insure that there is an ample future population to be carriers of the religious culture which the church propagates. Thus Communists as well as Catholics are interested in a sufficient birth rate. Also, motivations of power and prestige may play a role in the interest some church groups have in what happens to their families. Membership in a religious group is typically by families as units. If a family breaks up or loses its unity, the vitality of church membership is impaired at the same time. But religion, being essentially a system for the cultivation and practice of altruistic ideals, however these are couched in theological terminology, has an interest in family living which is primarily altruistic.

It is our concern to examine the interaction which takes place between religious institutions and family institutions. Often it is the same people who participate in both sets of institutions. We are then concerned with the interplay of religious ideas and practices, on the one hand, and family ideas and practices, on the other. Religion cultivates family goals and prescribes family practices. In turn, the family as an institution has an almost immeasurable impact on culture, including religion, since it is the chief transmitter of culture. What it does or fails to do in the development of children shapes the future course of human history. "The hand which rocks the cradle rules the world."

There are, moreover, things which happen to the family as a result of industrial living which in turn exert an influence upon religious institutions. The numerical size of the family, a falling birth rate, the mobility of families in changing residence, the separation of members of the family because of educational and economic pursuits and the instability of the family group engendered by the industrial revolution affect the magnitude of the tasks of the church as well as its resources for meeting these tasks.

One of the major theses of this text is that religious motivation is an energy system in competition with nonreligious motivations pressing for attention. The extent to which the energy system of religion is capable of imposing its aims upon the pattern of family living is an important research question. It is a question about which it is difficult to obtain carefully controlled scientific data for evaluating the extent of the influence of religious ideas and ideals. We begin by reviewing some of the concepts and plans which religious denominations have for family life.[1]

DENOMINATIONAL VIEWS OF MARRIAGE AND FAMILY

Jews

In Judaism the home of a family observing precepts of their religion is also regarded as the house of the Lord. He is omnipresent and continually reveals Himself in man's daily life as well as in nature and in history. Jewish ceremonial calls attention to this divine revelation and stresses the dependence of men upon God. Much of Jewish ceremonial is performed as part of activities in the home. Blessings are to be recited at mealtime and at frequent times during the day. Festivals such as Passover involve extensive participation by family groups in their homes. Jewish dietary laws perform more than a health function; they are part of a religious discipline to remind individuals of God.

Marriage in Judaism is considered an opportunity for human affection and happiness instituted by God. Mixed marriages between Jews and non-Jews are prohibited or discouraged. During the wedding ceremony the obligations assumed by bride and bridegroom toward each other are emphasized. A series of benedictions are said to express thanks to God for the experience of marriage and family living. The sexual relationship is regulated in Orthodox Jewish Law by being forbidden during menstrua-

[1] Among the numerous works which can be usefully consulted are: Sidney Goldstein, *Meaning of Marriage and Foundations of the Family, a Jewish Interpretation,* Bloch, 1942; Henry Bowman, *A Christian Interpretation of Marriage,* Westminster, 1959; J. L. Thomas, *The American Catholic Family,* Prentice-Hall, 1956; E. J. Mahoney, "Christian Marriage," in G. D. Smith, ed., *The Teaching of the Catholic Church,* 1949, Vol. II, pp. 1062–1100.

tion or for seven days afterward, and following this the wife takes a ritual bath in a pool of running water. Birth control has been recognized by Conservative and Reform rabbis to be appropriate in the marriage relationship.

The family carries considerable responsibility for religious instruction of children. To this end, the meaning of each detail in family ceremonials is explained to the growing child. Boys on reaching their thirteenth birthday and girls the twelfth go through a confirmation ceremony in which the boy, at least, participates in reading the Torah at a synagogue service. And at home there is a family celebration. These ceremonies mark the assumption of obligations to perform the commandments of God thereafter.

Divorce is granted by rabbis in Jewish Law only with the consent of both partners and after the civil courts have already approved a divorce. A complicated ritual to effect the divorce is performed by Orthodox and Conservative rabbis. In Reform Judaism a civil divorce is sufficient to terminate a Jewish marriage.

In summary, marriage in Judaism is an agreement of husband and wife to observe their obligations toward each other and to fulfill the commandments of God. As a consequence of doing these things they then experience the joys which marriage and family living provide for those who are faithful in their observance of divine requirements.

Catholics

The Roman Catholic view of marriage is that it is one of the seven sacraments, a permanent relationship of husband and wife for the performance of rights and duties. A sacrament is a procedure during which grace or supernatural help is given by God. Of course, whether sacramental grace is received depends upon a proper spiritual attitude of the recipient. Marriage is a state with special benefits bestowed by God, such as love and happiness, provided the marriage partners are faithful in performing requirements of the sacrament. Sexual activity divorced from procreation is regarded as a violation of divine law. Abstinence during the time of fertility as a means of birth control seems to be permitted, although Catholics are warned against abusing this procedure. The papal encyclical on marriage states:

> But no reason, however grave, may be put forward by which anything intrinsically against nature may become conformable to nature

and morally good. Since, therefore, the conjugal act is destined primarily by nature for the begetting of children, those who in exercising it deliberately frustrate its natural power and purpose sin against nature and commit a deed which is shameful and intrinsically vicious.

Small wonder, therefore, if Holy Writ bears witness that the Divine Majesty regards with greatest detestation this horrible crime and at times has punished it with death. As Saint Augustine notes, "Intercourse even with one's legitimate wife is unlawful and wicked where the conception of the offspring is prevented. Onan, the son of Juda, did this and the Lord killed him for it."[2]

Marriage between Catholics and non-Catholics is discouraged but is permitted provided the non-Catholic will sign an agreement that the requirements of the Catholic Church will be observed during the marriage. These requirements include the rearing of children in the Catholic faith.

In the marriage ceremony, the contracting partners are ministers of the sacrament of matrimony. The priest is present as a witness. The two people marry themselves by taking their vows and consummating their marriage.

Since, in Catholic doctrine, Christ raised marriage to the level of a sacrament and declared it to be indissoluble except by death, divorce is not permitted. However, for sufficient reason there may be a separation of husband and wife. In practice, the Catholic Church has in some cases involving civil divorce permitted a marriage to be annulled. In an annulment, the declaration is made that in one or more respects a valid marriage has not been undertaken. Fraud or entering a marriage under false pretenses are sufficient grounds for the granting of an annulment.

The Catholic Church is especially concerned for the satisfactory spiritual functioning of marriage and family life. An important and time-consuming responsibility of Catholic priests is to aid husbands and wives in the fulfillment of their family responsibilities toward each other and toward their children. This harmony between husband and wife is a matter for very serious concern of the church.

Parents are expected to begin the religious instruction of each child by teaching him to say his prayers and to trace the sign of the cross. Later he is taken to church and takes his first communion. In a Catholic home are found religious pictures, crucifixes, and other symbols of religious faith. These symbols link the home closely to the church.

Catholics, like Jews, seek to bring much of their religious ob-

[2] *Five Great Encyclicals,* Paulist Press, 1939, p. 92.

servances into the home. Religious objects, religious study, and family prayers are informal but important ways in which the sacramental system is supplemented by vital cultivation of religious motivation in family life. The spiritual basis of marriage has been summarized by J. Elliot Ross. "If a Catholic marries, it should not be through lust, but through the highest kind of conjugal love, in which natural inclinations are sublimated in the higher end of doing God's will, of acting as His agent in peopling Heaven, in giving to the new creatures of God the careful religious training which will insure the attainment of God's ultimate aim for human beings—the enjoyment by them of the Beatific Vision."[3]

In summary it may be said that in the Catholic view marriage, when properly undertaken, is a sacred ordinance of God. This ordinance imposes upon participants the obligation to bear and rear children and to maintain a loving and indissoluble union.

Protestants

The Protestant view of Christian marriage is less easily described since Protestants as well as Jews represent many shades of belief. All devout Protestants regard marriage as a religious affair with religious obligations to be performed. Orthodox Protestants believe that marriage, while not a sacrament, is sacred in the sense that it is to be performed according to God's will that husband and wife, and parents and children love one another and in that its spiritual fulfillment is made possible by the Spirit of Christ at work in the lives of the participants. A liberal view of Christian marriage described by a sociologist is given by Henry Bowman.[4] Liberal Christians are more inclined to spell out in detail techniques for achieving harmonious marriage and family experiences through application of the best insights available in psychology and sociology, rather than relying upon scriptural ideas. In any event, the teaching of Paul that it is better to marry than to be aflame with uncontrolled passion, but that it is better still not to marry at all, is largely forgotten by Protestant Christians, at least. The repressive attitude of Paul toward sex expression lingers in the thinking of a few Protestant church leaders, although the ideas of sex and marriage which Puritans brought with them are largely past history at the present time. Sexual expression is generally regarded as natural and desirable within

[3] L. Finkelstein, J. E. Ross, and W. A. Brown, *The Religions of Democracy,* Devin-Adair, 1949, p. 151.

[4] Bowman, *op. cit.*

the situation of stable marriage. The statement on the use of birth control, adopted by the Committee on Marriage and the Home of the Federal Council of Churches of Christ in America in 1931 expresses this view.

> A majority of the committee holds that the careful and restrained use of contraceptives by married people is valid and moral. They take this position because they believe that it is important to provide for the proper spacing of children, the control of the size of the family, and the protection of mothers and children; and because intercourse between the mates, when an expression of their spiritual union and affection, is right in itself. They are of the opinion that abstinence within marriage, except for the few, cannot be relied upon to meet these problems, and under ordinary conditions is not desirable in itself.[5]

More recent statements by the Department of Family Life of the National Council of Churches and by the Commission of the Churches on International Affairs of the World Council of Churches fortify and expand this point of view.

Protestant spokesmen, like Jewish and Catholic leaders, continue to support the scriptural injunctions against fornication and adultery, more commonly referred to today as premarital and extramarital coitus. However, a scientific defense of sexual continence outside of marriage is not usually adequately developed. Protestants together with Jews and Catholics are apt to fall back upon the simple declaration: "Thou shalt not."

Concerning the maintenance of religiously sanctioned sexual practices, the trend among Protestants is away from the repressive use of primary-group controls and legislation which prevailed until the past generation or two. Nevertheless, most sexual acts performed outside of marriage are defined by state laws as crimes or misdemeanors. The studies of the Institute for Sex Research, headed by the late Dr. Alfred C. Kinsey, indicate that very probably the majority of Americans during at least some episodes of their lives ignore these laws. Unfortunately, an occasional luckless victim is still singled out by smoldering religious opinion for punishment by mentally unhygienic and outdated laws pertaining to sexual activities in which there is mutual consent.

Opinion is increasingly divided among scientific students of sexual practices and marriage institutions as to whether the

[5] *New York Times,* March 21, 1931, p. 13. A thorough historical review of religious points of view on birth control is given by R. M. Fagley in *The Population Explosion and Christian Responsibility,* Oxford University Press, 1960.

restriction of coitus to marriage is necessary or desirable from the standpoint of mental health or individual happiness. Among thoughtful scholars whose views are those of sexual emancipation are unquestionably some persons who are sincere Christians. There appears to be increasing tacit acceptance, although still a decidedly minority one, among those speaking from the tradition of Protestantism, of the ethical appropriateness of coitus before marriage, especially when engaged in by those who expect to marry and whose family or economic circumstances make postponement necessary. Catholics, of course, continue stringently to reject sexual relationships outside of marriage, as far as official doctrine is concerned. In Protestantism today there is increasing tolerance of divorce, in many cases it being possible for divorced persons to remarry with the sanction of their church. Yet marriage between lifelong partners continues to be the aim and ideal in Protestant Christianity, as it is in other branches of religion in America.

As far as patterns of religious training and observance in the home are concerned, some Protestant groups, especially orthodox ones, still emphasize the importance of religious instruction of children and the practice of family prayers. While sufficient statistics are not available, it seems evident that in most Protestant homes responsibility for religious training and observance is left to the Sunday School and the church. Much the same might be said also of Catholic and Jewish homes where secular interests have pushed back religious interests into the confines of church or temple walls.

In summary, among Protestants marriage is viewed as an affair with religious or at least ethical responsibilities for mutual care of husband and wife and parents and children for each other. Except among Fundamentalists and those who are devout in their orthodoxy, a clear-cut religious definition of the marriage pattern is not given.

Effects of Religion on the Family

Our next task is to assess the effects of the religious forms which have been described upon marriage and family living in contemporary American culture. This assessment is difficult for a number of reasons. One of these is the lack of incisive and properly controlled data. Another difficulty is that prevailing patterns of attitudes and practices in sex and marriage are a result not only of contemporary religious viewpoints but also of religious doctrines effective in shaping people's thinking and acting during bygone generations. Another difficulty, and an important one, is the problem of separating the effects of the industrial revolution upon the marriage and family pattern from the effects of organized religion functioning at the same time. The interpretation given by sociologists and social economists of changes in family structure and functioning at the present time is largely an economic interpretation. The family is considered to be what it is as a result of industrial technology and the industrial way of life which has developed from this technology. Nevertheless, the author believes that the influences of religion or lack of religion upon the changing American family have been and are substantial ones. We will now endeavor to trace these influences.

In this tracing, a useful set of control data to be kept in mind for comparison is provided by the careful account given by Meyer Nimkoff of the Amish family pattern, cited as a case study in the introduction to Part V of this text. Among the Amish the peculiar trait of isolating themselves from outsiders has largely preserved their orthodox Christian ideas intact. This isolation appears to be less now than formerly. At the same time, they, together with other rural Americans, enjoy many of the benefits of industrial technology, such as tractors and farm machinery, although they reject riding in automobiles and such commercial entertainment as movies and television. The situation of the Amish, whose family patterns are strong and stable, can be duplicated by material from other cultures where the industrial revolution is far advanced but where religious influences continue to maintain a strong and traditional marriage and family pattern.

FUNCTIONS OF THE FAMILY

Analysis of the effects of religious ideas and practices on family life involves detailed consideration of the functions and structure of the family in American culture. The functions of the family as an institution refer to the things which are accomplished by members of the family acting together. Ultimately these refer to the experiences provided by family living which fulfill the wants of members of the family. Functions also refer to things which are essential means to such experiences. Food, clothing, and shelter produced by a peasant family for its own consumption are institutional functions. These things are essential to satisfactions experienced by the family.

The functions of the family have been undergoing fundamental changes since the onset of the industrial revolution. The traditional functions of the family in fulfilling the economic needs of its participants have largely been transferred to the economic order. Large numbers of people work together as industrial groups to accomplish the same economic functions once performed by individual families as work groups. Other functions of the family besides economic ones are also in a state of change and development. The ultimate shape which family living can be expected to assume in future generations is not entirely clear. Nevertheless, it is possible to list six basic functions of the family as an institution which continue to be very important to human beings at the present time. These are likely to continue as functions of the family for an indefinite time in the future, even though these functions may undergo changing expression and shifts in emphasis. This list of six includes: work, play, sex expression, childbearing, child rearing, and emotional security. The full meaning of the six categories for family living will appear when they are considered at some length, one by one.

The structure of an institution refers to the pattern of activities whereby its functions are accomplished. The concepts of function and structure refer in part to the same things. The concept of function refers also to the actions basic to the achievement of experiences sought. The two concepts also overlap in that the structure of the activities of a family terminates in the results produced by those activities. In spite of this duplication it is still useful to distinguish, apart from function, certain features of family structure, such as numerical size of the family, its permanence, the mobility of its participants from place to place or in and out of the home, the process of family decision, and the types of controls whereby the behavior of family members is regulated and decisions carried out. Some of these features of structure are the direct consequence of and are more easily examined in connection with particular functions of the family. Other features which affect the performance of all of the functions of the family are taken up in a succeeding section, "Family Harmony."

Closely related to the functions of the family are the motivating wants of its participants. If the functions are effective in satisfying the wants of participants, then there is a one-to-one correspondence between the experience of satisfying wants and the wants themselves. When an institution performs dysfunctions or fails to meet the needs of its participants, the correspondence breaks down. It is important to note that in the long run it is primarily the wants of people which determine the functions which their institutions perform, rather than the reverse. In examining the effects of religion upon family life one of the key avenues of influence is through altering the motivations of people. What people do as a family group during their leisure time is affected directly by the kinds of wants which have developed in their personality systems. Similarly, whether people approach their family situation in terms of altruistic aims or whether they approach their family situation in terms of individual pursuit of pleasure determines the kinds of things which people do together as a family and the types of experiences which family living provides for them.

Religion also affects family living by encouraging or prescribing the activities to be followed in achieving satisfaction of wants. If these specifications are closely related to family experiences, then they can be considered an influence upon family functions. If the prescription of activities relates rather to the pattern whereby members of the family work together or control each other's behavior, then this is an influence upon family structure.

Finally, it should be noted that religion goes beyond modifying or appealing to the wants of family members to follow activities which religion teaches. Religion also uses pressures and appeals which have little or no connection with what people want from family living. Thus churches at times use the social pressures of ostracism, excommunication, and boycott as a means of compelling people to act according to religious requirements. There is strong question of whether such pressure tactics are appropriate either to the idealistic purposes of a church or appropriate to the personal and social growth of members of families. Churches also make an effective appeal on the basis of loyalty of people to their own religion or religious group. Thus churches may encourage people to tithe a portion of the family income for religious work, rather than collect this money as if it were a compulsory tax. Through these various lines of influence organized religion as an institution molds and directs the functions and structure of the family.

Work and Play

Turning now to the six major functions of the family one by one, we endeavor to assess the relative influence of religious and economic factors in the changes which these functions have been undergoing since the rise of industrial technology. The reason why far fewer economic activities are performed by the family as a group instead of by people working together in industry is the much greater efficiency of the latter method of work. The advantages of industrial technology require that people develop economic specialities which they perform in combination with large numbers of people in a vast and intricate system of division of labor. The congregating of people in offices and factories to perform their economic tasks is an inevitable consequence of such labor-saving inventions as mechanical power, efficient transportation, the assembly line, and machines which perform intricate operations formerly performed laboriously and inefficiently by hand. Automation refers to a series of scientific and engineering procedures whereby the mind of the human operator is replaced by machines which respond automatically, just as if they had a human operator to guide them. However, automation replaces the memory activities of the human mind only, not its creative activities. It is still necessary for human minds to engage in the problem-solving and constructive activities necessary to design and instruct automation apparatus in the responses which it is to perform.

A large section of economic activities are still more satisfactorily performed in the home than outside of it. One of the main examples of this is provided by the care and maintenance of household possessions and equipment. More than this, people enjoy expressing their own individual preferences in home furnishings and interior decoration as well as in the preparation of their meals, even though these things can be done for people by automated industry. The family is the chief instrument for activities of buying and consuming. The economic function of social security has been assumed by the state, but the family is expected in religious thinking to supplement this in its personal care of the aged. Of much significance for the performance of family functions is the high standard of living made possible by industrial and then automated techniques of production. With a work week which approaches thirty hours instead of the sixty-hour work week characterizing preindustrial life, members of families have much more time to spend with each other and to do things together, if they are so disposed. Of greatest importance is the increased opportunity which people have for recreation together, either as family groups or as friends congregating in homes.

From an economic standpoint the advent of commercial entertainment has produced large inroads into the experiences which people as families have together. First, movie theaters took people outside of their homes to spectacles which they watched silently and alone as part of mass audiences. Now television permits them to watch the same shows seated comfortably in their own living rooms. The bodies of people have been brought back home by television, but not their minds and personalities.

Whether human beings use their vast reservoir of new-found leisure for cultural pursuits which are constructive for themselves and society depends considerably upon the ideals which they acquire from their experiences in schools and especially churches. The case study of the Amish shows the extent to which religion can limit family play activities to forms of recreation which provide satisfactions of group participation and social, rather than solitary, interests. If the importance of intellectual and religious development comes to be generally recognized by families in contemporary culture, much more time will be given to civic and educational pursuits, conversation on intellectual topics, and spiritual growth and development. Such activities can find natural and extensive opportunities for expression in the home, either by members of the family group or by friends who come together in each other's homes. More than these things, the perfection of human relationships, which requires thoughtful and sympathetic sharing of experiences and problems, can become a reality if the teachings of religion about human relationships gain ascendancy. Religion has traditionally been concerned with how people treat each other and how people find fulfillment in living for each other. As people gain greater appreciation of the importance of such ideals for personal relationships, it may be expected that religion will exercise a much wider influence over what people do together in their family living. Similarly, as people's sense of values change under the influence of religion, they may be expected to spend less time in the endless routine of trying to fix and polish up material aspects of their homes, possessions, and yards, which now claim such extravagant amounts of time in keeping up with the neighbors. Instead, they may be expected to spend much more time in polishing up important aspects of their personal relationships to each other.

Sex Expression

The love of husband and wife affords the most lasting experience of altruism which most human beings are able to find. While this altruism is expressed most of the time in what husband and wife do for each other at work or at play, the keenest expression for many years of their lives is found through their sexual relationship. Sexual fulfillment involves much more than sexual activity. Subtle shadings of feeling, desire, and spiritual purpose play a delicate yet immensely important role. It is with the psychological context in which sexual desire is expressed that religion has been primarily concerned.

To see in religious teaching merely a set of "thou-shalt's" and "thou-shalt-not's" is to miss the real significance of religious teaching about sexual love. Perhaps religion has been at fault for failing to make adequately clear its constructive psychological teachings about sex. Too often narrow-minded and intolerant moralists have imposed crudely repressive teachings in the name of religion while missing the spiritual significance of what religion can offer in aiding altruistic fulfillment through sex as well as through other aspects of human existence. At various times and places in religious history, spokesmen for some religious systems of living have preached ascetic practices at variance with contemporary ideals of conjugal love which are taught by many rabbis, priests, and ministers.

The elevation of these teachings to a set of principles fully documented by scientific research is an unfinished task. When we turn to psychology, sociology, and anthropology for the aid which they offer in an improved formulation of religious teaching, we reluctantly admit that science has as yet only partially explored the sexual side of human existence. It has done so primarily in terms of tabulations of behavior and has only started to probe the inward areas of social idealism and social feeling which accompany sexual activity. Yet if sex is to be satisfying and meaningful, this inward territory of what man thinks and feels concerning sexual activity must be surveyed before a scientific prescription for spiritually satisfying sex life can be formulated.

In drawing implications from factual studies of behavior, we must do so in terms of a conceptual system of human motivation. That is to say, we must interpret sexual activity by means of people's purposes and attitudes. Such interpretation is not "proved" by the statistical or case-study data. The data may disprove a system of principles and concepts, but they rarely affirm the alternative system conclusively. That affirmation depends upon the research judgment of the scientist or the intuition of the individual as he interprets for himself the factual results of behavior studies.

The system of concepts advanced by religion for interpreting the sexual side of human existence has no scientific originality. On the contrary, its traditional acceptance gives it verification by history. In every age and in every culture area leading thinkers have affirmed that man finds his greatest happiness and fullest emotional security in living for the group: his wife or husband, his children, his parents, his friends, and his community.

Throughout history there have been dissents from this spiritual view of how man finds his greatest fulfillment, and dissents from it arise today. The philosophy of wine, women, and wealth masquerades in each generation under the intellectual labels of the day as rationalizations of man's appetites. But the names of those who gain notoriety for "scientifically" justifying people's abandoning themselves to their desires are soon forgotten and their theories discarded as people learn by experience and grow up in the fullness of wisdom. In contrast, such passages as the writings of Jewish prophets, the Sermon on the Mount, and the *Bhagavad-Gita* have been a perennial source of inspiration and idealism to human beings as they seek to reap the full harvest of human love.

The goal of living for others instead of oneself is not a negation of one's happiness, but an affirmation of the means for experiencing it. The fundamental principle is that greater happiness results from fulfilling this goal than if one's pleasure were made the absorbing aim. The happiness comes as a concomitant of the creative process of planning and acting for the well-being of one's fellow men. Generally speaking, contemporary religions teach, not that the experience of pleasure is wrong, but that the pursuit of pleasure as an aim is wrong. Whatever comes as a concomitant of altruistic living in its fullest and highest sense is among the natural and expected things of life for human beings to enjoy rather than to avoid.

With this orientation toward accepting pleasurable experiences but rejecting pleasure as a pursuit, religion teaches that love between the sexes is to be fulfilled within a permanent marriage, not outside of it. Still less are sexual attachments sanctioned in which there is no enduring love between the partners. Observation of these regulations concerning sexual conduct is encouraged by a combination of inspiration, persuasion, argumentation, and imposition of social pressures. How effective are these regulations?

In Chapter 12 statistics from studies of sexual activities were cited which indicate substantial increases during the past generation or two in the amount of involvement of people in premarital and extramarital coitus. These statistics show rates of non-marital coitus for religiously devout women to be one-half that for non-religious women. In the case of men the rates for the religiously devout are not reduced by the same proportion but they are substantially lower than for the non-religious. Furthermore, it is significant that, according to the studies by the Institute for Sex Research, more than 80 percent of all sexual activity resulting in orgasm consists of marital coitus.[6] Marriage continues to provide most of the sexual experience of human beings.

Statistics are less available to show the precise extent of the changes in people's attitudes toward unconventional sexual behavior. If contemporary fiction is any indication, there is increasing tolerance of "midweek mistresses" and "week-end wives" accessory to an established marriage relationship. There appears to be an increasing tendency for husbands and wives to accept secondary sexual attachments made while a spouse is away from the home community. If such a trend should become well established, the resulting marriage situation would be comparable to that in some primitive societies where monogamy prevails with permissiveness of sexual partners outside of the marriage relationship. Where non-marital sexual relationships are entered upon for mutual pleasure and by common consent of the parties concerned, the strict monogamous teachings of religion encounter their sharpest test. What scientific line of reasoning can be advanced to demonstrate the unsoundness for a society or the individual of sexual love pursued outside of a durable marriage relationship? In particular, the attitude of many who have not yet married is one of: Why should we not take the physical opportunities for enjoyment which are ours? Why should sexual enjoyment be limited to marriage with a single lifelong partner?

To answer these questions from the standpoint of religion, the premise must first be acknowledged that altruistic living is superior to any other mode of life. By superior is meant that this way of life produces a deeper and more lasting sense of fulfillment for the individual as well as being most productive of the well-being of others. It is of course obvious that an individual who possesses little altruistic desire in his personality system will find more opportunities for satisfaction in pleasure seeking than in seeking the common good. However, the personality system is capable of development into one in which altruistic

[6] A. C. Kinsey, W. P. Pomeroy, C. E. Martin and P. H. Gebhart, *Sexual Behavior in the Human Female,* Saunders, 1953, pp. 305, 392, 424.

motivations are dominant and self-seeking motivations are minor in intensity. The contention of religion is that this transformed way of life affords the individual keener and more lasting enjoyment of life. The often reiterated conclusion of religious leaders from era to era is that the altruistic way of life enables people to find their deepest and most lasting sense of fulfillment. When the contention is examined more closely it is not that happiness becomes flawless, for some disappointments in life are inescapable. More realistically, the argument is that life becomes superior to what it otherwise would be for the individual. It is also conceivable that a supreme act of altruism may eventuate in physical suffering or death. In such extreme cases, which do not bear upon the issues of choice of sexual conduct, the individual may be sustained in his altruism by the conviction that the ultimate purposes in the universe will come to realization, whatever happens to the individual in his immediate span of life. Where a supreme act of sacrifice is called for, it can still be argued that the peace of mind of the individual for as long as he lives is necessarily increased by his self-negation.

The issue of pleasure seeking versus altruism comes into practical focus in relation to choice of sexual conduct. What religion then maintains, as expressed by many of its writers and spokesmen, is that both individual happiness and the welfare of the group are more fully served by fidelity to monogamy than by other patterns of sexual activity. Several points may be elaborated in this affirmation.

1. The aim of pleasure is self-defeating because of the conflict set up in the personality system between desire for the experience of enjoyment and the recurring occasions when enjoyment is absent. Such psychic conflict provides the occasion for psychic irritation and an unpleasant or even painful feeling tone much longer in duration than the moments of pleasure. Perhaps this thesis should be viewed as a theory for which scientific documentation is not yet entirely adequate. Yet it is a conviction born of the lives of many pleasure seekers who eventually found a sense of psychic harmony only through fidelity to their religious teachings. Goethe's Faust, who eventually turned from illicit pursuit of love to altruistic service as more enobling and deeply satisfying, is a case in point. The story is not merely that of Goethe; it is a folk story long ingrained in German culture.

2. Furthermore, it appears to those whose discernment of human nature stems from scientific study that the type of motivation most effective in producing an integrated and stable

personality system is altruistic. One of the reasons for cultivating this type of motivation is its contribution to personality stability and its contravention of mental and nervous disorder. While altruism is not a sure cure for all of the temperamental deficiencies stemming from heredity or faulty childhood conditioning, nevertheless it is a favorable influence lessening the deleterious effects of psychic handicaps. A long succession of psychoanalysts of world eminence, among them Alfred Adler and C. G. Jung, have testified from their clinical studies to the importance of altruistic love in fostering healthy personality development.

It is for the individual and for those who surround him with their own influences to choose whether altruistic or pleasure-seeking motivation is to be cultivated. In the realm of motivation man cannot effectively serve two masters. In the competition for dominance one or the other gains the upper hand and crowds out the other. If an equilibrium is reached, it is an uneasy one in which shifts in relative power are a recurring experience. What we are saying is that pursuit of the aim of pleasure takes place only at the expense of displacement of altruistic aims. Psychic energies are limited so that the more one form of motivation is followed, the less is there room remaining for the competing form. The integration of the personality system about the power of God requires the elimination of pursuit of pleasure as an aim.

3. If the foregoing psychic analysis is accepted, the question still remains of why those who are altruistically inclined should not seek to give each other pleasure in premarital or extramarital relationships. The answer to this question requires a careful examination of the psychic context in which sexual expression takes place. While altruistic love means giving happiness through the sexual relationship, something is missing if the sexual activity has no meaning beyond the pleasure which each receives. To aid the pleasure seeking of another rather than to fulfill durable social goals is on a level with pleasure seeking for oneself. What endow coitus with meaning beyond the giving and receiving of pleasure are the deeper purposes fused with it. One of these is the act of procreation, an experience of initiating a new life of immeasurable social and spiritual importance.

So sacredly is the act of procreation viewed in Catholic doctrine that sexual activity which does not at least provide opportunity for procreation is not acceptable. Yet, such an extreme view overlooks two important considerations. One of these is that sexual responsiveness and rapport are not a condition which can be turned off and on like running water. If husband and wife are mutually aroused to the point of sexual activity leading to procreation, then this has been preceded by an increasing crescendo of sexual preliminaries during courtship which help to establish mutual affection and sexual responsiveness. Following the procreative activity, the momentum of sexual interest and activity continues, even though another child is not immediately desirable. Moreover, Catholic doctrine acknowledges that sexual activity between husband and wife has other purposes besides procreation, such as mutual affection and happiness. But Catholic doctrine seeks to limit coitus to those situations where man has interposed no steps by his own design to circumvent the possibility of conception. In this doctrine it is not necessary that children be intended as a result of coitus. Concupiscence is acknowledged as a reason for marital coitus but steps must not be taken to prevent conception.

4. Another purpose apart from procreation is the symbolic role which coitus plays in married life. The symbolic meaning is far greater than that which results merely from indoctrination by ideas present in one's culture. The symbolic meaning is profoundly rooted in the physiological circumstances of the marriage partners. One of these is that the act of procreation of offspring in a setting of altruistic motivation inevitably implies parents who are devoted to each other and to their children. The renewal of coitus apart from procreation continues to symbolize the devotion of husband and wife to each other. The boy or girl with fine ethical sensibilities involuntarily reacts against coitus prior to marriage because of its emotional association with a permanent and socially sanctioned relationship of husband and wife.

The symbolic meaning of coitus as caring for each other has additional important roots. One of these is that from early childhood onward holding, embracing, and kissing mean loving care of one human being for another. In the marriage relationship coitus normally implies strong emotional acceptance of each partner by the other, since sexual responsiveness is a sensitive indicator of psychological as well as physical attraction toward one's mate. Where domestic conflict prevails, sexual responsiveness recedes or disappears, and inducement to form sexual attachments outside of the marriage relationship arises. Hence married people are reassured in a tangible and vivid way of their kindly affection for each other where warm sexual responsiveness prevails. Thus coitus symbolizes and directly expresses mutual feelings of altruistic love of husband and wife for each other. Protestant doctrine summarizes very well what we have been saying in this analysis, in the statement quoted previously that "intercourse between the mates, when an expression of their spiritual union and affection, is right in itself." Catholic doctrine would also accept this, but not to the extent that coitus as an expression of spiritual union and affection is to be engaged in when conception is prevented by human intention. Here Protestants and Catholics part company, most Protestants believing that coitus has such profound emotional meaning for husband and wife that it should be engaged in long after parents have been successful in adding an appropriate number of children to the family group.

However, the controversy between Protestants and Catholics over birth control is a lesser issue compared to the importance of grasping the spiritual significance of coitus in marriage. In a setting of altruistic ideals, it is a means of religious experience. Unless this significance is warmly and imaginatively felt, the performance of coitus becomes a meaningless pursuit of pleasure or merely a perfunctory act not expressive of the altruistic feeling of husband and wife toward each other.

The spiritual context in which contemporary religion typically places sex is the primary reason why premarital and extramarital coitus are unacceptable from the standpoint of maximum altruistic fulfillment. The point is that, accepting the social desirability of marriage as a lifelong relationship of two people caring for each other and their children, coitus symbolizes or, stronger still, expresses this type of emotional attachment. If the symbolism were no more than that of verbal conditioning, this argument from a religious standpoint would be without force and validity. Instead, the physiological and social circumstances of human beings inescapably endow coitus with this meaning for those who are altruistically motivated. To seek coitus outside of marriage therefore contradicts the spiritual purposes which coitus expresses in marriage. Also contradicting these purposes is the risk of pregnancy among the unmarried. On the basis of the prevailing proportion of births for the white population which are illegitimate, 2 percent, it can be estimated that approximately one female out of twenty in the white population gives birth to an illegitimate child during her lifetime. The incidence of pregnancy including that terminated by abortion is probably much higher, as indicated by data published by the Institute for Sex Research in *Pregnancy, Birth and Abortion.*

It is hardly surprising that a stable sexual relationship to which the marriage partners are faithful is the overwhelming pattern observed by most of the people most of the time in most human cultures. Sexual deviations from this pattern are plentiful from society to society, yet human beings usually look forward to or return to the monogamous relationship after their love affairs. This manifests the strong psychic disposition which human beings have for permanent sexual relationships, and which, if they were consistent, would not deviate from. Of course permanence is a matter of degree, and divorces and remarriages occur in many societies. At the moment what we are emphasizing is the normative as well as the ethical disposition of men and women toward a monogamous sexual relationship. Religion then merely argues that people recognize this disposition early rather than late and act consistently in accordance with it. Early in life human beings are influenced by many competing and conflicting motivations. As they move upward and through life their personality systems tend toward greater consistency and more harmonious integration about goals recognized as central.

Especially during the formative years does it seem important to moderate the sex drive. If altruistic motives are to be strong, they need opportunity to take firm root before sex is pursued. This applies to habits of work and character in general. If the structure of personality first is soundly established, then means are there for controlling and expressing sex in an idealistic way. Until habits of self-control and social purpose are acquired by the individual, he is not ready to maintain a family of his own. From a psychological viewpoint, his readiness for parenthood coincides with his readiness for sexual union.

The validity of this altruistic line of analysis receives statistical support from various studies made of factors associated with the achievement of happiness in marriage. Home, children, and love as motivations for marriage have been found to be favorably associated with marital satisfaction.[7] In contrast, such interests as commercial entertainment and enjoyment of drinking are unfavorably associated with marital happiness. An interest in religion is favorable for a happy marriage, and this seems un-

[7] H. J. Locke, *Predicting Adjustment in Marriage,* Holt, 1951, pp. 98, 257–258; P. H. Benson, "Familism and Marital Success," *Social Forces,* March, 1955, pp. 277–280; and Benson, "The Common Interests Myth in Marriage," *Social Problems,* July, 1955, pp. 27–34.

derstandable in view of the teachings of religion that love and children are important goals in marriage.[8] It is further significant that those who refrain from coitus until marriage find, on the average, greater happiness than those who are premaritally active.[9] The differences are less marked for premarital coitus between future spouses. Alfred Kinsey and his associates in the Institute for Sex Research report data to show that those women who engage in premarital coitus achieve orgasm more readily in marriage.[10] This may simply mean that women may require time to achieve full sexual response or that those tending to be more responsive are those who seek premarital coitus.

The foregoing data indicate the preponderant contribution to happy marriages from following traditional teachings of religion. A happy marriage relationship is a product of many things, and it cannot be argued that any particular deviation from religious teaching necessarily does irreparable harm to the quality of a marriage. One of the key concepts in religious teaching is that people have the capacity to grow beyond their past mistakes. Some religious groups recognize this with some form of confessional or absolution by which the psychological results of past misconduct are removed after the individual becomes committed to a sounder spiritual life course.

At all times it is important that those in the role of religious teachers or counselors advance their ideals without subjecting human personalities to the ordering and forbidding against which Freud made so cogent a protest. Sexual idealism is an affair to be induced by inspiration and enthusiastic teaching rather than by resort to punitive sanctions. The latter are not only psychologically harmful in arousing serious emotional conflicts, but they often have the effect of making the forbidden conduct more inviting than it would otherwise be. Prejudice against those whose sexual patterns deviate from religious standards is as much to be criticized as is prejudice shown against any group of human beings. The relative tolerance toward sexual deviation shown by a religiously devout group such as the Amish shows

[8] E. W. Burgess and L. S. Cottrell, Jr., *Predicting Success or Failure in Marriage,* Prentice-Hall, 1939, pp. 122–126; Locke, *op. cit.,* pp. 236–243; Benson, "Familism and Marital Success," *op. cit.;* for discussion of an exception see G. Karlsson, *Adaptability and Communication in Marriage,* Almquist and Wiksells, 1951, p. 107.

[9] L. M. Terman, *Psychological Factors in Marital Success,* McGraw-Hill, 1938, pp. 324–329; Locke, *op. cit.,* pp. 133–134; E. W. Burgess and P. Wallin, *Engagement and Marriage,* Lippincott, 1953, pp. 368–370.

[10] Kinsey, Pomeroy, Martin, and Gebhard, *op. cit.,* pp. 390–391.

a depth of wisdom and kindly feeling which all other religious groups would do well to emulate.

Childbearing and Child Rearing

The family function of producing offspring is one which is strongly encouraged by some religious groups, such as Catholics, because of the belief that bringing children into the world to become part of the divine kingdom is regarded as a religious responsibility. Most religious groups at least take the view that bearing and rearing of children afford a vital opportunity for creating something of great spiritual value. The thinking of Protestants in contrast to that of Catholics is apt to be tempered by considerations of adequate family income and, as far as the world scene is concerned, considerations of overpopulation. In the United States from 1870 to 1933 the birth rate fell from 38 babies born each year for each 1,000 inhabitants to a rate of 18 per 1,000. In the following decade the birth rate rose to 25 per 1,000 and has since continued in the vicinity of this figure. Because birth rates merely refer to the number of babies acquired in any given year, they are an unreliable indicator of the number of children couples will eventually have in the duration of their childbearing years. If the present high birth rate continues, a rapidly increasing population can be expected, since a birth rate of 16 would be sufficient to maintain a constant population with an average length of life of 67 years. It is impossible to predict in advance how many children parents in the future will desire to have. However, careful analysis of childbearing patterns in relation to age of parents indicates that the birth rate is unlikely to be sustained at its present high level, although it will probably continue at a figure large enough to produce an increasing population.

What parts are played by economic and religious factors in these trends in the birth rate? The reduction from seven or eight children born to a typical American mother in the eighteenth century to an average of three children in recent years is directly connected with changed economic circumstances of families. Formerly children were important to the family labor supply, since they took their place in the household economy at a young age. Now they require a decade or more of additional maintenance plus an expensive education before children are economically self-sufficient. Also of great economic consequence, mothers could formerly look after their children while continuing their usual employment in the household economy. Now wives must choose between a job which may double the family income or staying at home to take care of their children. Children are still much valued by most parents for social and psychological reasons. But parents find their desires for children are fulfilled after two or three rather than seven or eight.

In view of the economic impact of industrial technology on the family, it seems all the more remarkable that the long-run decline in the birth rate has been reversed and has leveled at a point which suggests that moderate if not large-sized families are still popular. A factor in the popularity of larger families among suburban dwellers may be the visible success and prosperity which well-clothed, well-fed, and well-possessioned children represent in the eyes of neighbors. An equally plausible reason is that the cultural values of success, conspicuous consumption, and individual happiness, stemming from the industrial revolution, are nearing the end of their ascendancy as people realize their futility and turn instead to the deeper and more lasting satisfactions connected with children and family living. These are the satisfactions advocated by religion. While it is difficult to determine the precise extent to which religion is responsible for the present level of familistic interests, it seems clear that this level is higher because of religion than it otherwise would be. Credit for maintaining a floor under the long-run downward trend in the birth rate is shared by religion.

The differential effects of religion on the birth rate are evident in comparing Catholic birth rates with those of Protestants, whose leaders are less emphatic in their insistence upon the family as an instrument for procreation. A study by the Milbank Memorial Fund of couples in Indianapolis disclosed 2.7 births per Catholic marriage, and 2.2 births per Protestant marriage.[11] However, A. J. Marx and Sue Mayer showed that in Hamtramck, Michigan, birth rates of the Catholic immigrant population progressively dropped to the level of the established population in Detroit.[12]

Parents occupy a vital role in preparing children to take their place in a new industrial society. That the upbringing of children takes place best in the sunshine of parental affection and care is the conclusion of most, if not all, child psychologists and child welfare workers in the U.S. Children, especially during their

[11] C. V. Kiser and P. K. Whelpton, "Social and Psychological Factors Affecting Fertility," *Milbank Memorial Fund Quarterly,* January, 1944, pp. 22–105.

[12] A. J. Marx and Sue Mayer, "Social Change, Religion, and Birth Rates," *American Journal of Sociology,* January, 1957, pp. 383–390.

helpless years, require tender loving care or "TLC," as pediatricians prescribe it for children emotionally and physically sick from lack of it. Infants are psychologically tied to their mothers as they were physically tied to the placenta for their sustenance. For many years of their lives children must have individual adults upon whom they emotionally depend and whom they feel are theirs as a permanent possession. A loving family is the crucible in which sentiments of altruism are forged for social living. For this reason experiments to rear children in state institutions fail unless permanent adults are provided for each three or four children, which in effect reconstitutes a family group.

The nurture of the personalities of children is the most critical function of the family from the standpoint of group welfare. Parents are responsible for equipping their children with interests and convictions needed for modern economic life. Families which are not self-sufficient can secure help from public funds; couples who divorce are usually able to provide for themselves even though they undergo emotional loss; and if families have fewer children than their neighbors, usually no one expresses concern. But if human beings are brought into the world and their minds and motivations are neglected, society pays an incalculable price in the wrecked lives of those who are criminal, neurotic, or psychotic. To cast this public-welfare view in theological terms, it can be said that no sin against God is greater than bringing into the world unfortunate children for whom adequate psychological provision is not made. The same can be said in an economic context of excessive numbers of children brought into families in countries where private or public resources are inadequate to care for these children at a level of health and decency. These comments highlight the difference between religious groups which consider unimpeded conception or an effort at sexual abstinence to be more important than what happens to children after they are born and those religious groups which place the quality of child rearing foremost.

At the same time, it is to be emphasized that Catholics, among others, possess a strongly family-centered religion in which the well-being of children is of very solicitous concern. However, many non-Catholics would part company with Catholics in the patterns of child discipline advocated. Scientific development of the personalities of children was referred to at some length in Chapter 11. It is sufficient at this point to say that non-Catholics seem to be more influenced by scientific knowledge in child psychology promulgated by figures such as John Dewey and

Dr. Benjamin Spock. It is difficult to determine the precise extent to which the patterns of religious obedience toward the church are replicated by insistence upon obedience of children toward their parents. In child care prescribed by contemporary psychology, the appropriateness of disciplinary requirements to each level of ability is stressed. It is regarded as more important to succeed in training and directing the motivations of children through tact, persuasion, and example than it is to insist upon conforming behavior whether the child's will is ready for it or not.

These generalizations concerning religious differences in child rearing are difficult to sustain from a factual standpoint. Part of the difficulty is the lack of systematic data collected concerning the effects of religion upon child-rearing practices. Another circumstance, and an important one, is that Catholics are increasingly influenced by psychological developments on the American scene. At the same time, devout Protestants or Jews may believe that firm obedience to God's laws must be maintained in the home. In individual cases the extent to which parental discipline is authoritarian may largely depend upon the extent to which parents project their own temperaments into the child-rearing situation. Those who are dominating or antagonistic by nature are apt to express these feelings toward children as well as toward others. Those who are calm and poised by temperament are likely to treat children as considerately as they treat their adult equals.

Emotional Security

The function of emotional security refers in a broad way to the aid which members of a family group give to each other in the guidance and control of motivation. Under conditions of acute stress people may react with inhibiting fear or destructive anger. The maintenance of poise and steady energy for life activities in place of these eruptions of emotion is emotional security in clear-cut form. In a less conspicuous way people in the close association of family or friendship relationships are able to encourage each other in those interests and activities which are constructive or necessary for personal accomplishment. Those motivations which are wasteful or which are carried to excess can be subordinated through the influence of people on each other. People respond in a sensitive manner to the encouragement of others. What they lack in motivational energy or control can often be provided through the stimulus of those with whom they are in sympathetic rapport. Not only do growing children depend considerably upon their parents for their development toward mature, adult goals, but adults, especially in times of crisis, are frequently able to supplement each other's motivational resources in valuable ways.

The mutual maintenance of emotional security of members of the family group depends upon much more than stimulating or appealing to worthwhile interests and aims. People need to accept circumstances which are beyond their control and to adjust their goals and expectations according to a realistic view of their circumstances. What people think about and believe plays a powerful role in whether they react emotionally to a frustrating or frightening situation. Beliefs of inferiority of self and lack of trust in others are deeply rooted in temperament resulting from hereditary tendencies and past experiences. The counseling and encouragement which people give each other go far in overcoming the mistaken beliefs which cause people to react emotionally with anxiety or in anger. Members of families and close friends are able to go further than this in assisting each other to keep emotional balance. They can modify the external circumstances in their situation which are emotionally provocative to others. It is expected by community understanding as well as in religious teaching that members of families have a special responsibility for helping each other gain and retain emotional security in their common life together.

Of subtle yet profound consequence is the degree of confidence which human beings have in each other and in the ultimate purposes of the universe as they discern these to be. Conviction in the power of love to bring out the best in others is an important aspect of emotional security. Belief that the human drama in the universe is essentially good and that it is leading toward something higher strongly colors one's outlook on life and the effectiveness with which one follows a program of activities for the good of all. These supports to emotional security are a basic part of a system of religious convictions. They are frequently matters of religious faith. But faith need not be thought of as believing what cannot be proved. In a more meaningful sense, faith refers to believing in that which has not yet come about, but which one accepts on the assurance of others whose competence one respects or as a result of one's own reasoning processes.

Religion of the kind which Freud criticized for imposing emotional stress on the functioning of personality or which sapped its vitality by inducing escape from life's problems is damaging to the emotional security of the individual. But this is not what religion typically does in the integration of the personality system. A military commander in the American Revolution is reported to have said that if he could find a Quaker who would fight he would rather have him under his command because of the equanimity with which a man of this type would face the hazards of battle. The pages of history contain many accounts of religiously devout persons whose morale in the face of personal danger was unbreakable.

The connection of religious belief and practice with emotional security is readily traced through the doctrines which become internalized in the personality system. It is also apparent without detailed study that human beings in family groups are frequently a source of emotional strength to each other. What is difficult to document is the precise extent to which the family function of providing emotional security is augmented by the influence of religion. Those families which are strong in their religious principles have the double resource of themselves and their religion in maintaining emotional stability. Where members of families are able to invoke religious resources in their common life, they are able to give each other emotional strength which personal encouragement alone would not provide. Even those families which are unaffiliated with a religious group derive benefit by sharing a common culture with those families for whom religion is a direct source of emotional security. People are continuously influenced by the beliefs and attitudes of others in the communities where they live. Thus religion has an effect, even if it cannot be accurately gauged, upon the emotional security of families indirectly, as well as directly, influenced.

Family Harmony

The characteristics of family structure whereby members of the family, especially husband and wife, work together effectively and permanently for the good of the family deserve attention beyond the review of family functions in relation to religion which has been given. Whether or not the functions of the family are performed well or at all depends upon the degree to which a harmonious relationship prevails in the family. By family harmony is here meant the presence of aims and interests and implementation of these in ways which lead to fulfillment of the members' life wants. One of the basic conditions of family harmony is the presence of altruistic desires. If each member of the family, or at least husband and wife, desires the welfare of others in the family, members are impelled by their motivation to function harmoniously. In contrast, if members of the family group are primarily motivated by self-interest, they face the difficult problem of overcoming the antagonism in their interests and in adjusting these interests to each other's requirements so that they can function as a family group.

The ultimate in disharmony occurs when husband and wife become divorced and the family is truncated or broken up altogether. The bereavement following divorce may exceed that of the death of one's partner because of the deep emotional involvement and the sense of remorse for what might have happened differently. In cases where both partners have become progressively alienated and have few bonds of love and affection, divorce is less of an immediate crisis for them, although in the long run it may considerably affect their psychological outlook as they progressively realize a sense of spiritual failure and futility. The emotional damage of divorce to children may be large. However, in exceptional circumstances this may be less for them than living in a home marked by cruelty and neglect. Marriage is a relationship meeting the needs of people to love and to be loved. These are needs which require a permanent relationship of two people caring for each other and their children to assure fulfillment of these needs.

Religion is closely connected with family harmony through the altruistic love which it teaches in marriage and family relationships. But altruistic intentions are not enough. People require the insights made possible by scientific study. A husband who finds his wife's emotional upsets disagreeable needs to search the strands in his personality system and her present environment which contribute to her upset condition. It is quite likely that the things which he says or does himself are important sources of the tears or tantrums of his wife. At the same time, a wife who is unhappy because of her husband's lack of self-confidence in business or personal affairs may unknowingly undermine his confidence through thoughtless things which she says or does. The emotional complexes in which two people can become entangled are not infrequently of such complexity that it requires the skill of a professional marriage counselor to untangle the chain reactions of antagonism and mutual reënforcement of hostilities and anxieties. The gifts of scientific study are necessary resources in the achievement of religious purposes. Considerable literature containing these resources has been published. The popular writings of David R. Mace may be taken as representative of the best in marriage counseling from a liberal religious standpoint.[13]

From what has been said concerning the connection of religion with family harmony, it would be expected that the presence or absence of religious affiliation would make a substantial difference in divorce rates, now at the ratio of one divorce for every four or five marriages. Three extensive studies disclose the divorce rate of couples without religious affiliation to be approximately three times the divorce rate of those who are affiliated with the same religious faith. Catholics have lower divorce rates than Protestants, and in one of the studies the divorce rate among Jews was lower than that among Christians.[14]

Divorce rates in these three studies were about as high for mixed marriages of a Catholic and a Protestant or of a Christian and a Jew as for couples without any religious affiliation. It is therefore clear that religious differences can be a highly divisive influence in family life. This is not so much a matter of differing theological beliefs as it is a matter of differing practices sanctioned or required by each religious system. Sex patterns, child-rearing methods, as well as rituals and ceremonials performed inside and outside the home, make mixed marriages difficult ones. Moreover, conflicts with in-laws arise. Even religious differences between members of a single denomination can be disruptive of family harmony.

Of considerable importance is a circumstance sometimes overlooked by those who criticize the Catholic Church for trying to keep the marriage a Catholic one. This is the circumstance that the natural unit of membership in a church is the family, which thereby receives spiritual counsel and encouragement for its total life. If the family is to receive maximum benefit from the practice of religion, members of the family should belong to the same church. This requirement does not seem convincing to those who take their religion lightly, yet if religion is regarded as a serious ally of family life, husband and wife will center their religious interests in the same congregational group. The family

[13] D. R. Mace, *Marriage, the Art of Lasting Love,* Doubleday, 1952; *Success in Marriage,* Abingdon, 1958. Also viewing marriage within a broad religious context are Henry Bowman, *Marriage for Moderns,* McGraw-Hill, 1954; and J. T. and M. G. Landis, *Building a Successful Marriage,* Prentice-Hall, 1958.

[14] H. M. Bell, *Youth Tell Their Story,* American Council on Education, 1938, p. 21; H. A. Weeks, "Differential Divorce Rates by Occupation," *Social Forces,* March, 1943, p. 336; Landis and Landis, *op. cit.,* pp. 242–245.

then becomes supported by other family units in the congregation as well as by religious leadership. In turn, such a family is able to support the spiritual life of other families.

Such mutual support is especially valuable in times of family crises, such as severe illness or death of a member of the family. At death the consolation of religion aids other members to retain their emotional stability and spiritual perspective. The amputation of an organically functioning member of the family leaves a wound which requires time and religious resources to heal.

Jesus said: "In my Father's house are many rooms."[15] Religious traditions teach that the present span of life is only one of these. Other rooms are attained when people succeed in finding places in the social worlds of others. One who dies physically still lives spiritually in that he has become an inseparable part of the personality systems and the culture of others. What he has done for their thinking and ideals endures as a permanent feature of their lives, as a wave on the sea moves endlessly into other waves. In a sense, the deceased is as much alive as are those who continue to live for the family and community purposes which are his.

The conviction frequently expressed by religious teaching and supported by philosophical reasoning is that those who pass from this life are taken to a larger existence, another room in the house of God. What people know of the present life convinces them that God sets a high value upon His children. While they know little of life hereafter, the trust they have learned to place in God leads them to believe that He will always care for them.

This line of thinking and feeling may be viewed casually by those who have not faced the physical fact of death. However, beliefs in social and personal immortality of the person lost are of immense encouragement to the bereaved ones in aiding them to continue life activities without interruption or impairment. Religion even teaches that death, unfortunate and unwelcome though it is, affords opportunities for people to undergo deeper spiritual growth. If spiritually disposed, they become carried to more fundamental levels of outlook and ideals. They become freed from encumbering baggage of self-will. They may then live more energetically in the building of an acceptable kingdom on earth. With St. Francis of Assisi they believe that in the immolation of self they are born to eternal life.

The full impact of religion upon the quality of family liv-

[15] *John* 14:2.

ing is not so much an actuality in contemporary culture as it is a potentiality. Family worship in the home is an art practiced by no more than a devout fraction of Jewish, Catholic, and Protestant families in contemporary culture. Yet such worship provides the means for daily appeal to spiritual power to upbuild and renew lives of loving affection.

How far family existence for many in America is removed from altruistic devotion to family and society as the ultimate meaning of life is poignantly depicted by John Keats. Author of *The Crack in the Picture Window,* he writes in an *Atlantic* article:

> Nick and Fran Baxter live, so to speak, with their three children in one of the five hundred three-bedroom houses of a real-estate nightmare we shall call Apple Drive. Neat, clean, wholesome, slightly vacuous, the Baxters look like one of those idealized suburban families you see in the full-color advertisements of the women's magazines. . . . Together with all others trapped in this development miles from nowhere, the Baxters are the prey of pressures less readily apparent to them, but which conspire to make suburban life somewhat disappointing. For one thing, Apple Drive, like most developments, is a jail of the soul, a wasteland of look-alike boxes stuffed with look-alike neighbors.
>
> Here are no facilities for human life, other than bedrooms and bathrooms. Here is a place that lacks the advantages of both city and country but retains the disadvantages of each. Each suburban family is somehow a broken home, consisting of a father who appears as an overnight guest, a put-upon housewife with too much to do, and children necessarily brought up in a kind of communism. For Apple Drive children, life is play school at age three, preschool at age four, kindergarten at age five. Thus do suburban mothers force their primary responsibilities upon someone else as soon as they can, in order to cope with the lesser but insistent needs to drive to the supermarket, clean the house, gabble on the telephone, and attend the *Kaffeeklatsch.* So, suburban children learn the dreary steaminess of group life as soon as they can walk, and after school they are plunked down before the television set to watch the slaughter in the late afternoon while mom thaws supper. In the evening the baby sitters arrive. . . .
>
> Here is certainly a milieu that shrieks for mitigation. It is absolutely different from any other society that America has ever produced, and it is new since the last world war. Its pressures are great, but rather than attempting to deal with these uncomfortable realities in any constructive way, most suburbanites, like the Baxters, try to drift away from them. The most prevalent form of escape can be called compulsive buying, and Nick is a practitioner and victim of it. . . .
>
> Nick and Fran Baxter never ask each other, "Do we really need this or do we just want it?" Nor do the sellers, who batten on customers

there is something eternal in religion which is destined to survive all the particular symbols in which religious thought has successively enveloped itself."[17]

When the author first traveled the scientific road and pondered whether God would be found in the temple at the end of the search, he experienced mounting suspense. What he and others found or failed to find would reflect the innermost nature of the universe such as the human race, under the impetus of science, must eventually discover it. When he found God at the end of the road he realized the warm and lasting glow which pervades human experience under the influence of His Spirit. He realized that, even though some might be engulfed by the whirlpools of nationalism and commercialism, the main stream of history would flow on to a greener plain of civilization.

> He shall judge between many peoples,
> and shall decide for strong nations afar off;
> and they shall beat their swords into plowshares,
> and their spears into pruning hooks;
> nation shall not lift up sword against nation,
> neither shall they learn war any more;
> but they shall sit every man under his vine and under his fig tree,
> and none shall make them afraid;
> for the mouth of the Lord of hosts has spoken.
>
> For all the peoples walk
> each in the name of its god,
> but we will walk in the name of the Lord our God
> for ever and ever.[18]

From time to time God, however we conceive of Him, rolls back the clouds of unknowing and allows His truths to shine through with new light as on Mount Sinai many years ago. Through scientific study of religion are provided fresh openings to the clear skies above.

[17] Emile Durkheim, *The Elementary Forms of the Religious Life,* Free Press, 1947, p. 427.
[18] Micah 4:3–5.

Index

Index of Names

Index of Subjects